P9-APV-910

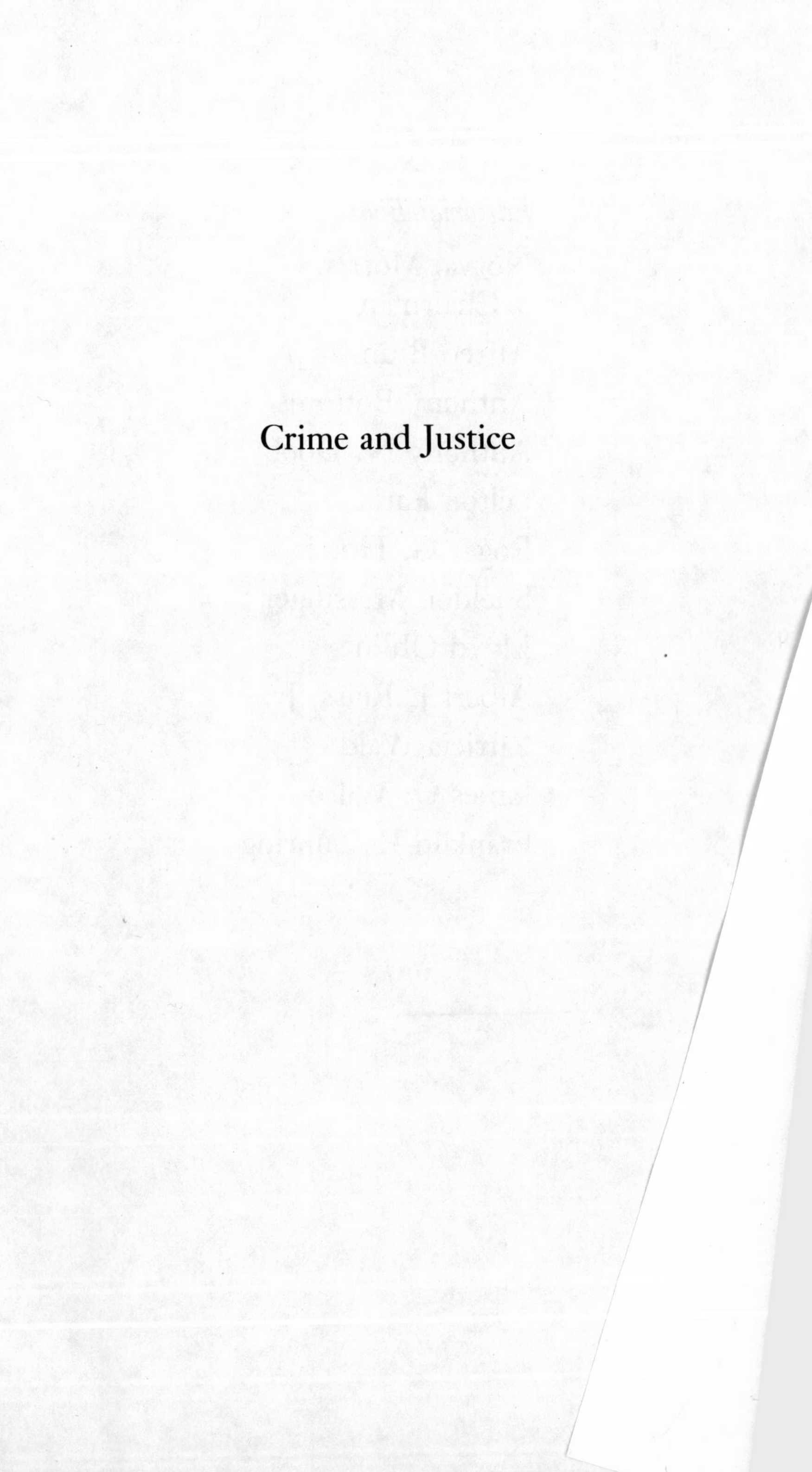

Crime and Justice

Crime and Justice
A Review of Research

Edited by Michael Tonry

VOLUME 14

The University of Chicago Press, Chicago and London

This volume was prepared under Grant Number 88-IJ-CX-0005 awarded to the Castine Research Corporation by the National Institute of Justice, U.S. Department of Justice, under the Omnibus Crime Control and Safe Streets Act of 1968 as amended. Points of view or opinions expressed in this volume are those of the editors or authors and do not necessarily represent the official position or policies of the U.S. Department of Justice.

The University of Chicago Press, Chicago 60637
The University of Chicago Press, Ltd., London

Printed in the United States of America

95 94 93 92 91 5 4 3 2 1

ISSN: 0192-3234

ISBN 0-226-80812-2

LCN: 80-642217

The paper used in this publication meets the minimum requirements of American National Standard for Information Sciences—Permanence of Paper for Printed Library Materials, ANSI Z39.48-1984. ♾

Contents

Preface

This is the first volume of *Crime and Justice* in which Norval Morris's name appears neither on the cover nor the title page. After serving as coeditor of the series for thirteen volumes, Norval has become chairman of the editorial board—a not unhappy improvement of condition inasmuch as it involves much less work but no less influence.

By the time this volume appears, fourteen years will have passed since a first organizational meeting for *Crime and Justice* was held in Reston, Virginia, at the initiative of Blair Ewing, then acting director of the National Institute of Justice, and Paul Cascarano, the institute's then-as-now assistant director. The establishing intent then, like the operating intent now, was a series of volumes of commissioned essays of high quality, written by writers from a multitude of disciplines, rigorously vetted by knowledgeable reviewers, and extensively revised for final publication.

Norval Morris undertook to give direction to *Crime and Justice* and for fourteen years has been setting its course and struggling to see that its ambitions are always attempted, if not always realized. It is with more than minor misgivings that I take on the editorial direction of *Crime and Justice* by myself.

This volume signals a major transition in the development of *Crime and Justice*, and it may not be inappropriate to step back and reflect a bit on the past. As we have acknowledged in every preface to every volume, *Crime and Justice* is supported by the National Institute of Justice. Each volume represents a separate grant; the series' assured future never extends further than the expiration date of the then-current funding. We have been remarkably fortunate in the continuing support of a series of directors and acting directors of the National Institute of Justice. In retrospect it is little short of astonishing that changes in policies, politics, and personalities at the National Institute of Justice and the U.S. Department of Justice did not long ago cut the string of grants that funded our efforts. We have been, and remain, grateful to NIJ directors and acting directors Blair Ewing, Harry Bratt, James Underwood, Bob Burkhart, and James K. Stewart and to Paul Cascarano, who was present at the creation and has remained to this day an enthusiastic supporter. Over the years numerous NIJ staffers have lent help, encouragement, critical reading, and succor. We are grateful to them all and particularly to Mary Graham, who has been our primary link to the National Institute of Justice for many years.

Passing of batons and changing of guards too easily become lugubrious affairs, and it may be appropriate to shift to more cheerful topics.

This is a volume of *Crime and Justice* of which we are particularly proud. Two of the essays, by Geoffrey Pearson and Ed Leuw, offer informed, comprehensive depictions of drug abuse policies in the United Kingdom and the Netherlands. These are the two countries to which reference is most often made when insights are sought concerning the drug policies of other nations. Both essays have been widely distributed privately and seem to fill a need for authoritative, balanced accounts of the experience in their respective countries.

Overviews of current knowledge of the incidence, prevalence, patterns, and prevention of burglary; of the psychology of violent robbers; of the roles of weapons in violent crime; and of the scope, operation, and effects of victim programs in the United States and elsewhere are all specimens of *Crime and Justice*'s staple—the informed state-of-the-art review. Essays by Lucia Zedner and David Garland offer, respectively, an overview of the history and historiography of attitudes and practices concerning the criminal justice system's handling of women offenders in the nineteenth century and a thoughtful synthesis of writing by social theorists on the functions and character of criminal punishment in modern society.

This is a volume that is representative of the values and standards that Norval Morris set for the series—to his vision in setting them, this volume is dedicated.

M. T.

Philip J. Cook

The Technology of Personal Violence

ABSTRACT

Over 30,000 deaths each year result from gunshot wounds. Two decades of systematic research on weapons and personal violence indicate a pervasive influence of weapon type on the patterns and outcomes of violent encounters. The likelihood that an assault will result in death depends (among other things) on the lethality of the weapon. The evidence that weapon lethality affects the likelihood of death in suicide is somewhat weaker. Assailants' weapon choice depends on a number of factors, including the relative vulnerability of the intended victim and the general availability of firearms. National Crime Survey data indicate that guns are used only about 80,000 times each year in self-defense.

The core issues for researchers concerned with the technology of personal violence were identified two decades ago in *Firearms and Violence in American Life* (Newton and Zimring 1969), a report of the National Commission on the Causes and Prevention of Violence. The first issue is to establish the causal importance of weapon type in influencing the volume, patterns, and lethality of personal violence. The second is to measure the effects of gun availability on the propensity to use guns in crime and suicide, where "availability" refers both to the prevalence of gun ownership and to the legal regulations governing transfer and use. The third core issue is to analyze how the threat of criminal victimiza-

Philip J. Cook is professor of public policy and economics, Duke University. Michael Rand of the Bureau of Justice Statistics provided unpublished data. Arthur Kellermann, Gary Kleck, Jacqueline Cohen, Albert J. Reiss, Jr., and Jeffrey Roth offered extensive and very useful comments on an earlier draft. Duke University's Fuqua School of Business provided an office and secretarial support.

0192-3234/91/0014-0003$01.00

tion influences the use of guns in self-defense, and to what effect. These were the central concerns of Newton and Zimring's seminal report, and they remain central today.

Obviously, these concerns are motivated by the ongoing debate over the proper regulation of guns. This policy context not only sets the agenda; it also tends to politicize scholarly interpretation and criticism of the results. In this context, it is too easy to lose sight of the fact that, at least in principle, research can be evaluated on the basis of its scientific merits independent of whether it seems more supportive of the "pro" or "anti" position on gun control. Furthermore, some of these issues are relevant to a basic scientific understanding of violence. This review aspires to apply the norms of science in evaluating research methods and results while taking note of the policy context.

There has been a shift in the emphasis of weapons research in the two decades since publication of *Firearms and Violence in American Life.* During the 1970s, the primary focus was on the criminal misuse of guns (Cook 1982; Wright, Rossi, and Daly 1983). But during the 1980s, the focus has broadened to include much greater attention to suicide and gun accidents. This shift is the result of the involvement of the public health research community as one aspect of its emerging concern with traumatic injury as a public health problem. Milestones in this new effort are the publication of *Injury in America: A Continuing Public Health Problem* by the Committee on Trauma Research of the National Research Council(1985) and the subsequent creation of a research program on intentional injury by the Centers for Disease Control (Mercy and Houk 1988).

The involvement of the public health community has a number of virtues besides generating increased scholarly attention to suicides and accidents. It also brings a new capacity to improve data collection on gunshot wounds and consideration of a variety of policy instruments for responding to this problem: improving emergency medical response to gunshot cases, encouraging physicians to advise their patients on how to prevent gun injuries in the home, and developing regulations on the design of guns to reduce accidental shootings. But even with the broader objectives dictated by the public health framework, the most important capacities for reducing gun violence continue to reside in the criminal justice system and government apparatus for regulating gun transfer, possession, and use.

My objective here is not to review the literature as much as to review and supplement current knowledge concerning weapons and violence.[1] While there are a few international comparisons offered, the bulk of the essay is limited to research using data from the United States. Section I charts trends in personal violence during the last two decades; since the early 1970s, there has not been much variation in death rates from homicide and suicide although there are interesting trends in the use of guns in personal violence during this period and a remarkable surge in homicide among black youths since 1984. Section II assesses the evidence on "instrumentality," concluding that the deadliness of the weapon used in a robbery or assault has an important effect on whether the victim lives or dies. The type of weapon also influences the likelihood that a robbery or assault will be "successful." Section III explores one logical implication of these findings, namely, that criminals who are equipped with a gun will be empowered to commit robberies or assaults on people who could defend themselves against attacks with less potent weapons; a gun is indeed the "great equalizer." The likelihood that a gun will be used is closely related to its relative value given the vulnerability of the victim. Section IV then considers how the general availability of guns influences their use in personal violence. There is considerable geographic variation in the prevalence of gun ownership, and the prevalence of gun ownership is highly correlated with the fractions of homicides, robberies, and suicides committed with a gun. Evidence is sketchy on whether regulations governing the possession, transfer, and use of guns have any additional effect. Section V reviews the evidence on the demand for and usefulness of guns in self-defense against crime and reports new results on the relative frequency with which guns are used in defense against burglars. The final section outlines a research agenda that identifies projects that appear feasible (given sufficient funding) and important from a policy perspective.

Virtually every issue discussed in this essay has been debated by partisans in the "great American gun war," and almost any conclusions concerning the scientific evidence would be controversial. Nonetheless, a number of policy-relevant conclusions are offered in this essay, albeit with what I hope is an appropriate degree of scholarly caution. These conclusions are briefly summarized in the next few paragraphs.

[1] This essay is an update and extension of Cook (1983*a*). The earlier review includes a discussion of the market for guns, a topic that is not included here, but this essay includes several new topics, most important, suicide and self-defense.

One familiar bumper sticker asserts, "Guns don't kill people: people kill people," meaning, perhaps, that it is the intent of the assailant rather than the type of weapon he uses that determines whether the victim lives or dies. But there is persuasive evidence that both intent and weapon matter. A policy that was successful in inducing a substitution of knives for guns in acts of interpersonal violence would save lives. It may be true that a resourceful person can always find a way to kill someone if he is determined to do so. But many homicides are not the result of a sustained, deliberate intent to kill but rather are etiologically indistinguishable from a larger set of assaults and robberies in which the victim does not die. The lethality of the weapon is a major independent determinant of the lethality of the attack. The importance of the weapon in this respect is perhaps the best-established finding relevant to the gun-control debate.

Another familiar bumper sticker reads, "When guns are outlawed, only outlaws will have guns." If this is not a tautology, then it expresses the belief that the violent criminals will always find a way to obtain guns, regardless of legal efforts to restrict availability. Undoubtedly, laws restricting gun possession, transfer, and carrying are difficult to enforce in the American context in which there are about 150 million firearms in private hands. However, it is notable that the tendency to use guns in crime differs widely among cities and is highly correlated with the local prevalence of gun ownership. A similar pattern holds in international comparisons. It is interesting that the prevalence of gun ownership does not appear to have much effect on the overall robbery rate; guns are simply substituted for other weapons when they are readily available. The consequence is not more robberies, but rather a higher death rate in those robberies that do occur. There is some evidence that assault is similar to robbery with respect to the effect of these weapons.

Are guns useful in self-defense? The answer is surely yes. Based on the best available evidence, the National Crime Survey (NCS), it appears that there are about 80,000 instances each year in which people attempt to defend themselves with guns against assault, robbery, rape, or burglary, and in most such cases they are successful. Unfortunately, guns are used far more often to perpetrate violent crimes—over 800,000 per year—than to defend against them. And guns acquired for self defense often end up being used to shoot family members, either accidentally or intentionally. One survey found that as many handgun owners reported being involved in a gun accident as reported using the gun in self-defense. In considering the social costs and benefits of the widespread ownership of firearms, the assertion that it produces a general deterrent effect on predatory crime is worth considering. But the evidence on this issue is inconclusive.

The rules of engagement over gun-control policy have been rewritten during the 1980s with the involvement of the public health community. The focus and perspective of public health officials on mortality and morbidity has the effect of reordering the implicit priorities in gun violence; in particular, suicide, which accounts for a majority of gunshot deaths each year, becomes much more important in a public health framework than in a criminal justice framework. And there is some evidence for "instrumentality" in suicide. The availability of deadly weapons that are acceptable in some sense to the suicidal person arguably plays an independent causal role in whether the person dies of self-inflicted injury. If suicide becomes a central focus of the debate over gun control, then much is changed. Those at greatest risk for suicide are the demographic mirror image of homicide victims (except with respect to sex), so that the "gun problem" becomes an affliction of the middle class and middle aged in this perspective. And there exist policies that arguably would make it more difficult for a suicidal person to obtain a gun but would be irrelevant to curtailing criminal violence: one such policy is counseling family members about keeping guns away from suicidal people.

The overarching conclusion from this essay is that the widespread involvement of firearms in personal violence is not just an incidental detail but, rather, has an important influence on the patterns and lethality of this violence.

I. Levels and Trends in Personal Violence

Over the last two decades, there has been little variation in death rates from intentional violence. Since 1970, the homicide rate per 100,000 has fluctuated within the range 8.1–10.6, while the suicide rate has varied between 11.6 and 13.3 per 100,000. The use of guns in homicide has declined in relative frequency since 1974, and increased in relative frequency for suicide, leaving the overall firearms fatality rate remarkably stable. Thus there seems to be little "news" in these trends. But no news in this case is bad news, at least in comparison with an earlier, more peaceful era.

The year President Kennedy was shot, the homicide rate was 4.6 per 100,000, about half the rate that has afflicted U.S. society during the

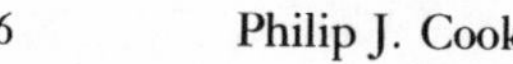

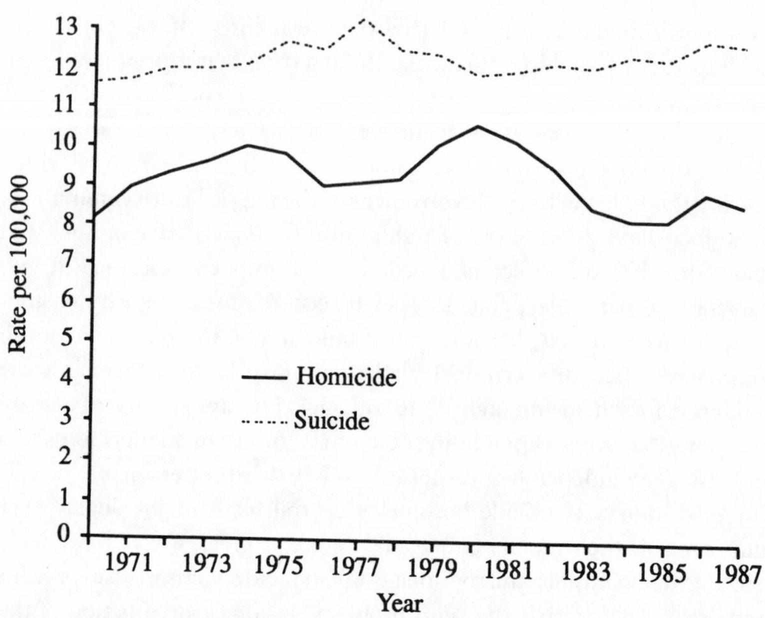

FIG. 1.—Trends in suicide and homicide rates, 1970–87. Sources: National Center for Health Statistics (1970–86, 1987).

1970s and 1980s. Indeed, this assassination came at an important turning point in the history of personal violence. Homicide rates began increasing rapidly in 1964. The data in figure 1 depict what has happened since 1970. There was a peak in 1980 at 10.6 deaths per 100,000, a subsequent reduction of 23 percent through 1985, and some increase since then.

Guns have been the leading instrument of death throughout this period, but they have declined in relative importance since 1974. In that year, 70 percent of homicides were committed with guns; by 1983, the gun fraction had declined to 60 percent, where it has remained since then (figure 2).

Suicide rates also increased during the 1960s, though less dramatically than for homicides. The postwar peak occurred in 1977, at 13.3 per 100,000, and after a small decline, the suicide rate has been gradually increasing since 1983 (figure 1). The relative importance of guns as instruments of suicide has increased during the same period that guns were of declining importance in homicide; between 1970 and 1981, the percentage of guns in contrast to other weapons or means increased 10

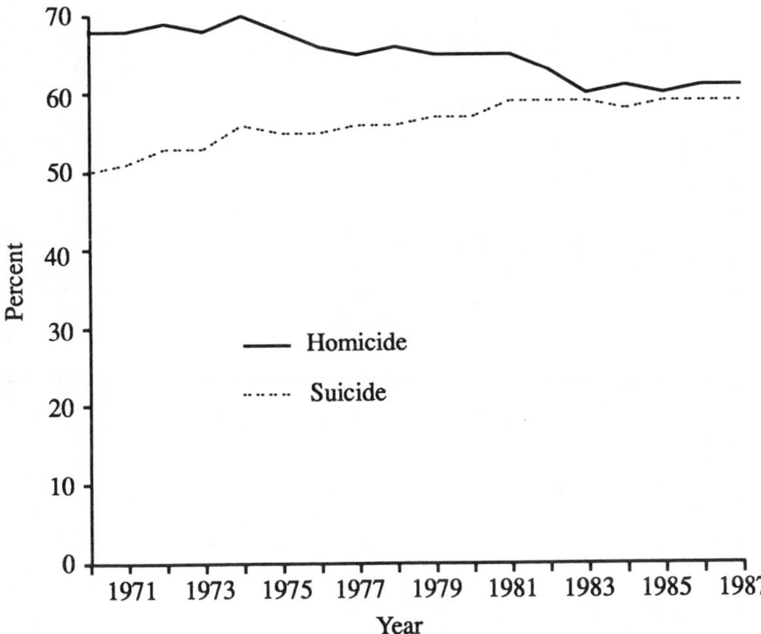

FIG. 2.—Trends in gun use in suicide and homicide, 1970–87. Sources: National Center for Health Statistics (1970–86, 1987).

percentage points to 59, where it has remained since then.[2] The opposite trends in the gun fractions for homicide and suicide, depicted in figure 2, pose an interesting conundrum. Whether weapon choice is a matter of availability or personal preference, there is no obvious reason why guns should be selected increasingly often by suicidal people and less often by assailants.

Figure 3 depicts the trends in firearm fatality rates from homicide, suicide, and accident.[3] The peak rate for gun fatalities was 15.3 per 100,000, in 1974. By way of comparison, the fatality rate due to motor vehicle accidents in 1974 was 21.0. It is also illuminating to compare

[2] Table 1 demonstrates a very similar temporal pattern of weapon choice for homicides and suicides involving youths age fifteen to twenty-four. The main exception is the upward surge in gun use in homicide after 1984, unique to this age group.

[3] The "total" rate exceeds the sum of gun accident, suicide, and homicide rates because each year there are several hundred gun fatalities for which there is insufficient information to allow assignment to one of these categories by the National Center for Health Statistics.

TABLE 1

Trends in Homicides, Suicides, and Gun Accidents, Rates per 100,000, among Victims Aged 15–24

	Rate of Homicide			Rate of Suicide				
Year	Total Deaths	No. of Gun Deaths	Gun Deaths/Total (Percent)	Total Deaths	No. of Gun Deaths	Gun Deaths/Total (Percent)	Rate of Gun Accidents	Rate of Total Gun Deaths*
1970	11.7	8.3	71	8.8	4.2	47	2.0	14.5
1971	12.7	8.9	70	9.4	4.7	50	2.1	15.7
1972	13.5	9.7	72	10.2	5.7	56	2.2	17.6
1973	13.4	9.5	71	10.6	5.9	55	2.2	17.6
1974	14.2	10.2	72	10.9	6.5	59	2.1	18.8
1975	13.7	9.6	70	11.8	6.9	58	1.9	18.4
1976	12.4	8.5	69	11.7	6.6	57	1.6	16.7
1977	12.7	8.6	68	13.6	8.1	60	1.6	18.4
1978	13.2	9.0	69	12.4	7.4	60	1.4	17.9
1979	14.9	10.0	67	12.7	7.8	61	1.6	19.4
1980	15.6	10.5	67	12.3	7.7	62	1.7	19.9
1981	14.7	10.2	68	12.3	7.7	63	1.5	19.2
1982	13.7	8.9	65	12.1	7.6	62	1.3	17.8
1983	12.4	7.8	63	11.9	7.3	62	1.3	16.5
1984	11.9	7.8	65	12.8	7.7	60	1.2	16.6
1985	12.2	7.9	65	12.7	7.5	59	1.3	16.8
1986	14.2	9.5	67	13.1	7.9	60	1.1	18.6
1987	14.0	9.8	70	12.9	7.7	59	1.1	18.5

SOURCE.—National Center for Health Statistics (1970-86 from published sources, 1987 by telephone).

* Includes International Classification of Disease (ICD) codes E922 (accident with gun), E955 (gun suicide), E965 (gun homicide), and E985 (gun death, uncertain whether accidental or intentional). Deaths by legal intervention are excluded.

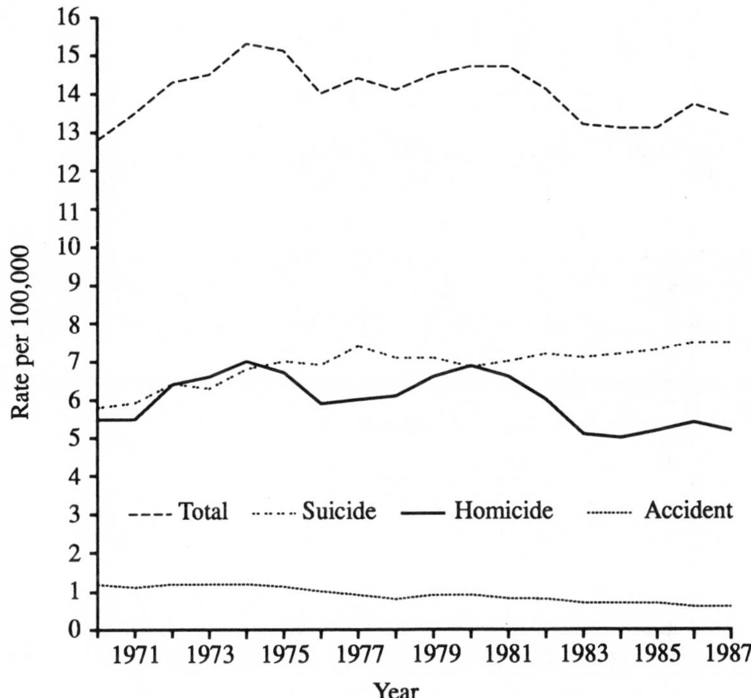

FIG. 3.—Trends in gun fatality rates, 1970–87. Sources: National Center for Health Statistics (1970–86, 1987).

the gun fatality rates with wartime fatalities. The gun death counts from suicide, homicide, and accident have totaled over 30,000 for every year since 1972. In terms of Americans killed, a year of gun misuse in the United States is the equivalent of the Korean War; a year and one-half yields a Vietnam, while nine years adds up to World War II.

Special interest focuses on the youthful victims of homicides and suicides (figure 4). The age group fifteen to twenty-four has been the object of particular attention by demographers because in recent decades this group has experienced exceptionally high rates of death due to trauma, which has prevented them from sharing in the general decline in mortality rates (see table 1). Homicide rates for this age group have been 40–50 percent higher than the population average, with a still wider gap (to over 60 percent) emerging in 1986 and 1987. The suicide rate for youths was lower than the population average until 1977 and has been about at the average since then; this is noteworthy since generally the suicide rate increases with age.

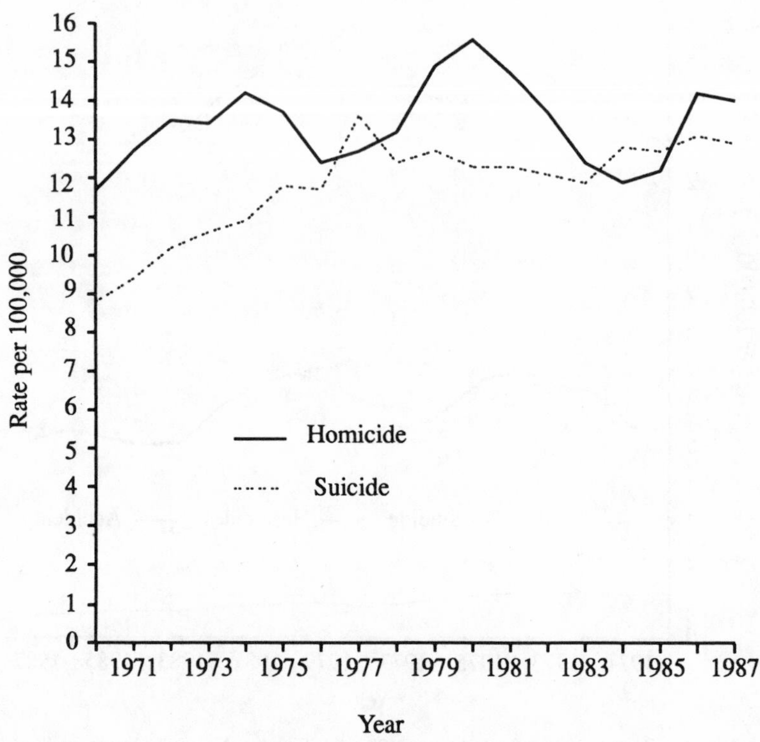

FIG. 4.—Trends in suicide and homicide rates, population age 15–24, 1970–87. Sources: National Center for Health Statistics (1970–86, 1987).

The fractions of youthful homicides and suicides involving guns have been close to the corresponding fractions for the population as a whole for most of the last two decades. But since 1984, there has been a sharp increase in the fraction of youth homicides involving guns at the same time that the overall youth homicide rate has been increasing. A closer look at these recent events indicates a divergence between blacks and whites: between 1984 and 1987, the number of black victims age fifteen to twenty-four increased 36 percent, while the number of white victims declined by 5 percent (figure 5). (This disparity widened still further in 1988.) An obvious hypothesis is that the vast increases in homicide rates for black youths, coupled with an increase in the fraction of these homicides involving guns, is a reflection of the increasing rates of violence related to the illicit drug trade during this period.[4]

[4] Recent trends in Washington, D.C., help document the lethal effects of the drug trade. According to the District of Columbia's Office of Criminal Justice Plans and

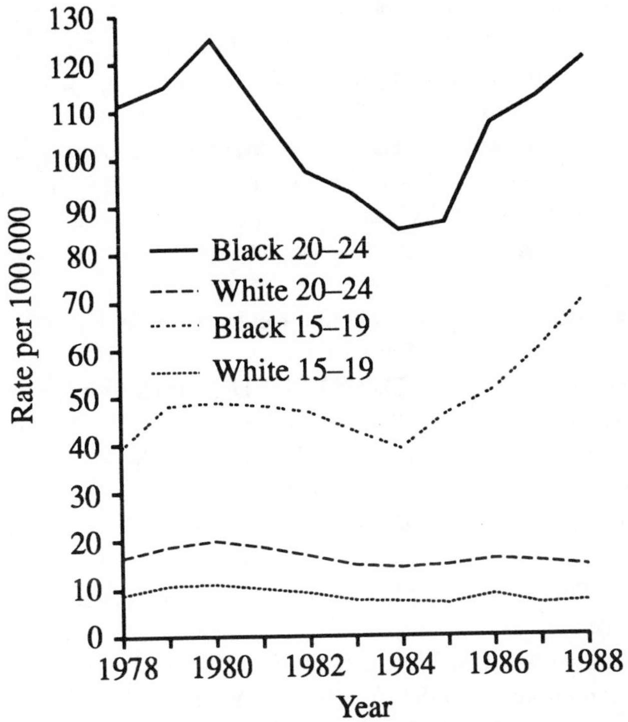

FIG. 5.—Trends in youthful male homicide rates by race, 1978–88. Sources: National Center for Health Statistics (1970–86, 1987); FBI (1989). The 1988 estimate presumes that the percentage increases in homicide rates for males in the specified age/race groups were equal to the percentage increases in the homicide rates for all people in the age/race groups.

For every person who is killed in a homicide, a suicide, or an accident there are several more who sustain a nonfatal injury. The number of such injuries is not tabulated or even estimated in any systematic fashion and must be guesstimated from rather sketchy evidence. The ap-

---

Analysis (1989), the number of homicide victims age eighteen to twenty-five increased from thirty-five in 1985 to sixty-five in 1987 and an annualized total of 110 during the first half of 1988. Most were black males. (While gender and race are not tabulated by age in the report, about three-quarters of all homicide victims in the District of Columbia were black males during this period. Indeed, there were only three white males killed during the first half of 1988 in the District of Columbia.) The Metropolitan Police Department classified most homicides by motive: the fraction classified as drug-related increased from 21 percent to 80 percent between 1985 and 1988. The homicide rate for black males age twenty to twenty-four was as high in 1980 as in 1988. But the earlier peak was coincident with a peak in the overall homicide rate, whereas the more recent pattern for young black males is unique to them.

proach used here is to multiply death counts (for 1987) by an estimate of the ratios of nonfatal injuries to deaths for each category. The estimates presented here are for gunshot wounds only (figure 6).

For assault, Cook (1985*a*) estimated a death rate of about 15 percent for gun assaults in which the victim was wounded; the data were special compilations from four law-enforcement agencies, with very similar results from each source. A death rate of 15 percent implies 5.7 nonfatal gunshot woundings for each fatality, or about 73,000 such cases in 1987.

The available data on suicide and accidents are much more sparse and unreliable. For lack of other sources, I requested and received a special tabulation from the Dallas Police Department some years ago, for the period November 1981–November 1982; the death rates in that sample were 76 percent for gun suicide attempts (N = 144), and just 2.6 percent for gun accidents (N = 152). If these rates are assumed valid for the nation as a whole in 1987, they imply 5,700 nonfatal injuries due to suicide attempts with a gun, and 60,800 nonfatal gun accidents. This last number has the greatest degree of uncertainty associated with it.

Combining assault, suicide, and accident, the total count of nonfatal gunshot woundings in 1987 is 139,000. This result is in line with an estimate generated by the Health Interview Survey (HIS) for 1971–72, of 155,000 nonfatal gunshot injuries for a twelve-month period (National Center for Health Statistics 1976). My approach yields an estimate of 163,000 injuries for 1971, which is well within the sampling error range of the HIS estimate. Wright, Rossi, and Daly (1983, p. 170) offer an estimate of 183,000 injuries in 1975, which is roughly consistent with mine when proper account is taken of changes in gun killings between 1975 and 1987.

If these estimates are in the right ball park, they suggest that nonfatal gunshot injuries outnumber fatal ones by a factor of four or five. Further, the relative importance of assaults, suicide attempts, and accidents is quite different in the case of nonfatal injuries than in the case of deaths; in particular, gun accidents form a much higher percentage of gunshot injuries than of deaths.

II. Instrumentality

Only a fraction of those who are shot, stabbed, cut, or bludgeoned in criminal assaults die of their wounds. That fraction is much higher for gunshot wounds than for wounds inflicted with other common

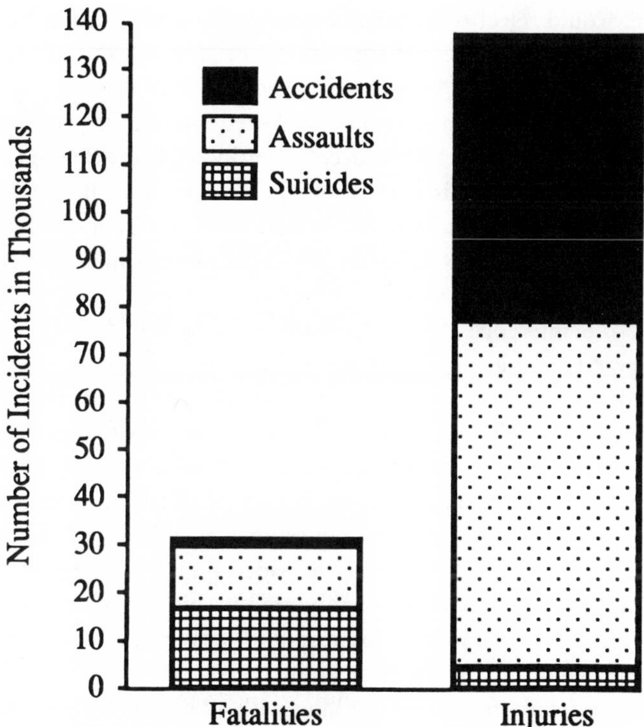

FIG. 6.—Fatalities and injuries from gunshot wounds, 1987. Source: National Center for Health Statistics (1987).

weapons. One interpretation of this weapon-specific difference in case fatality rates comes from Zimring (1968, 1972), who suggested that the death or survival of the victim of personal violence is largely a matter of chance, and that that chance depends in part on the lethality of the weapon used to inflict injury. This "weapon instrumentality effect," which ascribes causal importance to the type of weapon, is a fundamental tenet of gun-control advocates, and is, hence, one of the key points of debate in both the politics and the social science of this issue.

There is no question that case fatality rates for assaults, robberies, and other violent encounters are much higher when the assailant uses a gun than a knife, club, or bare hands; the controversy has focused on the interpretation of this finding. Marvin Wolfgang (1958, p. 83) states in his seminal study of homicide in Philadelphia that "it is the contention of this observer that few homicides due to shooting could be avoided merely if a firearm were not immediately present, and that the offender would select some other weapon to achieve the same destructive goal." Wolfgang believed that the choice of weapon by an assailant was an indication of his lethal intent, and that the relatively high case fatality rates for gun assaults simply reflected the relative prevalence of would-be killers among the gun users. Zimring's quite different conclusion was supported by his analysis of gun and knife assaults in Chicago; he found that gun assaults in his sample were five times as likely to result in death as knife assaults, despite the apparent similarity between gun and knife assaults in other observable respects. "These figures support the inference that if knives were substituted for guns, the homicide rate would drop significantly" (Zimring 1968, p. 728).

The debate over the weapon instrumentality effect can be clarified by a thought experiment. Imagine that it was possible to intervene just before the first blow was struck in a violent encounter, replacing the assailant's weapon with another that is less lethal, and then observe the outcome. In particular, Zimring's question was whether the death rate would be reduced in cases where a loaded gun was replaced with a knife. His affirmative answer is supported by his argument that many gun homicides are committed by people who have no clear intention to kill. If the assailant's intent were ambiguous or unsustained, then the fatality rate would fall because killing with a knife ordinarily requires greater strength and more sustained effort than killing with a gun. Indeed, despite his conclusion quoted above, Wolfgang suggested one mechanism for this possibility: "The offender's physical repugnance to engaging in direct physical assault by cutting or stabbing his adversary, may mean that in the absence of a firearm no homicide occurs" (Wolfgang 1958, p. 79). In other cases the assailant may cease the attack after inflicting a wound or two, simply because the violent urge that prompted the attack is satisfied. Rarely does the assailant administer the coup de grace that would ensure the victim's death. In Zimring's gun sample, only 16 percent of nonfatal cases and 19 percent of fatal cases involved more than one gunshot wound (1968, p. 737).

Wright, Rossi, and Daly (1983) provide the most prominent critique of Zimring's work on instrumentality. They focus on Zimring's conclusion that a large fraction of killers attack their victims with no clear intention of killing them and, in that respect, are similar to other assailants whose victims survive. Wright, Rossi, and Daly agree that *some* killers lack clear homicidal intent but do not accept Zimring's evidence as establishing that ambiguous intent characterizes a *large percentage* of homicidal attacks (Wright, Rossi, and Daly 1983, p. 192) and is hence so prevalent as to account for the large observed differences in weapon-specific case fatality rates.

The evidence in question is of three sorts. First, Zimring (1968) notes that homicides in Chicago in 1967 typically involved relatives or acquaintances caught up in altercations in which the assailant or victim had been drinking—circumstances that he asserts tend to be associated with ambiguous intent (p. 722). Second, he demonstrates that homicide cases are similar to serious assault cases with respect to the demographic characteristics of killers and victims, with greatly disproportionate involvement of males and blacks (p. 724). In that respect, then, fatal and nonfatal cases are similar, suggesting (says Zimring) that they may also be similar with respect to the assailants' state of mind. Third, he reports the results of a detailed study of the wounds inflicted in gun and knife attacks, concluding that despite the lower death rate in knife attacks, a greater percentage of knife than gun attacks appear to be "in earnest," based on the location and number of wounds inflicted (pp. 730–35). Zimring (1968) analyzed Chicago Police Department assault records for the period November 9–December 6, 1967. During this period there were 366 serious knife attacks, of which eight were fatal, and 247 serious gun attacks, of which thirty-four were fatal. He analyzed the number and location of wounds resulting from each of these attacks as a basis for judging the seriousness and intent of the assailant.

Wright, Rossi, and Daly's response to this evidence is that it is insufficient to offer persuasive support for Zimring's conclusion regarding ambiguous intent. However, Wright, Rossi, and Daly are impressed by Zimring's data on the seriousness of many nonfatal knife attacks, concluding that this evidence "does at least suggest that a substantial portion of knife attacks are indeed 'in earnest,' and this constitutes the strongest evidence yet encountered that the motives of gun and knife attackers may be similar" (Wright, Rossi, and Daly 1983, p. 200). The implication is that if these "earnest" knife attackers had used guns, a higher percentage of victims would have died; that is, Wright, Rossi, and Daly appear to accept the validity and importance of the weapon instrumentality effect while remaining unconvinced that Zimring's explanation for this effect (ambiguous intent) is correct.

Zimring buttressed the conclusions from his first study, which compared knife and gun attacks, with a later (1972) study comparing attacks with large- and small-caliber guns. The basic data for the caliber comparison came from an analysis of fatal and nonfatal firearm attacks reported to the Chicago Police between March 5 and July 22, 1970. In all, 1,115 gun attacks resulting in 156 fatalities were reported. For the purpose of comparing death rates by caliber, Zimring excluded from this sample all robberies and also all attacks with shotguns and large-caliber rifles and also excluded a number of cases (most of which were not fatal) in which the caliber of the gun was not known to police. The actual number of cases available for detailed study is not clear from Zimring's report.

He found that the fatality rate increased with caliber, as predicted by the weapon instrumentality effect. The alternative explanation takes the same form as in the case of guns versus knives: that assailants who use larger-caliber weapons tend to have more deadly intent, and that the fatality rate differential between large- and small-caliber guns reflects this difference in intent rather than the lethality of the weapon. This alternative explanation receives some support from the fact that shooters using a .38 or higher-caliber weapon were more likely to inflict multiple wounds than those using a .22-caliber weapon (26 percent vs. 11 percent) (Zimring 1972, p. 104). But the caliber-related differences in the death rate are large even when the number and location of wounds are controlled for. In any event, Wright, Rossi, and Daly (1983), despite their generally critical review of Zimring's work, are convinced by it that weapon lethality does have an independent causal effect on the probability of death: "One apparently certain implication of Zimring's result is that the substitution of higher-caliber for lower-caliber handguns would almost certainly cause the rate of handgun deaths to increase" (Wright, Rossi, and Daly 1983, p. 203).

While Zimring's work focused on weapon-specific case fatality rates for assaults, it is also of interest to observe how the weapon instrumentality effect fares in the context of other violent felonies. Homicides committed during the commission of a felony such as robbery, rape, or burglary account for about 20 percent of all criminal homicides, of which half are robberies (Cook 1985*b*). My studies of robbery violence offer support for the instrumentality effect in that context (Cook 1979, 1980*a*, 1987). Robbery is generally defined as theft or attempted theft by force or the threat of violence, including muggings and holdups. The overall robbery fatality rate is about one in 750 (Cook 1987), much lower than for serious assaults (where the rate is roughly one in 100).[5]

[5] The estimated number of aggravated assaults in 1987, based on the National Crime Survey, is 1.5 million (Bureau of Justice Statistics 1989*a*). There were about 20,000

But as in the case of assault, robbery fatality rates differ widely, depending on the type of weapon used. The fatality rate is four per thousand for gun robberies, which is about three times higher than for knife robberies and ten times higher than for robberies involving other weapons. Demonstrating that all or part of this difference in weapon-specific fatality rates is due to the weapon itself requires a statistical method for controlling for other factors that influence the probability that a robbery will result in the death of a victim.

One approach that I developed for testing weapon instrumentality in robbery was quite different from Zimring's. I reasoned that if the type of weapon had an independent causal effect on the probability of death, then a city's robbery murder rate should be more sensitive to variations in its gun robbery rate than to its nongun robbery rate. This prediction was confirmed in my study of changes in robbery and robbery murder in forty-three cities for the period 1976–83 (Cook 1987, p. 373). On the average, an additional 1,000 gun robberies produced an additional 4.8 murders, whereas an additional 1,000 nongun robberies added only 1.4 additional murders. These results are estimates of regression coefficients, where the dependent variable is the change in the robbery murder rate between two four-year periods (1976–79 and 1980–83), and the independent variables are the corresponding changes in the nongun robbery rate and the gun robbery rate. The purpose of studying intertemporal changes rather than working with a simple cross-sectional analysis is to obviate the need to develop a statistical explanation for the large permanent differences among cities with respect to robbery rates and gun usage in robbery. It is certainly possible that one or more of these differences among cities might affect both robbery rates and the robbery murder rate, thus creating a spurious association between the two. While in principle these "third cause" variables could be controlled for in a multiple regression format, in practice the correct choice of a specification for the regression is not obvious and adds a great deal of uncertainty to the estimates.

Of course, using change data does not eliminate the possibility that there is some third cause operating on both the changes in robbery rates and the changes in robbery murder rates. It is conceivable that the violent criminals in some cities became more vicious from one period to

criminal homicides in that year, of which about 20 percent were in felony circumstances (Federal Bureau of Investigation 1988). The remaining homicides would have been classified as aggravated assaults if the victims had survived.

the next and for that reason were more likely to use guns in robbery and to kill their robbery victims. One crude check on this possibility is to control for changes in the city's homicide rate (other than robbery murders), since viciousness would presumably spill over into other encounters if it were a general phenomenon. In any event, when I included a homicide change variable in the regression specification, it was statistically insignificant and had essentially no effect on other coefficient estimates. So I am quite confident in my causal interpretation of the results: that robbery murder is a direct, though fairly rare, result of robbery, that a change in the robbery rate will (other things equal) cause a corresponding change in the robbery murder rate, and that an increase in gun robberies has a larger effect on robbery murder than a similar increase in nongun robberies. It appears that, at this level of aggregation, murder can be viewed as a byproduct of robbery, the likelihood of which depends to an important degree on the type of weapon.

In sum, the weapons-specific differences in fatality rates in assault as well as for robbery have been clearly established; more lethal weapons are associated with higher fatality rates. Further, there is persuasive evidence that these differences in fatality rates are, in large part, the direct consequence of the differential lethality of the weapons, rather than simply a statistical artifact of some other causal process (such as differences in intent that influence both weapon choice and outcome). However, the various mechanisms that are responsible for the instrumentality effect have not been completely analyzed or documented.

The mechanism suggested by Zimring is that in a large percentage of violent attacks the assailant's intent is ambiguous. His data and those of others make clear that for every killing there are several other nonfatal attacks for which there was a real chance that the assailant's actions would cause death; for example, for everyone in his (1972) sample who died from a single gunshot wound in the chest, there were 1.8 others who suffered a single gunshot wound in the chest and survived. Surely the element of chance is important here, and in an unsustained attack, the lethality of the first blow will be a major determinant of the chance of death. But there are other mechanisms that may also be important in instrumentality.

In the mechanism suggested by Zimring, the key attribute of a gun is that it can kill without sustained effort; relatively small amounts of energy and time are sufficient. But another quality of firearms may also be relevant; it empowers someone to attack a stronger victim and kill him or her, which may be physically impossible with a less powerful weapon. Surely the power of a gun to overcome or forestall resistance helps explain why all successful presidential assassinations and over 90 percent of murders of police officers have been committed with a gun (Federal Bureau of Investigation 1979). Various other patterns of weapon use, discussed in Section III below, offer further support for the "power" explanation of instrumentality.

Whatever the mix of mechanisms that account for it, the instrumentality effect is not a complete explanation for observed weapons-specific differences in fatality rates. The death rate for assault may vary for reasons unrelated to weapon choice. For example, Swersey (1980) documented a large increase in the homicide rate in Harlem between 1968 and 1973 which was accompanied by a more than doubling of the fraction of gun attacks resulting in death; Swersey concluded that much of the change was due to an increase in intentional killings resulting from disputes involving narcotics activities. But the type of weapon, while not the sole determinant of the probability that a violent encounter will result in death, is one of the important determinants of this probability.

A. *Other Instrumentality Effects*

The effect of weapon type on the likelihood of death in a violent encounter is of paramount concern, but it is by no means the only weapon instrumentality effect. The type of weapon also influences the likelihood and severity of injury and the likelihood that the assailant will succeed in whatever purpose motivated the attack. As noted by Kleck and McElrath (1989), "The ultimate goal behind an act of violence is not necessarily the victim's death or injury, but rather may be money, sexual gratification, respect, attention, or the humiliation and domination of the victim." Their analysis of National Crime Survey data on assaults by strangers found that half of these cases were mere threats without any attack; in only about half of those cases where the assailant did attack was the victim injured. The type of weapon affects the likelihood of physical attack and injury in an assault, as well as the likelihood of "success."

Most of the previous research on this issue has focused on robbery. The principal role of a weapon in robbery is to aid the robber in coercing the victim (by force or threat) to part with his valuables. If the threat is sufficiently convincing, physical force is not necessary. For this reason, it is hardly surprising that the use of force is closely related to the weapon type in robbery, being very common in unarmed robbery and relatively rare in gun robbery. Using National Crime Panel data for twenty-six cities, I found that the likelihood of physical attack in a noncommercial robbery committed by one or more adult males differed with the type of weapon used as follows: gun, 22.1 percent; knife, 39.4 percent; other weapon, 60.4 percent; and strong-arm, 73.5 percent (Cook 1980*a*). As an immediate consequence, the likelihood of injury is less in a gun robbery than for robberies with other weapons (Conklin 1972; Cook 1976; Skogan 1978); indeed, the pattern of injury across the four weapon categories is exactly the reverse of the pattern of fatality rates. But if we confine our attention to injuries serious enough to require hospitalization, then this pattern largely disappears; when other factors are held constant (via a multivariate statistical analysis) gun and knife robberies are about equally likely to result in serious injury.[6] Thus more lethal weapons are less likely to be used to inflict injury, but when they are, the injury tends to be more serious. That is why the likelihood of death is much higher in gun robberies than in knife robberies, as noted above.

Kleck and McElrath (1989) report a similar analysis for assaults by strangers reported to the National Crime Survey during the years 1979–85. They found that the presence of a gun or knife reduces the likelihood that there will be any sort of physical attack during the assault; if there are lethal weapons present, it is more likely that the assault will terminate with a threat. Given that there is an attack during the assault by a stranger, it is less likely that the victim will sustain injury if the attack is perpetrated with a gun than with a knife, presumably because attack with a gun includes the possibility of shooting at but missing the victim, a possibility that has no analog for other types of weapons. If there is an injury, the probability that it will result in the death of the victim is much higher in the case of gunshot wounds than knife wounds.[7]

The inverse relation between weapon lethality and use of force is compatible with the notion that violence plays a tactical role in rob-

[6] "Serious injury" is defined here as "hospitalized overnight" (Cook 1987, p. 361). Robberies committed with clubs and other weapons (besides guns and knives) have the highest probability of serious injury.

[7] The authors were able to estimate "likelihood of death" equations by merging NCS data on nonfatal assaults with supplementary homicide report data. Kleck and McElrath (1989) do not replicate for assaults the analysis of robbery data reported in Cook (1986); that is, they do not estimate the effect of weapon type on the probability that the victim will sustain a serious injury given that there was an assault.

bery—that it is employed when the robber believes it is needed to overcome or forestall victim resistance, and that this need is less likely to arise when the robber uses a gun. (See Cook [1980*a*] for a complete discussion of this issue. Not all violence in robbery is tactical.) Thus, the type of weapon is an important determinant of the nature of the interaction between robber and victim.

The type of weapon is also important in determining whether a robbery is completed successfully. The powerful threat produced by the display of a gun generally ensures compliance. According to National Crime Survey data for 1987, success rates in noncommercial robbery ranged from 70 percent for gun cases down to 55 percent for knife robberies and 49 percent for robberies with clubs and other weapons (Bureau of Justice Statistics 1989*a*, p. 64). Furthermore, the value of items taken in completed robberies is over twice as high in gun robberies as for other armed robberies (Cook 1976).

B. Handgun versus Long Gun

Comparisons of fatality and injury rates across different categories of weapons conceal the potentially important diversity within each category. The "knife" category includes everything from scissors and penknives to large hunting knives, while "gun" incorporates homemade "zip" guns, assault rifles, and everything in between. Laws regulating the transfer and use of firearms incorporate certain distinctions among different types of firearm. For example, current federal law bans the transfer of automatic rifles and sawed-off shotguns and bans the importation of small cheap handguns commonly known as "Saturday Night Specials." State laws tend to regulate handguns more stringently than long guns (Cook and Blose 1981). If these legal distinctions affect the mix of guns used in assault and robbery, then they may thereby influence the fatality rate in these crimes.

Zimring's (1972) most persuasive demonstration of the instrumentality effect in assault used the finding that wounds made by larger-caliber bullets are more likely to result in death than were otherwise comparable wounds made by smaller-caliber bullets. Other characteristics of a bullet are also important in determining the lethality of a wound, including its shape and velocity. In particular, while tissue damage inflicted by a low-velocity bullet is primarily limited to the track of the bullet through the body, high-velocity bullets injure tissue distant from the bullet track, because of the large temporary cavity formed by the shock wave (Fackler 1988; Hollerman 1988).

Rifles are more deadly than handguns in part because of the difference in the velocity of the bullet. For example, a .22-caliber bullet fired from a rifle will travel at a muzzle velocity of about 1,700 feet per second, compared with a velocity of 950 feet per second for a bullet from the same cartridge fired from a handgun (Hollerman 1988, p. 238). The difference in velocity is the direct result of the difference in barrel length; a longer barrel provides a longer time for the force of the gunpowder explosion to accelerate the bullet. A corollary is that bullets fired from snub-nosed handguns have lower muzzle velocity than bullets fired from handguns with standard barrels.

Shotguns add a new dimension to the analysis of the intrinsic lethality of firearms since a single shotshell contains a number of projectiles. According to one expert, shotgun wounds are most commonly caused by a one-ounce load of no. 6 birdshot containing 225 pellets, fired from a twelve-gauge shotgun (Hollerman 1988, p. 241). The spread of the shot pattern and the trauma inflicted by multiple wounds enhance the case fatality rate for shotgun wounds.

Given a choice, one would prefer being shot at by someone using a handgun than a rifle or shotgun. This conclusion follows both from the wound ballistics information summarized above and because long guns are more accurate and easier to aim than handguns. A number of authors have considered the possible implications for the regulation of guns (Benenson and Kates 1979; Wright, Rossi, and Daly 1983; Kleck 1984*a*), concluding that a policy that regulates handguns more stringently than long guns may have the perverse effect of increasing the death rate from gun assaults. For example, if the only effect of a handgun prohibition were that shooters would use sawed-off shotguns instead, then there is no question that the result of the prohibition would be to increase the homicide rate. However, if the principal effect of the prohibition were to reduce the rate of gun assault, with only a relatively few cases in which another type of firearm was substituted for the handgun, then the homicide rate would fall. Note that "substitution" in this case is not a simple phenomenon; the elimination of handguns would presumably have some effect on all of the following: the rate of robberies and other potentially violent confrontations, the weapons deployed in these confrontations, the likelihood that if a gun were deployed it would be fired, the likelihood that if fired it would hit the intended victim, and finally, the likelihood that the wound would be fatal. There is no precise information on any of the links of this chain, and the net effect on the homicide rate is in doubt.

Those who favor more stringent regulation of handguns are impressed by the greatly disproportionate involvement of such guns in violent crime. There are more than twice as many long guns in private hands as handguns. Yet handguns were used in over 80 percent of the gun homicides in 1988 (Federal Bureau of Investigation 1989, p. 12) and over 90 percent of the noncommercial gun robberies in 1987 (Bureau of Justice Statistics 1989*a*, p. 64); among handgun crimes, most involve weapons with barrels that are shorter than the average of those in circulation (Cook 1981*a*). One consequence of the disproportionate use of handguns in crime is a rather high probability that a privately owned handgun has been or will be used in crime; by one estimate, a representative group of 100 handguns sold new in 1977 were, over the course of their lifetimes, involved in crime at the rate of .33 (one crime per three guns) (Cook 1981*b*).[8] This number is still higher for snub-nosed handguns. This relatively high rate of crime involvement, an order of magnitude higher for handguns than for long guns, suggests that handguns are especially well suited to criminal use and that the criminal use of guns would decline if handguns were somehow eliminated.

Kleck (1984*a*) has laid out a useful road map for estimating the effects of a handgun prohibition. If we knew the relative death rates for handgun wounds and long gun wounds resulting from criminal assault under current conditions of gun availability, then it would be possible to make at least a rough estimate of the effect of substitution on the homicide rate. Unfortunately, this information is not available. The overall death rate from gunshot wounds in assault is about one in seven (Cook 1985*a*), which can be viewed as an average of the long gun and handgun ratios. But data on gunshot wounds do not usually distinguish between long guns and handguns, so separate fatality rates cannot be calculated. Indirect methods employed by Kleck (1984*a*) suggest that the death rate for gunshot wounds inflicted by long guns may be three or four times as high as for wounds inflicted by handguns; the validity of these methods is not known due to the lack of direct evidence on this matter. The best evidence that is available is provided by Kleck him-

[8] This estimate is the ratio of crimes committed with handguns in 1977 (estimated from National Crime Survey data) to the number of new handguns sold in that year. This method of estimating the *lifetime* crime involvement of the 1977 cohort of new handguns is valid under the assumption that handgun sales and handgun crime rates are constant over time. It underestimates handgun crime involvement if crime increases after 1977 or if the 1977 cohort of new handguns turns out to be small relative to subsequent cohorts.

self, in a subsequent study (Kleck and McElrath 1989). He and his coauthor created a unique data set by combining the NCS reports of injuries resulting from stranger assaults with supplementary homicide reports of homicides by strangers for the year 1982. Based on these combined data, they estimated the effects of different weapon types on the likelihood of death, controlling for some other variables. Their estimates imply that the likelihood of death in handgun assaults is virtually identical to the likelihood of death in assaults with other guns.[9] They do not comment on this result, but the apparent implication is that other guns are no more lethal in practice than handguns.

One interesting aspect of the controversy concerning the possible effects of regulating some guns more stringently than others is that all parties to the debate seem to have accepted the validity of the weapon instrumentality effect. Thus there is a consensus among the researchers in this area that the type of weapon matters, not just as a signal of the intent or personality of the assailant, but as a distinct causal factor. Whether a shooting victim lives or dies depends in part on the length of the gun barrel and the size of the bullet.

C. *Suicide*

As with homicide, about 60 percent of suicides are committed with guns. And, as in the case of criminal attacks, there is evidence that the instrument chosen by suicide attempters affects whether the attempt proves fatal or not (Clarke and Lester 1989). Case fatality rates are much higher for gun attempts than for those involving other means that are frequently employed, such as drugs and razors; for example, Dallas Police Department data indicate a fatality rate of 76 percent for gun suicide attempts, compared with just 4 percent for all other means combined (table 2). In another study (Card 1974), it was found that 92 percent of suicide attempts by firearms were successful, compared with 78 percent for carbon monoxide, 9 percent for other gases, 78 percent for hanging, 67 percent for drowning, 23 percent for poisoning, and 4 percent for cutting. This impressive difference does not, of course, prove the instrumentality claim. It can be argued that the choice of weapon in a suicide attempt reflects the seriousness of purpose of the attempter and makes no independent contribution to the outcome. The

[9] In fact, in their probit estimate, the coefficient estimate for "handgun" is slightly higher than for "other gun," but the difference is small. It should be noted that Kleck and McElrath (1989), in constructing their data set, are forced, due to insufficient information, to omit over half of the homicides by strangers.

TABLE 2

Suicide Attempts and Fatality Rates, Dallas, November 1981–November 1982

Means	Suicide Attempts: Total	Unsuccessful	Successful	Fatality Rates (Percent)
Firearms	144	35	109	76
Other means:	857	823	34	4
Hanging	14	5	9	64
Drugs	652	643	9	1
Cutting	132	127	5	4
All other	59	48	11	19
Overall	1,001	858	143	14

SOURCE.—Special unpublished tabulation, Dallas Police Department (1983).

debate over instrumentality in suicide proceeds parallel to the debate over instrumentality in homicide.

The case for suicide instrumentality is weaker than for homicide. First, while Zimring's claim is plausible that a large fraction of the shooters in homicide cases have no clear intent to kill, a similar assertion for gun suicides is far less plausible. Surely someone who purposefully points a gun at a vital area and pulls the trigger expects to die. Further, if a gun is not available for some reason, then there are always alternatives that are nearly as lethal, including hanging and jumping from a high place (Card 1974). And while homicides are usually the result of transitory altercations or confrontations, we know that many suicides result from a chronic condition such as pathological depression or a terminal painful disease. In such cases, there is time to contemplate alternative means and select one that will succeed. It is noteworthy in this regard that Japan and some European countries have far higher suicide rates than the United States despite the fact that private ownership of guns is relatively rare in those countries and gun suicides make up only a small fraction of the total. Kates (1990, p. 42) tabulated suicide rates for various years in the mid-1980s. The U.S. rate was 12.2 per 100,000, compared with Japan (20.3), West Germany (20.4), France (21.8), Austria (26.9), Denmark (28.7), and Rumania (66.2).

Nevertheless, there is some evidence that the instrumentality effect is important in suicide. That some other countries have higher suicide rates despite the relatively rare use of guns does not undercut this conclusion. The argument here is *not* that the availability of lethal means is the *sole* determinant of suicide rates but, rather, that the availability of lethal means influences the extent to which suicidal impulses are translated into complete suicides. Depriving a suicidal person of a lethal and attractive means of self-destruction may well save his life. One telling case in point is the drop in British suicide rates during the 1960s. During that decade, the carbon monoxide (CO) was gradually eliminated from domestic gas. Before this changeover began, almost half the suicides in England and Wales were by CO; by 1970, the CO death rate had dropped to about one-sixth its level in 1962 (Kreitman 1976; Clarke and Mayhew 1988). During this period, there was very little change in the rate of suicide by all other means. As a result, the overall suicide rate fell by one-third during this period, suggesting that few of the people who would have killed themselves in 1970, had CO still been a component of their domestic gas, actually did so. However, the British experience has not been replicated in several other countries that eliminated CO from domestic gas at about the same time; in the Netherlands, for example, suicide by other means increased by more than enough to compensate for the reduction in CO deaths (Clark and Mayhew 1988; Sloan et al. 1990, p. 371).

The lessons from the coal gas story are not conclusive, but do encourage a closer look at the etiology of suicide. Kreitman (1976, p. 92) asks how the removal of a single agent of self-destruction could have a large effect on the suicide rate: "There is no shortage of exits from this life; it would seem that anyone bent on self-destruction must eventually succeed, yet it is also quite possible, given the ambivalence (or multivalence) of many suicides, that a failed attempt serves as a catharsis leading to profound psychological change. For others it may be that the scenario of suicide specifies the use of a particular method, and that if this is not available actual suicide is then less likely. Virtually nothing is known about such questions." His first suggestion receives support from Richard Seiden (1977), who followed up on over 700 people who were stopped from jumping off the Golden Gate or San Francisco Bay Bridges (both high enough to ensure a high probability of death). Only 4 percent had subsequently killed themselves. He asserts that "we know very well that suicidal people are typically very ambivalent . . . and that the risk period is transient, often directly related to acute stress situations" (Seiden 1977, p. 275).

Kreitman's second point, that the "scenario of suicide" may specify a particular weapon, is very important to the instrumentality argument. While lethal means are readily at hand even in the absence of a gun, some suicidal people may reject hanging, jumping, and drowning as too painful and uncertain, while not knowing enough about drugs to take that exit successfully. Boor (1981), notes the cultural specificity of suicide means, and concludes that a major determinant of suicide rates is the availability of a culturally accepted method of committing the act. For example, the majority of suicides in Sri Lanka are committed by ingesting pesticides (Berger 1988), but the availability of pesticides is not a suicide risk in the United States. But while there is some evidence that, if deprived of their favored means of death, some suicidal people may choose to live (e.g., Clarke and Mayhew 1988), this evidence is far from conclusive.

A recent study of risk factors in adolescent suicide is directly relevant to the issue of gun instrumentality and confirms (albeit for a small local sample) that suicidal youths are more likely to kill themselves if there is a gun in their home than otherwise (Brent et al. 1988). The authors conclude that "clinicians who work with suicidal adolescents should strongly advocate the removal of firearms from the home environment" (p. 587). This conclusion seems very reasonable, even in the absence of a definitive experiment. Sloan et al. (1990) used an entirely different method to reach a similar conclusion about youthful suicide: in their comparison of suicide rates in King County (Seattle) and Vancouver for the years 1985–87, they found that King County, with a much higher prevalence of gun ownership, had a 37 percent higher rate of suicide for youths age fifteen to twenty-four; King County had a much higher gun suicide rate for this group and a slightly lower nongun rate. However, the apparent importance of gun availability in influencing the overall suicide rate is limited to youths; for older people, the suicide rate was actually somewhat higher in Vancouver than in King County. It should be noted, in any event, that this comparison between two jurisdictions is not a reliable basis for making generalizations.

From what little is known of the suicide process, it appears plausible that there is an instrumentality effect, and in particular in the United States, where guns are the favored means, that depriving suicidal people of guns would save some lives. But the evidence available at this point is not strong and includes findings that contradict the instrumentality hypothesis. Nevertheless, if I had a deeply depressed teenage son or daughter, I would take care that there were no loaded guns in the house.

D. Conclusion

The discussion on instrumentality begins with the undeniable observation that death rates in assault, robbery, and parasuicide differ widely depending on the "instrument" used. The more lethal the weapon, the higher the fraction of injuries that prove fatal. The difficult question is how to interpret this empirical pattern. If the type of weapon in a violent encounter were chosen at random, then the significance of the observed pattern would be clear: the type of weapon has a direct influence on the outcome. But in practice, the choice of weapon in an assault or suicide attempt is not strictly random; to some extent it is a signal of intent, and other things equal, those with more deadly intent are more likely to kill. The debate over instrumentality, over whether the weapon "matters," is a debate over whether systematic differences in intent are sufficient to account for the large observed differences in weapon-specific death rates. While the evidence is mixed for suicide, it is more clear cut in assaultive crimes that the weapon does indeed matter.

This conclusion follows from close scrutiny of samples of assaults and from analysis of patterns in aggregate data. And it comports with common sense. The type of weapon matters in personal violence just as it does in warfare. If violent people did not have access to guns, there would still be as much violence in the United States as there is now, or more, but it would be much less deadly.

III. Patterns of Gun Use in Personal Violence

Firearms were used in 61 percent of the homicides, 33 percent of the robberies, and 21 percent of the aggravated assaults reported to the police in 1988 (Federal Bureau of Investigation 1989). These percentages have varied over time and differ across jurisdictions for reasons that are explored in subsequent sections. This section focuses on the patterns of gun use across the different circumstances in which these crimes occur. What characteristics of the assailant, the victim, and the immediate environment of the criminal act influence the likelihood that a gun is employed, rather than another type of weapon?

A gun has a number of characteristics that make it superior to other readily available weapons for use in violent crime: even in the hands of a weak and unskilled assailant, a gun can be used to kill. The killing can be accomplished from a distance without much risk of effective counterattack by the victim, and the killing can be completed quickly, without sustained effort, and in a relatively impersonal fashion. Furthermore, because everyone knows that a gun has these attributes, the mere display of a gun communicates a highly effective threat. In most circumstances, a gun maximizes the probability of success for a would-be robber or murderer.

Evidence that criminals who use guns are influenced by tactical considerations such as these comes from a survey of prisoners by James Wright and Peter Rossi (1986). They persuaded 1,874 convicted male felons in ten states to fill out questionnaires concerning their criminal histories and their use of weapons. This sample, it should be noted, is a sample of convenience, rather than a representative sample of all male prisoners, and no clear inferences can be drawn from the quantitative results. In the absence of other data, however, the Wright-Rossi survey is useful in providing a general qualitative impression. Respondents who had used guns in some of their crimes (almost all of whom admitted to committing robberies, among other crimes) cited a number of motives for this choice of weaponry. A majority indicated that each of the following reasons, related to their ability to forestall or overcome victim resistance and get away unscathed, was "very important" or "somewhat important": "chance victim would be armed," "prepared for anything," "ready to defend myself," "easier to do crime," "might need gun to escape," "need gun to do crime," "people don't mess with you." The *most* cited reason for using a gun was "don't have to hurt victim."

Given all these advantages, the obvious question is why only a minority of violent crimes are committed with a gun. Wright and Rossi asked felons in their sample who used weapons other than guns "why not carry a gun?" The most frequent reasons were "just asking for trouble," "get a stiffer sentence," "never needed a gun for my crimes." Lack of familiarity was important for a large minority of respondents, who checked "never owned a gun" or "don't like guns." One third of respondents checked "against the law for me to own a gun" as an important reason. Twenty-one percent of this group checked "too much trouble to get one." Thus, the respondents who used weapons other than guns were generally concerned about the legal consequences and other trouble resulting from carrying a gun to use in crime. Tastes, familiarity, and legal restrictions on ownership also played a role in their decisions. Availability is cited as an important consideration by only a few of the respondents, but that by no means "proves" that availability is generally unimportant. The respondents may have had a tendency to exaggerate their competence in obtaining whatever weapon they wanted. Further, the Wright-Rossi sample gives a highly distorted representation of the population of violent criminals; all respondents were prisoners, and prisoners tend to be older and perhaps more sophisticated about crime than the population of active criminals on the outside.

A variety of evidence gives clear indication that the decision about whether to go armed with a gun is closely linked to decisions about what crimes to commit and the likely success or failure of these crimes. The tool determines the task, and the task determines the tool. These links are clearly illustrated by the patterns of gun use in robbery, murder, and assault.

A. *Robbery*

The robber's essential task is to overcome the victim's natural tendency to resist parting with his or her valuables. A variety of techniques for accomplishing this task are used in robbery, including actual attack (as in muggings or yokings) and the threatening display of a weapon such as a gun, knife, or club. The objective is to gain the victim's compliance quickly or render him helpless, thereby preventing the victim from striking back, escaping, or summoning help. The amount of what could be called "power" (capability of generating lethal force) the robber needs to achieve a high probability of reaching these objectives depends on the characteristics of the robbery target (the victim) and, in particular, on the vulnerability of the target. The most vulnerable targets are people who are young, elderly, otherwise physically weak or disabled (e.g., by alcohol), or alone and without ready means of escape. The least vulnerable targets are commercial places, especially where there are several customers and clerks and possibly even armed guards—a bank being one extreme example.

A gun is the most effective tool for enhancing the robber's power. Unlike other common weapons, a gun gives a robber the capacity to threaten deadly harm from a distance, thus allowing him to maintain a buffer zone between himself and the victim and to control several victims simultaneously. A gun serves to preempt any rational victim's inclination to flee or resist. Skogan (1978) documented the effectiveness of a gun in forestalling victim resistance in his analysis of a national sample of victim-reported robberies: only 8 percent of gun robbery victims resisted physically in noncommercial robberies, compared with about 15 percent of victims in noncommercial robberies involving other weapons. Other types of resistance (arguing, screaming, fleeing) were also less common in gun robbery than in robbery involving other weapons.

It seems reasonable to assume, from the robber's viewpoint, that the value of employing a gun tends to be inversely related to the vulnerability of the target. A gun will cause a greater increase in the likelihood of success against well-defended targets than against more vulnerable targets. A strong-arm technique will be adequate against an elderly woman walking alone on the street—a gun would be redundant with such a victim—but a gun is virtually a requirement for a successful liquor store robbery. Skogan (1978) provides evidence supporting his claim: he finds little relation between robbery success rates and weapon type for personal robbery but a very strong relation for commercial robbery. He reports that success rates in commercial robbery were 94 percent with a gun, 65 percent with a knife, and 48 percent with other weapons.

In economic terms, we can characterize robbery as a production process (Cook 1979, pp. 752–53) with weapons, robbers, and a target as "inputs." The "output" of the production process can be defined as the probability of success. This probability increases with the number and skill of the robbers, the vulnerability of the target, and the lethality of the weapons. For a given robber and target characteristics, the "marginal product" of a gun can be defined as the increase in probability of success if the robber or robbers substitute a gun for, say, a knife. The evidence presented above suggests that the marginal product of a gun is small against vulnerable targets and relatively large against well-defended targets. We can go one step further and define the "value of a gun's marginal product" as its marginal product (increase in success probability) multiplied by the amount of loot if the robbery is successful. Since, for obvious reasons, targets with greater potential loot tend to be better defended against robbery, the value of the gun's marginal product is even more strongly related to target vulnerability than is its marginal product. It makes good economic sense, then, for gun use in robbery to be closely related to target vulnerability. Cook (1980*a*) demonstrates that this is indeed the case, on the basis of tabulating results of more than 12,000 robbery reports taken from victim survey data gathered in twenty-six large cities. These results are reproduced in table 3.

From the table (part A) we see that 55 percent of gun robberies committed by adults, but only 13 percent of other adult armed robberies, involve commercial targets. Those relatively few gun robberies

TABLE 3

Distribution of Robberies by Location and Victim Characteristics

A. Distribution of All Robberies across Locations by Adults (Percent)

Type	Gun	Knife or Other Weapon	Unarmed
Commercial	55.1	13.3	19.1
Residence	6.4	10.4	8.5
Street, vehicle, etc.	38.5	76.3	72.4

B. Distribution of Street Robberies by Victim Characteristics (Percent)

Victim	Gun	Knife or Other Weapon	Unarmed
Male victim aged 16–54	59.8	53.8	41.1
Two or more victims	10.5	5.8	3.7
All others (young, elderly, and/or female victims)	29.7	40.4	55.2

SOURCE.—Adapted from Cook (1980*a*), p. 43. The distributions are calculated from National Crime Panel victimization survey data of twenty-six cities.

NOTE.—Percentages sum to 100. All incidents involved at least one male robber age eighteen or over. Entries in the table reflect survey sampling weights.

that were committed against people on the street are concentrated on relatively invulnerable targets—groups of two or more victims, or prime-age males—while street robbery with other weapons was most likely to involve women, children, and elderly victims (part B). Skogan (1978) provides further detail for commercial robberies, reporting that the likelihood that a gun is present in such robberies is only 44 percent for commercial places that have only one employee but 68 percent for commercial places with two or more employees.

What is the causal process that produces these patterns in gun robbery? There are two plausible explanations, both compatible with the evidence presented above: robbers who aspire to well-defended, lucrative targets equip themselves with a gun in order to increase their chance of success; or robbers who happen to have a gun are more tempted to rob lucrative, well-defended targets than robbers who lack this tool. In short, the question is whether the weapon is chosen to suit the task, or rather that the available weapon helps define the task. There is doubtless some truth in both explanations. The first explanation suggests that the observed relation between gun use and target choice is the result of differences between the kinds of people who rob lucrative targets and those who commit relatively petty street robberies—a difference reminiscent of Conklin's (1972) distinction between "professionals" and "opportunists." Victim survey data suggest that gun robbers as a group have more of the earmarks of professionalism than other armed robbers: besides the fact that they make bigger "scores," gun robbers are older, less likely to rob acquaintances, and less likely to work in groups of three or more (Cook 1976; Skogan 1978). Cook and Nagin (1979, p. 25) demonstrated that the factors that determine a robber's choice of weapon have some tendency to persist: a cohort of adult men arrested for gun robbery in the District of Columbia showed a greater propensity to use guns in subsequent robberies than did the corresponding cohort of nongun robbery arrestees.

It seems reasonable to hypothesize, then, that robbers who engage in planning and who seek out big scores will take pains to equip themselves with the appropriate weapon—usually some type of firearm. The extent to which other, less professional robbers use guns, and hence the kinds of targets they choose, may be more sensitive to the extent to which such people have access to guns and are in the habit of carrying them, for whatever reason. Increased availability of guns may then result in some target switching by this group—substitution of more lucrative, better-defended targets for more vulnerable targets. Increased gun availability may also result in weapon substitution for a given type of target, implying an increase in the fraction of street robberies committed with a gun; that is, guns will be put to less valuable uses as they become "cheaper."

B. Murder

The qualities of a gun that make it the most effective robbery weapon, particularly against well-defended targets, are also of value to a killer. A decision to kill is easier and safer to implement with a gun than with other commonly available weapons—there is less danger of effective victim resistance during the attack, and the killing can be accomplished more quickly and impersonally, with less sustained effort than is usually required with a knife or blunt object. As in the case of robbery, a gun has greatest value against relatively invulnerable victims, and the vulnerability of the victim appears to be an important factor in determining the probability that a gun will be used as the murder weapon.

The least vulnerable victims are those who are guarded or armed. All presidential assassinations in U.S. history were committed with handguns or rifles. Almost all law-enforcement officers who have been murdered in recent years were shot: in 1978, ninety-one of ninety-three murdered officers were killed by guns (Federal Bureau of Investigation 1979, p. 309).

Physical size and strength are also components of vulnerability. For the period 1976–87, 67.5 percent of male homicide victims were shot, compared with only 50.6 percent of female homicide victims (Kellermann and Mercy 1990). The age pattern is strikingly regular: about 70 percent of victims aged twenty to twenty-four are shot, but this percentage drops off rapidly for younger and older—that is, more vulnerable—victims (Cook 1982).

Vulnerability is, of course, a relative matter. We would expect that the lethality of the murder weapons would be directly related to the difference in physical strength between the victim and killer, other things equal. This hypothesis can be investigated using the Federal Bureau of Investigation data coded from the supplementary homicide reports submitted by police departments. These data include the demographic characteristics of the victim and (where known) the offender, as well as the murder weapon, immediate circumstances, and apparent motive of the crime. Some patterns in these data offer support to the relative vulnerability hypothesis. First, women tend to use more lethal weapons than men to kill their spouses and intimate acquaintances: 99 percent of the women, but only 81 percent of the men, used a gun or knife during the years 1976–87 (Kellermann and Mercy 1990). The gun fractions alone are 70 percent and 66 percent—not a large difference, but one that is in the predicted direction. This result is especially notable since women typically have less experience than men in handling guns and are less likely to think of any guns kept in the home as their personal property.

Table 4 focuses on killings resulting from arguments and brawls in which both the killer and the victim were males. The gun fraction increases with the age of the killer and is inversely related to the age of the victim: the highest gun fraction (87 percent) involves elderly killers and youthful victims; the lowest gun fraction (48 percent) involves youthful killers and elderly victims. Since age is highly correlated with strength and robustness, these results offer strong support for the relative vulnerability hypothesis.

TABLE 4

Percent of Gun Use in Murders and Nonnegligent Homicides Resulting from Arguments or Brawls, Male Victim and Male Offender

	Offender Age		
Victim Age	18–39	40–59	60+
18–39	68.0 (91,906)	79.6 (368)	87.2 (47)
40–59	54.5 (398)	64.1 (245)	66.7 (57)
60+	48.3 (58)	49.2 (61)	63.3 (30)

SOURCE.—Federal Bureau of Investigation Supplementary Homicide Reports, fifty cities, 1976 and 1977 combined (unpublished microdata files). Reprinted from Cook (1982).

NOTE.—The sample size is in parentheses. Cases in which the age of the killer is not known are excluded.

Why are less vulnerable murder victims more likely to be shot than relatively vulnerable victims? A natural interpretation of this result is that intended victims who are physically strong or armed in some fashion are better able to defend themselves against homicidal assault than more vulnerable victims—unless the assailant uses a gun, the great equalizer. The "vulnerability pattern" can then be explained as resulting from some combination of three mechanisms: first, homicidal attacks are more likely to fail against strong victims than weak ones, and the difference in the likelihood of failure is greater for nongun attacks than attacks with a gun; second, the likelihood that an individual will act on a homicidal impulse depends in part on the perceived probability of success—the intended victim's ability to defend himself or herself acts as a deterrent to would-be killers, but this deterrent is much weaker if the killer has a gun; and, third, in the case of a planned murder, the killer will have the opportunity to equip himself with a tool that is adequate to the task. Against well-defended victims, the tool chosen will almost certainly be a gun, if one can be obtained without too much difficulty.

Each of these mechanisms is compatible with the prediction that a reduction in gun availability will cause a reduction in murder, a reduction that will be concentrated on killings that involve a victim who is physically stronger than the killer.

C. Assault

For a large percentage of violent crimes, it is in the assailant's interest to take care to *avoid* killing the victim. Robbery murder, for example, is a capital crime in many jurisdictions—even if the killing is an "accident" or a spontaneous reaction to victim resistance. Conklin (1972, p. 111) interviewed several robbery convicts who used an unloaded gun for fear that otherwise they might end up shooting their victims, and the same concern was reflected in some of the responses from Wright and Rossi's (1986) sample of prisoners. In other violent confrontations, such as fights between family members, this same concern may deter the combatants from reaching for a gun—even when there is one readily available. A loaded gun is not an appropriate weapon when the assailant's intent is to hurt, but not kill, the victim.

Some unknown fraction of assault cases is similar to robbery in that the assailant's objective is to coerce the victim's compliance—the assailant wants the victim to stop attacking him (physically or verbally) or stop dancing with his girlfriend or get off his favorite bar stool or turn down the stereo. Moreover, as in the case of robbery, the probability of a physical attack in such cases may be less if the assailant has a gun than otherwise, because the victim will be less inclined to ignore or resist a threat enforced by the display of a gun. (It may also be true that the assailant would be more hesitant to use a gun than another weapon to make good his threat.) In general support of these ideas, evidence from the National Crime Survey indicates that assaults with a gun are less likely to involve attack or injury than are assaults with other weapons (Kleck and McElrath 1989).

D. Conclusion

Consideration of the tactical concerns of criminals helps make sense of a number of patterns in weapon use in violent crime. A robber equipped with a gun can stage a successful robbery against a target that might effectively resist an assailant using a less powerful weapon. A woman who decides to kill a man who is larger and stronger than she will have a hard time of it with a knife, but a gun would do the job. Guns are most likely to be used where they have greatest value compared to other, less lethal weapons. This conclusion inspires an obvious question: if guns became more scarce, would there be relatively less violent crime of the sort for which guns are most valuable? In the case of robbery, for example, would there be a reduction in the victimization rate for commercial places? If so, would criminals substitute other targets or other types of crime for commercial robbery? These questions cannot be answered from the available literature but are relevant in assessing the policy-relevant effects from a change in gun availability. The research agenda offered in the concluding section includes specific recommendations for further work in this area.

IV. Availability

About one-half of the households in the United States possess at least one firearm, and the total number of firearms in private hands is on the order of 150 million. Nevertheless, guns are a scarce commodity, costly to obtain and to use. For a criminal, the costs may include not only the purchase price but also the various legal risks of obtaining, possessing, and using the gun in crime. These costs help explain why guns are not used in a higher proportion of violent crimes, as discussed in the previous section. For example, gun robberies tend to be considerably more lucrative than others, yet less than one-third of all robberies are committed with a gun.

Advocates of gun-control measures seek to make guns more scarce, especially to criminals and criminal use. "Gun control" generally encompasses three basic strategies (Zimring 1990): deprive dangerous people (convicted felons, mental patients) of guns; restrict high-risk uses (carrying concealed); and forbid commerce in certain kinds of firearms (machine guns, Saturday Night Specials). Evidence on the effectiveness of such measures in reducing the misuse of guns is sketchy. There have been only a few evaluations of specific ordinances, and these are reviewed below; more work has been done on how gun availability, defined generically, affects the prevalence of gun misuse.

The most obvious indicator of "availability" is the prevalence of ownership, which is the topic of the next section. Subsequent sections describe several operational definitions of "gun availability" and review empirical studies of the relation between availability measures and the incidence of suicide and violent crimes.

A. *Recent Trends and Patterns in Gun Ownership*

The number of firearms in private hands has been estimated both from survey data and from data on manufactures and imports. The most thorough study of this matter is by Wright, Rossi, and Daly (1983), who estimate that there were 100–140 million firearms in 1978, of which 30–40 million were handguns. Since then there have been 52 million firearms manufactured or imported into the United States for sale to households, businesses, and law-enforcement agencies (Bureau of Alcohol, Tobacco and Firearms 1989). Of the 52 million new guns, there were 6.6 million recorded exports (Bureau of Alcohol, Tobacco and Firearms 1989) and possibly millions more of illegal export. Further, some portion of the stock of guns existing in 1978 has been discarded, rendered useless by breakage and rust, or confiscated by authorities, so some of the new guns are "replacements" for older guns. If the stock in existence in 1978 depreciated by just 1 percent per year, then the total stock as of 1988 was 150 million give or take 20 million. (This estimate accepts the 100–140 million range for 1978 as correct and ignores illegal imports and exports since then.) While the trend probably continues upward, it is notable that fewer new guns were sold in the United States during the decade ending in 1988 than during the preceding decade.

The 1989 Gallup poll estimated 47 percent of households possessed a gun, a result that affirms one of the remarkable constants in American life: the fraction of American households owning a gun has remained at about one-half for at least the last three decades (Bureau of Justice Statistics 1989*b*, p. 232). There has, however, been a substantial increase in the fraction of households that own a handgun, from 13 percent in 1959 to about 24 percent in 1978 and thereafter; thus in recent years, about half of the gun-owning households own a handgun. Most gun-owning households have several guns, with an average of three as of 1978 (based on a poll of voters conducted by Decision Making Information, Inc. that year; see Wright 1981). Only one in six gun-owning households is limited to handguns; three-quarters of those who own a handgun also own a rifle or shotgun. These statistics are relevant to the question of how many guns are in private hands; between 1978 and 1988, the number of households increased by 12 million, while the fraction of households owning a gun remained roughly constant. These data support the conclusion that the total stock of guns in private hands has increased, but whether it has increased in proportion to the number of households depends on whether there has been any change in the average number of guns per gun-owning household during this period.[10]

The incidence of firearms ownership is not uniform across society.

[10] Gary Kleck (1990), in a personal communication, notes that data from a December 1989 poll imply that the average respondent who said there was at least one gun in the household had an average of 4.4 guns, considerably higher than the three-per-household estimate from a 1978 poll mentioned above.

The General Social Surveys conducted by the National Opinion Research Center have included an item about gun ownership since 1973; they consistently find that the fraction of households owning a gun increases with income, decreases with city size, is substantially higher for whites than blacks, and is highest in the South and lowest in the Northeast (Wright and Marston 1975; Bureau of Justice Statistics 1989*b*). An analysis of regional patterns of ownership for residents of large cities, using National Opinion Research Center polls taken in the mid-1970s, found a range for gun ownership from 10 percent for residents of large cities in New England and the Mid Atlantic up to 50 percent for the East South Central region (Louisville, Kentucky; Memphis and Nashville, Tennessee; Birmingham, Alabama). The South Atlantic, Mountain, and West South Central regions all had ownership rates of 40 percent or higher (Cook 1979).

B. *The Costs of Obtaining a Gun*

The density of gun ownership is one dimension of gun availability since gun owners obviously have more ready access to guns than do other people. The term "gun availability" also refers to the cost and difficulty of acquiring a gun. The purchase price of a new gun will differ widely depending on its characteristics. The trend in the average prices of new guns has followed the overall trend in consumer prices since 1960 (Cook 1982). Since about half of all gun transfers involve used guns (Blose and Cook 1980), it would also be relevant to assess price trends in that market. In the absence of any useful data on this subject, it seems safe to assume that prices in the second-hand market exhibit the same trend as prices in the market for new guns, as is true for autos and other consumer durables.

In addition to the purchase price, the cost of obtaining a gun may be increased by federal and state laws that regulate firearms commerce. What is required in this respect differs from state to state and sometimes also differs among jurisdictions within a state.

C. *Regulations Governing Transfers and Possession*

The Gun Control Act of 1968 established the framework for the current system of controls on gun transfers. All shipments of firearms are limited to federally licensed dealers who are required to obey all applicable state and local ordinances. This act also stipulates several categories of people who are denied the right to receive or possess a gun, including illegal aliens, convicted felons and those under indictment, and people who have at some time been involuntarily committed to a mental institution. People with a history of "substance abuse" are also proscribed from possessing a gun. Dealers are not allowed to sell handguns to people younger than twenty-one, or to sell long guns to those younger than eighteen, although there is no federal prohibition of gun possession by youths. Under the Gun Control Act, the various prohibitions are implemented by a requirement that the buyer sign a form stating that he does not fall into any of the proscribed categories.

The Gun Control Act imposed a national ban on mail-order purchases of firearms except by licensed dealers. There are also some restrictions on sales to people from out of state. The intended effect of these regulations was to insulate the states from each other so that the stringent regulations on firearms commerce adopted in some states would not be undercut by the greater availability of guns in other states.[11]

A number of states have adopted significant restrictions on commerce in firearms, especially handguns. Twenty-one states, including about two-thirds of the population, currently require that handgun buyers obtain a permit or license (or at least send an application to the police) before taking possession of the gun (Bureau of Justice Statistics 1989*b*, p. 169). Local jurisdictions in several other states have regulations of this sort in place. All but a few state transfer-control systems are "permissive," in the sense that most people are legally entitled to obtain a gun. In a few jurisdictions, however, it is very difficult to obtain a handgun legally. For example, Washington, D.C., stipulates that only law-enforcement officers and security guards are entitled to obtain a handgun (Jones 1981).

The effect of a permissive transfer-control system is to increase the effective cost of a legally purchased handgun by imposing a permit fee and a waiting period and by requiring applicants to do some paperwork and submit to a criminal-record check. These requirements may discourage some people from purchasing handguns and motivate others to evade the transfer regulations by purchasing from friends or other sources that lack a dealer's license. Of course, purchase from a nondealer may be costly and inconvenient in other ways.

[11] The McClure-Volkmer Amendments of 1986 eased the restriction on out-of-state purchases of long guns. Such purchases are now legal so long as they comply with the regulations of both the buyer's state of residence and the state in which the sale occurs.

D. Evading Regulations on Gun Transfers

Interstate differences in the stringency of transfer regulations produce a vigorous illegal commerce in guns moving across state lines (Bureau of Alcohol, Tobacco and Firearms 1976; Moore 1981). Even in jurisdictions that lack stringent regulations, there is an active market in stolen guns and off-the-book transfers. From their survey of prisoners, Wright and Rossi (1986, p. 185) report that few respondents acquired their guns by purchasing them from a licensed dealer. Of those who had owned a handgun, one-third reported having stolen their most recent one. For others, "family and friends" were the most common source of guns purchased, traded for, or borrowed. Many of the guns obtained from these sources had been stolen by someone else. These findings are suggestive although, as noted above, the Wright-Rossi study is based on a sample of convenience that is not representative of the population of active criminals.

It seems reasonable to conclude that gun availability to criminals has much to do with the ease of stealing a gun or obtaining one on the black market or from an acquaintance. Given these sources, the difficulty of obtaining a gun is presumably closely related to the density of gun ownership. For example, the fraction of burglaries that result in the theft of guns increases with the fraction of households that own guns (Moore 1981), so the black market for stolen guns will be more active in cities where gun ownership is prevalent. Further, criminals will find it easier (and perhaps cheaper) to buy or borrow a gun from an acquaintance in cities with high rates of gun ownership. Thus, the costs of obtaining a gun for those who are not inclined to buy from a dealer will depend on the general prevalence of gun ownership.

E. Carrying Guns in Public

Since most violent crimes occur away from the assailant's home, mere possession of a gun is not enough to guarantee that it is available for use when the occasion arises. Hence, the propensity to go armed in public is an important aspect of gun availability. Presumably, the prevalence of going armed is highly correlated with the prevalence of ownership across cities, but it may also be influenced by the vigor with which anticarrying laws are enforced and by other factors.

State and local legislation tends to make a sharp distinction between keeping a gun in one's home or business and carrying a gun in public. All but a few states either ban concealed weapons entirely or require a special license for carrying concealed weapons. One national survey found that 7 percent of respondents carried a handgun outside of their homes for protection (Wright 1981).

F. Measuring Gun Availability

The preceding discussion developed the notion of gun availability in terms of the prevalence of ownership, the costs of obtaining a gun, and the propensity to go armed in public. These three dimensions of availability are closely related, but it would be useful to distinguish among them in measuring the effects of gun availability on violent crime and suicide. Unfortunately, none of these dimensions can be measured directly from existing data. Instead, researchers make use of indicators that have some logical relation to availability, and are arguably correlated with one or more of the relevant dimensions of availability. But the interpretation of empirical studies of this sort is inevitably somewhat uncertain.

1. *Gun Use in Homicide as an Availability Measure.* Perhaps the most commonly used measure of gun availability is the fraction of criminal homicides committed with a gun. A number of authors have related this gun fraction to the homicide rate across jurisdictions or over time in a single jurisdiction. A positive correlation is interpreted as evidence that increased gun availability causes increases in the murder rate.

Brearley (1932), in perhaps the first study of this sort, analyzed a cross-sectional sample of states using this measure of availability. Fisher (1976) analyzed time series data for Detroit for the period 1926–68 while I sketched out a similar analysis for the United States as a whole (Cook 1982). Etzioni and Remp (1973) assessed cross-national patterns of homicide rates and gun involvement; Curtis (1974, pp. 103–13) did a more thorough analysis along the same lines. Each of these studies finds strong positive correlations, with the partial exception of Curtis. But none of these studies is particularly persuasive evidence of a direct causal link between availability and homicide; the gun fraction in homicide is a fairly primitive indicator of gun availability,[12] and there

[12] The gun fraction in homicide reflects other factors besides the general availability of guns. Within a particular city or region, some people will have greater access to guns or more motivation for using guns than others, and so the observed gun fraction in that locality will depend on who is doing the killing. For example, a city such as Washington, with a relatively low prevalence of gun ownership, can exhibit a high gun fraction in homicides during a year when most of the killings are by well-equipped gangsters. This measure of gun availability could, in principle, be refined by adjusting the crude gun fraction for circumstances and motives. In my work (Cook 1979), I took a step in that direction by excluding felony-type homicides in the calculation of the gun fraction.

are other plausible explanations for the observed correlations (Cook 1982, p. 266). There may, for example, be some "third cause" variable, such as a "culture of violence," that influences both the prevalence of guns and the rate of homicidal attacks.

The gun fraction in homicide is not the only available proxy for gun availability. Measurement theory suggests that we can obtain a more reliable indicator for this underlying trait by combining two or more proxy variables. One possibility in this regard is to average the gun fraction in homicide with the gun fraction in suicide (Cook 1979, 1985*c*). The latter also reflects the choices of a sample of people (suicides), and those choices reflect the ease of obtaining a gun, among other things (Clarke and Lester 1989). And the "sample" reflected in suicide statistics is quite different from the sample reflected in homicide statistics. In particular, the demographics of suicide and homicide are quite different, and in some ways are virtually mirror images. For example, the homicide death rate peaks in the third decade and drops sharply thereafter, while the suicide death rate tends to increase throughout the normal age span. The homicide rate for blacks is over six times as high as for whites, while the white suicide rate is almost double that of blacks. Most suicides occur at home, while most homicides occur away from home. Despite these differences and others, the use of guns in homicide and suicide exhibits a similar geographic pattern. For 1973 and 1974 data combined, the gun fractions for suicide and assaultive homicide were highly correlated across fifty large cities ($r = .82$), suggesting an environmental determinant of gun use. The validity of this interpretation was supported by comparing the regional pattern in this index with the regional pattern of urban gun ownership across eight regions (as measured by the National Opinion Research Center's [NORC] General Social Survey); the index proved compatible with the survey results.[13]

This index was then used as a measure of gun availability in a regression analysis of robbery rates. Controlling for other variables important

[13] The procedure for validating the index was as follows: Data for residents of large cities (over 250,000) were obtained from the National Opinion Research Center's General Social Survey files for 1973, 1974, and 1976. The results for the three years were combined to generate more reliable estimates. For each of the nine census regions, these data were used to estimate the prevalence of gun ownership among residents of large cities. Two of the regions (New England and the Middle Atlantic) were combined to increase sample size. The resulting estimates of gun prevalence in the remaining eight regions were compared with the corresponding values of the index for these regions. The correlation between the two was .94.

in explaining intercity differences in robbery,[14] the principal results were as follows: a 10 percent reduction in the prevalence of gun ownership in a city is associated with about a 5 percent reduction in the gun robbery rate and a 4 percent reduction in the robbery murder rate but has no discernible effect on the overall robbery rate. These results suggest that gun density influences the choice of weapon in robbery and its lethality but not the overall volume of robbery.

These estimates do not allow for the possibility that the prevalence of gun ownership is influenced in some way by the robbery rate. While it is true that a small fraction of guns are acquired for self-defense purposes (Kleck 1988; Smith and Uchida 1988), most of these are purchased by households that have acquired other guns for sporting purposes; three-quarters of those who own a handgun also own a rifle or shotgun (Wright 1981). The overall geographic pattern of gun ownership appears to have much more to do with regional culture than with the objective threat of crime.

While the geographic patterns of gun use in homicide and suicide are very similar, the same is not true for temporal patterns in gun use. As noted earlier, there has been a mild downward trend in gun use in homicide since 1975, while the trend in suicide has been toward somewhat greater use of guns (see also Cook 1985*c*).

2. *Survey Data.* Since there have been a number of national surveys that include items on gun ownership, an obvious question arises as to why the results cannot be used to measure geographic patterns of availability. The problem is that the national samples are too small to produce reliable estimates of ownership rates for cities or states. Markush and Bartolucci (1984) employed NORC survey data to estimate gun prevalence for each of nine regions; they increased the sample size and hence reliability of the estimates by combining data from four surveys. Their study was limited to suicide; across the nine regions, the suicide and gun ownership rates were highly correlated ($r = .81$). Unfortunately, with such a small sample, they are unable to take account of other factors besides gun availability that may also influence suicide rates, so the proper interpretation of their result is not clear (see also Lester 1988).

[14] The control variables include the following characteristics of the cities: percent of the population that are youthful black males; population per square mile; fraction of the standard metropolitan statistical area in the city; fraction of the population in relative poverty; number of Uniform Crime Report crimes per policeman; number of retail stores per capita; and an indicator for those cities in states with relatively stringent gun-control regulations.

The 1989 International Crime Survey (van Dijk, Mayhew, and Killias 1990) surveyed households in fourteen countries, and for the first time makes possible a valid international comparison of gun ownership and violent crime patterns. Killias (1990) looked at a subsample of eleven countries for which there were data on homicide by weapon type: for what it is worth, the correlation between the gun fraction in homicide and the prevalence of gun ownership is $r = .72$.[15]

3. *Manufacturing, Import, and Sales Data.* Newton and Zimring (1969) assembled a historical series on gun manufacture and import as a basis for estimating the current private stocks of handguns and long guns. These data are flawed by the facts (acknowledged by Newton and Zimring) that imports are not measured accurately, and data are lacking on exports, breakage, confiscation, and other removals from the stock. Nonetheless, this series has been used as a measure of gun availability by several researchers.

Four studies have analyzed the effect of the stock of guns, as estimated by the Newton-Zimring method, on temporal movements in the national homicide rate (Phillips, Votey, and Howell 1976; Kleck 1979, 1984*b*; Magaddino and Medoff 1984). All use multivariate statistical methods to control for some of the other variables that influence homicide rates, and all but Kleck (1984*b*) conclude from their analysis that the stock of guns has a positive effect on the homicide rate. The difficulty with this type of analysis, in addition to the flaws in the measure of gun availability, is the uncertainty concerning the proper specification of the statistical model; the social process that generates year-to-year changes in the homicide rate is poorly understood, and the estimates of how the gun stock affects homicide are sensitive to what assumptions are made about other factors. (It should be noted that specification uncertainty is also a problem in cross-sectional studies such as reported in Cook 1979.)

G. *Comparisons without Explicit Measures of Availability*

There is a tradition in debates over gun control to compare homicide rates across countries that are known to differ widely with respect to the private ownership of guns (Bruce-Briggs 1976). It is not necessary

[15] For these eleven countries, the percent of households possessing a firearm is as follows: Australia, 20.1; Belgium, 16.8; Canada, 30.8; England and Wales, 4.7; Federal Republic of Germany, 9.2; Finland, 25.5; France, 24.7; Netherlands, 2.0; Norway, 31.2; Switzerland, 32.6; and United States, 48.9. France is excluded from the correlation due to lack of homicide data.

to have a precise measure of availability to be sure that guns are much scarcer in Japan than in the United States. The problem with such comparisons is that countries that differ widely with respect to availability also differ with respect to various other factors that influence rates of personal violence. Japan, where few individuals own a gun, has a very low homicide rate and a high suicide rate by American standards. Kates (1990, p. 42) indicates that Japan's suicide rate was 20.3 per 100,000, compared to a U.S. rate of 12.2 in 1982; Japan's homicide rate was 0.9 per 100,000, compared with a rate of 7.6 in the United States. All we can safely conclude from this comparison is that guns are not the only thing that matters in personal violence.

A recent study by Sloan et al. (1988) claims to have solved the problem of finding two jurisdictions that are quite different with respect to gun availability but alike in other respects relevant to personal violence. Seattle and Vancouver share a common geography, climate, and history and are remarkably similar in terms of demographic and socioeconomic characteristics. But guns are more widely owned and more easily obtained in Seattle than in Vancouver, as indicated by differences in laws governing ownership, the number of gun permits issued, and the fractions of homicides and suicides committed with a gun. The two cities have similar rates of aggravated assault, but more of Seattle's assaults were committed with a gun. The homicide rate in Seattle averaged 11.3 per 100,000 (1980–86), compared with 6.9 for Vancouver; all the difference was in the rate of gun homicide. These results are intriguing, but there must remain some doubt about their proper interpretation.

In one view, the Seattle-Vancouver comparison should be considered a sort of natural controlled experiment, in which the people living in the two cities are two samples that have been "drawn" at random from the same population and assigned to either the Seattle "treatment" (more guns) or the Vancouver "treatment" (fewer guns). The probability statements in the article by Sloan and his associates only make sense in the context of a model such as this. There is certainly reason to doubt this model; the two "samples" are obviously not the result of random assignment (e.g., they differ substantially with respect to the ethnic composition of the nonwhite populations), and the two "treatments" differ in more ways than gun availability.

A quite different view of the Seattle-Vancouver comparison is that the relevant unit of observation is the city, rather than the individuals who make up the city populations. And in that perspective, the sample size here is just two. The fundamental finding is that the city with more guns also has a higher homicide rate, and that finding is compatible with the generalization that gun availability has a direct causal effect on the homicide rate. But with a sample of two, this conclusion is not persuasive. Quantifying the uncertainty in this case is difficult, and requires some careful thought about the appropriate model in which to view the two-city comparison.

H. Conclusions concerning Gun Availability Studies

Assessing the effects of gun availability on personal violence is made difficult by problems in defining and measuring availability as well as by the usual problems in interpreting results generated from nonexperimental data (Cook 1980*b*). It is clear from this work that the geographic differences in gun ownership are highly correlated with the fractions of homicides, suicides, assaults, and robberies involving guns. One explanation for this relation is that the weapon choices of violent and suicidal people are influenced by the ease of obtaining a gun.

Given the weapon instrumentality effect, greater use of guns in assaults and robberies is likely to increase the death rates from these types of violence. If an increase in gun availability produces an increase in the fraction of violent acts committed with a gun, then the end result will be more deaths. This conclusion is plausible and supported by a number of the studies reviewed above but difficult to document persuasively in the absence of a natural experiment. The case-control approach represented in the comparison of Vancouver and Seattle seems promising, though it is difficult, in practice, to identify suitable pairs of jurisdictions, and one pair is not enough. An alternative approach to assessing the effect of gun availability on personal violence is to evaluate the effects of legal interventions designed to reduce availability. Such evaluations are of particular interest because they are directly relevant to policy.

I. Evaluating Gun-Control Ordinances

Commerce in and use of firearms are subject to a variety of regulations; these regulations differ widely among states, and the effects of these regulations are mediated by the effort devoted to their enforcement. Research evaluating the effects of these ordinances has taken one of two approaches. Some studies employ a multivariate analysis in which one or more of the independent variables is an index of state regulatory stringency. A second approach focuses on the impact of the implementation of a new ordinance or a change in enforcement policy in a single jurisdiction.

1. *Cross-sectional Studies.* Several cross-sectional studies that attempt to measure the effectiveness of gun-control ordinances in reducing personal violence are noteworthy (Geisel, Ross, and Wettick 1969; Murray 1975; Medoff and Magaddino 1983; Magaddino and Medoff 1984). Each used cross-sectional data on the fifty states and reported regression results relating various measures of personal violence rates to a number of independent variables—including one or more indicators of the stringency of state gun-control legislation. Geisel, Ross, and Wettick reported that greater stringency, as measured by the index they devised, was associated with lower rates of suicide and homicide by gun. Medoff and Magaddino limited their analysis to suicide rates and reported that states requiring waiting times for handgun transfers had lower suicide rates than others, after controlling for relevant characteristics of the state population. Two other studies (Murray 1975; Magaddino and Medoff 1984), however, reported results that provide no support for the hypothesis that more stringent state gun-control laws are efficacious in reducing violent death rates.

All of these studies are problematic for several reasons (Cook 1982; Wright, Rossi, and Daly 1983). As with any statistical analysis of nonexperimental data, the results are sensitive to the specification of the model to be estimated. There are many plausible variables that may influence interstate variation in rates of personal violence, and the decision about which of these variables to include in the analysis is subject to a large and unquantifiable degree of uncertainty. Nevertheless, it is methodologically unacceptable simply to ignore the problem of multiple causation, as do Lester and Murrell (1982) in their study of the effect of gun-control ordinances on suicide rates. Further, none of the studies summarized above has even attempted to measure gun availability, even though most of the gun-control regulations influence rates of personal violence, if at all, by reducing the availability of guns. For example, if North Carolina and Connecticut have similar licensing systems for handguns and enforce them with equal vigor, gun availability will still remain far higher in North Carolina since a much higher percentage of households already own guns in that state. And finally, these studies code gun-control ordinances without regard to the vigor with which they are enforced and offenders are punished. In sum, it appears that the intrinsic difficulties with this approach virtually ensure against generating reliable, persuasive results that will be a useful guide to state legislators.

2. *Measuring the Impact of New Regulations.* The prognosis for evaluations of the impact of new regulations is more hopeful. Three major statutes have been subjected to systematic evaluation: the federal Gun Control Act of 1968 (GCA), the Bartley-Fox Amendment (Massachusetts), and the Firearms Control Act (District of Columbia). These three statutes represent three distinct strategies for reducing gun availability and hence personal violence involving guns.

As noted above, a major purpose of the GCA was to stop mail-order sales of guns to private individuals, and otherwise to interdict the interstate traffic in firearms. Zimring (1975, p. 176) observes that "if the Gun Control Act and its enforcement has led to a reduction in interstate firearms traffic, this reduction should be evident in New York City and Boston, the principal cities in the two most restrictive handgun-licensing states in the United States, because out-of-state handguns are a higher proportion of total handguns in these cities than in other metropolitan areas." Zimring finds that the trends in such variables as handgun homicides, firearm assaults, and the percentage of total homicides involving handguns provide no support for the hypothesis that the GCA reduced gun availability in New York City and Boston. All these variables trend upward during 1966–73, and these trends are not discernibly different from corresponding trends in Philadelphia or from the overall rates for large cities. Based on these findings and evidence from gun-tracing studies, Zimring concludes that the GCA had failed to diminish handgun migration or lethal violence.[16] Magaddino and Medoff (1984) employed a much different statistical approach but reached essentially the same conclusions concerning the GCA.

One explanation for this apparent failure is the lack of enforcement effort on the part of the Bureau of Alcohol, Tobacco and Firearms—the federal agency responsible for interdicting illegal interstate movements of firearms. This explanation received partial support from Operation D.C., in which the Bureau of Alcohol, Tobacco and Firearms enforcement staff in the District of Columbia was increased from seven to between thirty-five and fifty special agents for the first six months of

[16] However, the Gun Control Act (GCA) may have enhanced the capacity of the police to trace the ownership record of weapons used in crime.

1970. The gun murder rate dropped significantly during this period and rebounded thereafter, while the nongun murder rate remained roughly constant. The result is supportive of the claim that gun availability is sensitive to interdiction efforts and, further, that gun availability influences the gun murder rate and the overall murder rate.

Massachusetts's Bartley-Fox Amendment has received more scholarly scrutiny than any other piece of gun-related legislation. The amendment took effect on April 1, 1975, and established a minimum sentence of one year for an initial violation of Massachusetts's legal requirements for carrying a gun away from home or office. The amendment did not eliminate the possibility of charge bargaining in the prosecution of such cases but did effectively tie the hands of the sentencing judge. This mandatory sentence provision received tremendous publicity at the time it was implemented. The immediate impact was clear-cut: thousands of gun owners applied for licenses to carry (required to carry a handgun legally), and most gun owners obtained a firearms identification card required of all gun owners and sufficient for carrying a long gun legally. Indeed, 100,000 firearms identification cards were issued in April 1975—more than had been issued in all of 1973 and 1974 combined (Beha 1977).

James Beha's early analysis of the effect of this amendment found that the police and courts were making a conscientious effort to implement the spirit of the new law. It had little effect on the court processing of robberies and murders, but it did increase the likelihood of prison time for defendants accused of assault with a firearm. Most important, cases in which illegal carrying was the most serious charge had an increased chance of resulting in a prison term. Some indication was found (from interviews with law-enforcement officers and a few criminals in Boston) that the propensity of the "streetwise" to go armed had been reduced by the threat of the law (Beha 1977).

Pierce and Bowers (1979, 1981) assessed the impact of Bartley-Fox on violent crime through 1977. They constructed annual time series on a number of violent-crime measures for Massachusetts, Boston, and several comparison groups. They concluded that the short-term impact was to reduce the fractions of assaults and robberies involving guns and to reduce the criminal homicide rate. They noted that the effect on gun assault began one month prior to the effective date of the law, suggesting that offenders, at least initially, were responding to the publicity that accompanied the new law rather than to the actual imposition of severe sanctions that it engendered.

An alternative approach to evaluating Bartley-Fox was used by Deutsch and Alt (1977). They employed a stochastic modeling technique, applied to monthly time-series data on armed robbery, homicide, and gun assault in Boston (January 1966–October 1975). They found significant reductions in armed robbery and gun assault, but not homicide, during the first six months following implementation of Bartley-Fox. In a follow-up study of the same three violent-crime measures, utilizing thirty months of postintervention data, Deutsch (1979) found large reductions in all three series, which he attributed to the new law. It should be noted, however, that the rest of the country was also experiencing reductions in violent-crime rates during this period.

The District of Columbia implemented the strictest gun-control ordinance in the nation in February 1977. This ordinance, the Firearms Control Act, banned the acquisition or transfer of a handgun by any District resident, with the exception of law-enforcement officers and a few others. The only residents who could legally possess a handgun were those who acquired and registered them before the ordinance went into effect. To acquire handguns in the District, residents must steal them or make illegal purchases in the black market or in the neighboring states.

In contrast to Bartley-Fox, the crime-related effects of the Firearms Control Act would be likely to increase over time and to be quite small for the first few months or even years. This lack of a temporally concentrated impact increases the difficulty of evaluating this ordinance. The first evaluation that was attempted (U.S. Conference of Mayors 1980) compared average crime rates for a three-year period subsequent to implementation with corresponding rates for 1974–76. Rates of gun robbery, assault, and homicide were all lower in the postimplementation period. Jones (1981) extended this analysis in several respects. He found a reduction in the fraction of assaults and robberies committed with a gun following implementation. Further, he found a change in the distribution of criminal homicides across circumstances, with felony-type homicides becoming more important relative to homicides involving family members and arguments with acquaintances. This last finding is interesting given the enormous increase in homicides in the District of Columbia since 1985 (District of Columbia 1989). The doubling of this rate between 1985 and 1988 has been the result of drug-related conflicts, rather than increased prevalence of the altercations among family and friends. Homicides for which drug trafficking or use was a direct cause increased from twenty-one for all of 1985 to ninety-five for just the first six months of 1988, while the annual rate of other types of homicides was about the same (District of Columbia 1989). The fraction of homicides in which guns were used increased from 65 percent to 70 percent during this period. It is perhaps not surprising that the District's restrictions on handgun transfers have proven ineffective in stopping the tide of drug-related lethal violence.

V. Self-Defense

That one-half of American households own guns is primarily a reflection of the widespread involvement in hunting and target shooting. But for one-fifth of those who own a gun and two-fifths of handgun owners, the most important reason is self-defense at home (Wright, Rossi, and Daly 1983, p. 96). The concern reflected in this defensive demand for guns is quite reasonable, given the burglary statistics. During the period 1979–87, there was an annual average of one million residential burglaries in which a household member was present, yielding a household victimization rate of over 1 percent.[17] Thirty-four percent of these burglaries of occupied dwellings resulted in an assault, robbery, or rape. Thus the need to take precautions against intruders is real, and a gun seems to offer an inexpensive means of self-defense against intruders who are neither discouraged by locks nor deterred by the presence of someone in the home.

A number of studies have questioned whether a gun, in fact, offers much protection against burglars since most people who are burglarized while at home do not attempt to defend themselves with a gun even when there is one available. The larger issue is whether the presence of a gun in the home poses a risk to household members that outweighs whatever protection it may confer; a handgun obtained for self-protection may end up causing accidental injury or suicide (Kellermann and Reay 1986). There may, however, be a public benefit to the widespread ownership of guns, particularly in deterring burglary of occupied dwellings. And the use of guns for self-protection away from home raises the same issues; people who go armed in public may have a better chance to defend themselves against robbery and assault while at the same time increasing the rates of accidental shootings and other

[17] An unpublished tabulation provided the author by the U.S. Bureau of Justice Statistics estimated that, during the period 1979–87, there were 9.042 million burglaries in which a household member was present.

forms of misuse. Indeed, it is entirely reasonable that private gun ownership has mixed effects on personal violence and crime. This section documents these effects and reviews the evidence on their importance.

A. *The Demand for Guns for Self-Protection*

The qualities of a gun that make it effective in fending off assailants and intruders are the same as those that make it an effective tool in personal crimes of violence. A gun greatly enhances most people's capacity to intimidate or incapacitate an assailant. The defensive demand for guns extends even to those who routinely engage in violent crime; a majority of the gun-using felons who responded to Wright and Rossi's survey cited self-defense as an important reason for their practice of carrying a gun (Wright and Rossi 1986, p. 128).

As a means of defense against crime, guns supplement alarms, guard dogs, and "target-hardening" measures (door locks, window grilles, safes), both in residences and retail shops. A 1968 survey of small businesses found that the demand for guns and other protection devices increased with the threat of victimization. Businesses in the ghetto were more likely to have a gun than were those located in other areas of the central city, which, in turn, were more likely to have a gun than were businesses located in the suburbs (Kakalik and Wildhorn 1972). This pattern of gun ownership is not found among households since most people buy guns to hunt rather than for defending their homes; thus, urban households are less likely to own a gun than rural households. However, there is evidence that the propensity to obtain a gun specifically for self-protection is influenced by the threat of criminal victimization. Smith and Uchida (1988) demonstrate this result with data from a survey of three urban areas conducted in 1977. For the overall sample of 9,021 respondents, 14.3 percent reported that they or another member of their household had purchased a "gun or other weapon" for protection of home and family. The authors' multivariate analysis of these responses demonstrated that defensive weapon acquisition was more likely if a household member had been victimized in the last year, or if the respondent perceived an increase in his neighborhood's crime rate in the last year. They also found a strong negative association between weapon acquisition and the respondent's rating of police services. The authors conclude that obtaining a weapon for protection is a response to perceived vulnerability to crime. This result is surely credible though not definitive; the data do not allow them to distinguish between guns and other weapons and do not include any objective indicator of neighborhood crime rates.

B. *Use of Guns for Self-Protection*

If guns are obtained in part for self-protection, how often are they actually used for that purpose? Attempts to answer this question have relied primarily on survey data since there are no official records that are directly relevant.

Gary Kleck (1988) reviewed a number of surveys and other sources in an attempt to demonstrate the value of guns in defending against crime. He noted in particular the results of the 1981 Hart poll of registered voters; 4 percent of respondents said they or members of their household had used a handgun in the previous five years for self-protection or for protection of property at home, work, or elsewhere. (Respondents were instructed to limit their report to uses against people, as opposed to animals, and to exclude military and police-work uses.) On the assumption that respondents define "household" the same way as the Census Bureau, Kleck concludes that there were 3.2 million households (4 percent of 80 million) in which someone used a handgun to threaten or shoot at another person in an effort to defend life or property. Unfortunately, there are no details provided in the Hart poll concerning the distribution of circumstances for these events, nor any data on defensive uses of long guns. Kleck overcomes the latter problem by multiplying the incidence of handgun uses by a factor of 1.57. His justification is based on a poll conducted in 1978, which inquired whether guns in the home were owned primarily for self-defense. He concludes from the responses that there are 21 million handguns and 12 million long guns kept for self-defense, or .57 long guns for every handgun. He then assumes that long guns are used for self-defense in this same ratio (Kleck 1988, p. 4). He concludes that guns are used in self-defense about one million times each year.

The National Crime Survey (NCS) provides much more specific data on the use of guns in self-defense against personal violence. National Crime Survey data for 1979–85 yield an estimate of 386,000 instances in which victims of assault and robbery defended themselves with a gun (Kleck 1988). This implies an annual average of 55,000 defensive uses of firearms in crimes of violence, which is less than 6 percent of Kleck's estimate of the overall frequency of self-defense uses. The logical implication, if one believes Kleck's estimate, is that there are about 950,000 other "defensive" uses of guns that do not involve violent crimes. But Kleck comes to a different conclusion. He uses California survey data as a basis for arguing that most of the defensive uses of guns *do* involve crimes of personal violence, occurring primarily at home. His explanation for the seemingly gross inconsistency among his various statistics is that the NCS respondents underreport assaults occurring at home. The undercount would have to be vast indeed for this to be an adequate explanation, but perhaps it is: conceivably, respondents are so reticent about reporting domestic violence incidents to NCS interviewers that the NCS estimate misses all but 1 or 2 percent of them.[18]

Alternatively, or in addition, the Hart poll may be in error. The Hart poll on which Kleck's estimate is based requires respondents to recall events from years earlier and, in particular, to distinguish between those that occurred within five years and those that occurred earlier. Experiments conducted in the course of designing the National Crime Survey demonstrated that respondents made systematic errors in placing their personal victimization experiences in time; if asked to report victimizations occurring within the previous twelve months, they would tend to "telescope" in important experiences that had occurred outside of that time frame, while forgetting to mention other victimizations that occurred within the time frame (Penick and Owens 1976; Skogan 1981). The Hart poll asked respondents to deal with a time frame of five years, rather than one, and the question concerned experiences for any member of the "household," rather than just personal experience. Given these difficulties, it is likely that some of the respondents who gave a positive response were remembering events that, in fact, had occurred more than five years earlier or events that occurred to family members who were not members of the "household" as that term would be defined by the Bureau of the Census. In short, there are severe methodological problems with the Hart poll as a basis for estimating the prevalence of gun use in self-defense.

The National Crime Survey is a much larger and more sophisticated effort, based on questionnaires that have been devised and refined through a program of extensive testing to produce a reliable basis for

[18] The National Crime Survey (NCS) has encountered severe problems in counting repetitive crimes (known as "series incidents") and excludes them from its published estimates (Skogan 1990). This problem combined with the underreporting engendered by special sensitivities with domestic violence produces a considerable bias in estimates of household assaults (Bureau of Justice Statistics 1984). Presumably the Hart poll would suffer from the same problems.

estimating the volume of crime. Still, Kleck is correct in pointing out that the NCS data miss a large fraction of domestic assaults and the defensive uses of guns that may occur in that context. My conclusion is to accept the NCS-based estimate of 50,000 defensive uses per year against rape, robbery, and assault with the proviso that this figure excludes almost all defensive uses against members of the same household. The NCS data probably also miss most of the instances in which guns are used by criminals and others who are unlikely to cooperate with the National Crime Survey interviewers (Cook 1985*a*). Of course, there is no reason to believe that the Hart poll would do any better in this respect.

The National Crime Survey also offers some information on the frequency of gun use in protecting property. In particular, newly available results on burglaries provide the first direct measure of self-defense measures taken against burglars of occupied dwellings. Data from the National Crime Survey for the nine-year period 1979–87 were pooled to provide reliable estimates. Special tabulations were provided in personal correspondence to me from Michael Rand of the Bureau of Justice Statistics. During this period, there was an average of 6.8 million residential burglaries a year, of which in 1.0 million cases (14.7 percent), there was someone at home at the time. In about one-half of these burglaries (52.6 percent), some self-defense action was taken. Of greatest interest here is the use of weapons in self-defense: only 3.1 percent of occupants used a gun to defend against the intruder, while 2.0 percent used a knife or other weapon. Thus, there are about 32,000 instances each year in which someone uses a gun to scare off or defend against an intruder. In other words, a gun is used once in every 220 burglaries, or once in every thirty burglaries of an occupied residence.[19]

Given these results, it is possible to estimate the total number of defensive gun uses against burglary and violent crime. Of the 32,000 annual uses against burglary, about 9,000 involved violent crimes as well. Avoiding double counting, the total National Crime Survey–based estimate of gun uses against predatory crime is about 80,000 per year.

[19] About half (54 percent) of burglaries against an occupied dwelling are perpetrated by a relative or acquaintance of the victim. But only one-third of the instances of defensive gun use against intruders involve relatives or acquaintances. When a stranger burglarizes an occupied dwelling, the likelihood the victim will use a gun in self-defense is about 4.6 percent.

C. *Success and Failure in Self-Defense Efforts*

The statistical record suggests that people who use a weapon to defend against robberies, assaults, and burglaries are generally successful in foiling the crime and avoiding injury. In the case of burglary, the National Crime Survey sample for 1979–87 of burglaries of occupied residences indicate that gun defense is associated with a relatively low rate of successful theft (14 percent of gun-defense cases versus 33 percent overall). If we restrict the sample to those cases in which theft was actually attempted (41 percent of the total), there remains a large difference in success rates: 80 percent of all such attempts were successful in burglaries of occupied residences, but when the victim used a gun in self-defense, only 48 percent of attempts were successful. (The estimated theft success rate is only 46 percent when the victim defended himself or herself with a knife or other weapon.)

Robbery statistics also suggest the effectiveness of using a gun or other weapon in self-defense. Kleck's (1988) analysis of National Crime Survey data for the period 1979–85 found that the likelihood that a robbery would be completed successfully when the victim resisted with a gun was only 31 percent, the same as the rate for robberies where knives or other weapons were used to resist. (The overall rate of successful completion was 65 percent.) However, it was relatively rare for guns to be used to defend against robbery. Defense with guns occurred in only 1.2 percent of incidents, and knives or other weapons were used in another 2.3 percent of incidents. Proportionately, few victims have a gun handy when they are robbed, and most of those who do are surely not in a position to use it effectively. A skilled robber takes control of the victim quickly through violence or threats (Conklin 1972). Thus, the sample of robberies in which the victim uses a gun in self-defense is surely unrepresentative of the universe of robberies in a number of dimensions, including the competence of the robbers and the types of weapon they use. For that reason, the National Crime Survey tabulations are not a reliable guide to the costs and benefits of using a gun in self-defense in any specific robbery circumstances (Cook 1986).[20]

D. *Injury to Victims*

There is always a danger that victim resistance will provoke an assailant to greater violence and result in more serious injury to the victim

[20] Victims are much less likely to resist gun robbers than those with other weapons.

than if no resistance had been made. It is interesting that National Crime Survey data (Kleck 1988) suggest that physical attack and injury are much less likely to occur in robberies and assaults in which the victim is able to deploy a gun than in other circumstances. But that difference, in the absence of information on the sequence of events in the violent encounter, is subject to several interpretations (Cook 1986). It could be that resistance with a gun forestalls attack, or, alternatively, that an attack prevents the victim from deploying his gun. While both explanations may be valid, the latter is surely more important. In the usual sequence of events, the robber's attack on the victim *initiates* the encounter, as in a mugging or yoking. Thus instead of concluding that "gun resisters are unlikely to be attacked," it is more accurate to conclude that "victims who are attacked are unlikely to have the opportunity to deploy their gun."

The sparse National Crime Survey data on this subject say nothing at all about the likelihood that the victim will be killed since homicide is not a logical possibility in victim survey data. Police files on robbery murder do offer some information on the importance of resistance, however. I collected data from police files in Dade County, Florida, and Atlanta, Georgia, for several years in the mid-1970s (Cook 1980*a*). Out of thirty robbery murders in Dade County, there were just three in which the victim offered forceful resistance. In twenty-six robbery murders in Atlanta, there was evidence of forceful resistance in two cases, including one that involved a gun: a police officer was shot when he interrupted a robbery and attempted to draw his weapon (Cook and Nagin 1979, p. 33). It appears, then, that robbery murder is rarely the result of escalation of violence stemming from the victim's use of force.

In sum, while using a gun to resist a robber may sometimes result in serious injury or death to the victim, that result is not common. Only about 1 percent of victims of noncommercial robbery resist with a gun, and in those instances the resistance effort is usually successful. Of course, resisting with a gun is only possible if the robber fails to take immediate control of the situation and only prudent if the robber lacks a gun himself.

E. Deterrence and Other General Effects

While relatively few victims of burglary and personal violence attempt to defend themselves with guns, the possibility of encountering an armed victim poses a definite risk to predatory criminals. That risk may influence a number of crime-related decisions, including the kinds of crimes to commit, the selection of targets, the modus operandi, and even the decision of when to retire. The widespread availability of guns surely does have some influence on such decisions and, hence, on the overall volume and pattern of predatory crime. The pertinent question is whether these effects are large or small.

Wright and Rossi's (1986) survey of prisoners found a large minority with relevant personal experience. Overall, two-fifths said there had been one or more times in their life when they "decided not to do a crime because [they] knew or believed that the victim was carrying a gun" (p. 155). One-third had been "scared off, shot at, wounded, or captured by an armed victim." Wright and Rossi point out that there is an ambiguity in these results concerning the nature of the armed victim; no doubt some were law-abiding citizens, but others would be criminal associates of the respondent whom they fought or attempted to rob (p. 159). On the broader issue of deterrence, Wright and Rossi asked their respondents what felons worry about when contemplating criminal activity: "might get shot at by victim" was a frequent worry for 34 percent of the respondents, the same fraction as those whose concern was "might get shot at by police" (Wright and Rossi, p. 148). (By comparison, half of the respondents indicated that they worried about being caught.) These results, while based on a sample that is not representative of violent criminals, are at least suggestive that the threat of effective victim resistance is relevant in understanding criminal behavior.

The objective threat that armed victims pose to predatory criminals is difficult to measure. Wright and Rossi's (1986) data do not allow an estimate of the fraction who had been shot during the course of a crime. National Crime Survey data on self-defense do not include an item on whether the assailant was injured. Police departments file supplementary homicide reports with the Federal Bureau of Investigation that include cases of "civilian justifiable homicide"—instances in which a civilian killed a criminal in the act of committing a felony—but it is not always possible to determine the circumstances in which these homicides occur. One attempt to use these data focused on robbery (Cook 1979). I tabulated all such killings that occurred during robberies, 1973–74, in nineteen cities. The death rate per 100,000 exposures ranged from about four, for cities in the Northeast and Pacific regions, to a high of forty-eight for Atlanta. Assuming that the death rate from justifiable shootings in robberies is about 10 percent,[21] then an order-of-magnitude estimate for the risk a robber faces in a city with high gun ownership is 0.2 percent. This relative frequency is an average of commercial and noncommercial robberies; the former may be the more risky, given the presence of security guards in some cases. In any event, a probability on the order of 0.2 percent seems so low as to be readily ignored in a robber's calculations, yet for a robbery "career" of 100 robberies, the implication is an 18 percent probability of being shot at least once.

Do high rates of gun ownership have a deterrent effect on robbery? A multivariate analysis of city robbery rates, reported above, found that there was no statistically discernible effect of gun prevalence on the robbery rate (Cook 1979). Of course, "no effect" may be the net result of a negative deterrent effect and a positive effect stemming from the greater ease of robbers obtaining guns for use in crime.

There is a smattering of evidence on the likelihood that a residential burglar will be shot. The most often cited is Newton and Zimring's (1969, p. 63) order-of-magnitude estimate of 0.2 percent, based on a single city during a period when there were just seven justifiable homicides in burglaries. In any event, there is no evidence that higher gun ownership rates deter burglary. Indeed, I found that burglary rates tend to increase with gun ownership across large cities, other things equal (Cook 1983*b*). Presumably, this is the result of the greater average payoff to burglary in cities where guns are likely to be part of the loot.[22]

A number of authors have suggested that the threat of being shot by an occupant has the effect of deterring burglary of occupied dwellings (Kates 1983; Wright and Rossi 1986). In support of this proposition, Kleck (1988) observes that the occupancy rate for burglaries in the United States is far lower than in three countries for which the relevant burglary data exist (Canada, Great Britain, and the Netherlands) and where gun ownership is less prevalent.

[21] The "deterrence" explanation is speculative and should not be taken seriously until it is possible to rule out other explanations. As reported above, in the United States, it appears that burglary of occupied dwellings is a much different phenomenon than burglary of unoccupied dwellings. Half the former cases involve relatives or acquaintances, and, in most cases, their objective is something other than theft by stealth. Given this characterization, it is easy to believe that international differences in the relative frequency of burglary of occupied dwellings reflect societal differences.

[22] Alternatively, it could reflect the reverse causal process, in the sense that the demand for guns may be enhanced by a high burglary rate. However, as noted above, gun-ownership patterns are largely determined by the demand for use in hunting and other sports, rather than for use in self-defense.

There are two well-known instances in which a jurisdiction has implemented a policy of encouraging citizens to use guns in self-defense against crime. In both cases, short-term changes in crime statistics have been interpreted as evidence that the intervention had a large deterrent effect. Yet this interpretation of the data is open to serious doubt.

The first such intervention was in Orlando, Florida, where the police trained 6,000 women in the safe use of firearms between October 1966 and March 1967. The program was highly publicized as an anti-rape intervention. According to Kleck and Bordua (1983), the rape rate in Orlando dropped 88 percent from 1966 to 1967 and did not return to its former level until 1972. During that same period, the rape rate in the rest of Florida nearly doubled. But Green (1987) questioned the reliability of the Orlando Police Department's crime records as a basis for evaluating the effects of the gun training program. He pointed out that the recorded rape rate in Orlando fluctuated widely throughout the 1960s and actually dropped to zero in 1963. The pattern that is interpreted as a deterrent effect by Bordua and Kleck may be an artifact of poor data.

The second intervention was in Kennesaw, Georgia; in March 1982, the town council passed an ordinance requiring every household in the city to keep a firearm in their home. The law was enacted to make a public statement rather than to change behavior; there was no penalty for violation, and it exempted those who objected to firearms. Nevertheless, the burglary rate dropped sharply immediately following adoption of this ordinance, and it has continued to be touted as evidence of the crime-deterrent value of a well-armed citizenry (Kleck 1988; Kates 1989).

An analysis of the Kennesaw burglary data over the period from 1976 to 1986 suggests a different conclusion (McDowall, Wiersema, and Loftin 1989). They demonstrate that the burglary rate fluctuated widely from year to year (as one would expect in such a small city) but that there is no evidence that the gun ordinance produced a downward shift in the trend. They make a persuasive case that the ordinance had no effect on burglary rates in Kennesaw.

F. *Conclusion*

Despite the fact that there is a gun in half of American households, it is relatively rare for victims of burglary and crimes of violence to use them in self-defense. The National Crime Survey data suggest about 55,000 uses in robbery and assault each year, with an additional 25,000 uses against burglary. The National Crime Survey underestimates the volume of domestic violence, hence, underestimates the frequency with which guns are used to defend against family members. For other circumstances, however, the National Crime Survey estimates are a reasonable approximation of reality.

When guns are used in self-defense, the result is usually favorable; the victim is able to foil the robbery or assault attempt. There is little evidence that the use of a gun in self-defense tends to escalate violence, although it surely happens in some cases. Of course, an assailant who has obtained the upper hand quickly enough can forestall effective resistance, and the data reflect that fact.

The threat of a burglar or robber being shot by a civilian during the commission of a crime is small, on the average, though higher in more heavily armed jurisdictions than elsewhere. While predatory criminals are aware of this danger and surely adopt precautions in some cases, it is not true that jurisdictions with high gun ownership have lower robbery or burglary rates than others. The two famous quasi-experiments in Kennesaw and Orlando may have produced some deterrent effects, but the data are such as to vitiate confidence in this conclusion.

Finally, it is important to comment on the several studies (including Newton and Zimring 1969; Yeager 1976; Rushforth et al. 1977; Kellermann and Reay 1986) that demonstrate that guns kept in the home are far more likely to kill a family member or friend than an intruder. This is a strange comparison, in a way, since the defensive purpose of keeping a gun is not to kill intruders but to scare them off (Silver and Kates 1979). Wright (1984) has suggested that a more relevant comparison is between the likelihood of a gun accident and the likelihood of having occasion to use a gun in self-defense; based on one national survey, these appear to be approximately equal, on the average. But that comparison ignores the fact that a gun in the house may increase the risk that a household member will commit suicide. Thus the objective benefit of gun ownership is measured by the likelihood of using the gun to defend successfully against burglary and assault, whether or not the perpetrator is shot in the process. The cost of gun ownership is the risk of an accidental shooting, or, more problematically, of suicide. There is an asymmetry here: no cost is incurred unless there is injury, but the beneficial use of the gun does not require that anyone be injured.

Undoubtedly, anyone who is contemplating obtaining a gun should consider the risks, whose magnitude depends on how carefully a weapon is stored and handled, whether any family members are suicidal, and other factors. These risks can be compared to a realistic assessment of the benefit, that there is some small chance of being able to use the gun in self-defense if there were an intruder who could not otherwise be scared off. The upshot of this calculation will depend on the circumstances. Finally, the public benefit of having a heavily armed citizenry remains to be demonstrated.

VI. Directions for Future Research

Research on weapons and violence has provided some answers or partial answers to questions relevant to evaluating alternative gun-control strategies. At the same time, this research has demonstrated that the "technology" of personal violence is an important piece of the etiological puzzle. Further research in a number of areas would enhance our scientific understanding of personal violence and inform the policy debate on how best to combat this pressing problem. Below is a menu of promising and feasible projects.

A. *Data Collection*

There remains considerable uncertainty concerning the number of firearms in private households. This uncertainty could be greatly reduced by a carefully designed national survey that included items on whether there were any guns in the house, and if so, how many and of what sort. Other items of interest include information on how these guns are stored and used, who within the household has access to them, and how the guns were obtained.

There is a lack of information on the use of guns in self-defense. The National Crime Survey currently includes items that provide information on self-defense in violent confrontations and against burglars, but no information on other uses such as scaring trespassers away from private property. There is also need for better data on justifiable homicides than are currently available from the Federal Bureau of Investigation's supplementary homicide reports (Kleck 1988).

We need reliable estimates of the number of gunshot woundings in accidents, assaults, and suicide attempts, including detailed information on the type of gun. Without such data, it is not possible to develop a clear picture of the relative costs of gun misuse in different circumstances. The data that are currently routinely available, which are limited to fatal shootings, may tend to understate the importance of accidents (fatal or otherwise) relative to criminal or self-inflicted shootings. If this is true, then policy interventions directed specifically at reducing the accident rate are undervalued.

Finally, it is worth considering an expanded program of data collection on homicide and suicide, perhaps using the Fatal Accident Reporting System (FARS) as a model.[23] FARS is maintained by the National Highway Traffic Safety Administration, which collects detailed crash information from police records. Suicide and homicide data could be collected separately, or FARS could be expanded into a traumatic death reporting system; in either case, data elements would include information on the weapons that caused death, together with demographic characteristics, immediate circumstances, blood alcohol content of the participants, and so forth.

B. Measuring Gun Availability

Gun "availability" has been viewed by some researchers as virtually synonymous with the prevalence of gun ownership. It would be of great interest to evaluate this assumption by analyzing how violent people obtain their guns in a sample of jurisdictions that differ with respect to prevalence of ownership. Potential sources of information on this issue include traces of confiscated crime guns, police investigations of fences, drug dealers, and other black market operators, and interviews of the sort conducted by Wright and Rossi (1986), but with a broader and more representative sample.

In addition to this effort to develop better qualitative understanding of gun availability, it would be useful to conduct evaluations of various indicators of gun availability as a basis for studying the effect of availability on crime patterns. The most commonly used indicator, the percentage of homicides that are committed with a gun, is flawed by its sensitivity to differences in the composition of homicide over time and across jurisdictions.

The promising new effort to collect internationally comparable data on crime and the prevalence of gun ownership should be encouraged and broadened to include suicide. Casual international comparisons have long been a part of the rhetoric for and against gun-control measures, and it would be of value to be able to make these comparisons more systematically.

[23] Arthur Kellermann (1990) suggested this approach in a personal communication.

C. Methodology

The research on guns and crime that has received the most scholarly attention in recent memory is the comparison of homicide rates in Seattle and Vancouver, conducted by Sloan, Kellermann, and others (1988). There is an interesting methodological question about this type of comparison, relating to the degree of uncertainty that attaches to the results. Should this be viewed as a controlled laboratory experiment in which the two cities are identical in every relevant respect except gun availability? Or should this single comparison be viewed as an interesting anecdote that must be confirmed by results from many other pairs of cities before the result is well established in a statistical sense? I favor the second view but would welcome a careful analysis of the methodological issues here.

D. Evaluations of Policy Changes

Evaluations of the effects of changes in policies affecting gun availability and use offer the most direct evidence on the question of what generally can be accomplished through such measures. Of course, the consequences of any particular intervention will be influenced by the immediate context and the effort devoted to implementation, so there will always be a question about what generalizations can safely be drawn. But that simply argues for doing as many evaluations as possible and not resting strong conclusions on single cases.

Systematic evaluation of a policy change in one jurisdiction is relevant to predicting the consequences of a similar change proposed for another jurisdiction. In some cases it may also serve as a test of general propositions concerning guns and violence. A case in point is the Bartley-Fox Amendment in Massachusetts. Several studies found that its threat of severe punishment for carrying a gun illegally reduced illegal carrying and some types of violent crime, including homicide, although the nongun assault rate appears to have increased. In addition to providing information about the effects of this particular ordinance, this pattern of results is powerful evidence in support of the instrumentality effect.

These recommendations for research directions are not intended to exhaust the list of interesting possibilities but, rather, to suggest that there is much useful work that remains to be done. Indeed, even after two decades of systematic research on weapons and personal violence and results indicating the powerful and pervasive influence of weapon type on the patterns and outcomes of violent encounters, this area of research has yet to realize its great potential. Criminologists who set out to understand personal violence rarely devote much attention to weapons questions; they are apparently perceived as a distinct topic, which has not yet been "mainstreamed" into etiological research. Public health researchers appear to be moving more quickly in this respect, and guns have been established in the public health literature as a widely acknowledged environmental risk factor.

The type of weapon is more than an incidental detail of a violent encounter, and the general availability of guns in a community cannot be ignored when seeking to understand patterns of interpersonal violence and suicide. That is the bottom line and the basis for encouraging more research in this area.

REFERENCES

Beha, James A., III. 1977. "'And Nobody Can Get You Out': The Impact of a Mandatory Prison Sentence for the Illegal Carrying of a Firearm on the Use of Firearms and the Administration of Criminal Justice in Boston." *Boston University Law Review* 57:96–146, 289–33.

Benenson, Mark, and Don B. Kates, Jr. 1979. "Handgun Prohibition and Homicide: A Plausible Theory Meets the Intractible Facts." In *Restricting Handguns: The Liberal Skeptics Speak Out*, edited by Don B. Kates, Jr. Croton-on-Hudson, N.Y.: North River.

Berger, Lawrence R. 1988. "Suicides and Pesticides in Sri Lanka." *American Journal of Public Health* 78:826–28.

Blose, James, and Philip J. Cook. 1980. "Regulating Handgun Transfers: Current State and Federal Procedures, and an Assessment of the Feasibility and Costs of the Proposed Procedures in the Handgun Crime Control Act of 1979." Working paper. Durham, N.C.: Duke University, Institute of Policy Sciences.

Boor, M. 1981. "Methods of Suicide and Implications for Suicide Prevention." *Journal of Clinical Psychology* 37:70–75.

Brearly, Harrington C. 1932. *Homicide in the U.S.* Chapel Hill: University of North Carolina Press.

Brent, David A., Joshua A. Perper, Charles E. Goldstein, David J. Kolko, Marjorie J. Allan, Christopher J. Allman, and Janice P. Zelenak. 1988. "Risk Factors for Adolescent Suicide." *Archives of General Psychiatry* 45:581–88.

Bruce-Briggs, B. 1976. "The Great American Gun War." *Public Interest* 45:1–26.

Bureau of Alcohol, Tobacco and Firearms. 1976. *Project Identification: A Study of Handguns Used in Crime.* Washington, D.C.: U.S. Department of the Treasury.

———. 1989. "Ready Reference Statistics." Mimeographed. Washington, D.C.: U.S. Department of the Treasury.

Bureau of Justice Statistics. 1984. *Family Violence.* Bureau of Justice Statistics Special Report. Washington, D.C.: U.S. Bureau of Justice Statistics.

———. 1989*a*. *Criminal Victimization in the United States, 1987.* Washington, D.C.: U.S. Bureau of Justice Statistics.

———. 1989*b*. *Sourcebook of Criminal Justice Statistics—1988.* Washington, D.C.: U.S. Bureau of Justice Statistics.

Card, J. J. 1974. "Lethality of Suicidal Methods and Suicide Risk: Two Distinct Concepts." *Omega* 5:37–45.

Clarke, Ronald V., and David Lester. 1989. *Suicide: Closing the Exits.* New York: Springer-Verlag.

Clarke, Ronald V., and Pat Mayhew. 1988. "The British Gas Suicide Story and Its Criminological Implications." In *Crime and Justice: A Review of Research*, vol. 10, edited by Michael Tonry and Norval Morris. Chicago: University of Chicago Press.

Committee on Trauma Research, National Research Council. 1985. *Injury in America: A Continuing Public Health Problem.* Washington, D.C.: National Academy Press.

Conklin, John E. 1972. *Robbery and the Criminal Justice System.* Philadelphia: Lippincott.

Cook, Philip J. 1976. "A Strategic Choice Analysis of Robbery." In *Sample Surveys of the Victims of Crimes*, edited by Wesley Skogan. Cambridge, Mass.: Ballinger.

———. 1979. "The Effect of Gun Availability on Robbery and Robbery Murder: A Cross Section Study of Fifty Cities." In *Policy Studies Review Annual*, vol. 3, edited by Robert H. Haveman and B. Bruce Zellner. Beverly Hills, Calif.: Sage.

———. 1980*a*. "Reducing Injury and Death Rates in Robbery." *Policy Analysis* 6(1):21–45.

———. 1980*b*. "Research in Criminal Deterrence: Laying the Groundwork for the Second Decade." In *Crime and Justice: An Annual Review of Research*, vol. 2, edited by Norval Morris and Michael Tonry. Chicago: University of Chicago Press.

———. 1981*a*. "The 'Saturday Night Special': An Assessment of Alternative Definitions from a Policy Perspective." *Journal of Criminal Law and Criminology* 72:1735–45.

———. 1981*b*. "Guns and Crime: The Perils of Long Division." *Journal of Policy Analysis and Management* 1:120–25.

———. 1982. "The Role of Firearms in Violent Crime: An Interpretive Review of the Literature, with Some New Findings and Suggestions for Future Research." In *Criminal Violence*, edited by Marvin Wolfgang and Neil Weiner. Beverly Hills, Calif.: Sage.

———. 1983*a*. "The Influence of Gun Availability on Violent Crime Patterns." In *Crime and Justice: An Annual Review of Research*, vol. 4, edited by Michael Tonry and Norval Morris. Chicago: University of Chicago Press.

———. 1983*b*. "Does Gun Ownership Deter Burglary?" Mimeographed. Durham, N.C.: Duke University, Institute of Policy Sciences.

———. 1985*a*. "The Case of the Missing Victims: Gunshot Woundings in the National Crime Survey." *Journal of Quantitative Criminology* 1:91–102.

———. 1985*b*. "Is Robbery Becoming More Violent? An Analysis of Robbery Murder Trends since 1968." *Journal of Criminal Law and Criminology* 76:480–89.

———. 1985*c*. "Report on a City-specific Gun Prevalence Index." Mimeographed. Durham, N.C.: Duke University, Institute of Policy Sciences.

———. 1986. "The Relationship between Victim Resistance and Injury in Noncommercial Robbery." *Journal of Legal Studies* 15:405–16.

———. 1987. "Robbery Violence." *Journal of Criminal Law and Criminology* 78:357–76.

Cook, Philip J., and James Blose. 1981. "State Programs for Screening Handgun Buyers." *Annals of the American Academy of Political and Social Science* 455:80–91.

Cook, Philip J., and Daniel Nagin. 1979. *Does the Weapon Matter?* Washington, D.C.: Institute for Law and Social Research.

Curtis, Lynn A. 1974. *Criminal Violence*. Lexington, Mass.: Lexington.

Dallas Police Department. 1983. Personal communication with author.

Deutsch, Stuart Jay. 1979. "Lies, Damn Lies, and Statistics: A Rejoinder to the Comment by Hay and McCleary." *Evaluation Quarterly* 3:315–28.

Deutsch, Stuart Jay, and Francis B. Alt. 1977. "The Effect of Massachusetts' Gun Control Law on Gun-related Crimes in the City of Boston." *Evaluation Quarterly* 1:543–68.

District of Columbia. 1989. *Homicide in the District of Columbia*. Washington, D.C.: Office of Criminal Justice Plans and Analysis.

Etzioni, Amitai, and Richard Remp. 1973. *Technological Shortcuts to Social Change*. New York: Russell Sage.

Fackler, Martin L. 1988. "Wound Ballistics: A Review of Common Misconceptions." *Journal of the American Medical Association* 259(18):2730–36.

Federal Bureau of Investigation. 1979. *Crime in the United States, 1978*. Washington, D.C.: U.S. Government Printing Office.

———. 1988. *Crime in the United States, 1987*. Washington, D.C.: U.S. Government Printing Office.

———. 1989. *Crime in the United States, 1988*. Washington, D.C.: U.S. Government Printing Office.

Fisher, Joseph. 1976. "Homicide in Detroit: The Role of Firearms." *Criminology* 13:387–400.

Geisel, Martin S., Richard Ross, and R. Stanton Wettick, Jr. 1969. "The Effectiveness of State and Local Regulation of Handguns: A Statistical Analysis." *Duke Law Journal* 4:647–76.

Green, Gary S. 1987. "Citizen Gun Ownership and Criminal Deterrence: Theory, Research, and Policy." *Criminology* 25:63–82.

Hollerman, Jeremy J. 1988. "Gunshot Wounds." *American Family Physician* 37(5):231–46.

Jones, Edward D., III. 1981. "The District of Columbia's 'Firearms Control Regulations Act of 1975': The Toughest Handgun Control Law in the United States—or Is It?" *Annals of the American Academy of Political and Social Science* 455:138–49.

Kakalik, James S., and Sorrell Wildhorn. 1972. *The Private Security Industry—Its Nature and Extent*. Santa Monica, Calif.: RAND.

Kates, Don B., Jr. 1983. "Handgun Prohibition and the Original Meaning of the Second Amendment." *Michigan Law Review* 82:204–73.

———. 1989. "Firearms and Violence: Old Premises and Current Evidence." In *Violence in America: The History of Crime*, edited by Ted Robert Gurr. Newbury Park, Calif.: Sage.

———. 1990. *Guns, Murders, and the Constitution: A Realistic Assessment of Gun Control*. San Francisco: Pacific Research Institute.

Kellermann, Arthur L. 1990. Personal communication with author.

Kellermann, Arthur L., and James A. Mercy. 1990. "Sex, Lies and Safety: Should Women Buy Handguns for Self Defense?" Unpublished manuscript. Memphis: University of Tennessee, Department of Medicine.

Kellermann, Arthur L., and Donald T. Reay. 1986. "Protection or Peril? An Analysis of Firearm-related Deaths in the Home." *New England Journal of Medicine* 314:1557–60.

Killias, Martin. 1990. "Gun Ownership and Violent Crime: The Swiss Experience in International Perspective." *Security Journal* 1(3):169–74.

Kleck, Gary. 1979. "Capital Punishment, Gun Ownership, and Homicide." *American Journal of Sociology* 84:882–910.

———. 1984*a*. "Handgun-only Control: A Policy Disaster in the Making." In *Firearms and Violence: Issues of Public Policy*, edited by Don B. Kates, Jr. Cambridge, Mass.: Ballinger.

———. 1984*b*. "The Relationship between Gun Ownership Levels and Rates of Violence in the United States." In *Firearms and Violence: Issues of Public Policy*, edited by Don B. Kates, Jr. Cambridge, Mass.: Ballinger.

———. 1988. "Crime Control through the Private Use of Armed Force." *Social Problems* 35:1–22.

———. 1990. Personal communication with author.

Kleck, Gary, and David J. Bordua. 1983. "The Factual Foundation for Certain Key Assumptions of Gun Control." *Law and Policy Quarterly* 5:271–98.

Kleck, Gary, and Karen McElrath. 1989. "The Effects of Weaponry on Human Violence." Mimeographed. Tallahassee: Florida State University, School of Criminology.

Kreitman, Norman. 1976. "The Coal Gas Story: United Kingdom Suicide Rates, 1960–71." *British Journal of Preventive Social Medicine* 30:86–93.

Lester, David. 1988. "Research Note: Gun Control, Gun Ownership, and Suicide Prevention." *Suicide and Life-Threatening Behavior* 18(2):176–80.

Lester, David, and Mary E. Murrell. 1982. "The Prevention Effect of Strict Gun Control Laws on Suicide and Homicide." *Suicide and Life-Threatening Behavior* 12(3):131–40.

McDowall, David, Brian Wiersema, and Colin Loftin. 1989. "Did Mandatory Firearm Ownership in Kennesaw Prevent Burglaries?" Working paper. College Park: University of Maryland, Institute of Criminal Justice and Criminology.

Magaddino, Joseph P., and Marshall H. Medoff. 1984. "An Empirical Analysis of Federal and State Firearm Control Laws." In *Firearms and Violence: Issues of Public Policy*, edited by Don B. Kates, Jr. Cambridge, Mass.: Ballinger.

Markush, R. E., and A. A. Bartolucci. 1984. "Firearms and Suicide in the United States." *American Journal of Public Health* 74:123–27.

Medoff, Marshall H., and Joseph P. Magaddino. 1983. "Suicides and Firearm Control Laws." *Evaluation Review* 7(3):357–72.

Mercy, J. A., and V. N. Houk. 1988. "Firearm Injuries: A Call for Science." *New England Journal of Medicine* 319:1283–85.

Moore, Mark. 1981. "Keeping Handguns from Criminal Offenders." *Annals of the American Academy of Political and Social Science* 455:92–109.

Murray, Douglas R. 1975. "Handguns, Gun Control Laws, and Firearms Violence." *Social Problems* 23:81–93.

National Center for Health Statistics. 1970–86. *Vital Statistics of the United States*, vol. IIA: *Mortality*. Washington, D.C.: U.S. Government Printing Office.

———. 1976. *Persons Injured and Disability Days by Detailed Type and Class of Accident, United States, 1971–1972*. Vital and Health Statistics Series no. 10/105. Washington, D.C.: U.S. Government Printing Office.

———. 1987. Personal communication with author.

Newton, George D., Jr., and Franklin E. Zimring. 1969. *Firearms and Violence in American Life*. Washington, D.C.: U.S. Government Printing Office.

Penick, Bettye K., and Maurice E. B. Owens III. 1976. *Surveying Crime*. Washington, D.C.: National Academy of Sciences.

Phillips, Llad, Harold L. Votey, Jr., and John Howell. 1976. "Handguns and Homicide: Minimizing Losses and the Costs of Control." *Journal of Legal Studies* 5:463–78.

Pierce, Glenn L., and William J. Bowers. 1979. "The Impact of the Bartley-Fox Gun Law on Crime in Massachusetts." Unpublished manuscript. Boston: Northeastern University, Center for Applied Social Research.

———. 1981. "The Bartley-Fox Gun Law's Short-Term Impact on Crime in Boston." *Annals of the American Academy of Political and Social Science* 455:120–37.

Rushforth, N. B., A. B. Ford, C. S. Hirsh, N. M. Rushforth, and L. Adelson. 1977. "Violent Death in a Metropolitan County: Changing Patterns in Homicide (1958–74)." *New England Journal of Medicine* 297:531–38.

Seiden, Richard. 1977. "Suicide Prevention: A Public Health/Public Policy Approach." *Omega* 8:267–76.

Silver, Carol Ruth, and Don B. Kates, Jr. 1979. "Self-Defense, Handgun Ownership, and the Independence of Women in a Violent, Sexist Society." In *Restricting Handguns: The Liberals Skeptics Speak Out*, edited by Don B. Kates, Jr. Croton-on-Hudson, N.Y.: North River.

Skogan, Wesley G. 1978. "Weapon Use in Robbery: Patterns and Policy Implications." Unpublished manuscript. Evanston, Ill.: Northwestern University, Center for Urban Affairs.

———. 1981. *Issues in the Measurement of Victimization*. Washington, D.C.: U.S. Department of Justice, Bureau of Justice Statistics.

———. 1990. "The National Crime Survey Redesign." *Public Opinion Quarterly* 54:256–72.

Sloan, J. H., A. L. Kellermann, D. T. Reay, J. A. Ferris, T. Koepsell, F. P. Rivara, C. Rice, L. Gray, and J. LoGerfo. 1988. "Handgun Regulations, Crimes, Assaults, and Homicide. A Tale of Two Cities." *New England Journal of Medicine* 319:1256–62.

Sloan, J. H., F. P. Rivara, D. T. Reay, J. A. Ferris, and A. L. Kellermann. 1990. "Firearm Regulations and Community Suicide Rates: A Comparison of Two Metropolitan Areas." *New England Journal of Medicine* (forthcoming).

Smith, Douglas A., and Craig D. Uchida. 1988. "The Social Organization of Self-Help: A Study of Defensive Weapon Ownership." *American Sociological Review* 53(1):94–102.

Swersey, Arthur J. 1980. "A Greater Intent to Kill: The Changing Pattern of Homicide in Harlem and New York City." Unpublished manuscript. New Haven, Conn.: Yale School of Organization and Management.

U.S. Conference of Mayors. 1980. "The Analysis of the Firearms Control Act of 1975: Handgun Control in the District of Columbia." Mimeographed. Washington, D.C.: U.S. Conference of Mayors.

van Dijk, Jan J. M., Pat Mayhew, and Martin Killias. 1990. *Experiences of Crime across the World: Key Findings from the 1989 International Crime Survey*. Boston: Dordrecht.

Wolfgang, Marvin E. 1958. *Patterns in Criminal Homicide*. Philadelphia: University of Pennsylvania Press.

Wright, James D. 1981. "Public Opinion and Gun Control: A Comparison of Results from Two Recent National Surveys." *Annals of the American Academy of Political and Social Science* 455:24–39.

———. 1984. "The Ownership of Firearms for Reasons of Self-Defense." In *Firearms and Violence: Issues of Public Policy*, edited by Don B. Kates, Jr. Cambridge, Mass.: Ballinger.

Wright, James D., and Linda L. Marston. 1975. "The Ownership of the Means of Destruction: Weapons in the United States." *Social Problems* 23:81–107.

Wright, James D., and Peter H. Rossi. 1986. *The Armed Criminal in America: A Survey of Incarcerated Felons*. Hawthorne, N.Y.: Aldine.

Wright, James D., Peter H. Rossi, and Kathleen Daly. 1983. *Under the Gun: Weapons, Crime, and Violence in America*. Hawthorne, N.Y.: Aldine.

Yeager, Matthew G. 1976. *How Well Does the Handgun Protect You and Your Family?* Washington, D.C.: U.S. Conference of Mayors.

Zimring, Franklin E. 1968. "Is Gun Control Likely to Reduce Violent Killings?" *University of Chicago Law Review* 35:721–37.

———. 1972. "The Medium Is the Message: Firearm Calibre as a Determinant of Death from Assault." *Journal of Legal Studies* 1:97–124.

———. 1975. "Firearms and Federal Law: The Gun Control Act of 1968." *Journal of Legal Studies* 4:133–98.

———. 1990. "Firearms, Violence, and Public Policy." *Scientific American* (forthcoming).

Neal Shover

Burglary

ABSTRACT

Burglary is one of the most prevalent street crimes in the United States as well as in other countries. In the United States, the rate of burglary increased dramatically during the 1960s from 508.6 per 100,000 population before declining after 1975 and stabilizing near the 1984 rate of 1,263.7 per 100,000 population. Burglary rates are disproportionately low in the Northeast and high in the West and in cities, particularly those with large minority populations, high population mobility, and high income inequality. It occurs disproportionately in neighborhoods inhabited primarily by the young, minorities, and renters. Burglary is committed disproportionately by males, juveniles, and others who are unskilled offenders in or close to their home neighborhoods. A small group of burglars ranges over a wide territory, often searching out suitable targets. Although most victims sustain modest economic losses, the crime has serious psychological effects on some, particularly women who reside alone. General prevention programs aimed at burglary have met with uncertain success. Experience with neighborhood watch and target-hardening strategies points to the importance of better focused situational crime-prevention strategies.

The past twenty-five years have seen the publication of a substantial body of research that sheds light on burglary, burglars, and burglary victims. Some of this work was animated by the contention that improved understanding of the causes and consequences of crime can be gained through crime-specific analysis, while a less sizable but no less important set of investigations test theory-based predictions or explore decision making by street offenders. Burglary has attracted attention

Neal Shover is professor of sociology at the University of Tennessee, Knoxville.

0192-3234/91/0014-0001$01.00

not only because so much of it occurs but also because it ranks high among crimes that citizens fear most. Odds are high that today's urban resident, particularly in the United States, has been or knows a victim of burglars. A violation of private domains, burglary can have serious and long-lasting psychological effects on some victims. It is a serious problem for small, economically marginal businesses. By most ways of counting, burglary is a crime deserving of scholarly attention.

This essay reviews and assesses recent burglary-relevant theory and research. Section I defines burglary, notes changes in burglary law over time, and describes methods and sources of data used in studies of burglary. In Section II, I begin with comparative statistical data on the level of and trends in burglary in the United States and other countries and then move to a discussion of the epidemiology of burglary offenses and offenders. Section III summarizes and discusses the results of recent theory-driven efforts to explain the distribution of burglary. In Section IV, I describe burglary offenders, their social organization, criminal careers, and criminal activities. Section V presents data on victim and criminal justice responses to burglary, while Section VI discusses burglary prevention initiatives and their impact, chiefly neighborhood watch and target-hardening strategies. The essay concludes in Section VII with a brief assessment of theories employed to explain burglary and suggestions for research.

I. Burglary: Definitions and Data Sources

In common law, burglary was defined as "the breaking and entering of the dwelling of another in the nighttime with intent to commit a felony or petit larceny" (Perkins 1969, p. 212). Breaking meant creation of a breach or opening of a dwelling structure by disabling or putting aside any material part of it intended as security against intrusion. The importance placed on the time of the offense reflected an assumption that sleeping householders were least able to protect themselves by force of arms during the hours of darkness. Over two centuries the law of burglary has been reshaped to include all forms of attempted and unlawful entry regardless of how it is accomplished. Thus, it includes entries by trick or artifice, such as concealing oneself in a building prior to closing time; entering by false pretenses, such as claiming to be a delivery person; or conspiring with someone who has legitimate access to the structure. In addition, burglary now includes entry of buildings and structures other than dwellings and offenses committed in the daytime (Chappell 1965; Walsh 1980). In England, for example, enactment of the Theft Act of 1968 brought together older "breaking" offenses and other forms of unlawful entry. Today, the criminal codes of many states in the United States distinguish degrees of burglary by whether the burglarized structure was occupied when entered, the offender was armed, the offense was committed in the nighttime, or the victim or victims were assaulted. By establishing these statutory gradations, legislatures have tailored penalties to fit offenses of different levels of seriousness. Variation in state law notwithstanding, the Uniform Crime Reports program definition of burglary encompasses three criminal behaviors: forcible entry, attempted forcible entry, and unlawful entry (Federal Bureau of Investigation 1989, p. 27).

What we know about burglary is grounded in four types of data and research: information collected by official agencies that process burglary reports and offenders, victims' reports, reports and data from burglary offenders, and information available from trade groups and private industry. Since these data sources are familiar to most investigators, only a brief review of them is included here. Taken together they give a clear picture of many aspects of burglary, albeit one that is much better developed for its residential than for its nonresidential forms.

A. *Official Crime and Case-processing Data*

Agencies charged with responding to burglary complaints and processing apprehended burglary defendants generate a wealth of information on these matters. At the federal level, the Uniform Crime Reports (UCR) continues to be one of the most important of these (e.g., Federal Bureau of Investigation 1989). Defined as "the unlawful entry of a structure to commit a felony or theft," burglary is one of eight Index crimes on which UCR annually publishes incidence and prevalence data as well as limited demographic data on persons arrested. Until the advent of victimization surveys, it was the only source of information on trends in burglary. Similar national crime-reporting programs in other countries include Criminal Statistics from England and Wales (e.g., Home Office 1988). While several states—California is the best example—have well-developed uniform crime-reporting programs, they are exceptions, and these data have been used by few investigators (e.g., Pope 1977*a*, 1977*b*, 1977*c*). Police investigative and statistical reports have been used to examine characteristics of burglary incidents and police responses to them, usually in a single city (e.g., Chimbos 1973; Conklin and Bittner 1973; Rengert 1981; Eskridge 1983). State and local police occasionally analyze burglary data and publish their findings, but these are not disseminated widely, and they have found almost no use by investigators (Scarr 1973).

Drawing from the National Crime Survey and from its regular reporting programs, the Bureau of Justice Statistics (BJS) disseminates information about burglary, burglary victims, and the processing of burglary offenders (e.g., Bureau of Justice Statistics 1985, 1989*a;* Langan and Dawson 1990). Also at the federal level, the National Institute of Justice (NIJ) sponsors and publishes investigations of burglary and official responses to it (e.g., Eck 1983; Garofalo and Clark 1986). In Britain, the Home Office performs many functions similar to BJS and NIJ and, particularly in recent years, has supported or carried out very important studies of burglary and the effectiveness of burglary prevention programs (e.g., Elliott and Mayhew 1988; Forrester et al. 1988).

B. Victim Surveys and Accounts

After pioneering victimization surveys in the 1960s by the President's Commission on Law Enforcement and Administration of Justice and National Crime Panel surveys in twenty-six U.S. cities in the early 1970s, the ongoing National Crime Survey (NCS) began in 1973. The National Crime Survey defines burglary as "unlawful or forcible entry of a residence usually, but not necessarily, attended by theft . . . it includes attempted forcible entry. The entry may be by force . . . or it may be through an unlocked door or an open window. As long as the person entering had no legal right to be present in the structure, a burglary has occurred" (Bureau of Justice Statistics 1989*b*, p. 126). Surveys by the NCS for the years 1973–76 sampled commercial establishments as well as households; the commercial portion was discontinued during 1977. The National Crime Survey does not publish state-level or city-level data. This is an important shortcoming; it is all but impossible to use NCS data to examine determinants of areal variation in burglary.

National surveys in Britain began with specific questions about residential burglary in the General Household Survey of 1972 and evolved by 1982 into the ongoing British Crime Survey (Hough and Mayhew 1985; Mayhew, Elliott, and Dowds 1989). National surveys have been carried out in a growing number of countries, and local-level surveys are available from many more (Block 1984*a*). In early 1989, a comparative victim survey was completed in fifteen countries of Europe and North America (Block 1989). Reflecting variation in their sponsors' criminal code definitions of burglary, survey definitions of burglary are not invariant. For example, unlawful entry of outbuildings is not counted as residential burglary in all countries. Neither are survey methodology and procedures invariant. Differences in sampling, length of recall periods, and procedures for recording serial victimizations are examples. Given these design and procedural differences, raw comparison of survey findings is of dubious validity.

Although most investigations of burglary victims are based exclusively on survey methods, there are several excellent studies that are grounded in ethnographic approaches. Use of these approaches permits examination of burglary and victim experiences in greater detail and depth than survey methods allow. In addition to focused interviews with burglary victims (e.g., Maguire 1980; Walsh 1980), field observation and comparative site analysis of victimized and nonvictimized structures have shown how physical and environmental variables constrain the risk of burglary (e.g., Scarr 1973; Molumby 1976; Waller and Okihiro 1978; Winchester and Jackson 1982).

C. *Offender Accounts and Self-Report Surveys*

Victim reports and official crime and crime control data tell us a great deal about burglary but very little about those who commit it, their daily lives, or their criminal decision making. This information can be gained only from offenders. Past research on thieving and burglary includes a growing number of ethnographic studies of offenders, their criminal activities, decision making, and criminal careers. From life histories and focused interviews to field observation, the entire range of ethnographic techniques has been employed in the study of burglary (e.g., West 1978; Bennett and Wright 1984*a;* Rengert and Wasilchick 1985; Walsh 1986). Self-report survey investigations of incarcerated property offenders also have enhanced significantly understanding of issues as diverse as the social contexts of crime commission, offender motivation, individual offending rates, and criminal careers (e.g., Petersilia, Greenwood, and Lavin 1978; Figgie International 1988).

D. *Trade Organizations and Private Security Firms*

Data and materials available from trade organizations and private security firms hold potential for enhancing knowledge of burglary, but they have received only limited attention by investigators. We know, for example, that insurance industry policies and practices surely constrain empirical manifestations of burglary, but these links remain almost entirely unexplored (Litton and Pease 1984; Clark 1989; State

Farm 1989). Private police agencies have found increasing use by industry and government in recent years (Shearing and Stenning 1981), but they have been overlooked as research sites and sources of data on burglary.

II. Risks, Trends, and Distribution

Burglary is a commonplace crime and touches the lives of many citizens. In 1988, more than three million burglaries were reported to local police departments in the United States (Federal Bureau of Investigation 1989, p. 27). It is estimated that 72 percent of U.S. households will be victimized by burglars at least once over a twenty-year period (Koppel 1987). In England and Wales, the "average" household will be the target of an attempted or completed burglary once every thirty years (Hough 1984). The potential for physical harm to its victims places burglary near the top of offenses most feared by citizens.

All households and businesses do not have an equal chance of being victimized. Table 1 summarizes relations between household characteristics and the risk of victimization for U.S. households in 1987. The National Crime Survey defines household as the "occupants of separate living quarters . . . whose usual place of residence is the housing unit in question or . . . who have no usual place of residence elsewhere" (Bureau of Justice Statistics 1989*b*, p. 126). Table 1 shows that victimization rates are highest for renters, households headed by blacks, Hispanics, or young persons, and households located in central cities. National Crime Survey data for 1976, the final year commercial firms were surveyed, show that the highest commercial victimization rate was recorded by retail firms, particularly eating and drinking establishments, followed in decreasing order by service firms, wholesale businesses, and manufacturing firms (U.S. Department of Justice 1977).

A. Trends

Although official crime statistics remain the primary data for examining long-term burglary trends, the availability of NCS survey data since 1973 significantly enhances confidence about more recent changes and emerging trends. In 1960 the rate of reported burglary in the United States was 509 per 100,000 population, and by 1980 it more than tripled to 1,684 per 100,000 population (Bureau of Justice Statistics 1989*c*, p. 427). Except for one-year increases in 1975 and 1981, NCS data show that the percentage of households burglarized decreased overall by 30 percent from 1975 through 1984 and has not

TABLE 1

U.S. Household Burglary Victimization Rates (per 1,000 Households) in 1987

Variable	Burglary Victimization Rate
Household location:	
Metropolitan:	
Central cities	76.5
Outside central cities	54.3
Nonmetropolitan	53.9
Head of household:	
White	57.0
Black	94.4
Hispanic	73.3
Other	62.6
Head of household's age:	
12–19	173.5
20–34	85.0
35–49	65.5
50–64	45.1
65 or over	33.2
Form of tenure:	
Ownership or purchasing	47.8
Renting	85.3

SOURCE.—Bureau of Justice Statistics (1989*b*), tables 20, 21, 23, 24, 29, and 31.

changed significantly since (Bureau of Justice Statistics 1989*a*). There is disagreement over the reasons for the decline and stabilization of U.S. household burglary rates, but the decreasing size of youthful crime-prone age cohorts features prominently in all.

Comparison of UCR and NCS crime rates is a daunting exercise (Biderman and Lynch 1989). One reason is because each program uses different base measures to calculate burglary rates; UCR continues to use population size as the base in its reported burglary rate, while NCS uses the number of households. Also since UCR and other official crime rates reflect both citizen reporting and police recording practices, they can fluctuate independent of real shifts in the level of victimization. English data show, for example, that a 63 percent increase in the official rate of burglary involving loss during the 1970s far exceeds the increase of 15 percent measured by surveys (Hough 1984). Overall in the United States, about one-half of all household burglaries are reported to the police (Bureau of Justice Statistics 1988*a*).

National Crime Survey data show that in 1976 the rate of commercial burglary victimization was 2.4 times greater than the rate of household burglary (U.S. Department of Justice 1977, p. 12). Uniform Crime Reports data for 1980 show a ratio of five to one (Bureau of Justice Statistics 1983, p. 7). The fact that approximately 80 percent of commercial burglary victims report to the police while only half of residential victims do so probably explains some of this discrepancy (Reiss 1967; U.S. Department of Justice 1977; Williams and Lucianovic 1979).

Victimization surveys during 1965–76 paint a confusing picture, and, therefore, it is unclear whether the increase in residential burglary in the 1960s was matched by an increase in burglary of commercial structures. A 1967 national survey of businesses reported 270 burglaries per 1,000 establishments (U.S. Senate 1969, p. 3), while 1976 NCS survey results show a rate of 217.3 per 1,000 commercial firms (U.S. Department of Justice 1977, p. 12). This apparent counterintuitive decrease in the commercial burglary rate at a time when household victimization rates were increasing may stem from differences in survey design and procedures. Further confusing the picture, NCS surveys in the years 1973–76 show a 7 percent increase in the rate of commercial burglary but a 3 percent decrease in household burglary (U.S. Department of Justice 1977).

Because of variation in statutory definitions of burglary and in citizen reporting (Block 1989), use of police or other official data is of limited value for cross-national analysis of burglary (e.g., Kalish 1988). Survey data offer more promise here, at least so long as findings are adjusted to take account of methodological and procedural differences and simple ranks rather than precise comparisons are the objective. Block's (1984*b*) comparison of adjusted data from the Dutch National Crime Survey of 1977 and the U.S. National Crime Survey of 1976 shows a rate of household burglary in the United States more than five times higher than in the Netherlands. After adjusting for differences in survey design and procedures, Mayhew (1987) shows that U.S. burglary rates in 1981 were approximately 65 percent higher than in England and also higher than in Canada. It is worth noting that neither the post-1975 downturn nor the post-1984 stabilization of the household burglary rate in the United States has occurred in Britain (Mayhew, Elliott, and Dowds 1989).

B. Areal Variation

Studies in the United States over three decades have shown the rate of burglary is highest in the West and lowest in the Northeast (Shannon

1954; Harries 1974; Kowalski, Dittman, and Bung 1980). More recent UCR and NCS data show the burglary rate in the South is nearly the same as the West (Bureau of Justice Statistics 1988*b;* Federal Bureau of Investigation 1989). Unlike regional variation in homicide, this variation has attracted little attention from investigators.

In the United States, the risk of household victimization over a twenty-year period is 80 percent in urban areas, 70 percent in suburban areas, and 64 percent in rural areas (Koppel 1987). The urban-suburban-rural burglary gradient is similar in England, Canada, Australia, and the Netherlands (Block 1984*b;* Braithwaite and Biles 1984; Hough 1984; van Dijk and Steinmetz 1984). For reasons that are not understood, the gradient appears to be substantially larger in England and the Netherlands than in the United States (Block 1984*b;* Mayhew 1987). As with household burglary, a study by the U.S. Small Business Administration of a national probability sample of businesses shows an urban-suburban-rural gradient for commercial burglary (U.S. Senate 1969, p. 26).

The urban-suburban-rural gradient in burglary rates is not always smooth and uninterrupted. Instead, contiguous communities and areas can have very different burglary problems since location in wider ecological and spatial contexts constrains the burglary rate in constituent areas (Georges-Abeyie and Harries 1980). Maguire (1982) analyzed all offenses of burglary in dwellings recorded in three police sectors of the Thames Valley in 1975. Distinguished by marked differences in population, mix of housing types and value, average income, and proximity to major highways and rail transportation, the three communities attracted different kinds of burglars and developed different burglary profiles. This is evidenced in "householders' chances of being burgled, in the type and value of property stolen and in the sophistication of offenders. There was also some variation between areas in the physical circumstances of the offences—the times at which they were most often committed, the method of entry and the extent of disarrangement or damage to property—but not usually to a significant degree" (Maguire 1982, p. 44). Scarr (1973) shows that three communities, Washington, D.C., and two of its suburban areas, differed in the size and nature of their burglary problems. Eck (1983) describes differences in modal burglaries in three jurisdictions: a large, predominantly suburban area near Atlanta, Georgia (DeKalb County); a city populated disproportionately by elderly and retired citizens (St. Petersburg, Florida); and a midwestern industrial city (Wichita, Kansas). There were clear differences in average monetary loss from burglary, types of items stolen, and offender-victim relationship. We lack comparable descriptions and analyses of commercial burglary, although we know it also varies greatly across communities and neighborhoods (Boggs 1965; Reiss 1967; U.S. Senate 1969).

Apart from regional variation, statistical analyses consistently show that residential and commercial burglary rates vary substantially at the city level (U.S. Department of Justice 1975, 1976*a*, 1976*b;* Federal Bureau of Investigation 1989). Cross-sectional analysis of city-level UCR and U.S. Census data has identified social and economic correlates of intercity variation in the overall burglary rate. Population stability (Quinney 1966; Harries 1976; Worden 1980), income inequality (Danziger 1976; Jacobs 1981; Carroll and Jackson 1983), unemployment, and percent black are all related positively to the burglary rate in metropolitan areas or central cities (Danziger 1976; Carroll and Jackson 1983). The picture is more ambiguous where population density is concerned. Analyzing 1974 household victimization data for the twenty-six National Crime Panel cities, Shichor, Decker, and O'Brien (1979) found a strong inverse relation between population density and burglary ($r = -.64$). By contrast, Carroll and Jackson (1983) used UCR data and failed to find a relation between population density and crime.

There is little disagreement about the neighborhood population and structural correlates of residential burglary. It occurs disproportionately in transitional urban neighborhoods, many with "bad reputations," that are populated largely by minorities, young persons, and renters (Hough and Mayhew 1985). The rate of multiple victimization also is highest in these neighborhoods that produce disproportionately larger numbers of offenders as well. Homes and businesses located near these "dense pools of offenders" suffer high burglary rates (Boggs 1965; Baldwin and Bottoms 1976; Roncek, Bell, and Francik 1981).

C. *Temporal Variation*

Most forms of crime are not distributed evenly across the seasons, the week, or the day, and burglary is no exception. Compared to other types of street crime, however, it shows limited seasonal variation (Scarr 1973; Pope 1977*a;* Waller and Okihiro 1978). Unlawful entries increase significantly in June and July, perhaps reflecting increased opportunities for easy entry presented by windows and doors left open during the warm months. Attempted and completed forcible entry show much less seasonality (Bureau of Justice Statistics 1988*c*). Less is known about commercial burglary, but it apparently displays similar, minimal, seasonal variation (Gibbs and Shelly 1982*a*).

Since burglars ordinarily wish to avoid confrontations with victims, they tend to commit household burglaries when target premises are unoccupied, disproportionately on weekdays. Efforts to determine more precisely the time of day when burglaries occur are hampered by the fact that nearly one-third of victims do not know when their residence was entered. In reports from victims who can estimate with some precision when their household was victimized, 50 percent of burglaries occur between 6 A.M. and 6 P.M., 23 percent occur between 6 P.M. and midnight, and 16 percent occur between midnight and 6 A.M. The remaining 10 percent occur "sometime during the night" (calculated from Bureau of Justice Statistics 1989*b*, table 55). Commercial burglaries, by contrast, more often occur at night or on weekends, when businesses are closed (Gibbs and Shelly 1982*a*).

D. Targets

Within these temporal patterns, the world affords abundant poorly protected opportunities for burglars. This is suggested by the fact that unforced entries make up nearly 25 percent of completed household burglaries and also by what is known about the security of most households and businesses (Bureau of Justice Statistics 1989*b*, table 1). In a 1984 Victimization Risk Supplement to the National Crime Survey, respondents were asked about household use of three security measures, and interviewers also made a visual observation for security features. While one-third of household respondents reported at least one of three measures—a burglar alarm, property marking, or participation in a neighborhood watch program—only 7 percent had a burglar alarm (Whitaker 1986). Households and businesses that have alarms do not use them properly much of the time, and even when used properly the performance of burglar alarms leaves much to be desired. False alarms are commonplace (U.S. Senate 1969). A study of burglary in a suburban community found that alarms worked properly less than half the time, causing the investigators to estimate that an alarm will be present and will function properly in less than 5 percent of suburban burglaries (Conklin and Bittner 1973).

Although businesses are more likely than households to use burglary protection measures (Whitaker 1986), these often are not severe obstacles to determined thieves (Garofalo and Clark 1986). A study of 218 commercial thefts and burglaries investigated by the police in a small community located near the New York metropolitan area showed that in more than half the incidents the burglars' entry either was unforced or was gained simply by breaking a window or a lock (Gibbs and Shelly 1982*a*). Sophisticated methods of entry, such as cutting a hole in the roof or a wall or bypassing alarms, were employed in less than 1 percent of the cases. Surprised at discovering that nearly all the burglaries showed evidence of rather simple, straightforward, but effective techniques, the investigators remarked: "If there were alarms, they seem not to have worked; if there were guards, they seem not to have awakened. If gaining entry to these structures is as easy as it seems, why should it be expected that burglars would resort to more costly and complicated methods of gaining entry? Perhaps it is not the thieves in [the community] who are unsophisticated, but the owners of some of [the community's] commercial establishments" (Gibbs and Shelly 1982*a*, p. 7).

The proportion of time in the week that a structure is unoccupied and the rate of burglary in the surrounding neighborhood are major determinants of victimization risk. Beyond these powerful predictors, investigators have shown that measures of environmental risk modestly discriminate victimized and nonvictimized structures (Winchester and Jackson 1982). Multiunit dwellings without access security, corner houses or those located adjacent to parks or other open spaces, structures surrounded by view-obstructing foliage, and those located distant from other structures are at increased risk of burglary (Repetto 1974; Molumby 1976; Waller and Okihiro 1978). Houses located in neighborhood border blocks or near principal traffic arteries and through streets are at higher risk of burglary than houses on interior blocks or cul de sacs (Brantingham and Brantingham 1975; Maguire 1982). School buildings at high risk not only have more points of entry than nonburglarized schools but also are located on larger sites that afford less external surveillance (Hope 1982). When stealing from or scouting targets more distant from their home territory, burglars stick close to major traffic arteries and remain attentive for signs of potential high-yield targets (Rengert and Wasilchick 1985).

In one out of three U.S. household burglaries, nothing is stolen (Bureau of Justice Statistics 1989*b*, table 80). When offenders do steal something, they concentrate on cash, jewelry, and portable items, usually of low to moderate value (Conklin and Bittner 1973; Pope 1977*a*; Hough and Mayhew 1985; Bureau of Justice Statistics 1989*b*). Office equipment, video and sound equipment, clothing, cash, and small tools are popular targets of commercial burglars (Gibbs and Shelly 1982*a*). Preferred targets and theft items change with demand and supply (Gould 1969), which explains the current popularity of electronic and home stereo items as targets for burglars (Ferdinand 1972).

III. Explaining the Epidemiology of Burglary

The data problems involved in explanatory research on areal variation in burglary are substantial. In order to gain adequate sample sizes, investigators must use UCR crime data, which do not permit fine-grained analysis of relations among demographic, structural, and economic variables and more narrowly defined specific types of burglary. For example, nearly all studies use the overall burglary rate, residential and nonresidential combined, as the sole measure of burglary. There is reason to believe, however, that the two types of burglary vary independently of one another (Boggs 1965).[1] These data limitations combined with differences in study designs, samples, and analytic approaches limit confidence that we understand the complex of variables that determine intercity or neighborhood-level variation in the forms and incidence of burglary.

Two distinct but logically compatible approaches have dominated efforts to explain the epidemiology of burglary: deterrence theory and opportunity structure theory. The former draws support from studies of natural variation that show an inverse relation between measures of the objective certainty of punishment and the burglary rate in states and standard metropolitan statistical areas (e.g., Tittle 1969), even controlling for other presumably causal determinants of burglary (Danziger 1976). Assessing the evidence from studies of this type, a National Academy of Sciences panel notes: "Any conclusion that these negative associations reflect a deterrent effect, however, is limited principally by the inability to eliminate other factors that could account for the observed relationship, even in the absence of a deterrent effect" (Blumstein, Cohen, and Nagin 1978, p. 6). The ambiguous results from evaluation studies of campaigns to escalate punishment certainty also diminish confidence that more efficient control responses produce significant marginal deterrence (Zimring 1978; Cook 1980; Ross and LaFree 1986).

Research support for opportunity structure theory by contrast is not

[1] My calculations, using 1971–74 data from the twenty-six National Crime Panel cities, yield a correlation coefficient of .47.

nearly so equivocal. The core proposition of opportunity theory is that rates of theft are related directly to the volume of opportunities available for theft (Cook 1986). The theory takes for granted the existence of motivated offenders and assumes that the burglary rate will vary directly with the number of opportunities to commit burglaries (Cohen and Felson 1979; Brantingham and Brantingham 1980). Investigators have shown that the two indeed are positively related. Using St. Louis police data, Sarah Boggs (1965) examined census tract variation in four types of burglary: residential day, residential night, nonresidential day, and nonresidential night. She shows that the four types vary independently of one another to some extent and that each is related to the distribution of specific types of opportunities. Engstad's analysis (1975) of data from Edmonton, Canada, shows the predicted positive relation between neighborhood concentration of businesses and a combined rate of fraud, shop-breaking, and mischief. Investigations of intercity variation in burglary also have found support for propositions grounded in opportunity theory (Brantingham and Brantingham 1980).

Lifestyle (Hindelang, Gottfredson, and Garofalo 1978) and routine activities theories (Cohen and Felson 1979) are distinctive applications of the opportunity structure approach to crime. The causal focus in these theories is on social changes in post–World War II American life, such as increasing numbers of persons living alone and increasing female employment outside of the home. The altered lifestyles that parallel these changes have dispersed routine household activities away from the home, even as Americans have purchased increasing numbers of high-demand portable commodities, such as television sets, stereo sound equipment, and videocassette recorders. Since these consumer goods are left unprotected in unoccupied homes and apartments much of the time, opportunities for burglary have increased.

Cohen and Felson (1979) tested their theory over time for the period 1947–76 for the United States. They operationalized dispersion of household activities as the sum of the number of married, husband-present, female labor force participants and the number of nonhusband-wife households, divided by the sum of the total number of households. The resulting household activity ratio is a significant predictor of burglary and other street crimes and their increase even after controlling for percent unemployed and percent of the population aged fifteen to twenty-four. Jackson (1984) extends the Cohen and Felson analysis by showing that the dispersion of activities away from the home has a greater impact on burglary in larger cities than in smaller ones. A series of household-level studies also finds that measures of residents' weekly routine activities, particularly time away from home, predicts burglary risk (Hindelang, Gottfredson, and Garofalo 1978; Cohen and Cantor 1981; Cohen, Kluegel, and Land 1981; Maxfield 1987*a*, 1987*b*).

IV. Burglars

Overwhelmingly, burglary is a male enterprise; males were 91.4 percent of all persons arrested for burglary in the United States in 1988 (Federal Bureau of Investigation 1989, p. 173). The gender differential is greater for burglary than all other Index crimes except rape. This gender differential as well as differences in offense behavior of male and female burglars are well documented but unexplored and little interpreted by investigators (Pope 1977*c;* Rand 1987). Evidence from a self-report study of 589 Ohio prisoners shows that women offenders perceive burglary and other street crimes as riskier than do men offenders (Figgie International 1988).

Persons arrested for burglary are disproportionately male, young, and black. In 1988, 33 percent of persons arrested for burglary in the United States were under age eighteen, 67 percent were under age twenty-five, and 31 percent were black (Federal Bureau of Investigation 1989, pp. 184, 186). Although data on class origins are limited, burglars are products disproportionately of working-class and underclass backgrounds (Chimbos 1973). Since self-report surveys of the general population show similar albeit narrower class and racial differences (Braithwaite 1981; Elliott and Huizinga 1983), it is unlikely that discriminatory police practices or other explanations can account for all or most of this differential in burglary participation rates (Mawby 1981).

A. *Burglary Specialists?*

The image of "professional" burglars who specialize in their craft and commit infrequent, highly skilled crimes tugs persistently at popular and scholarly imaginations; a variety of data show it does not apply to the vast majority of contemporary burglars. Analysis of self-report data from eighty-eight incarcerated burglars showed minimal offense specialization (Shover 1971). A study of forty-nine imprisoned armed robbers in a California prison showed that they had committed three times more burglaries than robberies during their criminal careers (Petersilia, Greenwood, and Lavin 1978). Similar findings from a subsequent self-report study of 624 incarcerated felons in California prisons caused the investigators to conclude that "it can be misleading to describe and differentiate among offenders by their conviction offense" (Peterson and Braiker 1980, p. x). A self-report survey of 2,190 jail and prison inmates in California, Texas, and Michigan also found little evidence of offense specialization (Chaiken and Chaiken 1982).

Evidence of minimal specialization also comes from autobiographical data (Shover 1971), ethnographic interviews with offenders, and official data (Williams and Lucianovic 1979). English studies are consistent (Hood and Sparks 1970; Maguire 1982). Lest it be assumed that more successful and persistent offenders specialize more than inept ones, a study of police-identified "professional" thieves in three American cities likewise found little evidence of specialization in any offense (Gould et al. 1966), and Shover (1971) shows that criminal versatility actually increases with success at street crime. In sum, to the question, "How much specialization?" the answer for the overwhelming majority of burglars is, "Very little." Evidence on this point is diverse, substantial, and persuasive.

This does not mean the designation "burglar" lacks all denotative merit. Some offenders describe themselves as such and tend to restrict their criminal activities to burglary, at least for short periods of time. As opposed to rigid specialization, "[a] much more common pattern [is] what might be called 'short-term specialisation.' Many [subjects] recalled limited periods in which they had become involved in a specific type of crime to the virtual exclusion of others. However, these periods did not appear to follow any common sequence. . . . At the same time, habit, familiarity with techniques and personal preferences were always likely to draw them back towards their 'main line'—the type of crime they felt most at home with" (Maguire 1982, p. 80). Burglary is their "line," but this "is simply indicative of some consistency in one's choice of illegal activity" (Letkemann 1973, p. 36). Many self-described burglars follow this line because they prefer to avoid crimes that necessitate confronting victims, particularly armed robbery. In their view, confronting a potentially resistive victim with an undetermined number of deadly weapons in the mix is fraught with serious hazard. Many burglars also believe their odds of getting away are better for burglary than for other forms of street crime (Figgie International 1988). Except for their aversion to confrontational crimes and knowledge that burglary is a "safe" crime, burglars are not easily distinguishable from garden-variety street offenders. While they prefer burglary, most will commit other property crimes if a favorable opportunity arises.

B. Social Organization of Burglary

Burglary is an organized activity; more often than not, it is committed by two or more persons acting in concert (Pope 1977*c;* Eskridge 1983). Co-offending is attractive to many because, first, it can bolster courage and inattention or indifference to risk, thereby dampening apprehension and fear. Second, it facilitates management of the diverse practical demands of stealing. Third, it is also reassuring for some offenders to know that, if they are arrested, they will not have to endure it alone.

Beyond the internal social organization worked out by offenders while committing crimes, the activities of some are part of a larger, external social organization that provides them with information about potentially lucrative targets ("tipsters"), outlets for stolen goods ("fences"), and the services of bondsmen and attorneys when coping with inevitable arrests, criminal trials, and imprisonments (Shover 1973). None of these ties has received much attention. Although there are, for example, several excellent studies of people who traffic in stolen goods, we still do not know a great deal about criminal redistribution systems (Klockars 1974; Walsh 1977; Steffensmeier 1986).

C. Types of Burglars

Descriptions of thieves and burglars in the aggregate mask important diversity in their ranks. Some burglars take advantage of doors left unlocked or ajar to steal anything close at hand, while others employ elaborate techniques to defeat alarm systems and steal large sums of cash or high-value merchandise. A variety of thief and burglar typologies have been suggested as a means of identifying homogeneous subgroups of thieves, some containing two categories (Scarr 1973), others three (Shover 1971; David 1974), and others even larger numbers (Irwin 1970; Ferdinand 1972). Since most were developed post hoc as analytic devices and their predictive value is unclear, there is little to be gained from an extended tour of this taxonomic landscape.

Mike Maguire's three-category scheme (1982) has the advantage of grounding in a clear conception of how burglars' offenses and careers are limited by their connections. He highlights three fundamental problems faced by a thief: the contradiction between self-interest and the interest of the group, particularly in dealings with the police and other control agents; the contradictory desire to be recognized by one's peers as a competent thief and the need to keep one's activities secret; and the contradictory hedonistic lifestyle of thieves and the need for deferred gratification, prudence, and planning—in short, the need for rationality. Differential access to the social organization of burglary (i.e., connections) constrains individual solutions to these problems (Shover 1973).

The three categories of burglars distinguished by Maguire (1982) are differentiated on the degree of success at solving the fundamental problems of persistent burglary: low level, middle range, and high level. The ranks of low-level burglars are filled largely with juveniles, a smaller number of young adults, and a handful of adults. As with middle-range and high-level burglars, individual offending rates vary greatly. Their offenses often begin as spontaneous occurrences committed with friends for the expressed motives of fun or excitement or for the consumer items and small monetary rewards that seem princely in their world. Although co-offending is typical of low-level burglars, they lack significant commitment to crime or other criminals, and most do not think of themselves as "thieves." Those who use alcohol or other drugs as part of their burglary behaviors commonly do so to overcome inhibitions or to manage feelings of apprehension (Bennett and Wright 1984*b*). Low-level burglars often prey on those close at hand whose routines are known, and they often make target selections on the spur of the moment. Their attacks can generally be defeated by well-designed, locked entry points that are open to public view (Garofalo and Clark 1986). They usually gain entry by a door or window, grab visible cash and portable valuables, and leave quickly. Low-level burglars realize minimal take for their efforts, not only because they prey on victims who have little but also because they lack access to more sophisticated criminal peers, tipsters, and fences capable of handling diverse and large-quantity commodities. Many have juvenile arrest or confinement records, but, because of their youth, few low-level offenders have been tested by the experience of imprisonment. Their involvement in theft rarely lasts beyond a few years before the pull of conventional relationships and fear of more severe adult sanctions cause them to desist from further theft (Glassner et al. 1983).

Middle-range thieves usually begin their criminal participation as juveniles and move in and out of crime several times during their young adult years. Many vacillate between criminal and legitimate role identities (Irwin 1970; West 1978) or moonlight at crime (Holzman 1983). On average, they are older and more mobile than low-level burglars. Although many are daily users of alcohol and other drugs, the relation between this and their criminal participation is complex. On the one hand, some use drugs to diminish concern about the threatened penalties of acts they contemplate committing, while others use them immediately preceding their crimes in order to relax or to bolster courage. On the other hand, faced with the daily exigencies of managing a habit, those addicted to drugs are driven to commit crime and to do so with increased intensity (Ball, Shaffer, and Nurco 1983; Johnson et al. 1985).

Middle-range thieves search out targets over a wider area than low-level burglars, often traveling to or within suburban areas to commit crime (Rengert and Wasilchick 1985). Once intent on burglary and in an area of suitable targets, they are most concerned with choosing unoccupied structures with entry points that afford an obstructed view to potential witnesses (Repetto 1974; Walsh 1980; Maguire 1982; Bennett and Wright 1984*a*). More rational and experienced at theft than low-level burglars, they are a more determined adversary not easily defeated by common security measures.

Middle-range burglars also make target selections with an eye toward the potential payoff and are rewarded with higher aggregate average earnings. When they steal, most middle-range burglars concentrate less on what is close at hand than on valuable items located anywhere in a structure. They are more systematic than low-level burglars in disposing of stolen goods, but they usually do not have access to fences who can handle large quantities of goods.

Increasing age makes middle-range burglars more solitary in their criminal pursuits since this obviates the need to split criminal proceeds with others and, in the event of arrest, reduces the ability of police and prosecutors to pit crime partners against one another. Most middle-range thieves accumulate one or more jail and prison terms before desisting or changing their criminal line with advancing age (Meisenhelder 1977; Shover 1983*a*, 1985).

The diverse and occasionally complex tasks involved in high-level burglary make it a social enterprise (Shover 1973), and high-level burglars, therefore, are as likely as juveniles to steal with others (Gibbs and Shelly 1982*a*). These burglary crews operate democratically, but very few are mixed racially or ethnically. High-level burglars are connected with reliable sources of information about targets, they may travel long distances to work (Eskridge 1983), and they earn substantially more from crime than do less sophisticated thieves. Their task-force approach to organization and procedures bears similarities to military commando operations (McIntosh 1975; Shover 1983*b*). For example, careful arrangements for disposing of merchandise or other proceeds are made as part of the overall planning, and attention is paid to covering potential sticking points. Although they are capable of using more sophisticated techniques than other thieves, in many cases this is unnecessary. The external ties maintained by high-level burglars ensure access to the requisite technical expertise to commit burglaries and other crimes of varying complexity. Most are known to the police in their home territory as thieves or suspected thieves, but the details of their work, which is conducted elsewhere, remain unknown (Mack 1964, 1972).

Occupational and work metaphors have been the preferred approach to investigation and analysis of high-level burglary and its practitioners (Shover 1971; Letkemann 1973; Sparks 1982). This is evidenced not only in use of career metaphors but also in the attention paid to the appeal of crime and its attendant lifestyle as important payoffs for offenders. The lifestyle and criminal calculus of high-level burglars shows clearly the "seductions of crime" (Katz 1988, in this volume). Misfits in a world that values precise schedules, punctuality, and disciplined subordination to authority, high-level thieves value the autonomy to structure life and work as they wish. Gambling and drinking are popular pastimes in their world, and they live life in "the fast lane," albeit their enjoyment is interrupted periodically by imprisonment (Shover 1971; Mack 1972; Letkemann 1973; Gibbs and Shelly 1982*b*). Little is known about the later lives of high-level offenders, although some apparently become background operators (Mack 1975) as they get older (Shover 1983*b*, 1985). Only the infirmities of age and diminishing connections significantly dampen their criminal activities.

V. Victim and Criminal Justice Responses to Burglary

An unknown but presumably small proportion of burglaries go undetected even by their victims. Many of these probably are unlawful, unforced entries where the offender either finds nothing or takes flight prematurely without disturbing or taking anything. A household member was at home and saw the offender or offenders during 12.7 percent of all residential burglaries reported to the NCS during 1973–82 (Bureau of Justice Statistics 1985). The offender was an acquaintance in

25 percent of these cases; a spouse, ex-spouse, or other relative in 11.4 percent of the cases; and a person known only by sight in 5.6 percent of these cases. This means that upward to 42 percent of victims who chance to encounter a burglar in their home may discover the burglar is not a stranger. In 4 percent of household burglaries committed while a household member was at home, the victim also was raped, robbed, or assaulted (Bureau of Justice Statistics 1985).

Table 2 summarizes 1988 NCS data on relations between household characteristics and burglary reporting. Generally, the evidence more than confirms Sparks's observation that "victims' decisions to call the police are based mainly on a fairly rational assessment of the costs and benefits of doing this. . . . Every survey done to date has found that notification of the police is related to the 'seriousness,' in common-sense terms, of the incident in question. Thus, for example, the police are more likely to have been notified about completed crimes than about attempts . . . about crimes involving higher values of property stolen or damaged, or greater degrees of injury" (1981, pp. 22–23). Since forcible entry usually causes physical damage and financial loss and the likelihood of reporting increases as victim losses increase, it is not surprising that they are reported more often than unlawful entries and attempted forcible entries. Reporting rates are higher among middle- or higher-income victims. Generally, victims are less likely to report if their home is not disarranged (Kirchoff and Kirchoff 1984), if they recover their stolen objects independently, if they lack proof that a burglary occurred, or if they feel the incident is not important enough (Waller and Okihiro 1978; Bureau of Justice Statistics 1989*b*). In descending order of importance, victims who report to the police do so because they hope to recover property, to keep the same thing from happening again to themselves or to others, or because it was a crime and they feel a sense of duty to report it (Bureau of Justice Statistics 1989*c*, table 102). The likelihood of reporting increases as victim confidence increases that police could do something about the incident.

Confining attention to monetary losses sustained by victims, the great majority of burglaries are rather mundane affairs. Excluding losses caused by physical damage to dwellings, theft losses in half of burglaries are $250 or less (Bureau of Justice Statistics 1989*c*).

But financial loss is not the only way to assess the seriousness of burglary. Data from the 1983 British Crime Survey show that while nearly half of all burglary victims report minimal emotional problems following victimization, one in three suffers depression, sleeplessness,

TABLE 2

Percentage of U.S. Household Burglaries Reported to Police in 1987 by Characteristics of Offense and Household

Variable	Percentage of Households Reporting
Total (all burglaries)	52.1
Type of burglary:	
Forcible entry	76.6
Attempted forcible entry	31.5
Unlawful entry	43.4
Value of loss (in $):	
Less than 10	14.1
10–49	31.7
50–99	31.5
100–249	49.6
250–999	72.2
1,000 or more	89.5
Head of household:	
White	52.1
Black	52.6
Family income (in $):	
Less than 10,000	39.9
10,000–24,999	54.1
25,000–49,999	62.8
50,000 or more	56.5

SOURCE.—Bureau of Justice Statistics (1989*b*), tables 92, 99, 100, and 101.

or other health problems (Hough and Mayhew 1985, table J). Interviewed some four to ten weeks after the incident, 322 English victims of residential burglary were asked about their "first reaction" on discovering the burglary. The most common response by male victims was anger or annoyance; a much smaller proportion reported being upset, confused, or crying. Women victims most often reported a sense of shock, followed closely by being upset, confused, or crying (Maguire 1980, p. 262). Twenty-five percent of victims experienced acute or considerable stress; most of these were women (p. 263). When victims were asked to choose from a list of responses "the worst thing" about the burglary they sustained, 60 percent selected either intrusion on their privacy or emotional upset (pp. 266–67). Women victims more than men report personal feelings of revulsion and fear. Expressed in their use of words such as "pollution" and "violation," victims who experience the strongest sense of revulsion following household burglary are primarily women who live alone (Maguire 1980; Walsh 1980; Burt and Katz 1984).

Many have noted the apparent contradiction that burglary, a crime that rarely brings offenders and victims face-to-face and typically results in modest financial losses to victims, is feared by many citizens and evokes strong emotional reactions from its victims. In fact, except for victims' financial loss, as table 3 reveals, the experiences of burglary victims are very similar to the experiences of victims of robbery, a crime many consider more serious than burglary.

Most victims of burglary react to the experience by increased use of simple precautions or by installing marginally more resistant security hardware (Maguire 1980; Walsh 1980; Winchester and Jackson 1982). They may, for example, take care to simulate occupancy when the home is vacant or purchase and install improved door locks. Their heightened security consciousness and diligence in pursuing it generally diminish over ensuing months.

A. *Police*

Suspected and convicted burglars consume a major proportion of criminal justice attention and resources. The 300,000 persons arrested for burglary in 1988 constituted 16 percent of all arrests for Index crimes (Federal Bureau of Investigation 1989, table 33). The 14 percent clearance rate for burglaries is the lowest for the eight Index crimes (Federal Bureau of Investigation 1989, p. 159). Doubtless, the main reason for this is because burglars rarely are seen by victims and by the time the police are notified the trail is cold. The clearance rate declines rapidly as the time lag from incident to report increases, although a large number of burglaries are solved by questioning of offenders already in custody (Burrows 1986). The implication is clear: either offenders are apprehended at or near the crime scene, or they are not apprehended at all (Gibbs and Shelly 1982*a*). There is no quarrel with Conklin and Bittner (1973) who argue what is important is not police reaction time but detection of the crime soon after its occurrence.

"The vast majority of burglary . . . cases are investigated for no more than four hours, counting both the preliminary work by patrol officers and the follow-up by detectives" (Eck 1983, pp. xv–xvi). Police officers are the only official personnel most burglary victims will see, and their actions can be extremely important, particularly for the minority who are shaken severely by the experience. There is reason to believe that police do not always play this role well. The apparent reason is the

TABLE 3

Financial Loss and Problems Caused by Burglary and Robbery Victimization in England and Wales in 1983

Variable	Burglary (%)	Robbery (%)
Value of loss from property stolen (in £):		
Under 25	31	73
25–99	19	17
100–249	9	6
250+	40	4
Practical problems of victim:*		
None	42	68
Inconvenience	31	9
Financial problems	15	10
Difficulty dealing with police	7	1
Emotional problems:*		
None	47	51
Worry, fear, loss of confidence	31	28
Depression, stress, sleeping, health problems	8	8
Upset	9	13
Anger, frustration, annoyance	6	1

SOURCE.—Hough and Mayhew (1985), tables H, I, and J.

NOTE.—Percentages do not add to 100 due to rounding. In addition, "burglary" refers to incidents that exclude attempts, while "robbery" refers to incidents that include attempts.

* The percentages for this variable do not total 100 because "other answers" are not shown.

substantial gap between the importance of the crime as seen by victims and the police response to the same incident; burglary is both extraordinary and unsettling to the former but part of the daily routine to police officers. Unaware or unconcerned about this and limited police resources, victims may be surprised when investigating officers do not search for fingerprints or use complex evidence-gathering technologies. The "fundamental problem is that public expectations are probably out of line with what the police can actually do about many reported incidents" (Mayhew, Elliott, and Dowds 1989, p. 67). This may explain why victims who are dissatisfied with the police response believe they did not do enough, were not interested in the incident, or failed to keep them informed about developments in the case. Although few victims have serious complaints about their treatment by the police (Walsh 1980), many particularly regret this last point, the absence of follow-up contact (Maguire 1980).

B. Prosecutors, Courts, and Corrections

Williams and Lucianovic (1979) show that prosecution followed in 88 percent of 1973 Washington, D.C., burglary cases in which police arrested at least one adult suspect. In descending order of importance, the availability of witnesses, recovery of property or other evidence, use of a firearm during the offense, whether the offense was committed by strangers, and whether thirty minutes or less elapsed between the victim's report and the arrest affected the probability of conviction (Williams and Lucianovic 1979, p. 61). Convictions followed in 43 percent of the cases that were prosecuted. In 1986, 18 percent of felony convictions in U.S. state courts were burglary cases (Bureau of Justice Statistics 1989*d*).

Approximately 49 percent of convicted burglars are sentenced to prison confinement compared to 67 percent and 32 percent, respectively, for robbers and larcenists (Cunniff 1987, p. 5). On average, burglars are sentenced to fifty-seven months imprisonment (Bureau of Justice Statistics 1989*d*), approximately forty-six months for females and sixty-six months for males (Cunniff 1987, p. 31). These penalties exceed reported penalties for 1978 in England and Wales of nine months to three years (Maguire 1982, p. 153). It is difficult to know the origins and interpret the consequences for time served of this difference in the "going rate." Overall, the median time served by convicted U.S. burglars is about seventeen months, and the mean is twenty-one months (Minor-Harper and Innes 1987).

Convicted burglars are exceeded in numbers only by armed robbers in America's prison population (Innes 1988). They make up the largest group of prisoners released annually from U.S. prisons and they are among the most recidivistic of ordinary property offenders. This is true regardless of the measure of recidivism employed: rearrest, prosecution on new criminal charges, or reconviction (Beck and Shipley 1989). A three-year follow-up of 78,143 persons released from criminal justice custody anywhere in the United States in 1972 showed that nearly two-thirds of the cohort were rearrested at least once but burglars topped the list at 81 percent (Federal Bureau of Investigation 1976, pp. 42–46). Of all convicted burglars released from prison in eleven states in 1983, 54.6 percent were convicted of additional crimes within three years of release; only auto thieves and receivers of stolen property had higher failure rates (Beck and Shipley 1989, table 8). A three-year follow-up of 4,703 adults arrested in Washington, D.C., in a four-month period in 1976 showed that 61 percent of burglars were rearrested compared with

51 percent of robbers and 36 percent of the sample overall. Twenty-six percent of burglars, 25 percent of robbers, and 22 percent of the sample overall were reconvicted (Williams and Lucianovic 1979, p. 25).

VI. General Crime Prevention and Burglary

Two major approaches to general crime prevention have found favor in recent years, one emphasizing improved police response and the other emphasizing community crime control. Burglary prevention is one of their common objectives. Encouraged by the aggregate-level negative relation between punishment certainty and crime rates, the deterrence approach generally aims at reducing crime by increasing the objective risk of arrest and prosecution for offenders.

The High-Impact Anti-Crime Program stands as an example of the deterrence-based approach to crime reduction (Chelimsky 1976). Funded to the tune of $160 million, the program was inaugurated in 1972 by the U.S. Department of Justice in eight American cities with serious street-crime problems. The objective was to reduce the incidence of five specific crimes, including burglary. The target cities were given considerable latitude in determining how to spend the moneys they received, but slightly under half of all impact funds went to programs to increase deterrence through greater police presence or improved police and court operations. Each city's preprogram burglary rate was matched with the mean rate for six other cities that had similar burglary rates and trends. The experience in the matched cities between 1972 and 1974 was used as a baseline for comparing burglary performance in impact cities. Analysis of the program's effect showed that five of the impact cities had 1974 burglary rates lower than expected while three experienced no changes. Support for a deterrent effect was modest at best, and confidence was limited even more by poor program evaluation; the shortcomings of the evaluation design and methods were fundamental and substantial (Zimring 1978).

In the 1970s, political leaders and criminal justice administrators increasingly turned to citizens for assistance in controlling crime and, following now well-known efforts in the cities of Seattle, Portland (Oregon), and Hartford, community crime-prevention programs were established in many communities across the United States (Skogan 1988). Property marking, home-security surveys, and block or neighborhood watches are the backbone of most community programs (Feins 1983). After spreading rapidly in the United States, neighborhood watch programs spanned the Atlantic and spread with equal speed in

England and Wales (Husain 1988). By 1984, 7 percent of American households participated in neighborhood watch programs (Whitaker 1986, p. 2), and by 1988 an estimated 14 percent of households in Britain were members of similar programs (Mayhew, Elliott, and Dowds 1989, p. 51).

Home-security surveys reflect belief that subsequent property marking, improved locks, better lighting, and other target-hardening modifications of dwellings and businesses can make a burglar's task more difficult and successful burglary unlikely. Two types of investigations cast doubt on this assumption. First, imprisoned property offenders were asked to rate the likely effectiveness of fifteen security measures for preventing burglary. The four top-rated items—burglar alarms connected to law-enforcement offices, electronic window sensors, closed circuit television, and security patrols—are all very expensive measures unavailable to most private citizens (Figgie International 1988, p. 30). By contrast, the target-hardening measures promoted in most crime-prevention programs—local burglary alarms, deadbolt locks, timed interior lights—were rated as far less effective deterrents. Second, studies comparing attempted and successful burglaries report that occupancy at the time of the incident is the only variable that distinguishes successful and unsuccessful burglaries even for households with security measures (Garofalo and Clark 1986). Similarly, Titus (1989) analyzed data from the NCS Victim Risk Supplement survey and found that the two variables that best distinguish attempted and successful burglaries are location in a central city and whether a household member was home at the time of the incident. Reported presence of household security measures did not distinguish between attempted and completed burglaries.

Despite these findings, there is evidence that target-hardening strategies can reduce crime under specific conditions (e.g., Heal and Laycock 1986). The major question is whether communitywide target-hardening campaigns that rely on voluntary citizen participation can be as successful. At present there is no reason to dispute an earlier, mixed assessment of broad residential target-hardening strategies:

> Whatever benefits individual householders can achieve or be given from target hardening measures, any great impact on overall levels of burglary cannot be expected. . . . For understandable reasons, many people are currently lax about taking even the most elementary security precautions, or they apply security in

> piecemeal fashion; measures which have the biggest chance of success, too, are least likely to be adopted on any scale because of costs and acceptability. . . . This will leave a considerable number of properties, many of them risky because of easy access and poor surveillability, which burglars can choose instead of the minority of well-protected dwellings. [Mayhew 1984, p. 41]

The record with respect to neighborhood watch and its effectiveness is scarcely more encouraging. It is clear that neighborhood watch programs generally are plagued by persistent problems. Nationwide studies in both the United States and the United Kingdom point to difficulties particularly in program placement and maintenance (Garofalo and McLeod 1987, 1989; Husain 1988). Programs are least likely to be located in neighborhoods with serious burglary problems, and those at greatest risk of burglary are less likely to join even when programs are available in their neighborhood (Mayhew, Elliott, and Dowds 1989, pp. 53–54). Further, enthusiasm runs high and block meetings are lively and interesting during the early months of programs' existence, but interest and commitment wane as time passes. Experience with neighborhood watch programs makes it very doubtful that they can be routinized across the urban landscape with demonstrable and sustained impact (Rosenbaum 1986).

The effectiveness of neighborhood watch programs in preventing crime has been difficult to assess. Like evaluation studies of deterrence-based crime control programs, critical reviews of evaluation research on neighborhood watch programs have identified weak evaluation generally and imprecise specification of treatment variables as recurrent impediments to more confident assessment (Yin 1986; Rosenbaum 1988). Another problem for those who design and evaluate crime control programs is the possibility that crime will be displaced from program areas or targets to less secure ones (Repetto 1976; Gabor 1981; Hakim and Rengert 1981). This possibility must be addressed in program planning and evaluation, but it is only one of numerous complicating considerations surrounding the larger issue of program effectiveness (Rosenbaum 1988). It is worth noting that a recent careful quasi-experimental evaluation of neighborhood watch in areas of London found that crime increased slightly in program areas and remained constant or decreased in displacement and control areas (Bennett 1988).

Evaluation research on general prevention has taught us that broad-brush programs fail to take sufficient account of citizens' variable commitment to and ability to benefit from community crime-prevention programs. As we have learned that prevention efforts should take account of the variable nature of neighborhood burglary problems, the promise of situational crime prevention has become increasingly evident (Clarke 1980). This approach to crime control emphasizes measures "(1) directed at highly specific forms of crime (2) that involve the management, design, or manipulation of the immediate environment in as systematic and permanent a way as possible (3) so as to reduce the opportunities for crime and increase its risks as perceived by a wide range of offenders" (Clarke 1983, p. 225).

There is little doubt that this approach, when implemented in experimental programs infused by official commitment or concern, can reduce specific kinds of burglaries in well-defined target areas or target types (Laycock 1984, 1985; Hill 1986; Forrester et al. 1988). There is conditional evidence for the merits of crime-prevention programs and measures carefully devised to meet specific crime problems and profiles (Heal and Laycock 1986; Bennett 1988). A similar movement to more narrowly drawn target and program objectives has occurred in the area of deterrence-based approaches to burglary control. Thus, repeat-offender programs aimed at deterring and incapacitating high-rate offenders have become commonplace even as it is clear that they also pose problems of evaluation no less challenging than community crime-prevention programs (e.g., Martin and Sherman 1985).

VII. Concluding Remarks

Most theory-driven investigations of burglary over the past twenty-five years are grounded in opportunity structure theory. While this work has enhanced our understanding of the distribution of burglary, it is equally clear that tests of opportunity theory have been narrowly drawn and, therefore, are incomplete. While it is important to know that thefts increase when there are more opportunities for them to occur, causal variables at other levels of analysis must be added if we are to have a more complete explanation of burglary. For example, since the existence of offenders is treated as a "given," opportunity theory must be complemented by a theory that explains the variable size of the offender population. The emergence of world economic competition, declining federal expenditures for housing and welfare programs, and rapid international movement of corporate investment and production are obvious examples of macrolevel changes that may affect the size of groups with minimal stake in conformity located at the margin of conventional social arrangements. Carroll and Jackson (1983) show that proportionate increases in the household activity ratio are produced by increasing numbers of female-headed households, many with marginal incomes. Thus, dispersion of household activities may increase income inequality directly and burglary indirectly by increasing the supply of offenders.

Opportunity theory is compatible logically with deterrence theory and other rational-choice interpretations of crime that have found favor among public officials and scholars in recent years (Clarke and Cornish 1985; Cornish and Clarke 1986). Like most investigations of rational-choice theory, it is distinguished by failure to measure legitimate opportunities and their causal contribution to burglary and other street crimes (Piliavin et al. 1986). Aggregate-level tests of opportunity theory that move beyond exclusive focus on illicit opportunities must incorporate measures of legitimate opportunities and examine their effect on Index property crime.

The explanatory and predictive payoffs from a more complete and causally integrated theory of burglary will be enhanced considerably by analysis of intercity and neighborhood variation in offense rates. This will permit investigators to use samples large enough to examine the conjoint effects of opportunities and other structural and economic variables.

The core assumption of rational-choice theory is that individuals weigh the utilities and risks associated with behavioral options before choosing whether to commit a criminal act. Criminal participation is seen as a theoretically comprehensible decision-making process, with the probability of criminal participation increasing as the individual's expected net utilities from crime exceed some threshold.

For all the talk about criminal decision making, until recently there were more ad hoc models of the process than empirical studies (Manski 1978). A growing number of qualitative studies of persistent offenders show that real-life criminal decision making is substantially more complex than models suggest. While offenders sketched in decision-making models are alert to the risk of arrest and incarceration, their real-life counterparts oftentimes are blinded or indifferent toward it. Many persistent offenders weigh the potential outcomes of their crimes only casually and either refuse to consider the risk of arrest or dwell entirely on the usually exaggerated potential monetary return from a crime (Carroll 1982; Maguire 1982; Bennett and Wright 1984*a;* Feeney 1986; Shover and Honaker 1990). Offenders typically acknowledge a high probability of arrest "eventually," but they also know there is a low probability of arrest for any particular offense (Bennett and Wright 1984*a*). Collectively, studies "suggest that either (1) offenders are not utilizing a sensible cost-benefit analysis in committing crimes, or (2) the perceived costs of these crimes, especially the chances of going to prison, do not sufficiently outweigh the 'take' expected by offenders, thus making the expected profitability of [their] crimes relatively attractive" (Figgie International 1988, p. 25).

In sum, a variety of evidence strongly suggests that "effective assessments of risk are to some extent situationally-induced, transitory, and unstable" (Piliavin et al. 1986, pp. 115–16). Given the fact that most of the studies are limited to prisoners and ex-prisoners, the external validity of these findings is severely limited. They do, however, raise doubt about the likely impact on youthful persistent offenders of deterrence-based burglary prevention initiatives. There is a clear need for additional ethnographic investigations of offenders of different ages and types, particularly those who desist from crime before developing an appreciable criminal career.

There is serious danger of empirical sterility in too much of the decision-making approach to criminal participation. There is, to begin with, the apparent unconcern with the offender's motivation, that is, the purpose and the subjective meaning of a prospective criminal act. Surely this constrains the criminal calculus as when, for example, an act is viewed not as crime but as legitimate social control or self-help (Black 1983). Alternatively, consider how the presence of co-offenders (Reiss 1986, 1988) or prior use of alcohol or other drugs may distort the decision-making process (Cromwell, Olson, and Avary 1990). Finally, consider the importance of mood. Whereas the model criminal decision maker is never angry, desperate, or defiant, the moods of real-life decision makers can distort the criminal calculus severely and make offenders unconcerned about risk. Moreover, decisions to forgo crime similarly can result from mood or a belief simply that "things don't look right" rather than from a systematic, careful assessment of utilities and risks (Walsh 1986; Shover and Honaker 1990). Perhaps we would do well to follow Goffman's (1967) suggestion that crime be seen as one form of "action": behavior of problematic outcome and potentially serious consequences, such as high construction work, test piloting, or sky diving that is engaged in by choice. While it may be reasonable to approach criminal decision making as if it is little different from the decision to purchase a television set, theoretical dividends may come sooner if we focus for comparative purposes on specific forms of legitimate behavior that share some characteristics of criminal decision making.

Prospects for improving the effectiveness of burglary prevention programs are difficult to assess, but past efforts, even if interpreted optimistically, have met with limited success. Efforts to prevent burglary also could benefit from more attention to forces that determine the supply of offenders. As compared to the modest results from target-hardening approaches to burglary reduction, programs aimed at providing increased legitimate opportunities could be more effective by reducing the size of offender pools. As important, these programs are less likely to transform homes and businesses into fortresses in which fearful citizens cower. The task for burglary prevention programs seems clear: to learn more about the conditional effectiveness of diverse programs. This may offer protection from repetition of the "nothing works" response from investigators and public officials.

REFERENCES

Baldwin, John, and Anthony Bottoms. 1976. *The Urban Criminal*. London: Tavistock.

Ball, John C., John W. Shaffer, and David N. Nurco. 1983. "The Day-to-Day Criminality of Heroin Addicts in Baltimore: A Study in the Continuity of Offense Rates." *Drug and Alcohol Dependence* 12:119–42.

Beck, Allen J., and Bernard E. Shipley. 1989. *Recidivism of Prisoners Released in 1983*. Washington, D.C.: U.S. Department of Justice, Bureau of Justice Statistics.

Bennett, Trevor. 1988. "An Assessment of the Design, Implementation and Effectiveness of Neighbourhood Watch in London." *Howard Journal of Criminal Justice* 27:241–55.

Bennett, Trevor, and Richard Wright. 1984*a*. *Burglars on Burglary*. Aldershot: Gower.

———. 1984*b*. "The Relationship between Alcohol Use and Burglary." *British Journal of Addiction* 79:431–37.

Biderman, Albert D., and James P. Lynch. 1989. *Understanding Crime Incidence Statistics: Why the UCR Diverges from the NCS*. New York: Springer-Verlag.

Black, Donald. 1983. "Crime as Social Control." *American Sociological Review* 48:34–45.

Block, Richard L., ed. 1984*a*. *Victimization and Fear of Crime: World Perspectives*. Washington, D.C.: U.S. Department of Justice, Bureau of Justice Statistics.

———. 1984*b*. "The Impact of Victimization, Rates and Patterns: A Comparison of the Netherlands and the United States." In *Victimization and Fear of Crime: World Perspectives*, edited by Richard Block. Washington, D.C.: U.S. Government Printing Office.

———. 1989. "A Cross-national Comparison of Victims of Crime: Victim Surveys of Eleven Countries." Paper presented at the forty-first annual meeting of the American Society of Criminology, Reno, Nevada, November.

Blumstein, Alfred, Jacqueline Cohen, and Daniel Nagin, eds. 1978. *Deterrence and Incapacitation: Estimating the Effects of Criminal Sanctions on Crime Rates.* Washington, D.C.: National Academy Press.

Boggs, Sarah L. 1965. "Urban Crime Patterns." *American Sociological Review* 30:899–908.

Braithwaite, John. 1981. "The Myth of Social Class and Criminality Reconsidered." *American Sociological Review* 46:36–57.

Braithwaite, John, and David Biles. 1984. "Victims and Offenders: The Australian Experience." In *Victimization and Fear of Crime: World Perspectives,* edited by Richard Block. Washington, D.C.: U.S. Government Printing Office.

Brantingham, Paul J., and Patricia L. Brantingham. 1975. "The Spatial Patterning of Burglary." *Howard Journal of Criminal Justice* 14:11–23.

———. 1980. "Crime, Occupation, and Economic Specialization." In *Crime: A Spatial Perspective*, edited by Daniel E. Georges-Abeyie and Keith D. Harries. New York: Columbia University Press.

Bureau of Justice Statistics. 1983. *Report to the Nation on Crime and Justice: The Data.* Washington, D.C.: U.S. Government Printing Office.

———. 1985. *Household Burglary*. Washington, D.C.: U.S. Government Printing Office.

———. 1988*a*. *Households Touched by Crime, 1987.* Washington, D.C.: U.S. Government Printing Office.

———. 1988*b*. *Criminal Victimization 1987.* Washington, D.C.: U.S. Government Printing Office.

———. 1988*c*. *The Seasonality of Crime Victimization.* Washington, D.C.: U.S. Government Printing Office.

———. 1989*a*. *Households Touched by Crime, 1988.* Washington, D.C.: U.S. Government Printing Office.

———. 1989*b*. *Criminal Victimization in the United States, 1987.* Washington, D.C.: U.S. Government Printing Office.

———. 1989*c*. *Sourcebook of Criminal Justice Statistics—1988.* Washington, D.C.: U.S. Government Printing Office.

———. 1989*d*. *Felony Sentences in State Courts, 1986.* Washington, D.C.: U.S. Government Printing Office.

Burrows, J. 1986. "Investigating Burglary: The Measurement of Police Performance." Home Office Research Study no. 88. London: H.M. Stationery Office.

Burt, Martha R., and Bonnie L. Katz. 1984. "Rape, Robbery, and Burglary: Responses to Actual and Feared Victimization with Special Focus on Women and the Elderly." *Victimology* 10:325–58.

Carroll, John S. 1982. "Committing a Crime: The Offender's Decision." In *The Criminal Justice System: A Social-Psychological Analysis*, edited by V. J. Konecni and E. B. Ebbesen. San Francisco: Freeman.

Carroll, Leo, and Pamela Irving Jackson. 1983. "Inequality, Opportunity, and Crime Rates in Central Cities." *Criminology* 21:178–94.

Chaiken, Jan M., and Marcia R. Chaiken. 1982. *Varieties of Criminal Behavior*. Santa Monica, Calif.: RAND.

Chappell, Duncan. 1965. "The Development and Administration of the English Criminal Law Relating to Offenses of Breaking and Entering." Ph.D. dissertation, University of Cambridge.

Chelimsky, Eleanor. 1976. *High Impact Anti-crime Program*. Washington, D.C.: U.S. Department of Justice, National Institute of Law Enforcement and Criminal Justice.

Chimbos, Peter D. 1973. "A Study of Breaking and Entering Offences in 'Northern City,' Ontario." *Canadian Journal of Criminology and Corrections* 15:316–25.

Clark, Michael. 1989. "Insurance Fraud." *British Journal of Criminology* 29:1–20.

Clarke, Ronald V. 1980. "Situational Crime Prevention: Theory and Practice." *British Journal of Criminology* 20:136–47.

———. 1983. "Situational Crime Prevention: Its Theoretical Basis and Practical Scope." In *Crime and Justice: An Annual Review of Research*, vol. 4, edited by Michael Tonry and Norval Morris. Chicago: University of Chicago Press.

Clarke, Ronald V., and Derek B. Cornish. 1985. "Modeling Offenders' Decisions: A Framework for Research and Policy." In *Crime and Justice: An Annual Review of Research*, vol. 6, edited by Michael Tonry and Norval Morris. Chicago: University of Chicago Press.

Cohen, Lawrence E., and David Cantor. 1981. "Residential Burglary in the United States: Lifestyle and Demographic Factors Associated with the Probability of Victimization." *Journal of Research in Crime and Delinquency* 17:113–27.

Cohen, Lawrence E., and Marcus Felson. 1979. "Social Change and Crime Rate Trends: A Routine Activity Approach." *American Sociological Review* 44:588–608.

Cohen, Lawrence E., J. R. Kluegel, and Kenneth C. Land. 1981. "Social Inequality and Predatory Criminal Victimization: An Exposition and Test of a Formal Theory." *American Sociological Review* 46:504–24.

Conklin, John, and Egon Bittner. 1973. "Burglary in a Suburb." *Criminology* 11:206–32.

Cook, Philip J. 1980. "Research in Criminal Deterrence: Laying the Groundwork for the Second Decade." In *Crime and Justice: An Annual Review of Research*, vol. 2, edited by Norval Morris and Michael Tonry. Chicago: University of Chicago Press.

———. 1986. "The Demand and Supply of Criminal Opportunities." In *Crime and Justice: An Annual Review of Research*, vol. 7, edited by Michael Tonry and Norval Morris. Chicago: University of Chicago Press.

Cornish, Derek B., and Ronald V. Clarke, eds. 1986. *The Reasoning Criminal*. New York: Springer-Verlag.

Cromwell, Paul F., James N. Olson, and D'Unn Avary. 1990. "Residential Burglary: An Ethnographic Analysis." Report to the U.S. Department of Justice, National Institute of Justice. University of Texas at Permian Basin, Department of Criminology.

Cunniff, Mark A. 1987. *Sentencing Outcomes in 28 Felony Courts, 1985*. Washington, D.C.: U.S. Department of Justice, Bureau of Justice Statistics.

Danziger, Sheldon. 1976. "Explaining Urban Crime Rates." *Criminology* 14:291–96.

David, Pedro R., ed. 1974. *The World of the Burglar*. Albuquerque: University of New Mexico Press.

Eck, John E. 1983. *Solving Crimes: The Investigation of Burglary and Robbery*. Washington, D.C.: U.S. Department of Justice, National Institute of Justice.

Elliott, David, and Pat Mayhew. 1988. "Trends in Residential Burglary in England and Wales, 1972–1985." Home Office Research Bulletin no. 25. London: Home Office.

Elliott, Delbert S., and David Huizinga. 1983. "Social Class and Delinquent Behavior in a National Youth Panel." *Criminology* 21:149–77.

Engstad, P. A. 1975. "Environmental Opportunities and the Ecology of Crime." In *Crime in Canadian Society*, edited by R. A. Silverman and J. J. Teevan, Jr. Toronto: Butterworth.

Eskridge, Chris W. 1983. "Prediction of Burglary." *Journal of Criminal Justice* 11:67–75.

Federal Bureau of Investigation. 1976. *Uniform Crime Reports*. Washington, D.C.: U.S. Government Printing Office.

———. 1989. *Uniform Crime Reports 1988*. Washington, D.C.: U.S. Government Printing Office.

Feeney, Floyd. 1986. "Robbers as Decision-Makers." In *The Reasoning Criminal*, edited by D. B. Cornish and R. V. Clarke. New York: Springer-Verlag.

Feins, Judith D., with Joan Peterson, and Emily L. Rovetch. 1983. *Partnerships for Neighborhood Crime Prevention*. Washington, D.C.: U.S. Department of Justice, National Institute of Justice.

Ferdinand, T. N. 1972. "Burglary in Auburn, Massachusetts, 1960–1969." In *Politics, Crime and the International Scene*, edited by F. Adler and G. O. W. Mueller. San Juan, Puerto Rico: North-South Center Press.

Figgie International. 1988. *The Figgie Report Part VI—The Business of Crime: The Criminal Perspective*. Richmond, Va.: Figgie International.

Forrester, David, Mike Chatterton, and Ken Pease, with Robin Brown. 1988. "The Kirkholt Burglary Prevention Project, Rochdale." Home Office Crime Prevention Unit Paper no. 13. London: Home Office.

Gabor, Thomas. 1981. "The Crime Displacement Hypothesis: An Empirical Examination." *Crime and Delinquency* 27:390–404.

Garofalo, J., and D. Clark. 1986. "Attempted and Completed Crimes: A Study of Residential Burglaries and Personal Robberies." Draft final report to the U.S. Department of Justice, National Institute of Justice, Washington, D.C.

Garofalo, J., and M. McLeod. 1987. "Improving the Effectiveness and Utilization of Neighborhood Watch Programs." Report to the National Institute of

Justice. Albany: State University of New York, Hindelang Criminal Justice Research Center.

———. 1989. "The Structure and Operations of Neighborhood Watch Programs in the United States." *Crime and Delinquency* 35:326–44.

Georges-Abeyie, Daniel, and Keith D. Harries, eds. 1980. *Crime: A Spatial Perspective.* New York: Columbia University Press.

Gibbs, John J., and Peggy L. Shelly. 1982*a*. "Commercial Theft Studies: Theft in Two Cities." Draft report to the National Institute of Justice. Newark, N.J.: Rutgers University, Center for the Study of the Causes of Crime for Gain.

———. 1982*b*. "Life in the Fast Lane: A Retrospective View by Commercial Thieves." *Journal of Research in Crime and Delinquency* 19:299–330.

Glassner, Barry, Margret Ksander, Bruce Berg, and Bruce D. Johnson. 1983. "A Note on the Deterrent Effect of Juvenile vs. Adult Jurisdiction." *Social Problems* 31:219–22.

Goffman, Erving. 1967. *Interaction Ritual.* Garden City, N.Y.: Anchor.

Gould, Leroy C. 1969. "The Changing Structure of Property Crime in an Affluent Society." *Social Forces* 48:50–59.

Gould, Leroy C., Egon Bittner, Sol Chaneles, Sheldon Messinger, Kriss Novak, Fred Powledge, Howard Freeman, Stanton Wheeler, and Andrew Walker. 1966. "Crime as a Profession." Report submitted to the President's Commission on Law Enforcement and Administration of Justice. New Haven, Conn.: Yale University, Department of Sociology.

Hakim, Simon, and George F. Rengert, eds. 1981. *Crime Spillover.* Beverly Hills, Calif.: Sage.

Harries, Keith D. 1974. *The Geography of Crime and Justice.* New York: McGraw-Hill.

———. 1976. "Cities and Crime: A Geographic Model." *Criminology* 14:369–86.

Heal, Kevin, and Gloria Laycock, eds. 1986. *Situational Crime Prevention: From Theory into Practice.* London: H.M. Stationery Office.

Hill, Nigel. 1986. "Prepayment Coin Meters: A Target for Burglary." Home Office Crime Prevention Unit Paper no. 6. London: Home Office.

Hindelang, Michael J., Michael R. Gottfredson, and James Garofalo. 1978. *Victims of Personal Crime.* Cambridge, Mass.: Ballinger.

Holzman, Harold R. 1983. "The Serious Habitual Property Offender as Moonlighter: An Empirical Study of Labor Force Participation among Robbers and Burglars." *Journal of Criminal Law and Criminology* 73:1774–92.

Home Office. 1988. *Criminal Statistics, England and Wales, 1987.* London: H.M. Stationery Office.

Hood, Roger, and Richard F. Sparks. 1970. *Key Issues in Criminology.* New York: McGraw-Hill.

Hope, Tim. 1982. "Burglary in Schools: The Prospects for Prevention." Home Office Research and Planning Unit Paper no. 11. London: Home Office.

Hough, Mike. 1984. "Residential Burglary: A Profile from the British Crime Survey." In *Coping with Burglary*, edited by Ronald V. Clarke and Tim Hope. Boston: Kluwer-Nijhoff.

Hough, Mike, and Pat Mayhew. 1985. "Taking Account of Crime: Key Findings from the 1984 British Crime Survey." Home Office Research Study no. 85. London: H.M. Stationery Office.

Husain, Sohail. 1988. "Neighbourhood Watch in England and Wales: A Locational Analysis." Home Office Crime Prevention Unit Paper no. 12. London: Home Office.

Innes, Christopher A. 1988. *Profile of State Prison Inmates, 1986*. Washington, D.C.: U.S. Department of Justice, Bureau of Justice Statistics.

Irwin, John. 1970. *The Felon*. Englewood Cliffs, N.J.: Prentice-Hall.

Jackson, Pamela I. 1984. "Opportunity and Crime: A Function of City Size." *Sociology and Social Research* 68:172–93.

Jacobs, David. 1981. "Inequality and Economic Crime." *Sociology and Social Research* 66:12–28.

Johnson, Bruce D., Paul J. Goldstein, Edward Preble, James Schmeidler, Douglas S. Lipton, Barry Spunt, and Thomas Miller. 1985. *Taking Care of Business: The Economics of Crime by Heroin Abusers*. Lexington, Mass.: Heath.

Kalish, Carol B. 1988. *International Crime Rates*. Washington, D.C.: U.S. Department of Justice, Bureau of Justice Statistics.

Katz, Jack. 1988. *Seductions of Crime*. New York: Basic.

———. In this volume. "The Motivation of the Persistent Robber."

Kirchhoff, Gerd Ferdinand, and Claudia Kirchhoff. 1984. "Victimological Research in Germany: Victim Surveys and Research on Sexual Victimization." In *Victimization and Fear of Crime: World Perspectives*, edited by Richard Block. Washington, D.C.: U.S. Government Printing Office.

Klockars, Carl. 1974. *The Fence*. New York: Free Press.

Koppel, Herbert. 1987. *Lifetime Likelihood of Victimization*. Washington, D.C.: U.S. Department of Justice, Bureau of Justice Statistics.

Kowalski, Gregory S., Robert L. Dittman, Jr., and Wayne L. Bung. 1980. "Spatial Distribution of Offenses by States, 1970–1976." *Journal of Research in Crime and Delinquency* 17:4–25.

Langan, Patrick A., and John M. Dawson. 1990. *Profile of Felons Convicted in State Courts, 1986*. Washington, D.C.: U.S. Department of Justice, Bureau of Justice Statistics.

Laycock, Gloria. 1984. "Reducing Burglary: A Study of Chemists' Shops." Home Office Crime Prevention Unit Paper no. 1. London: Home Office.

———. 1985. "Property Marking: A Deterrent to Domestic Burglary?" Home Office Crime Prevention Unit Paper no. 3. London: Home Office.

Letkemann, Peter. 1973. *Crime as Work*. Englewood Cliffs, N.J.: Prentice-Hall.

Litton, Roger A., and Ken Pease. 1984. "Crimes and Claims: The Case of Burglary Insurance." In *Coping with Burglary*, edited by Ronald V. Clarke and Tim Hope. Boston: Kluwer-Nijhoff.

McIntosh, Mary. 1975. *Organization of Crime*. London: Macmillan.

Mack, John. 1964. "Full-Time Miscreants, Delinquent Neighbourhoods and Criminal Networks." *British Journal of Sociology* 15:38–52.

———. 1972. "The Able Criminal." *British Journal of Criminology* 12:44–54.

———. 1975. *The Crime Industry*. Farnborough, United Kingdom: Saxon House.

Maguire, Mike. 1980. "The Impact of Burglary upon Victims." *British Journal of Criminology* 20:261–75.

———. 1982. *Burglary in a Dwelling*. London: Heinemann.

Manski, Charles F. 1978. "Prospects for Inference on Deterrence through Empirical Analysis of Individual Criminal Behavior." In *Deterrence and Incapacitation: Estimating the Effects of Criminal Sanctions on Crime Rates*, edited by Alfred Blumstein, Jacqueline Cohen, and Daniel Nagin. Washington, D.C.: National Academy Press.

Martin, Susan, and Lawrence W. Sherman. 1985. *The Washington Repeat Offender Project*. Washington, D.C.: Police Foundation.

Mawby, R. I. 1981. "Police Practices and Crime Rates: A Case Study of a British City." In *Environmental Criminology*, edited by P. J. Brantingham and P. L. Brantingham. Beverly Hills, Calif.: Sage.

Maxfield, Michael G. 1987*a*. "Household Composition, Routine Activity, and Victimization: A Comparative Analysis." *Journal of Quantitative Criminology* 3:301–20.

———. 1987*b*. "Lifestyle and Routine Activity Theories of Crime: Empirical Studies of Victimization, Delinquency, and Offender Decision-Making." *Journal of Quantitative Criminology* 3:275–82.

Mayhew, Pat. 1984. "Target-Hardening: How Much of an Answer?" In *Coping with Burglary*, edited by Ronald V. Clarke and Tim Hope. Boston: Kluwer-Nijhoff.

———. 1987. *Residential Burglary: A Comparison of the United States, Canada and England and Wales*. Washington, D.C.: U.S. Department of Justice, National Institute of Justice.

Mayhew, Pat, David Elliott, and Lizanne Dowds. 1989. "The 1988 British Crime Survey." Home Office Research Study no. 111. London: H.M. Stationery Office.

Meisenhelder, Thomas. 1977. "An Exploratory Study of Exiting from Criminal Careers." *Criminology* 15:319–34.

Minor-Harper, Stephanie, and Christopher A. Innes. 1987. *Time Served in Prison and on Parole, 1984*. Washington, D.C.: U.S. Department of Justice, Bureau of Justice Statistics.

Molumby, Thomas. 1976. "Patterns of Crime in a University Housing Project." *American Behavioral Scientist* 20:247–59.

Perkins, Rollin M. 1969. *Criminal Law*. 2d ed. Mineola, N.Y.: Foundation Press.

Petersilia, Joan, Peter W. Greenwood, and Marvin Lavin. 1978. *Criminal Careers of Habitual Felons*. Washington, D.C.: U.S. Department of Justice, National Institute of Law Enforcement and Criminal Justice.

Peterson, Mark A., and Harriet B. Braiker. 1980. *Doing Crime: A Survey of California Prison Inmates*. Santa Monica, Calif.: RAND.

Piliavin, Irving, Rosemary Gartner, Craig Thornton, and Ross Matsueda. 1986. "Crime, Deterrence, and Rational Choice." *American Sociological Review* 51:101–19.

Pope, Carl E. 1977*a*. *Crime Specific Analysis: Characteristics of Burglary Incidents*. Washington, D.C.: U.S. Department of Justice, Law Enforcement Assistance Administration.

———. 1977*b*. *Crime Specific Analysis: An Empirical Examination of Burglary Offender Characteristics*. Washington, D.C.: U.S. Department of Justice, Law Enforcement Assistance Administration.

———. 1977*c*. *Crime Specific Analysis: An Empirical Examination of Burglary Offense and Offender Characteristics*. Washington, D.C.: U.S. Department of Justice, Law Enforcement Assistance Administration.

Quinney, Richard. 1966. "Structural Characteristics, Population Areas, and Crime Rates in the United States." *Journal of Criminal Law, Criminology, and Police Science* 57:45–52.

Rand, Alicia. 1987. "Mobility Triangles." In *Metropolitan Crime Patterns*, edited by Robert M. Figlio, Simon Hakim, and George F. Rengert. Monsey, N.Y.: Criminal Justice Press.

Reiss, Albert J., Jr. 1967. *Studies in Crime and Law Enforcement in Major Metropolitan Areas*, vol. 1. Washington, D.C.: U.S. Government Printing Office.

———. 1986. "Co-offender Influences on Criminal Careers." In *Criminal Careers and "Career Criminals,"* vol. 2, edited by Alfred Blumstein, Jacqueline Cohen, Jeffrey A. Roth, and Christy A. Visher. Washington, D.C.: National Academy Press.

———. 1988. "Co-offending and Criminal Careers." In *Crime and Justice: A Review of Research*, vol. 10, edited by Michael Tonry and Norval Morris. Chicago: University of Chicago Press.

Rengert, George F. 1981. "Burglary in Philadelphia: A Critique of an Opportunity Structure Model." In *Environmental Criminology*, edited by Paul J. Brantingham and Patricia L. Brantingham. Beverly Hills, Calif.: Sage.

Rengert, George F., and John Wasilchick. 1985. *Suburban Burglary*. Springfield, Ill.: Thomas.

Repetto, Thomas A. 1974. *Residential Crime*. Cambridge, Mass.: Ballinger.

———. 1976. "Crime Prevention and the Displacement Phenomenon." *Crime and Delinquency* 22:166–77.

Roncek, Dennis W., Ralph Bell, and Jeffrey M. A. Francik. 1981. "Housing Projects and Crime: Testing a Proximity Model." *Social Problems* 29: 151–67.

Rosenbaum, Dennis P., ed. 1986. *Community Crime Prevention: Does It Work?* Beverly Hills, Calif.: Sage.

———. 1988. "Community Crime Prevention: A Review and Synthesis of the Literature." *Justice Quarterly* 5:323–95.

Ross, H. Laurence, and Gary D. LaFree. 1986. "Deterrence in Criminology and Social Policy." In *Behavioral and Social Science Knowledge: Discovery, Diffusion, and Social Impact*, edited by Neil Smelser. Washington, D.C.: National Research Council.

Scarr, Harry A. 1973. *Patterns of Burglary*. 2d ed. Washington, D.C.: U.S. Department of Justice, National Institute of Law Enforcement and Criminal Justice.

Shannon, Lyle W. 1954. "The Spatial Distribution of Criminal Offenses by States." *Journal of Criminal Law, Criminology, and Police Science* 45:264–71.

Shearing, Clifford D., and Philip C. Stenning. 1981. "Modern Private Security: Its Growth and Implications." In *Crime and Justice: An Annual Review of*

Research, vol. 3, edited by Michael Tonry and Norval Morris. Chicago: University of Chicago Press.

Shichor, David, David L. Decker, and Robert M. O'Brien. 1979. "Population Density and Criminal Victimization: Some Unexpected Findings in Central Cities." *Criminology* 17:184–93.

Shover, Neal. 1971. "Burglary as an Occupation." Ph.D. dissertation, University of Illinois at Urbana-Champaign, Department of Sociology.

———. 1973. "The Social Organization of Burglary." *Social Problems* 20:499–514.

———. 1983*a*. "The Later Stages of Ordinary Property Offender Careers." *Social Problems* 31:208–19.

———. 1983*b*. "Professional Criminals: Major Offender." In *Encyclopedia of Crime and Justice*, edited by Sanford H. Kadish. New York: Macmillan.

———. 1985. *Aging Criminals*. Beverly Hills, Calif.: Sage.

Shover, Neal, and David W. Honaker. 1990. "The Criminal Calculus of Persistent Property Offenders: A Review of Evidence." Paper presented at the forty-second annual meeting of the American Society of Criminology, Baltimore, November.

Skogan, Wesley. 1988. "Community Organizations and Crime." In *Crime and Justice: A Review of Research*, vol. 10, edited by Michael Tonry and Norval Morris. Chicago: University of Chicago Press.

Sparks, Richard F. 1981. "Surveys of Victimization—an Optimistic Assessment." In *Crime and Justice: An Annual Review of Research*, vol. 3, edited by Michael Tonry and Norval Morris. Chicago: University of Chicago Press.

———. 1982. "Crime as Work: An Illustrative Example." Draft report to the National Institute of Justice. Newark, N.J.: Rutgers University, Center for the Study of the Causes of Crime for Gain.

State Farm Fire and Casualty Company. 1989. "Crime Statistics—Paid Loss Data." Letter to the author, August 7.

Steffensmeier, Darrell J. 1986. *The Fence: In the Shadow of Two Worlds*. Totowa, N.J.: Rowman & Littlefield.

Tittle, Charles R. 1969. "Crime Rates and Legal Sanctions." *Social Problems* 16:409–23.

Titus, Richard M. 1989. *Factors Relating to Completed vs. Attempted Forcible Residential Burglary*. Washington, D.C.: U.S. Department of Justice, National Institute of Justice.

U.S. Department of Justice. 1975. *Criminal Victimization Surveys in 13 American Cities*. Washington, D.C.: U.S. Government Printing Office.

———. 1976*a*. *Criminal Victimization Surveys in Chicago, Detroit, Los Angeles, New York, and Philadelphia*. Washington, D.C.: U.S. Government Printing Office.

———. 1976*b*. *Criminal Victimization Surveys in Eight American Cities*. Washington, D.C.: U.S. Government Printing Office.

———. 1977. *Criminal Victimization in the United States: A Comparison of 1975 and 1976 Findings*. Washington, D.C.: U.S. Government Printing Office.

U.S. Senate, Select Committee on Small Business. 1969. *Crimes against Small Business*. 91st Cong., 1st sess. Washington, D.C.: U.S. Government Printing Office.

van Dijk, Jan J. M., and Carl H. D. Steinmetz. 1984. "The Burden of Crime in Dutch Society, 1973–1979." In *Victimization and Fear of Crime: World Perspectives*, edited by Richard Block. Washington, D.C.: U.S. Government Printing Office.

Waller, Irvin, and Norman Okihiro. 1978. *Burglary: The Victim and the Public*. Toronto: University of Toronto Press.

Walsh, Dermot. 1980. *Break-ins: Burglary from Private Houses*. London: Constable.

———. 1986. *Heavy Business*. London: Routledge & Kegan Paul.

Walsh, Marilyn E. 1977. *The Fence*. Westport, Conn.: Greenwood.

West, W. Gordon. 1978. "The Short-Term Careers of Serious Thieves." *Canadian Journal of Criminology* 20:169–90.

Whitaker, Catherine J. 1986. *Crime Prevention Measures*. Washington, D.C.: U.S. Department of Justice, Bureau of Justice Statistics.

Williams, Kristen M., and Judith Lucianovic. 1979. *Robbery and Burglary*. Washington, D.C.: Institute for Law and Social Research.

Winchester, Stuart, and Hilary Jackson. 1982. "Residential Burglary." Home Office Research Study no. 74. London: H.M. Stationery Office.

Worden, Marshall A. 1980. "Criminogenic Correlates of Intermetropolitan Crime Rates, 1960 and 1970." In *Crime: A Spatial Perspective*, edited by Daniel E. Georges-Abeyie and Keith D. Harries. New York: Columbia University Press.

Yin, Robert K. 1986. "Community Crime Prevention: A Synthesis of Eleven Evaluations." In *Community Crime Prevention: Does It Work?* edited by Dennis P. Rosenbaum. Beverly Hills, Calif.: Sage.

Zimring, Franklin E. 1978. "Policy Experiments in General Deterrence: 1970–1975." In *Deterrence and Incapacitation: Estimating the Effects of Criminal Sanctions on Crime Rates*, edited by Alfred Blumstein, Jacqueline Cohen, and Daniel Nagin. Washington, D.C.: National Academy Press.

David Garland

Sociological Perspectives on Punishment

ABSTRACT

The sociology of punishment offers a framework for analyzing penal institutions that, potentially at least, can give a fuller and more realistic account than the punishment-as-crime-control approach of penological studies or the punishment-as-moral-problem approach of the philosophy of punishment. Sociological perspectives view punishment as a complex social institution, shaped by an ensemble of social and historical forces and having a range of effects that reach well beyond the population of offenders. The Durkheimian perspective interprets punishment as a morality-affirming, solidarity-producing mechanism grounded in collective sentiments. Marxist studies depict punishment as an economically conditioned state apparatus that plays an ideological and political role in ruling class domination. Foucault's work focuses on the specific technologies of power-knowledge that operate in the penal realm and links them to broader networks of discipline and regulation. The work of Norbert Elias points to the importance of cultural sensibilities and the "civilizing process" in the shaping of modern penal measures. Elements of these interpretive traditions can be brought together to produce a multidimensional account of punishment's social forms, functions, and significance that can, in turn, help promote more realistic and appropriate objectives for penal policy and a fuller framework for its normative evaluation.

The standard ways in which we think and talk about punishment are framed not so much by sociological theory as by two rather different discursive traditions, which might best be described as the "penological" and the "philosophical." The first of these ways of thinking—

David Garland is a reader in the Faculty of Law, University of Edinburgh.

0192-3234/91/0014-0006$01.00

which is as common among the lay public as it is among criminologists and criminal justice practitioners—views punishment more or less exclusively as a technique of crime control. Penal institutions and the processes of punishment are seen by penology as so many means to a fairly self-evident end: the reduction of crime rates and the restraint of individual criminals. Within this framework, the primary question is a technical one—"What works?"—and the critical tool for evaluating penal measures is the effectiveness study, which charts the impact of specific sanctions on patterns of offending and recidivism rates. Questions of "cost" are also part of the reckoning, and human costs may figure alongside financial and political ones, but the main thrust of the penological approach is to view criminal justice in instrumental terms as an apparatus whose overriding purpose is the management and control of crime (e.g., Walker 1969; Radzinowicz and Wolfgang 1971, pt. 2; Martinson 1974; Wilson 1975; Cook 1980).

The other way of thinking that standardly shapes our understanding of penal issues is "the philosophy of punishment"—a branch of moral philosophy that flourished during the Enlightenment and that has recently enjoyed something of a renaissance, as criminologists and jurists are led to reexamine the normative foundations on which the penal system rests. This tradition sets up punishment as a distinctively moral problem, asking how penal sanctions can be justified, what their proper objectives should be, and under what circumstances they can reasonably be imposed. Its central concern is not "What works?" but rather "What is just?" and its discursive style is based on ethical reasoning and moral appeal, rather than on empirical research or technical knowledge. Whether the appeal is to Kantian retributivism or Benthamite utility, to arguments for reform or to principles of denunciation, the framework supplied by this tradition leads us to pose punishment as a moral puzzle that can best be resolved by philosophical reflection and moral intuition (e.g., Hart 1968, chap. 1; Acton 1969; Feinberg and Gross 1975, pt. 5; Honderich 1976; Bean 1981).

Between the two of them, these penological and philosophical discourses account for most of the scholarly literature on punishment and shape much of our thinking about penal measures and criminal justice, not least because their arguments and evidence are routinely used in the rhetoric of penal reform and penal politics. To be an expert in penal matters or an authoritative voice on penal affairs is to be learned in one or both of these traditions and able to argue effectively within their terms. But despite the centrality and importance of these frameworks, and despite the stored-up wisdom and experience that, at their best, each of them represents, both traditions are marked by a number of serious limitations and actually amount to rather inadequate ways of thinking about the phenomenon. To view penal measures as technical instruments of crime control, to be evaluated in terms of efficacy and cost benefit, is no doubt a proper activity from the point of view of those charged with running the penal enterprise. But this penological approach fails to recognize that penal measures and institutions are never fully and rationally adapted to a single organizational objective of an instrumental kind. As sociological and historical studies show, penal measures and institutions have social determinants that have little to do with the need for law and order, social effects that go well beyond the business of crime control, and a symbolic significance that routinely engages a wide population, making it inappropriate to think of them in purely instrumental terms. The adoption of a penological approach thus tends to restrict the scope of inquiry and silence important aspects of the phenomenon. By taking the institution of punishment at its face value—as merely an instrument of crime control—penological studies produce data that may be useful to the enterprise, but at the cost of a more fundamental understanding that more adequately depicts its day-to-day operations and that might usefully challenge the institution's self-conceptions.

This instrumental way of thinking about punishment also helps create inappropriate and unrealistic expectations on the part of the public and the authorities, which add to the penal system's difficulties rather than resolving them. An instrumental technology, rationally and exclusively attuned to the goal of crime control, might reasonably be expected to work and generally to produce positive results, so it becomes difficult to account for the negative findings that are so consistently revealed by penological research. Penologists sometimes respond to this by blaming the penal system's difficulties on "extraneous" pressures—pointing to problems of underfunding, unwanted political interference, hostile mass media, irrational public attitudes, and so on. But in fact this response merely points up the limitations of the penological approach itself, for it is inconceivable that any penal system could be disengaged from social forces such as these, and it therefore makes little sense to view punishment as if it somehow stands outside of society and is only occasionally affected by it.

The philosophy of punishment, as currently conceived, is also marked by some serious limitations and by a similarly inadequate conception of the nature of penal practice. It is certainly important to subject penal institutions to moral scrutiny—not least because technical penology tends to shield punishment from searching moral questions by giving pride of place to effectiveness studies and taking it for granted that the institution is, in fact, a legitimate one. But the problem with much philosophy of punishment is that its philosophical foundations and the way in which it addresses the question of punishment tend to prevent it from mounting an effective evaluation of the actual details and different aspects of penal practice.

Most modern philosophizing about punishment begins with a rather idealized and one-dimensional image of punishment that treats the problem of punishing as a variant of the classic liberal problem of how the state should relate to the individual (see Garland 1983). Punishment is viewed primarily as an instance of state coercion and an infringement on individual freedom and therefore triggers a number of arguments about the general justifications of state power (usually some version of the social contract), about the circumstances justifying particular punishments (usually the perpetration of harm to others), and about the proper purposes of measures of this kind (usually the prevention of further harms). No doubt these are important issues, and philosophers have had important things to say about them, but by focusing so readily on the "civil liberty" aspects of the phenomenon, the philosophy of punishment often allows other aspects to be ignored. Conventional philosophy thus has little of substance to say about the actual methods of punishment that it is appropriate to use, about the nature of penal regimes and the quality of penal institutions. Key decisions about the acceptability of capital or corporal punishments, the use of electronic monitoring and close control regimes, solitary confinement or three prisoners to a cell consequently attract little comment or assistance from this brand of moral philosophy. Similarly, penal philosophy offers no help whatsoever in dealing with problems that take an aggregative rather than an individualistic form—such as the appropriate size of the prison population or the proportion of national resources that might be devoted to rehabilitative programs. Nor, finally, does it provide any developed means for evaluating the wider social and symbolic effects of punishment—the impact on sensibilities, solidarities, and social relations that punishments clearly have and that affect a population far beyond the offender in the dock or the inmate in a prison cell. These difficult issues tend to escape detailed moral scrutiny because they do not feature in the oversimplified conception of "punishment" that philosophers conventionally use: they are not part of the problem that this tradition has set out for itself. And yet these are often the most urgent and perplexing problems that assail those responsible for administering penal systems and legislating penal laws. If the philosophy of punishment often appears limited in its relevance and in its practical effect, this is because its basic conception of "punishment" has been shaped by traditional patterns of liberal thought (see Lacey 1988), rather than by close acquaintance with the characteristics of modern penal practice.

In recent years a third style of thinking about punishment has begun to develop and to offer a different framework for the analysis of penal issues. Instead of viewing punishment as a means to an end or a stock problem for moral philosophy, sociologists and historians have begun to conceptualize punishment as a social institution and to pose a series of questions that stem from this approach. In place of questions about punishment's effectiveness or its justification, these writers have been asking, "How do specific penal measures come into existence?" "What social functions does punishment perform?" "How do penal institutions relate to other institutions?" "How do they contribute to social order, or to state power, or to class domination, or to the cultural reproduction of society?" and "What are punishment's unintended social effects, its functional failures, and its wider social costs?" "Punishment" is thus understood as a cultural and historical artifact that may be centrally concerned with the control of crime but that is nevertheless shaped by an ensemble of social forces and has a significance and range of effects that reach well beyond the population of criminals. And the sociology of punishment—as I shall term this emergent tradition—has been concerned to explore the social foundations of punishment, to trace out the social implications of specific penal modes, and to uncover the structures of social action and webs of cultural meaning that give modern punishment its characteristic functions, forms, and effects (Ignatieff 1981; Garland and Young 1983; Jacobs 1983, chap. 1; Cohen 1985, chap. 1; Hirst 1986, chap. 7; Garland 1990*a*).

It is worth making clear, however, that this sociological tradition is by no means fully at odds with what I have termed the "penological" approach—indeed, it shares the same subject matter, adopts a similarly empirical or social scientific approach, and makes extensive use of penological materials in its analyses. The crucial difference is really one of analytical scope and parameters of study: whereas penology situates itself within penal institutions and seeks to attain a knowledge of their penological functioning, the sociology of punishment views the institutions from the outside, as it were, and seeks to understand their role as one distinctive set of social processes situated within a wider social network.

Nor does the sociological approach deny that penal institutions are, to a great extent, oriented toward crime control and shaped by that orientation. What it does deny, however, is that punishment and penal forms can be wholly understood in terms of this declared objective, simply because no social artifact can ever be explained in this way. Like architecture, or diet, or clothing, or table manners, the penal system has an instrumental purpose, but also a cultural style and an historical tradition, that shapes the ways in which that objective is pursued. The need to control crime in its various forms and to respond to the depredations of law breakers is thus only one of the factors that helps shape the institutions of penality. To the extent that penal systems adapt their practices to the problems of crime control, they do so in ways that are heavily mediated by independent considerations such as cultural conventions, economic resources, institutional dynamics, and political arguments—and it is precisely this interaction between the "social" and the "penological" that the sociological approach brings into focus.

It is also worth emphasizing that this sociological approach to punishment is not just an academic enthusiasm or a theoretical exercise without any practical payoff. Potentially, at least, it offers to provide an informed, empirical basis for understanding the ways in which penal systems actually operate in modern society and can thus help to develop more realistic expectations and objectives for penal policy and more appropriate strategies for putting policies into effect (e.g., Downes 1988). As we have seen, the conventional "penological" and "philosophical" approaches both base themselves on an implicit—and rather badly worked out—sociology of punishment, insofar as they rely on certain commonsense conceptions of what kind of institution punishment is and what kinds of social purposes it serves. To undertake a sociological analysis of punishment is thus to reinspect the basic presumptions that are normally made about punishment rather than simply to take them on trust. Properly done, the sociology of punishment should inform us about the social forces that condition penal processes and the various social consequences that these processes in turn produce. And rather than displacing the other traditions of thinking about punishment, or rendering them redundant, the sociological approach can be expected to revitalize and enrich them, inasmuch as its findings can provide the basis for a more sociologically informed penology and a more relevant and wide-ranging philosophy of punishment.

I. Sociological Perspectives on Punishment

Up to this point, I have talked about the sociology of punishment as a tradition of thinking about punishment, and to the extent that it represents a distinctive way of approaching the phenomenon—differing from penology and the philosophy of punishment—this is a reasonable way of presenting the matter. However, it would be quite misleading to continue to discuss the sociology of punishment as if it were a single, unified framework of thought (Garland 1990*b*). On closer inspection, the sociological and historical literature on punishment displays a range of theoretical approaches, analytical perspectives, and concrete interpretations that do not necessarily add up to form a single coherent or comprehensive account. Instead, what one finds is a set of competing interpretations, each one drawing on a different model of sociological explanation, each one going at the problem in a different way and for a different purpose, and each one highlighting a different characteristic of punishment and its social role. Like much of sociology, the sociology of punishment is characterized less by a settled research agenda and agreed parameters of study than by a noisy clash of perspectives and an apparently incorrigible conflict of different interpretations and varying points of view. One response to this situation has been to adopt a particular perspective—say, a Marxist approach, or a Durkheimian one—and to develop this analysis in critical disregard of other ways of proceeding. However, it is at least arguable that such an approach is less fruitful than one that tries to bring these different theoretical perspectives into conversation with one another, seeking to synthesize their interpretative strengths, to identify analyses that are complementary rather than contradictory, and to isolate specific points of disagreement so that one can endeavor to resolve them by means of further research or theoretical reflection.

What I do in this essay is to survey the major sociological interpretations of punishment and to give some sense of the resources that social theory offers for the understanding of punishment. I set out a number of perspectives in turn, dealing first with the more established traditions associated with the work of Durkheim, Marx, and Foucault and then with the perspective suggested by the work of Norbert Elias. In each case, I set out the distinctive questions that are posed, summarize the major interpretive themes associated with the perspective, and identify the kinds of insights each theory has to offer for the understanding of modern penality, as well as pointing to the weaknesses and limitations that affect each one. Inevitably a survey of this kind will flatten out nuances and fail to reflect the subtleties of the original works, but its main concern is to introduce readers to the central characteristics of each approach and point them to the texts themselves. The concluding section of the essay discusses the interrelationship of these perspectives and seeks to illustrate how a sociological approach to punishment can alter the way we think about certain penal issues.

A. *Punishment and Social Solidarity: The Durkheimian Perspective*

According to Emile Durkheim, punishment is above all a moral process, functioning to preserve the shared values and normative conventions on which social life is based. It is an institution that draws its motivating energies and support from the moral sentiments of the community; its forms symbolize and enact moral judgments; and its most important effect is to reaffirm and strengthen the moral order on which it is based. It is thus a part of the complex moral circuitry that creates and sustains social solidarity—a basic social institution with important moral functions, not just a regulatory mechanism for the control of crime. In effect, Durkheim's analysis insists that we must draw back from the immediacies of dealing with offenders and view punishment on a broader social plane if we are to appreciate the true characteristics of the institution and the forces that make it work (Durkheim 1933, 1973, 1983).

Durkheim argues that the criminal law of society is, for the most part, an embodiment of the basic moral values that society holds sacred, so that crimes that violate this "conscience collective" will tend to provoke collective moral outrage and a passionate desire for vengeance. These "passionate reactions" find expression in the legal practice of punishing offenders which, however much it becomes routinized and institutionalized, remains a mechanism for the channeling and expression of collective moral sentiment. So although the modern state now monopolizes the delivery and administration of punishment—and in doing so "graduates" the intensity of this reaction and renders it more uniform and predictable—Durkheim insists on two important points. First, that a much wider population feels itself to be involved in the act of punishing, thus supplying the state institution with its social support and legitimacy. Second, that despite all attempts to make punishment a rational, impassive, utilitarian process, it continues to be marked by the punitive sentiments and emotive reactions that are at the root of society's response to crime.

Punishment, therefore, is not an instrumental mechanism—or at least not primarily, since its deterrent and regulatory impact on offenders is, for Durkheim, severely limited. Rather it is an expressive institution: a realm for the ritualized expression of social values and the controlled release of psychic energy. And herein lies punishment's true functioning and social utility, for in reacting against violators of the *conscience collective*, penal institutions demonstrate the material force of basic social values and restore collective confidence in the integrity and power of the moral order. In Durkheim's view, the rituals of punishment are directed less at the individual offender than at the audience of impassioned onlookers whose cherished values and security had been momentarily undermined by the offender's actions. Punishment's significance is best conceived as social and moral rather than purely penological.

Punishment is thus an occasion for the practical realization of the moral values that make up the conscience collective. It responds to the criminal's attack on morality and solidarity by reaffirming the strength of that moral order, restating its terms, and reasserting its authority. It is able to do so because it can draw on the support of all those "healthy consciences" that are outraged by crime, a reaction that the ceremonial ritual of punishing helps to elicit as well as to express. Punishment thus transforms a threat to social order into a triumph of social solidarity. Instead of damaging the cohesiveness of society, crime sets in motion an elaborate moral circuitry that channels the energy of outraged sentiments into a socially binding ritual of moral affirmation (Durkheim 1933, pp. 70–111; Durkheim 1973, chaps. 11 and 12).

This sentiment-based, morality-affirming, solidarity-producing description of punishment is, according to Durkheim, as appropriate to modern penal systems as it is to premodern ones because it is only the *forms* of punishment that have undergone historical change, not the *functions* (Durkheim 1983). Modern sanctions—such as imprisonment—are considerably less severe than the terrible punishments of medieval or ancient societies, but this is because our modern *conscience collective* is more solicitous of the rights of individuals—even criminal individuals—and less dominated by religious or absolutist values. We have not ceased to react punitively when collective values are breached—it is rather that these values themselves dictate that punishments should be less destructive of human life. The suggestion that punishment might nowadays be directed toward nonpunitive ends—such as correction, rehabilitation, or prevention—is dismissed by Durkheim as a modern delusion reflecting the aspirations of penal administrators, not the actualities of their institutions (1933, p. 87).

This Durkheimian description of punishment undoubtedly has its limitations. It is very much a one-dimensional account, concerned to explicate punishment's moral content and moral consequences and to trace punishment's role in the maintenance of moral order. To the extent that punishment has other characteristics, other sources, and other effects, Durkheim's work has little or nothing to say of these. He offers, for example, very little analysis of the actual apparatus and instrumentalities of punishment. Penality's armory of carceral regimes, physical restrictions, monetary penalties, supervisory measures, and so on, are interesting to him only as so many means of conveying moral passions and moral messages to and from a watching public. Insofar as they operate as techniques for behavioral control or forms of disciplinary regulation, he no longer considers them truly moral phenomena, and they thus fall below the horizon of his analysis. Similarly, Durkheim has nothing to say about the ways in which penal institutions are influenced by all of those social forces—such as economic considerations, political ideologies, technical developments, scientific conceptions, or professional interests—that have little to do with moral passions or a collective conscience. But limitations of interpretive scope—which is what, in fact, these amount to—should not prevent us from seeing the intrinsic value and possibilities that Durkheim's work contains. As it turns out, all of the sociological perspectives that currently exist are limited in this way because neither Durkheim nor any of the others intended to develop a comprehensive theory of punishment's internal and external functioning. What is offered instead is an interpretive vision that, whatever its limitations, offers a way of understanding important aspects of this complex institution and connecting them to the other phenomena of social life, and it is in this sense that it ought to be considered.

Other criticisms of Durkheim do, however, have more force in the present context. His conception of the *conscience collective* is deeply problematic in a number of respects, as is his claim that penal sanctions and criminal laws are its faithful embodiment. To the extent that modern, pluralistic societies can be said to have a "totality of beliefs and sentiments common to the average citizen" (Durkheim 1933, p. 79), it seems more appropriate to think of this as the political achievement of the dominant cultural groups, whose particular vision of social order has achieved a measure of hegemony, rather than a given set of values that are somehow consensually shared. In this respect, institutions such as law and punishment should not be seen as merely reflecting values that everyone already holds. Rather, they are active, value-imposing agencies whose practices play a crucial role in winning support for the dominant morality.

Similarly, one must question Durkheim's easy assumption that penal measures somehow manifest or embody values that are generally held. As his critics have continually emphasized, it is not "society as a whole" that enacts laws and punishes offenders but, rather, legislative elites and professional functionaries, whose particular priorities and concerns may prompt an enacted version of social morality that is not universally shared (Spitzer 1975; Lukes and Scull 1983). And whatever the reality of the "passionate reactions" that Durkheim attributes to the public—and to the post-Freudian imagination these emotions seem a little too sanitized and well adjusted—they can only be indirectly effective in the formulation and enforcement of modern penal policies.

One might also argue—following Foucault and Elias—that Durkheim's stress on the public ritual of punishment is altogether misplaced in modern society since modern penal measures tend to be deployed "behind the scenes" of social life, located in closed institutions on society's margins, and are no longer conducted in public for all to see (Foucault 1977; Elias 1978). This, it seems to me, is an important criticism, as it points to a crucial division in modern penal systems between the *declaration* of punishment, which continues to take the form of a public ritual and which is continually the focus of public and media attention, and the *delivery* of punishment that now characteristically occurs behind closed doors and has a much lower level of visibility. Indeed, one might argue that modern punishment operates a two-pronged strategy—one aimed at expressing, educating, and reassuring public sentiment (which is the one Durkheim describes) and another aimed more directly at regulating deviant conduct, about which Durkheim has relatively little to say. If this is the case, then it amounts to another important limitation of Durkheim's analysis—confining this interpretation to a particular sphere of punishing rather than the whole system—but it is not a blanket refutation.

Durkheim's central argument about the solidarity-enhancing effects of punishment has also been a focus for criticism—even by writers such as Mead (1918), Garfinkel (1956), and Erikson (1966) who are usually seen as exponents of the Durkheimian interpretation of punishment. This body of work suggests that Durkheim is too ready to assume the very "functionality" that he sets out to prove. In contrast to his assertion that penal rituals always give rise to a single, solidarity-enhancing effect on a morally homogeneous and receptive community, these writers point to the possibility that punishment may evoke social divisions instead of solidarities, that it may achieve social bonding only by promoting feelings of hostility and intolerance, or even that the ritual may altogether fail to promote significant symbolic results. On this revised view, the processes of punishment do not necessarily promote "social solidarity." Rather, they should be regarded as a ritualized attempt by legal officials to reconstitute and reinforce already existing authority relations. Where there are limits to that authority, or contests of authority, the effects of penal rituals may be "functional," "dysfunctional," or simultaneously both.

Which leads us to a final criticism, regarding the basic argument that punishment is "functional" for society. Clearly punishment does perform certain "functions"—it sanctions certain kinds of rules, restrains certain kinds of conduct, expresses certain felt emotions, and reaffirms specific forms of authority and belief. But these rules, conducts, emotions, beliefs, and authorities may be the property of particular social groups rather than "society as a whole," and they need not be sanctioned in a way that necessarily promotes social harmony. One has to analyze punishment's effects in relation to specific interests, specific social relations, and particular outcomes—bearing in mind that what is "functional" from one point of view may be dysfunctional from another (Giddens 1978). Taken together, these are a formidable set of criticisms, and they could be extended were more space available. But their critical force is not to refute the Durkheimian perspective nor to reject the questions that it poses but instead to qualify the key terms of the perspective and to refine or modify the arguments that it makes. Thus, even if Durkheim's version of the *conscience collective* is unacceptable as it stands, it is nonetheless true that there is some correspondence between the moral rules that punishments enforce and the deeply felt beliefs of significant sections of the population, particularly in democratic societies, where popular sentiments help condition legal codes and decisions. And although his discussion of punishment's symbolic effects is marred by his functionalist assumptions, he is undoubtedly correct to point to the communicative and metaphoric propensities that punishments possess and thereby to alert us to the importance of what one might call the semiotics of punishment. As Durkheim makes clear, an act of punishment is also a sign that the authorities are in control, that crime is an aberration, and that the conventions that govern social life retain their force and vitality—which is why policies of crime control and punishment can so often become metaphors for political strength and take on a political significance out of proportion to their penological effect. (Ironically, Durkheim [1973] also makes it clear that punishment is used most frequently where authority is weakest—but in such cases it has least effect. A strong, legitimately established moral order requires only minimal sanctions to restore itself and to deal with violators—such regimes have little need of terroristic or force-displaying forms of punishment.)

For all its difficulties, Durkheim's analysis does succeed in opening up important dimensions of punishment that are not otherwise apparent. He shifts our attention from the mundane, administrative aspects of punishment (which form penality's modern self-image) to the broader social and emotive aspects of the process. Instead of seeing a utilitarian mechanism adapted to the technical business of crime control, we see an institution that operates on a different, symbolic register—and that resonates with meaning both for the social collectivity and for the individuals who compose it. The sense Durkheim gives of the sacred qualities claimed by authority, of the emotions that are stirred by crime and punishment, of the collective involvement of onlookers, of the role of penal rituals in organizing this, and, finally, of the social and moral significance of penal practices—all these interpretive insights can be shown to be important and relevant to an understanding of punishment today.

B. *The Political Economy of Punishment: The Marxist Perspective*

To adopt a Marxist perspective on punishment is to address a whole range of issues that are not dealt with at all by the Durkheimian tradition and to reinterpret many of those that are. Questions concerning the economic and political determinants of penal policy, the role of penal institutions in strategies of class rule, and the ways in which punishment serves class power—either symbolically or materially—now move to the forefront of attention, while the relations between punishment and popular morality, or between the state and the people, are reformulated to suggest ideological domination or even repression, instead of the implicit agreement that Durkheim suggests.

Marxist analyses of punishment are a product of recent "neo-Marxist" writings rather than of the original writings of Marx and Engels, and they reveal a variety of approaches to their topic. The problem of locating "punishment" within the Marxist conceptual framework has led some writers, such as Rusche and Kirchheimer (1968) or Melossi and Pavarini (1981), to stress the interconnections between penal institutions and the economic requirements of modes of production, while other writers, such as Pashukanis (1978) or Hay (1975), have preferred to stress the role of punishment in political and ideological class struggles and in the maintenance of state-power or ruling-class hegemony. We thus find some Marxist accounts dealing with punishment as an economic phenomenon that is ancillary to the labor market, others discussing its political role as a repressive state apparatus, and yet others conceiving it as an ideological institution that deals in symbols of legitimacy and the justification of established authority.

The most sustained and comprehensive Marxist account of punishment—and perhaps the most influential—is that developed by George Rusche and Otto Kirchheimer in their text *Punishment and Social Structure* (1968). In this historical account of penal development from the late Middle Ages to the middle of the twentieth century, the authors' primary concern is to explain why particular penal methods come to be selected and used at particular moments in time and to what extent the pattern of penal development is determined by "the basic social relations" (by which they mean the mode of production). In pursuing this historical question, they develop a number of theoretical propositions that can be abstracted from their account and stated in general terms. They thus propose that analysis should focus on historically specific penal practices and institutions rather than any general conception of "punishment as such"; punishment should be seen as a social phenomenon in its own right and not merely a technical response to crime. Specific penal practices are never determined solely by crime-control objectives, nor are their social effects exclusively "penological"; penal institutions are to be viewed in their interrelationship with other institutions and with nonpenal aspects of social policy. In effect, penal policy is taken to be one element within a wider strategy of controlling the poor; punishment should be understood not as a social response to the criminality of individuals but as a mechanism operating in the struggle between social classes; and official aims of penal agencies together with the philosophies of punishment that the judiciary espouse should be treated as ideological legitimations rather than prescriptions for actual practice. These "ideological veils and juristic appearances" must be stripped away to reveal the underlying (economic) relationships that really determine penal policy (Rusche and Kirchheimer 1968, pp. 3–7 and passim).

These, then, are the basic orientations of this Marxist analysis, and, one might note, they share with Durkheim an insistence that penal institutions are fully intelligible only on a wider social plane and by reference to wider social functions. Moving from this basic interpretive framework, Rusche and Kirchheimer go on to argue that it is the labor market which, in a variety of ways, has been the leading influence on the choice of penal methods and their pattern of use. To the extent that the labor of convicted offenders provides a potentially exploitable resource, its relative value has been a key consideration in penal policy. During periods when labor is in abundant supply, penal institutions can afford to be reckless with human lives, leading to the widespread use of corporal and capital punishments. However, where demand for labor threatens to exceed supply, then the state and its penal institutions have been less ready to dispense with the valuable resources that their captives represent. Penal measures such as galley slavery, transportation, forced labor, the early modern houses of correction, and even some twentieth-century prison regimes are all presented as clear instances where the exploitation of labor was the major determinant of penological developments.

Another, more immediate, way in which the labor market influences penal sanctions relates to the principle of "less eligibility" and the relative standards of penal institutions. Rusche and Kirchheimer insist that the penal system operates as a kind of coercive ancillary to the labor market, ensuring that the poorer classes are unable to sustain a living by criminal means, and threatening severe penalties for those who are tempted to try. In order to function in this role, it is vital that penal institutions adopt regimes that are markedly more unpleasant than the conditions of life experienced by the lowest strata living in "free society." Thus the discipline, the diet, the labor requirements, and the general living conditions of penal institutions are seen to be determined not by penological objectives but by the requirement that penality be "less eligible" than the labor market that it supports. As the authors argue in a chapter entitled "Modern Prison Reform and Its Limits," this concern for relative deprivation in punishment sets tight constraints on the possibilities of rehabilitative and humane regimes and is "the inner contradiction which underlies every reform programme" (1968, p. 159). It ensures that "all efforts to reform the punishment of criminals are inevitably limited by the situation of the lowest socially significant proletarian class" (Rusche 1980, p. 12).

Finally, in addition to shaping the options of the work force in general, modern punishments from the sixteenth century onwards are seen as attempts to shape the attitudes of the individual convict worker. Rusche and Kirchheimer suggest that a constant theme within penal institutions has been the concern to imbue prisoners with the disciplines and attitudes necessary for adaptation to the workplace. The modern prison—like its forerunners, the house of correction and the *hôpital général*—is, among other things, "a way of training new labour reserves," and even when labor can no longer be put to profitable use, prison inmates are still put to work as a kind of compulsory training for industry (1968, p. 63).

Rusche and Kirchheimer acknowledge that in the twentieth century it has become increasingly difficult to use convict labor in an economically effective way—whether because of resistance to the use of forced labor, or else because of the difficulties of operating modern production techniques in prisons—and consequently other considerations become central to the formation of penal policy. In particular, they point to the concern to minimize expenditure and to reduce the financial burden represented by punishment. This second-line fiscal consideration leads to the use of measures such as the fine, which in the twentieth century has come to be the most frequently deployed penal measure and "the epitome of rationalized capitalist penal law" (1968, p. 206). Moreover, the history of the use of the fine clearly indicates the dependence of penal policy on the economic status of the lower classes. As they point out, a generalized system of fining requires that the whole population should have access to an expendable monetary income. This was not always the case, and indeed the recurrence of serious unemployment and poverty can still lead to large-scale defaulting and the undermining of any penal system that relies heavily on financial penalties (1968, chap. 10).

A rather different Marxist interpretation of punishment is developed by the Russian jurist E. B. Pashukanis (1978), who argues that the penal institutions of capitalist societies are organized around a series of bourgeois values and ideological conceptions that tie punishment to the logic of capitalist economic relations rather than to the more appropriate logic of "scientific penology" (by which he means a social defense and treatment model). Thus, for instance, in the criminal court, individuals come to be seen as "legal subjects," bearing all the attributes of free will, responsibility, and hedonistic psychology that the standard bourgeois individual is deemed to possess, no matter how far the actualities of the case depart from this ideal. In the same way, what we would now call the "justice model" of sentencing and the philosophy of punishment that underlies it are shown to be structured by bourgeois principles and capitalist economic categories. According to Pashukanis, the essential idea in this style of sentencing is that punishment should be an "equivalent" of the offense, so that justice consists in a kind of fair trading that exchanges one harmful action for another that equals it. This idea of an equivalent—which Pashukanis traces back to the commodity form—makes punishment itself into an exchange transaction, in which the offender "pays his debt" and crime becomes "an involuntarily concluded contract." In dealing with offenders in this way, the courts help regenerate the basic ideological forms of capitalist society in the face of actualities such as inequality, unfreedom, and destitution.

The sanction of imprisonment is also seen by Pashukanis as a specifically bourgeois invention, utilizing conceptions of the person and of value that spring up from the capitalist mode of production and that reproduce bourgeois mentality in the process of punishing (1978, p. 181). Capitalist economic relations give rise to the idea of independent man as the possessor of labor power and liberty, both of which can be calibrated and measured in terms of time, and the modern prison owes its existence and extensive usage to these very notions. Thus, although the prison—and penal law more generally—has its uses as a repressive instrument of class domination, it also operates as an ideological apparatus, helping to reproduce the mental and cultural categories on which capitalist rule depends.

This view of punishment as a politicoideological instrument of the bourgeois state, structured by economically derived categories and used to promote ruling class power is developed and extended by other writers working in this tradition. The historical work of Douglas Hay (1975) likewise stresses the dual role of criminal law as ideological legitimation as well as class coercion. His study of eighteenth-century criminal law details the ways in which ruling class hegemony can be sustained by the strategic use of discretion in criminal justice, the careful management of symbols and ceremony, and the ideological appeal of a system that generally abides by its own legal ideals. For Hay, as much as for Pashukanis, penal law concerns itself with social authority and the governing claims of those in power. It reinforces these claims by means of coercive sanctions as well as symbolic displays, making punishment a form of power exercised as well as power expressed. Where social power and authority are structured on definite class lines, as they were in the eighteenth-century England that Hay describes, then punishment will reproduce the forms and figures of class even when its actions appear to transcend class divisions and protect those on the wrong side of the class divide.

These attempts by Marxist writers to explain penal practice by reference to the imperatives of class struggles and economic relations are open to important criticisms. Rusche and Kirchheimer undoubtedly overestimate the explanatory power of economic factors in the analysis of penal institutions, and the main weakness of their account of penal history is its failure to recognize the ways in which economic concerns are always tempered by other social forces—not just the kinds of political and ideological concerns noted by Hay and Pashukanis, but also by professional interests, institutional dynamics, criminological conceptions, and the religious and humanitarian reform programs that have played a crucial role in shaping penal practice (Ignatieff 1981; Spierenburg 1984*a;* Garland 1985; Beattie 1986; Innes 1987). To say this is not to dismiss the effectivity of modes of production in shaping penal systems, but it is to insist that any such causal effect is much more mediated and indirect—and therefore less "determinative"—than their account suggests. Historians such as Michael Ignatieff (1978) have demonstrated that one can combine a sensitivity to the specific interests and genuine concerns motivating actors in the penal process with a recognition that the shaping context for these ideas, and the practical constraints in which they operate, will be determined by the broader political and economic structure of the society in question—and such an approach would seem an important refinement of the Marxist case.

Similarly, it is insufficient to describe correlations between "economic interests" and penal outcomes, as Rusche and Kirchheimer tend to do, without also describing the mechanisms that allow these "interests" to be realized. This is particularly important in diversified, democratic societies, where penal decisions are undertaken by personnel who may be quite remote from the sphere of economic activity. If it is to be argued that economic imperatives are conveyed into the penal realm, then the mechanisms of this indirect influence must be clearly described, otherwise correlations can be seen as mere coincidence. It may be possible—as Steven Box has recently argued (1987)—that sentencers, prison authorities, and state officials come to recognize labor-market "needs" and "ruling-class interests" and then make decisions in accordance with them, but an analysis of this process would need to be much more complex than the one that Rusche and Kirchheimer supply.

Finally, the tendency of these analyses of punishment to describe criminal justice as a kind of class instrument used to regulate and control the working classes has had to contend with strong evidence that criminal law commands a wide degree of support among the popular classes, who frequently perceive it as protecting their interests as well as those of the ruling classes (Brewer and Styles 1980; Sparks 1980; Langbein 1983). Thus, if the Marxist argument is to be sustained, it must recognize—as many Marxists now do—that the criminal law's class functions are combined with genuine social functions, such as the prohibition of violence and the punishment of predatory criminals. Consequently, the key to understanding criminal law in class terms is not to deny its universal functions but rather to appreciate the ways in which particular interests are silently interwoven with more general ones. One might extend this point to argue that Pashukanis's rejection of "bourgeois legality" and the penal practices based on it fails to recognize the general protections that such principles can afford—a criticism made by fellow Marxists such as E. P. Thompson (1975)—and to point out that the legal ideals developed in capitalist societies may have a value that is independent of that particular socioeconomic context—as democratic socialists frequently assert. However, if this counterargument reduces the critical force of the Marxist position, it leaves intact the observation that the major principles, categories, and values to be found in the penal sphere are often direct homologies of cultural categories to be found in other areas of society, such as the polity and the economy.

If one bears in mind these criticisms and scales down Marxism's explanatory claims so that economic pressures and ruling-class interests are viewed as influential on, rather than wholly determinative of, penal policy, it seems clear that this kind of perspective can illuminate certain features of modern punishment. It can, for instance, go some way toward explaining contemporary penal phenomena such as the ideological importance of work in penal institutions, the continuation of "less eligibility" as a principle of administration, and the centrality of monetary penalties in most penal systems. Similarly, current policy developments such as the "privatization" of corrections, the movement toward "punishment in the community," and the utilization of new surveillance technologies, all have clear financial implications and repercussions for the labor market that would invite an analysis of this kind. The resilience and renewal of justice model thinking—throughout the era of rehabilitation and particularly since the 1970s—may also be better comprehended if we bear in mind the linkages identified by Pashukanis and look to the resurgence of market ideologies and the political decline of welfarism that has occurred in recent years. Finally, this perspective should make us prepared to analyze punishment not in the narrow terms of "the crime problem" but instead as one of the mechanisms for managing the urban underclass, together with social welfare regulations, policing strategies, housing, schooling, and employment policies. On this broader view, penal measures are shaped not just by patterns of criminality—themselves linked to the conditions of life of marginal groups and their relation to other classes—but primarily by governmental perceptions of the poor as a social problem and the preferred strategies for their treatment. These forms of treatment may involve aspects of caring and provision as well as coercion and control, but the embeddedness of these forms within wider strategies of rule is the point most crucial for their comprehension.

C. *Punishment, Power, and Knowledge: The Work of Michel Foucault*

I said of Durkheim that he told us little about the actual apparatus and instrumentalities of punishment. The same might be said of the Marxist perspective, which is primarily concerned to show how penal institutions come to be caught up in class divisions and shaped by economic and political structures. In contrast to these, Foucault's work takes us straight to the internal workings of the penal apparatus, focusing on the specific technologies of penal power and their mode of operation. His studies (Foucault 1977, 1978, 1980, 1990) analyze in detail the mechanisms whereby modern penal sanctions exert their specific forms of control, the principles of surveillance, inspection, and discipline on which they rely, and the penological knowledges and rationalities that inform these modes of exercising power. The result is a kind of phenomenology of penal control, showing the detailed ways in which the "microphysics of power" come into contact with the bodies of those subjected to it. And although he is concerned to show how penal technologies link up with other areas of governance and discipline and to situate them within a wider network of power relations, he insists that such matters cannot be understood by reference to general theories about how "society" is structured.

Foucault's *Discipline and Punish* (1977) sets itself the historical problem of how to explain the disappearance of one style of punishment—in which punishment operates as a public spectacle of bodily violence—and the emergence of another—in which the prison comes to be the standard penal method. He selects this problem in order to explore the wider (and more contemporary) theme of how power is exercised and individuals are governed in the modern world, and so, for the most part, the book is an analysis of the apparatus of power that the prison deploys and the forms of knowledge, technology, and social relationship on which this apparatus depends.

The emergence of the "modern" penal style that the prison epitomizes—and which Foucault locates between 1750 and 1820—is to be understood as a qualitative shift rather than a mere decrease in the quantity or intensity of punishment. In this transformation, the target of punishment is altered so that, although the body is still addressed by some penal measures, it is now as an instrument for transforming the soul rather than as a surface on which to inflict pain. At the same time, the objective of punishment undergoes a change so that the concern is now less to avenge the crime than to transform the criminal who stands behind it. This change in penal technology—from the scaffold to the penitentiary—signifies a deeper change in the character of justice itself. The new concern is to know the criminal, to understand the sources of his criminality, and to intervene to correct them wherever possible, so that the focus of judgment shifts away from the offense itself toward an assessment of the individual (see also Foucault 1990). This, in turn, requires the appointment of a variety of experts who become necessary in order to provide this knowledge, identify abnormalities, and help bring about a reformation. The result of these changes is a system of dealing with offenders that is not so much punitive as corrective and is more intent on producing normal, conforming individuals than on dispensing punishments and penalties.

On a wider scale, these developments represent for Foucault an illustrative model of how power tends to operate in modern society. Open physical force, the apparatus of violence, and the ceremonies of might are more and more replaced by a mode of power based on detailed knowledge, routine intervention, and gentle correction. The idea now is to regulate thoroughly, and at all times, rather than to repress in fits and starts, and by this means to improve troublesome individuals rather than to destroy them.

Foucault's way of looking at punishment is thus distinctive and quite specific. According to the principles of interpretation that he sets out, punishment is to be understood as a "political tactic" situated within the general field of power relations. It is to be studied with a view to its positive effects, however marginal or indirect, and not simply as a repressive mechanism. It is to be thought of as intimately and internally linked with the development of "the human sciences" (psychology, sociology, criminology, etc.) and not merely influenced by them from the outside. And, finally, the new concern with the individuality of the offender—with his "soul"—is to be conceived as the most recent chapter in a longer history of ways in which "the body" has been dealt with by political policies. Punishment is thus about power, particularly positive power; it is about knowledge—or rather power-knowledge; and it is about the ways in which technologies of power-knowledge come into contact with the bodies of offenders and exercise power in and through them.

Modern punishment—and especially the modern prison—deploys a distinctive kind of power that Foucault describes as "disciplinary" (1977, pt. 3). Discipline, for Foucault, is a method of mastering the human body and rendering it both obedient and useful. It operates on the smallest scale of control, paying attention not primarily to the whole body but to its individual movements and gestures, aiming to increase the efficiency of each movement and develop its coordination with others. This training of the body is accompanied by a constant, uninterrupted supervision that is alert to the slightest deviation and thus facilitates a meticulous control of the individual who is being disciplined.

This kind of close control was, in turn, dependent on certain organizational principles that had gradually been developed in various nonpenal settings from the seventeenth century onwards. Thus it was the army that did most to develop the art of distributing individuals in space—its ranks and files introducing a set orderliness into a mass of individuals, separating them one by one so that they could be individually viewed, supervised, and assessed. Similarly, the monastery developed the timetable—a means of imposing set rhythms to organize time and movement, specify a series of occupations, and regulate the cycle of repetition. On a smaller scale, the concept of "the manoeuvre" derives from both the barracks and the workshop. In this repeated routine the exact posture of the body, the positioning of the limbs, and the smallest of bodily movements were programmed to increase their efficiency and link them to the use of a weapon or the operation of a machine. By these means, bodies were to be put through their paces until they became docile, efficient, useful machines, programmed to carry out the functions for which they have been trained (Foucault 1977, pp. 135–70).

By way of enforcement, and in order to deal with deviance and disobedience, these disciplinary systems rely on a corrective method that Foucault calls "normalization." Normalization involves, first of all, a means of assessing the individual's performance in relation to a desired standard of conduct. Surveillance arrangements, case records, and examination procedures provide this knowledge, allowing incidents of nonconformity or departures from set standards to be recognized and dealt with, at the same time "individualizing" the different subjects who fall under this gaze. And since the object is to correct rather than punish, the actual sanctions used tend to involve exercises and training, measures that in themselves help bring conduct "into line" and make individuals more self-controlled. Implicated within this process of normalization are the new "human sciences"—such as criminology, penology, psychology, and sociology—since these sciences are only made possible by the production of detailed, systematic knowledge about individuals and, in their turn, are made to contribute to the normalizing power and control that is exercised over individuals (1977, pp. 107–95).

The "Panopticon" or "Inspection House" that Jeremy Bentham designed in 1791 is seen by Foucault as the very epitome of these power-knowledge principles—and as the prototype not just for prisons but for all institutions that implement regimes of surveillance and discipline. The Panopticon, in its ideal version, takes the form of a circular building with individual cells around its perimeter, the windows and lighting of which are arranged so as to make their occupants clearly visible to the central inspection tower, though it remains opaque to them. It is thus an architectural form designed to individualize bodies and to render these individuals constantly subject to the knowledge and power of the authorities who occupy its center. In time, this constant visibility and vulnerability is designed to induce self-control on the part of the inmates of the cells. Power no longer needs to unleash its sanctions, and instead its objects take it upon themselves to behave in the desired manner. Any remnant of physical repression is thus gradually replaced by a gentle but effective structure of domination (1977, pp. 195–209).

On the basis of this analysis, the prison and much of modern punishment are to be interpreted as specific aspects of that wider historical phenomenon, the development and generalization of the disciplines.

Key principles of modern penology—the investigation of "the criminal" behind the crime, the concern with correction and adjustment, the involvement of experts whose task is to observe, to assess, and to cure—are all hallmarks of this disciplinary process, as are the standard penitentiary techniques of isolation, work, individualized treatment, and the adjustment of sentence to reflect behavioral improvement. Moreover, the science of "criminology" comes to be viewed as an element within this normalizing, disciplinary system—with the implication that different regimes of power might give rise to rather different forms of criminological knowledge (and, of course, vice versa).

The structure of modern penal institutions is thus explained genealogically—in terms of the development of the disciplines—and structurally—in terms of the principles of operation and discursive rationalities that they employ. However, Foucault's account of the actual functioning of the prison stresses its hidden role in the wider field of political domination and general social control rather than its declared objectives of disciplining individuals. According to Foucault—and here he repeats the conventional wisdom—the prison has consistently failed in its penological objectives. Indeed, the defects of the prison—its failure to reduce crime, its tendency to produce recidivists, to organize a criminal milieu, to render prisoners' families destitute, and so forth—have all been recognized from as early as the 1820s. But this penological "failure" is reinterpreted by Foucault as a kind of unspoken political success. The creation of a recidivist delinquent class is deemed to be useful in a strategy of political domination because it works to separate crime from politics, to divide the working classes against themselves, to enhance the fear of prison, and to guarantee the authority and power of the police. By creating a well-defined delinquent class, the prison ensures that habitual criminals are known to the authorities and can more easily be managed, while the powers of surveillance, which this group necessitates, can be easily used for wider political purposes. On this account, the prison does not control the criminal so much as control the working class by creating the criminal, and, for Foucault, this is the unspoken rationale for the institution's persistence through nearly 200 years (1977, pp. 271–85; see also Foucault 1980).

The location and functioning of the prison in a more general "surveillance society" is most clearly brought out when Foucault describes the extensive network of normalizing practices in modern society. He describes how the frontiers between judicial punishment and the other institutions of social life, such as the school, the family, the workshop, and social welfare institutions came increasingly to be blurred by the development of similar disciplinary techniques in all of them, and the frequent transfers that take place from one institution to another. According to Foucault, there exists a kind of "carceral continuum" that covers the whole social body, linked by the pervasive concern to identify deviance, anomalies, and departures from the relevant norm. Within this overall framework, the process of punishing is not essentially different from that of educating or curing, and it tends to be represented as merely an extension of these less coercive practices, with the consequence that the legal restrictions that once surrounded the power to punish—tying it to specific crimes, determining its duration, guaranteeing the rights of those accused, and so on—tend to disappear. Penal law in effect becomes a hybrid system of control combining the principles of legality with the principles of normalization, and it is this transformation that extends the scope of its effective power, allowing it to sanction not just "violations of the law" but also "deviations from the norm" (1977, pp. 293–308).

This Foucauldian account of punishment, like any singular interpretation, has definite weaknesses and limitations. In focusing on the relations of power and knowledge that structure modern punishments, Foucault neglects other issues such as the sensibilities, moral values, and emotional forces that form the cultural framework in which penal power is exercised, the social support and political legitimacy on which penal measures depend, and even the day-to-day political struggles and negotiations that shape penal policies and institutional regimes. His account tends to identify modern punishment with disciplinary or normalizing methods, despite the fact that important contemporary sanctions, such as the fine and indeed the death penalty, are not, in his sense, disciplinary; despite the continuing tendency of criminal courts to utilize the language of moral censure and the logic of retribution; and despite the fact that, even where disciplinary techniques have been adopted, they are often in practice compromised by humanitarian and civil rights concerns, or even by an unreconstructed punitiveness (Bottoms 1983; Garland and Young 1983).

His assertion that the prison has consistently failed in its disciplinary project—whatever the plausibility of his alternative account of its functioning—also raises a theoretical problem for his approach: for if the prison is a concentrated, totalized form of discipline and it nonetheless fails in its disciplinary endeavors, what does this tell us about the conditions required for successful discipline? One possible answer is that the individual concerned must somehow share the goal of becoming disciplined—and that cooperation of this kind is infrequent in a punitive context. But to pursue this idea is to highlight the role of the subject-to-be-disciplined and his or her value orientation and, thus, to move away from the rather more automatic conception of discipline that Foucault implies. Also, his political explanation for the historical transformation of punishment seems to imply that the disappearance of the scaffold and physical sanctions coincided with the political sea change of the French Revolution, when in fact the decline of public penal violence seems to have been a much more gradual process, beginning at the start of the seventeenth century and continuing to the present day (Spierenburg 1984*b*).

A more contemporary criticism of Foucault's work might be that, although it describes very well the power-knowledge relations implicit within "rehabilitative" or "treatment-oriented" regimes of criminal justice, such strategies are no longer characteristic of penal policy in the 1980s and 1990s. In this "postrehabilitation" era—in which justice model thinking, retributive sentencing, and aims such as general deterrence and incapacitation have come to dominate penal policy—the phenomenology of penal control that Foucault presents might seem to relate to a system that no longer exists. However, such a criticism views Foucault's work much too narrowly and fails to understand the analytical level at which it aims. *Discipline and Punish* is not just an account of "positivist criminology" and "rehabilitative" policies: it is an account of more fundamental structures of penal modernity that have outlasted the policy objectives that first justified their introduction. Put in more Weberian terms, Foucault describes how punishment has become a rationalized, instrumentalized institution, dependent on expert knowledge, bureaucratic routines, and calculated techniques of fine-grain control. This historical process of professionalization, bureaucratization, and rationalization, of which the disciplines are a leading instance, has ensured that, whatever the judicial or political objectives of punishment, the institutions of penal control tend to adopt rationalized styles of regulation and risk-management procedures that rely on and refine the kinds of principles that Foucault describes. Contemporary policy options—such as selective incapacitation, and the identification of career criminals, dangerous individuals, or even appropriate cases for diversion—rely on the same principles of assessment, diagnosis, and prediction as did rehabilitative regimes (Floud and Young 1981; Greenwood 1982; von Hirsch 1985). "Panoptic" principles continue to inform not only modern prisons and reformatories but also spread out into the community via the new technologies of electronic surveillance and the various forms of house arrest and at-a-distance control that these make possible (Marx 1985). Normalization techniques continue to be utilized by the myriad of community-based criminal justice agencies that operate in the space between full imprisonment and unconditional liberty (Donzelot 1980; Cohen 1985; Harris and Webb 1987), and the importance of transfers along the carceral continuum is made vividly apparent by the fact that, in some jurisdictions, the number of individuals transferred into prison from parole agencies (as a result of parole violation) is now greater than that sent there directly by the courts (Messinger and Berecochia 1990). In other words, the eclipse of the rehabilitative ethos has done nothing to diminish the extensive network of investigative, classifying, and normalizing practices that were initially introduced under the rubric of "helping the offender" but that now form an essential part of the power-knowledge network of penal control.

Thus, although Foucault's account may overstate the importance of the disciplines and may neglect to deal with the counterdisciplinary forces and nondisciplinary forms that operate within the penal realm, he has nevertheless succeeded in identifying and analyzing certain characteristics of penal practice that are of major significance in the modern world.

D. *Punishment and Sensibilities: Norbert Elias and the "Civilizing" of Penal Methods*

The interpretive perspectives of Durkheim, Marx, and Foucault are by now well-established frameworks in the sociology of punishment and have prompted a considerable body of research and commentary. The final perspective that I discuss—that of Norbert Elias—is less well known and has only recently been shown to be relevant to the understanding of punishment and penal history.

The value of Elias's work for the sociology of punishment is that it provides a detailed account of certain cultural and psychic structures, which he terms "civilized sensibilities," that are characteristic of modern Western societies, and that can be shown to have major implications for the ways in which we punish. Although Durkheim touches briefly on this theme at one point, questions of "sensibilities" and "civilization" have not featured prominently in recent sociologies and histories of punishment. Indeed, Marxist and Foucauldian theorists have tended to exclude sensibilities from their explanatory framework, arguing that "humanitarianism" and "civilized sentiments" should be seen not as causal factors in penal change but instead as superficial rhetorics or ideologies concealing more basic economic interests or covert strategies of power and control (Ignatieff 1981). As a reaction to uncritical moral histories of penal progress, this skeptical approach was probably necessary, and it has certainly been illuminating in ways that I have already described. But it is increasingly apparent that this rejection of sensibilities and substantive moral convictions has been altogether too vehement. The revisionist emphasis on the implicit strategies of control and domination that operate through punishment has hidden the important role that cultural values and sensibilities play in giving shape and limits to the penal measures that may be deployed. Thus it may well be that hanging in chains, flogging bodies, or exposing offenders to crowd violence on scaffold or pillory no longer fit with the strategies of rule and the political relations of our time, and so their disappearance can be understood in political terms. But it is also the case that these measures would now be an affront to the normal sensibilities of individuals who have grown up in modern Western societies, and the reality and force of these sensibilities would soon be felt by any ruler who tried to reintroduce such "barbaric" methods within that cultural context.

The persuasiveness of the skeptics' account stems from their demonstration that the demands of "civilized" or "humanitarian" sentiments have sometimes coincided with interests of a political, economic, or ideological kind, as for example when humane measures also produced greater control and enhanced legitimacy. But on other occasions the two pull in opposite directions, and this is where the reality of sensibilities is best revealed: where they show themselves to be a genuine social force and not just "incidental music" (Geertz 1978). The ways in which we punish depend not just on political forces, economic interests, or even penological considerations but also on our conceptions of what is or is not culturally and emotionally acceptable. Penal policy decisions are always taken against a background of mores and sensibilities that, normally at least, will set limits to what will be tolerated by the public or implemented by the penal system's personnel. Such sensibilities force issues of "propriety" on even the most immoral of governments, dictating what is and is not too shameful or offensive for serious consideration.

There is thus a whole range of possible punishments (tortures, maimings, stonings, public whippings, etc.) that are simply ruled out as "unthinkable" because they strike us as impossibly cruel and "barbaric"—as wholly out of keeping with the sensibilities of modern, civilized human beings. Such judgments, based on the prevailing sensibilities, define the outer contours of possibility in the area of penal policy. Usually this boundary line has the unspoken, barely visible character of something that everyone takes for granted. It becomes visible, and obvious, only when some outrageous proposal crosses the line, or else when evidence from other times or other places shows how differently that line has been drawn elsewhere. It is therefore stating the obvious—but also reminding us of something we can easily forget—to say that punishments are, in part, determined by the specific structure of our sensibilities, and that these sensibilities are themselves subject to change and development.

The indispensable guide for any general analysis of civilized sensibilities is Elias's two-volume account of *The Civilizing Process* (1978 and 1982), first published in 1939. In the course of this historical study, Elias sets out a detailed description of the ways in which Western sensibilities have changed since the late medieval period, identifying a number of broad developmental patterns that seem to underlie the multitude of tiny, specific, and very gradual changes of attitude and conduct that the historical sources reveal. Having described this pattern of change and the typical directions that it has taken, Elias then sets out an explanatory account that links changes in sensibility and individual psychology with wider changes in social organization and modes of interaction. Unfortunately, Elias himself has little to say about the way in which the history of punishment fits into the broad developments which he describes. (He offers some brief remarks about the place of the gallows in the medieval world of the knight [it stands "in the background of his life. It may not be very important but at any rate, it is not a particularly painful sight"] and notes, on the very first page, that "the form of judicial punishment" is one of the social facts to which "civilization" typically refers [Elias 1978, p. 207 and p. 3]. Beyond this, nothing specific is said.) Nevertheless, it seems perfectly clear that Elias's analysis of the development and characteristics of modern sensibilities has a profound importance for the understanding of punishment, as the work of Pieter Spierenburg (1984*b*) and others has begun to make clear. In the remainder of this section, I set out the major themes of Elias's work and suggest how they can help us to understand the forms and cultural foundations of modern punishments. In doing so, I focus mainly on his account of modern sensibilities and the characteristic structure of fears, anxieties, and inhibitions produced in individuals by the controls and rituals of contemporary culture. It should be noted, however, that this psychic-cultural dimension forms only one aspect of Elias's general theory of social organization and development—a project conceived on the grand scale of Weber and Durkheim and synthesizing many of the arguments of these two writers.

In Elias's work, the concept of "civilization" refers to "a specific transformation of human behaviour" (1978, p. 151). Using a range of historical sources—but particularly etiquette manuals, pedagogical texts, and similar documents of detailed cultural instruction or description—Elias traces transformations of behavioral norms—and, eventually, of actual behavior—in several different spheres of social and personal life. Table manners, attitudes toward bodily functions, the proper methods of spitting or blowing one's nose, behavior in the bedroom, habits of washing and cleanliness, the expression of aggression, relationships between adults and children, the conduct of men in the presence of women, proper ways of addressing superiors or strangers—all these undergo important changes that Elias describes in rich and often fascinating detail. Moreover, he finds in this multitude of changes a number of recurring patterns and principles of development that give the whole movement a certain orderliness and direction. (One should add that this pattern is based not on any teleology of progress but on parallel developments in social organization—especially the formation of centralized nation-states with monopolies of legitimate violence and the increase in social differentiation and interdependence—that accompanied the transformation from feudal society, to court society, and, finally, to market society [Elias 1982].)

According to Elias, these changes in cultural demands and social relations eventually have an effect on the psychic organization of the individuals involved and, in particular, on the structure of their drives and emotions. Human beings gradually internalize the fears, anxieties, and inhibitions imposed on them by their parents and social environment, developing a superego that more or less effectively inhibits the expression of drives and aggressions in accordance with the demands of cultural life. There is thus a psychic corollary of cultural change—"the *psychical* process of civilization" (1978, p. xii)—that over the long term produces changes in the personality structure typically displayed by individuals, especially the development of self-controls, internalized restraints, and inhibiting anxieties such as fear, shame, delicacy, and embarrassment. Open displays of aggression, or indeed spontaneous emotion of any kind, are increasingly forbidden by force of law or by social prudence. To the extent that this process of socialization is successful, the emotions and behavior of the individual become more evenly ordered, less spontaneous, and less given to wild oscillation between extremes. Individuals are thus trained and psychologically equipped to sustain social conventions and to display a particular pattern of sensibility. Over time, these conventions tend to become more demanding, calling for greater levels of restraint and forbearance and producing ever-increasing thresholds of delicacy and sensitivity. Moreover there tends to be a diffusion of civilized manners from one social group to another, so that sensibilities and attitudes first developed within the social elite tend to spread outwards and affect ever-greater parts of the population. To the extent, then, that penal policies are conditioned by social attitudes toward violence, by emotional responses to the sight of pain and suffering, and particularly by elite conceptions of appropriate conduct and permissible behavior, Elias's account can be seen to be pertinent to our understanding of penal methods and their historical development.

Even more directly relevant is Elias's thesis that the civilizing process brings with it a move toward the "privatization" of disturbing events.[1] In the development of manners and cultural rituals, a key feature that Elias identifies is the process of privatization whereby certain aspects of life disappear from the public arena to become hidden behind the scenes of social life. Sex, violence, bodily functions, illness, suffering, and death gradually become a source of embarrassment and distaste and are more and more removed to various private domains such as the domesticated nuclear family, private lavatories and bedrooms, prison cells, and hospital wards. Lying behind this process is the tendency to suppress the more animalistic aspects of human conduct as being signs of the crude and the uncultivated. Such conduct comes to be defined as distasteful and unmannerly and individuals are taught to avoid shocking their superiors by displaying such behavior in their presence. Eventually this cultural suppression becomes more general and more pro-

[1] To avoid confusion, it should be noted that the term "privatization" as used by Elias has nothing to do with the kind of "privatization" mentioned earlier, which involves the transfer of the administration or ownership of penal institutions from state agencies to commercial corporations.

found. The sight of other people openly suffering, or defecating, or displaying their bodily functions becomes thoroughly distasteful and is banned from public places. Gradually, new and more private enclaves are developed "behind the scenes" in which such activities can be undertaken more discretely, withdrawn from the sight of others, and often surrounded by an aura of shame and embarrassment.

This concept of privatization is important, not just because it helps us understand the heavy reliance of modern society on institutional enclosures as its favored method of dealing with troublesome individuals. It also makes it clear that civilization involves a displacement and relocation of "uncivilized" behaviors, rather than their total suppression or disappearance. For example, one of the key characteristics of modern, state-governed societies is that violence is no longer a tolerated aspect of everyday, public life. However, as Elias points out, violence in society does not disappear. Instead, it is stored up "behind the scenes"—in the barracks, armories, and prison houses of the state—ready to be used in case of emergency and exerting an ever-present threat to possible violators of state norms and prohibitions (1978, p. 239). It is therefore unsurprising that those societies which are in every respect the most civilized are nonetheless capable of unleashing the massive violence of world wars, nuclear attacks, and genocide should the restraints of civility be for any reason abandoned.

As with other signs of brutishness, the sight of violence, pain, or physical suffering has become highly disturbing and distasteful to modern sensibilities. Consequently, it is minimized wherever possible. And where violence does continue to be used, it is usually removed from the public arena and sanitized or disguised in various ways, often becoming the monopoly of specialist groups such as the army, the police, or the prison staff that conduct themselves in an impersonal, professional manner, avoiding the emotional intensity that such behavior threatens to arouse.

The development of sensibilities, inhibitions, and cultural rituals that we equate with "civilization" took place over a long period of time and with all the unevenness and vicissitudes of any long-term process. However, Elias identifies what he calls a "typical civilization curve" that effectively summarizes the characteristic stages of this gradual development. An example of this developmental curve is given in his discussion of table manners and the socially sanctioned methods of carving animal meat:

> The increasingly strong tendency to remove the distasteful from the sight of society clearly applies, with few exceptions, to the carving of the whole animal. This carving . . . was formerly a direct part of social life in the upper class. Then the spectacle is felt more and more to be distasteful. Carving itself does not disappear, since the animal must, of course, be cut when being eaten. But the distasteful is removed behind the scenes of social life. Specialists take care of it in the shop or the kitchen. It will be seen again and again how characteristic of the whole process that we call civilization is this movement of segregation, this hiding "behind the scenes" of what has become distasteful. The curve running from the carving of a large part of the animal or even the whole animal at table, through the advance in the threshold of repugnance at the sight of dead animals, to the removal of carving to the specialized enclaves behind the scenes is a typical civilization curve. [1978, p. 121]

This quotation neatly summarizes much of Elias's discussion and illustrates several important points. But it also serves to suggest just how closely the history of punishment conforms to the general developmental pattern that Elias identifies. If one reads this passage bearing in mind the broad sweep of penal history, then a number of very significant parallels quickly emerge. Over the same period of time—from the sixteenth century to the twentieth—punitive manners have undergone a very similar series of changes. In the early modern period, capital and corporal executions were conducted in public, and both the ritual of judicial killing and the offender's display of suffering formed an open part of social life. Later, in the seventeenth and eighteenth centuries, the sight of this spectacle becomes redefined as distasteful, particularly among the social elite, and executions are gradually removed "behind the scenes"—normally behind the walls of prisons. Subsequently, the idea of doing violence to offenders becomes repugnant in itself, and corporal and capital punishments are largely abolished, to be replaced by other sanctions such as imprisonment (Spierenburg 1984*b;* Zimring and Hawkins 1986, pt. 1). By the late twentieth century, punishment has become a rather shameful activity, undertaken by specialists and professionals in enclaves (such as prisons and reformatories) that are, by and large, removed from the sight of the public.

This example serves to demonstrate that the cultural and psychic transformations which Elias describes as the origins of our present sensibilities may also have played an important part in shaping our institutions of punishment. If we accept the reality of the phenomena identified by this work—in particular, the intensification of "conscience," the increased restraints on violent behavior, the expansion of the individual's capacity to identify and empathize with others, the heightening of sensitivity to pain and suffering, and the broad cultural tendencies toward privatization and sanitization (for broadly supporting historical evidence, see Stone [1979]; Gatrell [1980]; Gurr [1981]; Beattie [1984]; and Thomas [1984]; for an opposing view, see Macfarlane [1981])—then we are obliged to include such variables in any account of penal history or the sociology of punishment. Of course, the role of sensibilities in determining punishments is in no sense an exclusive one: as Elias himself shows, these psychic and cultural phenomena are always bound up with social structures, class struggles, and organizational forms, all of which might be expected to contribute to the shaping of penal practices. Nor is there any need to accept Elias's account uncritically, or in every detail (see Giddens 1984; Lasch 1985; van Krieken 1989). But once we grant a reality and effectivity to the psychic and cultural phenomena that his work highlights, it seems clear that they must be included as an operative element in any social theory of punishment. Punishments can never be fully explained in terms of their instrumental purposes, their control potential, or their economic and political advantage because, as Elias's work shows, such possibilities will always be shaped and limited by cultural and psychic forces that define the basic contours of possibility in the realm of penal policy.

The importance of sensibilities in structuring modern penal practice is obvious if one considers the generalized refusal of Western societies to utilize what can, in some respects, be an efficient form of sanctioning, namely, corporal punishment. Unlike imprisonment (which is very expensive, difficult to manage, and which creates its own problems by bringing together large numbers of offenders under the same roof) and unlike the fine (which varies in effect according to the offender's means, and which frequently results in imprisonment for those who cannot pay) corporal punishments can be inexpensive, they can be precisely calibrated, their side effects can be minimized, and they can be delivered reasonably efficiently and uniformly. In these terms, at least, there are strong reasons to consider corporal punishments as a policy option within modern penal strategies. And yet penologists, by and large, do not even mention this possibility. (An exception to this is Newman [1983]. See the review by Simon [1985].) It is not an option on the modern penal agenda, but rather a fact of penal history, occasionally reinvoked for dramatic effect by reactionary politicians.

Why is this? The answer would seem to be that our modern sensibilities—or at least those of the sectors of society that are influential in policy-making—have been attuned to abhor physical violence and bodily suffering. Gross violence, deliberate brutality, the infliction of physical pain and suffering, all these are felt by many people to be intolerably offensive in themselves and to have no legitimate place within the public policy of a civilized nation. But it needs to be emphasized that this ban on violence and the infliction of pain is *not* a general one. On the contrary, an understanding of the human impact of some contemporary punishments makes it clear that government policy still permits the infliction of pain and public opinion still tolerates it—so long as it takes a particular form. It is well known to those with experience of imprisonment, for example, that incarceration, particularly for long periods of time, can produce acute mental and psychological suffering (Sykes 1958; Cohen and Taylor 1972). It can also bring about physical deterioration and the erosion of cognitive and social skills, and it frequently results in serious emotional and economic distress for the prisoner's family. But because these pains are mental and emotional rather than physical, because they are corrosive over an extended period rather than immediate, because they are removed from public view, and because they are legally disguised as a simple "loss of liberty," they do not greatly offend our sensibilities and they are permitted to form a part of public policy. In keeping with the demands of a "civilized" society, the experience of pain is ushered behind the scenes—whether this is behind the walls of a prison, or behind the "front" with which prisoners conceal their emotional distress.

The crucial difference between corporal punishments that are banned, and other punishments—such as long-term imprisonment—that are routinely used, is not a matter of the intrinsic levels of pain and brutality involved. It is a matter of the *form* which that violence takes, and the extent to which it impinges on public sensibilities. Modern sensibilities display a definite selectivity. They are highly attuned to perceive and recoil from certain acts of violence, but at the same time, they have particular blind spots, or sympathetic limitations, so that other forms are less clearly registered and experienced. Consequently, routine violence and the suffering of others can be tolerated on condition that it is discreet, disguised, or somehow removed from view. Because much of the public does not hear the anguish of prisoners and their families, because the discourses of the press and of popular criminology present offenders as "different" and less than fully human, and because penal violence is generally sanitized, situational, and of low visibility, the conflict between our civilized sensibilities and the often brutal routines of punishment is minimized and made more tolerable. Modern punishment is institutionally ordered and discursively represented in ways that deny the violence which continues to inhere in its practices.

One vivid illustration of this characteristic, which shows both the continued investment in penal violence and the limitations of public sensibilities, is the history of modern attempts to find an "acceptable" method of capital punishment. Throughout the modern period, governments have sought to discover new methods that might perform this ultimate act of violence while simultaneously concealing its brutal and painful aspects. At first the concern was to develop a means of ensuring death that would not depend on the skill of an individual executioner—hence the guillotine, the trapdoor gallows, and the firing squad. Later, in the nineteenth and twentieth centuries, the movement was toward elaborate technical devices—such as the electric chair and the gas chamber—that had the effect of distancing and dehumanizing the fatal act, rendering it as a technical scientific operation rather than one human being deliberately killing another. In effect, the moral question whether it was right to kill or not came to be translated into a question of aesthetics: could judicial killing be undertaken tastefully, in a manner that disguised the fact of its atrocity?

Given the gravity of a decision to kill another human being, it may well seem perverse and absurd to agonize over questions of decorum and presentation, but it is a fact of political life that these cosmetic aspects of punishment have been crucial in making judicial killing acceptable to (at least some sectors of) modern public opinion. Perhaps the high point in this search for a method that can kill without offending public sensibilities is the development of the "lethal injection" that is now used extensively in the United States. This technique of killing involves the injection of a lethal dose of "an ultra-fast-acting barbiturate" in combination with a paralytic agent into the veins of the offender. According to its proponents, this method is virtually painless and offers "an alternative, pleasanter, method of execution." It is represented as a quasi-medical procedure, to be undertaken not by executioners but by medical personnel, and of course in its form it imitates a routine, curative practice of modern health care (Zimring and Hawkins 1986, chap. 6).

This attempt to represent judicial killing as a form of euthanasia has been taken up by more than a dozen U.S. states during the last ten years. In practice, the distancing of the executioners from their victims has been further facilitated at the scene of the execution by the erection of a brick wall that separates the condemned from the technicians and permits the fatal dose to be administered through a tiny opening in the wall. The offender, who is strapped on a stretcher-trolley like a patient awaiting an operation, is put to death anonymously, under the guise of a medical procedure, by technicians who do not immediately witness the effects of their actions (Amnesty International 1987). This strange, and actually rather horrifying, scene encapsulates many of the important characteristics of modern punishment—its privatization, its sanitization, and the careful denial of its own violence—and shows very clearly the formal properties that modern sensibilities require of punitive action.

The value of Elias's work and the kind of approach that he has pioneered is that it trains our attention on the formal characteristics of modern punishment, identifies the kinds of sensibilities that create such forms, and helps us to trace their connection with the wider cultural and societal patterns that have brought them about. And if sensibilities do influence the forms that punishments take—and it seems clear that they do, though never directly or exclusively—then two consequences should follow. The first is the theoretical consequence that any analysis of penal forms or penal history must take these issues into account. We ought never to dismiss evidence of sensibilities as "mere ideology" in the way that Rusche and Kirchheimer and even Foucault tend to do. The second is a more practical point, namely, that cultural struggle, exposé journalism, and moral criticism—the traditional tools of the penal reformer—do have some measure of effectiveness in bringing about penal change. Penal forms are embedded within objective social structures *and* cultural frameworks. Political initiative, moral argument, the cultivation of sensibilities, and public awareness about what goes on "behind the scenes" all play a part in shaping the details and regimes of society's penal institutions. Even if we cannot see the immediate possibility of changing society's infrastructure of class relations, its dependence on capitalist forms, or its proliferation of power-knowledge networks, we can still look to the influence of moral and cultural struggles in the penal realm. Social institutions are more flexible than most structuralist sociology allows.

II. A Multidimensional Approach

These four broad perspectives that have been outlined—punishment as a moralizing mechanism, a component of class rule, an exercise of power, and an enacted cultural form—cannot be simply added together to provide some kind of grand overview of punishment and penal history. The danger of such eclecticism is that, in drawing on arguments made by different theorists about "punishment and society," one can too readily assume an identity of concerns where none in fact exists and end up in an intellectual tangle of incompatible premises, ambiguous concepts, and shifting objects of study. Trying to say everything at once, one can wind up saying nothing with any clarity or conviction. Any account of punishment drawing from more than one theoretical source must therefore be careful to avoid mixing up analyses and propositions that are theoretically incompatible. But while eclecticism has these risks, there is a definite explanatory strength to be found in theoretical pluralism, by which I mean a willingness to draw on more than one interpretive perspective and to construct multidimensional accounts of the phenomenon being investigated. What I have tried to suggest in this essay is that these different interpretations might be played off against each other—and against the factual research evidence that they help generate—in such a way as to overlay them, build them up, and use each one to correct and refine the others. Proceeding from one explanatory perspective to another, it becomes clear that each one asks slightly different questions about the phenomenon of "punishment," each pursues a different aspect, reveals a different determinant, and outlines a different connection.

Sometimes, of course, different theorists do address the same issue, only to interpret it in different ways—as when Marxists and Durkheimians disagree about the role of the state or of popular sentiments in the formation of penal policy. In such cases, one needs to argue out this disagreement and resolve it in favor of the best explanation—or else develop an alternative account that improves on them both. At other times, however, theoretical disagreement may, on closer inspection, turn out to be less substantive than it at first appears. Thus, as we have already seen, where Durkheim insists that modern punishment is irrational, emotional, and punitive, Foucault appears to argue that neither punitiveness nor vengeful emotion has any place in the rationalized disciplinary strategies of modern punishment—a direct contradiction of Durkheim's view. But in fact this statement misrepresents the scope of Foucault's argument. His analysis, unlike that of Durkheim, does not cover the whole social process of punishment, from prosecution through court trial to penal disposition. Instead he focuses on the practices of prisons and the rationalities that they employ. His is primarily an account of penal administration and technology—that is to say, of one crucial aspect of the penal process, rather than the whole process from beginning to end. And precisely because his purpose is to understand the mechanisms of positive, disciplinary power—rather than to understand "punishment" as such—his work makes no attempt to discuss the extent to which emotions and moral sentiments continue to structure the context in which imprisonment is used. Thus, what appears to be a direct contradiction can be viewed as a difference of interpretive focus and theoretical concern: Foucault, who seeks to understand the rationality of modern power, puts penal institutions into the foreground of his analysis, while Durkheim, concerned to understand social morality, bases his account on the courtroom ritual and the legislation of criminal law. Seen in this way, as interpretations grounded in different aspects of a differentiated process, the question should no longer be, Which one is correct, Foucault or Durkheim? Instead, we should enquire how the different tendencies that they describe interact with one another, how these conflicts are managed, and what effects these tensions have on the modern process of punishment.

In other cases, it may be that a particular theorist successfully identifies an element of penality that seems to escape the scrutiny of other theoretical accounts—as with Foucault on power-knowledge techniques, Durkheim on the role of the onlooker, Rusche and Kirchheimer on the role of the market, or else Elias on changing sensibilities. Here again, we are reminded that "punishment" is not a unitary thing but rather a complex and differentiated process, involving discursive frameworks of authority and condemnation, ritual procedures of imposing sentences, a repertoire of penal sanctions, institutions, and agencies for their administration, and a rhetoric of symbols and images with which the process is represented to its various audiences. One is therefore led to investigate how these different elements and aspects of punishment fit together to form a complex internally differentiated whole. At the same time, this realization allows us to better understand the diversity of interpretations that has been brought to bear on "punishment" and to acknowledge the possibility that these interpretations might be in some ways complementary and mutually confirming rather than mutually exclusive.

Thus, to give another example, although they start with quite different premises, both Durkheim and the Marxist writer Douglas Hay agree that punishment works through the forms of ritual display and symbolic representation and addresses itself to an audience of onlookers as much as to the offender in the dock. Both insist that such displays can be crucial to the generation and regeneration of a society's culture and the individual's commitment, whether by shoring up the claims of authority or else by dealing with social dangers. Despite radical disagreement over the interpretation of penal symbols and the nature of the societies that they depict, both accounts confirm the operation of punishments within this wider sphere of cultural and psychic life. Similarly, the Foucauldian and Eliasian accounts begin from very different positions in their analysis of penal history—one emphasizing the importance of sensibilities, the other insisting that these are merely a gloss concealing relations of power and knowledge—but their accounts of the removal of punishment from the public sphere into the privacy of institutional enclosures, administered by specialist functionaries in technical rather than emotive terms, can be seen as dealing with two dimensions of the same historical process and, thus, as mutually illuminating and reinforcing.

The theoretical conclusion that these considerations suggest is that a pluralistic, multidimensional approach is needed if we are to understand the historical development and present-day operation of the penal complex. If there is to be a sociology of punishment—and by this I mean a set of general parameters from which specific studies can take their theoretical bearings—then it should be the kind of sociology advocated by Marcel Mauss (1967, p. 78) when he talked about the need for a synthesis and consolidation of perspectives. It should be a sociology that strives to present a rounded, completed image: a recomposition of the fragmentary views developed by more narrowly focused studies.

One can rephrase this argument as a warning against reductionism in the analysis of punishment—by which I mean the tendency to explain penality in terms of any single causal principle or functional purpose, be it "morals" or "economics," "state control" or "crime control." Instead of searching for a single explanatory principle, we need to grasp the facts of multiple causality, multiple effects, and multiple meaning.

We need to realize that in the penal realm—as in all social experience—specific events or developments usually have a plurality of causes that interact to shape their final form, a plurality of effects that may be seen as functional or nonfunctional depending on one's criteria, and a plurality of meanings which will vary with the actors and audiences involved—though some meanings (or, for that matter, causes and effects) may be more powerful than others. The aim of analysis should always be to capture that variety of causes, effects and meanings and trace their interaction, rather than to reduce them all to a single currency.

The utility of the individual interpretive frameworks that I have discussed lies not in their creation of broad theoretical perspectives with which to view punishment—although these in themselves can sometimes change the ways in which we think about penal issues—but rather in their capacity to guide and inform more specific studies of penal practice and penal policy. For practical purposes, the kind of knowledge that is most useful is detailed, specific, local knowledge, focused on a particular problem, or institution, or policy question and informed about the specific cultural, political, and penological circumstances that apply. The best studies of this kind are nuanced, subtle, and complex; are able to see the phenomenon in all its complexity and yet at the same time clearly situate it within its social and historical context; and aim to unravel the details of its many determinants, dynamics, and consequences. Typically, works of this kind—whether historical or contemporary—tend to utilize the kind of interpretive pluralism I have been describing rather than rely entirely on one or other interpretive framework. Thus, for example, recent work by David Downes (1988) and by Zimring and Hawkins (1990) that attempts to explain differential rates of imprisonment have stressed the need to draw on a range of theoretical traditions and to construct a complex account of interacting variables and contributory factors. Similarly, the best historical studies in this field—such as those by Michael Ignatieff (1978) and by John Beattie (1986)—mobilize forms of analysis and lines of inquiry suggested by not one but several sociological perspectives and manage to bring them together in ways that do justice to the complexity of real events. As John Beattie has put it, summing up his magisterial study of penal change in early modern England:

> Changes in punishment are almost certain not to arise from a simple, one-dimensional effect. The forms of punishment

> employed by a society at any one moment are shaped by a variety of interests and intentions. They arise in response to what must often be antagonistic considerations, including the framework of law, what is technically possible, what seems desirable or necessary in the light of the apparent problem of crime, what society is willing to accept and pay for. Why one method of punishment loses favour over time and gives way to another is a complex question because penal methods evolve within a larger social and cultural context that in imperceptible ways alters the limits of what is acceptable and what is not. [1986, p. 470]

Sociological theories, such as those discussed in this essay, are useful in the understanding of punishment because they alert us to the kinds of constraints and structures within which policy is developed and to the kinds of social consequences that punishment can have. They point to the interconnections that link punishment to other spheres of social life and the functional role that it occupies in the network of social institutions. They can reveal institutional dynamics, characteristics, and effects that might otherwise go unacknowledged and of which policymakers themselves may be unaware. But only empirical research can determine how these conditioning circumstances come together at a particular moment to shape a course of action or define a particular event. Theory should be a set of interpretative tools for guiding and informing empirical inquiry—not a substitute for it.

III. Punishment as a Social Institution

What I have tried to do in this essay is to suggest how the theoretical tools of sociology can be used to help us think about punishment in its various aspects. Each of the different traditions of social theory provides a specific set of tools in the form of a specially adapted conceptual vocabulary, designed to explicate a particular aspect or dimension of social life. And, as I have tried to indicate, each of these interpretative vocabularies has its uses in understanding punishment and becomes more or less useful depending on the questions asked and the characteristics being explained. Thus, in some circumstances, and for some people (e.g., those groups for whom the law is merely superior force, coercively imposed), punishment is an exercise of raw power, best understood in vocabularies such as those supplied by Foucault or Marx. Yet at other points, and for other people—perhaps in the same society and the same penal system—punishment may be an expression of moral community and collective sensibility, in which penal sanctions are an authorized response to shared values individually violated. In these circumstances, the vocabularies of power and ideology need to be tempered by the rather different concerns articulated by Elias and Durkheim. The object of theoretical work in this area should not be to create a grand synthesis of these traditions, nor to construct some kind of overarching theoretical model. Rather, it should be to investigate how we might most usefully utilize the range of perspectives and vocabularies through which punishment can be variously understood and to develop a conception of punishment that can ground this multiplicity of interpretations and show how they interrelate.

These social interpretations might thus be used to enrich our understanding of punishment, leading us to conceive of it not just as a crime-control mechanism but instead as a distinctive and rather complex social institution that, in its routine practices, somehow contrives to condense a whole web of social relations and cultural meanings. This more developed, sociological conception of punishment can, I think, have important implications for the way we think about punishment and penal policy. By making the social dimensions of punishment explicit, and by showing the kinds of internal conflicts and social consequences that penal institutions entail, the sociology of punishment provides a more adequate empirical basis for policy evaluation, philosophical reflection, or political judgment in this area. As I suggested earlier, the evaluation of punishment is too readily cast in the narrow terms of instrumental utility. We are too prone to think of punishment as a simple means to a simple end—usually that of crime control—and to treat all other aspects of the institution as minor considerations. So, for instance, imprisonment, or probation, or rehabilitative policies, or even capital punishment, are all too frequently approached as if the major question to be answered concerned their technical efficacy as instruments of crime control. Their evaluation thus turns primarily on measures of recidivism, or deterrence, and on correlative crime rates rather than on judgments of their total worth as social practices. But, as each of these sociological perspectives makes clear, we can hardly begin to understand penal institutions if we insist on treating them as instrumentalities, geared to a single penological purpose—so the tendency to evaluate them in these terms seems misguided and unproductive.

Thus, to conclude with an illustration, we might consider the ways in which the institution of imprisonment tends to be evaluated in contemporary discussions. As every critical report reminds us, this institution signally fails to achieve the ends of crime control that, it is assumed, form its basic raison d'être (for a summary, see Mathiesen [1990]). Most prisoners are not reformed, new generations of criminals go undeterred, national crime rates are not forced into decline, so that by all these criteria the prison is deemed an inefficient instrument (though, it should be noted, not much more inefficient than many of its alternatives). This margin of failure—it is not suggested that prison has *no* success—is such that the prison and its present high frequency of use present a serious puzzle for social commentators and penal reformers alike. Theorists such as Foucault assume that the prison's failures must, in some covert sense, be "useful for power." Historians such as Lawrence Stone (1987, p. 10) assume it is a "vestigial institution" that has somehow outlived its usefulness. Liberal criminologists throw up their hands in despair at the "irrationality" of policy and urge governments to pay attention to penological research findings and the failures that these imply. But, in an important sense, this argument is misconceived, and the "puzzle" of imprisonment arises only because of the too-narrow starting points from which these analyses begin.

Neither the prison, nor any other penal institution, rests solely on its ability to achieve such instrumental ends. Despite recurring hopes and the exaggerated claims of some reformers, the simple fact is that no method of punishment has ever achieved high rates of reform or of crime control—and no method ever will. All punishments regularly "fail" in this respect because, as Emile Durkheim (1973, chaps. 10 and 11) and others have pointed out, it is only the mainstream processes of socialization (internalized morality and a sense of duty, the informal inducements and rewards of conformity, the practical and cultural networks of mutual expectation and interdependence, etc.) that are able to promote proper conduct on a consistent and regular basis. Punishment, so far as "control" is concerned, is merely a coercive backup to these more reliable social mechanisms, a backup that is often unable to do anything more than manage those who slip through these networks of normal control and integration. Punishment is fated never to "succeed" to any great degree because the conditions that do most to induce conformity—or to promote crime and deviance—lie outside the jurisdiction of penal institutions.

It will always be open to critics of the prison to point to its failures of crime control and use these as an argument for reform. But it seems altogether inappropriate for a sociologist or a historian to take these same arguments and draw from them the conclusion that the prison is a penological failure that owes its existence to some covert political strategy or else to the dead hand of history. Like all complex institutions, the prison simultaneously pursues a number of objectives and is kept in place by a range of forces. Crime control—in the sense of reforming offenders and reducing crime rates—is certainly one of these objectives but by no means the only one. As we have seen, the prison also serves as an effective means of incapacitation, securely excluding offenders from society, sometimes for very long periods, and containing those individuals who prove too troublesome for other institutions or communities. Unlike lesser penalties, it does not require much in the way of cooperation from the offender, so that it can deal with recalcitrant individuals, by force if necessary. In the absence of the generalized use of capital punishment, forced exile, or transportation, the prison thus forms the ultimate penalty for most modern penal systems, providing a compelling and forceful sanction of last resort. Most important, the prison provides a way of punishing people—of subjecting them to hard treatment, inflicting pain, doing them harm—that is largely compatible with modern sensibilities and conventional restraints on open, physical violence. In an era when corporal punishment has become uncivilized, and open violence unconscionable, the prison supplies a subtle, situational form of violence against the person that enables retribution to be inflicted in a way that is sufficiently discreet and "deniable" to be culturally acceptable to most of the population. Despite occasional suggestions that imprisonment is becoming too lenient—a view that is rarely shared by informed sources—it is widely accepted that the prison succeeds very well in imposing real hardship, serious deprivation, and personal suffering on most offenders who are sent there.

In terms of penological objectives then, the prison supports a range of them and is "functional" or "successful" with respect to some, less so with respect to others. Nor is there any need to argue that the prison's "failures" are somehow "useful"—as Foucault and others do. The fact that prison frequently reinforces criminality and helps produce recidivists is not a "useful" consequence desired by the authorities or part of some covert "strategy." It is a tolerated cost of pursuing other objectives such as retribution, incapacitation, and exclusion and is accepted in the same reluctant way that governments absorb the high financial costs entailed in the frequent use of imprisonment. So long as such costs appear to the authorities—and to the public—to be outweighed by the desirability of imprisoning offenders (and this desire has become an established element within public beliefs, institutional frameworks, and social traditions), then the prison remains a "functional" institution—and neither a puzzle nor an anachronism.

Consequently—and this is my point—if one wishes to understand and evaluate the prison as an institution—and the same arguments apply to the fine, probation, the death penalty, and the rest—it does little good to do so on a single plane or in relation to a single value. Instead, one must think of it as a complex institution and evaluate it accordingly, recognizing the range of its penal and social functions and the nature of its social support. Nor does this mean that one must abandon a critical approach because the prison is less irrational than it at first seems. One can challenge the institution by showing that the control of troublesome individuals can be undertaken in more humane and positive settings, that exclusion is anyway an unacceptable goal in a caring society, or that many prisoners are no real danger to the public and could, under certain conditions, be tolerated in the community. One could endeavor to expose the real psychological violence that exists behind the scenes of even the best prisons and argue that such violence is as retrograde and uncivilized in its way as the corporal and capital punishments that the prison replaced. Equally, one could challenge the cost of prison as a means of expressing punitive sentiments and exacting retribution against offenders and show ways in which funds and resources could be put to better use—for instance in compensating victims, in crime-prevention schemes, or in basic educational and social provision. In effect, the more one's understanding of an institution begins to capture its nuances and complexities—and its positive effects together with its negative ones—the more thoroughgoing, informed, and incisive will be the critique that one can mount.

Thinking of punishment as a social institution should change not only our mode of understanding penality but also our normative thinking about it. It should lead us to judge punishment according to a wider range of criteria and to bring to bear the kinds of demands and expectations that we customarily apply to social institutions. To say this is not to suggest that there is some universal normative approach that we always adopt toward social institutions—different institutions have distinctive functions and characteristics and give rise to diverse forms of evaluation. But, nevertheless, when we think of "the family" or "the law," "the government" or "the economy," and subject them to normative judgment, we do so in ways that are considerably more complex than our thinking about punishment tends to be. In none of these cases do we think it proper to judge these institutions according to purely instrumental criteria, nor do we suppose that they should serve a single end or affect only a particular sector of the population. Instead, they are all commonly viewed as if they were "total social facts" (Mauss 1967), the character of which is in some way constitutive of society's identity and character.

Perhaps the best example of this is the kind of thinking that emerges whenever a democratic society deliberately undertakes to reform its major social institutions by means of a written constitution. People do not ask of such a constitution merely that it should "work" with some degree of efficiency—although that is itself crucial. They also demand that its moral, political, economic, and cultural significance be considered and that these wider ramifications be made to conform, as far as is possible, to deeply held conceptions of what kind of people they are, how they wish to be governed, and what kind of society they wish to create. The implication of the sociological perspectives considered here is that punishment should be considered in the same kind of way and in the same kind of depth as other social institutions. We need an enriched form of penological thinking that considers penality as an institution through which society defines and expresses itself at the same time and through the same means that it exercises power over deviants (for an elaboration and development of this project, see Garland [1990*a*]).

To think of punishment in this way is to question the narrow, instrumental self-description that modern penal institutions generally adopt (and which technical penology tends to repeat) and instead to suggest more socially conscious and morally charged perceptions of penal affairs. By demonstrating the deeply social nature of legal punishment, and revealing the values and commitments that are embodied within its practices, the sociology of punishment tends to undermine any attempt to compartmentalize "the penal question" or to deal with it in a purely administrative way. By showing how penal issues pull together many diverse currents of political and cultural life, such an approach helps to reconstitute a more comprehensive social awareness and to counter the tendency of modern institutions to fragment consciousness and narrow perception. It gives a sense of the sociality of punishment—of the extended significance and depth of stored-up meanings that exist beneath the surface of this complex institution.

REFERENCES

Acton, H. B. 1969. *The Philosophy of Punishment*. London: Macmillan.

Amnesty International. 1987. *United States of America: The Death Penalty*. London: Amnesty International Publications.

Bean, P. 1981. *Punishment*. Oxford: Martin Robertson.

Beattie, J. M. 1984. "Violence and Society in Early Modern England." In *Perspectives in Criminal Law*, edited by A. Doob and E. Greenspan. Aurora, Ont.: Canada Law Book.

———. 1986. *Crime and the Courts in England, 1660–1800*. Princeton, N.J.: Princeton University Press.

Bottoms, A. E. 1983. "Neglected Features of Contemporary Penal Systems." In *The Power to Punish*, edited by D. Garland and P. Young. London: Gower.

Box, S. 1987. *Recession, Crime and Punishment*. London: Macmillan.

Brewer, J., and J. Styles, eds. 1980. *An Ungovernable People: The English and Their Law in the Seventeenth and Eighteenth Centuries*. London: Hutchinson.

Cohen, S. 1985. *Visions of Social Control*. Oxford: Polity.

Cohen, S., and L. Taylor. 1972. *Psychological Survival: The Experience of Long-Term Imprisonment*. Harmondsworth: Penguin.

Cook, P. J. 1980. "Research in Criminal Deterrence: Laying the Groundwork for the Second Decade." In *Crime and Justice: An Annual Review of Research*, vol. 2, edited by N. Morris and M. Tonry. Chicago: University of Chicago Press.

Donzelot, J. 1980. *The Policing of Families*. London: Hutchinson.

Downes, D. 1988. *Contrasts in Tolerance: Post-war Penal Policy in the Netherlands and England and Wales*. Oxford: Oxford University Press.

Durkheim, E. 1933. *The Division of Labor in Society*. Translated by G. Simpson. New York: Free Press. (Originally published 1893. Paris: Alcan.)

———. 1973. *Moral Education: A Study in the Theory and Application of the Sociology of Education*. Translated by E. K. Wilson and H. Schnurer. New York: Free Press. (Originally published 1925. Paris: Alcan.)

———. 1983. "The Evolution of Punishment." In *Durkheim and the Law*, edited by S. Lukes and A. Scull. Oxford: Martin Robertson.

Elias, N. 1978. *The History of Manners: The Civilising Process*, vol. 1. Oxford: Basil Blackwell. (Originally published 1939. Basel: Hans Zum Falken.)

———. 1982. *State Formation and Civilization: The Civilising Process*, vol. 2. Oxford: Basil Blackwell. (Originally published 1939. Basel: Hans Zum Falken.)

Erikson, K. 1966. *Wayward Puritans*. New York: Wiley.

Feinberg, J., and H. Gross. 1975. *Philosophy of Law*. Enrico, Calif.: Dickenson.

Floud, J., and W. Young. 1981. *Dangerousness and Criminal Justice*. London: Heinemann.

Foucault, M. 1977. *Discipline and Punish: The Birth of the Prison*. Translated by Alan Sheridan. London: Penguin.

———. 1978. *I, Piere Riviere*. Harmondsworth: Penguin.

———. 1980. "Prison Talk." In *Power/Knowledge: Selected Interviews and Other Writings, 1972–77*, edited by C. Gordon. New York: Pantheon.

———. 1990. "The Dangerous Individual." In *Politics, Philosophy, Culture: Interviews and Other Writings, 1977–1984*, edited by L. D. Kritzman. New York: Routledge.

Garfinkel, H. 1956. "Conditions of Successful Degradation Ceremonies." *American Journal of Sociology* 61:420–24.

Garland, D. 1983. "Philosophical Argument and Ideological Effect." *Contemporary Crises* 7:69–85.

———. 1985. *Punishment and Welfare: A History of Penal Strategies*. Aldershot: Gower.

———. 1990*a*. *Punishment and Modern Society: A Study in Social Theory*. Oxford and Chicago: Oxford University Press and University of Chicago Press.

———. 1990*b*. "Frameworks of Inquiry in the Sociology of Punishment." *British Journal of Sociology* 41:1–16.

Garland, D., and P. Young. 1983. "Towards a Social Analysis of Penality." In *The Power to Punish*, edited by D. Garland and P. Young. London: Gower.

Gatrell, V. A. C. 1980. "The Decline of Theft and Violence in Victorian and Edwardian England." In *Crime and the Law: The Social History of Crime in Western Europe since 1500*, edited by V. A. C. Gatrell, B. Lenman, and G. Parker. London: Europa.

Geertz, C. 1978. "Stir Crazy." *New York Review of Books*. January 26.

Giddens, A. 1978. *Durkheim*. Hassocks, England: Harvester.

———. 1984. *The Constitution of Society*. Oxford: Polity.

Greenwood, P. 1982. *Selective Incapacitation*. Santa Monica, Calif.: RAND.

Gurr, T. R. 1981. "Historical Trends in Violent Crimes: A Critical Review of the Evidence." In *Crime and Justice: An Annual Review of Research*, vol. 3, edited by M. Tonry and N. Morris. Chicago: University of Chicago Press.

Harris, R., and D. Webb. 1987. *Welfare, Power and Juvenile Justice*. London: Tavistock.

Hart, H. L. A. 1968. *Punishment and Responsibility*. Oxford: Oxford University Press.

Hay, D. 1975. "Property, Authority, and the Criminal Law." In *Albion's Fatal Tree: Crime and Society in Eighteenth-Century England*, edited by D. Hay, P. Linebaugh, and E. P. Thompson. Harmondsworth: Penguin.

Hirst, P. Q. 1986. *Law, Socialism and Democracy*. London: Allen & Unwin.

Honderich, T. 1976. *Punishment: The Supposed Justifications*. Harmondsworth: Penguin.

Ignatieff, M. 1978. *A Just Measure of Pain: The Penitentiary and the Industrial Revolution*. London: Macmillan.

———. 1981. "State, Civil Society, and Total Institutions: A Critique of Recent Social Histories of Punishment." In *Crime and Justice: An Annual Review of Research*, vol. 3, edited by M. Tonry and N. Morris. Chicago: University of Chicago Press.

Innes, J. 1987. "Prisons for the Poor: English Bridewells, 1550–1800." In *Labour, Law and Crime: An Historical Perspective*, edited by F. Snyder and D. Hay. London: Tavistock.

Jacobs, J. B. 1983. *New Perspectives on Prisons and Imprisonment*. Ithaca, N.Y.: Cornell University Press.

Lacey, N. 1988. *State Punishment: Political Principles and Community Values.* London: Routledge & Kegan Paul.

Langbein, J. 1983. "Albion's Fatal Flaws." *Past and Present* no. 98, pp. 96–120.

Lasch, C. 1985. "Historical Sociology and the Myth of Maturity: Norbert Elias' Very Simple Formula." *Theory and Society* 14:705–20.

Lukes, S., and A. Scull. 1983. "Introduction." In *Durkheim and the Law*, edited by S. Lukes and A. Scull. Oxford: Martin Robertson.

Macfarlane, A. 1981. *The Justice and the Mare's Tale: Law and Disorder in Seventeenth Century England.* Cambridge: Blackwell.

Martinson, R. 1974. "What Works?—Questions and Answers about Prison Reform." *Public Interest* 35:22–54.

Marx, G. 1985. "I'll be Watching You: The New Surveillance." *Dissent*, vol. 26.

Mathiesen, T. 1990. *Prison on Trial.* London: Sage.

Mauss, M. 1967. *The Gift: Forms and Functions of Exchange in Archaic Societies.* Translated by Ian Cunnison. New York: Norton. (Originally published in *L'annee sociologique* 1 [1923–24]: 30–186.)

Mead, G. H. 1918. "The Psychology of Punitive Justice." *American Journal of Sociology* 23:577–602.

Melossi, D., and M. Pavarini. 1981. *The Prison and the Factory.* London: Macmillan.

Messinger, S. L., and J. E. Berecochia. 1990. "Don't Stay Too Long but Do Come Back Soon: Reflections on the Size and Vicissitudes of California's Prison Population." Paper presented at the Conference on Growth and Its Influence on Correctional Policy, Berkeley, Calif., May.

Newman, G. 1983. *Just and Painful: A Case for the Corporal Punishment of Criminals.* New York: Macmillan.

Pashukanis, E. B. 1978. *Law and Marxism: A General Theory*, edited by C. Arthur, translated by Barbara Einhorn. London: Ink Links. (Originally published 1924. Moscow: Communist Academy.)

Radzinowicz, L., and M. Wolfgang. 1971. "The Criminal in Confinement." In *Crime and Justice*, vol. 3, edited by L. Radzinowicz and M. Wolfgang. New York: Basic.

Rusche, G. 1980. "Labor Market and Penal Sanction: Thoughts on the Sociology of Punishment." In *Punishment and Penal Discipline*, edited by T. Platt and P. Takagi. Translated by Gerda Dinwiddie. (Originally published in *Zeitschrift für Sozialforschung* 2 [1933]: 63–73.)

Rusche, G., and O. Kirchheimer. 1968. *Punishment and Social Structure.* New York: Russell & Russell. (Originally published 1939. New York: Columbia University Press.)

Simon, J. 1985. "Back to the Future: Newman on Corporal Punishment." *American Bar Foundation Research Journal* 4:937–41.

Sparks, R. F. 1980. "A Critique of Marxist Criminology." In *Crime and Justice: An Annual Review of Research*, vol. 2, edited by N. Morris and M. Tonry. Chicago: University of Chicago Press.

Spierenburg, P. 1984*a*. "The Sociogenesis of Confinement and Its Development in Early Modern Europe." In *The Emergence of Carceral Institutions*, edited by P. Spierenburg. Rotterdam: Erasmus University.

———. 1984*b*. *The Spectacle of Suffering: Executions and the Evolution of Repression*. Cambridge: Cambridge University Press.

Spitzer, S. 1975. "Punishment and Social Organisation: A Study of Durkheim's Theory of Evolution." *Law and Society Review* 9:613–37.

Stone, L. 1979. *The Family, Sex and Marriage in England, 1500–1800*. Harmondsworth: Penguin.

———. 1987. *The Past and the Present Revisited*. London: Routledge & Kegan Paul.

Sykes, G. 1958. *The Society of Captives*. Princeton, N.J.: Princeton University Press.

Thomas, K. 1984. *Man and the Natural World*. Harmondsworth: Penguin.

Thompson, E. P. 1975. *Whigs and Hunters: The Origins of the Black Act*. Harmondsworth: Penguin.

van Krieken, R. 1989. "Violence, Self-Discipline and Modernity: Beyond the Civilizing Process." *Sociological Review* 37:193–218.

von Hirsch, A. 1985. *Past or Future Crimes?* Manchester: Manchester University Press.

Walker, N. 1969. *Sentencing in a Rational Society*. London: Allen Lane.

Wilson, J. Q. 1975. *Thinking about Crime*. New York: Basic.

Zimring, F. E., and G. Hawkins. 1986. *Capital Punishment and the American Agenda*. Cambridge: Cambridge University Press.

———. 1990. *The Scale of Imprisonment*. Chicago: University of Chicago Press (forthcoming).

Geoffrey Pearson

Drug-Control Policies in Britain

ABSTRACT

The British approach to heroin addiction has been widely misunderstood. The "British system" did not break down in the 1960s under the pressure of an upsurge in heroin misuse. The 1960s heroin phenomenon was a relatively minor difficulty almost entirely confined to London and failed to dislodge the medical profession from its central role in the British response to serious drug misuse. During the 1980s, however, a major heroin epidemic spread rapidly through a number of towns and cities in the North of England and Scotland, concentrated mainly in areas of high unemployment and social deprivation. Government-sponsored responses have included high-profile mass media campaigns and a strengthening of the law-enforcement effort. Even so, the "British system" has remained essentially intact. In response to the threat of drug-related HIV transmission, public health remedies have reasserted themselves against the prevailing rhetoric of "law and order."

The "British system" of drug-control and treatment policies, allowing a central role for medical practitioners and treatment philosophies, has often been contrasted with the enforcement-driven policies in the United States. The contrasts are such as to invite myth and countermyth about the "British system" (Moore 1985). The aim of this essay is to review and clarify the background and continuing development of drug policies and drug problems in Britain, both of which often depart quite sharply from the received understandings of the "British system" that have developed over the years.

Geoffrey Pearson is Wates Professor of Social Work, University of London, Goldsmiths' College. I would like to thank Joy Mott of the Home Office Research and Planning Unit, the staff of the Institute for the Study of Drug Dependence, and the National Drugs Intelligence Unit for their assistance on points of detail.

0192-3234/91/0014-0002$01.00

The central misunderstanding concerns the developments in the 1960s when, according to one version of events, Britain was consumed by a major problem of heroin misuse that led to the abandonment of the "British system" and tight restrictions on the rights of medical practitioners to prescribe controlled drugs. In retrospect, we can see that what occurred in the 1960s was a "miniepidemic" of heroin misuse that was almost entirely centered on London. Medical practitioners, moreover, retained a large degree of discretion and flexibility in terms of their actual practice.

By contrast, since the early 1980s, there has been a heroin epidemic of unparalleled proportions by British standards that has reached far beyond London and is particularly concentrated in areas of high socioeconomic deprivation (Pearson, Gilman, and McIver 1985, 1986; Dorn and South 1987; Pearson 1987*a*, 1987*b*; Parker, Bakx, and Newcombe 1988). Cocaine, however, remains largely a "champagne drug" and is known only intermittently on the streets. But this, too, may soon change. In 1988, for the first time, more cocaine than heroin was found in drug seizures in Europe as a whole (National Drugs Intelligence Unit 1989). This is one fundamental way, among others, in which British drug problems differ from those of North America and can be easily misunderstood as a consequence.

This essay reviews the evolution and development of British drug policies. In Section I, I describe some of the historical background and the crucial recommendations of the "Rolleston Committee" in the 1920s that established the framework of law and medical practices that survived until the late 1960s. Section II examines what has often been understood as the "breakdown" in these arrangements in the 1960s and the policy discussions that led to the creation of the new system of drug-treatment centers or "clinics," which removed from ordinary medical practitioners the right to prescribe heroin and cocaine to addicts. Section III briefly describes how the new clinic system adapted itself in the 1970s at a time when drug misuse in Britain seemed to have stabilized. Section IV offers a more detailed account of a dramatic change during the early 1980s when Britain suffered a major heroin epidemic, largely associated with the novel practice of "chasing the dragon" in socioeconomically deprived neighborhoods. Section V describes how the British government attempted to respond to this new problem, particularly through a series of mass media advertising campaigns and a strengthening of law-enforcement efforts. In Section VI, a new threat is described in the form of HIV and AIDS, which has led to a further transformation in policy responses that involves an increasing emphasis on "harm-reduction" strategies and has given a new lease on life to maintenance prescribing of substitute drugs. Finally, Section VII offers pointers for the future by exploring contradictions in current drug-control strategy as these show themselves in two areas of concern: the trend toward increasing international cooperation in drug-enforcement efforts in the European context, and the likely influence of drug-related HIV risk on relevant policy matters. Taken as a whole, the essay indicates that there is a persistent thread of continuity through which the "British system" retains the possibilities of a flexible and adaptable approach to drug problems.

The context in which this essay is written is therefore one of unrelenting change in the past five to ten years. It is all the more remarkable, then, that what is usually meant by the "British system"—a degree of flexibility and pragmatism in the ways in which enforcement strategies can cohere with an emphasis on medical and social services for drug misusers—is essentially intact. This is most evident in the British response to HIV and AIDS, which has assumed the form of public health remedies intended to reduce the possibilities of HIV transmission through high-risk activities, such as sharing injecting equipment. It is equally important to stress by way of introduction, however, that, in terms of the potential and actual damage to the nation's health, alcohol misuse remains the "favorite drug" of the British Isles (Royal College of Psychiatrists 1986, 1987*a*). There are also large numbers of people who experience serious problems with medically prescribed "tranquilizer" drugs, with recent estimates indicating between 250,000 and 1.25 million people at risk (Lacey and Woodward 1985; Cooper 1987). Nevertheless, it is illicit drug misuse that concerns us in this essay and, more specifically, heroin misuse. Given the fast-changing events of the past decade we await with interest, and a certain degree of trepidation, what the next twist in the tail of Britain's evolving drug problem will be.

I. The Evolution of Drug-Control Policies: Medicine, Morality, and Penal Sanctions

The history of drug controls is largely relevant to the twentieth century. In Britain's case, it is customary to take the deliberations of the Departmental Committee on Morphine and Heroin Addiction—the "Rolleston Committee," which reported in 1926—as the point of departure for the development of the "British system" of drug-control policies. This is in many ways appropriate, although it should not deflect attention away from the historical undertow of nineteenth-century opiate use, even though drug misuse had remained subject to only spasmodic attempts at regulation.

A. *The Nineteenth-Century Legacy*

In common with North America and other parts of Europe, opiate use had been quite widespread in Britain during the nineteenth century (Musto 1973; Berridge and Edwards 1981). It involved a variety of patent medicines for common ailments, as well as forms of "recreational" or "stimulant" use. The issue extended well beyond celebrated cases such as Thomas De Quincey's *Confessions of an Opium Eater* (1971). References to opium and laudanum are scattered throughout nineteenth-century English novels, reflecting middle-class patterns of self-medication, experimentation with drugs in literary and bohemian circles, and working-class uses of opium as a cheap intoxicant or as an aid to routine physical labor (Berridge and Edwards 1981; Lindop 1985; Hayter 1988).

In agricultural areas, such as the Fenlands, opium had been well integrated into the popular culture in the nineteenth century, whether as a remedy for aches and pains among adults, as a comforter for children during the teething period in the form of poppyhead tea, or as a means to improve the health of farm animals (Berridge 1977). In the course of the industrial revolution, however, public health concerns came to center on the dangers of opium use among the urban working class. One focus for concern was the intoxicant use of opiates by adults in the manufacturing districts. Another was the practice of "infant doping" by the use of household remedies, which were widely marketed under trade names such as "Soothing Syrup," "Nurses' Drops," "Mothers' Quietness," "Infants' Quietness," and "Pennyworth of Peace." In the late nineteenth century, sensational accounts of the menace of the Chinese "opium den" in the East End of London provided another source of apprehension within a wider set of public anxieties about the morals of the working class (Pearson 1983).

According to Berridge and Edwards (1981, pp. 102–4), in their major study of this period, *Opium and the People*, these nineteenth-century anxieties focused almost entirely on working-class habits, to the neglect of equally widespread patterns of middle-class opiate use and self-medication. The British experience had therefore been directly similar to that of North America, where drug use in the nineteenth century had been regarded as largely unproblematic, but with a tendency for social concern to focus around wider preoccupations with low-status social groups (Musto 1973). One important difference, however, concerned Britain's imperialist role, in which British economic interests had been central in promoting and extending the opium problem in the Far East (Greenberg 1951; Johnson 1975*a;* Fay 1976; Guan 1987). By the beginning of the twentieth century, the issue of opiate misuse had almost entirely receded in Britain as a domestic concern. The legacy of imperialist interests, however, lingered on, and these global economic and political concerns played a major influence in Britain's subsequent role in international negotiations on drug controls (Stein 1985).

On the domestic front, Britain had inherited a somewhat haphazard system of regulation from the nineteenth century. The Pharmacy Act of 1868 had placed restrictions on the sale of morphine and opium derivatives through pharmacists, while prohibiting their sale through grocers and general stores, although patent medicines were not brought within this system of regulation until the Poisons and Pharmacy Act of 1908. The care and control of those who became dependent on opiates had not been brought under any effective regulation, in spite of various attempts by medical practitioners to extend the provisions of the 1888 Inebriates Act, which allowed for the voluntary detention of "habitual drunkards" or "inebriates." Those who were certifiably insane by virtue of their drug taking could be confined to a lunatic asylum, and the provisions of the 1890 Lunacy Act allowed for a form of guardianship in which patients were deemed incapable of managing their affairs and for their property to be controlled—a provision that was sometimes applied to drug addicts. Not until the 1913 Mental Deficiency Act, however, was specific legislative provision made by which "any sedative, narcotic, or stimulant drug" should fall within the definition of an "intoxicant," thus allowing for "moral imbeciles" to be either confined within an institution or placed under guardianship (Berridge and Edwards 1981, pp. 119–22, 165–69, 212–15).

B. *The "Cocaine Crisis" of the Great War*

In the eighteenth and early nineteenth centuries addiction had been regarded as a "bad habit"; in the second half of the nineteenth century the approach became more fully "medicalized" (Berridge 1979). By the outbreak of the First World War opinion in Britain was divided between those who saw addiction as a medical problem and those who saw addiction as a vice that should be controlled through penal sanctions (Berridge 1979; Smart 1984). Nevertheless, it is noticeable that the criminal law had not been invoked, and Britain was to remain a somewhat reluctant partner to the 1912 Hague Opium Convention in terms of introducing domestic legislation, which was required as a signatory to this agreement. Britain's agreement had been secured, in fact, not out of any concern with domestic drug problems. Rather, it was a matter of compliance with external pressure arising from a complex series of international and diplomatic interests (Stimson 1984; Stein 1985).

Britain first invoked an overtly penal strategy against illicit drug use in somewhat unusual circumstances, in response to a perceived threat to the war effort during the Great War of 1914–18. It was, however, to prove a decisive shift. Given what has already been indicated about the marginality of cocaine in Britain, it is also something of a historical irony that anxieties about the spread of cocaine use provoked Britain's entry into drug criminalization. In 1916, amidst public scandal and press hysteria concerning prostitution and the supply of cocaine to troops, a regulation was introduced under the emergency wartime powers allowed by the Defence of the Realm Acts (DORA 40B) that prohibited the unauthorized possession of cocaine, which could only be supplied on prescription (Berridge 1978; Stein 1985). It is an indication of the continuing marginality of the British "drug problem," however, that the public impact of this regulation paled in significance when set against the reaction to restrictions placed on liquor licensing and the opening hours of public houses through DORA regulations (Marwick 1965). In spite of the temporary nature of the cocaine "crisis" of 1916, however, regulation DORA 40B instated an emphatically "criminal" stamp on the subsequent history of British drug-control policy by bringing the Home Office into "the central controlling position" (Berridge 1978, p. 293).

In the years immediately following the 1914–18 War, the British government edged toward a largely American-inspired prohibitionist approach through the Dangerous Drugs Acts of 1920 and 1923. The possession of opiates and cocaine was made illegal, unless supplied by a doctor, while the Home Secretary was authorized to regulate the manufacture, distribution, and sale of these substances. These legislative enactments were undoubtedly inspired by a "criminal" rather than by a "medical" model of addiction, leading Stimson and Oppenheimer (1982, p. 25) to observe that the Home Office "had successfully claimed the problem as a criminal and policing one." Amidst a climate of continuing press sensationalism and calls in Parliament for the flogging of alien drug traffickers in the early 1920s, "the disease concept of addiction and all that it entailed was under serious attack" (Berridge 1979, p. 84).

C. The Rolleston Committee: Medicine in Partnership with the State

A question remained as to the circumstances under which it was legitimate for a medical practitioner to prescribe drugs that had now been placed outside of the law. To answer this question, the Departmental Committee on Morphine and Heroin Addiction was established in 1924 by the Ministry of Health—to be chaired by Sir Humphrey Rolleston, president of the Royal College of Physicians—with the following brief: "To consider and advise on the circumstances, if any, in which the supply of morphine and heroin . . . to persons suffering from addiction to those drugs may be regarded as medically advisable, and as to the precautions which it is desirable that medical practitioners administering or prescribing morphine or heroin should adopt for the avoidance of abuse" (Ministry of Health 1926, p. 2).

The Rolleston Committee's terms of reference thus seemed straightforward enough, even allowing for the possibility that the phrase "if any" betrayed the need to nod in the direction of the powerful emergence of prohibitionist attitudes not only in North America but also in the British Home Office (Stimson 1984). The committee's conclusions, which can be equally briefly stated, were to provide the foundation stone of the "British system": the prescription of heroin and morphine to certain classes of addicts (those requiring gradual withdrawal, and also those incapable of withdrawal or whose social habits deteriorated when not supplied with "regular allowances" of the drug) was to be deemed a "legitimate medical treatment." Moreover, the control of prescribing practices was to be by professional self-regulation through a medical panel.

It would be a mistake, however, to see this outcome simply as the victory of the professional autonomy of medicine over state and police regulation. In spite of the acceptance of the Rolleston Committee's recommendations, the Home Office retained a major stake in the administration of the system, and unauthorized possession of defined substances remained a criminal offense. "Doctors henceforth were in partnership with the state," is how Berridge (1979, p. 85) describes the resulting compromise. Smart (1984), drawing on the influential work of Michel Foucault, has suggested that a more useful way of approaching the history and evolution of British drug policies is to adopt a nuanced understanding of the ways in which medical, moral, and penal discourses have intersected to generate increasingly extensive systems of regulation and control—in which "medical" arguments might seem often to operate as no more than a rhetoric around which such regulation is enforced and articulated. One might reflect, of course, on the extent to which medicine more generally—particularly psychiatry—has come to arbitrate in moral disputes (Szasz 1961, 1963; Pearson 1975). Thus, the idea that the outcome of the Rolleston Committee's deliberations and the ensuing "Rolleston era" represented a medical dominance, pure and simple, must be qualified on a number of grounds. Indeed, it is unlikely that British responses to drug problems would have retained the flexibility that has been in evidence in much more recent history if the paramount interests of any single professional group had been dominant to such an extent as is implied both by those who idolize and by those who denigrate the so-called British system.

II. The Rolleston Era and Its "Breakdown" in the 1960s

The success of the "Rolleston era" is legendary. In 1932 the annual report to the League of Nations on *Opium and Other Dangerous Drugs* stated confidently that "drug addiction is not prevalent in Great Britain" (Spear 1969, p. 248). Moreover, the vast majority of those addicts who did come to notice "were persons who had become addicted in the course of an illness (of therapeutic origin) and an appreciable proportion of the addicts were members of the medical profession" (Spear 1969, p. 248). The pattern remained essentially unchanged through the 1940s and 1950s, in spite of small circles of heroin and cannabis use that were largely centered on jazz clubs and other entertainment facilities in London that catered to foreign seamen and soldiers (Spear 1969; MacInnes 1985). British difficulties with heroin in particular therefore failed to echo the problems experienced in North America in the postwar years in the 1950s and 1960s (Chein et al. 1964; Feldman 1968; Preble and Casey 1969; Hughes et al. 1972; Hughes 1977). And it was in such a context that the "British system" of heroin maintenance came to be applauded by North American commentators as a means by which drug-related crime and the growth of an illicit "street market" had been prevented (Schur 1964).

However, it is important to stress that medical dominance has been given such prominence in our understanding of the evolution and development of British drug-control policies only because prescription of maintenance doses of heroin and cocaine to addicts was at such variance to the practice in the United States. In spite of passionate endorsements of the "British system" from North America (Judson 1973; Trebach 1982), it is highly questionable either whether the role of the medical profession deserves such prominence or that the control of drug misuse in Britain was a consequence of policy. It is increasingly common to assert that the failure of a drug problem to emerge in Britain (for whatever reason) enabled the policy to survive. In one particularly outspoken attack on "the so-called British system" and the idea that doctors had single-handedly held at bay the development of an American-sized drug problem until the 1960s, Kay (1987, p. 12) has suggested that "only the medical profession could give rise to a myth of such stunning arrogance." Downes (1977, p. 89) had earlier offered the blunt judgment that the British system "has now been well and truly exposed as little more than masterly inactivity in the face of what was an almost nonexistent addiction problem."

In the mid-1950s there were already "the first signs of an emerging drug-subculture" in the West End of London, organized around the dealing activities of a young man referred to as "Mark" (Spear 1969, p. 254). Although this circle of heroin and cannabis users was still quite tiny, it prompted the Ministry of Health in 1958 to convene an Interdepartmental Committee on Drug Addiction to review existing policy. The committee, chaired by Sir Russell Brain, concluded that addiction to dangerous drugs "is still very small" and arrived at the conclusion that the increase in addiction (from a total of 260 known addicts in 1954 to 437 in 1960, of whom only sixty-eight were addicted to heroin with the large majority addicted to either morphine or pethidine) reflected "an intensified activity for its detection and recognition over the postwar period." Correspondingly, the view was taken that the illicit trade in dangerous drugs remained "so small as to be almost negligible" (Ministry of Health 1961, p. 9). Reaffirming the principle of the Rolleston Committee that "addiction should be regarded as an expression of mental disorder rather than a form of criminal behaviour," the Brain Committee concluded that there was no evidence to suggest that the right of medical practitioners to prescribe dangerous drugs to addicts had led to any increase in the problem of addiction and that there was no need for any major reconsideration of the Rolleston assumptions.

Within less than four years, however, the Interdepartmental Committee on Drug Addiction was reconvened in what was perceived to be a markedly different context (Stimson and Oppenheimer 1982, pp. 44–

48). A large amount of public concern in 1964 focused on the use of amphetamine drugs ("pep pills" and "purple hearts") by young people, together with cannabis use. The total number of known addicts had almost doubled in the early 1960s, from 437 in 1960 to 753 in 1964; there were also signs that the number of heroin addicts of nontherapeutic origin was increasing, from a mere forty-seven in 1959, rising to 222 in 1963, and then to 328 in 1964 (Ministry of Health 1965, p. 14). Finally, the committee described a "significant change" in the age distribution of addicts, with a tendency for known addicts to be younger than formerly.

The details of the second Brain Committee's deliberations are discussed elsewhere (Stimson and Oppenheimer 1982, chap. 3), and only the broad outlines need concern us here. While reaffirming its earlier view that the addict "should be regarded as a sick person . . . and not as a criminal," the committee also dismissed fears that an illicit trade in dangerous drugs had become established. There was "no evidence of any significant traffic, organised or otherwise, in dangerous drugs that have been stolen or smuggled into this country" (Ministry of Health 1965, pp. 6, 8). Rather, the major source of supply was identified as a small number of doctors in London who were prescribing excessively large amounts of heroin to addicts who were under their care. The relevant passage in the report is worthy of quotation since it establishes a necessary context for understanding the changes in policy that were to be recommended:

> We were informed that in 1962 one doctor alone prescribed almost 600,000 tablets of heroin (i.e., 6 kilogrammes) for addicts. The same doctor, on one occasion, prescribed 900 tablets of heroin (9 grammes) to one addict and, three days later, prescribed for the same patient another 600 tablets (i.e., 6 grammes) "to replace pills lost in an accident." Further prescriptions of 720 (i.e., 7.2 grammes) and 840 (8.4 grammes) tablets followed later to the same patient. Two doctors each issued a single prescription for 1,000 tablets (i.e., 10 grammes). These are only the more startling examples. . . . Supplies on such a scale can easily provide a surplus that will attract new recruits to the ranks of the addicts. [Ministry of Health 1965, p. 6]

The committee recommended that tighter controls were necessary on the supply of such drugs to addicts, although "we remain convinced that the doctor's right to prescribe dangerous drugs without restriction for the ordinary patient's needs should be maintained." These controls, it was suggested, should take the form of a system of notification of addicts whereby doctors would be under a statutory duty to notify a central authority of any unregistered addicts with whom they came into professional contact. Specialist drug-treatment centers should be established, at least in the London area, and only the staff of such treatment centers should retain the right to prescribe heroin and cocaine to drug addicts. Finally, the committee recommended that treatment centers should have powers to detain addicts for compulsory treatment where this was felt to be necessary.

With the exception of the question of compulsory treatment, the committee's recommendations were accepted by the Minister of Health and the Home Secretary, although it took more than two years before the Dangerous Drugs Act of 1967 was passed by Parliament, introducing the necessary legislation to implement the proposals. The major shift of emphasis implied by the second Brain report was that a responsibility would be placed on the medical profession not only to treat patients but also to control the supply of drugs and the spread of addiction, although the profession should not be dislodged from its central role in the management of drug addiction. This is taken by Stimson and Oppenheimer (1982, p. 52) to have involved a crucial reformulation of the medical model, which was to determine the path taken by the newly created drug-treatment centers in the course of the 1970s.

The recommendations of the second Brain Committee were received amidst a further intensification of public anxiety about drug misuse. In 1965, the grandson of the former Prime Minister Harold Macmillan died of an overdose in Oxford, and two years later Mick Jagger of the Rolling Stones was imprisoned for the possession of a small quantity of amphetamine sulphate. Further concern centered on the growing popularity of cannabis together with the question of LSD, which received massive publicity during 1967 with the appearance of the *Sergeant Pepper* "psychedelic" album by the Beatles. In the following year, agitation for the decriminalization of cannabis was given cautious encouragement by the Advisory Committee on Drug Dependence, which took the view that "the dangers of its use . . . and the risk of progression to opiates have been overstated, and that the existing criminal sanctions intended to curb its use are unjustifiably severe" (Home Office 1968*a*, p. v). Nevertheless, given the social climate the proposal predictably failed to make any headway. Although Britain's experience of the "flower power" and "hippie" movements never approached the scale of that in the United States, throughout Europe there were waves of student protest and increasing agitation around the war in Vietnam, through and beyond the events of May 1968 in Paris. The "youth question" was a matter of high public profile, and a concern with drug misuse was a constant accompaniment to this preoccupation that amounted to a sustained "moral panic" throughout the period (Halloran, Elliott, and Murdock 1970; Young 1971*a*, 1971*b*; Cohen 1972). It was in this social climate that, after a period of some hesitation and confusion about the status of the new drug-treatment centers, regulations were eventually introduced in April 1968 that prohibited ordinary medical practitioners from prescribing heroin and cocaine to addicts. This, according to one version of events, was the end of the "British system," which had broken down under the pressures of the 1960s. Or was it?

III. The New Clinic System of the 1970s

Even otherwise careful observers have sometimes overstated the scale of the changes that occurred in Britain during the 1960s, with a further consequence that subsequent developments have also been liable to misunderstanding. According to Laurie (1967, p. 20), for example, the second Brain Committee had been faced with "a sudden rush of new young addicts"; whereas, in fact, there were only forty known addicts under twenty years of age in the whole of Britain at this time (Ministry of Health 1965, p. 5). Similarly, Kaplan (1983, pp. 157–58), in an acerbic and methodical critique of heroin maintenance policies, describes the "breakdown of the system" in equally dramatic terms: "between 1961 and 1969 the number of British addicts increased more than fivefold," the "kind of addict changed dramatically," and this "quickly destroyed the British system." And yet, at the point when the drug-treatment centers were introduced in 1968, there were still fewer than 1,000 heroin addicts undergoing treatment in Britain, of whom only 147 were to be found outside of London (Home Office 1968*b*, p. 25). Moreover, the second Brain report asserted that "not more than six doctors" had been involved in the prescribing of excessive amounts of dangerous drugs to their patients (Ministry of Health 1965, p. 6). Can this in any meaningful sense be described as the "breakdown" of an entire system?

In retrospect, what happened in London in the late 1960s was a "miniepidemic" of almost negligible proportions in national terms. The immediate effect of the establishment of the drug-treatment centers (or "clinics" as they are more commonly known) was to lead to a further increase in the official numbers of heroin addicts as the notification system came into force. As a consequence, not much more than one-quarter of the 1,999 patients entering treatment during 1968 were previously known to the Home Office. Thereafter, the position rapidly stabilized with the numbers of newly notified addicts each year declining and a sharp fall in the number of addicts under the age of twenty years from 1969 onward (Johnson 1975*b*).

The subsequent development of the clinics has been charted in considerable detail by means of a ten-year follow-up study of one-third of addicts attending London drug-dependency units as outpatients in 1969 who were originally receiving prescriptions for heroin (Stimson 1973; Stimson and Oppenheimer 1982). At the end of this ten-year period, 38 percent of the original sample "had become abstinent from opiates and were leading reasonably ordinary lives with no major problems with other drugs"; 38 percent were still attending clinics and receiving prescriptions; and 15 percent had died. The remaining 9 percent were of "equivocal or uncertain status" (Stimson and Oppenheimer 1982, p. 5).

The clinics had moved swiftly in many cases in transferring patients from heroin to injectable methadone, later shifting toward oral methadone as a preferred method for treating heroin addicts—whether by means of a detoxification regime or maintenance prescriptions. These changes in treatment philosophy, as Stimson and Oppenheimer describe them, seem more likely to have been the result of frustrations and overwork rather than a planned policy. Having been initially overwhelmed by demands on the clinic system, medical personnel were faced with sometimes hostile and manipulative patients, and the quantity of drugs to be prescribed was regularly a focus for bargaining and argument. Staff were also confronted with a role conflict, between care and control, experiencing a growing dissatisfaction with maintenance regimes that simply preserved the status quo, but with no evident therapeutic benefits.

One illustration of these dynamics was the reception by clinic staff of research that contrasted the effectiveness of maintenance strategies using either injectable heroin or oral methadone (Mitcheson and Hartnoll 1978; Hartnoll et al. 1980). The research concluded that heroin prescriptions kept addicts in contact with the clinic and therefore might be a more effective system of "control," but the refusal to prescribe heroin suggested a more confrontational stance that might be thought to be conducive to "therapeutic" change. These changes were found to be unpredictable, however, in that, while they were associated overall with a higher abstinence rate, they also led to an increased amount of illicit drug involvement and criminal activity. These findings, Stimson and Oppenheimer (1982) noted, were widely misinterpreted by clinic staff in London, who used them to support their increasing dissatisfaction with maintenance as a "nontherapeutic" control strategy in favor of the increasing trend toward a more "confrontational" stance: "as so often happens in medicine and more generally in science, it did not matter to clinicians what the precise results were. What concerned them more, as several consultants indicated, was that here was scientific justification for a policy change that was already emerging from the work context" (Stimson and Oppenheimer 1982, p. 219).

Elsewhere, reflecting on thirty years' involvement in the drugs field, Connell (1986, p. 463) has advanced a similar view that, during the 1970s, "in the absence of research data, methods of treatment and management, whether inpatient or outpatient, were bound to reflect the whims, idiosyncracies and philosophical concepts of those in charge." The medical profession, as Connell also makes clear, had only reluctantly embraced "the notion of the 'stabilised addict' and of prescribing heroin and cocaine to addicts" in the wake of the second Brain report. Treatment policy, to put it bluntly, was being made on the hoof throughout the 1970s, with wide variations in approach and philosophy confirmed by a national survey of drug-dependence facilities conducted in 1982 (Smart 1985).

If the earlier "British system," to follow Downes (1977), had been one of masterly inactivity in response to a nonexistent problem, then what can we say of the clinic system during the 1970s? Looked at in its most general terms, the problem of heroin misuse had largely stabilized during the 1970s. If the official statistics of notified addicts showed a slight tendency to increase during this period, then this was offset by a leveling off in the numbers of people found guilty of drug offenses, together with an increase in the average age of newly notified addicts and an even more marked increase in the average age of drug offenders—from twenty-two years in 1973 to twenty-six years in 1980 (Home Office 1984). This would tend to suggest that both the medical and penal systems were coming into contact with an aging cohort of heroin users who had been washed ashore by the miniepidemic of the late 1960s. In a retrospective analysis of the ten-year period of operation of the new system, Edwards (1979) seemed entirely justified in taking the view that the British drug problem had become becalmed.

IV. The Heroin Epidemic of the 1980s

No sooner had these soothing retrospective judgments on the 1970s been announced than the storm broke, and this time it was for real: Britain was plunged into a heroin epidemic in the early 1980s from which it has yet to recover. In 1983, the number of heroin seizures doubled over the previous year, with a sixfold increase compared to the annual average for 1973–78. There was a 42 percent increase in the number of addicts notified to the Home Office, with a 50 percent increase in the number of new addicts notified in 1983 as against 1982 (Home Office 1984). The trend, which had already been established a year or two earlier although at a much less accelerated pace, was almost entirely confined to heroin misuse. And it was set to continue, so that by 1985 the number of newly notified heroin addicts had reached 5,930—a fivefold increase in the figure recorded in 1980, with a fourfold increase in persons found guilty of drug offenses in connection with heroin (Home Office 1987*a*). In 1986 and 1987, this trend appeared to level off, and there was even a recorded decrease in the number of newly notified heroin addicts to 4,082 by 1987. One would expect a heroin epidemic to "peak out" in this way (Hunt and Chambers 1976; Parker, Bakx, and Newcombe 1988), although it is not clear to what extent these declines might also have reflected alterations in the notification procedures that followed the introduction of a new computer system. Indeed, the numbers of drug addicts recorded as receiving notifiable drugs in treatment continued to increase, with the numbers receiving methadone almost doubling between 1984 and 1987 from 5,160 to 9,763, having already more than doubled between 1980 and 1984 (Home Office 1988*a*).

A. *Counting Heads: Uncertainties in the Notification System*

Taking a deep statistical breath, if one combines the figures for new notifications with those of renotifications of former addicts and those receiving treatment, there were something like 15,000 known drug misusers in Britain by the mid-1980s and more than 19,000 by 1988. Of course, the official statistics can only scratch the surface of the problem. Not only do many heroin users fail to register with doctors, but it is widely acknowledged that the notification system itself is imperfect. Two things need to be said about this.

The first is that important methodological developments have recently been made in attempts to estimate the actual numbers of drug users as against the numbers reflected in official statistics (Hartnoll et al. 1985*a*). Research in two areas of London in the early 1980s suggested that the number of notified addicts was approximately one-fifth of the actual number of regular opioid users in the local population (Hartnoll et al. 1985*b*). It is necessary to treat "multipliers" such as these with caution since they may well vary between different localities and across time. On these estimates, however, it is possible that there were already 50,000 regular opioid users in 1983 (Hartnoll et al. 1985*b*, p. 205). More recently, the Advisory Council on the Misuse of Drugs (1988, p. 13) has hazarded a guess that "there might have been between 75,000 and 150,000 misusers of notifiable drugs in the U.K. during 1986." This, it will be recognized, is a far cry from the "miniepidemic" of the late 1960s that, on some accounts, brought about the downfall of the "British system" (see fig. 1).

The second thing that has to be said is that, if by the "British system" one means the right of ordinary medical practitioners to prescribe notifiable drugs, then it was a peculiar kind of downfall. In spite of the restrictions on prescribing heroin and cocaine that came about with the creation of the clinic system, general practitioners continued to play a central role in the management of drug misuse and were still permitted to prescribe opioids such as methadone and Diconal (dipipanone). This continuing centrality of the role of general practitioners is one more issue that has often been overlooked by those who pronounce on the "breakdown" of the "British system" in the late 1960s. Through the 1970s there had actually been a steady expansion of the role of general practitioners, with the proportion of new notifications of addicts from this source increasing from 15 percent in 1970 to 53 percent in 1981 (Ashton 1987). A national survey conducted in 1985 estimated that, in a four-week period in England and Wales, there would be something in the region of 9,500 general practitioner consultations with patients who were misusing opiates (Glanz and Taylor 1986). This could mean that, from this source alone, there might be somewhere between 30,000 and 40,000 new addicts per year coming to notice, confirming that general practitioners had a major stake in the issue even if their activity was often hidden or overlooked. Surprisingly little is known about this fundamental area of service provision, although recent research has indicated that the work of general practitioners is beset with numerous difficulties when attempting to manage drug-misusing patients. These

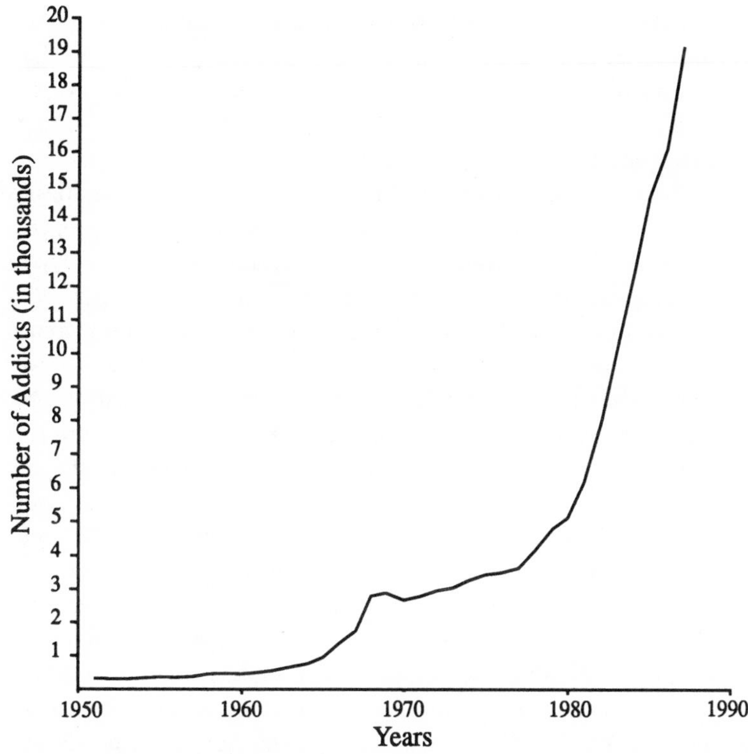

FIG. 1.—Addicts known to the Home Office, 1951–88. Source.—Spear (1969); Home Office (personal communication).

patients present a continuing challenge to the therapeutic identities of medical practitioners, tending to turn medical consultations into bargaining sessions about the quantity of drugs to be prescribed that can also be manipulative and hostile (McKeganey 1988; McKeganey and Boddy 1988).

In attempting to arrive at sound estimates of the actual numbers of those who misuse drugs, it is to be anticipated that the administration and efficiency of the notification system and, consequently, prescribing policies would be more variable where general practitioners were concerned. Indeed, in its 1982 report on *Treatment and Rehabilitation*, the Advisory Council had expressed deep concern about "profound differences in professional opinion on the prescribing of opioids," taking a view that "dubious practices have escaped the censure they merit" (Advisory Council on the Misuse of Drugs 1982, pp. 28, 57). There was certainly some evidence at this time of leakages of opiates into the street market through overprescribing (Advisory Council on the Misuse of Drugs 1982, p. 53; Burr 1983*a*, 1983*b*). Further concern centered on the security of controlled drugs held by retail pharmacists against the possibilities of burglary (Advisory Council on the Misuse of Drugs 1983; Laycock 1984).

The Advisory Council's worries therefore ran beyond difficulties in estimating the extent to which the notification system was properly used by general practitioners. In 1982 it was also found necessary to urge that restrictions on the right to prescribe controlled drugs should be extended to include Diconal, which had become a drug of preference in some localities (Pearson, Gilman, and McIver 1986; Gilman 1988*a*). As a consequence, new guidelines were subsequently issued on prescribing practices for medical practitioners (Department of Health and Social Security 1984). In response to the "dubious practices" of some medical practitioners, the Advisory Council (1982, p. 53) was also sufficiently moved to describe what it saw as "a recurrence of the problem that caused concern to the second Brain Committee"—namely, overprescribing practices fueling the illicit street market in opiates.

Saddled with this historically conceived preoccupation of regulating the means by which the medical profession supposedly controlled the supply of notifiable drugs, however, here at a crucial point in the development of the 1980s heroin epidemic, the Advisory Council was simply looking the wrong way. The explosion in heroin misuse that was already gathering pace had little to do with the medical profession, either in general practice or in the specialist clinics. Rather, it could be described as a consequence of failure in the area of drug-control policy that had been so neglected in Britain—that is, enforcement. The emergence of the 1980s heroin epidemic was associated with the arrival of heroin in cheap and plentiful supply through new distribution routes from Southwest Asia—Iran, Pakistan, and Afghanistan. One of the first warning shots about the new problem came from the trade union representing customs and excise staff, arguing that reductions in staffing levels as a consequence of government policies designed to contain public expenditure were damaging the effort to curb the importation of heroin and other illicit drugs (Society of Civil and Public Servants 1984*a*, 1984*b*). Insofar as heroin itself was concerned, field research has confirmed that, from 1979 or thereabouts, the drug started to become available in cheap and plentiful supply, sustaining a high level of purity, with street prices in London declining by something like 25 percent between 1980 and 1983 (Lewis et al. 1985).

B. The New Heroin Users: Geographical and Cultural Diversity

The change that was to overcome the British drug problem in the course of the 1980s was one of both scale and geographical variation. Heroin misuse became a serious problem in many towns and cities in the North of England and Scotland where heroin had been previously almost unknown. One of the earliest indications of the change was from Glasgow, where a sharp increase of heroin misuse was noted during 1981 (Ditton and Speirits 1981). At first this had appeared to be an isolated occurrence and even led to some controversy among drug specialists in Scotland that a "moral panic" was being fueled unnecessarily. However, subsequent research confirmed that not only was Glasgow a major site of heroin misuse, but also that epidemic forms of misuse had developed in other parts of Scotland such as Edinburgh (Haw 1985; Ditton and Taylor 1987; McKeganey and Boddy 1987; Morrison 1988).

A couple of years earlier, an unpublished fieldwork report had noted the appearance of imported heroin from Southwest Asia in the city of Bradford, in West Yorkshire in the north of England, at an absurdly low street price of thirty-five to forty pounds per gram at a time when the going rate was eighty to one hundred pounds per gram in London (Fox 1979). This was such an unusual occurrence that it had not led to any immediate or observable change in the local drug scene, and the report had commented that "most people felt that cheap heroin was just a flash in the pan." Late in 1983 and the early months of 1984, however, rumors began to circulate in Liverpool and the surrounding Merseyside region of an emerging heroin problem that came to be associated with young working-class people on socially deprived public housing estates—to the accompaniment of a substantial amount of sensational press coverage that dubbed Merseyside as "Smack City." Research subsequently established that, in both the city of Liverpool and the neighboring Wirral peninsula, there had been an explosion of heroin misuse (Parker, Bakx, and Newcombe 1986, 1988; Fazey 1987; Chadwick and Parker 1988). A certain amount of journalistic attention was also turned toward housing estates in deprived areas of inner London—such as Southwark, which lies south of the River Thames—where new words and phrases such as "skag" and "chasing the dragon" were perhaps first reported in Britain (Picardie and Wade 1985). Ethnographic fieldwork in the same areas of London has since provided details of the onset and development of this new phenomenon (Burr 1987, 1989).

By 1985, it was possible to confirm that local heroin epidemics were well established, not only in cities such as Liverpool and Glasgow but also in many other towns and cities of the north of England such as Sheffield, Carlisle, and Manchester (Pearson, Gilman, and McIver 1985, 1986). The scale of the changes should not be underestimated. In the Wirral peninsula alone detailed prevalence estimates indicated that, by 1987, there were some 5,000 regular heroin users; in 1980 there were fewer than a hundred people using opiates (Parker, Bakx, and Newcombe 1988, p. 76).

The problem nevertheless remained highly scattered and localized, with distinct regional variations and a tendency for heroin misuse to be densely concentrated in certain neighborhoods and not others (Haw 1985; Pearson, Gilman, and McIver 1986; Fazey 1987; Parker, Bakx, and Newcombe 1988). Some indication can be given of these variations. On the basis of broad-based surveys it is possible to estimate that, even among high-risk groups such as those aged sixteen to twenty-four years, the likelihood that someone had tried heroin even once would be no more than 0.5 percent (Plant, Peck, and Samuel 1985, p. 77). In some neighborhoods of Merseyside, however, as many as 2 percent of the entire sixteen to twenty-four years age group would be in treatment at the local clinic for drug addiction (Fazey 1987, p. 78). In one township in the Wirral peninsula where the problem was particularly severe, as many as 8.6 percent of the sixteen- to twenty-four-year-old age group were known heroin users, although not necessarily undergoing treatment (Parker, Bakx, and Newcombe 1988, p. 69).

One crucial determinant of this diversity was the tendency for heroin misuse to be associated with high levels of unemployment and other forms of social deprivation (Pearson 1987*b*). The heroin epidemic had developed, of course, at a time when unemployment was rapidly increasing in the British Isles, and a study of national trends had established a correlation between illicit drug use and unemployment (Peck and Plant 1986). These relations were even more marked at the neighborhood level, with a number of local and regional studies indicating a tendency for heroin misuse to be densely concentrated in areas of high socioeconomic deprivation (Haw 1985; Pearson, Gilman, and McIver 1986; Fazey 1987; Parker, Bakx, and Newcombe 1988). This is not to suggest that there is any simple causal relation between unemployment and heroin misuse, and the relations are undoubtedly no less complex than those existing between crime and unemployment (Hakim 1982; Box 1987; Carlen 1988). The role of housing markets and housing conditions is one crucial factor. These have a general significance in understanding local crime profiles (Bottoms and Wiles 1986) and are equally important in shaping the geographical clustering of heroin misuse alongside social deprivation (Pearson 1987*b*). Nevertheless, by whatever mechanism, the British experience in the 1980s confirmed the tendency in the United States in an earlier period for heroin use to be associated with areas of urban deprivation (Chein et al. 1964; Feldman 1968; Preble and Casey 1969; Johnson et al. 1985).

In other respects, however, the British heroin scene is significantly different from that of the United States. One major difference is the question of race and ethnicity. Although the new heroin users were drawn disproportionately from poor areas, the overwhelming tendency was for heroin users to be white, in spite of the aggravated circumstances of unemployment and social deprivation among black and other minority ethnic groups (Runnymede Trust 1981; Smith 1981; Brah 1986; Pearson 1987*a*, pp. 124–26). There has been little sustained research on the question of drug misuse and minority ethnic groups (Gabe and Thorogood 1986; Gabe 1988). It is nevertheless generally agreed that black people have been almost totally unknown within the heroin epidemic of the 1980s, possibly reflecting deep cultural taboos within the British Afro-Caribbean tradition against heroin as a "dirty white man's drug." The same is not true, of course, where cannabis is concerned, which remains not only the most commonly used illicit drug in Britain (Mott 1985) but has also accounted for 90–95 percent of all drug seizures in the period from 1977 to 1987 (Home Office 1988*a*). Questions of race and racism have figured prominently in public debates on the enforcement of cannabis legislation, and although crude stereotypes that depict the Afro-Caribbean community as uniformly devoted to "ganja" use are grossly inaccurate, it nevertheless remains true that both cannabis use and cannabis dealing have a well-established place within the "hustling" traditions of some black communities (Pryce 1979). The background to some instances of the social disorder that has visited inner-city areas of Britain during the 1980s—such as the riots in the St. Paul's area of Bristol in 1980, in the Brixton area of London in 1981, and in the Handsworth area of Birmingham in 1985—has involved accusations and counteraccusations of resistance by black youth to drug raids by the police and saturation policing by means of "stop and search" tactics directed against cannabis possession and dealing (Scarman 1981; Benyon and Solomos 1987; Solomos 1988). While many commentators have skirted around what is seen as the delicate issue of the policing of cannabis in black communities (Rex 1987, p. 109), it remains a highly contentious matter in some multiracial areas (Sampson et al. 1988; Pearson et al. 1989). Indeed, this only serves to underline the fact that, in spite of the high profile given to the policing of black communities in Britain, black and other minority groups were notable only by their absence during the heroin epidemic of the 1980s.

C. *"Chasing the Dragon": A New Style of Use and Drug-related Crime*

In addition to its clear association with social deprivation and uniform ethnic composition, undoubtedly the most distinctive feature of the heroin epidemic was its connection with the novel practice of smoking the drug through heating it on metal foil—"chasing the dragon," as it came to be known by some obscure linguistic dispersal of the expression from the Hong Kong Cantonese dialect, *Júi Lùng*. The older, much smaller heroin-using subculture of the 1960s and 1970s had been devoted to injection as a means of administration, and there had also been a further spread of injection practices in the "polydrug" phase of the later 1970s when the highly dangerous practice of injecting barbiturates had been fashionable in some localities including London (Ghodse 1977*a*, 1977*b;* Jamieson, Glanz, and McGregor 1984). The use of amphetamines (known colloquially as "speed" or "whizz") had also sometimes been associated with self-injection practices. However, the recognition in the early 1980s that the newly imported "brown" heroin could be smoked (it was, in fact, a Southwest Asian preparation of heroin intended for smoking) undoubtedly helped to accelerate the dispersal of the heroin habit within those communities where it had recently appeared since it removed a formidable cultural barrier against self-injection.

The question of injection was to assume a new significance, of course, in the context of HIV transmission and AIDS and is discussed in more detail in a later section. It is sufficient to say at this point that, although "chasing the dragon" was undoubtedly a predominant feature in the emergence of the heroin epidemic, in common with the widespread geographical variations already noted there were also crucial variations in some localities in the extent to which heroin was either smoked or injected. The "new" heroin could be rendered soluble for injection purposes if it was acidified, usually by means of a "jiff lemon," citric crystals, or a drop of vinegar. In areas such as Merseyside or Manchester, "chasing" was the dominant route of drug administration; in other areas self-injection was much more common even in the early stages of the epidemic.

A crucial determinant of these variations was whether injection techniques were already widely used within local drug subcultures prior to the first availability of heroin in plentiful supply between 1979 and 1981. Research undertaken in 1985 on behalf of the Health Education Council found widespread abhorrence and mistrust of needles and injection in many areas, indicating largely a fear of the unknown (i.e., self-injection) rather than any informed health awareness by drug users (Pearson, Gilman, and McIver 1986). Nevertheless, occasional experimentation with injection techniques—either in times of local scarcities of heroin when injection was a more economically efficient means of administration, or as a matter of curiosity—was probably quite common, even among those heroin users who preferred to smoke the drug (Pearson 1987*a*). By contrast, in those localities where there had been preestablished drug subcultures involving the injection of amphetamines and other drugs—known according to regional variation as "fixing," "shooting up," "jacking up," "jagging," or "having a dig"—it seemed much more likely that heroin would be injected as soon as it became locally available and that injection practices would be dominant. These local subcultural variations clearly have a considerable bearing on strategies intended to contain the threat of HIV infection among drug users.

Another significant question, both in terms of the overall character of heroin misuse and the relevance of service provision, is that of gender relations (Ettorre 1989). As might have been anticipated, the new heroin problem of the 1980s was largely a male phenomenon. Female drug misuse is much more likely to involve other substances, such as medically prescribed psychotropic drugs (Institute for the Study of Drug Dependence 1980). Estimates of the male to female ratio among heroin users as a consequence of the 1960s miniepidemic in London were that men outnumbered women by a factor of almost three to one (Stimson and Oppenheimer 1982). This appears to have been largely unchanged during the 1980s, although there are some indications of a larger proportion of women among notified addicts (Home Office 1988*a*). Research on Merseyside has confirmed a similar gender ratio, with a slight tendency for there to be more women among those heroin users unknown to official agencies (Parker, Bakx, and Newcombe 1988, p. 77). The specific circumstances of female heroin use remain largely unexplored (Rosenbaum 1981; Carlen 1988). It is nevertheless generally agreed that, when treatment services remain male-dominated in their orientation, many female drug misusers will be deterred from seeking help (Drugs Alcohol Women Nationally 1985; Ettorre 1989). This therefore poses a significant problem in relation to a number of issues, such as HIV preventive work, the relations between drug misuse and prostitution, and drug misuse and child protection (Parker and Chadwick 1987; Plant et al. 1989).

One final question that must be noted at this point is the extent to which the heroin epidemic was connected with increased levels of crime. The drugs-crime connection has, of course, long been established in North America (Inciardi 1981; Chaiken and Chaiken 1990). In Britain, by contrast, research evidence has not always supported such connections. The evidence has tended to suggest both that drug misuse is not inevitably linked to crime and that, even where such links can be established, a high proportion of heroin addicts were already involved in delinquent activity before they became involved in illicit drug misuse (Mott 1981). Analysis of the criminal careers of notified addicts and drug offenders has confirmed that both groups will tend to have a higher level of involvement in acquisitive crime (Home Office 1985*a*, 1987*b*). There is remaining uncertainty from these sources as to what extent drug use and crime are causally related, however, with further caution expressed by Mott (1986) about the degree to which one should place reliance on official notification records and formal criminal convictions when attempting to assess the relations between opioid use and crime.

To some extent, these remaining uncertainties reflect the fact that research into criminological aspects of drug misuse remains relatively undeveloped in Britain (Pearson 1989*a*). For example, of 161 current drug-related research projects known to the Institute for the Study of Drug Dependence research register in 1987, the number of these with a relevance to criminal justice and penal matters was still "strikingly low" (South 1987, p. 7). The immaturity of the British research tradition in this respect follows to some extent from the low profile given until recently to enforcement strategies within drug-control policies. As a result of the 1980s heroin epidemic, however, some interest in the drugs-crime connection has been stimulated.

There is continuing support for the view that "crime causes drug misuse." According to this account, when heroin initially became more readily available it assumed the form of a commodity within the "hidden economy." Those who were already involved in delinquent activities and more familiar with illicit economic transactions, such as the handling of stolen goods, would be more likely to come into contact with the drug; thus confirming the view that the drugs-crime connection resulted from people with previous criminal convictions subsequently becoming involved with heroin (Auld, Dorn, and South 1986; Burr 1987). Social processes such as these would also consolidate the tendency for heroin misuse to be densely concentrated in areas of high social deprivation as a consequence of both strong economic pressures leading to a greater demand for stolen goods and greater likelihood that young people involved in lifestyles that imply a high degree of risk taking will be attracted to the notoriety of heroin—thus once more replicating some aspects of the experience in ghetto areas of the United States (Feldman 1968; Preble and Casey 1969; Johnson et al. 1985; Burr 1987; Pearson 1987*b*).

Other recent British research has pointed to a direct and unqualified relation between heroin misuse and acquisitive crime, as a means by which heroin users finance their habits. A study of London-based heroin users, for example, has shown that their criminal convictions more than doubled following the onset of regular heroin use (Jarvis and Parker 1989). An earlier study in the context of the formidable heroin epidemic on the Wirral peninsula of Merseyside had indicated that the region had suffered an unparalleled increase in burglary offenses between 1979 and 1985 when set against national crime statistics (Parker and Newcombe 1987). The Wirral research found that a sample of young adults appearing before the court included a significant number of heroin users; these were both people whose criminal involvement had preceded the onset of their heroin use and a group whose criminal careers were highly atypical in that they had passed through the "peak age" for delinquency of sixteen years without receiving criminal convictions and had only subsequently become involved in acquisitive crime. This innovative research would therefore appear to have squared the circle, reconciling the two sides of the long-standing argument as to whether "heroin use causes crime" or "crime causes heroin use." Even so, this is not to everyone's satisfaction, with recent Scottish research once again calling the relation between opioid use and crime into question (Hammersley et al. 1989). One particularly significant finding from the Wirral project, however, was that no relation could be established within the individual criminal careers of heroin users with regard to typical nonacquisitive crimes such as vandalism and "joy riding," even though the local heroin epidemic had been associated with a dramatic and otherwise inexplicable increase in acquisitive crime (Parker and Newcombe 1987).

In summary, setting to one side remaining points of difficulty and argument, by the late 1980s it could be said with confidence that, in some areas of Britain at least, a pattern of criminal involvement by heroin users had become established that would be entirely familiar in North America. The heroin epidemic settled into areas of high social deprivation where there were few competing viable lifestyles available to young people. The means by which young people living in such neighborhoods came into contact with heroin was through friendship networks, rather than the discredited notion of "pushers" as the means by which people are first introduced to heroin (Hughes and Crawford 1972; Bennett and Wright 1986; Pearson 1987*a*). Once having established itself, the heroin habit moved rapidly through these networks and became associated with the hectic lifestyle of "taking care of business" (Preble and Casey 1969). Britain had been a late developer when set against the experience of the United States. Nevertheless, once its heroin problem had assumed maturity, the problems over which a previous generation had agonized—the so-called downfall of the "British system" in the late 1960s—began to fall into perspective.

V. Policy Responses in the 1980s: A New Emphasis on Prevention and Enforcement

Alarmed by some of the early indications of this upsurge in heroin misuse, the government appointed a ministerial subcommittee that first met in July 1984. In March of the following year a strategy document was issued, *Tackling Drug Misuse*, which has now appeared in its third revised edition (Home Office 1985*b*, 1988*b*). Simultaneous action was proposed on five main fronts: "reducing supplies from abroad; making enforcement even more effective; maintaining effective deterrents and tight domestic controls; developing prevention; and improving treatment and rehabilitation" (Home Office 1988*b*, p. 7). One important shift of emphasis was that enforcement measures were given a much higher priority than they had formerly assumed in British drug-control policies, at least insofar as they were firmly situated within what was intended as an interlocking strategy. If we set law-enforcement developments to one side for a moment, however, this strategy involved two broad initiatives on the domestic front: the enhancement of health education programs, including a series of high-profile mass media campaigns that began early in 1985, together with a Central Funding Initiative (CFI) to improve services for drug misusers.

A. Treatment and Prevention Strategies

Detailed reviews of the outcome of the Central Funding Initiative are to be found elsewhere (MacGregor, Ettorre, and Coomber 1987; MacGregor 1989). By 1987, the total sum allocated through the CFI was 17.5 million pounds, by means of 188 grants to local and regional projects that ranged "from clinics, drug-screening equipment and nurse training courses to counselling services, telephone help-lines, rehabilitation hostels and therapy services for drug misusers and their families" (Home Office 1988*b*, p. 31). Approximately two-thirds of this expenditure had been channeled through the statutory sector, with slightly more than one-half of it directed toward community-based projects. There was already experience of nonmedical community-based "street agencies" in some areas such as London (Dorn and South 1985), but the promotion of innovative community services was one important outcome of the government funding initiative, serving both as an alternative approach to the treatment and rehabilitation of drug users and also as a necessary adjunct to badly overstretched clinics (Strang 1989). A further consequence of the lack of adequate facilities in many areas had been the growth in the mid-1980s of grass-roots organizations such as parents' groups and other self-help and mutual aid community networks (Pearson, Gilman, and McIver 1986; Donoghoe et al. 1987; Dorn, Ribbens, and South 1987). In some localities, it was initiatives such as these that led to the establishment of formal systems of service provision (Social Services Inspectorate 1986).

Whatever the benefits of the CFI, there can be little doubt that the amount of funding made available (initially limited to a three-year pump-priming basis) was inadequate to meet the sharp increase in demand for treatment and rehabilitation resources. In Liverpool, for example, where a new outpatient clinic was established in 1985, it was almost immediately faced with operating difficulties owing to overwhelming demand (Fazey 1987). More generally, while noting that "existing services are woefully inadequate to cope with the increasing pressure" and demanding "an immediate, determined response from government," the Parliamentary Social Services Committee (1985, paras. 99, 105) regarded the CFI as "totally inadequate as a governmental response." Further doubt was placed against the government's stated intention to increase resources available to combat drug misuse when it became clear that any increased support of services for both drug misusers and AIDS initiatives should be funded out of savings in other sectors of health care. Fiscal concerns underlie a large amount of the current controversy within British professional drug circles, further reflected by the way in which the drugs and addictions research initiative announced by the Economic and Social Research Council in 1986 was subsequently abandoned due to lack of funding (Berridge 1988, 1989*a*).

The second line of attack adopted by the government was through a series of mass media campaigns that started in 1985 (Power 1989). The idea of some form of mass media campaign had first been raised in ministerial circles early in 1984 at the time of the first sensational news reports of the upsurge in heroin use. Professional responses to the proposal were initially guarded and cautious, however, warning against the lack of proved effectiveness of high-profile media campaigns in health education, with the serious possibility that such campaigns might even backfire and stimulate curiosity and experimentation with minority-pursuit drugs such as heroin. For these kinds of reasons the Health Education Council, a quasi-autonomous body centrally funded by government, found itself in opposition to the government proposals for a mass media campaign. This confirmed the view of the Advisory Council on the Misuse of Drugs, which in its report on *Prevention* had already warned of such a possibility (Advisory Council on the Misuse of Drugs 1984, p. 17).

The government broke this professional deadlock by placing a contract for developmental work on the project with a private market research organization, Andrew Irving Associates, which advocated a "low-key" advertising campaign (Andrew Irving Associates 1984). Eventually, however, the contract for a mass advertising campaign went to the Yellowhammer advertising organization, which had previously made its mark through high-profile campaigns on behalf of the ecological pressure group Greenpeace, and similar tactics characterized the resulting antiheroin campaign. They consisted of a series of highly dramatized television slots, advertising in the youth press, and a street-hoarding poster campaign with the slogans "Heroin Screws You Up" and "How Low Can You Get on Heroin?" A statistical evaluation of the campaign conducted by the Research Bureau Limited suggested that there had been a number of significant gains in hardening attitudes against heroin in the target group of thirteen- to twenty-year-olds (Research Bureau Limited 1986). A qualitative evaluation of the initial campaign provided by Andrew Irving Associates (1986, p. v) also confirmed the view that "the primary campaign objective: '*to reinforce young peoples' resistances to heroin misuse in order to discourage interest in trial'* has, to a large extent, been fulfilled."

Even so, there were controversies about the methodology of the evaluation (Marsh 1986; Dorn 1987), and other qualitative research suggested that the campaign might have helped to glamorize heroin use among some key groups of young people (Brown and Lawton 1988). In view of the continuing increase in heroin misuse through and beyond 1985, it would certainly be difficult to claim any immediate measure of success from this strategy. In a critical review of mass media drug-prevention campaigns by Power (1989, p. 142) it is regarded as "a sad irony . . . that, whilst the health and education services are under severe economic constraint, the Government sees fit to plough much-needed resources into a media campaign that has always lacked real justification." The same view was reflected in an unofficial report by senior police officers, which thought it "unfortunate that . . . the government has chosen to spend some of those scarce funds on an approach which gives an appearance of action, i.e. national publicity campaigns, rather than one which is committed to progress, i.e. a program of research which could establish the nature and scale of the problem and some validated solutions" (Police Staff College 1987, p. 13). Both of these statements reflect a remaining cynicism in professional circles that the government-sponsored media campaigns had been undertaken for political reasons, rather than on the basis of proven health education efficacy. Indeed, according to the initial report from Andrew Irving Associates, one key objective in the campaign should be to "reassure the public that the Government is taking effective action" (Andrew Irving Associates 1984, p. 1).

In spite of these and other criticisms, the advice to government was largely favorable and encouraged the further development of mass advertising campaigns (Tayler 1986). Nevertheless, even allowing for some success in reinforcing the attitudes of nondrug users against experimentation with heroin, Andrew Irving Associates (1986, p. vii) itself admitted that one unfortunate outcome of the initial campaign might have been that it increased "the demoralization of existing users . . . by encouraging them to feel even more negative about themselves" as a result of exposure to the advertising (Pearson, Gilman, and McIver 1986). A crucial issue here had been summarized by the Advisory Council in 1984, where two quite separate audiences and aims for drug education had been identified: "(a) to reduce the recruitment of individuals into patterns of drug involvement that involve illegality, and (b) to reduce the proportion of those taking drugs (legal or illegal) who suffer medical or social harm" (Advisory Council on the Misuse of Drugs 1984, p. 40).

It is highly questionable whether the advertising campaigns initiated in 1985 had thought through with sufficient clarity the distinction between an outright preventive campaign (e.g., "Just Say No") and one directed toward "harm reduction." The harm-reduction philosophy has gained steady ground in Britain, aiming to offer information to existing drug users that could help them to minimize the harm they might do to themselves; for example, not mixing drugs that might result in an unanticipated and potentially fatal overdose, or not sharing injecting equipment. Admittedly, there are difficulties in judging how to reconcile attempts to address these two quite distinct audiences (Pearson, Gilman, and McIver 1986, pp. 38–39; 1987, pp. 58–61). Within the advertising industry itself, moreover, there was continuing controversy about the logic and direction of Yellowhammer's "Heroin Screws You Up" campaign (Mason 1986).

The government was to press ahead, however, with later mass media ventures including a five million pound investment in 1987 in a blood-smeared "shock-tactic" campaign with the slogans "Don't Inject AIDS" and "Smack Isn't Worth It," and a two million pound package in late 1988 directed against the sharing of needles and syringes (Institute for the Study of Drug Dependence 1987, 1989). This latter campaign, with slogans "Don't Share Works" and "Sharing your mate's works means sharing with everyone he's ever shared with," involved a new twist in the evolution of media campaigning in that it appeared to make little attempt to discourage drug use itself. Indeed, it is one of the most significant indications of the steady movement toward "harm-reduction" tactics in the face of the threat of HIV infection and AIDS.

B. The Enforcement Strategy: A New Turn?

If both the government Central Funding Initiative and the mass media campaigns have provoked a large amount of controversy, the new emphasis given to enforcement measures within the government's overall strategy has not. In part, this reflects once more the prevailing assumptions of the "medicalized British system" that tended to marginalize or ignore the contribution of enforcement. The characterization of the "British system" as dominated by the medical profession (and hence by treatment ideologies, rather than by penal measures) is, however, difficult to uphold in the face of the available evidence. Even

TABLE 1

Persons Found Guilty or Cautioned for Drug Offenses, 1973–88

Year	Heroin	Cannabis	All Drugs
1973	435	11,476	14,977
1974	444	9,517	12,532
1975	393	8,987	11,846
1976	464	9,946	12,754
1977	393	10,607	12,907
1978	483	11,572	13,604
1979	520	12,409	14,339
1980	751	14,910	17,158
1981	808	15,388	17,921
1982	966	17,447	20,319
1983	1,508	20,006	23,341
1984	2,446	20,746	25,240
1985	3,227	21,337	26,958
1986	2,259	19,286	23,905
1987	2,151	21,733	26,278
1988	1,856	26,111	30,515

SOURCE.—Home Office (1987*a*, 1988*c*, 1989).

at the level of the bald facts of the known situation, a comparison of the treated incidence of narcotic addiction as against the numbers of drug offenders processed through the criminal justice system suggests something quite different than a medically inspired and dominated system: "For example, whilst in 1985 about 4,300 new patients were seen in drug addiction out-patient clinics, in the same year over 26,000 were convicted or cautioned for drug offences, and nearly 4,000 of these were for offences concerned with heroin and cocaine. In that year nearly 6,000 people received a custodial sentence for a drug offence. This side of the British response has tended to be neglected by those centrally involved in policy discussions and debate" (Stimson 1987, p. 38).

What these figures also reveal, of course, is that the major enforcement effort in Britain is directed against cannabis rather than heroin—with more than 21,000 convictions or cautions for cannabis offenses out of the total of approximately 26,000 recorded drug offenses in 1987. This reflects a trend within the criminal justice system that has been in evidence since the early 1970s (see table 1). It is one of the paradoxes of the "British system" that such a penal attitude toward cannabis possession rests alongside the traditional stance that opiate addiction should be viewed as a "sickness" rather than as a "crime." This paradox lends further weight to the view that more attention should be given to the effective deployment of scarce resources in the enforcement drive against serious drug misuse (Pearson 1989*b;* Gilman and Pearson 1990).

The neglect of any serious scrutiny of criminal justice and penal issues has, however, been particularly evident within the British research tradition on drug misuse. As already indicated, this is in part a reflection of the marginality of drug misuse in the generation of crime and juvenile delinquency in Britain. In spite of a long, connected history of concern with problems of street crime and violence such as "hooliganism" (Pearson 1983), there has been no tradition of social apprehension about drug-related violent crime, unlike the United States. The problem runs deeper, however, in that, although there is now an extensive body of British research on policing (Holdaway 1983; Reiner 1985; Smith and Gray 1985; Grimshaw and Jefferson 1987; Morgan and Smith 1989), there has been a surprising lack of curiosity about the policing of drug problems, with the result that there is no comparable work on drug enforcement to that undertaken in North America (Moore 1977; Wilson 1978; Manning 1980; Kleiman and Smith 1990). And this in turn reflects the low priority given to drug enforcement within the British police until recently, which makes the increased emphasis given to enforcement strategies and intelligence needs since the mid-1980s an even more significant change of emphasis in British drug-control policies.

The British police are organized on the basis of forty-three constabularies in England and Wales, including the Metropolitan Police, which serves the greater London area, and the City of London Police. There are also eight police constabularies in Scotland and the Royal Ulster Constabulary. Each of these fifty-two constabularies retains a constitutional separateness, which has been often fiercely defended by the police, in terms of both its operations and administration (Baldwin and Kinsey 1982; Jefferson and Grimshaw 1984). Against this territorial diversity, however, there has also been a steady procession of argument for greater centralization in the drugs field and elsewhere.

The first recognition of the need for a central drugs intelligence body (other than the Home Office register of notified addicts) had been in 1972 through the establishment of the Central Drugs and Illegal Immigration Unit, although the marginality of drug-enforcement issues was reflected in its alignment with illegal immigration (Home Office 1972). Subsequently, in 1974 the drug-enforcement aspects of this body were given a separate identity through the creation of the Central Drugs Intelligence Unit (CDIU) at New Scotland Yard, although CDIU's placement within the Metropolitan Police until 1985 only serves further to underline the lack of importance attached to national drug-enforcement policy and intelligence needs.

It was the dawning awareness of the emergence of a serious heroin problem in 1984 that spurred the next move, first by the National Drugs Conference and subsequently endorsed by the Association of Chief Police Officers (ACPO), by which the ACPO Crime Committee commissioned a report under the chairmanship of R. F. Broome, Chief Constable of Avon and Somerset. The "Broome Report" of 1985, which remains a confidential document, incorporated a number of significant recommendations that, having been accepted by the Home Secretary, led to an injection of resources and created a new structure of drug enforcement and intelligence (Home Office 1985*c*, 1988*b*).

Previously, the manpower strength and operational strategies of police drug squads had been a somewhat uneven development within the fifty-two constitutionally separate police constabularies. A central recommendation of the Broome Report was the establishment of "drug wings" to be attached to the nine regional crime squads that had a much larger territorial responsibility than the individual constabularies. Another fundamental development was that the National Drugs Intelligence Unit (NDIU) was created, which, although still located at New Scotland Yard, was under the command of a newly established post of National Drugs Intelligence Coordinator to be occupied by a senior-ranking police officer. The role of NDIU and its operations has been recently reviewed by Stockley (1988, p. 297), who summarizes this as "to gather, collate, analyse and disseminate drugs intelligence, whether emanating from within the United Kingdom or abroad, and to provide the essential link between the two enforcement agencies, police and customs." One crucial innovation in the establishment of NDIU was that it brought together officers from both H.M. Customs and the police in a shared organizational focus for the first time. Finally, as part of the government's declared strategy on *Tackling Drug Misuse*, the steering committee of the previous CDIU was replaced by a top-level Drugs Intelligence Steering Group (DISG) to oversee the work of the NDIU, which is chaired by a senior Home Office official and charged with keeping drug-enforcement strategies under review, maintaining effective liaison between customs and police, and offering strategic assessments to ministers (Home Office 1988*b*, p. 13).

There is little information, other than that of a confidential nature, on the subsequent development of NDIU and the wider drug-enforcement strategy. The establishment of the regional crime squad "drug wings" has certainly brought a greater degree of coordination into policing operations and, assisted through the support role of NDIU, has enhanced the intelligence capacities of both police and customs. Even so, the individual police constabularies still retain their own drug squads that have varying approaches and operational capabilities, so that there are remaining policy tensions in the relations between the local, regional, and national levels of drug-enforcement strategy (Wright and Waymont 1989). Relations between the police and customs, which had traditionally been characterized by mutual suspicion and professional rivalry, have also undoubtedly changed to a significant degree in spite of areas of residual tension (Fazey 1988). Other initiatives that can be mentioned here are that equipment needs commensurate with the newly enhanced role afforded to drugs intelligence have been identified, including the use of knowledge-based computer systems and artificial intelligence applications; greater attention is being given to such issues as the monitoring of precursor chemicals involved in illicit drug manufacture; and work is underway on the development of financial intelligence systems appropriate to the powers of asset confiscation and the investigation of cash movements embodied in the Drug Trafficking Offences Act of 1986.

The Drug Trafficking Offences Act (DTOA) is in itself another major innovation in British enforcement policy (Zander 1989; Dorn and South 1990*a*). The DTOA created a mandatory confiscation order for all offenders convicted of drug trafficking in a Crown Court. It requires the court to order that the offender should be deprived of all the proceeds of drug trafficking, not only on the specific offense for which he or she was convicted, but also in connection with drug trafficking over the previous six years. The DTOA also places a reverse obligation on the defendant to prove that any of his or her entire property does not represent the proceeds of drug trafficking. As Zander (1989, p. 11) describes it in a review of the Act and associated American law, the DTOA "is therefore an extraordinarily wide confiscation power." In addition to the powers of confiscation embodied in the DTOA, the act also allows the police and customs to investigate suspect bank accounts. It is therefore regarded as "a very useful investigative tool for operational officers and an important source of intelligence" (Stockley 1988, p. 299).

Given that the powers of the DTOA are only applicable in cases where proceedings were instituted on or after January 12, 1987, when the relevant section of the act came into force, it is undoubtedly too soon to judge its effectiveness. Nevertheless, the act has clearly experienced a number of teething difficulties, and in the short run its most important impact might well have been the investigative powers that it allows through the scrutiny of cash movements. In spite of the mandatory nature of the confiscation provisions, in 1987 the courts applied a confiscation order in only 200 cases (6 percent) out of a total of 3,560 sentenced offenders (Home Office 1988*c*, p. 141). Zander (1989, p. 52) suggests that this "astonishing statistic" probably reflects "not only ignorance of the new law but also considerable reluctance on the part of prosecutors and courts" to employ it. A further difficulty is that the DTOA applies to all drug-trafficking offenses, whatever the sums of money involved. One consequence of this provision is that of the 200 cases in 1987 where a confiscation order was applied, 135 of these (67 percent) involved sums of less than 1,000 pounds (Home Office 1988*c*, pp. 141, 163). It is hardly a matter of surprise, then, that Zander (1989, pp. 52–53) recommends both that it might be advisable to abolish the mandatory requirement of the DTOA and also that "the scarce expert skills of detection available to the police would . . . be better deployed in the more serious cases than in pursuing so many relatively minor offenders." A model for such an amendment might be the Criminal Justice Act of 1988, which allows for the confiscation of property in connection with any offense, but in which these powers only apply to sums in excess of 10,000 pounds.

In addition to these important developments in domestic drug-enforcement strategy, greater attention has also been paid to questions of international cooperation. The role of Drugs Liaison Officers who are situated in a number of European states, and also in producer nations, has been one significant development at an operational level. In terms of policy development there is a greater recognition of the need for a coordinated effort to combat drug misuse both within the European community and more widely (European Parliament 1986, 1989*a*, 1989*b*; Interpol 1989). Mutual Legal Assistance Treaties (MLATs) have been agreed on among the United Kingdom and a number of nation states, particularly as these relate to the provisions of the 1986 Drug Trafficking Offences Act—indeed, without MLAT agreements the 1986 Act would have little relevance to the global economy of illicit drugs trafficking. The movement toward a common European market in 1992 has undoubtedly accelerated these and other initiatives in the field of drug enforcement, in spite of some anxieties expressed by the British government, police, and customs concerning the relaxation of border controls (European Communities Commission 1987; European Parliament 1989*a*).

Some indication of the extent to which drug enforcement and intelligence operations have changed in Britain in recent years is that, although NDIU is no more than four years old, it is reported that police and customs officer referrals to the unit involve 346,000 search transactions annually, with approximately 500 operations currently registered with NDIU by operational officers (Stockley 1988, p. 302). This scale of activity, including the degree of mutuality and coordination between police and customs, simply would not have been possible among the existing police constabularies. In other words, coordinated law enforcement is now situated quite centrally within British drug-control strategies.

And yet, this is not all that has to be said about the evolution of British drug policy. Unquestionably, enforcement has achieved a new significance, and there are even signs of an awakening of research interest into crime-related aspects of drug misuse. The Home Office Research and Planning Unit has recently sponsored a major review of economic aspects of both illicit drug markets and enforcement measures (Wagstaff and Maynard 1988, 1989). The Police Foundation, with the support of the ACPO, has also sponsored an ongoing survey of comparative police strategies toward drug enforcement in the different regions of England and Wales (Wright and Waymont 1989). Some attention has been given to British drug problems in the context of the global economy of the trade in illicit drugs (Henman, Lewis, and Malyon 1985; Lewis 1989). Finally, we can note recent research that offers a more focused scrutiny of the structure and organization of drug distribution networks in Britain, which suggests the need for a radical rethinking of their mode of operation (Grieve 1986; Dorn and South 1986, 1990*b*). Although the dominant assumption is that drug markets tend toward a monopoly or cartel form, Dorn and South have identified a variety of "ideal types" of business organizations that operate as competitors within the market. These findings are fundamentally important for drug enforcement since each type of distribution network implies a different enforcement strategy (Dorn and South 1990*a*, 1990*b*).

Even so, in spite of recent and growing attention to this area of concern there are still a number of unanswered questions, whether in terms of how to situate the understanding of drug misuse within a criminological framework or the evaluation of the effectiveness of enforcement measures (Pearson 1989*a*, 1989*c*). As Wagstaff and Maynard (1989, p. 461) have described it, in spite of considerable resource inputs by government to antidrug measures, "none of these recommendations is based on any firm evidence that their adoption would represent an efficient deployment of resources." Wagstaff and Maynard also make it abundantly clear that there are considerable difficulties involved in arriving at a sound judgment on the effectiveness of drug-enforcement strategies, while remaining equivocal on the specific question of the effectiveness of the British enforcement effort. On one reading of the available evidence there is room for cautious optimism. Even so, there is a remaining ambiguity. While the levels of heroin seizures by customs officers fell sharply from their peak in 1985, giving some room for encouragement on the effects of international cooperation, they again showed an increase in 1988 (Home Office 1988*a;* National Drugs Intelligence Unit 1989). On another reading of the detailed evidence provided by Wagstaff and Maynard, however, British supply-side enforcement measures have failed (Peltzman 1989).

It is not possible here to develop a detailed argument about the most effective means to deploy police resources against problems of drug misuse. There are in any case general difficulties in establishing adequate performance indicators for police work (Clarke and Hough 1984; Burrows 1986; Horton and Smith 1988). The difficulty, as already indicated, is compounded by the neglect of criminological and penological aspects of drug problems in Britain, whether in terms of policy considerations or social research (Pearson 1989*a*). For the present, one can perhaps say no more than that, whereas evaluations of the effectiveness of drug-enforcement strategies tend to give priority to operations against major traffickers and bulk seizures (Wagstaff and Maynard 1988), there is compelling evidence to suggest that these policies have not been an unqualified success (Peltzman 1989). Low-level enforcement strategies deserve more focused attention, especially when aligned to multiagency community-based programs for offenders, as a means of coming to grips with drug problems at a neighborhood level (Pearson 1989*b*, 1989*c;* Gilman and Pearson 1990).

In summary, although law enforcement has been given a higher priority in recent years, it remains true that enforcement strategies cannot be said to have become dominant in British policy in that they coexist with a quite different line of thinking and action. This is predicated on policies that aim to reduce the harm done to individuals, families, and whole communities as a result of drug misuse—rather than simply enforcing the law and punishing wrongdoers. This emphasis on "harm reduction" offers a point of continuity within the "British system" as it is usually understood. It is also one that has recently flourished, and at precisely the same time that enforcement has assumed a new emphasis within British drug policy. The engine that drives this revitalization of harm-reduction strategies is, of course, the threat of HIV transmission and AIDS.

VI. HIV and AIDS: A New Threat, a New Policy?

At a point when the onset of the heroin epidemic was first coming to public notice, the Parliamentary Home Affairs Committee (1985, p. iii) in a distinctly proenforcement and pro-American report felt so moved as to describe drug misuse as "the most serious peacetime threat to our national well-being." Three years later, in a report that advanced a number of quite astonishing recommendations on the subject of *AIDS and Drug Misuse*, the Advisory Council on the Misuse of Drugs (1988, p. 1) trumped the Home Affairs Committee's exclamation in spades: "HIV is a greater threat to public and individual health than drug misuse." In spelling out the implications of such a stance, the Advisory Council offered a ritual endorsement of the view that "abstinence remains the ultimate goal" but far more significantly emphasized that "efforts to bring it about in individual cases must not jeopardize any reduction in HIV risk behaviour which has already been achieved." In a policy field that has simply refused to stand still for almost a decade there had been yet another change of gear. Most strikingly, the question of maintenance prescribing was back on the agenda with a vengeance.

The recognition that HIV transmission had become a central component of policy consideration in the drugs field was a transforming influence. Most significantly, the route of administration employed by drug users became the key target for a range of interventions rather than drug use itself. The government antiheroin campaigns of 1985 and 1986 had made no mention whatsoever of the risks of HIV infection, whereas the poster and television campaign initiated in 1988 was solely concerned with injection and the sharing of needles and syringes. One might characterize the message of the earlier campaigns as "Don't Use Heroin," whereas the later campaign was not specifically geared toward any specific drug substance, and while it did not condone drug misuse, neither did the campaign urge against drug use. Rather its message was "Don't Share Works."

As with much else in the drug field, there is a wide variation in the impact of HIV seropositivity within the British Isles. For reasons not entirely understood, there would appear to be a much higher rate of seropositivity among intravenous drug users in Scotland than elsewhere in the United Kingdom, and more particularly in Edinburgh and Dundee. High rates of HIV infection among intravenous drug users in Edinburgh, in excess of 50 percent, had been noted among both clinic samples and general practitioner samples by the mid-1980s (Brettle et al. 1986; Robertson et al. 1986). Establishing a more general estimate for Scotland of a 50 percent seropositivity among intravenous drug users in 1986, the Scottish Home and Health Department (1986) noted that this was in marked contrast to a figure of 11 percent seropositivity for England and Wales. Moreover, it was reported that, in some cities in the North of England that had been badly hit by the heroin epidemic, HIV seropositivity rates were approximating to zero. This would reflect the absence of any established concern about HIV and AIDS in those same cities at this time, where smoking ("chasing") was the predominant and preferred mode of drug administration (Pearson, Gilman, and McIver 1985, 1986).

Further evidence of the sharp difference between Scotland and the rest of the United Kingdom, in terms of the characteristics of those populations who were known to be HIV seropositive, serves to underline the extent of regional variations (Scottish Home and Health Department 1988*a*). Whereas in England, Wales, and Northern Ireland 51.8 percent of those known to be seropositive at the end of 1987 were homosexual or bisexual males, for example, in Scotland the figure was only 14.9 percent. In the rest of the United Kingdom, moreover, 15.2 percent of those known to be seropositive were hemophiliacs, as against only 5.4 percent in Scotland. Crucially, whereas merely 7.3 percent of those known to be HIV seropositive in the rest of the United Kingdom were intravenous drug users, the figure for Scotland was 57.3 percent. One final indication of these differences is that the male-to-female ratio among those known to be HIV positive in England, Wales, and Northern Ireland stood at 15.0 to 1 as against only 2.5 to 1 for Scotland (Scottish Home and Health Department 1988*a*, pp. 58–59).

In attempting to account for these differences, the Scottish Home and Health Department (1986, p. 7) suggested that two factors might have been important in establishing the extremely high rate of HIV infection in Edinburgh. The first was the role of the police in discouraging the sale of needles and syringes within the city, while also confiscating those items from people when found in their possession. This policy resulted in the "non-availability of sterile equipment in the city" that appeared "to have contributed to extensive sharing of equipment." The second reason advanced by the Scottish Home and Health Department was that locally there had been "medical opposition to maintenance prescribing." A third possibility not mentioned by the report was the previous pattern of drug use within local drug cultures, which were already inclined toward injection, a crucial variable in the North of England, as we have already seen (Pearson, Gilman, and McIver 1986).

One important characteristic of these subcultures of intravenous injection is that, to some extent at least, they remain substance nonspecific. Under these circumstances, one possible explanation is that the original injecting subculture had been formed during the 1970s in relation to various forms of polydrug use where amphetamines and barbiturates were sometimes predominant (Jamieson, Glanz, and MacGregor 1984). The arrival of the "new" heroin in the early 1980s would then involve a "substance transfer" of the inherited injection preference within the local subculture. And finally, in the case of Edinburgh, where heroin became extremely scarce around 1986 and 1987, heroin addicts switched to drugs available through medical prescription such as Temazepam, Temgesic, and DF118s. Indeed, by early 1988 a whole new subcultural folklore and vocabulary had evolved in this East Scotland (Edinburgh) region concerning tranquilizer drugs, which were now injected as substitutes for opiates (Morrison 1988). A similar switch by injecting drug users to the use of tranquilizers has been reported from Glasgow, and there are further indications of this trend in parts of the Northwest of England (Sakol, Stark, and Sykes 1989).

Faced with this developing problem the Scottish Home and Health Department (1986, p. 12) report on *HIV Infection in Scotland* had taken the view that "the prevention of spread [of HIV] should take priority over any perceived risk of increased drug misuse," through practical steps such as "substitution prescribing" and the provision of sterile injecting equipment to drug users. Its chairman, Dr. Brian McClelland (1987, p. 85) subsequently described how, for many professionals, such a policy raised "the concern that these policies may appear to be condoning drug abuse" and that "not surprisingly this has been robustly opposed by a number of groups." Harm-reduction strategies invariably raise controversies such as these (Pearson, Gilman, and McIver 1986).

As a result of the aggravated situation in some areas of Scotland with respect to HIV seropositivity one subsequent development, possibly designed to circumvent professional opposition to syringe-exchange schemes, was an instruction to health boards that they should ensure that there is an adequate availability of injecting equipment in each locality to be organized through sales by retail pharmacists (Scottish Home and Health Department 1988*b*). This is a potentially hazardous recommendation in Scotland, however, in that Scottish law includes a common-law crime of "reckless behaviour," with the attendant possibility that pharmacists might be subject to prosecution. However, the Lord Advocate has indicated that, although he would not give a general and unqualified undertaking of immunity before the law, he would not authorize prosecutions against medical practitioners or pharmacists if they observed the guidelines stated in this governmental circular (Scottish Home and Health Department 1988*b*).

More generally, the recognition of the risks of HIV transmission has led to a wholesale reconsideration of drug policies and practices. In two recent publications from the Advisory Council on the Misuse of Drugs (1988, 1989), a number of radical policy recommendations are made on service responsibilities with respect to HIV and AIDS, while some quite astonishing ideas are floated that indicate possible future agendas. The central, organizing principle of the Advisory Council's recommendations is that illicit drug users should not be deterred from making contact with services and that every effort should be made to keep them in contact. Maintenance prescribing, syringe-exchange schemes, health advice, safer-sex counseling, and community-based programs as alternatives to custody are among the directions advocated. Perhaps mindful of the Edinburgh experience, the police are encouraged to engage in multiagency consultations, to take such steps as necessary not to prevent the availability of sterile injecting equipment, and to avoid using such facilities as needle-exchange schemes for surveillance points (Advisory Council on the Misuse of Drugs 1988, p. 43). Social services departments are warned against taking the children of known drug users into public care, unless absolutely necessary, so as not to discourage drug users from using the available services (p. 33). Prisons are reminded of their own responsibilities where drug users are concerned, with both a recommendation that condoms should be made available to prisoners on a confidential basis (p. 65) and subsequently that the prescribing of oral methadone to prisoners should be considered as an option to discourage the dangerous practice of sharing injecting equipment that has been smuggled into prison (Advisory Council on the Misuse of Drugs 1989, p. 65). Such is the change of mood that the Advisory Council (1988, p. 65) even toyed with the idea of establishing syringe-exchange schemes in prisons. The paramount concern, however, should be to avoid imprisonment wherever possible through the expansion of community-based programs for drug offenders (Advisory Council on the Misuse of Drugs 1989, pp. 61–63; Gilman and Pearson 1990).

The increasing concern with HIV and AIDS has, therefore, already had a number of important consequences in the drug field. In particular, a lively controversy has been reengaged around the question of maintenance prescribing, which has been given a new source of legitimacy in the attempt to keep drug users in touch with services and to engage in harm-reduction education strategies (Connell 1986; Scottish Home and Health Department 1986, p. 12; Strang 1987; Advisory Council on the Misuse of Drugs 1988, pp. 47–48; Smith 1988). There have also been some strongly worded criticisms of the North American enforcement-led and prohibitionist approach to drug misuse, including one from the former Head of the Home Office Drugs Branch (Marks 1987; Parry and O'Hare 1988; Spear 1988). Harm-reduction strategies have been given a new prominence, particularly where there is an observable drift toward injecting in localities where smoking had been the preferred mode of using heroin at the outset of the epidemic (Dalton 1987; Carr and Dalton 1988; Chadwick and Parker 1988). Research has been initiated into the effectiveness of needle-exchange and syringe-exchange facilities in changing the behavior of drug users, particularly in terms of whether these methods can reduce the extent to which needle sharing is practiced (McDermott 1988; Monitoring Research Group 1988; Newcombe 1988*a;* Stimson, Dolan, et al. 1988; Stimson, Donoghoe, et al. 1988; Stimson et al. 1989; Aston and Tippell 1989).

The concern with AIDS and HIV has also stimulated various forms of outreach work in order to contact high-risk groups such as prostitutes who are not in touch with services (Parry 1988; Plant et al. 1989). The need for such work is emphatically demonstrated by research in one high-risk area of London (Earls Court) where within the same locality there is a highly youthful and mobile population, intersecting with an active gay scene, an extensive injecting drug subculture, and both female and male prostitution (Batliwala and Kneen 1987, 1988; Batliwala 1988).

One particularly interesting and welcome development is the experimentation with innovative forms of communication such as comic-strip cartoons and other devices to engage the street culture in the debate on HIV and AIDS, offering information on injection techniques and safer sex practices (Gilman 1988*b*, 1989; Newcombe 1988*b*). One by-product of this work is that it has revealed among other things a significant degree of suspicion among drug users about official mass media campaigns, which are regarded as being little more than "propaganda." Other experiments in this line include the use of local radio and the attempt to introduce health education messages on drug "wraps" used by dealers (Fraser 1988; Fraser and Gamble 1988). There are notable examples of police being prepared to cooperate with such initiatives, moreover, within a multiagency strategy (Metropolitan Police 1986; Drugs Misuse Unit 1988), even though, more generally, multiagency policing schemes have met with mixed success (Blagg et al. 1988; Sampson et al. 1988). The importance of outreach work and other innovative strategies has been emphasized by recent research that indicates the greater likelihood of drug users reducing the extent to which they engage in high-risk behaviors where they are in touch with services (Power, Hartnoll, and Daviaud 1988). The study of patterns of help seeking, together with those factors (real or imagined) in the structure of service provision that are likely to inhibit a problem drug user from making contact with service agencies, is another important area of concern in planning services and evaluating their effectiveness (Oppenheimer, Sheehan, and Taylor 1988; Drug Indicators Project 1989; Hartnoll and Power 1989).

It is important to stress that much of this innovative work has been of a "grass roots" character. The government strategy, while it has embraced high-profile mass advertising campaigns on the dangers of sharing syringes and needles, has not given much public encouragement to the far-reaching recommendations of the Advisory Council on the Misuse of Drugs reports on *AIDS and Drug Misuse* (Advisory Council on the Misuse of Drugs 1988, 1989; Newcombe 1988*c*). One particularly aggravated concern is the potential for HIV transmission within the prison system, where the government's low-key response rests uneasily against common knowledge of the widespread availability of a range of illicit drugs within the prison system at the same time that syringes and needles are in short supply, thus encouraging the practice of needle sharing (Newcombe 1987; Prison Reform Trust 1988; Rahman, Ditton, and Forsyth 1989; Carvell and Hart 1990). It is all the more worrying that, through the strengthening of deterrence measures, increasing numbers of drug offenders have been sentenced to imprisonment—from approximately 1,600 in 1977 to 4,000 in 1987; and this offers no way of estimating the numbers of drug users sentenced to imprisonment for other offenses. This trend is also reflected in the fact that one-fifth of all notifications of drug addicts in England and Wales in 1986 came from prison medical officers (Home Office 1988*a*). An increasing resort to the use of custody for drug offenses has also been identified in Scotland (Haw 1988), where research focused on a drug-using subculture in one Glasgow neighborhood has indicated that the experience of imprisonment can lead to dramatic increases in the readiness with which intravenous drug users will share injecting equipment (Rahman, Ditton, and Forsyth 1989).

It is here in relation to the question of the imprisonment of drug users that we find evidence of an emerging contradiction in current British drug policy in its most stark form. On the one hand, there exists a public health strategy that gives priority to the control of the spread of HIV infection, urging a paramount need to reduce the extent to which drug users are unnecessarily embroiled in Britain's vastly overcrowded prison system and the extension of noncustodial options to deal with drug offenders (Advisory Council on the Misuse of Drugs 1988, p. 67; 1989, p. 61). On the other hand, in spite of the government's own declared strategy to contain and reduce the reliance on custody in dealing with all classes of offenders (Home Office 1988*d*), there is a newly conceived prioritization of enforcement measures and deterrence, resulting in heavier sentences for drug offenders and increasing numbers of drug users entering the prison system. British drug policy finds itself, once again, on the horns of a dilemma.

VII. Back to the Future: Reconciling Contradictions in Policy Development

How can we understand this apparent contradiction in developments within the drugs field in Britain? In a recent and perceptive overview of British drug policies, Edwards (1989) has suggested that such policies have been informed by a number of apparently contradictory impulses: international influences, varieties of fear, medical entrepreneurship, and the tension between treatment versus control. These, Edwards argued, can be easily discerned in the history that shaped the "British system" and its aftermath. But equally, these same impulses can be seen as shaping and determining the continuing evolution of British drug policies, thus affording "a tentative connection between analysis of the past, understanding the present, and projection to the future" (Edwards 1989, p. 222).

If we take two of the key influences identified by Edwards—the British response to international influences and the extent to which policy has been driven by different varieties of fear—then some light can be cast on the apparently contradictory movements within the current development of British drug policies. On the international front, the new emphasis being given to European cooperation in a number of spheres of social and economic policy is clearly going to be a major consideration in the future. Quite apart from the continuing cooperation within the World Health Organization (WHO), Unesco, and similar international organizations, the accelerating pressures for European harmonization will provide a more specific influence on drug-control policies. Edwards (1989, p. 222) remarks somewhat dryly that, heretofore, "we have not bothered to know our European neighbours particularly well." He also suggests that "more subtle and congruent changes" might result if, "instead of the habitual comparisons in the policy debate continuing to be based only on dyadic matching (Britain and America), the debate comes also to be informed and enriched by a European stock of comparisons."

The movement toward European harmonization, however, contains its own contradictions. In spite of the shortage of any effective cooperation in comparative research, which makes it difficult to arrive at easy conclusions (Berridge 1989*b*), it is nevertheless possible to offer some indications of this terrain. I have already suggested that the European context has formed part of the new stress on enforcement strategies. At the same time, however, this European cross-fertilization includes an opposing influence toward a more liberal and tolerant emphasis.

It is customary to think in this respect only of the experience of the Netherlands, where there is both a tolerant attitude toward licensed cannabis use and also a tradition within the criminal justice system that places an extremely low reliance on imprisonment (Downes 1988; Leuw, in this volume). On the available evidence Dutch policy has resulted in a stabilization of the heroin problem in the 1980s that runs counter to the experience of many other European nations including Britain (Buisman 1988; Ghodse and Kaplan 1988; Englesman 1989). However, the Dutch experience touches on a wider current of feeling as evidenced by the European Parliament's committee of inquiry, which issued a curt expression of its view on the counterproductive influence of the use of custodial sentences for minor drug offenders (European Parliament 1986, p. 44). This can only give encouragement to the British government's own stated intention to constrain the growth of the prison population (Home Office 1988*d*). Moreover, this European dimension brings with it an even more explicit emphasis on the need to move away from policies based on enforcement and punishment. We see this in a variety of forms.

For example, there is the creation of the "European Movement for the Normalization of Drug Policy." The Minority Report of the European Parliament's committee of inquiry took the view that "the American method of drug prevention must be regarded as a failure in all respects," urging the need to develop "strategies to deal with drug problems in a new and unconventional manner," an argument that largely rested on a stance of decriminalization (European Parliament 1986, p. 96; Van der Valk 1986; Tongue 1988). There are echoes of this tendency elsewhere in Europe. In addition to the Netherlands, Spain has opted for a version of decriminalization in relation to drug possession. A recent federal commission report from Switzerland has also recommended the depenalization of possession offenses (Swiss Federal Commission 1989). And, finally, arguments have surfaced in France that suggest that drugs should be taken out of the criminal sphere and placed within a licensed national monopoly of production, importation, and distribution (Caballero 1989; Le Gendre 1989).

If European harmonization offers one clear example of how a single policy development involves internal contradictions, making available multiple interpretations of likely future outcomes, the other key policy issue for the future is undoubtedly how the impact of HIV and AIDS will influence drug-control measures. This has its own European dimension, of course, as well as much wider international implications (World Health Organization 1987). On the domestic front, however, Edwards (1989, p. 222) identifies the spread of HIV infection as "the dominant fear which now drives or engulfs British drug policies," involving its own multiple and sometimes contradictory effects. The fear of HIV and AIDS has had the effect in Britain as elsewhere of increasing public stigmatization of groups such as homosexuals and drug users (Vass 1986). It has, however, already produced an exceptional volatility in discussions of the agenda for future policy options on drug control and is a major vehicle through which a variety of liberalizations of existing policy are being argued—such as the extension of maintenance prescribing, the provision of syringe-exchange schemes, and the need to reduce the use of imprisonment.

Edwards (1989, p. 224) has also suggested that we are likely to witness a further contradictory twist in that the question of compulsory treatment for drug misusers is likely to return to the agenda, even though it is a matter that has never found wide acceptance within professional circles. A further straw in the wind is the current agitation and debate on whether there should be a new statutory provision of a compulsory community treatment order for the mentally ill (Royal College of Psychiatrists 1987*b;* Scott-Moncrieff 1988). This makes for an increasingly likely possibility that some form of compulsion might be introduced for those who persistently misuse drugs.

It is certainly arguable that some system of community-based compulsion would provide a means of resolving the contradiction between a sentencing trend that has seen an increasing number of drug misusers within the prison population at a time when the fear of HIV infection is gathering support for the position that there should be less reliance on custodial measures in dealing with drug users. The development of arrest-referral schemes and other forms of pretrial diversion projects, together with community-based programs of activity as alternatives to custody, would be a crucial step in this regard (Gilman and Pearson 1990). Initiatives such as these have been well tested in the sphere of juvenile justice in Britain, where they have helped to halve the population of young offenders in custody in the course of the 1980s (Children's Society 1988). This is also an area in which there is complete policy agreement between the Advisory Council on the Misuse of Drugs and the government's stated intention of reducing the reliance on imprisonment for young adult offenders, as represented in the Home Office "Green Paper" on *Punishment, Custody and the Community* (Advisory Council on the Misuse of Drugs 1988, 1989; Home Office 1988*d*). This tacit consensus between the interests of health care and criminal justice offers a real window of opportunity for the development of effective noncustodial measures, which serve the interests of both drug users and their families and the wider community in terms of crime reduction.

The relations between penal policy and health policy were, as we have seen, a crucial point of origin for the "British system" and the recommendations of the Rolleston Committee. In spite of the unprecedented nature of the AIDS epidemic, the system reasserts a remarkable line of continuity within British responses to drug problems, even allowing for many shifts of emphasis across historical time. It would therefore be a mistake to see the emergence of a public health strategy to combat HIV infection as an entirely new departure. Indeed, the recommendations of the second Brain committee, which have usually been understood as signaling the end of the "British system," were themselves organized around public health concepts and the assumption that "addiction is after all a socially infectious condition" (Ministry of Health 1965, p. 8). Even allowing for the likelihood that syringe-exchange schemes and other "harm-reduction" strategies will continue to provoke controversy in some professional circles, such innovations nevertheless cohere with a traditional line of response to drug problems in Britain and will in all probability remain in the ascendancy as the organizing principle of future policy developments.

One final consideration needs to be entered here, which is that, although HIV and AIDS have come to dominate British thinking on drug problems, it is no doubt likely that at some point in the future there will be a further recognition of the potential dangers of only seeing the problem of drug misuse through the prism of HIV and AIDS. The trigger to such a development could well be if cocaine misuse (in the form of "freebasing" or "crack") comes to be more widespread than it is currently in Britain, a possibility that has been forecast now for some years in view of the trend of increasing quantities of cocaine seized by enforcement agencies (Home Office 1988*b;* Turner 1988; Home Affairs Committee 1989; National Drugs Intelligence Unit 1989). It is an open question whether such a turn of events would deeply unsettle the extremely adaptable British policy response to drug control. As the 1980s heroin epidemic and the subsequent responses to the problem of HIV and AIDS have demonstrated, there is much more flexibility and heterogeneity in the actually existing responses to drug misuse in Britain than might be imagined from a naive reading of the directions resulting from the reforms of the late 1960s. It was not, as has often been stated, that the "British system" had broken down; rather, under the pressure of events it had been transformed, finding new sources of renewal and growth from a diverse range of influences.

REFERENCES

Advisory Council on the Misuse of Drugs. 1982. *Treatment and Rehabilitation.* London: H.M. Stationery Office.

———. 1983. *Security of Controlled Drugs.* London: Home Office.

———. 1984. *Prevention.* London: H.M. Stationery Office.

———. 1988. *AIDS and Drug Misuse, Part I.* London: H.M. Stationery Office.

———. 1989. *AIDS and Drug Misuse, Part II.* London: H.M. Stationery Office.

Andrew Irving Associates. 1984. *Heroin Misuse Publicity Campaign: A Qualitative Study Designed to Guide the Targetting and Development of an Effective Mass Media Campaign.* London: Andrew Irving Associates.

———. 1986. *Anti-heroin Misuse Campaign: Qualitative Evaluation Research Report.* London: Andrew Irving Associates.

Ashton, M. 1987. "Treatment Trends." *Druglink* 2(5):12–13.

Aston, F., and S. Tippell. 1989. *A Report on the Development and Operation of a Syringe Exchange Scheme Based at the Community Drug Project.* London: Community Drug Project.

Auld, J., N. Dorn, and N. South. 1986. "Irregular Work, Irregular Pleasures: Heroin in the 1980s." In *Confronting Crime,* edited by R. Matthews and J. Young. London: Sage.

Baldwin, R., and R. Kinsey. 1982. *Police Powers and Politics.* London: Quartet.

Batliwala, Y. 1988. "A Community Tailor-made for AIDS? Problematic Drug Use in the Earls Court Area of London." Paper presented at the Drug Questions Research Conference, Institute for the Study of Drug Dependence, London, April.

Batliwala, Y., and J. Kneen. 1987. *Drug Abuse Research Team: Problematic Drug Use and Service Provision in S.W.5. Interim Report.* London: Drug Abuse Research Team.

———. 1988. *Drug Abuse Research Team: A Strategy for Future Service Provision of Drug Misuse in the Riverside Area (with Particular Reference to Earls Court): Recommendations.* London: Drug Abuse Research Team.

Bennett, T., and R. Wright. 1986. "The Drug-taking Careers of Opioid Users." *Howard Journal of Criminal Justice* 25(1):1–12.

Benyon, J., and J. Solomos, eds. 1987. *The Roots of Urban Unrest.* London: Pergamon.

Berridge, V. 1977. "Fenland Opium Eating in the Nineteenth Century." *British Journal of Addiction* 72:275–84.

———. 1978. "War Conditions and Narcotics Control: The Passing of Defence of the Realm Act Regulation 40B." *Journal of Social Policy* 7(3):285–304.

———. 1979. "Morality and Medical Science: Concepts of Narcotic Addiction in Britain, 1820–1926." *Annals of Science* 36:67–85.

———. 1988. "Coordinating Drugs Research in Britain." *British Journal of Addiction* 83:1013–18.

———, ed. 1989*a*. *Drugs Research and Policy in Britain.* Aldershot: Gower/Avebury.

———. 1989*b*. *Drug Research in Europe: A Report to the WHO.* London: Institute for the Study of Drug Dependence.

Berridge, V., and G. Edwards. 1981. *Opium and the People: Opiate Use in*

Nineteenth Century England. London: Allen Lane. 2d ed., New Haven, Conn.: Yale University Press, 1987.

Blagg, H., G. Pearson, A. Sampson, D. Smith, and P. Stubbs. 1988. "Inter-agency Cooperation: Rhetoric and Reality." In *Communities and Crime Reduction*, edited by T. Hope and M. Shaw. London: H.M. Stationery Office.

Bottoms, A. E., and P. Wiles. 1986. "Housing Tenure and Residential Community Crime Careers in Britain." In *Communities and Crime*, edited by A. J. Reiss, Jr., and M. Tonry. Vol. 8 of *Crime and Justice: A Review of Research*, edited by M. Tonry and N. Morris. Chicago: University of Chicago Press.

Box, S. 1987. *Recession, Crime and Punishment*. London: Macmillan.

Brah, A. 1986. "Asian Youth and Racism: Asian Youth on the Dole." In *The Experience of Unemployment*, edited by S. Allen, A. Waton, K. Purcell, and S. Wood. London: Macmillan.

Brettle, R. P., J. Davidson, S. J. Davidson, J. M. N. Gray, J. M. Inglis, J. S. Conn, G. E. Bath, J. Gillon, and D. B. L. McLelland. 1986. "HTLV-III Antibodies in an Edinburgh Clinic." *Lancet* 1(8489):1099.

Brown, C., and J. Lawton. 1988. *Illicit Drug Use in Portsmouth and Havant: A Local Study of a National Problem*. London: Policy Studies Institute.

Buisman, W. R. 1988. "Drug Prevention in the Netherlands." Paper presented at "The Anglo-Dutch Debate: Responding to Drug Problems," Royal Society of Medicine, London, September.

Burr, A. 1983*a*. "The Piccadilly Drug Scene." *British Journal of Addiction* 78:5–19.

———. 1983*b*. "Increased Sale of Opiates on the Black Market in the Piccadilly Area." *British Medical Journal* 287:883–85.

———. 1987. "Chasing the Dragon: Heroin Misuse, Delinquency and Crime in the Context of South London Culture." *British Journal of Criminology* 27:333–57.

———. 1989. "An Inner-City Community Response to Heroin Use." In *Drugs and British Society*, edited by S. MacGregor. London: Routledge.

Burrows, J. 1986. *Investigating Burglary: The Measurement of Police Performance*. Home Office Research Study no. 88. London: H.M. Stationery Office.

Caballero, F. 1989. *Droit de la drogue*. Paris: Dalloz.

Carlen, P. 1988. *Women, Crime and Poverty*. Milton Keynes: Open University Press.

Carr, J., and S. Dalton. 1988. "Syringe Exchange: The Liverpool Experience." *Druglink* 3(3):12–14.

Carvell, A. L. M., and G. J. Hart. 1990. "Risk Behaviors for HIV Infection among Drug Users in Prison." *British Medical Journal* 300:1383–84.

Chadwick, C., and H. Parker. 1988. *Wirral's Enduring Heroin Problem*. Liverpool: University of Liverpool, Misuse of Drugs Research Project.

Chaiken, J. M., and M. R. Chaiken. 1990. "Drugs and Predatory Crime." In *Drugs and Crime*, edited by M. Tonry and J. Q. Wilson. Vol. 13 of *Crime and Justice: A Review of Research*, edited by M. Tonry and N. Morris. Chicago: University of Chicago Press.

Chein, I., D. Gerard, R. Lee, and E. Rosenfeld. 1964. *The Road to H: Narcotics, Delinquency and Social Policy*. London: Tavistock.

Children's Society. 1988. *Penal Custody for Juveniles: The Least Line of Resistance.* Report of the Children's Society Advisory Committee on Penal Custody and Its Alternatives for Juveniles. London: Children's Society.

Clarke, R. V., and M. Hough. 1984. *Crime and Police Effectiveness.* Home Office Research Study no. 79. London: H.M. Stationery Office.

Cohen, S. 1972. *Folk Devils and Moral Panics: The Creation of the Mods and Rockers.* London: MacGibbon & Kee.

Connell, P. H. 1986. "'I Need Heroin.' Thirty Years' Experience of Drug Dependence and the Medical Challenges at Local, National, International and Political Level. What Next?" *British Journal of Addiction* 81:461–72.

Cooper, J. 1987. "Benzodiazepine Prescribing: The Aftermath." *Druglink* 2(5):8–10.

Dalton, S. 1987. "Wirral Injectors." *Mersey Drugs Journal* 1(3):11.

Department of Health and Social Security. 1984. *Medical Working Group on Drug Dependence. Guidelines on Good Clinical Practice in the Treatment of Drug Misuse.* London: Department of Health and Social Security.

De Quincey, T. 1971. *Confessions of an Opium Eater.* Harmondsworth: Penguin.

Ditton, J., and K. Speirits. 1981. *The Rapid Increase in Heroin Addiction in Glasgow during 1981.* Background Paper no. 2. Glasgow: University of Glasgow, Department of Sociology.

Ditton, J., and A. Taylor. 1987. *Scotland Drugs Resource Book: 1980–1984.* Glasgow: University of Glasgow, Criminology Research Unit.

Donoghoe, M., N. Dorn, C. James, S. Jones, J. Ribbens, and N. South. 1987. "How Families and Communities Respond to Heroin." In *A Land Fit for Heroin? Drug Policies, Prevention and Practice,* edited by N. Dorn and N. South. London: Macmillan.

Dorn, N. 1987. "Media Campaigns." *Druglink* 1(2):8–9.

Dorn, N., J. Ribbens, and N. South. 1987. *Coping with a Nightmare: Family Feelings about Long-Term Drug Use.* London: Institute for the Study of Drug Dependence.

Dorn, N., and N. South. 1985. *Helping Drug Users: Social Work, Advice Giving, Referral and Training Services of Three London "Street Agencies."* Aldershot: Gower/Avebury.

———. 1986. "Criminology and Economics of Drug Distribution in Britain: Options for Control." *Journal of Drug Issues* 16:523–35.

———, eds. 1987. *A Land Fit for Heroin? Drug Policies, Prevention and Practice.* London: Macmillan.

———. 1990*a*. "Profits and Penalties: New Trends in Legislation and Law Enforcement concerning Illegal Drugs." In *Policing and Prescribing: The British System of Drug Control,* edited by P. Bean and D. K. Whynes. London: Macmillan.

———. 1990*b*. "Drug Markets and Law Enforcement." *British Journal of Criminology* 30:171–88.

Downes, D. 1977. "The Drug Addict as a Folk Devil." In *Drugs and Politics,* edited by P. Rock. New Brunswick, N.J.: Transaction.

———. 1988. *Contrasts in Tolerance: Postwar Penal Policy in The Netherlands and England and Wales.* Oxford: Oxford University Press.

Drug Indicators Project. 1989. *Study of Help-Seeking and Service Utilisation by Problem Drug Takers*. London: Institute for the Study of Drug Dependence.

Drugs Alcohol Women Nationally. 1985. *A Survey of Facilities for Women Using Drugs (including Alcohol) in London*. London: Drugs Alcohol Women Nationally (DAWN).

Drugs Misuse Unit. 1988. *Report of the Southwark Drugs Misuse Unit, 1987/88*. London: London Borough of Southwark.

Edwards, G. 1979. "British Policies on Opiate Addiction: Ten Year Working of the Revised Response and Options for the Future." *British Journal of Psychiatry* 134:1–13.

———. 1989. "What Drives British Drug Policies?" *British Journal of Addiction* 84:219–26.

Engelsman, E. L. 1989. "Dutch Policy on the Management of Drug-related Problems." *British Journal of Addiction* 84:211–18.

Ettorre, B. 1989. "Women, Substance Abuse and Self-Help." In *Drugs and British Society*, edited by S. MacGregor. London: Routledge.

European Communities Commission. 1987. *Europe without Frontiers: Completing the Internal Market*. Luxembourg: Office for Official Publications of the European Communities.

European Parliament. 1986. *Committee of Enquiry into the Drugs Problem in the Member States of the Community*, rapporteur Sir Jack Stewart-Clark, Document A 2-114/86.

———. 1989*a*. "Resolution on Measures to Combat Drugs." *Official Journal of the European Communities*, no. C 47/51, 27.2.89.

———. 1989*b*. "Resolution on Drug Trafficking." Document A 2-349/88. *Official Journal of the European Communities*, no. C 47/53, 27.2.89.

Fay, P. W. 1976. *The Opium War, 1840–1842*. New York: Norton.

Fazey, C. S. J. 1987. *The Evaluation of Liverpool Drug Dependency Clinic: The First Two Years, 1985 to 1987. A Report to Mersey Regional Health Authority*. Liverpool: Mersey Health Authority.

———. 1988. "Policy on Drug Misuse: Too Little Too Late?" In *Crime U.K. 88*, edited by A. Harrison and J. Gretton. Newbury: Policy Journals.

Feldman, H. W. 1968. "Ideological Supports to Becoming and Remaining a Heroin Addict." *Journal of Health and Social Behaviour* 9:131–39.

Fox, A. 1979. *Yorkshire Report*. London: Hungerford Project.

Fraser, A. 1988. "Wraps against AIDS." *Druglink* 3(4):13.

Fraser, A., and L. Gamble. 1988. "Local Radio as a Strategy in Reducing Drug Related Harm." In *Drug Questions: An Annual Research Register*, issue 4, edited by N. Dorn, L. Lucas, and N. South. London: Institute for the Study of Drug Dependence.

Gabe, J. 1988. "'Race' and Tranquilliser Use." In *Drug Questions: An Annual Research Register*, issue 4, edited by N. Dorn, L. Lucas, and N. South. London: Institute for the Study of Drug Dependence.

Gabe, J., and N. Thorogood. 1986. "Prescribed Drug Use and the Management of Everyday Life: The Experiences of Black and White Working Class Women." *Sociological Review* 34(4):737–72.

Ghodse, A. H. 1977*a*. "Drug Dependent Individuals Dealt with by London Casualty Departments." *British Journal of Psychiatry* 131:273–80.

———. 1977*b*. "Casualty Departments and the Monitoring of Drug Dependence." *British Medical Journal* 1:1381–82.

Ghodse, A. H., and C. Kaplan. 1988. "Anglo-Dutch Responses to Drug Problems." *Journal of the Royal Society of Medicine* 81:497–98.

Gilman, M. 1988*a*. "DIY Diconal?" *Mersey Drugs Journal* 1(5):15.

———. 1988*b*. "Comics as a Strategy in Reducing Drug-related Harm." In *Drug Questions: An Annual Research Register*, issue 4, edited by N. Dorn, L. Lucas, and N. South. London: Institute for the Study of Drug Dependence.

———. 1989. *Comics as a Strategy in Reducing Drug-related Harm*. Manchester: Lifeline.

Gilman, M., and G. Pearson. 1990. "Lifestyle and Law Enforcement: Using Criminal Justice to Help Drug Users." In *Policing and Prescribing: The British System of Drug Control*, edited by P. Bean and D. K. Whynes. London: Macmillan.

Glanz, A., and C. Taylor. 1986. "Findings of a National Survey of the Role of General Practitioners in the Treatment of Opiate Misuse: Extent of Contact with Opiate Misusers." *British Medical Journal* 293:427–30.

Greenberg, M. 1951. *British Trade and the Opening of China, 1800–1842*. Cambridge: Cambridge University Press.

Grieve, J. G. D. 1986. "Law and Enforcement: Policing and Drug Related Crime in Urban Areas." Paper presented at the conference of the Royal Society for the Promotion of Health, London.

Grimshaw, R., and T. Jefferson. 1987. *Interpreting Policework: Policy and Practice in Forms of Beat Policing*. London: Allen & Unwin.

Guan, S. 1987. "Chartism and the First Opium War." *History Workshop* 24:17–31.

Hakim, C. 1982. "The Social Consequences of High Unemployment." *Journal of Social Policy* 11:433–67.

Halloran, J. D., P. Elliott, and G. Murdock. 1970. *Demonstrations and Communication: A Case Study*. Harmondsworth: Penguin.

Hammersley, R., A. Forsyth, V. Morrisson, and J. B. Davies. 1989. "The Relationship between Crime and Opioid Use." *British Journal of Addiction* 84:1029–43.

Hartnoll, R., E. Daviaud, R. Lewis, and M. Mitcheson. 1985*a*. *Drug Problems: Assessing Local Needs*. London: University of London, Birkbeck College, Drug Indicators Project.

Hartnoll, R., R. Lewis, M. Mitcheson, and S. Bryer. 1985*b*. "Estimating the Prevalence of Opioid Dependence." *Lancet* 1(8422):203–5.

Hartnoll, R. L., M. C. Mitcheson, A. Battersby, G. Brown, M. Ellis, P. Fleming, and N. Hedley. 1980. "Evaluation of Heroin Maintenance in Controlled Trial." *Archives of General Psychiatry* 37:877–84.

Hartnoll, R., and R. Power. 1989. "Looking for Help." *Druglink* 4(2):8–9.

Haw, S. 1985. *Drug Problems in Greater Glasgow*. London: Standing Conference on Drug Abuse.

———. 1988. "The Sentencing of Drug Offenders in Scottish Courts." Paper presented at the Drug Questions Research Conference, Institute for the Study of Drug Dependence, London, April.

Hayter, A. 1988. *Opium and the Romantic Imagination: Addiction and Creativity in De Quincey, Coleridge, Baudelaire and Others.* Rev. ed. Wellingborough: Crucible. 1st ed., London: Faber & Faber, 1968.

Henman, A., R. Lewis, and T. Malyon, eds. 1985. *Big Deal: The Politics of the Illicit Drugs Business.* London: Pluto.

Holdaway, S. 1983. *Inside the British Police.* Oxford: Blackwell.

Home Affairs Committee. 1985. *Misuse of Hard Drugs: Interim Report*, HC 399. London: H.M. Stationery Office.

———. 1989. *Crack: The Threat of Hard Drugs in the Next Decade (Interim Report)*, HC536. London: H.M. Stationery Office.

Home Office. 1968*a*. *Cannabis: Report by the Advisory Committee on Drug Dependence*. London: H.M. Stationery Office.

———. 1968*b*. *The Rehabilitation of Drug Addicts: Report of the Advisory Committee on Drug Dependence.* London: H.M. Stationery Office.

———. 1972. "Drugs and Illegal Immigration: Establishment of Central Intelligence Units and Cooperation with Immigration Branch." Home Office Circular HO173/72. London: Home Office.

———. 1984. *Statistics of the Misuse of Drugs, United Kingdom, 1983*. Home Office Statistical Bulletin 18/84. London: Home Office.

———. 1985*a*. *Criminal Convictions of Persons First Notified as Narcotic Addicts in 1979–81*. Home Office Statistical Bulletin, 19/85. London: Home Office.

———. 1985*b*. *Tackling Drug Misuse: A Summary of the Government's Strategy*. London: Home Office.

———. 1985*c*. "Increased Resources to Counter Drug Misuse." Home Office Circular H067/85. London: Home Office.

———. 1987*a*. *Statistics of the Misuse of Drugs, United Kingdom, 1986*. Home Office Statistical Bulletin, 28/87. London: Home Office.

———. 1987*b*. *Criminal Careers of Persons Convicted of Drug Offences in 1980–81*. Home Office Statistical Bulletin, 31/87. London: Home Office.

———. 1988*a*. *Statistics of the Misuse of Drugs, United Kingdom, 1987*. Home Office Statistical Bulletin, 25/88. London: Home Office.

———. 1988*b*. *Tackling Drug Misuse: A Summary of the Government's Strategy*. 3d ed. London: Home Office.

———. 1988*c*. *Criminal Statistics: England and Wales 1987*. Cmnd. 498. London: H.M. Stationery Office.

———. 1988*d*. *Punishment, Custody and the Community*. Cmnd. 424. London: H.M. Stationery Office.

———. 1989. "Statistics on the Misuse of Drugs: Seizures and Offenders Dealt with, United Kingdom, 1988." Home Office Statistical Bulletin, 30/89. London: Home Office.

Horton, C., and D. J. Smith. 1988. *Evaluating Police Work: An Action Research Project*. London: Policy Studies Institute.

Hughes, P. H. 1977. *Behind the Wall of Respect*. Chicago: University of Chicago Press.

Hughes, P. H., N. W. Barker, G. A. Crawford, and J. H. Jaffe. 1972. "The Natural History of a Heroin Epidemic." *American Journal of Public Health* 162:995–1001.

Hughes, P. H., and G. A. Crawford. 1972. "A Contagious Disease Model for Researching and Intervening in Heroin Epidemics." *Archives of General Psychiatry* 27:189–205.

Hunt, L. G., and C. D. Chambers. 1976. *The Heroin Epidemics: A Study of Heroin Use in the United States, 1965–75*. New York: Spectrum.

Inciardi, J. A., ed. 1981. *The Drugs-Crime Connection*. London: Sage.

Institute for the Study of Drug Dependence. 1980. *Prevalence of Psychotropic Drug Taking amongst Women in the UK*. London: Institute for the Study of Drug Dependence.

———. 1987. "Gloves Off in Anti-injecting Campaign." *Druglink* 2(6):4, 10–12.

———. 1989. "New Drugs Ads Focus on Sharing." *Druglink* 4(1):5.

Interpol. 1989. *International Meeting on Assets Derived from Crime: Reference Documents*. Saint Cloud, France: Interpol.

Jamieson, A., A. Glanz, and S. MacGregor. 1984. *Dealing with Drug Misuse: Crisis Intervention in the City*. London: Tavistock.

Jarvis, G., and H. Parker. 1989. "Young Heroin Users and Crime: How Do the 'New Users' Finance Their Habits?" *British Journal of Criminology* 29(2):175–85.

Jefferson, T., and R. Grimshaw. 1984. *Controlling the Constable: Police Accountability in England and Wales*. London: Frederick Muller.

Johnson, B. D. 1975*a*. "Righteousness before Revenue: The Forgotten Moral Crusade against the Indo-Chinese Opium Trade." *Journal of Drug Issues* 5:304–26.

———. 1975*b*. "Understanding British Addiction Statistics." *Bulletin on Narcotics* 27(1):49–65.

Johnson, B. D., P. J. Goldstein, E. Preble, J. Schmeidler, D. S. Lipton, B. Spunt, and T. Miller. 1985. *Taking Care of Business: The Economics of Crime by Heroin Abusers*. Lexington, Mass.: Lexington.

Judson, H. 1973. *Heroin Addiction in Britain*. New York: Harcourt Brace Jovanovich.

Kaplan, J. 1983. *The Hardest Drug: Heroin and Public Policy*. Chicago: University of Chicago Press.

Kay, L. 1987. "Prescription or Proscription? The New Maintenance Myths." *Mersey Drugs Journal* 1(3):12–13.

Kleiman, Mark A. R., and Kerry Smith. 1990. "State and Local Drug Enforcement: In Search of a Strategy." In *Drugs and Crime*, edited by M. Tonry and N. Morris. Vol. 13 of *Crime and Justice: A Review of Research*, edited by M. Tonry and N. Morris. Chicago: University of Chicago Press.

Lacey, R., and S. Woodward. 1985. *That's Life! Survey on Tranquillisers*. London: BBC/Mind.

Laurie, P. 1967. *Drugs: Medical, Psychological and Social Facts*. Harmondsworth: Penguin.

Laycock, G. 1984. *Reducing Burglary: A Study of Chemists' Shops*. Crime Prevention Unit Paper no. 1. London: Home Office.

Le Gendre, B. 1989. "La drogue dans tous ses etats." *Le monde* (August 21), p. 14.

Leuw, Ed. In this volume. "Drugs and Drug Policy in the Netherlands."

Lewis, R. 1989. "European Markets in Cocaine." *Contemporary Crises* 13(1):35–52.

Lewis, R., R. Hartnoll, S. Bryer, E. Daviaud, and M. Mitcheson. 1985. "Scoring Smack: The Illicit Heroin Market in London, 1980–1983." *British Journal of Addiction* 80:281–90.

Lindop, G. 1985. *The Opium-Eater: A Life of Thomas De Quincey*. Oxford: Oxford University Press.

McClelland, B. 1987. "HIV Infection in Drug Abusers in Scotland." In *Future Trends in AIDS,* edited by the Department of Health and Social Security. London: H M. Stationery Office.

McDermott, P. 1988. "Harm Reduction and AIDS Prevention: An Evaluation of Attitudes, Lifestyle and Behaviour of Syringe Exchange Clients." *Mersey Drugs Journal* 1(5):10–12.

MacGregor, S., ed. 1989. *Drugs and British Society: Responses to a Social Problem in the 1980s.* London: Routledge.

MacGregor, S., B. Ettorre, and R. Coomber. 1987. *Summary of the First Phase of Research: An Assessment of the Central Funding Initiative on Services for the Treatment and Rehabilitation of Drug Misusers.* London: University of London, Birkbeck College.

MacInnes, C. 1985. *City of Spades.* London: Alison & Busby.

McKeganey, N. 1988. "Shadowland: General Practitioners and the Treatment of Opiate-abusing Patients." *British Journal of Addiction* 83:373–86.

McKeganey, N., and F. A. Boddy. 1987. *Drug Abuse in Glasgow: An Interim Report of an Exploratory Study*. Glasgow: University of Glasgow, Department of Child Health and Obstetrics.

———. 1988. "General Practitioners and Opiate-abusing Patients." *Journal of the Royal College of General Practitioners* 38:73–75.

Manning, P. K. 1980. *The Narcs' Game: Organizational and Informational Limits on Drug Law Enforcement*. Cambridge, Mass.: MIT Press.

Marks, J. 1987. "The Paradox of Prohibition." *Mersey Drugs Journal* 1(1):6–7.

Marsh, C. 1986. "Medicine and the Media: Government Campaign on Misuse of Drugs Report." *British Medical Journal* 292:895.

Marwick, A. 1965. *The Deluge: British Society and the First World War*. London: Macmillan.

Mason, T. 1986. "The Yellowhammer Anti-heroin Work in New Blow as Report Explodes Addiction Myth: Are the Government's £2m Ads Working?" *Campaign* (September 26), pp. 16–17.

Metropolitan Police. 1986. *Drug Abuse: A Guide for Divisions on the Formation of Multi-agency Cooperation*. London: New Scotland Yard.

Ministry of Health. 1926. *Report of the Departmental Committee on Morphine and Heroin Addiction*. London: H.M. Stationery Office.

———. 1961. *Drug Addiction: Report of the Interdepartmental Committee*. London: H.M. Stationery Office.

———. 1965. *Drug Addiction: The Second Report of the Interdepartmental Committee*. London: H.M. Stationery Office.

Mitcheson, M. C., and R. L. Hartnoll. 1978. "Conflicts in Deciding Treatment within Drug Dependency Clinics." In *Problems of Drug Abuse in Britain*, edited by D. J. West. Cambridge: Institute of Criminology.

Monitoring Research Group. 1988. *Injecting Equipment Exchange Schemes: Final Report*. London: University of London, Goldsmiths' College.

Moore, M. H. 1977. *Buy and Bust: The Effective Regulation of an Illicit Market in Heroin*. Lexington, Mass.: Lexington.

———. 1985. "Regulating Heroin: Kaplan and Trebach on the Dilemma of Public Policy." *American Bar Foundation Research Journal* 3:723–31.

Morgan, R., and D. J. Smith. 1989. *Coming to Terms with Policing: Perspectives on Policy*. London: Routledge.

Morrison, V. 1988. "Drug Misuse and Concern about HIV Infection in Edinburgh: An Interim Report." In *Drug Questions: An Annual Research Register*, issue 4, edited by N. Dorn, L. Lucas, and N. South. London: Institute for the Study of Drug Dependence.

Mott, J. 1981. "Criminal Involvement and Penal Response." In *Drug Problems in Britain: A Review of Ten Years*, edited by G. Edwards and C. Busch. London: Academic Press.

———. 1985. "Self-reported Cannabis Use in Great Britain in 1981." *British Journal of Addiction* 80:37–43.

———. 1986. "Opioid Use and Burglary." *British Journal of Addiction* 81:671–77.

Musto, D. F. 1973. *The American Disease: Origins of Narcotics Control*. New Haven, Conn.: Yale University Press.

National Drugs Intelligence Unit. 1989. *Drug Seizure Statistics 1989*. London: National Drugs Intelligence Unit.

Newcombe, R. 1987. "Prisoners and HIV Infection." *Mersey Drugs Journal* 1(4):10–11.

———. 1988*a*. "The Liverpool Syringe Exchange Scheme for Drug Injectors: Initial Evidence of Effectiveness in HIV Prevention." *Mersey Drugs Journal* 1(6):4–5.

———. 1988*b*. "Serious Fun: Drug Education through Popular Culture." *Druglink* 3(6):10–13.

———. 1988*c*. "Drugs and AIDS: Radical Proposals Shelved." *Mersey Drugs Journal* 1(6):10–13.

Oppenheimer, E., M. Sheehan, and C. Taylor. 1988. "Letting the Client Speak: Drug Misusers and the Process of Help Seeking." *British Journal of Addiction* 83:635–47.

Parker, H., K. Bakx, and R. Newcombe. 1986. *Drug Misuse in Wirral: A Study of Eighteen Hundred Problem Drug Users Known to Official Agencies. The First Report of the Wirral Misuse of Drugs Research Project*. Liverpool: University of Liverpool.

———. 1988. *Living with Heroin: The Impact of a Drugs "Epidemic" on an English Community*. Milton Keynes: Open University Press.

Parker, H., and C. Chadwick. 1987. *Heroin Use, Mothers and Child Care.* Report of the Misuse of Drugs Research Project. Liverpool: University of Liverpool.

Parker, H., and R. Newcombe. 1987. "Heroin Use and Acquisitive Crime in an English Community." *British Journal of Sociology* 38(3):331–50.

Parry, A. 1988. "HIV and Drugs: Outreach Work in the Mersey Region." *Mersey Drugs Journal* 2(3):7–9.

Parry, A., and P. O'Hare. 1988. "This Means War! Drug Education the American Way." *Mersey Drugs Journal* 2(1):7–11.

Pearson, G. 1975. *The Deviant Imagination: Psychiatry, Social Work and Social Change.* London: Macmillan.

———. 1983. *Hooligan: A History of Respectable Fears.* London: Macmillan.

———. 1987*a*. *The New Heroin Users.* Oxford: Basil Blackwell.

———. 1987*b*. "Social Deprivation, Unemployment and Patterns of Heroin Use." In *A Land Fit for Heroin? Drug Policies, Prevention and Practice*, edited by N. Dorn and N. South. London: Macmillan.

———. 1989*a*. "Drugs, Law Enforcement and Criminology." In *Drugs Research and Policy in Britain*, edited by V. Berridge. Aldershot: Gower/Avebury.

———. 1989*b*. "The Street Connection." *New Statesman and Society* (September 15), pp. 10–11.

———. 1989*c*. "Low-Level Drug Enforcement: A Multi-agency Perspective from Britain." Paper presented at the conference "What Works: An International Perspective on Drug Abuse and Prevention Research," New York, October.

Pearson, G., M. Gilman, and S. McIver. 1985. "Heroin Use in the North of England." *Health Education Journal* 45(3):186–89.

———. 1986. *Young People and Heroin: An Examination of Heroin Use in the North of England.* London: Health Education Council. 2d ed., Aldershot: Gower/Avebury, 1987.

Pearson, G., A. Sampson, H. Blagg, P. Stubbs, and D. Smith. 1989. "Policing Racism." In *Coming to Terms with Policing*, edited by R. Morgan and D. J. Smith. London: Routledge.

Peck, D. F., and M. A. Plant. 1986. "Unemployment and Illegal Drug Use: Concordant Evidence from a Prospective Study and National Trends." *British Medical Journal* 293:929–32.

Pelzman, S. 1989. "The Failure of Enforcement." *British Journal of Addiction* 84:469–70.

Picardie, J., and D. Wade. 1985. *Heroin: Chasing the Dragon.* Harmondsworth: Penguin.

Plant, M. A., D. F. Peck, and E. Samuel. 1985. *Alcohol, Drugs and School-Leavers.* London: Tavistock.

Plant, M. L., M. A. Plant, D. F. Peck, and J. Setters. 1989. "The Sex Industry, Alcohol and Illicit Drugs: Implications for the Spread of HIV Infection." *British Journal of Addiction* 84:53–59.

Police Staff College. 1987. *Drugs: A Review of the Government Strategy "Tackling Drug Misuse" from a Police Perspective.* Report of the Drug Topic Group, Twenty-fourth Senior Command Course. Bramshill: Police Staff College.

Power, R. 1989. "Drugs and the Media: Prevention Campaigns and Television." In *Drugs and British Society*, edited by S. MacGregor. London: Routledge.

Power, R., R. Hartnoll, and E. Daviaud. 1988. "Drug Injecting, AIDS, and Risk Behaviour: Potential for Change and Intervention Strategies." *British Journal of Addiction* 83:649–54.

Preble, E., and J. J. Casey. 1969. "Taking Care of Business: The Heroin User's Life on the Street." *International Journal of the Addictions* 4(1):1–24.

Prison Reform Trust. 1988. *HIV, AIDS and Prisons*. London: Prison Reform Trust.

Pryce, K. 1979. *Endless Pressure: A Study of West Indian Lifestyles in Bristol*. Harmondsworth: Penguin.

Rahman, M. Z., J. Ditton, and A. J. M. Forsyth. 1989. "Variations in Needle Sharing Practices among Intravenous Drug Users in the Possil (Glasgow)." *British Journal of Addiction* 84:923–27.

Reiner, R. 1985. *The Politics of the Police*. Brighton: Wheatsheaf.

Research Bureau Ltd. 1986. *Heroin Misuse Campaign Evaluation: Report of Findings*. London: Research Bureau Ltd.

Rex, J. 1987. "Life in the Ghetto." In *The Roots of Urban Unrest*, edited by J. Benyon and J. Solomos. London: Pergamon.

Robertson, J. R., A. B. V. Bucknall, P. D. Welsby, J. J. Roberts, J. M. Inglis, J. F. Peutherer, and R. P. Brettle. 1986. "Epidemic of AIDS Related Virus (HTLV III/LAV) Infection among Intravenous Drug Abusers." *British Medical Journal* 292:527–29.

Rosenbaum, M. 1981. *Women on Heroin*. New Brunswick, N.J.: Rutgers University Press.

Royal College of Psychiatrists. 1986. *Alcohol: Our Favourite Drug*. London: Tavistock.

———. 1987*a*. *Drug Scenes: A Report on Drugs and Drug Dependence by the Royal College of Psychiatrists*. London: Gaskell.

———. 1987*b*. *Community Treatment Orders: A Discussion Document*. London: Royal College of Psychiatrists.

Runnymede Trust. 1981. *Employment, Unemployment and the Black Population*. London: Runnymede Trust.

Sakol, M. S., C. Stark, and R. Sykes. 1989. "Buprenorphine and Temazepam Abuse by Drug Takers in Glasgow: An Increase." *British Journal of Addiction* 84:439–41.

Sampson, A., P. Stubbs, D. Smith, G. Pearson, and H. Blagg. 1988. "Crime, Localities and the Multi-agency Approach." *British Journal of Criminology* 28(4):478–93.

Scarman, Lord. 1981. *Report of an Inquiry into the Brixton Disorder, 10th–12th April 1981*. London: H.M. Stationery Office.

Schur, E. M. 1964. "Drug Addiction under British Policy." In *The Other Side: Perspectives on Deviance*, edited by H. S. Becker. New York: Free Press.

Scottish Home and Health Department. 1986. *HIV Infection in Scotland, Report of the Scottish Committee on HIV Infection and Intravenous Drug Misuse*. Edinburgh: Scottish Home and Health Department.

———. 1988*a*. *Health in Scotland 1987*. Edinburgh: H.M. Stationery Office.

———. 1988*b*. *AIDS and Drug Misuse: Sale of Injecting Equipment by Retail Pharmacists*. National Health Service Circular (GEN) 19, June.

Scott-Moncrieff, L. 1988. "Comments on the Discussion Document of the Royal College of Psychiatrists regarding Community Treatment Orders." *Bulletin of the Royal College of Psychiatrists* 12(June):220–23.

Smart, C. 1984. "Social Policy and Drug Addiction: A Critical Study of Policy Development." *British Journal of Addiction* 79:31–39.

———. 1985. "Drug Dependence Units in England and Wales: The Results of a National Survey." *Drug and Alcohol Dependence* 15:131–44.

Smith, D. J. 1981. *Unemployment and Racial Minorities*. London: Policy Studies Institute.

Smith, D. J., and J. Gray. 1985. *Police and People in London: The PSI Report*. Aldershot: Gower.

Smith, M. 1988. "Prescribing Policy and Normalisation." *Mersey Drugs Journal* 1(5):16–17.

Social Services Committee. 1985. *Misuse of Hard Drugs: Fourth Report of the Social Services Committee*. London: H.M. Stationery Office.

Social Services Inspectorate. 1986. *Project on Drug Misuse*. London: Department of Health and Social Security.

Society of Civil and Public Servants. 1984*a*. *Customs Controls in the United Kingdom. Evidence to Support a Claim for Additional Customs Staff Submitted to the Board of Customs and Excise, March 1984*. London: Customs and Excise Group of the Society of Civil and Public Servants.

———. 1984*b*. *Customs Controls in the United Kingdom. Updated Evidence to Support a Claim for Additional Customs Staff Submitted to the Board of Customs and Excise, September 1984*. London: Customs and Excise Group of the Society of Civil and Public Servants.

Solomos, J. 1988. *Black Youth, Racism and the State*. Cambridge: Cambridge University Press.

South, N. 1987. "Editorial." In *Drug Questions: An Annual Research Register*, issue no. 3, edited by N. Dorn, L. Lucas, and N. South. London: Institute for the Study of Drug Dependence.

Spear, H. B. 1969. "The Growth of Heroin Addiction in the U.K." *British Journal of Addiction* 64:245–55.

———. 1988. "Drug Policy: Time for a Change." *Mersey Drugs Journal* 2(3):12–14.

Stein, S. D. 1985. *International Diplomacy, State Administrators and Narcotics Control: The Origins of a Social Problem*. Aldershot: Gower.

Stimson, G. V. 1973. *Heroin and Behaviour*. Shannon: Irish University Press.

———. 1984. "Drugs and Social Policy: The Establishment of Drug Control in Britain, 1900–30." *British Journal of Addiction* 79:17–29.

———. 1987. "The War on Heroin: British Policy and the International Trade in Illicit Drugs." In *A Land Fit for Heroin? Drug Policies, Prevention and Practice*, edited by N. Dorn and N. South. London: Macmillan.

Stimson, G. V., K. Dolan, M. Donoghoe, and L. Alldritt. 1988. "Syringe Exchange 1." *Druglink* 3(3):10–11.

Stimson, G. V., K. Dolan, M. Donoghoe, L. Alldritt, and R. Lart. 1989. "Syringe Exchange 3: Can Injectors Change?" *Druglink* 4(1):10–11.

Stimson, G. V., M. Donoghoe, L. Alldritt, and K. Dolan. 1988. "Syringe Exchange 2: The Clients." *Druglink* 3(4):8–9.

Stimson, G. V., and E. Oppenheimer. 1982. *Heroin Addiction: Treatment and Control in Britain*. London: Tavistock.

Stockley, D. 1988. "National Drugs Intelligence Unit." *Police Journal* (October), pp. 295–303.

Strang, J. 1987. "The Prescribing Debate." *Druglink* 2(4):10–12.

———. 1989. "A Model Service: Turning the Generalist on to Drugs." In *Drugs and British Society*, edited by S. MacGregor. London: Routledge.

Swiss Federal Commission. 1989. *Aspects de la situation et de la politique en matière de drogue en Suisse. Rapport de la sous-commission "Drogue" de la Commission Fédérale des Stupefiants*. Berne: Office Fédéral de la Santé.

Szasz, T. S. 1961. *The Myth of Mental Illness*. New York: Harper & Row.

———. 1963. *Law, Liberty and Psychiatry*. New York: Macmillan.

Tayler, F. S. 1986. *COI Management Summaries of Completed Research Projects: DHSS Anti-heroin Campaign Evaluation, Research Stages I–III*. Memorandum RS2096. Central Office of Information Research Unit.

Tongue, C. 1988. "The Failures of Prohibition." *Druglink* 3(1):7.

Trebach, A. S. 1982. *The Heroin Solution*. New Haven, Conn.: Yale University Press.

Turner, D. 1988. "Figuratively Speaking: The Statistics of the Misuse of Drugs for 1987." *SCODA Newsletter* (August/September), pp. 1–9.

Van der Valk, P. 1986. "A Different Way of Thinking: An Explanation of the Constitution of the European Movement for the Normalisation of Drug Policy." *Newsletter of the European Movement for the Normalisation of Drug Policy* 1:5–10.

Vass, A. A. 1986. *AIDS: A Plague in Us*. St. Ives: Venus Academica.

Wagstaff, A., and A. Maynard. 1988. *Economic Aspects of the Illicit Drug Market and Drug Enforcement Policies in the United Kingdom*. Home Office Research Study no. 95. London: Home Office.

———. 1989. "Economic Aspects of the Illicit Drug Market and Drug Enforcement Policies in the United Kingdom: Summary of the Report." *British Journal of Addiction* 84:461–67.

Wilson, James Q. 1978. *The Investigators*. New York: Basic.

World Health Organization. 1987. *AIDS among Drug Abusers: Report on a WHO Consultation*. Copenhagen: World Health Organization.

Wright, A., and A. Waymont. 1989. "Studying Drug Law Enforcement Policies in England and Wales with Special Reference to Intelligence Needs: Preliminary Report on the Police Foundation Project." Paper presented at the Police Foundation conference on "Drug Law Enforcement Strategies and the Implications of 1992," Windsor Great Park, London, February.

Young, J. 1971*a*. "The Role of the Police as Amplifiers of Deviance, Negotiators of Reality and Translators of Fantasy." In *Images of Deviance*, edited by S. Cohen. Harmondsworth: Penguin.

———. 1971*b*. *The Drugtakers*. London: Paladin.

Zander, M. 1989. *Confiscation and Forfeiture Law: English and American Comparisons*. London: Police Foundation.

Ed Leuw

Drugs and Drug Policy in the Netherlands

ABSTRACT

National drug abuse policies in the Netherlands reject law enforcement as the primary drug abuse strategy except in regard to higher levels of trafficking in hard drugs. Dutch policy can be characterized as normalizing, pragmatic, and nonmoralistic. It accepts the existence of the use of illegal drugs as inevitable in modern society. Official reactions are directed at reduction of social and personal harms. The drug policy is based on the revised Opium Act of 1976 that aims at separating the markets and the social contexts of soft drugs (cannabis), and hard drugs. It focuses law-enforcement efforts on the higher levels of the supply system. Retail trade in cannabis is tolerated in numerous "coffee shops." The use of hard drugs is primarily considered a public health problem. Policy components concerning hard-drug use include easily accessible social assistance programs, methadone maintenance, other drug treatment facilities, and needle exchange.

The Dutch parliament enacted the revised Opium Act in 1976. This penal law is part of the policy framework of Dutch drug policy that includes tolerance for nonconforming lifestyles, risk reduction in regard to the harmful health and social consequences of drug taking, and penal measures directed against illicit trafficking in hard drugs. This multifaceted approach established the basic principles and operating practices of contemporary social and criminal drug policy in the Netherlands.

Dutch drug policy is pragmatic and nonmoralistic. Govert van de

Ed Leuw is senior researcher in the Ministry of Justice, Scientific Research and Documentation Center. He thanks Charles D. Kaplan, Dirk Korf, and Theo Bot for their helpful comments and Marisca Brouwers and Jo-Ann Wemmers for their English-language editing.

0192-3234/91/0014-0008$01.00

Wijngaart has conceptualized Dutch drug policy within a "normalizing" model of social control (aiming at depolarization and integration of deviance) as opposed to a "deterrence" model of social control (aiming at isolation and removal of deviance) (van de Wijngaart 1990, pp. 83–104). Within this ideology of normalization, illegal drugs are seen as a limited and manageable social problem rather than an alien threat forced on an otherwise innocent society.

The existence of deviant drug use is widely accepted as inevitable in modern Dutch society. To a certain extent the phenomena of drug addiction and low levels of drug distribution have been allowed to become visible and relatively undisturbed by law-enforcement efforts. This reflects a conscious choice to aim at reduced risks of drug addiction, rather than at the wholesale eradication of drug use. Wholesale eradication has been rejected as unrealistic because it is inevitably futile and because repressive attempts to eradicate drug use are believed likely to produce social damage, rather than to prevent or cure it. A rigorous law-enforcement strategy is likely both to breed a violent and subterranean illicit drug market and to marginalize drug users and minor traffickers more than they already are. According to the Dutch philosophy of drug policy, both processes will exacerbate clearly undesirable secondary problems.

The Dutch drug policy has resulted in the effective legalization of soft drugs (hashish and marijuana). This may be understood as partial "decriminalization" of use and small scale trade. Although formally these activities are misdemeanors, in practice, there exists an all but full decriminalization of these manifestations of cannabis. The hard-drug problem, by contrast, is treated as a public health problem in which law enforcement plays a restricted and secondary role.

Modern drug policy in the Netherlands has consistently been flexible and reflects an attempt at social control by nonmoralistic and adaptable means. This essay describes and explains the content, development, and implementation of Dutch drug policy. Section I describes the extent and seriousness of drug problems in the Netherlands. Comparisons are made with other Western countries. The existing penal law legislation and the current law-enforcement approach are discussed. Section II presents the recent history of drug policy formulation, including the arguments and proposals of two national advisory committees on drug policy and the parliamentary discussions preceding the adoption of the revised Opium Act. In Section III Dutch drug policies are contrasted to those of other countries. Section IV discusses the evolution of nonjudicial ways of social reaction to drug problems. The illusions of being able to solve the problem of hard drugs by just relying on tolerance and sociomedical care were abandoned. Instead a more sober approach was adopted that accepted the inevitability of drug addiction and aimed at the reduction of the risks involved. Section V provides a short case history of Amsterdam as a renowned center of the drug phenomenon. Section VI offers concluding remarks.

I. Drug Policies and Drug Problems

Although the Netherland's drug policies may be unusual, drug taking in the Netherlands is not. The kinds of drugs used and the prevalence of drug dependence are not atypical for Western European countries. This section describes current drug laws and prosecutorial policies, reviews what is known about the prevalence of drug use, and describes drug-related social problems in the Netherlands.

A. *Drug Law-Enforcement Policy*

The revised Opium Act of 1976 is a compromise between outright prohibition and attempted normalization and social integration of drug use. Compared with previous Dutch drug laws, the 1976 penal law revision embodied the following changes: reduction of all penalties regarding soft drugs; reduction of penalties for possession for use (e.g., possession for own use of hard drugs could be penalized by up to four years under the old Opium Act of 1928 compared to one year under the present Opium Act); differentiation of maximum penalties for different aspects of drug trafficking; and an *increase* of maximum penalties for trafficking in hard drugs, from four years to twelve years.

The partly decriminalized status of cannabis (marijuana and hashish) is the most explicit expression of the normalizing approach. The act includes two schedules. Schedule 1 lists a number of substances (opiates, cocaine, amphetamines, LSD) under the heading "drugs presenting unacceptable risks." Schedule 2 mentions cannabis only, without mention of unacceptable risks. Penalties for forbidden actions pertaining to schedule 2 are considerably lower than those for schedule 1.

Laws in practice are, however, more relevant than laws in books. The social reality of modern penal law involvement with illegal drugs may be described as de facto abolition in regard to use of small quantities of all illegal substances. Normally for the use of hard drugs, as for the use of soft drugs, there are no investigations, arrests, or criminal prosecutions (Rüter 1988). For marijuana, there has been a de facto legalization of the retail market. Hashish and marijuana are openly permitted (though not officially "licensed") to be traded in limited quantities. During the past decade, this has taken the form of small commercial outlets, "coffee shops," which operate openly, similar to "normal" bars or coffee shops (Jansen 1989).

For commercial trafficking in drugs, Dutch policies and practices resemble those of most Western countries. The Dutch drug policy conforms to the international agreements to combat drug importation, exportation, and transportation (Rüter 1988; van Kalmthout 1989). A recent publication of the U.S. Embassy in the Netherlands observes: "Dutch attitudes toward trafficking closely mirror those of the United States government and of the neighboring states in the European Community" (U.S. Embassy 1989, p. 2).

Law-enforcement policy in the Netherlands operates within the framework of general national drug policies, except concerning large-scale drug trafficking, where law-enforcement agencies act autonomously. In other realms of the drug problem, such as the control of street markets for hard drugs, meeting places for drug users, and the supervision over commercial establishments for the sale of soft drugs, crime control interests are coordinated with public order, public health, and welfare interests. Typically police and justice authorities work with municipal authorities to integrate law-enforcement activities into the central priorities of local drug policies.

The flexibility of drug law-enforcement approaches is warranted by the "expediency principle," which authorizes the prosecution office to decide whether to prosecute or initiate criminal investigations. Those decisions can be made "in the public interest." They are ultimately based on the political responsibility of the Minister of Justice.

In 1976, guidelines for the investigation and prosecution of drug offenses under the revised Opium Act were issued by the Ministry of Justice. Prosecutors have the authority to direct police investigation activities within their districts by stipulating police priorities in regard to specific violations of the law. For instance, the police operate on the basis of the "stumble principle" when small but commercial amounts of cannabis (thirty grams or less) are involved. The police will not initiate investigations of such violations but may act if they stumble on such an amount (Rüter 1988). In 1987 the commissioner of police in Amsterdam wrote all "coffee shop" keepers in the city, warning them of possible police actions if they traded in quantities larger than thirty grams (de Beaufort 1989, p. 74).

The guidelines give prosecutors some latitude regarding small-scale dealers of hard drugs who provide for their own use. Those cases are presumed appropriate for prosecutorial demands of imprisonment, although no standards for length of imprisonment are specified. For all other hard-drug offenses the guidelines stipulate police and prosecutorial actions, including minimum terms of imprisonment to be demanded by the prosecutor. Under the guidelines, offenses of possession and use of hard drugs, however, do not require specific police investigation or pretrial detention or prosecution (Rüter 1988).

Starting in 1976, law-enforcement practices have developed on the basis of these guidelines. Prosecution policies are illustrated by a study of 1,042 drug offenses that came to the knowledge of the public prosecutor in 1982. Cases were randomly sampled from the files of the prosecution offices in six of the nineteen Dutch judicial districts (Rook and Essers 1987). The authors concluded that prosecutorial practices were more lenient for both hard and soft drugs than was provided under the guidelines. Of all possession-for-trade cases in which unconditional demands for imprisonment were made, 64 percent were below the one-year term designated by the guidelines. "Manufacturing hard drugs" is specified by the guidelines to be met with a demand for imprisonment of at least two years. In 73 percent of cases, the actual demand was less. Similarly, 56 percent of the demands for imprisonment for international hard-drug trafficking were more lenient than the two years of imprisonment directed by the guidelines. In many cases, the leniency of prosecutorial practices could be explained by the small quantities of hard drugs (i.e., ten–fifty grams) (Rook and Essers 1987, p. 39). The sample included sixty-three cases of cannabis trafficking in amounts exceeding 3,000 grams in which an unconditional demand for imprisonment was made by the prosecutor. In 50 percent of those cases, the demanded prison sentence was less than three months (Rook and Essers 1987, p. 37).

The Rook and Essers study does not indicate the sentences actually imposed. It has to be noticed however that judges are not subject to the authority of the minister of justice and are not bound by the guidelines.

Very large cases of international cannabis trafficking, for instance amounts over 1,000 kilograms, will normally be met with a demand for two to four years imprisonment. Large-scale international trafficking cases involving hard drugs will be met by prison sentences of about six to ten years. Of course these figures should be compared to Dutch sentencing standards; in that context, they are very severe. In recent years the median length of unconditional prison sentences in the Netherlands has been about two months. Prison sentences of more than one year occur in only 10 percent of all prison sentences (Jaarverslag Openbaar Ministerie 1987).

In 1984 a working group was appointed by the assembly of heads of prosecution offices of all the judicial districts in the Netherlands and directed to update the 1976 prosecutorial guidelines. The working group concluded that the guidelines for prosecution and criminal investigation of drug offenses should be revised. Its report reaffirmed the policy of partial decriminalization and the restrained application of law enforcement in regard to drug problems in the Netherlands as formalized by the revised Opium Act. "In comparison with criminal law practices abroad there is no need to withdraw from those basic principles. This certainly is not necessary in view of the fact that the policy that has been conducted—and which should be continued—has not resulted in a disproportionate spread of drug use . . . [but has] . . . on the contrary probably contributed to the relatively low level of physical damage in the population of addicts" (Werkgroep Vooronderzoek Vervolgings—en Straftoemetingsbeleid Inzake Opiumwetdelicten 1987, p. 16). The working group observed that the practice of prosecution and criminal investigation had generally been more lenient than was originally intended by the guidelines. Arguing that the original guidelines, if followed, would have caused serious capacity problems for all law-enforcement institutions, the working group proposed that the official guidelines be brought more in line with the more lenient practice that had evolved in recent years.

The everyday operating practices of the police are probably even more important for the control of drug problems than the bureaucratic policy decisions of the prosecution offices. The functioning of the police is determined by many factors, of which criminal policy is just one. How police react to illegal drug problems is influenced by local traditions, official local policies, the policies of public health and social service agencies, the demands of local citizens and specific interest groups, and other situational conditions. Police practices in regard to drug problems in Amsterdam are described in Section V.

B. Extent and Nature of Illegal Drug Taking

The number of addicts in the Netherlands increased sharply from 1974 until the present level was reached around 1980. According to most estimates, there are between 15,000 and 20,000 "addicts" who use opiates, cocaine, or both. This number has been stable for the last ten years, and the average age of this population has substantially increased (Buning 1990; van de Wijngaart 1990, p. 56). This indicates that fewer young people are becoming addicts and that earlier cohorts are aging.

Unfortunately, estimates of numbers of drug addicts in European countries are not based on "objective," comparable, or reliable research procedures. They represent in each country informed estimates of a probable range of incidence. National drug policy officials in West Germany estimate between 60,000 and 70,000 drug addicts in that country. In England, the estimate ranges between 75,000 and 100,000 (Engelsman 1990). Converted to rates, these numbers suggest 100–133 Dutch addicts per 100,000 population; the German rate of 99–115 is slightly lower; the English rate of 132–175 is slightly higher. The Dutch figure is probably substantially inflated by the inclusion of foreign drug addicts (see Sec. V). Due to the relatively "friendlier" Dutch situation for drug addicts, the "foreign element" is probably more significant than in the other countries.

The few sources available suggest that epidemiological developments in several European countries have been comparable (Hartnoll 1986). The stabilization of the number of drug addicts may have occurred somewhat earlier in the Netherlands than elsewhere. For instance, drug addiction in Italy, Western Germany, and England sharply increased until the middle of the 1980s (Hartnoll 1986).

The Dutch prevalence figures for deviant drug use are probably reasonably reliable because of the easy accessibility of social service and medical agencies for drug addicts. It is unlikely that the Dutch figures are an underrepresentation relative to other countries.

In Europe, although cocaine has become more widely available since the beginning of the last decade, present deviant drug use is still primarily a matter of opiates. There is a strong concurrence of heroin and cocaine use in the Dutch junkie scene. A recent field study on drug use and income patterns in Amsterdam, based on a sample of 150 hard-drug users, showed that 70 percent of frequent heroin users (thus excluding those who use legally supplied methadone) also used cocaine (Grapendaal 1989).

There is, however, very little indication of hard-drug users who use only cocaine, to the exclusion of heroin. This suggests low levels of primary deviant cocaine addiction in the Netherlands—a conclusion that is probably also true for other European countries. Deviant, subcultural, and marginalized use of cocaine seems to be restricted to a portion of the heroin addict population. This deviant subcultural form of cocaine use is to be distinguished from recreational patterns of cocaine use. Cocaine use is part of a lifestyle characteristic of some young urbanites, who spend evenings in social gatherings, in private settings, or in fashionable disco bars. A recent study in Amsterdam concluded that among this partying population cocaine is used almost exclusively by way of snorting, in contrast to the junkie scene where cocaine is either injected or freebased (Cohen 1989). Cocaine is traded in these recreational settings, whereas the junkie market for cocaine is integrated into the deviant hard-drugs market. This same study found that nonsubcultural use of cocaine is generally characterized by well-controlled frequency and intensity of use patterns (Cohen 1989, pp. 21–39). Social or mental health consequences were found to be relatively limited and unproblematic. The highest figures for prevalence of cocaine use in the general population may be expected to be found in Amsterdam.

A recent population survey on drug taking in Amsterdam, based on face-to-face questionnaires ($N = 4{,}371$), showed a prevalence of cocaine use at least once a month of 0.6 percent, and of 1.2 percent in the twenty- to twenty-nine years age group, in which cocaine use appeared to be most common (Sandwijk, Westerterp, and Musterd 1988). This is a low figure compared to the 1988 estimate that 1.5 percent of the general population of the United States used cocaine within the month preceding the survey (National Institute on Drug Abuse 1989).

Finally, but not unimportant, there are as yet few signs of crack on the Dutch drugs market.

For both theoretical and practical reasons, comparative figures for cannabis use in the Netherlands and other countries may be of special interest. Because cannabis use is much more common in representative populations than is hard-drug use, its prevalence can be investigated by more reliable epidemiological methods. Consequently, cannabis use prevalence data are probably more reliable than corresponding data for hard drugs. One major question is whether the de facto decriminalization of cannabis in the Netherlands has produced relatively higher prevalence figures than in other countries. A recent analysis combined the results of more than twenty Dutch "ever used" prevalence studies since 1970. The figures were compared with the results of comparable studies in Norway, Sweden, and the United States (Driesen, van Dam, and Olsen 1989). Table 1 summarizes the main results for the mid-eighties in adolescent populations around eighteen years of age. The

TABLE 1

Prevalence of Cannabis Use in the Mid-1980s among Adolescents and Young Adults

Country	Percent
The Netherlands (18-year-olds)	17
The Netherlands (15-year-olds)	9
Sweden (15-year-olds)	7
Norway (15–21-year-olds)	18
United States (18-year-olds)	57

SOURCES.—Hauge (1985); Stockholm Skolförfaltning (1985); Johnston, O'Malley, and Bachman (1987); Johnston (1988); and Driessen, van Dam, and Olsen (1989).

data for the Netherlands represent average results of national school surveys with a response rate of at least 99 percent. The data for the other countries derive from trend studies among similar populations.

Taking survey findings over the last twenty years into account, the authors conclude: "The results of the analysis show that the prevalence of [Dutch] cannabis use since 1970 decreased, whereas the policy became more tolerant. Since 1979 a slight increase in the use of cannabis can be observed. A comparison with data from countries with a more restrictive policy reveals that the use of cannabis in the Netherlands is on the same level as in Sweden and Norway, but far lower than in the U.S. However, the downward trend in these three countries since 1984 did not occur in the Netherlands" (Driesen, van Dam, and Olsen 1989, p. 11).

C. Drug-related Social Problems

Drug abuse and drug abusers are likely to exist in Western societies, irrespective of the character of national drug abuse policies. The comparative data on drug-use prevalences cited above suggest that the extent of the drug problem may not be substantially affected by the drug control policies directed against it. But what about the intensity of individual drug problems?

A number of indicators of the effects of drug abuse for addicts or for society are available: the social marginality of drug users, health conditions of users, criminality, and social consequences for public health, public order, and livability.

A number of health indicators are available. Sixty to 80 percent of

Dutch drug addicts are estimated to be in regular contact with specialized health and welfare institutions (Wever 1989). This may have some relevance for the general observation of many foreign visitors that Dutch addicts appear relatively well and sound. In itself this is, of course, very hard to substantiate and can only be taken at face value.

Mortality of drug users is a firmer indication of the level of social and medical problems in connection with the use of hard drugs. Between 1979 and 1986, an average of 38.4 Dutch citizens died each year from overdoses of heroin. In West Germany, the corresponding annual number is 377. Adjusted for population size, deaths by overdoses are 2.3 times as probable in Germany as in the Netherlands (6.2 vs. 2.7 per 100,000) (Korf 1989). This ratio may well be related to hard-drug use conventions in the Dutch context that may promote safer ways of hard-drug use. In the Netherlands, 40 percent of users are estimated to use drugs intravenously (Buning 1989*a*); in Germany this proportion has been estimated to be at least twice as high. Although reliable quantitative research data do not seem to exist for modalities of heroin use in Germany, it is generally assumed that virtually all German heroin users will eventually use intravenously. A qualitative study of German heroin users showed that 57 percent injected even on their first experience with heroin (Berger, Reuband, and Widlitzek 1980). Different socialization processes of drug use in both countries are also suggested by the finding that "drug deaths" among German users in Amsterdam are about six times as probable as among Dutch users.

The relatively low levels of intravenous drug use in the Netherlands may have beneficial effects for the AIDS epidemic. Among eleven countries of the European Economic Community, the Netherlands ranks eighth with 2.7 intravenous-drug-using AIDS patients per million inhabitants; the mean for those countries is 9.4 (Buning 1989*b*).

The threat of diffusion of HIV infection by drug users has recently overshadowed the long-standing concern for drug-related criminality as a harmful consequence of drug use for society. There is a close connection between addiction to illegal drugs and income-producing criminality. People addicted to expensive illegal substances normally cannot provide for them by legal means (Wish and Johnson 1986). According to records of the Ministry of Justice in 1987, more than one-third of the incarcerated population in the Netherlands were known by the medical prison services to be problem users of hard drugs before incarceration. Dutch users are no exception to the rule of strong correlation of drug problems and delinquency. According to recent figures of the Amster-

TABLE 2

Annualized Sources of Cash Income of Heroin Users in New York and Amsterdam

Source of Income	Amsterdam (N = 150)	New York (N = 201)
Nondrug crime (%)	22	43
Any drug business (%)	18	17
Prostitution, pimping, etc. (%)	22	7
Public support (%)	28	11
Work (%)	4	9
Other legal sources (%)	5	12
Average annual income ($)	23,000	11,290

SOURCES.—For Amsterdam, Grapendaal (1989), p. 40; for New York, Johnson et al. (1985), p. 99.

NOTE.—Percentages do not total 100 due to rounding.

dam probation office, which organizes assistance to drug addicts among arrestees in police cells, about 35–40 percent of this population are users of hard drugs (Meertens 1990).

The social context of illegal drug taking, which to a large extent is produced by the nature of drug control policies, may have important effects on the level and nature of drug-related criminality. What is known about the Dutch drug control policies effects on crime? Only international comparative data would be relevant to answering this question, and unfortunately these are very scarce. The results of the previously mentioned field study of Amsterdam hard-drug users (Grapendaal 1989) might be compared with those from a similar study in New York (Johnson et al. 1985). The Amsterdam study was based on the same methodology—repeated self-reports of concurrent economic behavior—for the purpose of making it comparable to the New York data. The Dutch data are preliminary, based on one of the seven weeks that will eventually be included in the completed project (Grapendaal 1989, p. 25). Table 2 reports the data from the two studies. It suggests that Dutch addicts resort to relatively less socially harmful ways to produce income than do their New York counterparts. According to a comparable study of income sources, similar conclusions can be drawn for the generally more problematic subgroup of foreign hard-drug addicts in Amsterdam (Korf 1987).

One other dimension of criminality related to the illegal drug problem in the Netherlands should briefly be mentioned. Violence seems to be as inescapably connected with the supply of illegal drugs as is income-providing criminality with its consumption. Violence is commonly and instrumentally used as a means of disciplining business relations on all levels of the drug markets (Preble 1983; Adler 1985). Similarly, it is used to protect business interests from invasion by rivals and penal law enforcement. Perhaps most damaging, it is a means of terrorizing the community (e.g., the neighborhood in which the drug market is settled) into condoning the drug trade.

It has widely been observed that the Dutch drug market is relatively peaceful. The use of guns is rare at all but the top levels. During the nine-year period 1980–88, fifteen criminal offenses resulting in death in Amsterdam were attributed to conflicts in the drug distribution system. In another thirty-two cases, there was a possible connection with the illegal drug market. Altogether, 135 criminal deaths occurred during that period (Gemeentepolitie Amsterdam 1988).

More important in regard to public order and livability is the comparatively low level of violence in consumer markets for hard drugs in the Netherlands. During the last eight years, there have been only two fatal injuries of Amsterdam policemen in connection with the drug scene. Fist fights and incidental knife fights sometimes occur in the marketplace of street dealers and drug addicts. Open use of soft drugs and some times of hard drugs seems as typical of the Dutch drug situation as low levels of violence.

The relative tolerance of hard-drug use in the Netherlands offers a probable explanation for low levels of violence. The police are not especially interested in small-time street dealers. Police practices, such as undercover purchases or pressuring junkies to serve as police informers, are normally not employed at the retail level of the hard-drug market (van Gemert 1988). Consequently, the paranoia and retaliation so characteristic of drug scenes elsewhere exist to a moderate degree only.

II. The Development of the Dutch Drug Policies

Two advisory groups appointed around 1970 influenced the formulation and execution of what in recent years has come to be known as the "Dutch model" of drug policy. These groups were established in an era and in a society where drug use had come to the public consciousness against a background of relatively mild disputes over lifestyles and value systems and not against a background of criminality, pathology, and deeply rooted social conflict. Those elements certainly entered

Dutch drug policy debates in later years, but by then the traditions of nonmoralistic accommodation and pragmatic risk management were firmly established.

A. *The Initial Problem Definition*

Although opiate and cocaine use had to a limited extent been present in Dutch society since the mid-nineteenth century, drug taking became a significant social concern around 1965 (De Kort 1989). Public concern for addiction and substance use as a social problem was until then primarily focused on alcohol. Drug taking and addiction were rare phenomena of personal misfortune that could be dealt with by the medical profession and by appeals to self-evident morality. There appeared to be no more need for social policy debates on drug taking than on suicide, heart disease, or insanity.

Beginning around 1965, the situation changed rapidly and radically. Drug taking as a social problem came to the public consciousness in a much broader cultural context of diversification of lifestyles and value systems. During that period, a broad variety of traditional moral constraints and normative expectations were successfully challenged. The challenges involved lifestyles, sexual behavior, and conventions of public appearance. They also involved lessening of traditional power differentials between groups in society, such as between the generations or the sexes or socioeconomic and political status groups.

Perhaps because drug taking was closely identified with countercultural lifestyles and values, the initial approaches to drug taking as a social problem in the Netherlands were fundamentally ambivalent. They included both the approval of personal freedom and tolerance and disapproval of deviance, pathology, and immorality. The 1960s phenomenon of "drug taking," which in practice meant the use of cannabis, fell within the gambit of the relative tolerance of Dutch society, as did other moral and normative innovations, including legalized abortion and pornography, and the more uninhibited manifestations of prostitution, homosexuality, and hedonistic sexuality.

By 1970, illicit and licit drug use (LSD and amphetamines were not yet outlawed) had spread sufficiently to generate widespread confusion, anxiety, and, in some quarters, moral outrage. The public dispute mainly centered around the almost defiantly conspicuous use of cannabis and LSD by a young nonconformist, but nonmarginal avant-garde (Cohen 1975). Later, with the "flower-power" revolution well on its way, those groups could comfortably be typed as hippies. Social reaction increased when it became clear to parents, educators, and legislators that the hippie lifestyle was appealing to broad segments of the "normal" young population.

These developments were met with contradictory and ambivalent reactions. By some they were welcomed as a humanistic liberation from worn-out moral and social constraints. The hash-blowing "hippies" had many supporters among liberally minded elites, such as the young university graduates who were taking positions in the rapidly expanding worlds of mental health, welfare, and social policy. To many in this increasingly influential group of policymakers, the hippies appeared as the bearers of the key to a better world of love, understanding, and carefree hedonism.

At the same time, other groups in Dutch society were ideologically opposed to the hippie lifestyle and drug taking. Typically they included older moral conservatives who were affronted by fashionable tolerance and moral pluralism. They appeared as unglamorous embodiments of a cultural ancien régime of medical doctors, parents, educators, and law-enforcement officials. The one cabinet minister (R. J. H. Kruisinga, a Christian Democratic secretary for public health, and a physician by profession) who actively sided with this conservative moral opposition was cheerfully mocked by the flourishing underground press and by one of the major public radio networks.

Apart from the rapidly growing numbers of cannabis experimenters and users, in 1970 more serious drug problems remained rare. "Ever used" prevalence rates of cannabis in adolescent populations in the beginning of the seventies varied around 20 percent (Buikhuisen and Timmerman 1971; Leuw 1972; Buikhuisen, Timmerman, and de Jong 1973). Social dropouts, health troubles, and drug-related criminality were reported in the context of some LSD, opium, and amphetamine use. But these cases, although they were seen as a disturbing prospect by many social policy officials, numbered no more than several hundred.

B. *The Initial Formulation of Drug Policies and the Construction of the Revised Opium Act*

Until the enactment of the revised Opium Act in 1976, the legal status of psychotropic substances was regulated by the Opiate Act of 1928. This act prohibited virtually any conceivable action involving opiates, cocaine, and cannabis. The only exception was for strictly controlled licensing of some opiates for specified medical application by authorized physicians. The act of 1928 did not differentiate the penal law statuses of the different substances and set a maximum prison sentence of four years for any intentional violation (Werkgroep Verdovende Middelen 1972).

In 1969 and 1970, two scientific committees were appointed and charged to consider social policies toward illegal drug use. The committees have since become best known by reference to their chairmen's names: hence, the "Hulsman Committee" and the "Baan Committee."

The committees completed their work in about two years, and each produced a concise report that can easily be read in less than two hours. The committees, each in its own way, exerted much influence on the development of a legal framework and the execution of drug policy to the present day. The committees' reasoning and conclusions were not unlike the results of similar contemporaneous working groups in the United States, Canada, and the United Kingdom (Advisory Committee on Drug Dependence 1968; Commission of Inquiry into the Nonmedical Use of Drugs 1972; National Commission on Marihuana and Drug Abuse 1973). It might be noted that, even in the U.S. commissions' official name, cannabis was distinguished from "drugs." The real difference between the Dutch and the Anglo-Saxon commission reports, in retrospect, is that the Dutch reports were taken seriously by policymakers.

1. *The Hulsman Committee: Defining Basic Social Attitudes.* In 1969, the state-sponsored Institution for Mental Health appointed a drug policy working group chaired by Loek Hulsman, a law professor reputed for his abolitionist views. The fourteen-member committee included representatives of scientific disciplines, high-ranking officials from law enforcement and the Ministries of Justice and Public Health, and directors of mental health and welfare institutions. Five were social scientists. This committee had no official political status.

The Hulsman Committee based its risk analysis of illegal drugs mainly on the dependency-producing potential of different substances including legal recreational drugs and medical drugs. While stressing the potential dangers of opiates, amphetamines (the possibility of cocaine becoming a problem was not foreseen because this drug was virtually absent), and barbiturates, it characterized the pharmacological risks of cannabis as much less serious. The committee observed that "tobacco undoubtedly has stronger addictive properties than cannabis" (Stichting Algemeen Centraal Bureau voor de Geestelijke Volksgezondheid 1971, pp. 19–20). The committee rejected the "stepping-stone" thesis of cannabis noting that "one of the most important causes of escalation from cannabis to other, more dangerous drugs is the fact that cannabis is included in the Opium Act" (Stichting Algemeen Centraal Bureau voor de Geestelijke Volksgezondheid 1971, p. 53).

The Hulsman Committee viewed cannabis use as a subcultural phenomenon, fitting into a certain lifestyle, which in a modern pluralist society should not be judged by the norms and values of the majority culture. The committee reasoned that moral rejection and repressive social control measures would marginalize members of the youth and countercultural subcultures: "The government should not take a censuring position based on the fact that a certain behavior does not fit into the life-concept of those who are holding state-power" (Stichting Algemeen Centraal Bureau voor de Geestelijke Volksgezondheid 1971, p. 40). The report warned against the potentially harmful effects of law-enforcement practices in this respect.

Philosophically the report was based on the principle that the state should refrain as much as possible from interference with behaviors that have consequences only for the individual. In the committee's view, this philosophy precluded use of repressive social control for cannabis as for cigarettes and alcohol: "Although it is highly probable that the smoking of cigarettes will yearly make thousands of victims in this country, it can't well be imagined that the state would take forceful action against the tobacco-smoker" (Stichting Algemeen Centraal Bureau voor de Geestelijke Volksgezondheid 1971, p. 39).

The Hulsman Committee warned against putting more than nominal reliance on the penal law in controlling drug problems; the threat of law enforcement would not only fail to deter people from engaging in vice in their private lives, it would also fail to control the supply side of the drug market. When penal law action is considered, the committee reasoned, its possible or actual benefits should always be weighed against the costs, both in terms of money and resources and in terms of the harmful social effects of law enforcement. Among those latter predicted side effects of a prohibitionist drug control strategy, the committee identified the amplification of deviance and social marginalization among drug-using subcultures, the symbiotic development of vigorous and violent specialized police forces and drug traffickers, and the gradual undermining of civil liberties as well as the legitimacy of penal law.

With hindsight the committees' speculation on the risks of a predominantly law-enforcement approach to drug-control policy may have been remarkably accurate:

> The narcotic department of the police force will develop into a big, well trained, and excellently "armed" unit, which will have to be improved and increased permanently, to keep up with the never-ending escalation. The undoubtedly more vicious character of the drugs problem that will develop will deplete the administration of other options to react to the problem. The dealer of marijuana as we know him now will only survive as a memory of how it all started, in the romantic Sixties and Seventies. [Stichting Algemeen Centraal Bureau voor de Geestelijke Volksgezondheid 1971, p. 49]

The commission specified the social risks of relying primarily on law enforcement: "This instrument will fail again and again, which will induce its proponents to further increase the repressive measures . . . law enforcement will increasingly have to intrude into the spheres of private life . . . [that] . . . will further the polarization between several groups in society and may thus lead to increasing violence" (Stichting Algemeen Centraal Bureau voor de Geestelijke Volksgezondheid 1971, p. 51).

Although the Hulsman Committee's policy recommendations (which are discussed below) were less radical than its rhetoric might suggest, the committee may have reflected the high tide of moral pluralism that dominated Dutch society around 1970. Sexual morals and corresponding legal practices changed drastically. Homosexuality, abortion, and pornography were more openly accepted. Traditional authority relations between the sexes and the generations were challenged, as was the authority of religious and political institutions. During that period, crowds of young American backpack tourists congregated to share their joints openly on Dam-square or in Vondelpark. Sex and abortion tourists from southern European countries descended on Amsterdam. On Friday nights, airplanes from London crowded with gay people set out to party in the gay bars of Amsterdam.

2. *The Baan Committee: Defining Basic Social Reactions.* This fifteen-member "Working Group on Narcotic Substances" was composed mostly of high-ranking administrators of the Ministries of Public Health and Justice and included more penal law officials than did the Hulsman Committee.

The working group's original assignment from the state secretary of social affairs and public health was clearly premised on a traditional prohibitionist framework. The charge mentioned three main topics. Two were the causes of the increasing use of illegal drugs and the correct medical and social treatments of those addicted to such substances. The remaining more extensively qualified topic read as follows: "The counteracting of the irresponsible use of those substances by: (a) efficient criminal investigation of illegal trade channels, (b) efficient criminal investigation of and appropriate ways of dealing with users, (c) education on the dangers . . . of use" (Werkgroep Verdovende Middelen 1972).

The Baan Committee did not indulge in philosophical or ideological digressions but straightforwardly tackled two main issues: first, whether a strictly prohibitionist approach should be retained for all drugs outlawed by the then existing national and international legislation; and second, whether an integrated social policy model could be devised in which diverse control measures could be linked to available policy options like psychological, medical, and welfare measures and education.

The working group's central notion was that the levels of coercion and social reaction to using and trading drugs should relate closely to a risk analysis of the kind of drugs and behaviors involved. The working group devoted special attention to cannabis and concluded that it should not be included in the category of drugs presenting "unacceptable risks." It argued that the social costs of criminal law approaches to use and low-level trafficking of cannabis would outweigh the possible benefits.

The working group stated that "penal law policy should take into account the more general aims of social drug policy" (Werkgroep Verdovende Middelen 1972, p. 67). Drug policy, according to the working group, should aim at primary and secondary risk prevention. The report stated that "socially integrated use of drugs may be possible. . . . This does not mean that no risks are involved, but that those risks could be acceptable" (Werkgroep Verdovende Middelen 1972, p. 66).

The two committees' recommendations were substantially similar. They presented their penal law reform proposals in similar frameworks. They distinguished between cannabis and the other illegal drugs and between using and trading drugs. The Hulsman Committee proposed that use of cannabis should be legalized and that trade in cannabis on any level should be made a misdemeanor punishable only by a fine. Similar misdemeanor handling was also proposed for possession and use of illegal drugs other than cannabis. Trafficking in those drugs was, however, recommended to remain a criminal offense.

The Baan Committee recommended that use and "small scale trade" (up to 250 grams) of cannabis should be made a misdemeanor, for which detention of not more than one month would be the maximum sentence. Trading of quantities exceeding 250 grams should remain a felony but should not be threatened by imprisonment of more than one year. Using and trading other illegal drugs were proposed to remain felonies. The Baan Committee observed, however, that "a penal law approach toward drug users is inadequate" (Werkgroep Verdovende Middelen 1972, p. 68) but urged for the foreseeable future that criminal statutes would be needed as a means of exerting pressure on chronic users to seek treatment and as a symbolic warning for prospective or experimental users.

The conclusions in the 1972 report were almost fully adopted by the center/conservative government that was then in office. A revised form of the strictly prohibitionist 1928 "Opium Act" was constructed by the center/left-wing government that took office in 1973. This bill was not brought before parliament until 1975. The four years between the law reform proposal and passage of the legislation were probably socially constructive because the proposed decriminalization and relaxation of drug control were already introduced in practice during this period. So before official new legislation was adopted, its effects were first to be tested in practice. This accorded with the Baan Committee's view that a drug policy framework should be created in which experimentation was possible. From those experimental conditions, observation and evaluation of ensuing developments should be made: "when sufficient faith in the safety of new positions exists, then the old ones can be left" (Werkgroep Verdovende Middelen 1972, p. 74).

In 1975, a new cabinet in which the (more left-wing) Social Democrats had replaced the Conservatives in a coalition with the Christian Democrats presented the new bill, a revised form of the existing Opium Act, to the parliament. The bill proposed by the government was somewhat less liberal than the Baan Committee had intended. The general recommendations of the Baan Committee had been transformed to concrete provisions. The government stated three goals of this law reform: a more severe criminalization of the trade in amphetamines; a maximal separation between the trade in cannabis and the trade in drugs with "unacceptable risks"; and, finally, the reduction from felony to misdemeanor of the possession of cannabis for personal use.

3. *Parliamentary Acceptance of Pragmatic Policies.* In 1976, the bill was discussed in parliament. Although formally a penal law bill, the Minister of Public Health, Social Democrat Irene Vorrink, was the cabinet member responsible for its defense. The Minister of Justice, the Christian Democrat Dries van Agt, played a less important role in the bill's defense. This order reflects the central notion in Dutch drug policy that this problem is primarily a public health and welfare issue, in which criminal law and law enforcement are of secondary importance. The bill passed in parliament, not without some passionate discussions, but in the end emerged almost unscathed, with two minor criminalizing provisions being added.

The conservative opposition (mainly christian fundamentalist parties plus some members of the Conservative Party) voted against the bill. It was adopted by a three to one majority. The Social Democrats, and two Christian Democratic parties, the parties making up the coalition government, unanimously supported the bill.

There was broad acceptance of the central notion that the use of hard drugs (such as opiates) is not a problem primarily to be controlled by criminal law. A spokeswoman for a Christian Democratic party went even further than the Social Democrats in urging an eventual decriminalization of all drug use. The spokesman for a Christian Democratic opposition party that opposed the bill agreed with the government's view that the threat of criminal law against users of hard drugs should be moderate and only be used to put some pressure on them to seek treatment: "there is a limit beyond which execution of punishment serves no reasonable end. This limit is reached when truly addicted people are concerned . . . we favour medical treatment instead of criminal prosecution" (Handelingen Tweede Kamer 1976, p. 3021). The left-wing opposition agreed with the depenalization of the use of hard drugs but instead of forced treatment advocated the possibility of medical prescription of heroin to addicts. There was little disagreement about considerable increases proposed for maximum penalties for wholesale illicit trafficking in drugs with unacceptable risks, although the Social Democrats and some left-wing parties warned against the social risks of escalating the war against the drug trade. The minister of justice, Dries van Agt, acknowledged that such undesirable effects as more violence, more aggressive marketing tactics, higher prices, and consequently more criminality might occur. But that would be no reason not to fight more forcefully against the suppliers of illicit hard drugs, he stated, and he added that a balanced two-track policy against both the supply of, and the demand for, hard drugs would be necessary.

The bill's opponents mainly argued against it because of the proposed reduction to misdemeanor status of the use and small scale trade of cannabis. This suggests that this symbolic issue was at the heart of the value dispute this new drug policy reflected. Generally the opponents contested the government's conclusion that the individual and social risks of cannabis were "not unacceptable." A small but familiar battle of "scientific proofs" about the possible psychomedical and social harmfulness of cannabis raged in parliament. Only two small religious parties admitted their conviction that official "approval" of any kind of drug use was unacceptable for moral reasons.

Apart from the main question of whether cannabis should be legalized, there remained three controversial issues that were heavily contested: the thirty-gram limit, the "house dealer," and the "Stock Exchange Reports." In one of those, the government was beaten.

There was some opposition against an allegedly too liberal allowance of the quantity of cannabis that could be possessed before felony status would apply. The thirty-gram limit was based on the calculation that this would allow a personal supply sufficient for two weeks that would also enable the user to share some with his friends. Some skeptical representatives rightly assumed that this would protect small scale dealers of cannabis from serious law enforcement. The government did not try to refute this argument but said that such a consequence should be accepted. The later development of the "coffee shop" phenomenon was based on this arrangement. A proposed amendment against the thirty-gram limit was rejected by a two-thirds majority.

Animated discussions were devoted to the phenomenon of the so-called house dealer. This is a person who is permitted by the staff and the board of a recreational or educational youth center to sell limited quantities of cannabis to the members or visitors of such a youth center. This practice had for some years been adopted by a small number of youth centers on the preventive rationale that some of their visitors used cannabis as a part of their recreational activities within the center. Some were attracted to other drugs and consequently there was a substantial risk that dealers of those harder drugs would try to develop a market in the youth center. The house-dealer practice served to prevent the risk of hard-drug use diffusing into vulnerable groups of adolescents. The parliamentary opponents' objections pertained not only to criminal law (as the "house dealer" would probably violate the thirty-gram limit) but also to the fact that those youth centers were fully funded by public means.

As the parliamentary discussions unfolded, criminal proceedings were taking place against a house dealer in The Hague. The Minister of Justice argued that the dilemmas involved in this case could not be solved by law or by a central policy. Decisions should be made by law-enforcement authorities, who, on the basis of the expediency principle, could decide whether to act against a specific house dealer in specific circumstances. The minister affirmed, however, that this practice could be very useful in realizing a central aim of Dutch drug policy, namely the separation of the markets and social contexts of hard and soft drugs. For this reason, he said that "law enforcement should take into account the interests of public health and welfare" when deciding about the legal position of the house dealer (Handelingen Tweede Kamer 1976, p. 3116).

Shortly after the adoption of the new Opium Act, this issue became a subject of practical drug policy consultation at local levels between administrative and law-enforcement authorities. Since then, no more house dealers seem to have been prosecuted. The issue would have been forgotten completely had not an overzealous municipality near the German border adopted the idea of appointing a house dealer, who had operated for some years in one of their youth centers, as an officially licensed cannabis dealer. This was more than the eastern neighbors were prepared to take, and it resulted in diplomatic confrontations between West Germany and the Netherlands (Kaplan 1984).

In the last of the three controversial cannabis issues, the government backed off. The dispute around the "Stock Exchange Reports" was highly symbolically charged. It concerned a weekly feature in a very popular radio program for young people. Information was given on drug issues, including nonmoralistic warnings against the risks of hard drugs; most controversially, the program announced the market prices of different brands of hashish and marijuana. The feature always ended by a reference to the home grown weed variety as " 'Lowlands Weed,' our national pride." The radio performer was the chief editor of a flourishing "underground" magazine and was often alluded to as "the emperor of the alternative youth culture."

This issue showed where the broad consensus on more tolerance for the social phenomenon of cannabis use ended. The "Stock Exchange

Reports" were disapproved by many in parliament, including many who favored the new decriminalizing drug policies. They were deemed to be blatant propaganda for drug use.

Over the government's opposition, section 3b was added to the revised Opium Act, which made illegal "any publication aimed at promoting the sale or delivery" of all illegal substances. The "Stock Exchange Reports" however were never met by any law-enforcement action and continued on the air for five more years. Then the feature died a natural death because of a lack of interest as the prices of soft drugs were beginning to be published on the "menus" of the "coffee shops."

In June 1976, the new Opium Act was adopted. Apart from the parliamentary amendments already mentioned, it contained only technical alterations from the bill that was originally proposed.

III. Ideological Principles and Some Consequences of Pragmatic Drug Policy

In 1976, Irene Vorrink, the minister of public health, summarized before parliament the most important elements of the government drug policy: "the central aim is the prevention and amelioration of social and individual risks caused by the use of drugs; a rational relation between those risks and policy-measures; a differentiation of policy-measures which takes into account the risks of legal recreational and medical drugs; a priority of repressive measures against [other than cannabis] drug trafficking; the inadequacy of criminal law with regard to any other aspect of the drugs problem" (Handelingen Tweede Kamer 1976, pp. 3088–89). Those basic ideas have generally been adopted by the predominantly more conservative administrations that have been in power since 1976. The policy has consistently been implemented and executed, although, as is discussed in Section IV, it has been adapted or modified.

A. *Rejecting a "War on Drugs"*

A broad conviction exists in Dutch society that the problems of drug use are far too serious to tackle with a single-minded "war on drugs." The importation of the American crack epidemic would be widely deplored, but no more than the importation of primarily law-enforcement-based solutions to the drug problem.

This basic societal attitude to the problem should not be misunderstood as a wishful construction cherished by Dutch liberals or leftists.

In the Netherlands, the issue of drugs has never worked very well as a means of promoting political or moral power, nor has it served the specific institutional interests of law-enforcement agencies. Political speeches elaborating on abhorrence for illegal drugs have seldomly been staged. They would appear quite out of place in the Dutch political culture. Consequently there are no votes to be won or positions to be conquered by rallying on the antidrug theme.

A comparative analysis of the development of drug policies in the Netherlands and West Germany concluded that "a low degree of politicalization of the issue was the most important prerequisite for successful decriminalization" in the Netherlands (Scheerer 1978, p. 603). In the decisive years for setting the tone of drug policies, around 1970, the general public in both countries was assumed to be quite similar in its moral rejection of cannabis use. Thereafter, according to Scheerer, social policy reactions strongly diverged. In West Germany, the political parties, the police, and the medical profession used the drug issue to further their own institutional objectives by a process of problem amplification. The Social Democrats who formed the major political party in the German coalition government for reasons of political expediency competed with the Christian Democrats in being tough on drugs. In West Germany, a major drug law reform was enacted in 1981; all maximum penalties were increased and the range of punishable acts was enlarged. Cannabis is included in the same legal category as heroin or cocaine (Albrecht 1989, pp. 176–77). Forced treatment of addicts has been adopted and implemented with limited numbers of addicts (Kreuzer 1989). Until recently, even methadone maintenance has been illegal in West Germany (Albrecht 1989, pp. 186–87).

A contrary process occurred in the Netherlands. The Social Democrats were allowed to realize their "liberal" interests in moral issues because their Christian Democratic partners in the coalition cabinet did not choose to use the drugs issue "as a self-serving sociopolitical symbol" (Scheerer 1978, p. 595).

Adoption of a pragmatic social policy on drug use need not imply a blind eye to the limitations and the basic contradictions of attempts to reach practical solutions. A study of "the Dutch approach" observed that, within the Ministry of Public Health, which bears the primary responsibility for national drug policy formulation, there is no such concept as "solving the problem." Instead, policy efforts are understood as attempts to cope, which means minimizing the risks and the damaging effects of drug use and preparing society to "optimally live with the drugs phenomenon" (Baanders 1989). Positively, this pragmatism acknowledges moral and lifestyle pluralism in modern Western societies. Negatively, it requires a clear dissociation from the stringent moral approach of the prohibition perspective.

The recognition of different risks posed by different kinds of drugs and kinds of drug use is a basic element of pragmatic Dutch drug policy. Perhaps most important, this model of social control tries to account for the ultimate paradox of all drug policy, which is that attempts to limit the availability of drugs tend to increase their damaging social effects as well as their psychological and economic attractions. The more drugs are tabooed and forcefully repressed, the more their users will become marginalized, criminal, bearers and sources of diseases, and the more the world of drug use will offer attractive opportunities for earning money and living a meaningful life in deviant subcultures. A number of mainly American sociological and ethnographic drug studies, based on the tradition of the classic "Taking Care of Business" (Preble and Casey 1969), document this essential paradox.

The challenge for a pragmatic drug policy is to strike a balance between limiting the availability of "dangerous substances" and augmenting their secondary risks. Pragmatic drug policy allows for a policy stance in which responsibility for drug taking is not one-sidedly fixed to drugs, drug takers, or even drug dealers but also acknowledges the effects of social adversity. Socioeconomic, ethnic, and cultural adversity coincide with drug taking and drug dealing. This essentially makes the whole concept of problem solving by a predominantly repressive drug policy rather paradoxical. "The more a society succeeds in protecting its members from poverty and hopelessness, being one of the breeding grounds for drug use, the more it will succeed in reducing the demand for drugs" (Engelsman 1988).

In Amsterdam's "program toward an integrated approach to hard drugs," (Gemeente Amsterdam 1985), the drug problem has been put into the context of social rehabilitation programs for poor neighborhoods. In the most troubled drugs area of Amsterdam, more intensive police surveillance has been put into practice to contain the presence and the impact of the street market for hard drugs within manageable limits. At the same time, an extensive program for renovation of houses for local citizens in this same neighborhood and for economic rehabilitation are being carried out.

Ultimately, there is no way to recast the social order in such a way that basic structural and cultural tensions within any given society will be solved for the sake of solving symptomatic consequences like drug problems. The basic limitations of Dutch national drug policy are acknowledged by one of the key figures in its formulation: "a coherent set of policy objectives and the required means are not available. Often policy objectives are conflicting. In other words: in trying to alleviate the risks for the individual, his direct environment and society as a whole, one is confronted with a lot of unintentional effects of drug policy" (Engelsman 1986).

As yet, the Dutch approach has not gone beyond certain clear limits. There is a continuing debate on the feasibility of radical abolition of all criminal law interference with drugs. This option has some prominent proponents, notably among penal law professors, law-enforcement authorities, and local politicians (Rüter 1986; Baanders 1989). Nationally and officially, however, the flexibility of Dutch drug policy has stopped short of formal legalization or even further practical decriminalization of illegal drugs. Engelsman (1988) described the "Dutch model" as a "compromise between a 'war on drugs' and legalization," to which he added that the Netherlands wants to operate within the boundaries of the international drug conventions. A comparative study of national drug laws of several Western European countries concluded, perhaps surprisingly, that apart from the partially decriminalized status of cannabis, the Dutch Opium Act is not the most liberal (Meyer 1987, pp. 784–88; van Atteveld 1988). Penal law handling of "possession for own use" in Italy, Spain, and Switzerland were more liberal than in the Netherlands.

B. *The Impact of Drug Policy on the Appearance of Drug Problems*

That health or welfare interests take precedence over the criminal law has important consequences for the ways in which drug problems surface in Dutch society. The purposely restrained role of "the law" has led to high visibility of manifestations of drug use. This has strongly shaped the image that has been established of the nature of drug problems and drug policy in the Netherlands, an image which may be quite misleading when its background is not understood or is ignored. Visibility signals failure if maintaining appearances is an important aim of drug policy. It may indicate success, however, if drug policy aims at minimizing the marginalization of drug addicts. "Foreign visitors may complain about the junkies they encounter in the shopping areas or entertainment centers of Amsterdam—but the fact that they encounter them there is, strange as it may sound, one of the triumphs of the policy" (van de Wijngaart 1990, p. 115).

Overt drug taking in the Netherlands shows itself either in its recreational or in its problematic forms. This may be the uninhibited smoking of hash on sidewalk terraces or on the steps of the National Monument in Amsterdam. This may also be the rather more embarrassing shooting of speedballs by down-and-out junkies in the littered alleys of the vice district in Amsterdam, or perhaps the somewhat frightening and volatile gatherings of small crowds of users and sellers of horse and coke, circling around each other.

Those manifestations, provocative or alarming as they may appear, may easily be understood as indicating anarchy, laissez-faire, or defeatism on the part of Dutch drug policy. To critics or skeptics, such conclusions may seem quite evident. They may even be correct from a moralistic frame of reference. They are quite beside the point, however, when those phenomena are judged within the context of the purposes of Dutch drug policy. Similarly, it would also be unwarranted to infer from visible manifestations that the Netherlands is plagued with relatively more drug taking, drug dealing, and drug problems than other comparable countries in Western Europe. As was noted in Section I, the incidence of drug taking is similar to or less than in most of those other countries. Absence of visible signs of drug problems is probably as good an indicator for its presence in society as the (former) absence of political demonstrations was for the level of political discontent in the Soviet Union. Due to a much lesser extent of drug law enforcement in the Netherlands, there is a correspondingly smaller ratio between overt and hidden drug phenomena than in other Western countries.

The hard-drug manifestations described above are the price that Dutch society pays for a policy that will not marginalize problematic drug users more than is necessary. Dutch policy does not encourage the problematic drug takers to move underground, where they will drift out of reach of health institutions and where their subcultures may uncontrollably "infect" other local or social areas in the city. Similarly, Dutch policy will not allow a street market of hard drugs in any other part of the town than where it is expected and can be contained within limits by the permanent presence of the police. This social control policy toward hard-drug manifestation is not different from and serves the same ends as the long-existing policy toward the traditional forms of prostitution in the Netherlands.

In the case of soft-drug use the situation is even simpler. Young American or German tourists smoking hashish on Dam-square will not be put in jeopardy by forcing them to use or buy cannabis in the alleys of the vice district, from dealers who may then have soft drugs in one pocket and hard drugs in the other. Instead they will buy cannabis in decent "coffee shops" that are closely monitored by the police and city officials for not dealing anything other than soft drinks and soft drugs. Legally operating hash cafés can be found throughout the country. In Amsterdam, approximately 300 such small-scale commercial establishments exist. They fill a gap between outright legalization, which will inevitably lead to aggressive commercial marketing of the product, and futile prohibition. The "coffee shops" have been accepted as normal urban facilities that do not offer any special threat to public order or livability (Jansen 1989; Leuw 1989).

IV. Public Health and Welfare Policy

Some twenty years after the first social construction of the drug problem, it is easy to see that the problems of drug taking in society have reached quite different dimensions. We have to recognize that it now involves more than a rather amusing, frivolous battle of "good taste" and value orientations.

A. *Reaching the Limits of Tolerance*

Holland, like the rest of the Western world, has to face the "real" problems of drug use in modern society: addiction, income-providing criminality, the attraction that a drug life offers to the "lowest" socioeconomic strata, the livability of cities, the violence of the drugs trade, the powerlessness and impending corruption of law-enforcement institutions, threats to the legitimacy of the legal system, and most recently the threat of proliferation of AIDS.

The soft-drugs part of the Dutch problem, in retrospect, has been reduced to something that seems hardly relevant for further worrying by simply refraining from moral judgment and withdrawing law enforcement from users and the retail market. The links between soft and hard drugs were effectively broken. No significant health problems ensued nor did a significant increase in prevalence of use, manifestations of "concerned parents," and unnecessary alienation of young people with different habits.

In a letter to parliament in 1983, the state secretary for welfare, health and cultural affairs repeated the major principle of Dutch drug policy: "The basic aim has not been to combat drug use itself or to prosecute persons because they are drug users, but to reduce these risks" (State Secretary for Welfare, Health and Cultural Affairs 1983, p. 2). For the implementation of this aim there has been a heavy reliance on existing or especially created social work and medical institutions. Due to the traditions of the welfare state and to the booming economy of the sixties and early seventies, there existed an extensive, easily accessible network of medical and social assistance facilities in the Netherlands. Inexpensive and comprehensive public insurance covers the expenses for virtually all people.

In Dutch society, there has been some illusion that hard-drug problems could be handled in a similar way as soft-drug problems; this illusion was common in the seventies and particularly manifested itself in Amsterdam. In the seventies, there was a strong contrast between a more or less traditional medical approach for dealing with problematic drug users and an approach that was based on the views of newly professionalized social work groups. According to the medical perspective, addicts were sick people who should be medically treated until their addiction was cured. According to the social work point of view, persons addicted to hard drugs should be supported, cared for, and shielded from moral and social expulsion from conventional society. This latter approach for a time gained considerable influence and may very well be considered the Dutch version of madness in drugs policy.

Countless groups of providers of social assistance and care for problem drug users succeeded in convincing local or national authorities that they understood addicts and should be subsidized to rehabilitate them. Especially in Amsterdam, this led to the establishment of several day-care centers, "drug cafés," and social clubs for hard-drug users (Leuw 1984). The use of hard drugs was officially tolerated in these facilities, while hard-drug dealers were officially banned from the premises. In practice, dealers soon displaced the social workers from control of the daily course of events. One story from the rich Amsterdam drugs folklore, dating to the late seventies, may be illustrative. A well known day-care center (Het HUK) for heroin addicts organized a bus trip for their clients to an exotic bird park. The bus was to leave at 11 A.M. One hour later, many of the expected day-trippers had arrived, but still there was no way of departing because the heroin dealer was not yet there and the junkies refused to leave without this necessity being met. When "The Man" finally arrived, the party took off. The same story further relates the perplexity of a restaurant keeper when, before lunch could be served, half of the company, armed with their soup spoons, rushed to the lavatory to prepare their overdue shots of heroin.

The drug cafés were meant to be shelters where addicts could find rest and protection that would enable them to reverse their path. However, it soon appeared that these settings were often exploited by addicts. The addicts were not so much directed toward rehabilitation as reinforced in lifestyles of deviant drug use. It took several years for the institutions themselves and for the municipal and national authorities to find out that this approach of "limitless tolerance" was a failure (Downes 1988). It had allowed an uncontrolled increase of expensive but inadequate help-providing institutions. In the end, this approach could not survive the confrontation with the harsh realities of increasing numbers of hard-drug users, increasing drug-related crime, and, perhaps most important, the threat of hard-drug scenes to public order and livability in the cities.

After some years, both policy models for the realization of risk reduction had to be reappraised: the traditional medical institutions were basically unable even to reach the addicts and the "alternative" institutions were aggravating the problem. In the early years of the 1980s, this rather sad situation was officially recognized and new ways of pursuing risk reduction were attempted. It was recognized that the social strategy of tolerance and full integration that had worked so well for cannabis could not as easily be applied to hard drugs.

The concept of risk reduction as the core of drugs policy addresses three sets of risks: to the addicts themselves, to their immediate environment, and to society as a whole. The last two sets encompass undesirable effects on public order, livability, public health, and drug-related criminality. The reconsideration of drug policy in the early eighties resulted in a more sober and less idealistic outlook. The first element of risk reduction lost the predominance over the other two that it had enjoyed in practice. The day-care centers, social clubs for addicts, and the like, were abolished under a pledge of "never again."

Not accidentally, this development coincided with the onset of harder economic times and a more business-like "no-nonsense" social climate in general. The officially redefined drug policy in Amsterdam was proclaimed in 1983 as a "two-track policy," which meant that the interests of society would be considered equal to the interests of addicts. To put it in less abstract terms, the revised strategy meant that addicts would receive some well-defined assistance and would not be chased by the police, unless they would cause nuisances for their environment (Gemeente Amsterdam 1985).

B. Reformulation of Drug Policy

Dutch national policy on drug use developed along the lines of the 1983 letter to parliament already mentioned (State Secretary for Welfare, Health and Cultural Affairs 1983). Two years later, the reconsidered national policy was explained in a report published by the Ministry of Welfare, Health and Cultural Affairs entitled "Drug Policy in Motion: Towards a Normalisation of Drug Problems" (Interdepartementale Stuurgroep Alcohol—en Drugsbeleid 1985). This report relied heavily on a sociological study, funded by this same ministry, about meanings and functions of deviant drug use for groups of problematic drug takers in Dutch society and about the career patterns of those same groups (Janssen and Swierstra 1982). The report's analysis has largely governed the philosophy and practice of social policy on drug use to the present day.

The aims and strategies of treatment and social assistance as an answer to drug problems were reappraised. The state secretary argued that aiming at abstinence and complete rehabilitation was generally unrealistic and inefficient: "Addicts who do not, or do not primarily, feel the need to 'kick the habit' or are not capable of doing so will remain beyond the reach of assistance" (State Secretary for Welfare, Health and Cultural Affairs 1983, p. 7). The secretary stated that effective social policy aiming at reduction of the risks of drug use will have to acknowledge that deviant drug use has important functions for the addict. Thus, conceiving no alternative for acceptance of drug addiction in many individual cases, the report argued that "there must be increasing scope for forms of assistance which are not primarily aimed at curing the addiction as such, but at improving the social and physical functioning of addicts" (State Secretary for Welfare, Health and Cultural Affairs 1983, p. 7).

Based on this perspective, in recent years a stronger accent has been put on operating low-threshold facilities that offer limited but easily accessible services for a broad population of drug addicts: free medical care, free large-scale methadone programs, free needle exchange programs, material support (free meals, housing projects), and social guidance programs. Some practical characteristics of such programs are briefly discussed in Section V on the drug situation in Amsterdam. Nationally, methadone programs form the core of most treatment programs for drug addicts. Registration figures of the ministry in charge indicate that the strategy of establishing regular, frequent contacts between the hard-drug using population and sociomedical institutions has been fairly successful. "Methadone has proved itself an instrument for establishing contact. Concomitant social assistance is tailored to the needs of the clients, both with regard to content as well as intensity. Assistance varies from incidental contacts concerning one-time problems, to referral to intensive treatment services" (van de Wijngaart 1988*a*).

The estimated number of heroin users in the Netherlands since the beginning of the last decade has stabilized at between 15,000 and 20,000 (10–20 percent foreigners included). According to information obtained from the ministry, "daily" contacts of methadone dispensing institutions with individual addicts have gradually increased from less than 3,000 in 1981 to 6,800 in 1988.

Those numbers include both maintenance and reduction programs. An unknown additional number of addicts receive methadone from family doctors. By conservative estimates, the majority of the Dutch population of hard-drug users has been partly retrieved from the societal spheres of anonymous, hidden deviance.

The prominent role of methadone provision may be understood as an expression of the rather modest and sober "normalization" approach. Janssen and Swierstra (1982) found that deviant drug users have "good reasons" for their problematic drug use and that those reasons for and functions of drug use are closely linked to moralizing, stigmatizing, and criminalizing social reactions. Drug users were found to use drugs "because," in comparison to their expectations of conventional society, the drug subculture offered attractive alternatives that mainly exist under the conditions of criminalization: adventure, excitement, friends, and illegal economic perspectives.

The policy report *Drug Policy in Motion* adopted the fundamental conclusion of this study that "a gradual cultural integration of heroin use" will be a rational and feasible aim of social drug policy (Interdepartementale Stuurgroep Alcohol—en Drugsbeleid 1985, p. 13). This implies that drug use will have to be accepted as a reality in modern society that cannot be eradicated, but that can "be reduced to a problem of individual addicts" (Interdepartementale Stuurgroep Alcohol—en Drugsbeleid 1985, p. 20).

This objective is to be attained by the "normalization of drug problems." In practice, this means a policy of aiming at reducing secondary drug problems and the secondary attractions and rewards of illegal drug use. Secondary problems are considered to result primarily from the level of criminalization of drugs. They are "the price that has to be paid for limiting primary [trafficking and consumption of drugs] drug problems" (Interdepartementale Stuurgroep Alcohol—en Drugsbeleid 1985, p. 9). The reduction of secondary problems involves a process of destigmatization, while the reduction of secondary rewards and attractions calls for a process of demythologization. The report proposes a sober and unemotional attitude toward illegal drug taking in which users are as far as possible not morally judged, are minimally criminalized, and are minimally marginalized. They can expect to receive assistance attuned to their motivation and ability to rehabilitate or even kick the habit. The report explicitly states that, under those conditions, addicts should be held responsible for their own choices. Assistance will be offered on the basis of reciprocity, and their addiction will not exempt them from responsibility for their acts. The director of the ministerial drug policy department involved summarized the basic notion as follows:

> Being a "junkie" should be de-mythologized and de-glamorized. By pursuing drug policy in the way at present favoured by most countries a specific "meaning" is attached to drug use. The less "meaning" authorities attach to the drug phenomenon, the less "meaning" it generates for addicts. This indicates that drug takers or even addicts should neither be seen as criminals, nor as dependent patients, but as "normal" citizens of whom we make "normal" demands and to whom we offer "normal" opportunities. [Engelsman 1989, p. 215]

This pragmatic and nonmoralizing drug policy has thus far operated within clear limits, although the limits at times have been seriously challenged. The report reaffirms some basic positions that have been taken since the introduction of the new Opium Act. Three possible alternatives for the proposed cultural integration of illegal drug use are mentioned: forced treatment of drug users, large-scale medical prescription of heroin, and legalization. Each was rejected as not fitting within the basic philosophy of Dutch drugs policy.

Forced treatment has been discussed since the beginning of the hard-drugs era. The idea has often received warm support from various groups in the population, ranging from groups of parents of drug users to policemen and trade unions. Among policymakers and perhaps more important among staff members of drug treatment facilities, however, this proposal has been rejected (Sijes 1987). The policy report *Drug Policy in Motion* (Interdepartementale Stuurgroep Alcohol—en Drugsbeleid 1985) arrived at the same conclusion on the basis of incompatibility of coercion with the principle of the addict's acceptance of responsibility. A later report welcomes the idea of applying some pressure to enter treatment as has been an ongoing practice in suspending sentences for addicts brought to court for drug-related crime. The idea of "contract treatment" has recently been promoted by the government (State Secretary for Welfare, Health and Cultural Affairs and the Minister of Justice to the States-General 1987).

The radical alternative of legalization is widely viewed as a theoretical option, with quite a few theoretical advocates. For several compelling reasons—most important and perhaps even sufficient that Holland is a small country in the geographical center of the Western world—legalization has never been considered as a practical option.

Several years ago there was a serious debate on large-scale regulated prescription of heroin. In 1983, as part of the aftermath of the disillusionment with policies of "limitless tolerance" in Amsterdam, the city administration adopted a plan for large-scale prescription. A small-scale medical-psychiatric experiment was initiated with prescription of morphine to a stringently defined group of thirty-seven addicts (Derks 1990).

Proposals were made to the central government for starting an experiment beyond strictly medical purposes with 300 addicts. Some people envisaged such an experiment as the first phase of further policy development that would lead to prescription of heroin to all 7,000 established users in Amsterdam at the time. There is little doubt that the city administration would have introduced this scheme had the central government not categorically rejected it. In a report to the parliamentary commission for drug policy, the government interpreted the Amsterdam proposal as an attempt at "pseudo-legalisation." It further stated that such a policy would be unwise in regard to the unpredictable social side effects, unnecessary in regard to the treatment facilities that were already available or would become available in the near future, and harmful in regard to Dutch international relations in the context of the Single Convention (Tweede 1984–85). More recent drug policy reports from Amsterdam indicate that schemes of large-scale legalized prescription of hard drugs have been abandoned.

V. A City Coping with a Problem: The Case of Amsterdam

Amsterdam is a special case. The city is the largest in the country, the most cosmopolitan, and the main cultural center. It has its own atmosphere, history, and traditions that may all be relevant both to the character of its drug problems and social reactions. Amsterdam easily qualifies as the drug capital of the country. It has the largest concentration of drug users, some 40 percent of the total Dutch number, the highest visibility of drug use, the highest level of social debate on the phenomenon and, to put it neutrally, the strongest reputation. Since 1981, the estimated number of deviant drug users has stabilized around 7,500. In 1989, the drug addict population in Amsterdam consisted of three groups: foreigners (48 percent), Dutch autochtons (33 percent), and Dutch ethnic minorities (19 percent) (Buning 1990). Among the ethnic groups, black people from Suriname constitute about 80 percent. Among the foreigners, Germans and Italians are especially heavily represented. These figures derive from epidemiological estimates based on contacts with addicts in police cells and in the methadone-providing institutions. Since 1981, the average age of the population of heroin addicts has gradually increased from 26.8 years to 31.6 years in 1989 (Buning 1990, p. 12). This has been interpreted as indication that levels of entry into heroin addiction among the Dutch population may be declining.

A. *The Retail Market for Hard Drugs*

Many a visitor arriving in the central railway station of Amsterdam seems attracted to a part of town just left of the main boulevard that leads directly through the city center. The visitor then enters the most visible location of the Amsterdam drug scene, an area known as "de Wallen." In this area of half a square kilometer, the drug subculture has joined prostitution which has "always" been the traditional vice in that part of the city. The visibility of Dutch drug problems and the corresponding dubious international reputation of Amsterdam as the "drugs Mecca" of the Western world is largely based on the existence of de Wallen. The availability of drugs and the opportunities to consume them on the spot make up the major attractions of this vice area to drug takers. Although, as is described below, the levels of tolerance have varied considerably, de Wallen has always been a place where drug takers interested in heroin, cocaine, or pharmaceuticals (including illicit methadone), could relatively safely obtain substances of reasonable quality for reasonable prices at any hour day or night. Horse and coke, which have an average purity of 60 percent (Gerechtelijk Laboratorium 1985), can be bought for an average price of F 150 ($70) a gram.

Apart from being a copping area, de Wallen is an agreeable place to hang around for people who have lots of time but little money. It has traditionally been an attractive part of the inner city where tourists, small business enterprises, university students, sailors, and local inhabitants mix with the participants and the observers of the commercial sex scene. The drug scene has over the last fifteen years quite naturally established its retail market in this setting. This of course does not imply that the drug scene has been welcomed. To the contrary, many people despise the drug scene for spoiling a hitherto pleasant area of city life.

Amsterdam's official drug policy has mainly operated by setting limits on manifestations of the drug market. Thus, over all else, it has aimed at preserving public order and achieving an acceptable level of livability in this part of the city. Different amounts of policing pressure have been put into practice to produce the varying levels of control that were considered as necessary or as feasible at different times during the last fifteen years. During some periods, large crowds of addicts were left undisturbed while they occupied parts of the area and openly traded and consumed hard drugs. In other periods, often responding to protests and demonstrations of the "normal" inhabitants of this and neighboring city areas, tolerance was reduced. During these periods of low tolerance, the petty participants in the retail trade were deterred out of visibility, their clients were forced to keep moving, and those who had succeeded in obtaining drugs were discouraged from overt consumption. The policy of control for the sake of maintaining public order has, however, stopped short of forcing the hard-drug scene from its "natural" habitat. This could easily be achieved in such a limited area. There is, however, a recognition that if undesirable realities are suppressed in one part of the town, they will pop up in another. Some decades ago, there was an unhappy attempt to put pressure on prostitution in this same vice area. In no time, street walkers appeared in the most unexpected parts of town.

In a control policy that aims at striking a balance between reasonable tolerance and necessary suppression, law-enforcement objectives, such as arresting and prosecuting persons in possession of hard drugs and persons participating in the retail trade, may receive a lower priority. A municipal report stated that police actions against the hard-drug scene should be evaluated in light of whether "a more stringent enforcement of the Opiate Act would produce less public nuisance and violent crime than a less stringent enforcement" (Gemeente Amsterdam 1985, p. 25). In an evaluation, the head of a subdivision of the Amsterdam Narcotic Squad operating in the drugs area rejected the idea of more intensive police actions against the drug-using population. According to his experience, this would only lead to adaptations in the drug market, making it still more elusive. "Instead of removing the rotten parts of a drug organisation the police would relapse to 'junkie hunting' as before" (Gemeentepolitie Amsterdam 1986).

Looking back over the last fifteen years, there has been a clear tendency toward decreasing official tolerance for the hard-drug market in the drugs quarter of Amsterdam. The city administration has appeared to be responding to two kinds of pressure in adopting a less lenient policy. International media reports on the alleged drugs anarchy in the area have had some impact, mainly because of a concern that they would damage the city's reputation as an international trade and tourist center. The growing indignation of local interest groups concerned with safety and livability in this part of town has probably played a more important role. Shopkeepers and the "normal" dwellers of the affected neighborhoods have put increasing pressure on the police and the city administration to act against the drug market.

In the early eighties, a policy was initiated of rolling back the well-established power of the drug trade in "the Zeedijk," a street in the drugs area. For several years, this street had been dominated by collaborating bar owners and drug dealers. The hard-drug trade operated openly in numerous bars on the Zeedijk. The Surinamese drug dealers and customers were constantly present. This attracted many more addicts who could be assured of successful transactions any time they wanted. The city administration started a policy of revoking business licenses of all commercial establishments where involvement with the drug trade could be proved. Simultaneously, a city development corporation for the "Economic Rehabilitation of the Zeedijk" was established which gained the ownership of the former "drug buildings."

Within three years, all drug bars were closed down and large-scale reconstruction activities were started as the first phase of a comprehensive program to restore normal economic and living conditions. By 1989, the program had been partially realized. Although no one would dare to claim the absence of other aspects of the hard-drug trade in the area, there were in 1989 no drug bars on or around the Zeedijk. The concerted actions of the city administration and the police had a clear impact on the drug market. Some of the effects may be considered as favorable, others are definitely not. Hard-drug dealing in the drugs area has become a much more fragmented, volatile, and elusive phenomenon; in effect this represents an adjustment by the drug trade to protect itself against interference from law enforcement (van Gemert 1988).

Selling and buying at street level is no longer a two-party phenomenon, but may involve as many as five persons, each playing a partial role. The number of persons being involved in the retail market has thus vastly increased. The drug market is being kept on the move (in the most literal sense of the word, scores of addicts promenading the area in countlessly repeated circles) by the constant presence of the police. New public order regulations directed against the drug markets have been issued, including prohibition of possession of knives in the area. The police have been equipped with new authority, such as temporarily expelling addicts from the area. Local citizens, both shopkeepers and residents, have taken their own actions against the drug market, some discouraged by the city administration and some supported. Intimidating actions by hired musclemen have been resisted by the city, whereas an attempt to remove pill peddlers from a bridge by erecting a pastry stall on the spot has been supported (Leuw 1987).

All this may have diminished de Wallen's attraction to the addicts, but it has probably also resulted in a higher level of paranoia and aggression in the retail market (Verbraeck 1988). It has also been observed that drug markets started to develop in other parts of town after this attempted "cleaning up" of the central areas. Drug problems may successfully be chased around town. Unfortunately there seems to be no way to chase them out of existence.

B. Sociomedical Care for Drug Takers in Amsterdam

Since abandonment early in this decade of the "limitless tolerance" approach to hard-drug users, Amsterdam's social policy has been built on an extensive and easily accessible methadone provision. The Municipal Health Service (MHS) in Amsterdam has a specialized division for drug addiction, which organizes and operates a network of sociomedical aid facilities for drug users. There are in addition therapeutic, social work, and rehabilitation programs. The Public Health Department coordinates the functioning of the methadone-providing institutions and the psychosocially oriented institutions. Here I limit discussion to the large-scale methadone programs.

In 1987, an estimated 4,000 individual heroin addicts received methadone on prescription. More than 70 percent were supplied by one of the methadone maintenance programs of the MHS. Some addicts received methadone from family doctors or as arrestees in police cells. A Central Methadone Registration is operated to prevent addicts from receiving multiple prescriptions (Buning 1990). The maintenance programs have two methods of methadone prescription. The first level consists of two "methadone buses," each with a schedule of three or four stops at fixed times and places throughout the city. The second consists of three polyclinical facilities located in nonmedical settings in different parts of the city. These are referred to as "community posts." The two modalities provide for about equal numbers of addicts.

There are also separate facilities for methadone provision and sociomedical support for specific categories of drug users such as prostitutes and "extremely problematic drug users" (epd's). The needs and problems of these groups are considered to be too specific to be handled by the more common programs. The epd's are down-and-out addicts in the end stages of a drugs career. Many are in bad shape, mentally as well as physically. In the epd's methadone program, they receive more intensive support such as food and shelter facilities. For this group, a special scheme has been set up to manage the welfare allowance. Like other unemployed citizens (in Dutch conditions nearly all addicts are unemployed), they are entitled to a monthly allowance of about $500. The scheme, which can be entered on a voluntary basis, hands out the allowance in weekly portions, after subtraction of rent and some other essential expenditures. It thus prevents the clients from spending the whole monthly sum on drugs in a few days. More intensive support and guidance for those specific groups is also motivated by concern for the diffusion of AIDS infection. This, of course, especially applies to the heroin prostitutes.

The bulk of methadone maintenance in Amsterdam is executed by either the buses or the community posts. Until recently, the methadone buses were adapted, but old and worn out, vehicles of the Amsterdam public transport company. In the spring of 1989, two specially designed new buses were festively introduced by presenting them on Dam-square, where they could be visited by the Amsterdam public.

The buses are the most easily accessible part of the programs. Anyone who can prove to be using heroin regularly may enter the program. Participation will not create any demands on the drug user as far as his lifestyle is concerned. There are no checks on further illegal drug use or criminal behavior. The only condition is that the client present himself at least three out of the seven days a week. The addicts are registered in either one of the buses, which have fixed stops from roughly 11 A.M. to 6 P.M. The buses provide a maximum dose of sixty milligrams per client. The clients are free to visit the bus at any stop. They will receive methadone in liquid form, which is supposed to guarantee that they consume it on the spot. Of course, some clients outsmart the staff in one way or another. Recently, instances have been discovered of clients who shoot the methadone they manage to smuggle out of the buses. This has triggered a discussion in the MHS whether, for purposes of AIDS prevention, injectable methadone should be offered on demand. Apart from methadone, the bus programs offer only basic medical attention. When addicts want more support or guidance, they have to apply to the community posts.

The community posts, however, make some demands on the clients in return for the extra services they provide. Addicts can be "promoted" to this community program if they are prepared to abstain from heroin and cocaine. Once or twice a week, clients are tested for use of those substances. In practice, however, the clients are not thrown out of the program as long as their illegal substance use stays within certain limits. The facilities are closed on weekends, for which clients receive their methadone in the form of pills. When going on holidays, clients are allowed to obtain pills for several weeks. The maximum dose of methadone, 100 milligrams, is higher than in the buses (sixty milligrams). Social workers are connected to the program. They regularly meet with the clients, offering a variety of practical or psychosocial support, ranging, for instance, from assistance in finding adequate housing to weekly consultations or introduction to various therapeutical schemes.

This discussion of implementation of municipal drug policy in Amsterdam has been limited to those forms that characterize the Dutch drug policy approach. Of course, many other therapeutic schemes exist: detoxification programs, psychosocial therapies, social rehabiliation programs, and drug-free therapeutic communities. They are obviously very important facilities, but probably not very different from similar kinds of institutions that operate in the Western world.

There is, however, one more typical arrangement that should be mentioned. In 1984, a free needle exchange program started on the initiative of the "Junky Union," an organized and subsidized self-help group of drug users (van de Wijngaart 1988*b*). The program was established because pharmacists no longer wanted to sell syringes to addicts, and consequently the hazard of an increase of hepatitis B infection was feared. One year later, it became all too clear that AIDS was a much more menacing basis for concern about needle sharing. It stimulated other institutions, of which the methadone programs of the MHS are the most important, to participate in this scheme of needle exchange. Judged by the numbers, the exchange program has fared very well. In 1984, 25,000 needles/syringes were exchanged; in 1986, the number had risen to 400,000; and in 1989, to 820,000 (Buning 1990). Obviously, success of such a program should be measured by other intrinsic and external criteria as well. From the founding of this program, it has been deemed essential that it should be an exchange program and not a dispensing program. In regard to the risks of infection, it is vital that used syringes be returned and safely destroyed. For this reason, addicts can obtain only as many free syringes as they return. In 1985, the return rate was estimated at 80 percent (Buning 1989*a*). Because there is no limit to the number of syringes to be exchanged, there was an incentive for the junkies to cheat. A syringe has a value of about $0.50 to $2.00 in the streets of Amsterdam. Consequently, some junkies would put one hundred used syringes in a plastic bag and claim that there were 125. They stood a fair chance of success of claiming the difference because the exchange staff was not inclined to muddle in a bag of used needles. In 1988, a new foolproof and safe system for receiving used syringes was introduced, in which the objects can be counted one by one. The return rate has increased to 87 percent (Buning 1990). Observers of the Amsterdam junkie scene know several enterprising addicts who make a living by roaming the streets and parks in search of used needles and trading the new ones they receive in return. They thereby not only purge the city of biological boobytraps but also participate in the distribution of safe syringes.

Some external effects of the exchange program have been studied by the MHS. There appeared some clear indications that needle exchange did not stimulate drug use, that it decreased the incidence of needle sharing, and, most important of all, that it decreased the diffusion of injection-related infections in the hard-drug population. No decrease of needle stick accidents with thrown away syringes could be demonstrated (Buning 1989*b*).

VI. Concluding Remarks

Drug problems may be conceived on three levels. The first level is centered around the incidence of drug use and its primary consequences for users. The second concerns the social consequences and seriousness of drug problems. The third concerns the functions of public policy reactions to drug use.

On the primary level, relatively "simple" and objective questions can be asked about the epidemiology and the psychomedical characteristics of substance use. People derive pleasure and relaxation from drug use, but not without paying a price. The price consists of potentially damaging effects of drugs, including their toxicity and addictiveness.

The incidence of addiction to substances and the primary mental and physical consequences of substance use are the most basic and objective dimension of the drug problem. Neither the extent nor the acuteness of drug problems in this sense appear to be much affected by specific drug policies. Western European countries exhibit comparable socioeconomic and cultural conditions and a comparable incidence of drug taking, notwithstanding quite different approaches to drug policy. This may suggest that the nature of drug problems is largely determined by fundamental structural and cultural characteristics of societies. Prevailing lifestyles and consumption patterns are relevant, together with the classical symptoms of structural and cultural strain such as poverty, unemployment, ethnic tension, the decline of core values and institutions, and the alienation and experimentalism of adolescents.

This analysis also suggests that the level of diffusion of illicit drug use is largely unrelated to the operation of vigorous drug law-enforcement efforts, or to the existence of a more tolerant social policy of accommodation. Countries like Singapore or Malaysia, which impose severe punishment including the death penalty, have not "solved" their drug problems. Nor have Western countries like West Germany or the United States that rely heavily on drug law-enforcement strategies. At the same time, the Dutch approach has not "tolerated" drug addiction out of existence.

On the second level of the drug problem, different drug-control policies seem to produce substantially different results. Apart from psychopharmacological effects on users, the hazards of drug taking mainly derive from social reactions to drug use. The more severe and stigmatizing the drug policy, the greater the extent to which drug users are marginalized in delinquent subcultures, the more they suffer and spread diseases, and the more they disturb their social surroundings. Drug policy generates the secondary effects of drug taking. A prohibitionistic policy creates conditions for a drug-using lifestyle that symbolizes protest and opposition to mainstream culture and offers attractive economic opportunities.

On the supply side, the problem-generating effects of prohibitionistic drug policies are more direct and obvious. The "monetarization of risks" is easily expressed in hard figures (Wisotsky 1989). The violence of the drug trade and its capacity to corrupt law enforcement and other institutions are well known.

The Dutch approach has by no means resolved this devastating paradox of drug control, but it has had some success in making drug use less hazardous, alluring, and fateful. By virtue of its successful separation of soft and hard drugs, Dutch social policy is removing the socially created "stepping-stone" mechanism. At the same time, the "decriminalization" of soft drugs has conveyed the important message that the restriction of hazardous substances is not motivated by moral or political expediency. Official concerns about hard-drug taking may thus appear more legitimate and credible, even in the eyes of drug users.

The relatively accommodating Dutch drug policy is not, however, without drawbacks. The intensive and accessible welfare culture in which drug addiction is embedded obviously generates its own secondary rewards. Treating drug addicts as objects of social care is likely to reinforce their dependency and passivity and undermine incentives to break away from the addict lifestyle. The retired, pacified, but perpetual "junkie" may thus become a typically Dutch phenomenon (Swierstra 1990).

On the third level of the drug problem, drugs and addiction may be no more than a fortuitous vehicle for expression of significant cultural processes. Symbolic meanings both of drug use and of social reactions to it may be more important than the actual behaviors and processes. In the early seventies, countercultural use of cannabis had overwhelming symbolic meanings; the real issue was not cannabis but the "cultural revolution" that its use expressed. Most of the social and legal reactions to cannabis had substantial symbolic meaning in the eyes of those who saw the "counterculture" as a serious threat to traditional mainstream values and lifestyles.

The recent Dutch experience has shown that cannabis has largely lost its mythical qualities. Its use no longer challenges basic values of the conventional world. Cannabis is no longer a potent symbol of conflict between generations or proponents of different social and cultural values. Similarly, use of heroin is not preponderantly associated with a romantic subculture of bohemianism and unconventionality but with a dependent population of social welfare recipients. Dutch experience with deescalation of risks and rewards of drug problems indicates that a pragmatic approach may be a viable alternative to approaches that rely mainly on law-enforcement strategies.

REFERENCES

Adler, P. A. 1985. *Wheeling and Dealing: An Ethnography of an Upper-Level Drug Dealing and Smuggling Community*. New York: Columbia University Press.

Advisory Committee on Drug Dependence. 1968. *Cannabis*. London: H.M. Stationery Office.

Albrecht, H. J. 1989. "Drug Policy in the Federal Republic of Germany." In *Drug Policies in Western Europe*, edited by Hans-Jörg Albrecht and Anton van Kalmthout. Freiburg: Max Planck Institut.

Baanders, Arthur. 1989. *De Hollandse Aanpak, Opvoedingscultuur, Druggebruik en het Nederlandse Overheidsbeleid*. Assen: Van Gorcum.

Berger, H., K. H. Reuband, and H. Widlitzek. 1980. *Wegen in die Heroin Abhängigkeit: Zur Entwicklung Abweichender Karrièren*. Munich: Juventa Verlag.

Buikhuisen, W., and H. Timmerman. 1971. "De Ontwikkeling van Druggebruik onder Middelbare Scholieren." *Nederlands Tijdschrift voor Criminologie* 13:193–210.

Buikhuisen, W., H. Timmerman, and J. de Jong. 1973. "De Ontwikkeling van Druggebruik onder Middelbare Scholieren Tussen, 1969 en 1973." *Nederlands Tijdschrift voor Criminologie* 15:259–68.

Buning, E. C. 1989*a*. "Effects of Amsterdam Needle and Syringe Exchange." Paper presented at the conference on "Drug Abuse Research and Policy: A Dutch-American Debate," The Hague, June.

———. 1989*b*. "The Role of Methadone in Amsterdam's AIDS Policy." Paper presented at the first Scottish National Symposium on Caring for AIDS, Glasgow, January.

———. 1990. *De GG&GD en het Drugprobleem in Cijfers, Deel IV*. Amsterdam: Gemeentelijke Geneeskundige en Gezondheids Dienst.

Cohen, Herman. 1975. *Drugs, Drugsgebruikers en Drug-Scene*. Alphen aan de Rijn: Samsom.

Cohen, Peter. 1989. *Cocaine Use in Amsterdam in Non Deviant Subcultures*. Amsterdam: University of Amsterdam.

Commission of Inquiry into the Non-medical Use of Drugs. 1972. *A Report of the Commission of Inquiry into the Non-medical Use of Drugs*. Ottawa: Information Canada.

de Beaufort, L. A. R. J. 1989. "Strafrechtelijke Marktbeheersing." In *Nederlands Drugsbeleid in Westeuropees Perspectief*, edited by M. S. Groenhuijsen and A. M. van Kalmthout. Arnhem: Gouda Quint.

De Kort, M. 1989. *De Problematisering van het Druggebruik in Nederland, 1850–1940*. Rotterdam: Erasmus Universiteit.

Derks, J. 1990. *Het Amsterdamse Morfine Verstrekkings Programma.* Utrecht: National Centrum voor de Geestelijke Volksgezondheid.

Downes, David. 1988. *Contrasts in Tolerance: Post-war Penal Policy in the Netherlands, England and Wales.* Oxford: Clarendon Press.

Driesen, F. M. H. M., G. van Dam, and B. Olsen. 1989. "De Ontwikkeling van het Cannabisgebruik in Nederland, Enkele Europese Landen en de VS Sinds 1969." *Tijdschrift voor Alcohol, Drugs en Andere Psychotrope Stoffen* 15:2–15.

Engelsman, E. L. 1986. "Drug Policy: Is the Cure Worse than the Disease? To a Process of Normalisation of Drug Problems." Paper presented at the fifteenth annual meeting of the ICAA International Institute on Prevention and Treatment of Drug Dependence, Noordwijkerhout, April.

———. 1988. "Responding to Drug Problems: Dutch Policy and Practice." Paper presented at the International Conference on Drug Policy Reform, Washington, D.C., May.

———. 1989. "Dutch Policy on the Management of Drug-related Problems." *British Journal of Addictions* 84:211–18.

———. 1990. Personal communication with author.

Gemeente Amsterdam. 1985. *Nota Hard Drugs, een Aanzet Tot een Geïntegreerd Beleid.* Amsterdam: Gemeente Amsterdam.

Gemeentepolitie Amsterdam. 1986. "Evaluatie Afdeling Lokale Handel." Unpublished manuscript. Amsterdam: Gemeentepolitie Amsterdam.

———. 1988. *Kriminaliteitsbeeldanalyse, E. D. Zaken, 1980–1988.* Amsterdam: Gemeentepolitie Amsterdam.

Gerechtelijk Laboratorium. 1985. *Verdovende Middelen Jaarverslag 1985.* Amsterdam: Gerechtelijk Laboratorium.

Grapendaal, M. 1989. "De Tering Naar de Nering: Middelengebruik en Economie van Opiaatverslaafden." *Justitiële Verkenningen* 15:23–47.

Handelingen Tweede Kamer. 1976. "Proceedings of the House of Representatives." The Hague: Staatsuitgeverij.

Hartnoll, R. L. 1986. "Current Situation Relating to Drug Abuse Assessment in European Countries." *Bulletin on Narcotics* 28:65–80.

Hauge, R. 1985. "Trends in Drug Use in Norway." *Journal of Drug Issues* 15:321–31.

Interdepartementale Stuurgroep Alcohol—en Drugsbeleid. 1985. *Drugbeleid in Beweging: Naar een Normalisering van de Drugproblematiek.* The Hague: Ministerie van Welzijn, Volksgezondheid en Cultuur.

Jaarverslag Openbaar Ministerie. 1987. "Year Report of the Prosecution Office." The Hague: Staatsuitgeverij.

Jansen, A. C. M. 1989. *Cannabis in Amsterdam, een Geografie van Hashish en Marihuana.* Muiderberg: Dick Coutinho.

Janssen, O. J. A., and K. Swierstra. 1982. *Heroïnegebruikers in Nederland, een Typologie van Levensstijlen.* Groningen: Criminologisch Instituut Rijksuniversiteit.

Johnson, B. D., P. J. Goldstein, E. Preble, J. Schmeidler, D. S. Lipton, B. Spunt, and T. Miller. 1985. *Taking Care of Business: The Economics of Crime by Heroin Abusers.* Lexington, Mass.: Lexington Books.

Johnston, L. D. 1988. "Summary of 1987 Drug Study Results." Media statement at a national news conference in Washington, D.C., at the offices of the Secretary of Health and Human Services, January 13.

Johnston, L. D., P. M. O'Malley, and J. G. Bachman. 1987. *National Trends in Drug Use and Related Factors among American High-School Students and Young Adults, 1975–1986*. Rockville, Md.: U.S. Department of Health and Human Services, National Institute on Drug Abuse.

Kaplan, Charles D. 1984. "The Uneasy Consensus, Prohibitionist and Experimentalist Expectancies behind the International Narcotics Control System." *Tijdschrift voor Criminologie* 26:98–109.

Korf, Dirk J. 1987. *Heroïnetoerisme II: Resultaten van een Veldonderzoek Onder 382 Buitenlandse Dagelijkse Opiaatgebruikers in Amsterdam*. Amsterdam: Universiteit van Amsterdam, Instituut voor Sociale Geografie.

———. 1989. "Herointoten in den Niederlanden und in der Bundesrepublik Deutschland." Unpublished manuscript. Amsterdam: Universiteit van Amsterdam, Criminologisch Instituut "Bonger."

Kreuzer, A. 1989. "Therapie und Strafe, Versuch einer Zwischenbilanz zur Drogenpolitik und zum Betäubungsmittelgesetz von 1981." *Neue Juristische Wochenschrift* 42:1505–12.

Leuw, Ed. 1972. *Cannabis en Schooljeugd, Een Onderzoek naar Achtergronden en Betekenis van Gebruik en Niet-Gebruik van Cannabis Onder Leeerlingen van het Voortgezet Algemeen Vormend Onderwijs in de Provincie Zuid-Holland*. Amsterdam: Stichting Wetenschappelijk Onderzoek Alcohol—en Druggebruik.

———. 1984. "Door Schade en Schande: De Geschiedenis van Drugs-Hulpverlening als Sociaal Beleid in Amsterdam." *Tijdschrift voor Criminologie* 26:149–67.

———. 1987. "Illegal Drug Problems and Criminality in Amsterdam and Its Consequences for the Inhabitants." Paper presented at the meeting of the Council of Europe on "Reduction of Urban Insecurity," Barcelona, November.

———. 1989. "The Normalised Retail Trade of Cannabis in Amsterdam." Paper presented at the European Colloquium on Criminology and Criminal Policy, Freiburg, October.

Meertens, A. 1990. Personal communication with author, Amsterdam Probation Foundation.

Meyer, Jürgen. 1987. "Comparative Analysis." In *Betäubungsmittelstrafrecht in Westeuropa*, edited by J. Meyer. Freiburg: Max Planck Institut.

National Commission on Marihuana and Drug Abuse. 1973. *Second Report of the National Commission on Marihuana and Drug Abuse*. Washington, D.C.: U.S. Government Printing Office.

National Institute on Drug Abuse. 1989. *National Household Survey on Drug Abuse: Population Estimates 1988*. Rockville, Md.: U.S. Department of Health and Human Services, National Institute on Drug Abuse.

Preble, E. 1983. "Aggressive Accounting in the Illegal Drug Market." In *Alcohol, Drug Abuse and Aggression*, edited by E. Gottheil, K. Druley, T. Skoloda, and M. Waxman. Springfield, Ill.: Charles C. Thomas.

Preble, E., and J. Casey. 1969. "Taking Care of Business: The Heroin User's Life on the Street." *International Journal of the Addictions* 4:1–24.

Rook, A., and J. Essers. 1987. *Vervolging en Strafvordering bij Opiumwet Delicten*. The Hague: Ministerie van Justitie/Staatsuitgeverij.

Rüter, C. F. 1986. "Drugs and the Criminal Law in the Netherlands." In *Criminal Law in Action: An Overview of Current Issues in Western Societies*, edited by J. van Dijk, Ch. Haffmans, and F. Rüter. Arnhem: Gouda Quint.

———. 1988. "Die Strafrechtliche Drogenbekämpfung in den Niederlanden: Ein Königreich als Aussteiger." *Zeitschrift für Strafrechtwissenschaft 100 heft* 2:121–39.

Sandwijk, J. P., I. Westerterp, and S. Musterd. 1988. *Het Gebruik van Legale en Illegale Drugs in Amsterdam, Verslag van een Prevalentie-Onderzoek Onder de Bevolking van 12 Jaar en Ouder*. Amsterdam: Universiteit van Amsterdam, Instituut voor Sociale Geografie.

Scheerer, Sebastian. 1978. "The New Dutch and German Drug Laws: Social and Political Conditions for Criminalization and Decriminalization." *Law and Society* 12:585–605.

Sijes, M. 1987. "Gedwongen Behandeling van Druggebruikers in West-Duitsland en Zweden." *Justitiële Verkenningen* 13:28–43.

State Secretary for Welfare, Health and Cultural Affairs. 1983. "Policy on Drug Use." Paper presented at the annual meeting of the Special Committee on Drugs Policy, The Hague, June.

State Secretary for Welfare, Health and Cultural Affairs and the Minister of Justice to the States-General. 1987. "Notitie Dwang en Drag." Letter from the State Secretary for Welfare, Health and Cultural Affairs and the Minister of Justice to the States-General. The Hague: State Secretary for Welfare, Health and Cultural Affairs.

Stichting Algemeen Centraal Bureau voor de Geestelijke Volksgezondheid. 1971. *Ruimte in het Drugbeleid*. Meppel: Boom.

Stockholm Skolförfaltning. 1985. *1984-ars ANT-vane Untersökning, Arskurs 9 Grundskolan, Arskurs 2 Gymnasiet*. Stockholm: ANT Information.

Swierstra, K. 1990. *Drugscarrieres, van Crimineel tot Conventioneel*. Groningen: Rijks Universiteit Groningen, Onderzoekscentrum voor Criminologie en Jeugdcriminologie.

Tweede Kamer. 1984–85. Files of the House of Representatives, no. 18600 nr. 45. The Hague: House of Representatives.

U.S. Embassy. 1989. "A Report on Drug Policy in the Netherlands." Unpublished manuscript. The Hague: U.S. Embassy.

van Atteveld, J. M. A. 1988. "Het Nederlandse Drugsbeleid in Vergelijking met Andere Westeuropese Landen: Liberaal?" *Tijdschrift voor Alcohol, Drugs en Andere Psychotrope Stoffen* 14:3–11.

van Gemert, Frank. 1988. *Mazen en Netwerken: De Invloed van Beleid op de Drugshandel in de Amsterdamse Binnenstad*. Amsterdam: Universiteit van Amsterdam, Instituut voor Sociale Geografie.

van Kalmthout, Anton M. 1989. "Characteristics of Drug Policy in the Netherlands." In *Drug Policies in Western Europe*, edited by Hans-Jörg Albrecht and Anton M. van Kalmthout. Freiburg: Max Planck Institute.

van de Wijngaart, Govert F. 1988*a*. "Methadone in the Netherlands: An Evaluation." *International Journal of the Addictions* 23:913–25.

———. 1988*b*. "Heroin Use in the Netherlands." *American Journal of Drug and Alcohol Abuse* 14:125–36.

———. 1990. *Competing Perspectives on Drug Use: The Dutch Experience*. Utrecht: Rijks Universiteit Utrecht.

Verbraeck, Hans T. 1988. *De Staart van de Zeedijk: Een Bliksemonderzoek naar Enkele Effecten van het Zomerplan 1987 in het Wallengebied*. Amsterdam: Universiteit van Amsterdam, Instituut voor Sociale Geografie.

Werkgroep Verdovende Middelen. 1972. *Rapport van de Werkgroep Verdovende Middelen*. The Hague: Staatsuitgeverij.

Werkgroep Vooronderzoek Vervolgings—En Straftoemetingsbeleid Inzake Opiumwetdelicten. 1987. "Opsporings-, Vervolgings—en Strafvorderingsbeleid Inzake Opiumwetdelicten." Unpublished manuscript. The Hague: Werkgroep Vooronderzoek Vervolgings—En Straftoemetingsbeleid Inzake Opiumwetdelicten.

Wever, L. J. S. 1989. "A National Policy Programme on Aids and Drug Use in the Netherlands." The Hague: Ministry of Welfare, Health and Cultural Affairs.

Wish, E. D., and B. D. Johnson. 1986. "The Impact of Substance Abuse on Criminal Careers." In *Criminal Careers and "Career Criminals,"* vol. 2, edited by A. Blumstein, J. Cohen, J. Roth, and C. Visher. Washington, D.C.: National Academic Press.

Wisotsky, Stephen. 1989. "Recent Developments in the U.S. War on Drugs." In *Drug Policies in Western Europe*, edited by Hans-Jörg Albrecht and Anton van Kalmthout. Freiburg: Max Planck Institut.

Jack Katz

The Motivation of the Persistent Robber

ABSTRACT

There is a group of offenders who are unusually persistent in robbery, even after serving lengthy prison terms. Three lines of inquiry clarify their motivations. First, the practical situational demands of robbery militate against an election of the offense as the outcome of a rational process of cost-benefit calculations. Appreciation of interactions between the conduct of robbery offenders and victims clarifies the inherent openness of the offender's situational desires. Second, the persistent offender's commitment to robbery is an aspect of the open-ended, interlocking character of the deviant social environment in which he operates. Third, persistent robbers have a distinguishing attraction to the use of violence; their attraction to robbery reflects a fascination with imposing transcendent control on a range of chaotic circumstances. Once research interests shift from generic "robbery" to the characterization of the persistent offender, ethnographic materials and ethnomethodological inquiries become essential.

The motivations that animate robbery vary so greatly that they seem to defy generalization. Keeping in mind a loose definition of robbery as the taking of something of value by force or threat of force, then the offense is found quite commonly in childhood. Much of the "bully's" behavior might be seen as robbery, as might much of the unkindness that gives sibling rivalry its bad reputation.

The personal consequences and social dimensions of robbery are so disturbing that an allusion to the nasty and rough play of early childhood may seem frivolous. Yet biographies of hard-core robbers describe early offenses that occur close to home, if not against kin, then

Jack Katz is professor of sociology at the University of California, Los Angeles.

0192-3234/91/0014-0007$01.00

within local social circles and on local streets.[1] These mean and predatory actions do not seem to warrant the archetype of "robbery," perhaps because they are more clearly expressive than economic projects: intimidating a classmate to "give" pocket change; using a tough posture to deflect requests by a friend that he be repaid money that was, some time before, handed over as a "loan;" seizing an item of clothing from another youth because it represents membership in an enemy group; approaching strangers in public spaces with a humble monetary "request" that subtly but quickly becomes recognized as an arrogant and inexorable demand.

Robbery is often a group activity for young, officially apprehended offenders (Zimring 1981). In recent surveys, crime victims report that they were attacked by multiple offenders in about 25 percent of the robberies in which the offenders appeared to be between the ages of twelve and twenty, compared to about 8 percent of robberies in which the offenders seemed to be thirty or over (Bureau of Justice Statistics 1989, table 47, p. 52). The group character of youth robberies suggests that, qualitatively, the details of individual offenses will display numerous moments of interactional fireworks. The following case, drawn from Chicago police information, illustrates what youths might well deem to be a "cool" strategy for drawing a victim, as well as a pattern of spontaneously and interactively escalating violence.

> Four teenagers planned to rob a pizza delivery man. They called in an order, and when the delivery man reached their area, the youngest of the group, a 14-year old, approached him on foot and declared, "This is a stickup, don't make it a murder." The victim, 55 years old, threw up his hands and dropped the money he was holding. The 14-year old then asked, "Where is the rest of the money, man?" The victim ran to his car, got inside, and started it, but the two of them jumped in and began to struggle with him. Then one pulled a shotgun from his overcoat and shot the victim in the throat and chest. The four split with $27 to divide. [Katz 1988, p. 186]

Materialistic interests, playful maneuvers, and intensely hostile emotions all swirl around in the motivations governing youthful robbery. Indeed, a series of colloquialisms ("stickup," "wilding," "mugging,"

[1] Farrington (1986, p. 233) suggests "that more attention should be given to 'offending' before the age of criminal responsibility."

"yoking," "purse snatching") has emerged to grasp street distinctions among behaviors that statutory law may treat equally as "robbery."

But if robbery has a widely experienced and highly varied appeal to children and male adolescents, the appeal is usually not very deep, at least not for officially recognized instances of the offense. Robbery arrests have often been found to peak in late adolescence or the early twenties (Miller, Dinitz, and Conrad 1982); in recent arrest data, robberies peak at ages seventeen and eighteen (Federal Bureau of Investigation 1987, table 33, p. 174; Federal Bureau of Investigation 1988, table 33, p. 178). Historical research on arrest data indicates that robbery has become increasingly concentrated among the young. The peak age of robbery has declined from nineteen in 1940 to seventeen in 1980; in age distributions of robbery arrests, the age at which the number of arrests is at half the number produced by the peak age was twenty-nine in 1940, dropped to twenty-seven in 1960, and dropped to twenty-four in 1980 (Steffensmeier et al. 1989, table 2, p. 815). In national U.S. data on arrests for robbery, within the five-year age set of males forty to forty-four, there is an average of about 500 robbery arrests for each year, compared to almost 7,000 arrests of eighteen-year-old males (Federal Bureau of Investigation 1988, table 34, pp. 180–81). Various studies indicate that many young people who are intensely active in thieving cultures during their adolescence are vividly aware that penalties will increase when they reach the age of majority; their desistance appears to be a response (West 1978; Sullivan 1983). These age-related data suggest that those who persist with robbery late in their twenties or into their thirties are likely to be a rather special set of criminal actors.

Over the last decade, several studies have documented the existence of a relatively small number of unusually persistent offenders who commit a disproportionate number of robberies. Variously labeled "violent predators," "heavies," "habitual," "chronic," and "career" robbers, these persistent offenders are not crime specialists. Typically they also commit nonviolent property crimes, undertake assaults independent of acquisitive objectives, and, at one or another phase of their criminal careers, participate intensively in vice (drug, prostitution, illegal gambling) markets. A famous self-report study of 2,200 U.S. jail and prison inmates identified a set of "violent predators" who reported that they commit robbery, deal drugs, and assault persons. Ten percent of "violent predators" reported committing an average of 135 robberies per year of release time, compared to 90 percent of robbers who reported that they did not deal drugs or commit assaults and who committed an average of ten robberies per year (Chaiken and Chaiken 1982, p. 55). A team of researchers in French Canada classified a sample of thirty-five armed robbers into "chronic" and "occasional" offenders and found that the former had committed an average of twenty to fifty robberies, compared to an average of one to six for the latter group. The occasionals were specialists in crime, while the chronics were generalists, although with a special aversion for fraud crimes (Gabor et al. 1987, p. 55). And in a national U.S. sample of over 1,800 felons in state prisons, Wright and Rossi (1986, p. 76) identified through self-reports a set of handgun "predators" who constituted 17 percent of the sample but were responsible for over 50 percent of the total crimes committed by the sample, leading in nonviolent as well as the violent types of crime.[2]

These studies might be read to suggest that a commitment to the use of violence, in robbery and personal relations, is an inevitable response to the chaos that characterizes the lives of street criminals, except that the same studies have also documented the lack of significant involvement in robbery on the part of many who persist in nonviolent theft and vice activities. If robbery is not sufficiently rewarding to maintain the involvement of most young offenders who try it, and if robbery is not necessary to persist through young adulthood in a life of street crime, what motivates the small set of persistent robbers?

Utilitarian or materialistic explanations that point to the offender's lack of legitimate economic opportunities or suggest that he is immune from punishment are not very helpful. As to employment opportunities, offenders may not have economically attractive legitimate alternatives, but the rewards of street robbery are often minimal. Gas station robberies averaged a loss of $303 in 1986 (Federal Bureau of Investigation 1986); convenience store robberies averaged a loss of $344 in 1988 (Federal Bureau of Investigation 1988, p. 19); only 15 percent of noncommercial victims reported losses of $500 or more in 1987, and in 40 percent of the robberies the victims reported theft losses of less than $100 (Bureau of Justice Statistics 1989, tables 82 and 83, pp. 74, 76). And given the familiarity of persistent robbers with nonviolent theft and rich vice markets, materialistic factors cannot explain their specialization in a violent form of criminal career. As to punishment, the career criminal data, combined with the biographical accounts, indicate

[2] See also Petersilia, Greenwood, and Lavin (1977) and Haran (1982).

that persistent robbers continue despite lengthy periods of incarceration during youthful years. When offenders desist in their late twenties or in their thirties, it is usually after a number of stretches in confinement had failed to provoke desistance, and it cannot be that, after years of imprisonment, their legitimate economic opportunities exceed what they were before they compiled a lengthy criminal record.

Gender differences in robbery offense rates also indicate the inadequacies of utilitarian or materialistic explanations. The pressures of poverty are equal, if not greater, on females than they are on males, yet males recurrently make up about 90 percent of those counted in arrest data (Federal Bureau of Investigation 1988, table 37) and in conviction records of bank robbers (Haran 1982); in the national victims survey for 1987, victims identified only 7 percent of single offender robbers as female (Bureau of Justice Statistics 1989, table 39, p. 46; see also Hindelang 1981).

A difference by sex in anxiety about physical danger cannot fully explain the gender difference in robbery. Criminal practices that are more attractive than robbery to poor women, such as prostitution and drug dealing, are not obviously safer. Nor can a psychobiological male tendency toward violence account for the enormous gender disproportion in robbery. The male-to-female ratio in assaults is much smaller than it is in robbery. In victim survey data organized to permit comparisons within race, Laub and McDermott (1985, table 2, p. 90) found a male-to-female ratio of between 3:1 and 4:1 for "assaultive violence without theft"; within arrest data they found a male-to-female ratio of about 3:1 for "simple assaults." And in domestic criminal homicides, in several American cities it is almost as likely, in some times and locations more likely, that the female will be the one who survives and is arrested (Riedel and Zahn 1985, p. 41).

Differences in the representation of ethnic groups in robbery statistics also militate against materialistic explanations. In Canada, predominantly French Quebec has had armed robbery rates that are two to three times the rates in the English provinces, even while the rates of nonrobbery violent crimes and nonviolent property crimes have been lower in French than in English Canada (Gabor et al. 1987, pp. 13, 23).

Ethnic group comparisons are more meaningful when they attempt to control for economic status. Although neither arrest nor victim-based data provide information on the offenders' economic status, if we assume that robbery offenders come from poverty populations, we can easily generate useful ethnic comparisons. Because the historical mixture of Hispanic and black populations in the Caribbean is significantly represented in eastern and midwestern U.S. cities, ethnic comparisons among poverty populations in the U.S. Southwest, where Hispanics are primarily of Mexican and Central American origin, give a more clear-cut picture. In Southern California, the rate of robbery arrests of poor blacks is four to five times that of poor Hispanics; for homicides (violence usually without theft) as well as for burglaries (theft without violence), the black rates are only about twice the Hispanic rates (Katz 1988, p. 240, table 7.1).

In sum, a variety of patterns indicates that persistent robbers have motivations that distinguish them from other persistent offenders, that are sufficiently powerful to transcend heavy costs of punishment, and that are apparently not grounded in sex or race dispositions either toward violence in particular or toward crime in general. One way to explore the motivations of persistent robbers is to try to identify uniquely correlated background factors—some bizarre form of abuse in early childhood, an odd feature in contemporaneous socioeconomic ecology, or a deep predisposition measurable on psychological inventories. No such factors have as yet been identified, and several considerations point to the futility of a research strategy focused on background factors. Involvement in robbery changes over the life course and from moment to moment within an offender's day on the streets, while the offender's socioeconomic context and psychologically formative experiences remain constant. More important, the attractions of persisting in robbery are so peculiar that to pursue a significant, discrete background cause, even presuming it exists, would be to search for a needle in a haystack. To justify such a search, one must have faith that some form of evil genius in biology or social organization cunningly guides offenders to a peculiar form of criminality that is quite rare even among persistent or "career" criminals.

We might better appreciate the contributions of demographic research, not by looking for age, race, sex, social ecological or other background causes, but by acknowledging an implication of the gross character of demographic correlations: the motivation to rob is relatively rare and obviously not easy to sustain. We are then led to wonder *how* persistent robbers overcome the many discouragements to their "careers." The inquiry into criminal motives becomes a question of understanding what makes robbery attractive for those few who persist in it or, more precisely, how offenders construct and sustain the attractions of robbery. If a search for background explanations for such a rare form of criminality implies theories of evil genius in nature or social organization, it must be admitted that an inquiry into the methods by which offenders themselves make robbery attractive indulges a humanistic prejudice.

Methodologically, an emphasis in motivational inquiry on the "how" of a form of criminality turns research attentions from statistical data describing biographical and ecological background factors to life histories and narratives of crimes that describe the foreground of robbery. The foreground of a crime consists of its situational practice, the contemporaneous biographical context from which an offender's participation in the crime emerges, and the distinctive attraction of the offense to the offender. Section I reviews cases of offenders' *behavior in crime situations*. They indicate that the motives that actually guide the offender's conduct typically are not and often could not be planned or predisposed but emerge as the offense transpires. In Section II, I examine materials showing the offender's *contemporaneous biographical context*. They indicate that, for persistent offenders, motivational drives do not simply press from external sources or psychological complexes; they are, figuratively and often literally, embodied in a way of life that makes illicit motivation sensually immediate. In Section III, through analyzing biographical materials in search of *the distinctive meaning* that draws offenders persistently to robbery, I find that mean violence has overriding attractions. In a concluding section, I stress the contributions to the study of robbery, including the outlines of a theory of desistance, that become visible when situational and biographical forms of evidence are integrated; and I outline various general methodological advantages of indulging the humanistic prejudice and studying the "how" of criminality: the symbolically creative, sensually complex, and situationally detailed ways in which offenders construct lines of criminal action.

I. Situational Challenges and the Rational Robber

When asked, robbers often define themselves as rational actors, doing crime "to make money the best way I know how" and using violence prudently by attacking victims only when they resist. But a close examination of interaction within robberies indicates that this is not the sort of "job" that, through weighing costs and benefits, one can sensibly elect to make one's career. And the suggestion that offenders typically monitor their use of violence according to a utilitarian calculus about the means of intimidation that they possess (bare arms, knives, guns) and the minimal use of force necessary to control victims ignores the nonrational commitment that is essential for persistently committing the offense (e.g., Skogan 1978; Luckenbill 1980; Feeney 1986).

Data describing high correlations between victim resistance and violence by robbery offenders have frequently been reported. In perhaps the first significant study that bore on the question, Conklin (1972, p. 115) found, in two Boston samples totaling 1,242 robberies, that offenders used force in less than half the cases where victims did not resist and in almost two-thirds of the cases where victims did resist.[3] Luckenbill (1981) reconstructed 257 robbery events from police records in a Texas city and found that, although gun-armed offenders always began with a threat alone, in those cases in which the victim resisted, half the time the offender would abandon the scene and half the time he would shoot. Block (1977) examined over 1,000 robberies as described in Chicago police reports and found that, in robberies by gun in which the victim did not resist, only 7 percent of victims were injured, while 78 percent of resisting victims were injured.

As Philip Cook (1986) has stressed, any inference that victim conduct can control offender violence depends on a questionable reading of causal direction. Does victim resistance provoke violence by offenders? Or does incipient violence by offenders provoke resistance by victims? In his study, Block (1977, p. 81) addressed this issue and found that two-thirds of resisting victims resisted *before* the robber used force. But in close examinations of police files, offenders sometimes appear so wild or so bent on "vicious" conduct (Cook 1980, p. 31) that a reasonable victim might well "resist" just before or just as the offender begins to launch his attack. It is not clear that routine police records, created for law enforcement purposes and examined after the fact for evidence on a question of causal direction that a researcher brings to and imposes on them, can provide data of sufficiently high quality to resolve the matter.

More significant, the subtly interactive nature of each party's conduct creates substantial difficulties for interpreting causal direction in any given case. Not only are victims intensely concerned to read offenders' posture and gestures to anticipate being attacked, offenders enter the scene geared to read their victims for signs of likely resistance. Just as with victims who see the offender provide a cue for a preemp-

[3] For evidence from victim survey data, see Hindelang, Gottfredson, and Garofalo (1978).

tory strike, offenders who strike victims who had not resisted may simply be trying to strike first. More complex still, we cannot be sure of the accuracy of these readings: offenders and victims alike may strike first on a mistaken belief that the other is about to act.

The subtlety and complexity of social interaction in robbery, and the risk of a fateful misreading, is a problem not only for the researcher but, initially, for the robber. Offenders who discover the intrinsic difficulties of rationally managing violence within robbery have reason to abandon the offense. Those who persist must either be especially skilled in dramatizing violent behavior or unusually indifferent to the dictates of reason.

Biographical evidence indicates that ironically both are true. "Career" robbers recall adolescent years dedicated to the perfection of "badass" identities, the key to which is the portrayal of a personal character that is committed to violence beyond calculations of legal, material, or even physical costs to oneself. They learn that what wins in a showdown with another "badass" is not so much superiority in fighting skill or firepower but escaping the ghost of reason and continuing to attack when an opponent, haunted by anticipations of injury or imprisonment, will back off (see Keiser 1979; Dietz 1983).

That the criminal predator's career is originally shaped through adolescent peer testing creates fundamental problems for analyzing the common forms of statistical data in order to understand the relationship between offender violence and victim resistance. Such data, whether compiled from police records or victim reports, are seriously biased against including robberies committed against victims who are similar to offenders in social identity. If robbery offenders are engaged in vice and other, nonviolent activities, they have special reasons for not reporting their own victimization in robberies to the police, and they are likely to be living in ways that make them especially inaccessible to phone surveys that attempt to identify victims. And if conventional citizens, when faced with an offender, may sometimes detect cues that seem to them to justify anticipatory resistance, the offender's mirror-image peers must quite often provide heavy-handed cues that they will try preemptive strikes.

Violent predators typically reside near other violent predators, on ghetto streets and in state confinement. It is revealing that the research literature on victim-offender interaction in robbery makes virtually no mention of the absence from its statistical data base of offenses conducted within confinement settings. If one's interest is in advising conventional citizens how to behave within robberies, this neglect is understandable. But for an understanding of offenders' motivations, it is essential to appreciate the contexts for robbery that are familiar to them. Research on gun possession indicates that, in order to seize emergent opportunities but also in order to defend against surprise attacks, violent predators maintain a constant readiness for violence, often literally sleeping with a weapon under the pillow and driving with a gun in the glove compartment (Wright and Rossi 1986, p. 14). In the context of this lifestyle, there are so many good reasons for anticipating situationally unprovoked attacks that a complementary, nonrational commitment to violence would itself be rational.

The rational basis for the persistent robber to become committed beyond reason to violence appears even stronger if we appreciate the many prudent, practical considerations that recommend unprovoked violence to robbers. Although it is common to consider "victim resistance" as a "reason" for offender violence, and "unprovoked violence" as an indicator of nonrational behavior, the "resistance" concept is much more open than is usually appreciated, with the result that "unprovoked violence" often has a readily located, reasonable, practical, and utilitarian basis for the offender.

Thus, whether a victim is resisting or not depends on how ambitious and elastic are the offender's expectations and desires. In the research literature, "resistance" is variously applied to cover physically expressed protests, attempts to flee and calls for help, and failures to comply quickly with offenders' demands. But, however facile the researcher's coding of the phenomena, the judgment of victim resistance from the offender's perspective is often quite ambiguous. The offender, after all, will usually not know what the victim has to offer in exchange for the offender's withholding of violence; "unprovoked" violence may serve to reveal valuables that an initial request did not uncover. Faced by an offender who seems violently impatient, victims may discover valuables to offer that they otherwise would not consider to be part of the criminal exchange. A phrase currently popular among armed robbers, "Give it up!" contains a denotative ambiguity that neatly serves the exploratory aspects of the robber's crime.

Because contemporary robberies are commonly "spur-of-the-moment" affairs with little advance planning of methodology or "casing" of targets (Dietz 1983; on bank robberies, see Johnston 1978), the robber will often be determining the limits of what he is willing to demand within the robbery interaction itself. Victims initially targeted for their cash or drugs may, on closer inspection, wear jewelry, clothing, or even gold fillings that might as well be demanded (Katz 1988, p. 190). Unprovoked violence is also useful for the offender to gauge just how compliant the victim is willing to be. Although such events are rare, offenders may discover other, nonmonetary desires that victims might serve, and offenders may perceive in victim compliance an invitation to extend the robbery relationship beyond its initial setting, for example, through kidnapping the victim and using him or her as a guide to treasures stored at home.

First, then, the rationality of unprovoked offender violence is an open matter because, for the offender, what the victim has to offer and what the offender himself desires are both phenomena that emerge within the robbery situation. For both reasons, a robber is well-advised to appear to be at least somewhat outside the limitations of reason. A robber who appears too civil might not effectively convey his commitment to back demands with force; a robber who articulates his desires too precisely might miss valuables that a victim might supply in an effort to identify and satisfy the desires of a brusque, crude assailant.

Second, the rational basis of offender violence is unclear even when the victim *does* resist first. If offenders often have empirically justifiable reasons to employ violence when they are not provoked, the inverse also holds: offenders often lack firmly based reasons to use violence when victims do resist. When victims resist, they rarely threaten to disable the offender physically or to block his escape (an indication of just how rare is given in Katz 1988, p. 186). Given the minimal amount of investment robbers usually make in setting up a particular offense, when victims resist, the rational course of action for offenders would not be to respond with violence but to abandon the immediate crime scene for another they could easily find and enter. Were robbers truly rational or solely instrumental in their use of violence, they would commonly use some violence *before but rarely after* victims resist.[4]

Cool, retrospective statements by offenders that they limit violence to practical necessity (Allen 1978; Feeney 1986) misrepresent their motivation by obscuring the wild possibilities of the interaction. Offenders know that they do not know what victims will do; some report a self-conscious paranoia that victims will counterattack with guns.

[4] Compare Zimring and Zuehl (1986, pp. 30–31), who advise victims not to resist armed robbers, implying that robbers restrain their violence unless given practical reasons to unleash it, but who also offer the observation that "'recreational violence' seems to us not only evocative but descriptive of a large number of . . . [robberies]."

When they act with confederates, they often have good reasons to believe that the confederates may not be reliable partners because of their potential for unreliable conduct within the robbery, vulnerability to law enforcement pressure related to other offenses, or inclination toward predatory attacks on colleagues.

Building on all the other uncertainties and most difficult to control is the offender's uncertainty as to how he, himself, will respond within the robbery scene. Those who act under the influence of intoxicating substances are not unaware that their strategic ability may be affected. And while persistent offenders often decry the "stupid" or "hotheaded" practices of novice robbers, their posture of professionalism is belied by detailed accounts of their own mature offenses. They relate crimes in which they attacked what they regard as low-status targets, such as gas stations, out of loyalty to overly spontaneous colleagues (Allen 1978, p. 192); their pride in knowingly taking on unusual risks by acting with colleagues they regard as weak willed, just for the ironic purpose of demonstrating their superior self-control (Taylor 1985, p. 72); and a retrospective awareness of their own tendencies toward explosive violence.

Novice offenders may be unaware of all these uncertainties and fantasize robbery as an occasion for enacting an efficient, cold-blooded control. They may be lured in by street comments that recommend robbery as "easy," a way to get money within a matter of moments, virtually whenever one needs it, without requiring any special skills; a rhetoric that celebrates the crime as a neatly bounded task, something one can "get in, get out, and get away with" quickly; a deviant culture that portrays the crime as a routine matter analogous to going shopping. But persistent robbers know intimately that the crime is shot through with uncertainties and uncontrollable risk. Thus, although they may enjoy distinguishing themselves as more sophisticated and business-like about the crime than amateurs and those who start robbing and then soon desist, they know that neither the payoffs from the crime nor the offender's conduct within it can be systematically managed to make sense on a utilitarian calculation.

Against this background knowledge, seemingly gratuitous violence becomes sensible to the persistent offender for a reason that specifically overrides situational risk calculations. In order to persist as a robber, it is necessary to steel oneself against utilitarian thinking, becoming, in one contemporary street phrase, a "hardhead" who is impervious to attacks of reason. For some careers, the commitment to persist depends on accepting the gambler's maxim that one should not throw good money after bad. Professional card players, for example, protect their career commitments by sacrificing their earlier stakes when an unexpected turn of the cards shows that the risk of loss has suddenly increased. But "professional" robbers cannot afford routinely to abandon offenses when victims resist and simply move on to the next crime scene. The adoption of such a finely calculating perspective on crime would block them from doing robberies in the first place. Much of the "gratuitous violence" in robberies makes sense within the uniquely demanding needs of "career" robbery offenders. By leaping over a retail counter, putting a gun to the side of a clerk's head and slamming him to the floor, an offender sends a strong message to the victim, and to himself as well, that material profit may not be all that the event is about. And by taking victim resistance as a "reason" for a violent response, offenders ritualize their criminal commitments in ceremonies that sometimes portray intentions in blood.

In sum, the study of interaction within robbery events indicates that, in order to conduct robbery persistently, one must commit oneself spiritually and emotionally beyond what material and mundane calculation can recommend. "Nonrational" violence makes sense as a way of committing oneself to persist in robbery in the face of the risks and chaos inherent in the criminal event. The next question is, What makes that commitment, unusual even among "career criminals," effectively attractive?

This question requires a broader biographical investigation than situational analysis of robbery interaction can provide. Working out from robbery events to the overall way of life of the offender, it is possible to track along several lines of inquiry. Methodologically, it is feasible to examine where the offender was coming from before and where he went to after the event, his prior and subsequent relations to others who accompanied him or remained on the peripheries of the event, the ways in which he drew on social ties as resources for entering the event, and the ramifications of the event within his social networks. For evidence, it is necessary to rely heavily on the handful of self-report interview studies that statistically relate persistence in robbery with other lifestyle patterns, on details in police files that indicate the connection of robbery events to other relationships and pursuits in the offenders' lives, and on biographical and autobiographical accounts focusing extensively on individual offenders (Brown 1965; Keiser 1965; Shaw 1966; Miller and Helwig 1972; Thomas 1974; Willwerth 1974;

Carr 1975; Rettig, Torres, and Garrett 1977; Allen 1978; Mancini 1980; Dietz 1983; Pileggi 1985; Taylor 1985; Wideman 1985).

These materials support two relevant themes. One is that the attraction of robbery to persistent offenders emerges as a continuation of the themes of illicit action that they diffusely embed in their lives. Persistent robbers are not attracted to the offense through cold, materialistic calculations, nor as a result of independently existing pressures from a difficult socioeconomic environment, but in response to dynamics of deviant action that, in corporeal and metaphoric senses, they have already made central to the body of their lives. The second is that, in contrast to nonviolent "career" criminals, persistent robbers are distinctly attracted to imposing a hard, relentless order on what others fear as overwhelming chaos.

II. The Embodiment of Deviant Motivation

Young offenders often combine many forms of extraneous illicit action with robbery (Katz 1988, pp. 197–98). They engage in group attacks that gratuitously humiliate victims. They sometimes combine sex or sadistic pleasures with the property-acquisition purpose of the event. They may engage in particular robberies as part of a "spree" conducted within a drug-animated mood.

Persistent robbers often disdain such behavior as unprofessional, as signs of immaturity or of emotional imbalance. But the difference between the novice and the experienced robber is less clearly a matter of the type of motivation than of the way deviant motives are woven into an overall lifestyle. The novice combines robbery with other forms of illicit action directly within the robbery events themselves. Experienced offenders accomplish a similar combination, but more diffusely, through multiple and intertwined connections of robberies to other relationships that build illicit action into their overall lives. The themes that appear within particular offenses committed by young, relatively inexperienced offenders, as emotionally wild, suddenly emergent, gratuitously destructive dynamics, reappear as patterns within the broader life worlds of more experienced, older offenders.

The quantified results of self-report and official records studies have established that persistent robbery offenders are not crime specialists but are also recurrently engaged in illegal substance abuse and marketing, nonviolent theft and fraud, and assault independent of theft (Petersilia, Greenwood, and Lavin 1977; Chaiken and Chaiken 1982; Gabor et al. 1987). It would be artificial to seek an understanding of the robber's motivation by ignoring this larger context of criminal involvement, for example, by calculating the rewards and risks of their robberies alone. Offenders do not shape the rest of their lives to facilitate their commitment to robbery; they shape their involvement in robbery to fit in with the deviant character of their social life in general.

Biographies of persistent offenders, whether they be robbers, safecrackers, fences, or professional thieves, often contain remarks that scoff at conventional lifestyles with an attitude of presumptive sensual superiority.[5] While they may acknowledge to interviewers that they suffer extensive barren periods when locked up, and that they must often endure deep pain from substance addiction, long-term offenders frequently claim to enjoy a more compelling way of life than do their "straight" counterparts. They make isolated, particular claims that their sex lives are more glorious than those of respectable married men, that the joys offered by the hedonistic substances they use transcend the modest pleasures of conventional alcohol use, and that the manly challenges and material rewards of their criminal offenses make the image of the working man's life pale by comparison. Indeed, rhetorical flourishes with which offenders dub crime their "business" and robberies as "getting paid" should be appreciated for their mocking undertones (cf. Sullivan 1989). But more generally, and underlying such particularized boasts, they devote themselves to living what they regard as a hyperreal life, a life more alive, even if, in a final accounting, less materially rewarding, than "straight" life.

Disdaining the life of the "straight John" as superficial because it too systematically bounds sensual involvements from work commitments, offenders routinely run into difficulties for managing their criminal work in a strictly "professional" fashion. Thus, it is not unusual for robbers, even those who claim to be especially sophisticated, to act with heavily drug-dependent associates and to fail to separate carefully their own use of intoxicating substances from their criminal acts (Haran 1982; Wideman 1985). In effect persistent offenders work elaborately to make their lives more profound by giving them more body, a project which has literal dimensions, such as associating drug and sexual "partying" with criminal acts, as well as less tangible themes.

Through property crimes, sexual adventures and partying, and illicit drug use and gambling, the persistent offender embeds his criminality

[5] In addition to the life histories cited above, see King and Chambliss (1984) and Jackson (1972).

in a lifestyle that operates in parallel to sensual processes of the body and in juxtaposition to the image of the constricted conventional self that he mocks. The "straight John's" life is divested of fullness by work, family, recreation, entertainment, and other respectable institutions that allocate different "roles" to distinct units of time and place. In contrast to this image of an identity broken by social expectations into unconnected fragments, the offender devotes himself to realizing a more fully embodied life by engaging society more in line with the rhythms of his body's sensualities. Through our bodies we live an integrated world sustained by a multitude of ongoing processes—respiration, circulation, digestion, hormonal stimulation, flow of consciousness—any one of which may, at any moment, move unexpectedly to the foreground of our attention, with the others continuing in the background. The various forms of illicit action in the criminal lifestyle are distinguished specifically by a twofold analogy to the sensuality of the body: they are ongoing processes with characteristic rhythms in the offender's life; each may, at virtually any moment and with stunning surprise, emerge to dominate the offender's experience.

Thus, the habitual use of some form of intoxicating substance, whether legal or illegal and whether physically addictive or not, influences the active criminal life phases of virtually all persistent robbers. Robbers' biographies variously show their practiced ingestion of alcohol, of opiates with narcotic effects, of stimulants like cocaine or amphetamines, or of some combination of intoxicating substances (Willwerth 1974; Rettig, Torres, and Garrett 1977; Allen 1978; Mancini 1980; Pileggi 1985; Wideman 1985). While some have argued that addictions produce economic needs for crime or feelings of omnipotence that reduce hesitations against committing crimes, these substances vary radically in their physiological, psychological, and emotional effects and they have varied radically in their costs.

Rather than simply imputing unique etiological significance to one or another illegal substance, we will develop a more generally valid understanding of the robber's motivation by appreciating that the habitual use of illicit substances fits into the careers of robbery offenders in a variety of ways. For some, robbery and addictive heroin use emerges in their lives long after they had been heavily involved in nonviolent, criminal vice, or theft activities; opiate addiction is a product rather than a cause of a deviant lifestyle, and then becomes a cause of relatively imprudent criminal acts such as street robbery, which lead to imprisonment. Here drug addiction ends rather than promotes a criminal career. For some, the use of cocaine is related to the practice of robbery as a means of enhancing courage and celebrating success. In some ways, underground markets in illegal substances create opportunities to commit nonrobbery crimes; and contraband street markets produce especially attractive potential victims, luring experienced robbers from legitimate to criminal commercial targets and luring previously nonviolent offenders into the practice of robbery.

The one constant, across chemical differences in intoxicating substances, across their costs and accessibility in different times and places, and across the biographical ways they relate specifically to the practice of robbery, is the offender's use of a substance that, in one manner or another, recurrently stimulates subjective awareness of his physical being. Habitual intoxication by means of alcohol, opiates, cocaine, amphetamines, and other consciousness-affecting substances provides a means of making an extraordinary, provocatively sensual experience of a wide range of otherwise conventional actions (walking, talking, driving, making a routine retail purchase); a culture (a characteristic form of humorous commentary on everyday events and an aesthetic of hedonism, such as the "player's" style); and a series of problems due to physical and legal consequences of use that implicate wide swaths of one's life in momentary acts of ingestion. Disdaining the subordination in contemporary society of personal life and private interests to the work role, persistent offenders labor hard to counter the suppression of bodily awareness that modern science and the contemporary diet make possible. In effect, persistent offenders recreate through the use of intoxicating substances the virtually constant awareness of corporeal pleasures and pains, and the cyclical emergence of hallucinatory or hyperreal worlds, that, in previous centuries in the West, was conventionally available for the poverty population in the form of cycles of hunger and disease (see Camporesi 1989).

The contemporary example of bulimia reminds us that even as seemingly innocent a feature of the conventional environment as food can, if used in a sufficiently willful manner, produce cycles of euphoria and discomfort, and a constant preoccupation. But if the individual with bulimia must work diligently to convert food into a resource for an unconventionally continuous awareness of his or her body, the substances used by the persistent violent property offender make this preoccupation with the body much easier. This is, of course, the special virtue of alcohol, heroin, cocaine, and the like: they have chemical properties that, if ingested in appropriate but relatively small amounts, can be relied on to produce exceptional sensual experiences. For some users, these drugs will require changing levels and methods of usage in order that they retain their exceptional power. But in comparison to food and cigarettes, which typically produce corporeal effects that fade far into the backgrounds of their users' awareness, alcohol and contraband drugs easily produce unconventional sensual self-awareness in a temporally episodic form.[6] At some point, continued ingestion requires that one get "into" the experience so deeply that one must, sometime later, come "out" of it.

It is useful to specify the common and distinctively corporeal self-awareness created by the chemically diverse substances that the offender exploits in order to appreciate that it is the sensual texture of his daily experience, not the dictates of cool reason nor the pressures of a materially deprived background, that animates the offender. For the persistent offender, intoxicating substances are conveniently transportable ingredients for episodic hedonism. They make for neat adventure kits and, in an even more conveniently transportable form, so does the offender's sexuality.

Persistent offenders structure their sexual involvements along lines analogous to those governing their drug and alcohol use, in intense and episodic relationships. The available evidence on marital history, parental status, and residential career indicates strongly that robbers typically move frequently from one to another partner without creating enduring commitments, often maintaining more than one sexual liaison at a time, and rarely sleeping in the same place for more than a matter of months (Haran 1982). The biographies and autobiographies of especially hard-core, repeat offenders are full of accounts of "partying," a general celebratory, multiday episode involving illegal drugs and short-term understandings with prostitutes or with girlfriends interested in sharing the fruits of some recent crime (Katz 1988, pp. 200–202). Research on a small sample of thirty-nine French Canadian armed robbers indicates that the "chronic" offender was especially prone to spend his

[6] Cigarettes have been a popular, literally handy, socially unbiquitous device for stimulating awareness of an ongoing corporeal process, namely breathing. It is instructive that, in the United States, cigarettes are quickly being reinstitutionalized along the social lines that govern alcohol use—to a vaguely deviant, if legal, status; as a substance to be used freely only outside the collective workplace; and increasingly, as in airport bars, to be used in the same confined public places where alcohol is permitted. Gum chewing, which public schools must still take pains to prohibit among their students, has long been relegated by the social class sentiments to the lower social levels of workplaces. Within this historical and cultural context, "substance abuse," when mixed with any form of work, legitimate or criminal, continually takes on increasingly deviant character.

criminal income quickly on drug purchases, alcohol, and night clubs (Gabor et al. 1987, pp. 81–83).

Like his use of intoxicating substances, the offender's sexual lifestyle is particularly useful as a way of promoting a subjective awareness of his corporeal being. Hanging out on street corners, the young offender may use physical gestures and graphic language to point to his genitals, keeping in virtually continuous, figurative if not literal, contact with his sexual identity. During terms of confinement, the deprivation of heterosexual interaction and the charging of male relationships with a potential for humiliating dominance heighten the interplay of eroticism and power, intensifying the offender's awareness of masculine sexuality. The emphasis on body building in contemporary prisons promulgates a series of provocative messages about seduction and its resistance, creating a continuing drama in which sensuality struggles continuously to triumph over will.

To some commentators, the heavy alcohol and illicit drug use of serious offenders will seem causally crucial; to others, the offenders' transient sexual partnerships and their extreme "macho" style in posture and culture will stand out. But both lifestyle patterns help to maintain an adventuresome, sensually emphatic quality throughout the offender's life, and this appears to be more fundamental motivationally than either considered alone. Moreover, and almost completely ignored by contemporary commentators and by the research literature, is a parallel relevance for the gambling metaphor. The parallelism is suggested by the interchangeability of terms among drug use, sexual practice, and gambling events (e.g., drug dealers, craps players, and sexual partners seek "action," trying to "score" when they "go down" or "get down"); by evidence in the biographies of persistent robbers of gambling in their lives and in the lives of older men who were significant models for them (Katz 1988, pp. 207–9); and by the magical power of gambling to make a stretch of life into "action," something more fully embodied and more intensely realized than ordinary, mundane life.

Compared to the forms of "action" that may be sought in adventuresome sex and through the use of illicit drugs, gambling is an especially protean resource. Drugs and sex run up against physiological limits, but the number of gambles one can have "in play" is limited only by economic resources. As with drugs and sex, gambling has an episodic structure, with a phase for making an irrevocable commitment, a phase in which one's fate is suspended, and a phase that provides a definitive resolution of the bet, with the potential for extraordinary rewards; but the gambles one has in play may be overlapped temporally so that one has "something going" twenty-four hours a day. And, while the objective requirements for sex and drug use are fairly specific, one can gamble, not only in many different forms of play but with many different types of tokens, including people, drugs, and sex relationships. Indeed, formal betting aside, a type of gambling ubiquitously relevant to contemporary offenders is inherent in the personal associations they maintain.

One relatively simple gamble is involved in paying for a "tip" on a valuable target for robbery. If the tip proves accurate, the offender's rewards will be in fabulous ratio to the investment made to get the crucial information. If the tip proves false, the offender may realize that he has become the victim in a "game" that was "run on" him. The "gaming" theme is richly represented in portraits of offenders' street lives, the game being a form of gamble in which one puts up something of value by taking a risk on another's honesty. What is bet may be money, on the promise that drugs will be delivered; drugs, on the inverse promise; or one's presence, as when an offender is induced to accompany another on what the latter promises will be a big "score" (e.g., Thomas 1974, pp. 80–81; Allen 1978, p. 112). When payoffs come, they may take anticipated forms, or they may come at unexpected times and in surprising forms, for example, as gifts of cocaine to be shared in celebration of an acquaintance's criminal successes.

Two pervasive patterns in the lives of persistent offenders combine to guarantee that they will experience a series of high-stakes gambles. One is that, when they enjoy large "takes" or windfalls, they spend heavily and quickly, with the result that, whether or not they formally gamble, they live the boom-and-bust cycles that are characteristic of the gambler's life. Biographical accounts describe showy spending on clothes, gifts to women, luxury cars, and stunning acts of largess to parties of friends, acquaintances, and strangers. Money is frequently spent so quickly as to suggest that the money is attacked, or "burned," so as to avoid giving an impression that the offender's criminal motivation is materialistic.

The second relevant pattern is the overlapping of the social networks in which the offender pursues drug, sex, "partying," gambling, and property crime activities. His boom-and-bust cycles place the offender alternatively in the position of investor-benefactor and debtor-supplicant, and, in either financial position, they induce him to be eager to entertain a variety of high-risk propositions. These may come from a robber-confederate who becomes aware of an investment opportunity to move into a marketing position in an illicit drug market; from a thief–drug customer who, to forestall pressure to pay for drugs already obtained, offers information pointing to the robbery of a vulnerable "fence"; from a girlfriend who is employed in a fast-food restaurant and who, feeling denigrated by the manager, anticipates the pleasures of revenge as she imagines her boyfriend robbing the place.

The gambling attitude of persistent offenders is also represented by their tendency to enter risky ventures with bare acquaintances. Thus it is not uncommon for a member of a group arrested for robbery to be unable to report the last name or the legal first name of one or more of his confederates.[7] To an appreciation of the interlocking character of the offender's various lines of illicit action must be added an appreciation of the open nature of each line: girlfriends, drug suppliers, and customers, confederates within given offenses—all are subject to frequent change. This unique social structure creates a life shot through with "action." Not only may an invitation to a high-risk adventure begin at any moment, even the most mundane acts could become a retrospectively appreciated first critical act on the way to a fateful course of action. So, riding with a friend in his car may take on special meaning when a police car passes and the offender realizes that he is carrying an illegal weapon and that one of the rear lights of the car is out of service, that the registration is not current, and that the car itself might well be stolen.

Thus, even when nothing particularly significant seems to be happening, the offender who lives in an interlocking, open-ended social network of illicit activities frequently has reason to suspect the presence of profound implications. As the offender uses drugs and sex to promote, in a literal sense, an exceptionally full-bodied world of experience, so he develops his career within the context of social networks that invite an overlay of consequentiality onto what otherwise would be unremarkable moments in everyday, mundane life. From the offender's perspective, he is not providing the distinctive motive forces in his world. They come *to* him, from the drugs themselves, from what he experiences as the inherent attractions of comely females, in the forms of irresistible suggestions from acquaintances and of troubles that suddenly emerge as unavoidable obstacles in his path. The motive forces in his world are in front of him, all around him, and calling to him; yet at

[7] For an example, see Keiser (1965, p. 205).

the same time, they are the products of his elaborate preparations and they speak to him intimately, in the embodied form of "gut" reactions.

III. A Transcendent Commitment to Violence

A similar social fabric of illicit action can be found in the careers of nonviolent and violent, persistent property offenders. While it is essential to appreciate how violent predators may use drugs, sexual relationships, gambling, and robbery offenses to embody their desires in a social world that will then promote their persistent criminality, their motivations contain a more distinctive theme. In juxtaposition to the self-consciously sensual dynamics they work into their lives is their generalized commitment to violence, a commitment that serves the emphatically disembodied purpose of being mean.

Violent predators appear to become distinguished from nonviolent "career" criminals at an early age. Their biographies reveal their experience of an early, critical test. However strong they may be—and they do not describe themselves uniformly as particularly capable of physical aggression—they come to realize, through battles with peers, that fighting skills or weapons possession will never be sufficient to guarantee dominance. Battles, they learn, are decided ultimately by a fierceness of will that has no substantive objective other than dominance itself: the victor is the one who manages best not to be concerned about his own legal liability or physical survival; conversely, so long as there is a possibility of continuing to attack, or returning another day to attack again, the loser is ultimately defined as the one who begins to worry and then backs off. In a phrase, they learn that they must be mean, to insist that their meaning or definition of the situation prevail regardless of its utility for any further purpose. Much of the culture of the "badass" that is popular in high-crime areas celebrates the substantively purposeless yet highly expressive styles and symbols of being mean (Katz 1988, pp. 99–112).

The challenges of humiliating dominance that are represented in early adolescence primarily by insults from neighboring peers become constant and more diffuse for the persistent offender in his young adult years. The life histories of violent and nonviolent "career" thieves alike show them recurrently struggling against powerful chaotic forces that threaten to make fools of them, to abuse them physically, to lock them up, or to kill them. Habitual participation as a customer and as a seller in drug markets has its well-known risks. Jealous and vengeful, abandoned mistresses appear to be valuable resources for law enforcement investigators. If confederates in property crimes are pressured by the police, the contemporary offender has little basis to anticipate that traditions of honor will protect him. In addition to the chaos stimulated by boom-and-bust financial cycles, by the complexities of managing multiple and shifting intimate relationships, and by episodic abandonment to the powers of intoxicating substances, the persistent offender keeps in mind that, because of the variety of his previous criminal involvements, he may currently be sought by the police and seized in connection with any of a number of offenses he no longer keeps in mind.

Against this background of chaos, persistent violent property offenders are known in a variety of cultural contexts as "hard-legged," "hard-headed," and "hardmen." What distinguishes robbery from sneak, con, and other surreptitious forms of theft is the offender's demand that everyone on a scene in effect "shut up" and comply to his will. The relatively broad appeal of robbery to young offenders suggests the attractiveness of this posture; and the relatively narrow appeal of persisting in robbery indicates that, as costs and benefits begin to weigh in, career motivation comes to depend increasingly on the personal importance of overtly demanding compliance without giving reasons.

That a posture of readiness to use violence is significant to violent predators not only as a discretely applied criminal skill but as a generalized personal stance toward chaotic circumstances is indicated by data describing their common, extensive assault histories and their virtually continuous maintenance of weapons close at hand (Wright and Rossi 1986). Scenes from life histories vividly convey a readiness to settle disagreements over personal debts with a show of force that brooks no protest; to silence discordant mates with sudden, overwhelming acts of violence; and to abuse small children verbally and physically with a quick and cold indifference (Willwerth 1974; Carr 1975; Allen 1978; Dietz 1983).

In several respects, the robber exploits in his crime the specifically transcendent potential of criminal violence. He creates and transcends chaos by first establishing fearful victims, overcoming any resistance they may mount, and either freezing the scene or transforming victims into compliant accomplices who locate valuables and clear paths for escape. As a stunning physical act, an offender's violence goes one significant step beyond the career criminal's effort to embody his acts with a sensual self-awareness: the offender's violence dramatizes the dominance of his purpose unforgettably in another's body. And in light of the multitude of uncertainties that block a calculated election of robbery as a rational offense, the offender's violence becomes invaluable as a ritual to sustain a will always threatened by the temptations of reason. While robbery may not fare well in materialistic cost-benefit comparisons with other lines of criminal involvement, the robber's generalized embrace of violence has the special virtue of helping steel oneself continually to "get over" the omnipresent threat of chaos in contemporary, urban, street criminal life.

IV. Reflections on Methodology

For about twenty years, the explanation of criminal motivation has been given a relatively low priority in criminological research. Academic social scientists occasionally examine the explanatory potential of background conditions, such as biology or economic class status, for a wide and often undifferentiated range of crimes; and they routinely and prolifically exploit the information that governmental census and law enforcement units, influenced by their own historical commitments and institutional imperatives, happen to gather systematically. Meanwhile, policy-driven research provides offense-specific evidence that describes various facets of criminal behavior and careers, but with only fragmentary relevance to what is perhaps the primary question of criminal motivation: what is it that offenders find distinctively compelling in committing a particular type of offense?

One of the purposes of this essay is to suggest that researchers who are interested in understanding criminal motivation will find it particularly useful to join what have been largely separate lines of research by combining situational analysis with "career," life-history, and biographical research. The connection to situational analysis provides career studies, particularly the qualitative forms of life-history studies, with an enhanced and clarified relevance for criminology. And the study of situated criminal action, as represented here by the review of offender-victim interaction in robberies, takes on new significance when placed within a biographically longer inquiry into motivation.

For situational analysis, the perspective of biographical evidence provides cautions against potentially fundamental misreadings of offender behavior. Thus, for many years, a series of studies correlating offender violence and victim resistance within robberies has promoted the dubious impression that offenders govern their violence according to the dictates of instrumental rationality. Life-history sources caution the researcher to recognize the biases in police and victim-survey data sets that fail to capture many of the robbery offenses that occur among peers, within prison, and within street criminal life. Biographical studies that trace the offender as he moves into given offenses and builds a personal reference set of prior offenses help to keep the analyst sensitive to the emergence of "victim resistance" and of "offender violence" as definitions generated within situated interaction. What may seem, to a researcher inspecting police records describing now-cold criminal events, as independently identifiable and quantifiable acts of aggression and resistance, may, when viewed from within the lived dynamics of the scene, often seem inherently interconnected. Resistance by victims does not necessarily presuppose their perception of emerging offender violence; nor does violence by offenders necessarily presuppose their perception of victim resistance; but sometimes they do.

Life-history materials, with their temporal character, encourage the analyst to appreciate the processual nature of interaction. They also encourage caution on the interpretation of offender goals. In coding victim resistance, researchers have often implicitly presumed that they know what the offender's objectives were, an assumption that itself assumes that the offender knew what his objectives were. But biographical evidence indicates that the robber's objectives are often quickly changing and that at any moment they may be somewhat inarticulate and undisciplined. The offender's experience of the victim as resisting or not will depend on the offender's understanding of the victim's grasp of the offender's demands, which may not have been expressed with legal precision and which may be changing even as the victim tries to firm up his definition of their nature.

If the connection of biographical and situational research should grow stronger, it is the biographical side that especially needs nourishment. For an understanding of the motivation of robbers, perhaps the most strategic, needed line of research is to carry life-history studies into phases of desistance. When prison, incapacitating drug dependency, mortality, or physical disability do not take offenders out of recurrently committing robbery, what mechanisms and forces usher their exit?

It is tempting to read the distribution of police statistics across age groups for a connection between the peaking of robbery and the peaking of male sexual drives, but only if, like the criminal justice system, we discount much of the aggressive behavior of early and late childhood as not worthy of serious consideration. If physiological explanations are not clearly indicated, neither are economic, materialistic theories.

Legitimate economic alternative opportunities should not increase with age and criminal record, although illegitimate, nonviolent opportunities may increase with age. But if older offenders assess the costs of violent crime as outweighing the benefits,[8] an explanation citing economic rationality is not very helpful because it merely transforms the question into one about how offenders come finally to give in to materialistic calculations. It appears that, for aging robbers, it becomes increasingly difficult to "do the time"; for "chronic" armed robbers in French Canada, "as gratifying and attractive as [the criminal 'milieu' and their friends] were before, they lose their allure as the offender ages" (Gabor et al. 1987, p. 73). But why?

I would suggest that the impact of age is not primarily through hormonal influences or changes in economic circumstances but through the offender's increasing awareness of the inevitable and regrettable fact that as he becomes older, others become younger. A "hardhead," "badass" posture that conveyed an inspiring indifference to practical consequences at age seventeen may lose its seductive appeal as one moves through the twenties and on up through the thirties and increasingly encounters this style of bravado being put on display by teenagers. With guns readily available, the physical exertions practically required within robbery scenes by offenders at age forty are not significantly greater than the demands at age twenty; but the pressures of casually associating with ever-younger offenders who are quick with challenging taunts and mocking humor must become much larger. With age, a "hardman" reputation that was once a source of arrogant pride may become evidence of a humiliating inability to differentiate oneself from an increasingly larger, increasingly younger, "naive," "foolish," and "hotheaded" mass.

If these questions seem to call for "psychological" explanations, there is no call for the methodologically troublesome practice frequently associated with that rubric, the invocation of invisible causal forces. I have tried to demonstrate that a falsifiable explanation of the robber's motivation can be developed without relying on theories that locate causal forces as buried in psychic locations but, rather, by focusing on the offender's construction and maintenance of causal forces during his criminally active life. In testing such an explanation, there is no need

[8] On nonviolent, aging criminals, see Shover (1985); for quantitative evidence that, when asked about the attractions of crime, younger criminals cite thrills and older criminals' profit, see Petersilia, Greenwood, and Lavin (1977); for an elaborate model, see Wilson and Herrnstein (1985, pp. 146–47).

for the researcher to "get into the mind" of the offender or to speculate about "subjective" factors that are not amenable to documentation by "objective" evidence. The basic stuff of data is the same as that conventionally incorporated into quantitative and qualitative social research: what people say, the physical movements they make, the relationships they create between the situations they come from and go to, and the problems they confront with others. The researcher takes an unusual focus in motivational inquiry, but what is unusual is not interpretive license but the interactional detail and the biographical breadth of evidence that is included as a resource for disciplining theory.

The materials for criminology become ethnographic, and the questions become ethnomethodological, that is, questions about the methods by which offenders construct the appeal, the practical details, and the situationally specific meanings of their crimes. Attention to "background" factors is not abandoned but is made specific to the *immediate* background or context of the offender's action. Motives do not become forces hidden within the actor, nor are they considered external to the actor. The ways in which the offender's conduct becomes interrelated with changes in his environment become the subject of study, and motivational forces, such as those from drugs, from networks of opportunity in social relations, and from economic lifestyle pressures, are appreciated as creatively *embodied* by the offender. And the researcher's pursuit of the meaning that criminality has for offenders is not a matter of determining what they "think" but of specifying a distinctive *quality of the way they act*.

As soon as criminology, in an attempt to understand the motivations of finely discriminated forms of criminality, narrows its focus from vague notions of "criminal personality," from global conceptions of "deviance," and from the overly broad, statute-based categories used in law enforcement processes, progress in motivational research quickly becomes dependent on qualitative materials and on lines of inquiry about the lived quality of offenders' experience. These changes in explanatory perspective and in data are not the result of a bias against quantitative methods and data; they result from the empirical irrelevance of larger scale, temporally more distant life events and social structures. If there is a relevant bias, it is humanistic: a bias toward appreciating the variously creative ways in which people can construct compelling lives around committing crimes. Because of their importance within the contemporary crime problem, persistent robbers are especially fitting targets for discriminating inquiry, but no less so than are street-level drug dealers, mate batterers, and savings-and-loan fraud artists or, to put the challenge more precisely, than are the empirically valid subtypes of such criminals that qualitative study may help us perceive.

REFERENCES

Allen, John [pseudonym]. 1978. *Assault with a Deadly Weapon*, edited by Dianne Hall Kelly and Philip Heymann. New York: McGraw-Hill.

Block, Richard. 1977. *Violent Crime*. Lexington, Mass.: Lexington.

Brown, Claude. 1965. *Manchild in the Promised Land*. New York: New American Library.

Bureau of Justice Statistics. 1989. *Criminal Victimization in the United States, 1987*. Washington, D.C.: U.S. Department of Justice, Bureau of Justice Statistics.

Camporesi, Piero. 1989. *Bread of Dreams*. Chicago: University of Chicago Press.

Carr, James. 1975. *Bad*. New York: Herman Graf.

Chaiken, Jan M., and Marcia R. Chaiken. 1982. *Varieties of Criminal Behavior*. Santa Monica, Calif.: RAND.

Conklin, John E. 1972. *Robbery and the Criminal Justice System*. Philadelphia: Lippincott.

Cook, Philip. 1980. "Reducing Injury and Death Rates in Robbery." *Policy Analysis* 6:21–45.

———. 1986. "The Relationship between Victim Resistance and Injury in Noncommercial Robbery." *Journal of Legal Studies* 15:405–16.

Dietz, Mary Lorenz. 1983. *Killing for Profit*. Chicago: Nelson-Hall.

Farrington, David P. 1986. "Age and Crime." In *Crime and Justice: A Review of Research*, vol. 7, edited by Michael Tonry and Norval Morris. Chicago: University of Chicago Press.

Federal Bureau of Investigation. 1986. *Uniform Crime Reports*. Washington, D.C.: U.S. Government Printing Office.

———. 1987. *Uniform Crime Reports*. Washington, D.C.: U.S. Government Printing Office.

———. 1988. *Uniform Crime Reports*. Washington, D.C.: U.S. Government Printing Office.

Feeney, Floyd. 1986. "Robbers as Decision-Makers." In *The Reasoning Criminal*, edited by Derek B. Cornish and Ronald V. Clarke. New York: Springer-Verlag.

Gabor, Thomas, Micheline Baril, Maurice Cusson, Daniel Elie, Marc LeBlanc, and André Normandeau. 1987. *Armed Robber: Cops, Robbers, and Victims*. Springfield, Ill.: Charles C. Thomas.

Haran, James F. 1982. "The Loser's Game: A Sociological Profile of 500

Armed Bank Robbers." Ph.D. dissertation, Fordham University, Department of Sociology.

Hindelang, Michael J. 1981. "Variations in Sex-Race-Age-specific Incidence Rates of Offending." *American Sociological Review* 46:461–74.

Hindelang, Michael J., Michael R. Gottfredson, and James Garofalo. 1978. *Victims of Personal Crime*. Cambridge, Mass.: Ballinger.

Jackson, Bruce. 1972. *Outside the Law*. New Brunswick, N.J.: Transaction.

Johnston, D. A. 1978. "Psychological Observations of Bank Robbery." *American Journal of Psychiatry* 135:1377–79.

Katz, Jack. 1988. *Seductions of Crime*. New York: Basic.

Keiser, R. Lincoln. 1965. *Hustler! The Autobiography of a Thief*. New York: Doubleday.

———. 1979. *The Vice Lords*. New York: Holt, Rinehart & Winston.

King, Harry, and William Chambliss. 1984. *Harry King, A Professional Thief's Journey*. New York: John Wiley.

Laub, John, and M. Joan McDermott. 1985. "Young Black Women." *Criminology* 23:81–99.

Luckenbill, David. 1980. "Patterns of Force in Robbery." *Deviant Behavior* 1:361–78.

———. 1981. "Generating Compliance: The Case of Robbery." *Urban Life* 10:25–46.

Mancini, Janet K. 1980. *Coping in the Inner City*. Hanover, N.H.: University Press of New England.

Miller, Billie, and David Helwig. 1972. *A Book about Billie*. Ottawa: Oberon Press.

Miller, Stuart J., Simon Dinitz, and John P. Conrad. 1982. *Careers of the Violent*. Lexington, Mass.: Heath.

Petersilia, Joan, Peter W. Greenwood, and Marvin Lavin. 1977. *Criminal Careers of Habitual Felons*. Santa Monica, Calif.: RAND.

Pileggi, Nicholas. 1985. *Wiseguy*. New York: Simon & Schuster.

Reidel, Marc, and Margaret Zahn. 1985. *Nature and Patterns of American Homicide*. Washington, D.C.: U.S. Department of Justice.

Rettig, Richard P., Manual J. Torres, and Gerald R. Garrett. 1977. *Manny: A Criminal Addict's Story*. Boston: Houghton Mifflin.

Shaw, Clifford. 1966. *The Jack-Roller*. Chicago: University of Chicago Press.

Shover, Neal. 1985. *Aging Criminals*. Beverly Hills, Calif.: Sage.

Skogan, Wesley G. 1978. "Weapon Use in Robbery." In *Violent Crime: Historical and Contemporary Issues*, edited by James A. Inciardi and Anna E. Pottieger. Beverly Hills, Calif.: Sage.

Steffensmeier, Darrell J., Emilie Andersen Allan, Miles D. Harer, and Cathy Treifel. 1989. "Age and the Distribution of Crime." *American Journal of Sociology* 94:803–31.

Sullivan, Mercer L. 1983. "Youth Crime: New York's Two Varieties." *New York Affairs* 8:31–48.

———. 1989. *Getting Paid*. Ithaca, N.Y.: Cornell University Press.

Taylor, Laurie. 1985. *In the Underworld*. London: Unwin.

Thomas, Piri. 1974. *Down These Mean Streets*. New York: Vintage.

West, W. Gordon. 1978. "The Short Term Careers of Serious Thieves." *Canadian Journal of Criminology* 20:169–90.

Wideman, John Edgar. 1985. *Brothers and Keepers*. New York: Penguin.

Willwerth, James. 1974. *Jones*. New York: M. Evans.

Wilson, James Q., and Richard J. Herrnstein. 1985. *Crime and Human Nature*. New York: Simon & Schuster.

Wright, James D., and Peter H. Rossi. 1986. *Armed and Considered Dangerous*. New York: Aldine de Gruyter.

Zimring, Franklin E. 1981. "Kids, Groups and Crime: Some Implications of a Well-known Secret." *Journal of Criminal Law and Criminology* 72:867–85.

Zimring, Franklin E., and James Zuehl. 1986. "Victim Injury and Death in Urban Robbery: A Chicago Study." *Journal of Legal Studies* 15:1–40.

Lucia Zedner

Women, Crime, and Penal Responses: A Historical Account

ABSTRACT

In the eighteenth and nineteenth centuries, women were more commonly convicted of crimes than they are today. Their crimes appear to have been determined more by their socioeconomic situation than by any innate sex differences. Contemporaries reacted very differently to female offenders. Male prison regimes emphasized discipline and deterrence; female prisons developed individualized programs of "moral regeneration." In the latter years of the nineteenth century, biological explanations of crime grew increasingly popular. They were found particularly plausible in explaining female crime long after they had been discredited in relation to men. In the early years of the twentieth century the growing influence of psychiatry focused attention on mental inadequacy as a cause of crime. Many female offenders were reassessed as "mad" rather than "bad." For mainly historical reasons, penal policy continues to be dominated by the belief that women prisoners are likely to be mentally disturbed or inadequate.

This essay examines the dimension of gender in perceptions, explanations, and responses to crime during the nineteenth and twentieth centuries. It owes two major intellectual debts. The first is to the recent development of social histories of punishment that have opened up an exciting area of historical research and developed an analytical framework for understanding the development of crime control. The second is to the development of feminist criminology that has highlighted the concentration of criminological studies almost exclusively on men and

Lucia Zedner, lecturer in law, London School of Economics, University of London, and honorary research fellow, Centre for Criminological Research, Oxford, is grateful to Roger Hood for comments on earlier drafts. This essay is based on research carried out as a prize research fellow, Nuffield College, Oxford.

0192-3234/91/0014-0004$01.00

has sought to redress this imbalance by focusing both specifically on the study of female criminality and, more generally, on the issue of gender. These developments, in both historical and feminist criminology, have made major contributions to our understanding of crime and its control. In North America they have already resulted in valuable research into the history of the incarceration of women and girls in industrial schools, reformatories, and prisons (Schlossman 1977, 1978; Brenzel 1980; Hahn 1980*a*, 1980*b*; Rosen 1980; Freedman 1981; Rafter 1983*a*, 1983*b*, 1985*a*, 1985*b*). In Britain to date there has been little work of comparable depth and quality (though see Dobash, Dobash, and Gutteridge 1986). There has been no empirical research into the perceptions and explanations of female criminality that shaped the development of penal institutions for women.

In this essay I show that up to the mid-nineteenth century the predominant approach to female criminality was moralistic. Women criminals were judged against a highly artificial notion of the ideal woman—an exemplary moral being. Women's crimes not only broke the criminal law but were viewed as acts of deviance from the "norm" of femininity. Prison regimes focused on individual women's failings of character and sought—through external management, educational provision, or self-discipline—to restore inmates to the ideal of femininity.

Toward the end of the nineteenth century attention focused increasingly on the constitution of the offender and particularly on the internal attributes that, it was believed, made people criminal. Criminality in women became the focus of considerable concern not least because, in their role as mothers, they were identified as the biological source of crime and degeneracy. Victorian notions of women as the "weaker sex" made them particularly susceptible to a process of medicalization that has endured into the twentieth century. Biological, and later psychological, interpretations of female criminality were suffused with a highly moral view of what constituted deviance and what constituted normality in women. The apparent shift from moralizing about crime to scientific investigation was rather less marked, therefore, than many have assumed. By building on Victorian assumptions about women's supposed moral weaknesses and by seeking to endow them with quasi-scientific status, these constitutional explanations found greater and more enduring plausibility in relation to female than to male criminality.

Section I of this essay begins by acknowledging the intellectual developments on which it builds—most notably, recent social histories of the prison, the development of historical criminology, and the growth of writings by feminist criminologists. Section II provides, as a benchmark, a brief survey of what is known about the nature and extent of female crime in the eighteenth and nineteenth centuries. For all the well-known weaknesses of official criminal statistics, these provide some basis against which to assess changing views of crime. Section III examines those views, beginning with the development of theories of female criminality in the early nineteenth century. It considers why moralistic approaches to female criminality predominated for much of the nineteenth century and examines to what extent such approaches demanded differential treatment of women in prison. I suggest that this moralizing approach both exacerbated concern about female crime and drew attention to "crimes of morality" committed by women, such as prostitution or public drunkenness. Section IV examines the emergence of biological theories of crime in the late nineteenth century, culminating in the writings of Cesare Lombroso—the most famous proponent of biological positivism. This section looks in detail at the context and the content of such writings. I suggest that they were less novel and certainly less scientific than has generally been thought. Section V traces the emergence of psychological theories that laid stress instead on the incidence of mental defect, again particularly among female offenders. It asks why the growing intervention of psychiatry into the penal sphere focused primarily on female offenders and with what results for those women who were identified as mentally inadequate. Section VI argues that, until relatively recently, the twentieth century has seen remarkably little advance in the understanding of female criminality. Today, penal responses to female crime remain locked within the turn-of-the-century view of criminal women as mentally ill or otherwise inadequate. If anything, this view has spread to encompass not just a group of identifiably deficient women; it suggests that all women who offend are likely to be in some way psychologically disturbed. The continuing prevalence of such a view is explicable only by understanding the extent to which Victorian moral concepts of "normal" and "deviant" women underpin modern psychiatric analysis.

I. Intellectual Acknowledgments

In recent years there has been considerable valuable research into the history of crime in both Europe and America. The major areas of historical interest and controversy have been the development of the police and of custodial institutions: the prison, the reformatory, and the asylum (Foucault 1967, 1977; Rothman 1971, 1980; Ignatieff 1978; Scull 1979, 1981; Bailey 1981; Harding et al. 1985). These writers have looked critically at traditional interpretations that presented the growth of crime control in terms of gradual progress motivated by humanitarian idealism. They have questioned to what extent the aims of late eighteenth and nineteenth century penal reformers were actually achieved; they have looked beyond the rhetoric of reform to examine social, economic, and political forces behind the expansion of crime control and changes in penal policy; and they have focused particularly on the relations between penal institutions and wider mechanisms for maintaining social discipline and asked why the prison emerged as the preeminent punitive solution.

In Europe many of these so-called revisionist writers have worked more or less self-consciously in the shadow of the French philosopher Michel Foucault. His *Discipline and Punish* (1977) developed a schematic vision of the emergence of the "carceral archipelago," in which the prison was only the most extreme of a series of institutions designed to maintain discipline throughout society. Foucault suggested that the conception of power as knowledge formed the basis of this disciplinary order. Penal institutions were primarily observatories in which offenders could be watched, known, and thereby controlled (Foucault 1977, chap. 2). Foucault's thesis suggests an intimate relationship between the history of the prison and the development of criminological knowledge. Only by examining how criminality was perceived and explained can we fully understand the development of institutions designed for its control.

Following Foucault, while explicitly rejecting his more extravagant visions, a generation of writers has sought to delineate the development of the modern apparatus of "penality" (see Cohen and Scull 1983 for a collection of the best of such writings). Writers such as Michael Ignatieff and Patricia O'Brien in England, and David Rothman, Andrew Scull, and Nicole Hahn Rafter in the United States, among others, have produced important works on the history of prisons, reformatories, asylums, and other agencies set up to control deviance (Beattie 1975; Ignatieff 1978, 1983*a*, 1983*b*; O'Brien 1978, 1982; Scull 1979, 1981; Bailey 1980; Hay 1980; Rothman 1980; Cohen and Scull 1983; Rafter 1983*b*; Cohen 1985; Rudé 1985; Radzinowicz and Hood 1986). Penal institutions have been seen as epitomizing a much more generalized encroachment of the state, imposing discipline and controlling more and more aspects of social life. The converging interest of historians, sociologists, and criminologists has thus provided for a fruitful cross-fertilization of ideas and a genuinely critical reappraisal of the development of state control of crime.

This intense concentration of interest in the development of institutions and agencies of crime control has tended to be at the expense of Foucault's parallel interest in the construction of the "power-knowledge spiral" (Foucault 1977, chap. 3). Until recently, relatively little has been written about the accumulation of criminological knowledge over the course of the nineteenth century, about the birth of criminology as a distinct academic discipline around the turn of the century, or about its effect on changing penal policy. In England the vast, pioneering work of Sir Leon Radzinowicz (Radzinowicz 1948, 1956*a*, 1956*b*, 1966, 1968), was the only notable attempt to understand changes in conceptions of crime or in the apparatus of punishment. Only in the past few years have criminologists as a group been admonished that "its [their discipline's] history and development have escaped the close and critical scrutiny usually afforded to powerful forms of social knowledge" (Garland 1985*a*, pp. 109–10). Attempts to redress this oversight have been initiated in the main not by historians but by historically minded criminologists anxious to understand the theoretical framework within which the discipline of criminology emerged (Garland 1985*a*, 1985*b*, 1988; Radzinowicz and Hood 1986). Garland described his own work as an "account of the theoretical formation of the criminological program, its internal characteristics and its relationship to its social conditions of emergence" (Garland 1985*a*, p. 110). In tracing the emergence of criminology in Britain in the latter years of the nineteenth century, he has mapped out the relationship between the formation of criminological understanding and the development of penal ideologies and institutions that it supported. He recognized that the most important of criminology's precursors was the "ecclesiastical law of penance," which focused attention not on the offense but on the sinfulness of the offender. The birth of positivist criminology rested on a fundamental shift of focus so that "the basis of crime no longer lay in sin or in faulty reasoning but in an aberration or abnormality of the individual's constitution" (Garland 1985*a*, p. 111).

This essay takes up Garland's notion of a general shift in criminological understanding from the "moral" to the "medical." It suggests that, in relation to female offenders, this shift was rather less marked than has been thought. For, in relation to female criminality at least, the questions, methods, and, indeed, findings of the new medical and psychiatric approaches to crime remained bound by the traditional moral framework. I argue later that these new interpretations achieved their greatest currency in relation to female criminality for the very reason that they appeared to provide "scientific" confirmation of existing assumptions about "normal" and "deviant" women. As a result, medicine, particularly psychiatry, has continued to inform responses to female criminality through the twentieth century.

As yet there has been very little interest among historical criminologists in the question of gender (Zedner 1988). Probably the main reason is the feeling, common to members of many academic disciplines, that women are marginal to the big, important questions. Criminal men were, indeed, the primary target of the development of formal policing and the proliferation of prisons—and the histories have reflected this. Yet little attention has been paid to the question of how far gender informed these developments; the degree to which notions of appropriate male behavior colored definitions of male criminality; how far emerging explanations of crime were differentiated according to the sex of the offender; the extent to which penal institutions were identifiably masculine in their culture and orientation. In sum, the history of criminality and its control has been documented with remarkably little regard to the issue of gender (with a few important exceptions: for example, O'Brien 1978, 1982; Freedman 1981; Rafter 1983*a*, 1983*b*, 1985*a*, 1985*b;* Hartman 1985).

Differential perceptions of men's and women's characters, roles, and statuses were far more important in nineteenth-century society than they are today. This essay examines the ways in which gender, particularly as constructed in notions of masculinity and femininity, informed early criminological theories. It suggests that female offenders were perceived and treated very differently from men. In Britain the lack of interest in the history of female criminality is doubly surprising given that women made up a far larger proportion of those coming before the courts and going into prison than they do today. While women comprise only 3 percent of the daily average prison population in England and Wales today, a hundred years ago they made up over 17 percent.

Whether as prison doctors, chaplains, governors, or matrons, many of those who dealt with criminals took an intense interest in the criminality of their wards. As they studied and published their findings, they came to be respected as informed commentators, and some were even recognized as experts on crime. Many of these observers and investigators were deeply interested in female criminality and especially in the inmates of women's prisons; as Dobash, Dobash, and Gutteridge (1986, p. 101) have recognized, "Some developed elaborate theories about the nature of criminal women, and the ideas of a few gained considerable prominence." The leading commentators on crime were commonly concerned about female criminality, writing articles, substantial sections in larger works, and occasionally entire monographs on the subject (for example, Carpenter 1858, 1864*a*, 1864*b*; Crofton 1867, 1873; Morrison 1891; Adam 1914; Thomson 1925; Mayhew 1968). To give just an indication of the scope of other writings that had something to say about female criminality, the authors may usefully be divided up into groups. Many works were written by prison chaplains (Field 1846; Kingsmill 1854; Clay 1861; Horsley 1887, 1898, 1913; Merrick 1891). Men and women who worked with prisoners, for example, as prison directors, police court missionaries, or aftercare specialists also wrote about their experiences (Griffiths 1884, 1894, 1904; Davenport-Hill 1885; Holmes 1900, 1908; Bedford 1910; Gordon 1922). Learned societies such as the Social Science Association attracted a variety of contributors and published reports of their proceedings (Frazer 1863; Jellicoe 1863; Safford 1867; Nugent 1877; Wells 1877; Wilson 1878). More specifically, philanthropic ladies who visited women inmates produced books and pamphlets, often as a means of raising funds for their work (Wrench 1852; Hill 1864; Meredith 1881; Scougal 1889; Steer 1893; Orme 1898; Higgs 1906; see also the fictitious works by "A Prison Matron" 1862, 1864, 1866). Unfortunately, very few women wrote about their own experiences as prisoners; two who did were Americans: Mrs. Maybrick (1905), a Southern belle suspected of poisoning her husband, and Susan Willis Fletcher (1884), an upper-class American lady spiritualist accused of theft by deception. In addition, many lesser figures, including a great many anonymous writers, contributed to the journals and periodicals of the day. Such writers merit closer attention than they have so far received, for they are important to understanding responses to female crime both historically and today.

In large part, the questions posed here arise out of, and build on, a wealth of research by social historians and historical criminologists. However, the agenda of this essay owes a second intellectual debt. In the past decade or so, feminist criminologists in America, and more recently in Europe, have sought to pinpoint and to explain differences in female crime and responses to it. Given the huge growth of such writings, any list of writers is bound to be incomplete (to cite just a selection: Giallombardo 1966; Brodsky 1975; Smart 1976, 1977; Vicinus 1977, 1980; Bowker 1978; Crites 1978; Klein 1978; Smart and Smart 1978; Hutter and Williams 1981; Morris and Gelsthorpe 1981; Leonard 1982; Rafter and Stanko 1982; Heidensohn 1985; Morris 1987; Gelsthorpe and Morris 1988). Feminists have criticized existing criminology for its failure to address female criminality, emphasizing the inadequacy of any account that does not encompass gender. As Gelsthorpe and Morris (1988, p. 233) have insisted, "Theories are weak if they do not apply to half of the potential criminal population . . . whether or not a particular theory helps us to understand women's crime better is of fundamental, not marginal, importance for criminology."

In Britain, Carole Smart's *Women, Crime and Criminology* (1976) is generally regarded as the starting point of feminist criminological studies, setting an agenda that has been explored and expanded by subsequent writers (see Gelsthorpe and Morris [1988] for a critical overview of the development of feminist criminology in Britain since Smart). It is not without significance that Smart began her work with an entire chapter devoted to historical studies of female criminality in an attempt to uncover the roots of current attitudes toward female crime. She was immediately criticized by one leading British sociologist who condemned the inclusion of such a lengthy historical section as "the true work of exhumation. It resembles the activities of the resurrection men, the disinterring of the buried for the purposes of clinical analysis" (Rock 1977, p. 394). And yet, as many subsequent feminist criminologists have concurred, it is only by looking at the past that we can begin to understand the genesis of modern views of criminal women. The primary interest of feminist criminologists has been, therefore, less in history per se than in the extent to which the legacy of historical understanding continues to exert an influence over contemporary thinking. Unfortunately, this interest has not yet encouraged empirical historical research but has led, rather, to a general reliance on received historical wisdom.

Carole Smart set the birth of the criminology of women in 1893 with the publication in Italy of Lombroso and Ferrero's *La Donna Delinquenta*—a massive study of the biological characteristics of criminal women. It quickly appeared in an English version in 1895 as *The Female Offender* and, as I show later on, had an influence on explanations of female crime that endured long after Lombrosian positivism had been discredited in mainstream criminology (i.e., that relating to men).

Smart saw *The Female Offender* as a "pioneer" study and thus established a presumption among subsequent feminist criminologists that there had been no interest in the criminality of women before Lombroso (Klein 1978; Pollock and Chesney-Lind 1978). Following Smart, the British sociologist Frances Heidensohn has argued that criminologists concentrate on Lombroso and Ferrero because they "actually wrote about women . . . when their contemporaries were silent" (Heidensohn 1985, pp. 111–12). Similarly, the American writer Eileen B. Leonard (1982) suggests that Lombroso marked the beginning of "scientific" criminology. As the purposes of these works were not primarily historical but looked to the past only insofar as it informed present thinking, it is, no doubt, inappropriate to criticize their historical research. However, in this essay I seek to put forward a rather more historically grounded view based on extensive research into earlier writings on female crime to show that interest in female offenders long predated Lombroso (Zedner 1988). His studies were only part of a longer shift from early moralistic understandings of crime to the rise of secular, scientific, and increasingly exculpatory interpretations and responses to female criminality.

The lack of research into explanations of female crime prior to 1895 has led to a common overstatement of Lombroso's influence on criminological thinking at that time. The very reason why many, especially outside continental Europe, were skeptical of his ideas was because they had already developed sophisticated theories of their own. Perhaps, more important, the lack of research masks the reasons why biological positivism has endured. Dorie Klein (1978, p. 8) is right to note that "the road from Lombroso to the present is surprisingly straight." What is needed now is some explanation of why biological and psychological explanations of female criminality were so readily accepted at the time and why they persist long after constitutional explanations of criminality have lost currency in relation to male crime. Put simply, why has the view endured that the female offender is likely to be sick or inadequate?

Building on this feminist criminological scholarship and extending my account of the historical development of women and crime back beyond Lombroso, I hope to trace the roots of these views of the female offender. I suggest that their enduring influence is not simply attributable to the persuasive powers of Italian positivism but harks back to an older and far wider assumption that all women are morally weak because they are biologically and psychologically inferior to men.

II. The Extent and Nature of Female Crime in the Eighteenth and Nineteenth Centuries

Before the development of criminological knowledge concerning women can be assessed, it is essential to establish some picture of women's crime itself. Official criminal statistics can scarcely be said to provide an accurate picture of "real" crime, so great is the unreported and unrecorded "dark figure." Even if official figures are used only as a benchmark rather than as an accurate representation, it is important to note that changing attitudes, the development of formal policing, and changes in court administration and sentencing policy can all have a major effect on the figures recorded. The fact that the statistics give a better indication of perceptions and responses to crime than of criminal activity itself may be less of a problem, however, if the primary interest is in changes in crime control. Bearing these caveats in mind, what follows is an attempt to draw in broad brush strokes a picture of known female crimes in England during the eighteenth and nineteenth centuries.

In eighteenth-century England, mobility was highly restricted for most women: they were confined for much of their time to the home and to the duties of child care; they spent little time in the public sphere and had relatively few opportunities to meet with other women. By comparison, men spent far more time in public, frequented pubs or bars, and congregated on the streets where they could both devise and commit crimes. Women living in rural communities were likely to be particularly limited in their movement and closely observed in public. Their apparent lack of criminal propensity may well have been due largely to a simple lack of opportunity. Urban life, conversely, not only provided fewer effective checks, less security, and more irregular work but also obvious temptations such as gambling, drinking, and opportunities for prostitution. The Canadian historian J. M. Beattie (1975) has investigated the amount and type of crime of which women were convicted in eighteenth-century England. By statistical analysis of the extent to which women accounted for recorded crime, he provides an important benchmark against which to set historical beliefs and, most important, to measure the gap between widely held assumptions about female criminality and actual levels of recorded crime committed by women. Beattie has found that not only was the crime rate for women living in urban areas far higher than for those remaining in rural Britain, but that city women tended to commit more serious property offenses than their rural counterparts. While the relative passivity of country women may be partly explained by reference to the greater strictures and closer surveillance over their lives, it may also be that rural rebels simply migrated to the city.

Broadly speaking, Beattie found that men outnumbered women in nearly all types of criminal convictions but that women were engaged in roughly the same range of crimes as men and followed similar patterns of offending behavior within this range. Beattie did find qualitative differences between the types of crime for which men and women were convicted: for example (perhaps not surprisingly), he found that women who committed assault were generally less violent than men. More significantly, he confounded many common assumptions about the different nature of female crime. He suggested that women did not, as it was assumed, rely on the supposedly feminine attributes of stealth and deception any more than men did; nor did female murderers necessarily favor poisoning as they were believed to do (Beattie 1975, p. 83). Indeed, Beattie concluded that differences between female and male criminality were determined as much by social situation as by gender.

Surveying the extent and nature of crime over the nineteenth century indicates the relatively high rates of participation by women compared with today. The following figures are taken from the official figures or "Judicial Statistics" published annually in Britain (Judicial Statistics 1857–92). For much of the nineteenth century, women made up nearly a fifth of summary convictions and over a quarter of those committed for trial on indictment (a remarkably high proportion as compared to today). As in the eighteenth century, patterns of crime by men and women were broadly similar to one another with the exception of a number of sex-specific offenses, most notably relating to prostitution.

The largest single category of summary convictions for both sexes was for drunkenness. Perhaps surprisingly, drunkenness accounted for an even larger proportion of female convictions than it did of male convictions. It may well be, however, that a drunken woman attracted more opprobrium and was more likely to find herself arrested than was a man found drunk in public. The second largest category of summary offense for which both men and women were convicted was common assault. Surprisingly, this again made up a larger proportion of female than male crime. Anecdotal evidence suggests that assaults committed by women were often drink related, for example, brawls between women outside pubs or assaults by prostitutes resisting arrest, against drunken clients, or seeking to defend their pitch from rival trade (Jones 1982, p. 105). Of course, this is not to suggest that women were necessarily more violent than men. Fights between men may have been ignored by the police as inoffensive "manly" behavior (unless they seriously threatened public order or the lives of those involved), whereas women fighting in the street would quickly attract police attention. Both sexes were convicted of proportionately fewer assaults over the second half of the nineteenth century, perhaps reflecting the increasing stability of late Victorian society.

For women, the next most common summary offense was prostitution. It is interesting that the proportion of female convictions made up by prostitution was not as high as Victorian literary sources would lead us to believe. As a percentage of female summary convictions, prostitution fell from 13 percent in 1857 to barely 7 percent by 1890. It may well be, however, that many of those convicted of drunkenness, disorderly behavior, or theft were, in fact, prostitutes arrested in the course of their business.

Besides these main categories of summary convictions, a mass of petty offenses such as vagrancy, begging, breach of the peace, and offenses against local acts and bylaws brought both men and women before the courts. Convictions for such offenses were common among the poor living both in rural areas and, increasingly, on the streets of the growing towns and cities. One offense for which convictions of women consistently outnumbered those of men was "offenses against the Pawnbroker's Act by persons unlawfully pledging and disposing." Women working in the sweated trades sometimes pawned the raw materials given them by their employers in order to buy food and then found themselves unable to redeem the goods in time to return them as finished garments or goods. The preponderance of women convicted of this offense tells us much both of the role of women in managing and attempting to eke out an inadequate household budget and also of the place of petty crime in the economy of the urban female poor. Beattie's (1975) conclusion that female crime in the eighteenth century was primarily determined by their socioeconomic situation would seem, therefore, to hold good also for the nineteenth century. Women's offenses, like those of men, were determined largely by the habitat, opportunities, and difficulties of life especially in the growing urban slums inhabited by the very poorest sections of the population.

More serious offenses were tried on indictment. Unfortunately, we do not have statistics for convictions broken down by sex and are forced to rely, therefore, on figures for committal to trial. Women formed a large, though declining, proportion of those proceeded against by indictment—falling from 27 percent in 1857 to only 19 percent by the final decade of the century. By far the largest category of trials on indictment was for larceny. For much of the second half of the nineteenth century women made up nearly a quarter of those tried for "simple larceny," well over a third of those tried for "larceny against the person," and nearly a third of those tried for larceny "by servants."

The next largest category for which both men and women were tried on indictment was "offenses against the person." These made up an increasing proportion of trials on indictment of both sexes—8 percent of female and 13 percent of male at midcentury, rising to 13 and 20 percent, respectively, by the end of the century.

It is perhaps significant that for much of the nineteenth century women made up a striking 40 percent of all those tried for murder. Since murder is probably the least likely of all offenses to go undetected, this figure raises interesting questions about the amount of other serious female crime which was perhaps not so readily detected and counted in the crime statistics. In the last decades of the nineteenth century, statistics for murder were grouped by the age of the victim with the result that women fell to less than a quarter of those offenders tried for the murder of victims over one year but made up nearly all of those tried for the murder of infants. Infant murder was distinguished from "concealing the birth of infants," under which many cases of suspected infanticide were tried (Hoffer and Hull 1981). Given the difficulty of establishing whether the baby was born dead, died during delivery, or was deliberately killed, women were often found guilty only of failing to prepare responsibly for the impending birth of their child—obviously a much lesser charge than the capital offense of child murder. Not surprisingly, nearly all those tried for this crime of "concealment" were women.

Women made up much smaller proportions of other categories such as offenses against property with violence, or forgery, or offenses against the currency. The only other offense for which commitments of women consistently outnumbered men was that of "keeping disorderly houses" or brothels, for which women were between 54 and 70 percent of all those tried.

In the main, then, women were tried on indictment for financially motivated crimes. These were often planned, organized, and entailed some degree of skill. Such findings tend to belie the widely held notion of female criminals as sexually motivated or driven by impulse to commit irrational, behavioral offenses.

III. Moral Approaches to Female Crime in the Nineteenth Century

It is important to bear the preceding figures in mind as the writings and responses of nineteenth-century social scientists and early criminological observers are examined. For it quickly becomes apparent that, while all writings about crime can only be understood within the more general framework of Victorian morality, responses to female crime were deeply embedded in an even more complex value structure, at the heart of which was the highly artificial construct of ideal womanhood. Men who committed many of the less serious forms of crime could be seen as displaying attributes not too far removed from Victorian notions of masculinity: entrepreneurial drive, initiative, courage, physical vigor, and agility were all thought to be appropriate male traits. Although male criminals undoubtedly broke the law, they did not necessarily deviate from accepted notions of "manliness." By contrast, the literature surveyed in this section suggests that criminal women were seen to repudiate revered qualities of femininity. In doing so, they offended not only against the law, but against their ascribed social and moral roles.

The Victorian construction of femininity has generated an entire historiography of its own (Klein 1946; Houghton 1957; Cominos 1963; Basch 1974; Christ 1977; Delamount and Duffin 1978; Banks 1981; Gorham 1982; Davidoff 1983; Showalter 1987). This literature has explored the extent to which, well into the nineteenth century, Victorian social thought was heavily influenced by the legacy of the medieval view of woman as virginal, pure, asexual, and an uplifting influence. Yet, at the same time, women were also seen as Eve-like, both corrupt and corrupting. This duality largely explains the many apparent contradictions in nineteenth-century views of women. Women were lauded as honest, restrained, sober, innocent, and yet they were also feared to be deceitful, designing, avaricious, and dangerously susceptible to corruption. This gap between the feminine ideal and the feared potential for female immorality could only be breached by enforcing an elaborate code of prescribed feminine behavior which might suppress the "darker self" beneath.

The female criminal, the prostitute, and the female drunk were held up as the very negation of the feminine ideal, a warning to other women to conform (Gorham 1982; Walkowitz 1982). And the seriousness of female crimes was measured primarily in terms of women's failure to live up to the requirements of the feminine ideal. Note, for example, the description of criminal women by Henry Mayhew (1862, p. 464), a famous English journalist and social investigator: "in them one sees the most hideous picture of all human weakness and depravity—a picture the more striking because exhibiting the coarsest and rudest moral features in connection with a being whom we are apt to regard as the most graceful and gentle form of humanity." For the most part, criminal women were viewed not so much as economically damaging, physically dangerous, or destructive of property but as a moral menace. Mary Carpenter (1864*b*, 1:31–32), an influential philanthropist and penal reformer generally sympathetic to the plight of women in prison, nonetheless argued: "the very susceptibility and tenderness of woman's nature render her more completely diseased in her whole nature when this is perverted to evil; and when a woman has thrown aside the virtuous restraints of society and is enlisted on the side of evil, she is far more dangerous to society than the other sex." Descriptions of crime frequently referred to the female offender's past sexual conduct, marital status, abilities as a wife and mother, lack of regret, or apparent "shamelessness." In sum, discussion of crime by women went far beyond the offense committed to build up a damning portrait of the character of the offender.

The following contribution by one writer in the popular *Cornhill Magazine* perhaps gives a flavor of a common view of the character of criminal women. "The man's nature may be said to be hardened, the woman's destroyed. Women of this stamp are generally so bold and unblushing in crime, so indifferent to right and wrong, so lost to all sense of shame, so destitute of the instincts of womanhood, that they may be more justly compared to wild beasts than to women" (Owen 1866, p. 153).

It can be seen from quotes such as these that, although male criminals were also seen as sinners, women who offended provoked a quite different response—not least an extraordinary sense of moral outrage. The moralizing approach to crime that predominated in the early nineteenth century clearly distinguished, therefore, according to sex. While the male offender was merely immoral, his female counterpart was likely to be seen as utterly depraved irrespective of any actual, objective difference between them.

Just how far such attitudes affected judgments made about women actually on trial, to what extent courts demanded information about female defendants' moral credentials, and how far they passed sentence on the basis of this strictly irrelevant information remains unknown.

How far differential views of male and female offenders affected penal policy regarding women and were translated into institutional practice has been largely overlooked by historians. Most prison histories have ignored the extent to which treatment of offenders was differentiated by sex, and one British study has gone so far as to assert, "Prison was a man's world; made by men, for men. Women in prison were seen as somehow anomalous: not foreseen and therefore not legislated for. They were provided with separate quarters and female staff for reasons of modesty and good order—but not otherwise dealt with all that differently" (Priestley 1985, p. 69). In fact, women prisoners were seen as quite different creatures from men, requiring special treatment appropriate to their sex. The result was that, at both local and national levels, penal policymakers recognized the need to modify regimes for women.

Given that, throughout the early Victorian era, perceptions and explanations of crime were highly moralistic, it is perhaps not surprising that penal policy focused on the central aim of reform. Policymakers in Britain were divided between those who advocated the "silent system" of prisons (in which prisoners were allowed to work communally but not to talk to one another) and those who advocated the "separate system" (in which prisoners were isolated in individual cells and their solitary confinement was to be broken only by visits from the chaplain). These systems gained prominence in England only after the visit of two highly eminent prison inspectors, William Crawford and Whitworth Russell, to America to investigate the rivalry between the silent associated system, evolved at Auburn Penitentiary, New York, and the separate system, which was rather harshly enforced at the Western Penitentiary, Philadelphia. Both regimes isolated inmates from wider society and prevented communication between prisoners with the ultimate aim of securing their moral reform (Forsythe 1987). While strenuous efforts were made to limit contact among all prisoners, the benefits of isolation were held to be even greater in the case of women. As Whitworth Russell insisted, "With Women . . . I would have Silence and Separation strictly observed, for Women contaminate one another even more than Men do" (Russell 1835).

The silent system was widely criticized by those in Britain who felt that it would be impossible to enforce silence on prisoners without continual recourse to punishment. Since women were considered to have lesser powers of self-discipline, imposing silent association on them was seen to be both more difficult and possibly more damaging to their more delicate nervous health. The separate system was much more popular with British policymakers and prison administrators (Henriques 1972). It fitted well with the prevailing view of criminals as sinners incapable of self-control and was seen as a more likely means of achieving spiritual and moral reform (Forsythe 1987). In Britain, although prisoners were isolated in separate cells, they were to be visited regularly by the chaplain, the scripture reader, and warders (Field 1846; Kingsmill 1854; Clay 1861; Mayhew 1862). In this respect, the rigors of separation were mitigated rather more than in the American model.

Many argued that the central aim of securing moral reform by isolating prisoners from one another was even more important in the case of women than of men. For women were believed to be more impressionable than men and, therefore, at the same time, both more easily corrupted and more susceptible to reformatory influences. One county prison chaplain applauded the benefits of separation arguing that women who "under the old system, must have gone out corrupted and ruined by association with the most depraved and basest of their sex, have under that now in operation been discharged from prison impressed with better principles, and possessed of a real desire to retrieve their characters and to become useful members of society" (Chaplain of Stafford County Gaol 1854, p. 42).

In Britain, the mass of offenders were sentenced to short periods of a few weeks or months in one of over a hundred small local prisons scattered across the country. Until 1877, these prisons were under local government, often poorly organized, and commonly overcrowded (DeLacy 1986). Women composed just over a fifth of the local prison population but, with the exception of two or three special institutions, were housed in wards or wings within male prisons. Removing women to separate accommodation was all too often regarded as impractical on grounds of expense, so women were fitted in wherever practical, often in conditions far worse than those suffered by men convicted of like offenses. Provision was generally maintained at a minimum so even a small rise in the number of commitments could overburden existing accommodation intolerably. In many local prisons, separation was not even attempted—for example, in 1857, prison inspectors at Carmartheon Jail found fourteen women and two children sharing only five beds in filthy conditions. In the face of such inadequate resources, prison administrators put great emphasis on the role of female prison staff in creating a regime suitable for women. "Successful treatment of female criminals . . . largely depends on the tone and disposition of female prison officers. Harshness and impatience . . . are only calculated to aggravate violence and insubordination. Despair and hopelessness fill the minds of the most criminal women: the antidote to which is the feeling of hope" (Bremner 1874, p. 282).

While petty offenders were sentenced to local prisons, more serious ones were transported to the colonies as "convicts." The increasing reluctance of the colonies to take British convicts in the first half of the nineteenth century generated a period of intense innovation in penal theorizing as policymakers struggled to come up with an alternative form of punishment. The ending of "transportation" in the 1850s thus led to the establishment of a second tier of national or "convict" prisons (many of which are still standing and in use today). These held prisoners for long terms of "penal servitude" set originally at a minimum of five years, though this was later reduced to three. The need to hold prisoners for such long periods meant that regimes, purposes, and priorities of convict prisons were necessarily very different from those in local prisons.

Although the development of penal policy for convicts was primarily male oriented, it was widely accepted that women must be treated differently from men. As the prison inspector Whitworth Russell (1835, p. 124) insisted, women required "a very different System of Penal Discipline . . . I hardly see anything in common between the Case of a Male and a Female Convict." There were, of course, leading and highly influential women in the field of penal reform, such as Elizabeth Fry (1827*a*, 1827*b*), Susanna Meredith (Lloyd 1903), and Mary Carpenter (1864*a*, 1864*b*, 1872). Yet even they were less than confident about how the prison regime could best be adapted for women, as Carpenter (1864*b*, 1:31) herself admitted, "It is well known to all persons who have the care of criminals, whether old or young, that the treatment of females is far more perplexing than that of males. It demands, indeed, peculiar consideration and comprehension of the special difficulties to be grappled with."

Women convicts were held initially at three prisons, all in London, at Millbank, Brixton, and Fulham (though other convict prisons were set up over the century at Parkhurst, Woking, Aylesbury, and Holloway). The difficulties of holding women for long periods of penal servitude were seen to be even greater than for men. Not only was it feared that women would "not have the same physical and mental powers which enable them to bear up against the depressing influence of prolonged imprisonment" (Jebb 1855), but for practical reasons "females must of necessity be employed chiefly indoors, and will have neither the varied work, nor the complete change afforded to Male Convicts by removal to the public works" (Jebb 1855). That is, whereas male convicts passed their days outside the prison at hard manual labor on "public works," female convicts were to be held permanently, and monotonously, within the prison itself. As a result, whereas male-convict prisons were primarily concerned with inculcating work discipline, the predominant goal of the female prison was to achieve some degree of "moral regeneration." The emphasis on moral reform in female prisons sprang partly from the belief that female offenders were generally more depraved than male prisoners and had, therefore, greater moral ground to recover. Paradoxically, the very fact that they were considered to be more impressionable also gave greater hope for reform. More pragmatically, it was recognized that, while men could generally get some sort of rough work after release, most respectable work for women, particularly if it were in domestic service, required testimonies as to their character and conduct. The creator and head of the English convict prison system, Major Joshua Jebb (1854, p. 64), recognized that "the difficulties in the way of a woman of the character of the majority of these prisoners returning to respectability are too notorious to require description. They beset her in every direction the moment she is discharged."

Whereas in male-convict prisons regulations were enforced with militaristic precision, the regimented and uniformed convicts marching lockstep to and from their work, in women's prisons, inmates were subject to a more individualized, manipulative regime. The superintendent of Brixton Prison described the discipline in her prison accordingly: "although it is in strict accordance with the rules laid down, yet it varies in some degree according to the disposition and habits of the prisoner. Indeed, without this individual treatment the attempt to reform them would be most superficial" (Surveyor-General 1857–58, p. 50). Though the emphasis was on "treatment" rather than discipline, it would be wrong to assume this necessarily created a more lenient regime. Male prisoners were expected only to work hard and refrain from breaking prison rules; every aspect of women prisoners' appearance, manner, and conduct was required to conform to highly artificial constructions that made up the ideal femininity. As a result, a much higher level of surveillance prevailed in women's prisons, raising tensions, inviting rebellion, and so increasing the punishment rate (Carpenter

1864*b*, 2:426). It might well be instructive to compare this situation with that in modern prisons where the current rate of punishment of women prisoners for rule infractions is proportionately more than twice that of men (Morris 1987, p. 122).

Over the second half of the nineteenth century, faith in the efficacy of moral reform was badly shaken. "Habitual offenders," who defied all reformatory efforts and returned to the prison time and again, forced even the most ardent supporters of reform to admit that this group, at least, was irredeemable. The atmosphere of moral regeneration and religious awakening that had prevailed under the leadership of Joshua Jebb now disappeared under the regime of Sir Edmund Du Cane (director from 1865 to 1898; see Du Cane 1876, 1885), to be replaced by an emphasis on discipline and deterrence. Prisons had become dumping grounds for the socially inadequate, and prison officials were disturbed to find that there was a sizable core of criminal women who appeared almost immune to the pains of imprisonment. Although women formed less than a fifth of all prisoners, they actually outnumbered men in the class of those who had ten or more previous convictions—the so-called hardened habituals. Du Cane (1885) argued that the repeated reappearance of the same core of offenders signified a measure of success in that it indicated that new "recruits" were being deterred from entering the prison system. Indeed, over the second half of the nineteenth century, the number of women committed to penal servitude steadily declined from an annual high of 1,050 in 1860 to a mere ninety-five in 1890 ("Women Convicts" 1887, p. 473; Johnston 1901). The obvious success of deterrence was, however, at the expense of any attempt to reform those who did end up in prison. For the later years of the nineteenth century saw a marked decline in the confidence of those who had once propounded moral reform, particularly in relation to women. For example, in its annual report for 1880, the leading reform agency, the Howard Association, admitted that "it is well known that the least hopeful subjects of moral influence are habitual criminals, and most of all, criminal and debased *women*" (Howard Association 1880, p. 11).

The apparent inability of the prison to reform clearly caused even greater anxiety in the case of female prisoners than of male. This was mainly because women were supposed to act as a potential moralizing force in society. Among the urban poor, especially, women were seen as a means to police those communities least susceptible to more formal controls. In *The Policing of Families* (1979), Jacques Donzelot has traced the genesis in France during the eighteenth and nineteenth centuries of the "social sector." This he defines as the process of identifying social problems and establishing personnel qualified to combat them, of specialist institutions, and of social programs as a means of both preventive and remedial control. In these developments, Donzelot sees the family as the crucial point of intersection between the private and social spheres. The family, with a woman at its heart, was both the focus of state intervention and itself held up as a moralizing agent. Donzelot's thesis can be usefully applied to much of western Europe where the pace of industrialization led to intense pressure on the family to withstand the demoralizing effects of urbanization, to lessen the corrupting effects of overcrowding, and, above all, to police its own members. Women, as wives and mothers, were central figures in this endeavor (Summers 1976; Christ 1977; Roberts 1984). Not surprisingly, if they then repudiated their supposedly moral duty, by failing to act as feminine exemplars of respectability, it caused intense anxiety. Note the following observations, all made during the middle years of the nineteenth century. "Female crime has a much worse effect on the morals of the young, and is therefore of a far more powerfully depraving character than the crimes of men . . . the influence and example of the mother are all powerful: and corruption, if it be there, exists in the source and must taint the stream" (Symons 1849, p. 25). "The conduct of the female sex more deeply affects the well-being of the community. A bad woman inflicts more moral injury on society than a bad man" (Hill 1864, p. 134). "There is domestic purity and moral life in a good home, and individual defilement and moral ruin in a bad one" (Gibb 1875, p. 334). Or, finally, and most dramatically, "Woe to that country in which men are not able to consider women as living lives on the whole more sober, righteous and godly than their own!" (Horsley 1887, p. 62).

It was commonly held that corruption or criminality in mothers was a major source of juvenile delinquency (Carpenter 1858, 1864*b*). Women who led their children into crime were doubly condemned, for they were seen not only to have offended against their maternal instincts but to have repudiated their responsibilities to society in general. Even crime among grown men was traced back to the corrupting influence of a woman—a single prostitute became "the seducer of virtue, not in one, but in hundreds of young men: [she] robs them of their strength, their money, their character" (Kingsmill 1854, p. 64). This biblical notion of the sinful woman leading men astray was pervasive throughout mid-nineteenth-century criminological literature and, perhaps not surprisingly, was even adopted by male criminals anxious to displace blame. One influential prison chaplain interviewed hundreds of male prisoners and recounted the explanations they gave for their crimes: one asserted that "a bad wife was the first cause of all my trouble," another blamed "bad company, particularly female," and another claimed that "one female so persuaded me to adopt her life that, in order to gratify her wishes . . . I was led to steal" (Kingsmill 1854, pp. 285 ff.). The supposed potential for criminal women to lead others into crime thus amplified the costs of female criminality far beyond the offenses committed by women alone. The criminal woman not only disavowed her role as a benign moral influence but, infinitely worse, became a source of "moral contagion."

The moralizing role ascribed to women was instrumental not only in responding to female criminality but also in designating what types of crime were regarded as most serious when committed by women. As the historian David Jones (1982, p. 129) has noted, mid-nineteenth-century Britain witnessed a rising obsession with "crimes of morality": sexual offenses, prostitution, drunkenness, vagrancy, and illegal gambling. To the middle classes, the urban poor seemed to be turning their backs on precepts of respectability, self-restraint, and sobriety (Symons 1849; Mayhew 1861–62; Greenwood 1981). A growing body of wealthy philanthropists decided to sponsor statistical research into the problems of Victorian society with a view to seeking their solution. "Ameliorism," as this movement was known, viewed most social problems as being caused by the combination of two main factors: the strains of difficult social environments and the moral weakness of the individual. The conjunction of social circumstance and individual failure was held up as the cause of all the major social problems of the day (for more detailed discussion of Ameliorism as a movement, see Abrams 1968, pp. 33–52; Radzinowicz and Hood 1986, chap. 3, "The Ameliorative Creed").

While this concern with immorality informed views of crime generally, it became a veritable obsession in defining female criminality. An apparent rise in the proportion of female offenders in the first half of the century was regarded as indicative of the "increasing demoralisation" of the population as a whole (Symons 1849, p. 25). Links were made between female crime and sexual morality, not least because all female sexual activity outside the bounds of marriage was seen as an undesirable and particularly damaging form of deviance. This thinking had the effect, first, of encouraging the Victorians to search for a sexual element in all female crime, even that which had no obvious sexual content and, second, of placing special emphasis on sexual misdemeanors committed by women. The Victorian tendency to compound female sexuality with deviancy in women has attracted a quite distinct historical literature of its own (Cominos 1963; Marcus 1966; Finnegan 1979; Walkowitz 1980; Weeks 1981; Mort 1987).

The prostitute attracted most attention for she epitomized what Peter Cominos (1963, pp. 166–68) has identified as "The Tainted Model." Although prostitution itself was not illegal, it was responded to and policed in much the same way as crime. Throughout much of continental Europe and, to a lesser extent, in Britain (until the repeal of the Contagious Diseases Acts in 1883), prostitutes were subjected to strict regulation. Prostitution was the most commonly recognized and carefully documented area of female deviance, and it is significant in early criminological literature that little distinction was made between female criminality and unchastity. This was partly because observers tended to confound sexual delinquency with crime in women but also because many women who engaged in prostitution supplemented their income by other offenses. For example, in their massive study of London lowlife, the social investigators Henry Mayhew and John Binney declared, "We found it impossible to draw an exact distinction between prostitution and prostitute thieves"; of the lower-class prostitutes, they maintained, "Most of them steal when they can get an opportunity" (Mayhew 1968, 4:355–66). In a subsequent study, Mayhew (1862, p. 462) worked from the assumption that "it will, we believe, be found to be generally true that those countries in which the standard of female propriety is the lowest, or where the number of prostitutes is the greatest, there the criminality of the women is the greatest."

Opportunities for crime were seen to arise in the course of the prostitute's daily activities: petty theft from the person or burglary of their homes, assault or even murder of difficult clients, or the fencing of articles stolen by less honest ones. Prostitution as a motivational cause of crime was explained with unwitting reference to the moral code enforced against women. Since women were believed to need social approbation for their self-respect, once a woman became a prostitute, she was thought to collapse under the burden of shame. She was said to become reckless in her actions and turn to crime in desperation. Significantly, the overriding concern with the moral costs of prostitution meant that even the prostitute whose original motivation was economic and who used her trade primarily for the purposes of petty theft, was, nevertheless, seen as a sexual deviant without economic rationale. The legacy of such views in the tendency to sexualize female criminality continues today and has been recognized by modern feminist criminologists (Heidensohn 1985; Morris 1987).

Undoubtedly the most important attempt to question these assumptions about prostitution was William Acton's massive 1857 study *Prostitution, considered in its Moral, Social, and Sanitary Aspects.* Acton's work differed from other contemporary studies of prostitution not merely in its size and scope but in its attempt to move beyond the imagery of the "harlot" as the negation of all that was good in woman. Instead, he saw prostitution "as an inevitable attendant upon civilized, and especially closely-packed, population" (Acton 1972, p. 3). His relative restraint from moralizing allowed for far more systematic investigation than had been achieved before. For example, Acton challenged the common assumption that prostitutes necessarily followed a downward path through destitution, drunkenness, and disease to the hospital or the pauper's grave. He maintained instead that most prostitutes returned eventually to ordinary life, to respectable work, or to marriage.

This interpretation of the role of prostitution in the economy of the female poor has been reexamined by several historians (Finnegan 1979; McHugh 1980; Walkowitz 1980, 1982). Following Acton, Walkowitz (1980, p. 25) has suggested that prostitutes were far from cut off from the society of the urban poor and that prostitution represented a means by which young working-class women could retain their independence during periods of hardship. However, that women chose to turn to prostitution does not necessarily support any romanticization of their lives but may merely attest to their lack of power, to the limited opportunities open to them. Historian Frances Finnegan (1979, p. 215), on the basis of an in-depth study of the lives of prostitutes in one nineteenth-century city, has argued, "The criminality and drunkenness of York's prostitutes reveals conclusively that they were brutalized and degraded by the occupation, that they suffered both physically and mentally and that they were regarded both by society and themselves as social outcasts." The contrast between the two views of nineteenth-century prostitution presented by Walkowitz and Finnegan is not easily resolved. Yet what stands out and unites both studies is the gap between the ideals of Victorian middle class morality and the realities of working-class life.

Alongside prostitution, alcoholism was a major preoccupation of

Victorian moralists. Public houses, spirit shops, and dancing saloons, and the drunkenness that accompanied them, were seen as sources of corruption, degradation, and, ultimately, of criminality. Drunkenness originally attracted the attention of social observers primarily as a moral issue. Pubs tempted both men and women out of the home and away from their families. Drink was thought to lessen self-control, to encourage promiscuity, and to lead women into prostitution. Many prostitutes claimed to have been seduced first when drunk, alcohol being used to break down resistance and to excite sexual passion in both men and women. Moreover, drinking halls provided a trading ground for potential clients.

The links made between prostitution and alcoholism are worth observing for they epitomize the moralizing approach to female criminality more generally. For example, Dr. Norman Kerr (1880, p. 9), a leading medical and social reformer, assumed that "by drink, the 'unfortunates' deadened their conscience and stifled stirrings of remorse, thus fortifying themselves to ply their hideous calling." The Reverend G. P. Merrick, Chaplain to Millbank Prison, London, conducted a massive study of 14,100 prostitutes in prison. He ascribed even greater importance to alcoholism in overcoming what he assumed to be women's natural resistance to a "wicked and wretched mode of life," asserting that prostitutes: "loathe it, and their repugnance to it can only be stifled when they are more or less under the influence of intoxicating drinks" (Merrick 1891, p. 29). How far this supposed hatred was genuinely felt, merely professed for the benefit of a pious prison chaplain, or blithely ascribed by observers insensitive to the equal misery of alternative forms of employment is unclear. What is striking is the apparent readiness of observers to see alcohol consumption not as part and parcel of urban working-class life, where supplies of uncontaminated water were scarce and expensive, but as indicative of a more general moral decline.

Alcoholism in women was seen to have particularly serious moral consequences given women's responsibilities for home life and child care (MacLeod 1967). Toward the latter years of the nineteenth century an increasing number of writers concerned themselves with the social and moral consequences of female alcoholism. The prominent campaigner, Dr. Norman Kerr (1880, p. 142), insisted "that the female parent is the more general transmitter of the hereditary alcoholic taint I have little doubt." Female alcoholism was considered to be potentially far more damaging than that in men, for example, if a woman was drunk during conception, or if she continued to drink during pregnancy. Numerous studies (many of which were published in medical journals or a specialist periodical, the *British Journal of Inebriety*) were devoted entirely to investigating the extent and effects of maternal alcoholism. Debates raged about the effects of alcoholism on fertility rates and on infant health (Kerr 1880, 1888; Sullivan 1906; Kelynack 1907; Scharlieb 1907). While some suggested that long-term alcoholism made women sterile, others feared that drunken women were giving birth to an "ever-increasing multitude of social failures." This literature was highly moralizing in tone, condemning the inebriate mother for her irresponsibility or her deliberate defiance of maternal duties. Women who drank were condemned for failing to clean, feed, clothe, or care for their infants; for leaving them at home to fend for themselves; and for spending the household budget on drink (Alford 1877; Kerr 1880, 1888; Holmes 1903; Westcott 1903; Zanetti 1903; Kelynack 1907). The lack of sympathy for women who sought to escape the miseries of destitution in drink is all the more marked when one notes the relative lack of comparable censure of men.

In these writings the moral implications of women's behavior were further exacerbated by the costs of their drunkenness for future generations. Yet one must also wonder how far concern ostensibly about the genetic implications of female alcoholism was fed by the threat to traditional morality such women posed. For example, during the second half of the nineteenth century, women increasingly went into pubs to drink (Scharlieb 1907). Their presence there signified a direct violation of a traditional male bastion and the invasion of an arena which had previously operated outside and, in many ways, in opposition to the ideal of domesticity. The extent to which moral fears and genetic concerns fed off each other in the minds of contemporary observers is illustrated by the following condemnation of the trend toward women drinking in public: "Women have shown an unforeseen facility for adopting masculine vices, without the saving grace of masculine self-respect. When they give way at all they are lost: and the temptation to which they are thus exposed by the removal of conventional safeguards is much greater than that which assails men, by reason of the physical weakness and emotional sensibility peculiar to their sex" (Shadwell 1902, p. 76).

The combined concerns of medical lobbyists and moral reformers proved to be a powerful interest group. They were highly influential in drawing attention to the problem of women alcoholics, to the futility of sending them repeatedly to prison for short terms, and to the need for more appropriate provision. Successive legislation to provide for inebriates in the 1870s and 1880s singularly failed to address the plight of poor, mainly female, inebriates whose repeated reappearance before the courts represented a growing public scandal (one apparently notorious woman, Jane Cakebread, had achieved 278 police court appearances by 1895). A new consensus that compulsory, long-term commitment to publicly funded, specialist institutions was the only hope of reform led to the introduction of a two-tier system of certified and state reformatories under the Inebriates Act of 1898. The act identified two main, though not necessarily discrete, groups: habitual drunkards and those who committed serious offenses while drunk. It was hoped that if placed in a sufficiently propitious environment and subjected to benign moral influences these drunkards could be "cured" of their addiction. Significantly, women were overwhelmingly the subjects of this legislation—by 1904 over 90 percent of those admitted to certified reformatories were women.

Unlike most female prisons, which were generally located in the hearts of the areas from which they recruited their clients, reformatories for alcoholics were built almost exclusively in rural locations (e.g., at Farmfield in Surrey; Aylesbury in Buckinghamshire; Ashford in Middlesex). In their organization, regime, and even in the goals they pursued they were remarkably similar to the reformatories set up to socialize and domesticate wayward women in later nineteenth- and early twentieth-century America (Brenzel 1975; Freedman 1981; Rafter 1983*b*). Established in rural settings, they were organized around large country houses or groups of cottages designed to maximize the potential for curing and domesticating women in an environment far removed from the potential temptations of modern city life. Both American and British institutions provided "protection" for the women in their care. Their avowed aims were to encourage self-respect and to promote an active interest and competence in feminine pursuits through domestic training. More often, reformatories on both sides of the Atlantic resorted to systems of petty rewards and sanctions in an attempt to rehabilitate their "wayward" charges, effectively infantilizing them in the process.

The form and means adopted by the reformatory endeavor suggested a fulsome rejection of women's increasing invasion of the public sphere, particularly in the growing towns and cities. In establishing reformatories in the countryside where women could be returned to a nostalgic version of rural domestic life, penologists reflected the growing belief that female emancipation necessarily led to increased rates of female crime. Such fears prompted comparative studies of crime rates in different areas that were used to demonstrate that the extent of women's movement into the public sphere correlated directly with the number of crimes they committed (Ellis 1890; Morrison 1891). The emerging "new woman" quickly became a scapegoat, held responsible for the decline of the family, and a forcible argument for resisting further movement of women outside the home. "One thing at least is certain, that crime will never permanently decrease till the material conditions of existence are such that women will not be called upon to fight the battle of life as men are, but will be able to concentrate their influence on the nurture and education of the young" (Morrison 1891, p. 157). Modern-day criminologists will recognize in such dramatic prophesies parallel predictions made with equal force in response to the second wave of the women's movement in the second half of the twentieth century (see, e.g., Adler 1975).

The growing concern about female alcoholism reflects how, in the middle years of the nineteenth century, traditional moralistic explanations of offending behavior were increasingly overlaid with a rising obsession with physiological causes. Views of crime as the product of individual moral choice were gradually replaced by a newer and more disturbing perception of criminals as an almost separate species, distinct from the rest of the population in constitution and appearance. This perception was, in part, the product of large-scale migration to industrial cities that raised fears about the health of the nation's stock and generated theories of hereditary national decline. The historian Gareth Stedman Jones has shown how the Victorian middle classes feared that the vast and ever-increasing urban population would sink further into the so-called residuum or outcast classes with each successive generation (Stedman Jones 1971; Soloway 1982).

The extraordinary growth of writing on crime over the course of the nineteenth century suggests a preoccupation with the failure of prison regimes to deter a substantial core of "habitual offenders." Even in England, where in the second half of the century official returns seemed to suggest that crime was decreasing (Gatrell, Lenman, and Parker 1980; Radzinowicz and Hood 1986, pp. 113–24), social commentators and researchers in the nascent discipline of criminology focused attention on that group of criminals who seemed to be impervious to "civilizing" or reformative influences. Journalists and other social researchers ventured into the slum areas to investigate what were feared to be "criminal areas" of dense, frenetic criminal activity (e.g., Carpenter 1864*b;* Greenwood 1869; Morrison 1891; Mayhew 1968; Mearns 1970). They focused particularly on the costs of overcrowding in unsanitary and demoralizing living conditions that it seemed could only degrade those who suffered them. Women were seen to be especially impressionable and ill-equipped to resist the degradation of their environment. One prison chaplain observed "the indiscriminate herding together of the poor of all sexes and ages in their cramped, comfortless and inconvenient houses has a necessary tendency to sap that instinctive modesty and delicacy of feeling which the Creator intended to be the guardians of virtue, and which are more especially necessary for the defense of the female character" (Rogers 1850, p. 45). As a result, it was feared women were most likely to succumb to promiscuity, to alcoholism, and to crime.

The reformer Mary Carpenter (1864*b*) categorized slum dwellers as falling into two distinct social groups—the "perishing and dangerous classes," that is, those at risk from demoralization and those who had already turned to crime. Women in the latter group caused Carpenter particular concern. "Convict women usually spring from a portion of society quite cut off from intercourse with that in which exists any self-respect, and they are entirely lost to shame or reputation . . . [they] . . . belong to a pariah class, which exists in our state as something fearfully rotten and polluted" (Carpenter 1864*b*, 2:208). This notion of pollution may be seen as arising from an organic view of society as the "Body Politic" (Davidoff 1983)—a body of interdependent parts with the middle-class male as its head, the middle-class female as its heart, and the working classes as its hands. Criminal women, and prostitutes especially, represented various unmentionable and distasteful bodily functions. Consequently two interrelated, if somewhat contradictory, biological images of criminal women arose—one as pathological, rotten, and corrupting; the other as a necessary drain of society's "effluvia" protecting the purity of middle-class wives and daughters at the expense of their own. Whichever view prevailed, the end result was the same—to set criminal and "fallen" women apart as a distinct, debased group within society.

IV. Late Nineteenth-Century Biological Theories of Female Crime

It is clear that, although this period saw traditional moralizing interpretations replaced by newly emergent "scientific" conceptions of human behavior, the very impetus to this new body of research was firmly grounded in Victorian morality. Although the rise of the "scientific" represented an attempt at a higher understanding—a search for the rational, for the clinically testable—such theories were in no sense value free. A growing number of physicians and biologists took an interest in social problems, yet the very way in which they defined these problems and the range of solutions they proposed remained bounded by a value-laden normative framework.

Figures like Auguste Comte and Herbert Spencer were highly influential in arguing that it was possible to derive principles of social organization and action on the basis of biological models (see Conway 1970). They inspired doctors working in the prison service to argue that it was possible to develop laws of criminality parallel to those of natural science. Attention turned to the internal or constitutional attributes believed to make people into criminals. Whatever their true scientific status, new "specialisms" like physiognomy became extremely popular (Sturma 1978). In Britain writers indulged in lengthy discussions about the physiognomy of female offenders, subjecting their facial traits to endless analysis broken only by exclamations of horror. For example, the writer Frederick Robinson observed of one woman, "[A] physiognomist might have guessed much of her character from her countenance—it was so disproportionate and revolting" ("A Prison Matron" 1862, 1:284). It is notable how often supposedly scientific observation of female facial features descended to impassioned comparison with some ideal of feminine beauty—against which many ill-nourished, filthy, or elderly female offenders fared very poorly. While physiognomy was also avidly applied to criminal men, there was no comparable standard of male appearance against which men were judged. This is especially important since facial features were taken to be the outward signs of "moral corruption and weak character."

In these accounts we see the beginnings of what was to become a veritable obsession with the constitutional characteristics of the female offender, the strength of which can only be understood by looking back to earlier Victorian assumptions about female biology. As the historian Roger Smith (1981*b*, p. 143) has pointed out, for the Victorians, "Conceptions of women's social position were integrated with naturalistic descriptions of disease types and deterministic explanatory schemes. It was relatively easy to objectify women as part of physical nature." All women were seen to be closely bound to their biology, and their psyche was thought to be intimately connected with the reproductive cycle, the health or pathology of which directly determined their mental health (see discussions in Skultans 1975, p. 4; Showalter 1987). Pioneering sociologists like Herbert Spencer suggested that the reproductive cycle so taxed women's energies that they had little surplus for other activities (Conway 1970). Even in the normal woman, the round of biological crises—from puberty through menstruation, pregnancy, and labor to menopause was fraught with dangers for her mental health. The influential "alienist" Henry Maudsley catalogued the range of disorders attendant on these biological crises: from the hysterical melancholy of pubescent girls to the recurrent mania liable to be provoked by menstruation (Maudsley 1870). To the extent that a woman could be seen as a prisoner of her biology she could deny her culpability even for serious offenses. Maudsley (1874, p. 163) later affirmed: "cases have occurred in which women, under the influence of derangement of their special bodily functions, have been seized with an impulse, which they have or have not been able to resist, to kill or to set fire to property or to steal."

Deviant behavior could also be explained as the product of a series of mental conditions: delicate nerves, emotional disorder, or mental defect all of which were related back to woman's biology. Havelock Ellis (1904, p. 293), pursuing a strong interest in the nascent discipline of criminal anthropology, argued that women were so much victims of their monthly cycle that "whenever a woman has committed any offense against the law, it is essential that the relation of the act to her monthly cycle should be ascertained as a matter of routine."

A more damaging view was that the criminal woman's constitution was inherently pathological. This suggested a far more dangerous type of criminal woman who lacked the inner resources to overcome the tremendous pull of degeneracy. Seeking to identify the attributes of such a type, scientifically minded observers, such as British prison doctors G. Wilson, J. Bruce Thomson, and David Nicolson, began to investigate and to describe in minute detail the physical characteristics of prison inmates (Prewer 1974; Radzinowicz and Hood 1986, pp. 3–11). Typographies of offenders were developed for both men and women but were all the more extreme and grotesque in the case of women. Havelock Ellis (1890) claimed that women guilty of infanticide were endowed with excessive down on their faces, that female thieves went grey more quickly, were uglier, and exhibited more signs of degeneracy (especially of the sexual organs) than ordinary women. Although Ellis was writing before the publication of *The Female Offender* in 1895, he drew heavily on the research already carried out by Lombroso and Ferrero. He went so far as to proffer an extraordinary explanation of the low levels of female crime based on a crude model of sexual selection. "Masculine, unsexed, ugly, abnormal woman—the woman, that is, most strongly marked with the signs of degeneration, and therefore the tendency to criminality—would be to a large extent passed by in the choice of a mate, and would tend to be eliminated" (Ellis 1890, p. 217).

While Ellis claimed that his conclusions were based on the work of professional criminal anthropologists including Lombroso, it is not difficult to call into question the validity of such findings. The attributes that he supposed were innate are more likely to have been the products of poor environment, meager diet, or inadequate access to light and clean water. Together these would account for the stunted growth, deformities, and sickly physical appearance of the many women who turned to crime not out of "innate depravity" but for the very reason that they were poor. Ellis failed to consider the possibility that poverty and poor environment, rather than innate pathology, had determined the appearance of many criminal women.

It is striking how far the physical characteristics attributed to criminal women, when taken together, represent an uncanny negative to Victorian imagery of feminine beauty and propriety. It is almost as if observers chose to "see" traits in female offenders that represented the antithesis of the feminine ideal. Moreover, the frequency with which the research studies discussed by Ellis noted the "masculine" appearance of criminal women indicates how far the supposedly scientific process of observation was tightly bound by culturally determined expectations of femininity. As Carole Smart perceptively pointed out in 1977: "where gender appropriate behavior is seen as biologically determined, women who adopt 'masculine' forms of behavior become labeled 'masculine' themselves and this has connotations of 'maleness' which are seen to be linked to hormonal or genetic abnormalities" (Smart 1977, p. 93).

Ellis's *The Criminal* (1890), a potboiler of existing criminal anthropology, was hugely popular in Britain. It passed through four editions, the latter two being substantially revised and enlarged. Outside continental Europe, Ellis was one of the few to take up criminal anthropology and was largely responsible for the promotion of Lombrosian positivism in the English-speaking world. Recent feminist commentators have not recognized the extent to which Lombroso was preceded by Ellis's proselytizing endeavors. Yet if it had not been for Ellis's fascination with the subject it seems unlikely that Lombroso and Ferrero's *The Female Offender* would have received much attention beyond the Continent.

In *The Female Offender*, Lombroso elaborated on the established conception of female criminality as biologically determined. He endorsed the view of criminal woman as atavistic. According to him she was even more biologically primitive than criminal man (Lombroso and Ferrero 1895, p. 107). And yet when Lombroso tried to investigate the physical characteristics of women criminals, he found it extremely difficult to confirm his hypothesis (Lombroso and Ferrero 1895, pp. 54 ff.). Instead of abandoning his theory as unfounded, Lombroso invoked the generally held belief, described above, that all women were biologically inferior to men. If all women were, to a degree, atavistic, he argued, it would obviously be more difficult to discern atavism in criminal women because the distinguishing signs would be relatively less marked. Following Lombroso's own logic through, Frances Heidensohn (1985, p. 112) has pointed out that this assertion of women's biological inferiority ought to mean that "a much higher crime rate would be predicted for women than for men." Given that this was evidently not the case, the only explanation of this apparent illogicality is that Lombroso did not differentiate between crime and sexual delinquency in women. Seeing prostitution as the most "natural" outcome of female degeneracy, it could legitimately be included in any assessment of overall levels of female delinquency. This would then push the female level up to match rates of male crime (Heidensohn 1985, p. 114). This interpretation seems to be born out by Lombroso's having "found" the prostitute to be the epitome of primitive woman. He claimed that she was abundantly endowed with atavistic traits masked only by the plumpness of her youth and her elaborate makeup.

Closer investigation of the traits Lombroso claimed to have observed reveals how far his supposedly scientific objectivity was colored by culturally determined conceptions of what constituted normality and deviance in women. Moreover, he evidently found it impossible to confine his explanation to the supposedly inherent or pathological qualities of his subjects and referred constantly to their social background, sexual history, and marital status. The claims of Lombroso's research to impartiality were further marred by his patent desire to seek confirmation in biology of his social judgment of woman, namely that she was in all respects inferior to man, as can be seen in the following quotation: "The normal woman is deficient in moral sense, and possessed of slight criminal tendencies, such as vindictiveness, jealousy, envy, malignity, which are usually neutralized by less sensibility and less intensity of passion. Let a woman, normal in all else, be slightly more excitable than usual, or let a perfectly normal woman be exposed to grave provocations, and these criminal tendencies will take the upper hand" (Lombroso and Ferrero 1895, p. 263). In this and in other descriptions of criminal women as "masculine," even "virile" in appearance, coarse voiced, and unusually strong, his sense of distaste was barely concealed (Lombroso and Ferrero 1895, pp. 93–99).

In this scarcely dispassionate frame of mind, Lombroso conducted his famous anthropometric measurements. He was severely hampered by the difficulty of testing those of criminal women against any "control" or "normal" women—"it not being too easy to find subjects who will submit to the experiment" (Lombroso and Ferrero 1895, p. 56). This was hardly surprising since most women, inculcated with a deep sense of modesty, not unreasonably objected to Lombroso's requests to take his measuring instruments to their necks, thighs, and legs. In the end he was obliged to confine his sample of "normal women" to only fourteen—a tiny number that rather belies the weight often attributed to his lengthy and detailed findings. Undaunted, Lombroso presented his catalog of supposedly anomalous characteristics as certain proof of atavism in the criminal woman. For example, he claimed that, whereas normal women had markedly different skulls than men, the skulls of criminal women "approximate more to males, both criminal and normal, than to normal women" (Lombroso and Ferrero 1895, p. 28) and most closely resembled those of ancient man. Thus, argued Lombroso, criminal woman was proved to be a throwback to an earlier, less civilized, age.

In line with the then current vogue for classification, Lombroso subdivided criminal women into various supposedly distinct groups: the "occasional," the "hysterical," the "lunatic," the perpetrator of "crimes of passion," and the "born female criminal." Only the relatively small class of born female criminals, "whose criminal propensities [were] more intense and more perverse than those of the male prototypes," clearly fitted Lombroso's conception of degeneracy (Lombroso and Ferrero 1895, p. 147). The born female criminal was the very antithesis of femininity, "excessively erotic, weak in maternal feeling, inclined to dissipation, astute and audacious" (Lombroso and Ferrero 1895, p. 187). She was even endowed with masculine characteristics, such as her love of violence and vice and "added to these virile characteristics [were] often the worst qualities of woman: namely, an excessive desire for revenge, cunning, cruelty, love of dress, and untruthfulness" (Lombroso and Ferrero 1895, p. 187). Lombroso condemned the born female criminal as "completely and intensely depraved," as "more terrible than any man."

That his condemnation derived from an ideology which demanded higher qualities of women than of men is only too evident from Lombroso's (Lombroso and Ferrero 1895, p. 152) most damning exclamation: "As a double exception, the criminal woman is consequently a monster." As was true of writings half a century earlier, responses to the female offender were determined by the fact that she was seen not only to have flouted the criminal law but, more heinously still, the norms of femininity. It would seem, then, that Lombroso's writings were in many ways far less novel than subsequent commentators have suggested. While vigorously expounding his anthropometric theories, Lombroso remained squarely within the moral framework of his day.

Of course, Lombroso's wilder theories about criminal women did not have to wait until the emergence of feminist criminology in the late twentieth century to face criticism. Even at the height of his influence in Italy and Germany, Lombroso's brand of criminal anthropology met with considerable skepticism in France and particularly in English-speaking countries. In the United States one of the first people to put Lombroso's findings systematically to the test was the sociologist Frances Kellor (1901). Her work is discussed in detail in the context of emerging American criminology in Estelle Freedman's *Their Sisters' Keepers* (Freedman 1981, pp. 111–15). Kellor replicated Lombroso's work on a much larger scale using as her sample fifty-five white female students and ninety black and sixty white female criminals, applying his anthropometric measures to every aspect of these women's bodies. In addition she introduced psychological tests of faculties, senses, memory, and color and collected detailed sociological data including family background, occupation, religion, education, "amusements," "conjugal conditions," and environment. Unable to confirm Lombroso's findings, she severely criticized the conclusions that he had derived from such tests and refuted his interpretation of female criminality as biologically determined. Kellor (1901, quoted in Freedman 1981, p. 113) criticized Lombroso for ignoring the "tremendous force of social and economic environment" and pointed out that Lombroso's methods would tend to confuse ethnic and national traits with criminal ones. The extent to which Lombroso operated within the prevailing double standard was also recognized by Kellor (1901, quoted in Freedman 1981, p. 115). "We say that a woman is worse, but we judge her so by comparison with the *ideal* of woman, not with a common ideal."

A decade later in England, Hargrave Adam, the author of a major monograph, *Women and Crime* (1914), launched probably the most scathing attack on *The Female Offender*. Lombroso's thesis was, he said, "an utter fallacy" with no foundation in fact and counter to common sense. "What nonsense it all is. As if we do not know that prostitutes are of all sizes and shapes, from the very thin to the very fat. . . . The mystery is how such a fallacy ever came to be taken seriously" (Adam 1914, p. 23).

Lombroso's influence in Britain and America was certainly limited by such criticism. However, in the case of female criminality it proved obstinately enduring. Women's primary role as mothers remained at the heart of concern about female crime and ensured a continuing preoccupation with the physiology of female offenders. This, together with the enduring belief that women were biologically inferior to men, ensured that the constitution of the female offender remained central to criminological explanation long after biological positivism had been derided and discarded in explanations of male crime. The continuing effect of biological positivism lay primarily in its influence on the development of psychological approaches to female criminality.

V. Early Twentieth-Century Views of Female Crime as the Product of Innate Defect

The general rejection of Continental biological positivism was by no means wholesale for it was mitigated in large part by the development of the "eugenics" movement (Searle 1976; Freeden 1979, 1986; Soloway 1982). This movement sought to draw attention to the dangers to society of hereditarily transmitted defects and to promote means of controlling the mental and physical qualities of future generations. "Negative eugenics," as it was called, focused particularly on the need to prevent the criminal, the weak, and the defective from reproducing. These groups were reproducing at a faster rate than the middle classes. If not curtailed they would, it was argued, eventually swamp society with increasing numbers of enfeebled offspring.

The growth of this concern about degeneracy can only be understood with reference to its wider historical context. For example, in Britain, by the close of the nineteenth century, Victorian optimism had been badly shaken by economic crisis and the rise of foreign competition—both commercial and military. Eugenic theories of hereditary degeneration provided ready explanations for the relative decline of Britain's international status. The Edwardians, disillusioned with the preoccupation with biological positivism in continental Europe, focused instead on mental defect as the root of a whole range of pathological conditions. This trend toward psychiatric interpretation grew in large part out of the continuing vogue for "objective" scientific observation of the peculiarities of prison inmates. It was also heavily influenced by studies such as *The English Convict*, a massive work by Charles Goring (1913) in which he studied nearly 4,000 male convicts. Goring resoundingly denied the existence of a physically distinctive criminal type along the lines described by Lombroso. Although the proper interpretation of Goring's findings was a matter of considerable controversy, they did seem to point to a greater incidence of defective intelligence among convicts. Many eugenicists were quick to pick up on Goring's work as a basis for substantiating their claim that mental degeneracy could be observed in a significant proportion of the casual poor, slum dwellers, and the prison population. The origins, and particularly the political implications, of this rising concern with mental degeneracy has attracted considerable historical interest (Stedman Jones 1971; Searle 1976; Nye 1984; Bynum, Porter, and Shepherd 1985; Garland 1985*b;* Freeden 1986; Radzinowicz and Hood 1986; Harris 1989).

Eugenicism inevitably focused on women, for it was feared that the "degenerate women" of the slum-dwelling "dangerous classes" were innately promiscuous and, despite their weak constitutions, highly fertile. If allowed to continue to breed unchecked, the so-called unfit would increasingly outnumber the "fit" (Rentoul 1906; Tredgold 1909). If women were alcoholic, sexually promiscuous, or mentally or otherwise deficient, it was believed that their failings would be multiplied in the next generation. Social observers like Hargrave Adam began to explore the extent to which female alcoholism, prostitution, and crime were products of mental defect. He called for investigation into "the intimate connection which exists between nervous disorders and crime" (Adam 1914, p. 34). Interest in mentality was widespread: analyses of body type and skull dimension were largely replaced by studies of psychological characteristics and the investigation of mental deficiencies in both men and women (in Britain, Tredgold 1908, 1909, and 1910; Meredith 1909; Devon 1912). However, just as physical explanations of criminality had once been found particularly plausible in relation to women, new interest in the weaknesses and abnormalities of the criminal mind gained most credibility as a means of explaining female criminality. For these theories fitted only too well with the long-standing belief that criminal women not merely broke the law but tended to exhibit fundamental flaws of character. Note the observation by Hargrave Adam (1914, pp. 3–4) that some criminal women were "almost entirely devoid of any gentle or redeeming trait; some . . . indeed, are, in baseness, cunning, callousness, cruelty, and persistent criminality far worse than the worst male offender known to law."

The search for hard "scientific" evidence for the causes of crime was strongly influenced by the methods of the psychiatric profession. Increasingly prestigious, it provided criminology with a quasi-medical status. In its early years British criminology borrowed heavily from psychiatry the vocabulary, theories, categories, and strategies of what was then commonly known as the medical speciality of "alienism" (Walker 1968; Walker and McCabe 1973). Criminological interest in psychiatric interpretation was reflected in the growing numbers of medical men within the penal system who entered into debates in "mental science" journals (Guy 1863, 1869; Thomson 1870*a*, 1870*b;* Nicolson 1873). It was largely from this discourse that new diagnoses of offenders as mentally deficient were to be drawn.

The relationship between criminology and psychiatry was by no means one way. By informing and directing the development of criminology, psychiatry sought to expand its influence into the judicial and penal arena. Both David Garland and Roger Smith ask to what extent psychiatric intervention should be seen as empire building by a group of specialist professionals anxious to assert their status (Smith 1981*a;* Garland 1985*b*). Psychiatrists certainly did not see themselves in that way but rather as impartial observers, elevating criminological understanding with their techniques of observation and classification. Rothman (1980, p. 133) suggests that in America intervention by psychiatrists into the penal sphere was quite popular with prison officials. The early twenties saw an influx of psychiatric professionals into American prisons so that, by 1926, sixty-seven institutions employed psychiatrists and forty-five employed psychologists. How to interpret the growth of psychiatric intervention in deviance control remains the subject of much historiographical controversy (Skultans 1975; McCandless 1978; Rothman 1980; Smith 1981*a*, 1981*b;* Garland 1985*a*, 1985*b*). Should one see turn-of-the-century psychiatrists merely as unscrupulous entrepreneurs? As innovative scientists? As guardians of the moral order? Or, as Vieda Skultans (1975) suggests, as agents of social control?

Given prevailing beliefs in the physiological inferiority of women, and given the assumption that women's mental health was more closely tied to their biology than men's, it was perhaps not surprising that psychologically informed views of female deviance became popular (Thomson 1870*a*, 1870*b*; Nicholson 1873). Manifestations of mental disorder or even insanity were not merely unsurprising but almost to be expected in a constitution innately predisposed to upheaval and crisis. Nor was this view of female psychology tied only to her reproductive functions, it found even greater currency in relation to traditional concerns about wayward sexuality. Middle-class norms of propriety set the female sexual appetite at zero and established complete passivity, bordering on indifference, as the healthy sexual state for women. Any deviation from this condition of sexual apathy could be seen, therefore, as indicative of a disordered mind. Almost any expression of sexual desire by a woman could be interpreted as pathological and clinically described as nymphomania. Henry Maudsley (1870, p. 82) characterized nymphomania as "the irritation of the ovaries or uterus . . . a disease by which the most chaste and modest woman is transformed into a raging fury of lust." Premarital sex, infidelity, or even open expressions of sexual desire, might also be seen as symptoms of this dangerous sexual mania and so justify drastic psychiatric or even surgical intervention.

With the ascendancy of "scientific" discourse around the end of the century, outraged vilifications of the sexually active woman were increasingly replaced by apparently clinical discussion of her sexual exploits as symptomatic of cerebral disorder. Yet the technical language of these discussions barely conceals the extent to which conventional morality continued to infuse supposedly scientific thinking and underpin arguments about what constituted "normality" in women.

The extent to which new psychiatric concepts were built onto traditional moral concerns is illustrated by the work of Hargrave Adam (1914) who investigated the "the sex question" (prostitution) in relation to mental defect. Denying the traditional assumption that prostitutes were victims of male lust or perverted by modern life, he argued that the majority were quite simply nymphomaniacs. And this notion of deviant women as driven by sexual mania was carried over to explain more serious female crimes. Poisoners, murderesses, and vitriol throwers were, according to Adam (1914, p. 34), primarily sexually motivated. "Sexual mania" was, he suggested, a widespread cause of female deviance. That sexual desire in women thus came to be identified as a disease depended on a moral code that insisted that women were without such impulses.

Psychiatric discourse was employed not only to explain the clearly criminal but also to establish standards of mental normality. It was particularly influential in defining the margins between acceptable behavior and that which, by contravening accepted norms of propriety, could be classed as abnormal (Tredgold 1908, 1909, 1910; Meredith 1909; Melland 1911; Devon 1912). The prevailing belief that women were mentally as well as physically weak ensured that they were more readily and enduringly integrated into the psychiatric model. Categorizations of women as abnormal, mentally weak, "feebleminded," or insane were then as much a product of contemporary values as were earlier explicitly moral and social interpretations.

While eugenicists sought to draw attention to the general problem of mental deficiency among prisoners, their investigations led to the identification of a group who were classified as "feebleminded." These were that portion of the prison and reformatory population who were apparently incapable of submitting to discipline and impervious to all attempts to appeal to their moral sense. Seen cynically, the "discovery" of feeblemindedness provided a means of explaining the failure of prisons and reformatories to reform. It is, indeed, debatable whether feeblemindedness represented some actual, identifiable medical condition, or whether it was merely a label for a section of society. Significantly, it had no precise medical definition but was used as a generic term to encompass all those who were unable to make "correct" moral judgments. The feebleminded were that dangerous subsection of the mentally deficient who were not so impaired as to show external signs of deficiency but who seemed, nonetheless, to be incapable of surviving in normal society. Outside the prison they lived on the margins, often destitute and homeless, relying on charity or petty theft to survive.

That, in Britain, women were the majority of those labeled and confined as feebleminded has so far been largely overlooked (with a few notable exceptions, e.g., Simmons 1978; Radzinowicz and Hood 1986). The predominant concern with feeblemindedness in women raises a number of questions that have yet to be studied in depth by historians or criminologists. Were women prisoners actually more commonly mentally deficient than men or were they simply more likely to be diagnosed as such? What were the social costs of allowing feebleminded women to live outside custody? Why did contemporaries fear such women enough to demand their long-term or even permanent segregation (Meredith 1909)?

It is, perhaps, significant that feeblemindedness in women was defined as much by reference to moral as mental considerations. Assessments of a woman's moral conduct, her apparent degree of self-control, or lack of it, were taken as evidence of her mental state. By far the largest single group of feebleminded women were assumed to have become prostitutes, not because they were thought to be sinful, but because "many of these women, sometimes even mere girls, are possessed of such erotic tendencies that nothing short of lock and key will keep them off the streets" (Rentoul 1903; Tredgold 1910, p. 270). This tendency to confound mental deficiency with sexual immorality in women greatly exacerbated fears about its potential results.

Many articles in early twentieth-century editions of *The Eugenics Review* and the *British Medical Journal* focused on the supposed fertility of feebleminded women. Ostensibly scientific analyses of relative fertility rates were used to substantiate highly dramatic visions of hoards of feebleminded women producing multitudes of defective children (Potts 1905; Tredgold 1910). Moreover, it was asserted that "when illegitimate children are borne by such young women, the chances are enormously in favor of their turning out to be either imbeciles, or degenerates, or criminals" (Royal Commission on the Care and Control of the Feeble-minded 1904–8, p. 120). Significantly, this commentator apparently did not feel it necessary to clarify why he thought that the "illegitimate" offspring of the feebleminded would be more susceptible to their mother's mental condition than those born within marriage. The questionable logic of these views did not prevent their having a significant effect on the ensuing legislation. Under the 1913 Mental Deficiency Act, a woman receiving poor relief (state aid) when pregnant with, or at the time of giving birth to, an illegitimate child could be labeled "feebleminded," even if there was no medical evidence of any mental deficiency. As a result, she could be incarcerated in a mental hospital indefinitely simply because she acted outside the conventions of marriage and had the misfortune to get pregnant without a male provider for her child.

Often feebleminded women charged with neglect or cruelty to their children were subsequently found to be "mentally incapable of taking care of them" (Devon 1912, pp. 56–58). Some women thus charged were, on assessment, judged to be so defective as to be certifiable; far more were simply deemed feebleminded.

There was much concern, even sympathy, for the plight of the women themselves. Their lives were portrayed as often wretched, existing in poverty and filth on the margins of society. They were seen as easy prey, incapable of escaping the attentions of men who sought to exploit their weak will. Much of the evidence given to the Royal Commission on the Care and Control of the Feeble-Minded (1904–8) emphasized the need to extend control over feebleminded women in order to save them from sexual violation. The dangers of attack, of prostitution, of disease and the need, therefore, to protect such women were invoked to justify incarceration (Royal Commission on the Care and Control of the Feeble-Minded 1904–8). In a debate in the House of Commons in 1912, one M.P., Dr. Chapple, argued: "To obtain control early of such a woman is humanitarian, and it is the bounden duty of the State to mitigate the sufferings of such women by getting them early under proper control. They are not in prison when under control."

Dr. Chapple's reference to prison was highly pertinent since the presence of feebleminded women within the penal system was one of the main motivating factors behind calls for legislation. Feebleminded women committed to prison tended to receive lighter sentences in recognition of their condition. While in prison they were less able to comply with the structures of the regime and inevitably undermined any attempt to impose uniform discipline. Held for only a few weeks or months, they were released unimproved and unaided into a world whose demands they could not meet. All too often they fell to the margins of society, resorting to prostitution or petty theft to survive. Returned to the prison on a new charge after the shortest of intervals, they were liable to enter into a round of repeated short-term sentences from which they were unlikely ever to escape. The immediate costs of their recidivism were amplified by the fact that this continual round of imprisonment and temporary release created stresses that aggravated existing mental inadequacies.

It is not surprising that prison governesses, visitors, and administrators all called for the removal of the feebleminded from the prison to specialist institutions. The English prison commissioners, in their report for 1909, declared that feebleminded women "constitute one of the saddest and most unprofitable features of prison administration" (Prison Commissioners 1909, p. 158). To a degree, these demands for the removal of the feebleminded from the prison system, by rejecting the penal in favor of the medical sphere, constituted a tacit decriminalization of those women who could be judged mentally deficient.

After several years of heated debate, both inside and outside Parliament, the Mental Deficiency Act was passed in 1913. It included provision for the removal of the feebleminded from prisons, workhouses, and reformatories to be held instead in special institutions. Women who could be judged in any way defective were liable to be removed from prison, and those who were deemed violent were sent to new institutions where any pretension to reform or rehabilitation was replaced by long-term containment, ostensibly "not to punish but to protect" (Board of Control 1916, p. 40). Removed from the penal sphere, diagnosed as sick rather than sinful, even these most dangerous women were effectively decriminalized.

VI. The Legacy in the Twentieth Century

Over the first half of the twentieth century, the numbers of women sent to prison in Britain decreased remarkably. In 1913, the year of the Mental Deficiency Act, 33,000 women were committed to prison. Within eight years of the act, the number had fallen to 11,000 and by 1960, it had declined to less than 2,000. These figures are, in part, attributable to the growing view that many women who committed crimes were mentally or socially inadequate and so were not deserving of punishment. Many female offenders were sufficiently inadequate to require protection and treatment in suitable nonpenal institutions. However, there remained large numbers who were not certifiable under the 1913 Mental Deficiency Act (or under the subsequent Mental Deficiency Act of 1927). These women occupied the "borderland" of sanity, incapable of surviving unprotected in wider society yet entirely inappropriate for imprisonment. Repeatedly sentenced to prison for petty offending or public disorder, their continued presence there was a constant cause of disruption and a source of anxiety to prison commissioners throughout the interwar years (Smith 1962, pp. 230–36).

The concern that the prison was a wholly unsuitable environment for many women inmates led eventually to the Mental Health Act (1959) which, in repealing the 1913 act, sought to expedite the further removal of mentally deficient women from prisons. Significantly, the preoccupations motivating this reform seem to have changed little from those that had prompted the original legislation half a century earlier. Note, for example, the observations of one commentator writing just after the

1959 act was passed: "Social inadequacy and social inefficiency which are typical of mental defect often influence women to commit the types of crime to which their sex is particularly prone. . . . The majority of such women are quite unable to take advantage of any training offered in prison. They disrupt the routine, and hamper the progressive schemes for work and education. Even borderline cases who can profit by some form of training require care and protection, not imprisonment" (Smith 1962, p. 231).

In the second half of the twentieth century, the view that much female crime is the product of mental inadequacy has become commonplace, infiltrating the mainstream prison system itself. Significantly, the most important of the prisons for women in Britain today, the new Holloway prison in north London, was designed on the assumption that "most women and girls in custody require some form of medical, psychiatric or remedial treatment . . . [Holloway] will be basically a secure hospital to act as the hub of the female system. Its medical and psychiatric facilities will be its central feature and normal custodial facilities will comprise a relatively small part of the establishment" (James Callaghan, then British home secretary, speaking in 1968, quoted in Morris 1987, p. 109). As Carole Smart observed in 1977: "The assumption underlying this policy is that to deviate in a criminal way is 'proof' of some kind of mental imbalance in women" (Smart 1977, p. 96). The new Holloway was intended to replace punishment with psychiatric treatment related to the perceived psychological "needs" of each woman. It has been argued that the supposedly symbiotic relation between mental inadequacy and criminality in women sets up psychological disturbance as an "alternative" to crime for women. While the rather simplistic conclusion that mental illness in women is equivalent to male criminality begs more questions than it answers, there can be little doubt that assumptions about the propensity of women to mental illness have had a profound effect on the organization and regimen of female prisons.

While Holloway has remained more punitive than was perhaps originally intended, its special facilities for mentally disturbed prisoners are testament to continuing psychiatric interpretations of female criminality. What began as a view that a proportion of criminal women were inadequate now extends to envelop views of the female prison population as a whole. Today psychotropic drugs are dispensed in far larger quantities in female prisons than in those for males (Heidensohn 1985, pp. 73–75), ostensibly in response to women prisoners' greater mental problems. The tendency to self-mutilate has at times become almost endemic in female prisons but there seems to be no self-destructive equivalent among male prisoners. That women in British prisons have a punishment rate for disciplinary violations roughly double that of men is also cited as evidence of their greater psychiatric disturbance. The expectation that women in prison are likely to be in some way inadequate is now accepted among many penal policymakers. The possibility that women, for a host of social rather than psychiatric reasons (not least the fact that many are mothers forced to leave their children outside), simply find prisons harder to take has yet to be fully explored.

Until the relatively recent developments in feminist criminology, theories of female crime have altered remarkably little. If one considers the huge and rapidly changing array of theories concerning male criminality, the lack of advance becomes all the more striking (see discussions in Heidensohn 1981; Leonard 1982; Morris 1987). The birth of feminist criminology contains the promise of new gender-based theories that may radically alter our understanding of both male and female criminality (e.g., see Gelsthorpe and Morris 1988). For the moment, however, our criminal justice programs and penal systems rest on understandings of female criminality that continue to be dominated by theories preeminent around the turn of the century. The resolute persistence of these ideas is explicable only if we appreciate the extent to which psychological responses to female crime are founded on earlier, deeply moralistic theories about what constitutes normality and what deviance in women. If the mass of women in prison are seen as "sick" and prison regimes are organized around therapy and treatment, this then presupposes some notion of the "healthy," the "natural," the "good" woman. We must ask where, or, indeed, when, such notions derive?

VII. Conclusion

Victorian perceptions, assessments, and explanations of female crime are explicable only in relation to their wider moral and social context. The finding that these views about criminal women related directly to prevailing notions of femininity raises important questions about the extent to which male behavior was also assessed in relation to parallel constructs of masculinity. Whereas male criminals often acted out supposedly manly traits, criminal women not only broke the law but also contravened various prescriptions about femininity deemed essential to the moral order of Victorian society. The extent to which female crime was seen to repudiate feminine moral duties partly explains the high level of anxiety it seems to have provoked. Anxiety about female crime sprang directly from the preoccupations of the day: urban filth and overcrowding, disease and degeneration, and the threat posed by urbanization to community and family. These were major concerns that partly explained, but also exacerbated, the costs of female crime. By studying attempts to control crime historically, this essay has shown how concern about crime is a mirror for the wider problems that preoccupy society at any given time. As such it has important implications for present-day criminology.

Around the turn of the century, links drawn between criminality, alcoholism, and insanity crystallized long-standing eugenic fears about deviance in women. Female crime came to be seen less as the deliberate contravention of social norms or laws but instead as the manifestation of innate pathology. For those women who could be seen as sick or mad, rather than bad, punitive responses came to be seen as less appropriate than specialized treatment outside the penal sphere. Although the intervention of medicine, particularly psychiatry, tended to decriminalize female deviancy, paradoxically, in stressing its hereditary aspects psychiatrists also amplified its perceived costs. The new reformatories for alcoholics and asylums for the so-called feebleminded catered overwhelmingly to women. Whether women were really so much more mentally deficient than men is questionable, for assessments of normality and abnormality in women were measured against a continuing notion of the feminine ideal. Whatever the case, it does seem likely that the smaller scale of female imprisonment allowed for experimentation not possible in the much larger male system.

This essay has traced a path, albeit uneven and patchy, from moralizing attitudes and responses to female criminality that prevailed until the mid-nineteenth century to the development of medicalized interpretations and endeavors around the opening of the twentieth century. The aim was to remove inadequate or "incorrigible" women from the penal sphere altogether to new specialist institutions. In these, moral reform gave way to medicalized "treatment" and the indefinite segregation of those who could not be "cured."

The nineteenth-century view that criminal women were distinct creatures requiring differentiated treatment appropriate to their sex has endured into the twentieth century. "Sex" not only "remained the basis for the difference in institutional response for most of the 19th century" as historian Patricia O'Brien has argued (1978, p. 516) but has continued to do so in the twentieth. Therapeutic approaches to female criminality have become commonplace. But the extent to which these ostensibly scientific, medicalized responses were erected on the foundation of older, culturally derived assumptions about women's character and behavior has been largely overlooked. Only by historical research can we expose how far this model of femininity determined what was later to be seen as natural and what unnatural, dangerous, or deviant in women. By looking to the past in this way, we can begin to recognize how far, and in what guises, Victorian assumptions about women continue to inform penal policy today.

REFERENCES

Abrams, Philip. 1968. *The Origins of British Sociology: 1834–1914*. Chicago: University of Chicago Press.

Acton, William. 1972. *Prostitution: Considered in Its Moral, Social, and Sanitary Aspects in London and Other Large Cities and Garrison Towns*. London: Frank Cass. (Originally published 1857. London: John Churchill & Sons.)

Adam, Hargrave. 1914. *Woman and Crime*. London: T. Werner Laurie.

Adler, Freda. 1975. *Sisters in Crime*. New York: McGraw-Hill.

Alford, Stephen S. 1877. "The Necessity of Legislation for the Control and Cure of Habitual Drunkards." In *Transactions of the National Association for the Promotion of Social Science 1876*. London: Longmans.

Bailey, Victor. 1980. "Crime, Criminal Justice and Authority in England." *Society for the Study of Labour History Bulletin* 40:36–46.

———. 1981. *Policing and Punishment in Nineteenth Century Britain*. London: Croom Helm.

Banks, O. 1981. *Faces of Feminism*. Oxford: Martin Robertson.

Basch, F. 1974. *Relative Creatures*. London: Allen Lane.

Beattie, J. M. 1975. "The Criminality of Women in Eighteenth Century England." *Journal of Social History* 8:80–116.

Bedford, Adeline M. 1910. "Fifteen Years' Work in a Female Convict Prison." *Nineteenth Century and After* 68(404):615–31.

Board of Control. 1916. *Report of the Board of Control*. Parliamentary Papers. London: H.M. Stationery Office.

Bowker, Lee H., ed. 1978. *Women, Crime and the Criminal Justice System*. Toronto: Lexington.

Bremner, John A. 1874. "What Improvements are Required in the System of Discipline in County and Borough Prisons?" In *Transactions of the National Association for the Promotion of Social Science 1873*. London: Longmans.

Brenzel, Barbara. 1980. "Domestication as Reform: A Study of the Socialization of Wayward Girls, 1856–1905." *Harvard Educational Review* 50:196–213.

Brodsky, Annette M. 1975. *The Female Offender*. Beverly Hills, Calif.: Sage.

Bynum, W. F., R. Porter, and M. Shepherd, eds. 1985. *The Anatomy of Madness: Essays in the History of Psychiatry*. Vols. 1–2. London: Tavistock.

Carpenter, Mary. 1858. "Reformatories for Convicted Girls." In *Transactions of the National Association for the Promotion of Social Science 1857*. London: Longmans.

———. 1864*a*. "On the Treatment of Female Convicts." In *Transactions of the National Association for the Promotion of Social Science 1863*. London: Longmans.

———. 1864*b*. *Our Convicts*. 2 vols. London: Longmans.

Chaplain of Stafford County Gaol. 1854. "Nineteenth Report of the Prison Inspectors." *Parliamentary Papers*. Vol. 34. London: H.M. Stationery Office.

Christ, Carol. 1977. "Victorian Masculinity and the Angel in the House." In *A Widening Sphere*, edited by Martha Vicinus. Bloomington: Indiana University Press.

Clay, W. L. 1861. *The Prison Chaplain: A Memoir of the late Revd John Clay*. London: Macmillan.

Cohen, Stanley. 1985. *Visions of Social Control: Crime, Punishment and Classification*. Cambridge: Polity.

Cohen, Stanley, and Andrew Scull, eds. 1983. *Social Control and the State: Historical and Comparative Essays*. Oxford: Martin Robertson.

Cominos, Peter. 1963. "Late Victorian Sexual Respectability and the Social System." *International Review of Social History* 8:18–48, 216–50.

Conway, Jill. 1970. "Stereotypes of Femininity in a Theory of Sexual Evolution." *Victorian Studies* 14(1):47–62.

Crites, Laura. 1978. *The Female Offender*. Lexington, Mass.: Lexington.

Crofton, Walter. 1867. "Female Convicts, and Our Efforts to Amend Them." In *Transactions of the National Association for the Promotion of Social Science 1866*. London: Longmans.

———. 1873. "Female Criminals—Their Children's Fate." *Good Words for 1873*. London: W. Isbister & Co.

Davenport-Hill, Florence. 1885. "Art. II. Women Prison Visitors." *Englishwoman's Review* 16(152):536–46.

Davidoff, Leonore. 1983. "Class and Gender in Victorian England." In *Sex and Class*, edited by Judith Newton. London: Routledge & Kegan Paul.

Delacy, Margaret E. 1986. *Prison Reform in Lancashire, 1700–1850: A Study in Local Administration*. Manchester: Manchester University Press.

Delamount, Sara, and Lorna Duffin, eds. 1978. *The Nineteenth Century Woman: Her Cultural and Physical World*. London: Croom Helm.

Devon, James. 1912. *The Criminal and the Community*. New York: John Lane.

Dobash, Russell P., R. Emerson Dobash, and Sue Gutteridge. 1986. *The Imprisonment of Women*. Oxford: Basil Blackwell.

Donzelot, Jacques. 1979. *The Policing of Families: Welfare versus the State*. Translated by Robert Hurley. London: Hutchinson.

Du Cane, E. F. 1876. "Address on the Repression of Crime." In *Transactions of the National Association for the Promotion of Social Science 1875*. London: Longmans.

———. 1885. *The Punishment and Prevention of Crime*. London: Macmillan.

Ellis, Havelock. 1890. *The Criminal*. London: Walter Scott.

———. 1904. *Man and Woman: A Study of Human Secondary Sexual Characters*. 4th ed. London: Walter Scott.

Field, J. 1846. *Prison Discipline*. London: Longmans.

Finnegan, Frances. 1979. *Poverty and Prostitution: A Study of Victorian Prostitutes in York*. Cambridge: Cambridge University Press.

Fletcher, Susan Willis. 1884. *Twelve Months in an English Prison*. Boston: Lee & Shepard.

Forsythe, William James. 1987. *The Reform of Prisoners, 1830–1900*. London: Croom Helm.

Foucault, Michel. 1967. *Madness and Civilisation: A History of Insanity in the Age of Reason*. Translated by Richard Howard. London: Tavistock.

———. 1977. *Discipline and Punish: The Birth of the Prison*. Translated by Alan Sheridan. London: Penguin.

Frazer, Catherine. 1863. "The Origin and Progress of the British Ladies' Society for Promoting the Reformation of Female Prisoners, Established by Mrs. Fry in 1821." In *Transactions of the National Association for the Promotion of Social Science 1862*. London: Longmans.

Freeden, Michael. 1979. "Eugenics and Progressive Thought: A Study in Ideological Affinity." *Historical Journal* 22(3):645–71.

———. 1986. *The New Liberalism—an Ideology of Social Reform*. Oxford: Oxford University Press.

Freedman, Estelle B. 1981. *Their Sisters' Keepers: Women's Prison Reform in America, 1830–1930*. Ann Arbor: University of Michigan Press.

Fry, Elizabeth. 1827*a*. *Observations on the Visiting, Superintending, and Government of Female Prisoners*. 2d ed. London: John & Arthur Arch.

———. 1827*b*. *Sketch of the Origins and Results of Ladies' Prison Associations, with Hints for the Formation of Local Associations*. London: John & Arthur Arch.

Garland, David. 1985*a*. "The Criminal and His Science: A Critical Account of the Formation of Criminology at the end of the Nineteenth Century." *British Journal of Criminology* 25(2):109–37.

———. 1985*b*. *Punishment and Welfare—a History of Penal Strategies*. Aldershot: Gower.

———. 1988. "British Criminology before 1935." *British Journal of Criminology* 28(2):131–47.

Gatrell, V. A. C., Bruce Lenman, and Geoffrey Parker, eds. 1980. *Crime and the Law: The Social History of Crime in Western Europe since 1500*. London: Europa.

Gelsthorpe, Loraine, and Allison Morris. 1988. "Feminism and Criminology in Britain." *British Journal of Criminology* 28(2):223–40.

Giallombardo, Rose. 1966. *Society of Women: A Study of a Women's Prison*. New York: Wiley.

Gibb, David. 1875. "The Relative Increase of Wages, of Drunkenness, and of Crime." In *Transactions of the National Association for the Promotion of Social Science 1874*. London: Longmans.

Gordon, Mary. 1922. *Penal Discipline*. London: Routledge & Kegan Paul.

Gorham, Deborah. 1982. *The Victorian Girl and the Feminine Ideal*. London: Croom Helm.

Goring, Charles. 1913. *The English Convict*. Report. London: H.M. Stationery Office.

Greenwood, James. 1981. *The Seven Curses of London—Scenes from the Victorian Underworld*. Oxford: Basil Blackwell. (Originally published 1869. London: Stanley Rivers & Co.)

Griffiths, Arthur. 1884. *Memorials of Millbank and Chapters in Prison History*. London: Chapman & Hall.

———. 1894. *Secrets of the Prison-house or Gaol Studies and Sketches*. 2 vols. London: Chapman & Hall.

———. 1904. *Fifty Years of Public Service*. London: Cassell.

Guy, W. A. 1863. "On Some Results of a Recent Census of the Population of the Convict Prisons in England; and Especially on the Rate of Mortality at Present Prevailing among Convicts." In *Transactions of the National Association for the Promotion of Social Science 1862*. London: Longmans.

———. 1869. "On Insanity and Crime; and on the Plea of Insanity in Criminal Cases." *Journal of the Statistical Society* 32:159–91.

Hahn, N. F. 1980*a*. "Female State Prisoners in Tennessee, 1831–1979." *Tennessee Historical Quarterly* 39(4):485–97.

———. 1980*b*. "Matrons and Molls—the Study of Women's Prison History." In *History and Crime*, edited by James Inciardi and Charles E. Faupel. Beverly Hills, Calif.: Sage.

Harding, Christopher, Bill Hines, Richard Ireland, and Philip Rawlings. 1985. *Imprisonment in England and Wales: A Concise History*. London: Croom Helm.

Harris, Ruth. 1989. *Murders and Madness—Medicine, Law, Society in the Fin de Siècle*. Oxford: Clarendon.

Hartman, Mary S. 1985. *Victorian Murderesses: A True History of Thirteen Respectable French and English Women Accused of Unspeakable Crimes*. London: Robson.

Hay, Douglas. 1980. "Crime and Justice in Eighteenth- and Nineteenth-Century England." In *Crime and Justice: An Annual Review of Research*, vol. 2, edited by Norval Morris and Michael Tonry. Chicago: University of Chicago Press.

Heidensohn, Frances. 1981. "Women and the Penal System." In *Women and Crime*, edited by Allison Morris and Loraine Gelsthorpe. Cropwood Conference Series no. 13. Cambridge: Cambridge University, Institute of Criminology.

———. 1985. *Women and Crime*. Basingstoke: Macmillan.

Henriques, Ursula. 1972. "The Rise and Decline of the Separate System of Prison Discipline." *Past and Present*, no. 54, pp. 61–93.

Higgs, Mary. 1906. *Glimpses into the Abyss*. London: King.

Hill, Rosamond. 1864. "XXII.—A Plea for Female Convicts." *English Woman's Journal* 13(74):130–34.

Hoffer, Peter C., and N. E. H. Hull. 1981. *Murdering Mothers: Infanticide in England and New England, 1558–1803*. New York: New York University Press.

Holmes, Thomas. 1900. *Pictures and Problems from the London Police Courts*. London: Nelson.

———. 1903. "The Criminal Inebriate Female." *British Journal of Inebriety* 1(2):69–72.

———. 1908. *Known to the Police*. London: Edward Arnold.

Horsley, Canon J. W. 1887. *Jottings from Jail: Notes and Papers on Prison Matters*. London: Unwin.

———. 1898. *Prisons and Prisoners*. London: Pearson.

———. 1913. *How Criminals are Made and Prevented: A Retrospect of Forty Years*. London: Unwin.

Houghton, Walter E. 1957. *The Victorian Frame of Mind, 1830–1870*. New Haven, Conn.: Yale University Press.

Howard Association. 1880. *Annual Report*. London: Howard Association.

Hutter, Bridget, and Gillian Williams, eds. 1981. *Controlling Women: The Normal and the Deviant*. London: Croom Helm.

Ignatieff, Michael. 1978. *A Just Measure of Pain: The Penitentiary in the Industrial Revolution, 1750–1850*. London: Macmillan.

———. 1983*a*. "State, Civil Society and Total Institutions: A Critique of Recent Social Histories of Punishment." In *Social Control and the State*, edited by Stanley Cohen and Andrew Scull. Oxford: Basil Blackwell.

———. 1983*b*. "Total Institutions and Working Classes: A Review Essay." *History Workshop* 15:167–73.

Jebb, Joshua. 1854. "Report of the Surveyor-General for the Year 1853." *Parliamentary Papers*. Vol. 33. London: H.M. Stationery Office.

———. 1855. "Letters to Henry Waddington." Unpublished papers held at the University of London, London School of Economics.

Jellicoe, Anne. 1863. "A Visit to the Female Convict Prison at Mountjoy, Dublin." In *Transactions of the National Association for the Promotion of Social Science 1862*. London: Longmans.

Johnston, M. F. 1901. "The Life of a Woman Convict." *Fortnightly Review* 75:559–67.

Jones, David. 1982. *Crime, Protest, Community and Police in Nineteenth Century Britain*. London: Routledge & Kegan Paul.

"Judicial Statistics." 1857–92. Parliamentary Papers. Vols. 37–72. London: H.M. Stationery Office.

Kellor, Frances. 1901. *Experimental Sociology: Descriptive and Analytical*. New York: Macmillan.

Kelynack, T. N., ed. 1907. *The Drink Problem: In Its Medico-sociological Aspects*. London: Methuen.

Kerr, Norman. 1880. *Female Intemperance*. London: National Temperance Union.

———. 1888. *Inebriety: Its Etiology, Pathology, Treatment and Jurisprudence*. London: Lewis.

Kingsmill, Joseph. 1854. *Chapters on Prisons and Prisoners and the Prevention of Crime*. London: Longmans.

Klein, Dorie. 1978. "The Etiology of Female Crime: A Review of the Literature." In *The Female Offender*, edited by Laura Crites. Lexington, Mass.: Lexington.

Klein, Viola. 1946. *The Feminine Character—History of an Ideology*. London: Routledge & Kegan Paul.

Leonard, Eileen. 1982. *Women, Crime and Society*. London: Longmans.

Lloyd, M. A. 1903. *Susanna Meredith: A Record of a Vigorous Life*. London: Hodder & Stoughton.

Lombroso, Cesare, and William Ferrero. 1895. *The Female Offender*. London: Unwin.

McCandless, Peter. 1978. "Liberty and Lunacy: The Victorians and Wrongful Confinement." *Journal of Social History* 11(3):366–86.

McHugh, Paul. 1980. *Prostitution and Victorian Social Reform*. London: Croom Helm.

MacLeod, Roy M. 1967. "The Edge of Hope: Social Policy and Chronic Alcoholism, 1870–1900." *Journal of the History of Medicine* 22(3):215–44.

Marcus, Steven. 1966. *The Other Victorians: A Study of Sexuality and Pornography in Mid-Nineteenth Century England*. London: Weidenfeld & Nicolson.

Maudsley, Henry. 1870. *Body and Mind: An Inquiry into Their Connection and Mental Influence*. London: Macmillan.

———. 1874. *Responsibility in Mental Disease*. London: P.S. King & Son.

Maybrick, Florence Elizabeth. 1905. *My Fifteen Lost Years*. New York: Funk & Wagnalls.

Mayhew, Henry. 1862. *The Criminal Prisons of London and Scenes of Prison Life*. London: Griffin & Bohn.

———. 1968. *Those That Will Not Work*. Vol. 4 of *London Labour and London Poor*. London: Dover. (Originally published 1861–62. London: Griffin & Bohn.)

Mearns, Andrew. 1970. *The Bitter Cry of Outcast London: An Inquiry into the Condition of the Abject Poor*. London: Frank Cass. (Originally published 1883. London: London Congregational Union.)

Melland, Charles H. 1911. "The Feeble-minded in Prisons." *Report of the National Conference on the Prevention of Destitution*. London: P. S. King & Son.

Meredith, M. 1909. "Women and the Nation—the Outcasts II: The Feebleminded." *Englishwoman* 2(4):406–22.

Meredith, Susanna. 1881. *A Book about Criminals*. London: James Nisbet.

Merrick, G. P. 1891. *Work among the Fallen as Seen in the Prison Cell*. London: Ward & Lock.

Morris, Allison. 1987. *Women, Crime and Criminal Justice*. Oxford: Basil Blackwell.

Morris, Allison, and Loraine Gelsthorpe. 1981. *Women and Crime*. Cambridge: Cambridge University, Institute of Criminology.

Morrison, W. D. 1891. *Crime and Its Causes*. London: Swan Sonnenschein.

Mort, Frank. 1987. *Dangerous Sexualities: Medico-moral Politics in England since 1830*. London: Routledge & Kegan Paul.

Nicolson, David. 1873. "The Morbid Psychology of Criminals." *Journal of Mental Science* 19(86):222–32, 398–409.

Nugent, James. 1877. "Incorrigible Women: What are We to Do with Them?" In *Transactions of the National Association for the Promotion of Social Science 1876*. London: Longmans.

Nye, Robert A. 1984. *Crime, Madness and Politics in Modern France: The Medical Concept of National Decline*. Princeton, N.J.: Princeton University Press.

O'Brien, Patricia. 1978. "Crime and Punishment as a Historical Problem." *Journal of Social History* 11(4):508–20.

———. 1982. *The Promise of Punishment—Prisons in Nineteenth Century France*. Princeton, N.J.: Princeton University Press.

Orme, Eliza. 1898. "Our Female Criminals." *Fortnightly Review* 69:790–96.

Owen, M. E. 1866. "Criminal Women." *Cornhill Magazine* 14:153.

Pollock, Joy, and Meda Chesney-Lind. 1978. "Early Theories of Female Criminality." In *Women, Crime, and the Criminal Justice System*, edited by Lee H. Bowker. Toronto: Lexington.

Potts, W. A. 1905. "Causation of Mental Defect in Children." *British Medical Journal* 2:946–48.

Prewer, R. R. 1974. "The Contribution of Prison Medicine." In *Progress in Penal Reform*, edited by Louis Blom-Cooper. Oxford: Oxford University Press.

Priestly, Philip. 1985. *Victorian Prison Lives: English Prison Biography, 1830–1914*. London: Methuen.

Prison Commissioners. 1909. *Report of the Prison Commissioners for 1909*. Parliamentary Papers. Vol. 45. London: H.M. Stationery Office.

"A Prison Matron" (pseudonym, attributed to Frederick William Robinson). 1862. *Female Life in Prison*. 2 vols. London: Hurst & Blackett.

———. 1864. *Memoirs of Jane Cameron*. 2 vols. London: Hurst & Blackett.

———. 1866. *Prison Characters Drawn from Life with Suggestions for Prison Government*. 2 vols. London: Hurst & Blackett.

Radzinowicz, Leon. 1966. *Ideology and Crime: A Study of Crime in Its Social and Historical Context*. London: Heinemann.

———. 1948, 1956*a*, 1956*b*, and 1968. *A History of English Criminal Law and Its Administration from 1750*. 4 vols. London: Stevens & Son.

Radzinowicz, Leon, and Roger Hood. 1986. *The Emergence of Penal Policy*. Vol. 5 of *A History of English Criminal Law and Its Administration from 1750*. London: Stevens & Son.

Rafter, Nicole Hahn. 1983*a*. "Chastizing the Unchaste: Social Control Functions of a Women's Reformatory, 1894–1931." In *Social Control and the State*, edited by Stanley Cohen and Andrew Scull. Oxford: Basil Blackwell.

———. 1983*b*. "Prisons for Women, 1790–1980." In *Crime and Justice: An Annual Review of Research*, vol. 5, edited by Michael Tonry and Norval Morris. Chicago: University of Chicago Press.

———. 1985*a*. "Gender, Prisons, and Prison History." *Social Science History* 9(3):233–47.

———. 1985*b*. *Partial Justice*. Boston: Northeastern University Press.

Rafter, Nicole Hahn, and Elizabeth Anne Stanko. 1982. *Judge, Lawyer, Victim, Thief: Women, Gender Roles, and Criminal Justice*. Boston: Northeastern University Press.

Rentoul, Robert Reid. 1903. *Proposed Sterilisation of Certain Mental and Physical Degenerates*. London: Walter Scott.

———. 1906. *Race Culture; or, Race Suicide? (A Plea for the Unborn)*. London: Walter Scott.

Roberts, Elizabeth. 1984. *A Woman's Place: An Oral History of Working Class Women, 1890–1940*. Oxford: Basil Blackwell.

Rock, Paul. 1977. "Review Symposium." *British Journal of Criminology* 17:390–95.

Rogers, Foster. 1850. "Reports of the Governors and Chaplains of Middlesex Prisons." Unpublished manuscripts. London: Greater London Record Office.

Rosen, Ruth. 1980. *The Lost Sisterhood: Prostitution in America, 1900–1918*. Baltimore: John Hopkins University Press.

Rothman, David. 1971. *The Discovery of the Asylum—Social Order and Disorder in the New Republic*. Boston: Little, Brown.

———. 1980. *Conscience and Convenience—the Asylum and Its Alternatives in Progressive America*. Boston: Little, Brown.

Royal Commission on the Care and Control of the Feeble-minded. 1904–8. *Parlimentary Papers*. Vols. 35–39. London: H.M. Stationery Office.

Rudé, George. 1985. *Criminal and Victims: Crime and Society in Early Nineteenth Century England*. Oxford: Clarendon.

Russell, W. 1835. "Select Committee of the House of Lords on Gaols and Houses of Correction, Minutes of Evidence." *Parliamentary Papers*. Vol. 11. London: H.M. Stationery Office.

Safford, A. Herbert. 1867. "What are the best means of preventing Infanticide?" In *Transactions of the National Association for the Promotion of Social Science 1866*. London: Longmans.

Scharlieb, Mary. 1907. "Alcoholism in Relation to Women and Children." In *The Drink Problem*, edited by T. N. Kelynack. London: Methuen.

Schlossman, Steven L. 1977. *Love and the American Delinquent: The Theory and Practice of "Progressive" Juvenile Justice, 1825–1920*. Chicago: University of Chicago Press.

———. 1978. "The Crime of Precocious Sexuality: Female Juvenile Delinquency in the Progressive Era." *Harvard Educational Review* 48:65–94.

Scougal, Francis (pseudonym for Felicia Mary Francis Skene). 1889. *Scenes from a Silent World or Prisons and Their Inmates*. London: William Blackwood.

Scull, Andrew. 1979. *Museums of Madness: The Social Organisation of Insanity in Nineteenth-Century England*. London: Allen Lane.

———, ed. 1981. *Madhouses, Mad-Doctors and Madmen: The Social History of Psychiatry in the Victorian Era*. London: Athlone.

Searle, G. R. 1976. *Eugenics and Politics in Britain, 1900–1914*. Leyden: Noordoff International.

Shadwell, Arthur. 1902. *Drink, Temperance and Legislation*. London: Longmans, Green.

Showalter, Elaine. 1987. *The Female Malady: Women, Madness, and English Culture, 1830–1980*. London: Virago.

Simmons, Harvey G. 1978. "Explaining Social Policy: The English Mental Deficiency Act of 1913." *Journal of Social History* 11(3):387–483.

Skultans, Vieda. 1975. *Madness and Morals: Ideas on Insanity in the Nineteenth Century*. London: Routledge & Kegan Paul.

Smart, Carole. 1976. *Women, Crime and Criminology: A Feminist Critique*. London: Routledge & Kegan Paul.

———. 1977. "Criminological Theory: Its Ideology and Implications concerning Women." *British Journal of Sociology* 28(1):89–100.

Smart, Carole, and Barry Smart, eds. 1978. *Women, Sexuality and Social Control*. London: Routledge & Kegan Paul.

Smith, Ann. 1962. *Women in Prison*. London: Stevens & Son.

Smith, Roger. 1981*a*. "The Boundary between Insanity and Criminal Responsibility in Nineteenth Century England." In *Madhouses, Mad-Doctors and Madmen*, edited by Andrew Scull. London: Athlone.

———. 1981*b*. *Trial by Medicine: Insanity and Responsibility in Victorian Trials*. Edinburgh: Edinburgh University Press.

Soloway, Richard. 1982. "Counting the Degenerates: The Statistics of Race Deterioration in Edwardian England." *Journal of Contemporary History* 17(1):137–64.

Stedman Jones, Gareth. 1971. *Outcast London—a Study in the Relationship between Classes in Victorian Society*. Oxford: Clarendon.

Steer, Mary H. 1893. "Rescue Work by Women among Women." In *Woman's Mission*, edited by Baroness Burdett-Coutts. London: Sampson, Low & Marston.

Sturma, Michael. 1978. "Eye of the Beholder: The Stereotype of Women Convicts, 1788–1852." *Labour History* 34:3–10.

Sullivan, W. C. 1906. *Alcoholism: A Chapter in Social Pathology*. London: James Nisbet.

Summers, Anne. 1976. *Damned Whores and God's Police: The Colonisation of Women in Australia*. Victoria, Australia: Penguin.

Surveyor-General. 1857–58. "Report of the Surveyor General for 1856–57." *Parliamentary Papers*. Vol. 29. London: H.M. Stationery Office.

Symons, Jelinger C. 1849. *Tactics for the Times: As Regards the Condition and Treatment of the Dangerous Classes*. London: John Olivier.

Thomson, Basil. 1925. *The Criminal*. London: Hodder & Stoughton.

Thomson, J. B. 1870*a*. "The Hereditary Nature of Crime." *Journal of Mental Science* 15(72):487–98.

———. 1870*b*. "The Psychology of Criminals." *Journal of Mental Science* 17(75):321–50.

Tredgold, A. F. 1908. *Mental Deficiency*. London: Baillere, Tindall & Cox.

———. 1909. "The Feeble-minded—a Social Danger." *Eugenics Review* 1(2):96–104.

———. 1910. "The Feeble-minded." *Contemporary Review* 97(534):717–27.

Vicinus, Martha. 1977. *A Widening Sphere—Changing Roles of Victorian Women*. Bloomington: Indiana University Press.

———, ed. 1980. *Suffer and Be Still: Women in the Victorian Age*. London: Methuen.

Walker, Nigel, ed. 1968. *The Historical Perspective*. Vol. 1 of *Crime and Insanity in England*. Edinburgh: Edinburgh University Press.

Walker, Nigel, and Sarah McCabe, eds. 1973. *New Solutions and New Problems*.

Vol. 2 of *Crime and Insanity in England*. Edinburgh: Edinburgh University Press.

Walkowitz, Judith. 1980. *Prostitution and Victorian Society: Women, Class and the State*. Cambridge: Cambridge University Press.

———. 1982. "Male Vice and Feminist Virtue: Feminism and the Politics of Prostitution in Nineteenth Century Britain." *History Workshop* 13:77–93.

Weeks, Jeffrey. 1981. *Sex, Politics and Society: The Regulation of Sexuality since 1800*. London: Longmans.

Wells, Ashton. 1877. "Crime in Women; Its Sources and Treatment." In *Transactions of the National Association for the Promotion of Social Science 1876*. London: Longmans.

Westcott, W. M. Wynn. 1903. "Inebriety in Women and the Overlaying of Infants." *British Journal of Inebriety* 1(2):65–68.

Wilson, John Dove. 1878. "Can any Better Measures be Devised for the Prevention and Punishment of Infanticide?" In *Transactions of the National Association for the Promotion of Social Science 1877*. London: Longmans.

"Women Convicts." 1887. *Englishwoman's Review* 18(173):473–74.

Wrench, Matilda, ed. 1852. *Visits to Female Prisoners at Home and Abroad*. London: Wertheim & Macintosh.

Zanetti, Frances. 1903. "Inebriety in Women and Its Influence on Child-Life." *British Journal of Inebriety* 1(2):47–57.

Zedner, Lucia. 1988. "The Criminality of Women and Its Control in England, 1850–1914." Ph.D. dissertation, University of Oxford.

Mike Maguire

The Needs and Rights of Victims of Crime

ABSTRACT

The "victims' movement" can claim considerable success in putting the interests of crime victims on the political agenda in North America and Europe. Pioneering groups of volunteers and activists laid the groundwork for financial, practical, and psychological support services that are now funded by government on a significant scale. In the United States, legislation creates rights for victims to participate in the criminal justice process. It has not been firmly established how many (and what kinds of) victims are seriously in need of assistance, or what form this should take: research findings are contradictory and confusing, plagued by methodological and definitional problems. Service delivery also presents difficult dilemmas because many victims will not ask for help; high take-up rates emerge only when a personal approach is made. Although there is evidence of high levels of client satisfaction with victim services, research has not established that service provision greatly affects recovery from the effects of crime.

Over the past twenty years, but especially during the last decade, the rhetoric of North American and European criminal justice has been increasingly permeated with concern for the rights and welfare of "the victim." In their everyday decision making, police officers, prosecutors, judges, probation officers, and parole boards are frequently enjoined—and, increasingly, compelled—to pay heed to victims' interests as well as to those of the community and the offender. Legislation has granted new rights to victims to participate in court processes and

Mike Maguire is lecturer in criminology and penology at the University of Wales, Cardiff. He is grateful to Claire Corbett for helpful comments, and to Wesley Skogan for a sight of his forthcoming book, edited with Robert Davis and Arthur Lurigio.

0192-3234/91/0014-0005$01.00

to claim compensation. National and local government agencies have funded programs of victim and witness assistance. Voluntary organizations are providing services on a significant scale. Research projects and academic books on victims have become a growth industry. And, hardly mentioned in university courses even ten years ago, the needs and rights of victims have become regular topics of discussion in undergraduate classes in criminology.

Two brief illustrations of the scale of these developments are provided by figures from the National Organization for Victim Assistance (NOVA) and the National Association of Victim Support Schemes ("Victim Support"), the leading victims' organizations in the United States and Britain, respectively. In the United States, according to NOVA (1985*a*, 1988), there are about 5,000 separate victim assistance programs, covering a wide range of aims and practices and staffed variously by volunteers, paid workers, and professionals. The National Organization for Victim Assistance also estimates that over 5,000 separate pieces of legislation conferring rights or benefits on victims have been passed by local or federal governments in recent years and reports that forty-three states have established victim compensation programs. In Britain, the number of registered "victims support schemes" increased from thirty in 1979 to 350 by mid-1989. Between April 1988 and March 1989, 400,810 victims were referred by the police or other agencies to these British schemes that, between them, boasted nearly 10,000 volunteers. During the same twelve-month period, £2.5 million ($5.2 million) was disbursed in direct central government grants to fund local schemes—an exceptionally high contribution to a voluntary organization from a cost-cutting government (Victim Support 1989*a*).

The literature on victims is already vast, and it would be foolhardy to attempt to cover every aspect in the space available here. Most writers have focused on one of two broad themes, *victims' rights* and *services to victims.* Those interested primarily in rights—many of them academic lawyers—have tended to concentrate on the relations between victims and the criminal justice system, in particular, on entitlements to compensation or restitution and the extent to which victims should have a say in prosecution, bail, or sentencing decisions. Writers on services—who span a wider range of backgrounds and include almost as many practitioners as researchers and academics—have devoted most of their energies to assessing the material and psychological effects of crime and the most efficacious ways of identifying and satisfying victims' needs. To keep this essay within manageable bounds, I have opted to deal principally with the latter body of literature. However, victims' rights and services are interrelated issues and problems of service provision can be properly understood only within a broader social and political context. Hence, though it is not covered comprehensively here, the important literature on victims' rights is accorded at least some of the prominence it deserves.

My three main objectives in the essay are to outline the history of the recent unprecedented growth of interest in victims, drawing attention to the tensions as well as the good will that have accompanied this burgeoning interest; to provide a critical overview of research findings on the effects of crime and the needs of victims; and to describe and evaluate some of the service programs that have been designed to meet the perceived needs. I restrict the focus mainly to North America and Great Britain, although reference is made at times to continental European countries (for a fuller review of recent developments in Europe, see Maguire and Shapland [1990]).

The essay is structured as follows. Section I contains an account of the origins and growth of what has become known as the "victims' movement," charting its manifestations in a wide variety of new organizations, official policies, and legislation. The concatenation of a number of different trends and events produced within a short period a climate exceptionally favorable to the reemergence of the victim as a significant actor in the criminal justice process. Initially, the various campaigning organizations, voluntary groups, and professional agencies involved had little in common beyond a professed "concern for the victim," but more recently the differences have been reduced by an increasing institutionalization and professionalization of victim services and the emergence of certain orthodoxies. This is a particularly marked trend in the United Kingdom, where the key organization, Victim Support, which works very closely with the police, has largely succeeded in setting the agenda and defining the kinds of victimization that should receive priority attention.

Section II contains a summary of research findings on the effects of crime on victims. The quality of research on this subject is very variable, and caution often has to be exercised in interpreting the results. Nevertheless, some general conclusions can be drawn with a fair degree of confidence, most important, that major crimes such as rape and robbery are frequently psychologically damaging to victims over the long term, and that victims' suffering is often exacerbated by official or community neglect.

In Section III, I review the state and quality of knowledge based on research and practical experience about the nature and level of need for services. In the light of this knowledge, I ask what conclusions can be drawn about the effectiveness of services currently provided by victim assistance programs in the United States and United Kingdom, considering the extent to which they reach the "right" victims; the appropriateness of the services offered; and whether intervention can be said to work in the sense of ameliorating the effect of crime. I argue that, while there are possible mismatches between needs and the services provided and while there is no firm evidence of changes in victims as a result of intervention, the many methodological weaknesses and confusions in the literature make it premature to draw solid conclusions. There may be invisible or long-term benefits not easily measured by the narrow approaches so far adopted. In this section, I also consider an area in which disagreements about the appropriate form of assistance have been particularly strong: that of services to rape victims. It is argued that the diversity may be a positive advantage, as different women may benefit from the different kinds of services provided by professional counselors, feminists from rape crisis centers, and volunteers from victims support schemes.

In the final section, I draw the strands together, arguing that, although the victims' movement has clearly established itself and has persuaded many influential people and organizations that victims' interests should be provided for, the actual form that this provision will take in the future remains in doubt. Where welfare services are concerned, questions about the level of need, the precise kinds of service that should be offered, and the best ways of delivering them demand clearer answers, while it is politically important to provide evidence that services make a difference to victim recovery. Where the position of the victim vis-à-vis the criminal justice system is concerned, caution is needed before illiberal steps are taken that seriously undermine the rights of offenders.

I. Origins, Growth, and Consolidation of the Victims' Movement

The phenomenon in question has often been referred to as the "victims' movement," but the label, though convenient, is somewhat misleading. Despite a common professed desire to improve the lot of crime victims, the many individuals, groups, and organizations that have played a part have been motivated by a wide variety of interests, aims, and ideologies and have included some very strange bedfellows (C. Smith 1985; van Dijk 1988). Radical feminists, right-wing "law-and-order" groups, legislators, lawyers, psychologists and psychiatrists, welfare workers, churches, groups of ex-victims, criminal justice agencies, and academics from many different disciplines have all contributed to the debate and action. While their common concern for "victims" has often obscured their differences, the field is a wide one, and discord is by no means absent.

The birth of the "movement" is generally agreed to have occurred during the early 1970s in the United States. At that time, the activities of a number of voluntary groups, government agencies, and researchers began to draw public attention to the severe psychological and material effects that crime could inflict on victims and to a widespread neglect of victims' needs and interests by the police, prosecutors, courts, welfare services, and government in general. Before considering the various contributions of these pioneering groups, it is essential to ask why such a high level of interest and activity in a previously ignored area should have emerged so suddenly and taken root so quickly at this particular time.

A. *A Climate for Change*

At one level, it can be argued that the rise of the victims' movement represents an inevitable (and overdue) correction in a long-term historical trend. Writers such as Schafer (1968), Christie (1977), and Harding (1982) have noted that, before the growth of the modern state, victims obtained redress from offenders in a direct manner, originally by vengeance or force of arms but later through negotiated or arbitrated settlements. While this tradition continues, through the redress of wrongs under the aegis of civil law, the development of the criminal law gradually allowed the state, in a widening range of cases, to "steal the conflict" (Christie 1977) from the two parties directly concerned. Fines replaced compensation, thus severing the links between restitution and punishment. The victim was excluded from dealings with the offender and relegated to the marginal role of reporter of offenses and witness in court. The new movement can thus be seen as a belated reaction, an attempt, that was bound to have occurred at some time, to regain lost ground.

The speed with which, when it finally emerged, this counteroffensive by victims began to prosper reflects the existence of several factors that made the early 1970s an unusually propitious time for winning public sympathy and support. The United States, like most Western democracies, had experienced exceptional rises in crime rates during the sixties, and "law and order" was already a major political issue. At the same time, the civil rights movement had stimulated a period of gains in the rights of suspects, accused persons, and prisoners (Berger 1980; Morgan and Bronstein 1988). In reaction to both trends, the question, "What about the victim?" struck a particularly sympathetic chord. A rather different factor was the growth of feminism, which, in raising the general level of consciousness about male oppression, prepared a climate more receptive to calls for action against rape, the most extreme expression of this oppression. It also helped to open people's eyes to uninformed attitudes toward (and sometimes humiliating treatment of) rape victims displayed by the police and courts—a problem experienced, to a lesser degree, by victims of all kinds.

B. Pioneers

The early manifestations and growth of the victims' movement have been described many times but mainly in introductory passages to books on wider themes (see, e.g., Galaway and Hudson 1981; Karmen 1984; Elias 1986; Mawby and Gill 1987). A comprehensive international history has yet to be written, although Rock (1986, 1988, 1990) has produced valuable reconstructions of the policy debates and pressure group activities leading to major government initiatives in Canada and Great Britain.

In the United States, at least two distinct strands of development can be identified, although in recent years they have come closer together and, to some extent, have merged. One is associated primarily with agency-based initiatives set up by government and criminal justice–related institutions, whose initial concern was to tackle the problem of lack of cooperation by victims in reporting crime and giving evidence in court. The other, much more fragmented and diverse, was begun by voluntary groups, some of them deliberately avoiding collaboration and contact with officialdom. Their main goals were to establish more legal rights for victims, to demand better treatment by the police and courts, or simply to alleviate suffering through the provision of special welfare services. A growing band of academic, government, and independent researchers and writers materialized, bridging these two strands of the movement and playing an increasingly important role in legitimizing their claims to attention.

1. *Early Government Initiatives.* Government action on behalf of vic-

tims was rare before the 1970s, although there were scattered initiatives in the area of compensation during the previous decade. Compensatory payments by the state to victims of crime were pioneered by New Zealand (1963) and Great Britain (1964), followed shortly thereafter in the United States by California (1965), New York State (1966), and Hawaii (1967). Most of these schemes awarded ex gratia compensation to victims of serious criminal assault but under rules and arrangements that considerably restricted the numbers of beneficiaries (Edelhertz and Geis 1974). While generally welcomed at the time, they were subsequently subjected to considerable criticism as symbolic products of opportunistic politics (to attract the law-and-order vote) rather than as serious attempts to identify and meet victims' needs and wishes (Miers 1978; Elias 1983, 1986; Shapland 1986; Walklate 1989).

Another significant train of events was set in motion in the United States in 1967, when the President's Commission on Law Enforcement and Administration of Justice expressed concern that many victims were reluctant to cooperate with judicial proceedings and testify in court (see also Lamborn 1970; Ash 1972). Further evidence of victims' alienation from the criminal process came in the same year from the first experimental "victim surveys," conducted by Biderman et al. (1967) and Ennis (1967). The results of these experiments, as of their full-blown successor, the National Crime Survey,[1] showed that, even where some of the more serious offenses were concerned, more than half went unreported; many victims clearly felt that they had little to gain by calling in the authorities.

Growing concern about the lack of cooperation by witnesses in particular persuaded the Law Enforcement Assistance Administration (LEAA) in the early 1970s to begin funding a number of "victim-witness assistance" programs, based principally in prosecutors' offices. By 1975, the LEAA had invested over 22 million dollars in setting up such projects (Schneider and Schneider 1981). By 1978, there were almost 100 programs, and by 1980—the peak before LEAA began to be wound up in the early eighties—the number had rocketed to 400 (Karmen 1984). The programs were designed to provide better information to victims about cases and court appearances, protection from intimidation, more comfortable and secure waiting-room facilities, and assis-

[1] Beginning in 1972, respondents from a panel of 60,000 households were interviewed at intervals to determine whether they had recently been a crime victim. This survey spawned a regular flood of publications, providing a valuable alternative measure of crime rates to the Uniform Crime Reports (see, e.g., U.S. Department of Justice 1975, 1979).

tance with transportation, baby-sitting, and claims for fees and expenses (Rosenblum and Blew 1979; Viano 1979). However, as several commentators pointed out, they were geared first and foremost to the institutional imperative of producing more witnesses in court, rather than to the needs or wishes expressed by victims themselves, and there was mounting evidence of dissatisfaction and disappointment (Dussich 1976, 1981; Even-Zohar et al. 1976; Bolin 1980; Cronin and Bourque 1981). Even so, these schemes were far in advance of developments in other countries. In Britain, for example, similar concerns surfaced only in the mid-1980s. Following research studies (e.g., Shapland, Willmore, and Duff 1985; Shapland and Cohen 1987) and some effective lobbying (National Association of Victims Support Schemes 1988), the government moved to improve court facilities and to ensure better provision of information to victims.

2. *Campaigners and Service Providers.* At the vanguard of the grassroots part of the movement in the United States were groups of feminists who, from the early 1970s, began to campaign strongly on behalf of victims of sexual assault. In 1972, the first rape crisis centers were set up in California and Washington, D.C. These were designed not only to offer comfort and advice but also to disseminate a radical critique of the male oppression that was seen to underlie both the prevalence of the offense and the inadequate responses of the community and the criminal justice system to women who had been raped (including tendencies to disbelieve women and even to blame them for "inviting" attack). Many of the centers refused to cooperate in any way with the police or other agencies. They offered confidential counseling, advice, and practical help—mainly via telephone "hotlines" but sometimes in person—to any women who wished to call them. They also tended to avoid the use of the word "victim," which was felt to have undertones of passivity, preferring the more positive term "survivor" (Gornick, Burt, and Pittman 1983; Schwendinger and Schwendinger 1983). A fuller account of their aims, practices, and achievements is presented in Section III.

Feminists were also instrumental in drawing attention to forms of crime and victimization that had remained largely hidden from official view. While government attention was focused on the victims of "conventional" crime (i.e., predatory offenses such as robbery, burglary, and theft, most of which are committed by strangers), feminists began to redefine the boundaries by pointing out that vast numbers of women were victims of repeated violence from male partners within their own homes. Social work agencies were reluctant to provide alternative accommodation, while if the woman called the police, firm action was rarely taken and she was likely to face retaliation from the perpetrator (Friedman and Schulman 1990). From the early seventies, women's groups began to establish emergency shelters and "refuges" to provide sanctuary for such battered women (Fleming 1979; Walker 1979; Roberts 1982). These leads were soon followed by women in Britain and elsewhere in Europe (Gilley 1974; Pizzey 1974; Pahl 1978, 1985; London Rape Crisis Centre 1979). Many of the original refuges were precariously small and underfunded and lasted only a few years. Others have gradually expanded and become integrated into officially funded welfare services. At the same time, there has been a shift in emphasis among feminists away from providing shelter for women to advocating firmer police action and the removal of offending men from the home.

Another type of "hidden" crime that began to attract increasing attention in the 1970s was that of child abuse, both physical and sexual. Although the number of cases of physical abuse processed by child protection officers or other professionals was relatively small—in the region of 60,000 a year, according to the National Center on Child Abuse and Neglect in 1978—responsible observers estimated the true annual incidence of violence to children in the United States at over one million (Straus, Gelles, and Steinmetz 1980). Equally dramatic figures were produced for the incidence of sexual abuse (e.g., Colao and Hosansky 1983; Russell 1983), although this was much more difficult to measure and estimates varied widely. One of the most reliable studies is that of Finkelhor (1979), who calculated from interviews with adults that at least 9 percent of females had been sexually abused by a relative when they were children. Similar figures have since emerged in Britain (Baker and Duncan 1985).

In both countries, publicity about child abuse, together with increased sensitivity to the issue by doctors, teachers, and social workers, had the effect of bringing many more cases to light. For instance, the National Society for the Prevention of Cruelty to Children (1987) reported a 137 percent increase in known cases of sexual abuse in Britain in 1986 alone. This trend has not only put tremendous pressure on the resources of the relevant agencies (Morgan 1988) but has focused attention sharply on the sensitive issue of how to respond. Studies showed that sexual abusers of children were less likely to be prosecuted or imprisoned than those whose victims were adults (B. Smith 1983;

Chapman and Smith 1988), and, as with wife batterers, campaigns were launched to bring higher proportions to justice.

By the early eighties, a growing number of voluntary organizations were being formed in the United States to support and fight on behalf of victims of other specific types of offense. These "victim advocate" projects, as they were often called, were, in many cases, created and run by people who had suffered themselves and whose anger was often apparent in their choice of acronym. Prominent examples were Mothers Against Drunk Driving (MADD), Victims of Child Abuse Laws (VOCAL), and Parents of Murdered Children. The last named, which originated in Ohio in 1980, soon became a well-established national organization and is now represented in most states through over 250 local "chapters" (Davis and Henley 1990). As with many other victim advocate projects, its emphasis has been on self-help, with regular meetings of bereaved parents, led by a trained counselor who has himself or herself lost a child (National Organization for Victim Assistance 1985*a*). Similarly, MADD, which claimed to have over 6,000 active volunteers nationwide by 1986, has generally relied on victims for its counseling, fund-raising, and campaigning activities (Mawby and Gill 1987). While accepting government grants to supplement their charitable income, both have remained private and independent organizations, often critical of official policies.

Several victim-advocate organizations achieved national visibility through an aggressive law-and-order campaigning approach, demanding rights for specific types of victim, including compensation, a say in prosecution and parole decisions, and heavier sentences for offenders (Du Bow and Becker 1976). This is particularly true of MADD, which claims to have stimulated changes in over 400 drunk-driving laws (Davis and Henley 1990). Other organizations geared their efforts more toward "welfare" work. These included an increasingly important category adopting a "generalist" approach. Concerned about what they saw as a major gap in existing social services, they began to offer free assistance to victims of all kinds.

The most prominent was the Victim Services Agency (VSA) in New York, a corporation set up in 1978 by then-Mayor Edward Koch. The VSA played, and continues to play, a leading part in the development of service practice in the United States. It employs a large, trained staff, one of whose main tasks is "crisis intervention" during the first few days or weeks after a serious crime. This includes emotional support and counseling, the provision of emergency shelter, and help with transportation, medical treatment, repairs, and insurance or compensation claims. In some cases, longer-term support is given, and staff may accompany victims to court. The VSA also offers legal or security advice and information about the criminal justice system to anyone who requests it. Victims are either referred by the police or other agencies, or they can use a twenty-four-hour telephone hotline to ask for help. Finally, the organization has sponsored or produced a considerable amount of research on the needs of victims and has evaluated different types of service delivery (Victim Services Agency 1986). Other early projects in this tradition (for brief descriptive accounts, see Baluss 1975; Schneider and Reiter 1975; Gordon 1977; Lowenberg 1981) varied widely in size, expertise, financial resources, and working practices. While some employed professionals (Salasin 1981; Schneider and Schneider 1981; Ziegenhagen and Benyi 1981), a great deal of work was, and continues to be, undertaken by paraprofessionals or volunteers who have attended training courses in counseling (Barkas 1978; Friedman 1985; Finn and Lee 1987). Yet while such groups have begun to flourish over the last few years, it is noteworthy that the welfare-oriented, generalist model took root earlier and more readily in other countries, notably Britain, Canada, and Holland (Rock 1986; Mawby and Gill 1987; Maguire and Pointing 1988).

In Britain, the development of the victims' movement has been virtually synonymous with that of "victims support schemes"—a network of groups that, until recently, restricted their activities almost entirely to the provision of welfare services (Maguire and Corbett 1987). The first scheme was set up in Bristol in 1974, under the auspices of the National Association for the Care and Resettlement of Offenders, an independent organization with strong probation service connections (Gay, Holtom, and Thomas 1975; Holtom and Raynor 1988). The scheme received excellent cooperation from the local police who passed on the names and addresses of victims of a variety of offenses, consisting mainly of theft and burglary. Many of these victims were visited the same day by volunteers offering to assist them with repairs, insurance claims, or security measures or simply providing a "listening ear" for their anger, fears, or distress. By 1979, there were about thirty schemes in existence, of varying sizes and backgrounds, but almost entirely staffed by lay volunteers and heavily reliant on charitable donations. In that year, the groups agreed to form the National Association of Victims Support Schemes (NAVSS, recently renamed "Victim Support"). Within a short time, NAVSS not only encouraged an impressively rapid expansion of schemes (to 67 member groups by 1980, 194 by 1984, and 256 by 1985) but in 1986 attracted the promise of £9 million ($15 million) in government funding to support their work over the next three years.

Early Canadian initiatives took the theme of cooperation with the police even further. In three important pioneering schemes, the Calgary Victim Crisis Unit (set up in 1977), the Edmonton Victim Services Unit (organized in 1979), and the Kitchener-Waterloo Victim Services Program (organized in 1982), trained staff and volunteers were based in offices within police departments so that victims in need of help or support could be identified as quickly as possible. The largest scheme, the Edmonton Victim Services Unit, operated with a staff of six police officers and about seventy trained volunteer advocates. The unit provided immediate crisis counseling, mainly to victims of burglary, robbery, and assault, but occasionally to victims of accidents or other noncriminal incidents. It also routinely sent letters to victims informing them of the progress of cases, arranged the prompt return of recovered stolen property, and offered crime prevention and other advice. This model was influential in the development of major government-funded programs in the mid-1980s (see Canadian Federal-Provincial Task Force 1983; Stuebing 1984; Rock 1986).

3. *The Effect of Research.* Research in the victims area has been variable in quality and is frequently conducted by people with a strong commitment to the victims' movement, raising questions about its objectivity. Even so, there is little doubt that research into the effects of crime on victims has been of considerable importance in legitimizing the claims of victim assistance groups about the need for their services. In particular, it has had a considerable effect on the seriousness with which government has taken victims' claims and has provided a strong lever in demands for funding (see, e.g., Rock 1986, 1990).

Academic interest in victims can be traced back to the work of "victimologists" such as Von Hentig (1948) and Mendelsohn (1947, 1974), but their concerns—primarily to explain the generation of crime patterns through the "precipitation" of offenses by victims—were far removed from those of a later generation of writers and researchers, who began to examine the effect of crime on individuals and the treatment of victims by the police and criminal justice system. Several of the latter moved away from purely academic writing into the practical world of advocacy of reform. Some, such as Emilio Viano, Paul Separovic, Irvin Waller, and Leroy Lamborn, became prominent in international organizations set up to promote greater awareness of victims' issues (notably the International Institute on Victimology and the World Society of Victimology). They, as much as practitioners in victim assistance and victim advocacy, have helped to maintain the momentum. Irvin Waller in particular, characterized by Rock (1986) as a key "moral entrepreneur" in the victims arena, became interested in the subject initially through a fairly conventional study of burglary (Waller and Okihiro 1978) but subsequently put academic caution and neutrality behind him (cf. emotive titles of papers, such as Waller 1986). His previous status as a researcher became a powerful weapon in successful campaigns to put victims higher on the agenda not only of the Canadian government (Rock 1986) but of the United Nations as well (Waller 1988).

Most of the earliest studies of the impact of conventional crime, which appeared in the early 1970s, were heavily influenced by psychological papers on the emotional damage suffered by survivors of the holocaust, prisoners of war, and victims of terrorism. They focused on serious violent offenses and used the language particularly of "crisis" theory (Caplan 1964; Parad 1965) to explain their effects on victims. For example, the effects of rape were analyzed by Sutherland and Scherl (1970) and Burgess and Holmstrom (1974*a*, 1974*b*), the latter defining a specific set of reactions which they called "rape trauma syndrome." Similar approaches to violence in general were adopted by Symonds (1975), Cohn (1976), and Fields (1981). Such literature, some of it presented in popular books with large sales (e.g., Bard and Sangrey 1979) has subsequently been criticized in some quarters for overdramatizing the scale of the problem (see, e.g., Mayhew 1985), but it certainly contributed to keeping victims in the public eye, as well as creating more interest among clinicians and mental health professionals.

In the late seventies and early eighties, social researchers, using surveys and interviews, rather than clinical methods, produced findings suggesting that lesser offenses such as residential burglary and street robbery quite often had a serious effect on victims' lives, as well as being very costly in terms of financial loss, time off work, and general inconvenience (Bourque et al. 1978; Waller and Okihiro 1978; Brown and Yantzi 1980; Maguire 1980; Stookey 1981; Friedman et al. 1982; for reviews, see Maguire 1985; Mayhew 1985). For example, Friedman et al. (1982, p. 5) asserted that three-quarters of a sample of burglary and robbery victims were affected by "psychological problems including fear, anxiety, nervousness, self-blame, anger, shame, and difficulty sleeping." Whatever doubts may be expressed about the validity of such findings (see below), studies of this kind were particularly useful to victim assistance groups, not only for guidance on where to direct their services but to help make their case to funding agencies for increased financial aid as well.

Researchers also provided support for campaigns to improve agency responses to victims. Mounting evidence was adduced of the problem of "secondary victimization" or "the second injury" (Symonds 1980)—the exacerbation of victims' distress by unsympathetic reactions, even blame for inviting the incident (Pagelow 1977), from the police, other agencies, and the local community (Chelimsky 1981; Stuebing 1984; Shapland, Willmore, and Duff 1985; Villmow 1985). Similarly, confirmation was produced of victims' feelings of alienation resulting from insensitive treatment, underlining the need for effective victim-witness assistance programs (Knudten et al. 1977; Holmstrom and Burgess 1978; Knudten and Knudten 1981). More important, however, from the mid-seventies onwards, the whole relationship between victims and the criminal justice system began to be examined in a more systematic way, raising fundamental questions about the role of the victim and his or her rights to a hearing or other form of participation in the criminal justice process. This rapidly became one of the focal concerns of the victims' movement, spawning a large body of theoretical and research literature (prominent early examples being McDonald [1976*a*] and Ziegenhagen [1977]).

C. Consolidation: Organization, Legislation, and Funding

While a great deal was achieved in the 1970s in putting the problem of victimization "on the map," most of the voluntary initiatives suffered from limited funding, limited official support or encouragement, and limited public awareness. At the same time, the better-funded compensation and victim-witness assistance projects were underused and subject to considerable criticism. During the last decade, by contrast, victim issues have become quite prominent in the criminal justice policy agenda, attracting more effective agency initiatives, new legislation, greater financial support for service programs, and continuing attention from the media and the academic world. It is important, too, that the separate strands of the victims' movement have come closer together, and even some of the most radical groups have developed good working relationships with the police and other official agencies.

1. *The United States: Services, Rights, and Compensation.* One of the enabling factors behind this consolidation has been the formation of strong national organizations that have lobbied successfully for legislation, funds, and policy changes. The key organization in the United States has been the National Organization for Victim Assistance (NOVA), set up in 1976 in Washington, D.C. (Carrington and Nicholson 1984; Young 1988). Originally conceived principally as a coordinating body and information center, it welcomed member groups of all ideological and political persuasions—a policy it has maintained despite becoming increasingly important as a campaigning and lobbying organization (Edmunds et al. 1985; Mawby and Gill 1987). Partly as a result of its campaigning activities, President Reagan announced in 1981 the first "National Victims of Crime Week." The National Organization for Victim Assistance was also influential in shaping the recommendations of the President's Task Force on Victims of Crime (1982), which called for radical new legislation to create victims' rights (including the abolition of the *Miranda* exclusionary rule decision and the granting of public access to parole hearings), advocated reforms of victim-witness assistance schemes, and recommended the institution of a federal "crime victims fund," to be financed mainly from fines and bond forfeitures.

The President's Task Force was extremely important in maintaining the impetus in the victims' movement at a time when LEAA funding, which had previously supported many individual projects in addition to the major expenditure on the victim-witness assistance programs, was being phased out. Some of the Task Force's proposals were enacted later in the same year (see below). Perhaps more significant, the recommended Crime Victims Fund was set up two years later, under the Victims of Crime Act of 1984 (42 U.S.C. Sec. 10601). By 1987, the fund had been used to support nearly 1,400 separate projects (Lurigio, Skogan, and Davis 1990). The legislation allowed for the disbursement of up to $110 million in any one year; in fiscal year 1985–86, $68 million was distributed, and in 1987-88 this figure rose to $77 million (Beard 1988). All but 5 percent of the total was earmarked for spending on state rather than federal schemes, and was split fairly evenly between compensation programs and victim assistance and child abuse projects.

A further source of funding has come from state block grants originating under the provisions of the Justice Assistance Act of 1984. While not specifically earmarked for victim assistance, many states have used these funds partly for this purpose. By the end of 1987, over 200 victim groups had received grants; although there were cuts in the program the next year, it remained a useful supplement to the Crime Victims Fund (Beard 1988).

These national developments helped to consolidate advances that were being made in many states in three main victim-related areas: welfare services; legislation of rights vis-à-vis offenders; and compensation, restitution, and mediation. It is worth looking briefly at each in turn.

First, in the area of services to victims, the fragmentation and ideological differences which had characterized the 1970s became less acute, and voluntary and official agencies moved closer together in aims and practices. For example, many of the plethora of small private schemes in New Jersey listed in a twenty-seven-page directory by Grayson (1983) are now plugged into official networks and receive regular referrals from the state-funded victim-witness assistance programs. Other groups throughout the country are cooperating with, and receiving cooperation from, local police departments, giving their staff and volunteers more immediate access to victims and allowing them to become involved in training programs to educate officers about the needs of victims. Furthermore, the practice of physically locating civilian-run victim assistance programs within police departments is becoming quite common. Three fairly typical examples of police-based services in Florida are given by Mawby and Gill (1987), all of which concentrate primarily on offering immediate assistance to victims of violence, provided either by paid "victim assistants" or by trained volunteers. Victims are usually visited or telephoned on the recommendation of police officers, with priority likely to be given to the elderly.

Rape crisis centers and domestic violence advocacy groups have achieved greater credibility in police and other official eyes, especially since the advocacy groups received high-level "blessing" in the report of the U.S. Attorney General's Task Force on Family Violence (1984). Many now receive substantial grants from state governments or other sources of public funding. Mawby and Gill (1987) describe the Refuge House in Tallahassee, Florida, which began as a small volunteer-based project of the women's center but now operates on an annual budget of over $150,000, employing eight full-time staff members and accommodating over 300 women and children per year for an average of twelve days each. While what were formerly regarded as the extreme ideas held by such groups are now taken seriously, the other side of the coin is that, in order to attract official cooperation and state funding, they are increasingly having to demonstrate their suitability to receive public money by instituting improvements in their standards of administration and training (Davis and Henley 1990).

A second and more controversial area in which the victims' movement has consolidated its strength in the 1980s is that of legislation creating specific victims' rights vis-à-vis offenders. The main trigger for the spate of local lawmaking in this area was the passing, in 1982, of the Omnibus Victim and Witness Protection Act (96 Stat. 1248 [1982]). This act, covering federal criminal cases, introduced greater protection from intimidation for witnesses, increased courts' powers to order restitution from offenders, imposed stricter bail conditions, and required sentencers to consider "victim impact statements" before making their decisions.

The National Organization for Victim Assistance estimates that, subsequently, around 5,000 separate pieces of legislation (many of them, it should be pointed out, fairly minor) have been passed by local or federal governments, conferring rights or benefits on victims. One common development has been the right to make a "victim impact statement," which now exists in at least forty-three states (Davis and Henley 1990). Many states also require probation officers to include comments on the impact in their pretrial reports. Impact statements are used partly to determine possible restitution, which is now a constitutional right in Michigan, Rhode Island, and California (Hillenbrand 1990) but may also be taken into account in fixing the sentence. A stronger version is the "victim statement of opinion," in which the victim is entitled to make a statement on what sentence he or she would like to see passed. Another fairly common legislated right (currently in at least twenty-three states) is for victims to be consulted before any plea bargaining takes place, although, as Kelly (1990) points out, this is restricted in some states to the most serious crimes and in others (e.g., Arizona) simply requires the prosecutor to notify the victim of his or her plans and to consider any written objection. Similar rights are accorded in a few states before parole is awarded.

A somewhat different area in which the legal rights of victims have been strengthened is that of domestic violence. During the early eighties, women's groups put concerted pressure on legislatures and the police to treat spouse abuse as a crime and to arrest and prosecute offenders (Humphreys and Humphreys 1985; Yllo and Bograd 1988).

This campaign has achieved considerable success over the last five years, with some major changes in laws, attitudes, and practices. One important factor was the success of litigants in court actions, most notably the case of *Thurman v. City of Torrington* (59 F.Supp. 1521 [1984]), in which a woman was awarded huge damages against the police for failing to respond effectively to her requests for assistance. Another was the unequivocal recommendations of the U.S. Attorney General's Task Force on Family Violence (1984) that the police should treat domestic violence calls as priority matters and that their preferred response should be to arrest. A third factor was research findings indicating that arrest is more effective than the "crisis intervention" approach in preventing further violence (Sherman and Berk 1984; Elliott 1989). Subsequent legislation has removed obstacles to arrest in nearly all states, and in several it is now *mandatory* to arrest in the case of an alleged felonious attack (Victim Services Agency 1986).

The third and final aspect of consolidation has been the expansion of compensation, restitution, and mediation. Most of the funding for compensation schemes has come from state governments. In 1982, only about half the states ran such schemes (Elias 1983; McGillis and Smith 1983), but now all but five provide some payments from their tax revenue to victims of violence (Hillenbrand 1990). In recent years, it is estimated, about $100 million has been distributed annually, of which the Crime Victims Fund has contributed about $35 million (Beard 1988). Even so, evaluations of compensation schemes have generally concluded that they reach only a tiny proportion of those eligible. The increases, though not insignificant, are nowhere near the levels required to change the picture dramatically.

The concept of restitution came in for much academic discussion in the 1970s, gaining support both as a positive alternative to imprisonment and, more idealistically, as a means of reproducing the relationship between offender and victim that existed before the state "took over" through criminal prosecutions (see, e.g., Hudson and Galaway 1975; Christie 1977; McDonald 1976*b;* Harland 1983). However, relatively little restitution, in the form of compensatory payments from offender to victim, was actually ordered by the courts during this period, despite the existence by 1979 of eighty-two state-funded restitution programs designed to encourage just that (Hudson and Galaway 1980). Moreover, even when it was ordered, offenders often defaulted. Significant changes began to occur only when, following recommendations from the President's Task Force on Victims of Crime in 1982, the Omnibus Victim and Witness Protection Act authorized restitution in federal cases "in addition to or in lieu of any other penalty" and required judges to state reasons whenever it was *not* granted. By 1987, virtually every state had enacted new restitution legislation, although, in many cases, the rights of victims were couched in rather vague terms (Hillenbrand 1990).

Another variation of the concept of restitution can be found in victim-offender reconciliation or mediation programs. The basic model involves a mediated discussion between victim and offender, following which the latter agrees to pay compensation, to perform work or services, or simply to tender an apology. First experimented with in Kitchener, Ohio, in 1974, the idea had been implemented in eighty areas of North America by 1986 (Mawby and Gill 1987). Programs vary in kind, ranging from schemes that divert offenders entirely from the court process to those in which mediation forms a condition of the sentence—the latter being much more common (Zehr and Umbreit 1982).

2. *The United Kingdom: Police, Compensation, and Victim Support.* A period of consolidation of the strength of the victims' movement also occurred in Britain during the 1980s, although there are differences in the areas in which the most significant developments have occurred. One of the key factors in the movement's success in the United Kingdom has been the relatively enthusiastic response of the police, in particular their willingness to take a degree of responsibility for the welfare of victims. (While this is also evident in Canada, it has been much less consistently the case in the United States.) Little of the police role has been legislated in the United Kingdom, but it is spelled out in numerous force policies and instructions to officers. For example, following adverse publicity in the late 1970s about the treatment of women who reported that they had been raped, as well as critical semiofficial reports in both Scotland (Chambers and Millar 1983) and England (Blair 1985), all forces have reviewed their policies. It is now general practice to examine rape victims in areas away from the uncongenial surroundings of charge rooms and cells (in some forces, in specially designed "rape examination suites"), to encourage officers to be less hasty in disbelieving women, and to pay more attention to victims' feelings rather than simply gathering evidence (Corbett and Hobdell 1988). Again, the police have adopted a very active role in victims support schemes, with senior officers being obliged to attend monthly meetings and to facilitate the schemes' work as much as possible.

Criticism of unsympathetic attitudes by officers attending the scenes of crimes and failures to inform victims of the progress of investigations (Howley 1982; Maguire 1984; Shapland, Willmore, and Duff 1985) have also been taken seriously. Courses on handling victims are now a common feature of training programs for police recruits, and by 1987 about half of all forces in England and Wales claimed to have instituted systems designed to keep victims better informed (Shapland and Cohen 1987). Further progress was made in the latter area in 1988, when the British government issued a circular instructing forces to provide all victims with feedback on their cases and also to furnish courts with information about victims' material losses in order to encourage greater use of compensation orders.

Where compensation and restitution are concerned, three developments deserve mention. First, some efforts have been made to improve the operation of the Criminal Injuries Compensation Scheme. Although considerable sums (in recent years, the equivalent of over $80 million per annum) have been distributed to victims of violent crime, the scheme has received persistent criticism on a number of scores. These include its low public profile (leading to proportionately more claims made on behalf of members of well-informed organizations, such as the police or transport unions, than by unattached individuals); the limiting of expenditure through the setting of high minimum awards (currently £750—roughly $1,500), which effectively excludes the majority of victims; the arbitrary disqualification of victims not perceived as wholly "innocent" (including people with a criminal record of violence, even if innocent on this occasion); and bureaucratic delays, often extending to over a year before any money is paid (Samuels 1973; Miers 1978; Shapland, Willmore, and Duff 1985; Maguire 1986). More staff personnel have recently been appointed, and the police have been instructed to issue leaflets to all victims of violence (Home Office 1990). The Criminal Justice Act (1988) also contains clauses under which the scheme can be put on a statutory footing, although there are doubts whether this will be implemented. The proposed changes will not fully dispel the charge put most strongly by Miers (1978) that the system is concerned more with appearances than with actually meeting victims' needs, but the new publicity should lead to a significant increase in the number of applicants.

Second, the Criminal Justice Act requires sentencers to give reasons if they do not award financial restitution from the offender, in the form of a "compensation order," in any case in which an identifiable victim suffered loss, damage, or injury (Home Office 1990). Compensation orders have been permitted as sentences in their own right (i.e., not simply attached to another penalty) since 1982, taking priority over a fine when the offender's resources are low, but have been used less than intended, owing partly to conservatism among sentencers and partly to a lack of information on the basis of which to set the level of payment. The new requirement that the police furnish such information is intended to overcome these obstacles.

Third, following British researchers' interest in American experience of reconciliation programs (Harding 1982; Marshall 1984), the Home Office funded and monitored experiments with different varieties of reparation and mediation in four cities. The accounts so far available of these and other locally funded schemes suggest that much more caution has been exercised than in the United States, both in the numbers and types of offenders allowed to take part. Most participants have been young property offenders without a serious criminal record (Blagg 1985; Marshall and Walpole 1985); in one scheme, as few as six offenders were referred by magistrates over a twelve-month period (Davis, Boucherat, and Watson 1987). Moreover, the idea has not been endorsed by the influential Victim Support, which is wary of its being geared to the interests of offender rehabilitation or diversion from courts, rather than to the needs and interests of victims. Nevertheless, there remains a steady level of enthusiasm for the concept, which is being promoted by a private organization, the Forum for Initiatives in Reparation and Mediation (FIRM), and by committed writers such as Martin Wright (1982, 1985).

Despite these developments, it should be stressed that the relationship of victims to offenders and the courts has so far played a relatively small part in the victim debate in Britain. Generally speaking, it remains one of the countries with the least appetite for change in this area, and there are few loud demands for the introduction of victim impact statements or similar opportunities for victims' direct participation in the criminal justice system. A British research project based on interviews with large samples of victims of violence also found little desire among them for an active role in decision making, although most were anxious to be kept well informed about the progress of their case (Shapland, Willmore, and Duff 1985). The only serious court-related campaigning by a victims' organization—much of it conducted in private discussions with government officials (Rock 1990)—has been NAVSS's recent efforts to bring about improvements in waiting facilities, the provision to sentencers of information relevant to compensation orders, and the provision to victims of information about dates and results of cases (National Association of Victims Support Schemes 1988).

The courts have been the most resistant of all criminal justice agencies in the United Kingdom to attempts to change their treatment of victims. A nationwide survey of court administrators (Shapland and Cohen 1987) found lukewarm responses even to the idea of improving waiting facilities for victims; several argued that victims should be treated no differently than other witnesses, including defense witnesses.

The major trend in the United Kingdom has been toward the expansion and improvement of welfare services to victims. As mentioned earlier, the dominant force has been Victim Support, whose national association now represents over 350 individual schemes with 6,300 volunteer visitors and a further 3,600 committee members (Victim Support 1990). Despite some resistance from local schemes, the association has gradually encouraged the centralization and, to some extent, the "professionalization" of what was originally very much a grass-roots movement and has introduced an increasingly standardized model of organization, service, and approach (Reeves 1985; Maguire and Corbett 1987). The main elements of its approach are outreach (in the form of letters, telephone calls, or unannounced visits offering services to large numbers of victims), the use of volunteers, and the availability of the backup services of networks made up of other statutory and voluntary agencies in the local area, many of which will be represented on the scheme's management committee. This model has begun to have a strong influence on developments in continental Europe. For example, the Vereiniging Landelijke Organisatie Slachtofferhulp in Holland (Vereiniging Landelijke Organisatie Slachtofferhulp 1989), has established close links with NAVSS and has borrowed a great deal from the British model, as has the network of more than 150 schemes set up in France over the last few years (Waller 1988; Maguire and Shapland 1990).

The reasons for the astonishingly rapid growth of victims support schemes are complex. Apart from a general climate of sympathy toward victims similar to that in the United States, they had, from the beginning, the advantage of the strong tradition of voluntarism in the United Kingdom. In stark contrast to the victims' movement across the Atlantic, NAVSS has generally avoided political activity or overt campaigning and, in particular, has consistently refused to make public statements about sentencing policy (Corbett and Maguire 1988).[2] This has had two advantages from the point of view of recruitment. First, it has allowed schemes to tap into the army of people in Britain anxious to help others through any kind of voluntary service. Gill and Mawby (1990) show that the majority of volunteers recruited into victims support schemes, unlike volunteers who assist the police as special constables, have no special previous interest in crime or criminal victimization per se: many join after being approached by a friend, or offer their services to a general volunteer bureau. Second, the absence of a "law-and-order" ethos has served to keep within the fold many individual probation officers and social workers whose primary commitment has traditionally been to the rehabilitation of offenders. These professionals have assisted in forging strong links with local statutory agencies, which continue to provide valuable facilities as well as specialist knowledge, counseling skills, and input into training courses.

The presence of such institutional support—which was vital to schemes in their formative period—can also be seen, more cynically, as a function of problems within the agencies concerned. Victim support has offered some agencies a new strategy for protecting their budgets at a time of crisis. The probation service, in particular, has suffered since the mid-seventies from a general decline of faith in the rehabilitative ideal and, consequently, in its effectiveness: involvement with victims provides an excellent opportunity for demonstrating its pursuit of new objectives, such as the promotion of cooperative initiatives in the local community (Pointing and Maguire 1988).

Above all, however, the success of victims support schemes was sealed in 1986 by the decision of the government to commit 9 million pounds to their development—primarily for the payment of administrative staff (Corbett and Maguire 1988). Given a conservative government generally committed to cuts in public expenditure, the grant of such a sum to a voluntary organization was a striking achievement. The background to the decision is described in detail by Rock (1990), who gives a fascinating account of the behind-the-scenes lobbying of influential Home Office figures by the director of NAVSS and of the important roles played by researchers and other outsiders. The event

[2] For example, NAVSS withdrew its membership in the World Society of Victimology in 1985, when the WSV proposed a UN charter recommending a greater role for victims in the sentencing process.

was also a clear demonstration of the extent to which, in Britain at least, the support of victims had become an established item on the political agenda. There is every indication that this funding, which has recently been renewed and increased to 4 million pounds per year, will continue for the foreseeable future. Victim Support was mentioned in the manifesto of each of the main political parties in the 1987 general election, and at present it would be difficult for any party to renege on its commitment (Phipps 1988).

A final but very important point to be made in this context is that, while Victim Support has consolidated its position, other organizations concerned with victims do not have the ear of government ministers and remain without significant funding. Many rape crisis centers, indeed, have deliberately chosen neither to court official funding nor to collaborate with victims support schemes or the police, thus maintaining their distinct ideological approach (Maguire and Pointing 1988). They also have no national organization, in order to preserve local autonomy. Similarly, women's refuges have generally remained small, suspicious of other agencies, and overtly feminist in philosophy and approach, seeing their role as one of political education as well as of the provision of welfare (Daniels 1977; Rose 1978). The few that have sought and been granted state funding have tended to shift toward more conventional welfare concerns and practices (Gill 1986).

This imbalance in size and resources has important implications for the philosophy and practice of victim assistance in the United Kingdom, including the relative degree of attention given to different categories of victim. For example, it is the policy of most victims support schemes not to take referrals of domestic violence (NAVSS having argued that this is the province of the statutory social services and that volunteers are insufficiently trained to handle the difficult and dangerous situations that can arise). However, women's groups argue that a serious problem is being neglected: the underfunded refuges cannot meet the national need, and virtually every study of the problem has criticized the lack of adequate action by the police, social workers, and housing agencies (Pahl 1978; Dobash and Dobash 1979; Binney, Harkell, and Nixon 1985). In a nutshell, victim support definitions of "the problem" are tending to dominate. These focus on "conventional" crime, predatory offenses such as burglary, robbery, stranger rape, and street theft, which are mainly one-shot events committed by strangers. As schemes rely heavily on the police for referrals, they focus also on *recorded* offenses of these kinds. The danger is that this police-influenced view of the nature of crime and victimization prevails to such an extent that other less visible but equally damaging forms such as repeated domestic assault or racial or sexual harassment remain too far out of the purview of agencies equipped to help (for further discussion of this issue, see Corbett and Maguire 1988).

II. Research on the Effects of Crime

In this section, I review research findings on the practical and emotional effects of crime on different categories of victims. First, however, a strong note of caution is injected concerning the methodological problems and weaknesses that abound in this type of research and, equally important, the tendency of writers committed to "the cause" to make excessive claims for the potentiality of some of the findings to be generalized. Despite these pitfalls, the available data allow some general conclusions to be drawn with reasonable confidence.

A. *Sources of Knowledge and Reliability of Data*

Research into the effects of victimization can be divided into three main categories: clinical studies of the psychological consequences of catastrophic events, criminal and noncriminal in origin, in people's lives; in-depth interview studies of the victims of selected types of offense (most often at the "medium to serious" end of the spectrum of recorded crime); and survey data on the financial, practical, or emotional effects of a range of personal and household crimes, both reported and not reported to the police.

The longest-established tradition of victim research is clinically based work on the aftereffects of major, life-threatening events. Early studies of survivors of the holocaust (e.g., Eitinger 1964) and of "brainwashing" camps in Korea and China (e.g., Lifton 1961) influenced subsequent work on the survivors of terrorist attacks (Ochberg 1980; Symonds 1982) and disasters (Parad, Resnick, and Parad 1976; Weisaeth 1985). Gradually, a literature built up linking the findings of such studies and postulating general theories about the consequences of traumatic life events of all kinds (see, e.g., Horowicz 1980; Silver and Wortman 1980; Salasin 1981; Janoff-Bulman and Frieze 1983). More important for our purposes here, several of the concepts developed, particularly the notions of "crisis" and "stress" (Appley and Trumbull 1967), "helplessness" (Seligmann 1975), and loss of faith in a just world (Lerner 1980) were adopted and adapted by the authors of studies of the victims of more common criminal events, especially rape and sexual assault. Probably the most influential of these were Burgess and Holmstrom (1974*a*) who defined the condition of "rape trauma syndrome"—recognized in 1980 as a subset of "posttraumatic stress disorder" in the Diagnostic Standards Manual of the American Psychiatric Association—and Bard and Sangrey (1979), who popularized some of the more dramatic findings in a widely read book about crime victims in general.

While this literature has been of immense political value to the victims' movement and has fostered greater interest in crime victims among the mental health profession, the empirical base for some of the conclusions reached is relatively thin. Fields (1981), who herself worked with many survivors of torture, natural disasters, and terrorism, points out serious limitations in the methodologies used by clinical researchers. Too much reliance has been placed on laboratory experiments, case studies, and anecdotal evidence, in most cases referring to only small groups of subjects. There are rarely any reliable data on pretrauma conditions to use as a baseline. There is a lack of longitudinal evidence, and too little account has been taken of extraneous factors (e.g., among former political prisoners, to what extent is the observed psychological disturbance a result of captivity or of subsequent refugee status?). Moreover, the field is plagued by confusions and ambiguity in terminology: for example, the word "stress" has been applied indiscriminately to the consequences of events as disparate as rape, torture in captivity, and regular commuting in traffic jams.

There are notable exceptions. Eitinger and Strom's (1973) studies of concentration camp survivors in Israel were based on a large sample, used both psychological and physiological measurements, were longitudinal in design, and had the advantage of baseline data in the form of service records. However, few of the clinically based studies of victims of rape or other violent crime have approached this level of sophistication. Burt and Katz (1985), in a review of the literature on rape and robbery, found the rigorous use of nonvictim control groups to be surprisingly rare and identified only one study (Orlando and Koss 1983) using the distinction between rape and lesser sexual assaults in the analysis. Samples have often been small, and there are few longitudinal studies (Shapland, Willmore, and Duff [1985] is an exception).

Despite these problems, the literature has, as Burt and Katz (1985, p. 328) put it, "succeeded in generating detailed and rich descriptions of the multiple psychological, behavioral, physical and material effects of rape." Psychiatrists and psychologists have certainly acquired useful knowledge about patterns of reaction exhibited by *some* victims. However, as the kinds of cases they deal with are, almost by definition, the most serious, there are doubts about how much they can tell us about the incidence of disturbance in the whole "victim population." Mayhew (1985, p. 90), in a challenging review of research for the European Committee on Crime Problems, warns against "the more emotive pro-victim writings" which, by generalizing from the findings of such studies, "may, with more emotion than judgement, have exaggerated victims' needs."

Nonclinical researchers have been more interested in the incidence of different kinds of effects and, from the practical policy viewpoint, in the level of "need" for victim services. The most common methodology used for these purposes has been the "in depth interview" (Maguire 1985). This relies on samples of victims being asked to report in some detail, usually a few weeks or months after the event, the effect that a particular crime has had on their lives. Sometimes the self-reporting technique has been supplemented with more objective measures such as the completion of standard general health questionnaires. Many of these studies have been based on samples of victims of rape, robbery, assault, or burglary that reflect the kinds of cases typically dealt with by generalized victim-assistance programs.

As illustrations of the above points, it is worth briefly describing the design of two of the larger studies in this tradition, the results of which are referred to several times in the next section.

Friedman et al. (1982), in a project sponsored by the Victim Services Agency and funded by the National Institute of Justice, interviewed 274 victims of recorded offenses of burglary (63 percent of the total), robbery (29 percent), and assault (8 percent). One of the main methodological problems with the study was the low response rate, the researchers having started with a pool of 1,919 crime reports from police records in three contrasting neighborhoods of New York. The interviews were conducted by telephone, and 63 percent of nonresponses were due to failure to contact the victim, 19 percent to refusals. It appears from the socioeconomic structure of the interviewed population (40 percent having college education) that the response rate was highest among more affluent victims. Nevertheless, almost half were Blacks or Hispanics. Victims were interviewed as soon as possible after the offense, and a longitudinal element was included by reinterviewing two-thirds of the sample four months later. In addition, 152 "supporters"—friends, relatives, or others named by the victim as having rendered assistance—were interviewed.

The interviewers' questions were designed mainly to elicit information about the initial and longer-term effects of the incident, victims' perceptions of their own needs, and the views and reactions of the supporters. An "Affect Balance Scale" (containing measures of joy, contentment, vigor, and affection, as opposed to anxiety, guilt, depression, and hostility) was also included to throw more light on psychological reactions to the crime. However, the finding that victims were significantly more anxious and depressed than a sample of college students has to be treated with caution, considering the social makeup of the interviewed group. The research was geared ultimately toward learning lessons of use to the VSA to improve their service delivery, and several conclusions were reached on this score.

Maguire and Corbett (1987), in a two-year study in England funded by the Home Office, interviewed in person 265 victims of burglary, robbery, rape, assault, and street "snatch" theft (51 percent were burglary victims). These were drawn from a combination of police and victim support scheme records in six contrasting areas of England. The researchers emphasized that the full 265 cases could not be treated as a random sample of all victims of these offenses because some came from schemes where referrals consisted of victims selected by the police as likely to need assistance. However, they created a "composite sample" of 175 cases, using only those from areas where referral to schemes was automatic and nonselective, combined with those randomly selected from police crime reports. This sample was also weighted to represent the relative incidence of burglary, robbery, assault, and snatch theft (for other reasons, violent offenses had been deliberately oversampled). It could therefore be said to be reasonably representative of recorded offenses of these kinds. The response rate for interviews was quite high (67 percent), considerable effort having been made, by telephone, letter, and house call, to contact people. Sixty-six percent of the full interviewed population had been visited by a victim support volunteer, and one of the purposes of the study was to probe their reactions to this contact, as well as to compare their current state of mind with that of people who had had no contact with a scheme.

Most of the interviews were conducted between three and six weeks after the offense, although, in order to look at longer-term effects, a subsample was interviewed three to four months after the event. A variety of methods were used to rate the impact of the crime, including victims' unprompted descriptions, precoded lists of possible effects, a general self-rated scale of "upset," and a standardized measure, the

General Health Questionnaire. Maguire and Corbett were also given space in the 1984 British Crime Survey for a number of questions about the impact of crime and views about victim support, and the responses provided helpful data to compare with the interview results. Finally, they analyzed records at the National Association of Victims Support Schemes and in the offices of eight local schemes, which, together with interviews with scheme members, police officers, and the victims, allowed them to make a broad evaluation of the work of the organization.

There are clearly a number of questions to be raised about this kind of methodology and the conclusions that can be drawn from it. First of all, nearly all the studies are based on samples of victims of crimes recorded by the police. Moreover, they have tended to concentrate on the more serious end of the spectrum. They cannot, therefore, legitimately claim to reflect the consequences of "crime" in general. Unfortunately, some of the research literature and, even more, literature quoting research findings at second hand, is permeated by loose statements of the order, "*x* percent of victims experience emotional distress," omitting a precise definition of the population of "victims" being referred to, let alone what counts as distress (Maguire 1985; Mayhew 1985).

Second, it has to be asked how much credence can be attached to victims' own perceptions of how badly they have been affected by one event that took place some time ago. There is some evidence (Leymann 1985) of reasonably strong correlations between subjective data of this kind and data from objective physiological measures of stress, such as hormone secretions and cardiac activity. Maguire and Corbett (1987) also found a broad similarity between crude ratings by victims on scales of how badly they had been affected ("very much," "quite a lot," etc.) and results from a standard measure of anxiety levels. However, caution still has to be exercised. More problematic are weaknesses similar to those identified above in relation to clinical studies, namely, a lack of valid control samples of nonvictims, an absence of data on previctimization states of mind, and difficulties in dealing with extraneous factors that may have contributed to the "effects" found.

Finally, a major problem in those studies that have gone further and made attempts to assess the level of "need" for victim services—findings discussed in Section III—has been a lack of clarity about the meaning of this concept, reflected especially in a tendency to confuse "needs" and "effects." Writers in other areas of social policy (e.g., Culyer, Lavers, and Williams 1972; Armstrong 1982) have, for years, been drawing attention to the ambiguities inherent in the concept of need, which can be defined according to an arbitrary standard, an expert's judgment, the subject's own perceptions, or the actual take-up rates for a service on offer. As Shapland, Willmore, and Duff (1985, p. 112) write in the context of crime victims: "Expressed needs are to some extent culturally based. They are related to the expectations of victims as to the potential effects of the offence and to their knowledge of what remedies exist."

Most researchers in the victims field have based their assessments of need on victims' own statements about what services they required after the offense, without taking account of this basic point. Statements of the order, "*x* percent of victims had unmet needs" are not uncommon (e.g., Brown and Yantzi 1980; Stuebing 1984), the percentage being derived from adding together a set of disparate services (e.g., counseling, repairs, and legal advice) which individuals said they had felt in need of. When one compares the results of different studies of this kind, it is clear that they vary considerably according to how the questions were put: where interviewees were prompted, or given a list of "needs" from which to choose, the levels of "unmet need" have emerged as much higher (see Maguire 1985).

The third distinct source of information on the effects of crime covers a much wider range of victims. Household victimization surveys have been conducted regularly in the United States since the early 1970s and in at least twenty European countries during the 1980s (e.g., U.S. Department of Justice 1975; Breen and Rottman 1985; Hough and Mayhew 1985). Recently, too, van Dijk, Mayhew, and Killias (1990) have produced an ambitious international crime survey, covering fourteen different countries. At first, such surveys were designed mainly to obtain information about the "dark figure" of unreported crime, but they have increasingly been used to assess the impact of crime and the attitudes of victims.

Their main advantages are the very large samples (for example, the British Crime Survey covers 11,000 households, of which about 5,000 contain self-reported "victims"), the inclusion of a wide variety of offense types and, of course, knowledge about offenses not reported to the police. Their deficiencies include the omission of many important crimes (e.g., murder, fraud, crimes against children, and crimes against organizations); the gross undercounting of sexual offenses; the undercounting of victims not easily contacted by interviewers (particularly the homeless and the underprivileged); difficulties in dealing with "multiple victims" (Genn 1988); and their questionable ability to provide precise estimates of victimization over specific time periods. Moreover, while these surveys have produced valuable data on the financial and practical consequences of crime, they have generally skirted the emotional impact and the psychological needs of victims (Mayhew 1985).

B. Main Findings

The variety of research methods described above, the methodological problems and, indeed, the ideological commitment of many writers and researchers, have combined to produce an overall picture of confusing, and, superficially at least, conflicting answers to questions about the effects of crime and the needs of victims. In this section, I look first at findings in relation to the more common types of crime, and then at homicide and rape, which are widely agreed to produce among the most devastating effects on victims' and loved ones' lives.

1. *The More Common Offenses.* A casual reader may be forgiven for becoming confused, when reading on the one hand, Mayhew's (1985, p. 72) conclusion that crime in its most typical form is "a relatively trivial event . . . part of life's vicissitudes, not ineffectively coped with by victims with help from family, friends and insurance premiums" and, on the other, Friedman et al.'s (1982, p. 266) account of their experiences in interviewing victims: "We were stunned at the general impact of crime on the victim's psychological state, and at the alterations in daily life which were so often part of the victimization experience."

The difference is largely a function of the types of research in which these two parties have been involved. Patricia Mayhew, a senior researcher in the Home Office, was taking as her main frame of reference offenses identified by the British Crime Survey, while Friedman's group had recently completed interviews with a sample of victims of relatively serious offenses recorded by the police.

To illustrate the scale of the difference this makes, as well as the importance of the specific methodology employed, we may compare findings from the 1984 British Crime Survey with those of the in-depth interview study by Maguire and Corbett (1987), described above. In both projects, the same question was put to victims: "Thinking back over the first few days after it happened, how much would you say the incident affected you or your household at that time: very much, quite a lot, a little, or not at all?" Table 1 shows the responses. At the

TABLE 1

Victims' Ratings of Level of Effect on Themselves or Household by Selected Groups of Respondents

Source of Data and Type of Respondent	Rating of Level of Impact: Very Much Affected (%)	A Little/Not at All Affected (%)	Unweighted N*
British Crime Survey, victims of:			
All incidents	12	71	4,882
Incidents known to police only:			
All offense categories	21	55	1,927
Burglary, robbery, wounding, snatch theft	36	36	345
"In Depth" Interviews' of victims of burglary, robbery, assault, snatch theft:			
Composite sample reflecting crimes recorded by the police	66	18	175
All those visited by scheme volunteers	79	8	151

SOURCE.—Adapted from Maguire and Corbett (1987), p. 42.
* Percentages given are based on weighted data.

extremes, while only 12 percent of all victims identified by the survey replied that they had been "very much affected," this answer was given in the interview study by 79 percent of the victims of burglary, robbery, assault, or snatch theft who had been visited by scheme volunteers. The survey-based percentage climbs to 21 percent when one includes only those victims who reported the offense to the police (reflecting the point that reported crime is generally more serious than nonreported crime; see Hough and Mayhew [1985]). Not surprisingly, it climbs further, to 36 percent, when one looks only at the group of more serious offenses included in the Maguire and Corbett study—although it is noteworthy that it still falls well short of the 66 percent level Maguire and Corbett found among their "composite sample," reflecting all such crimes recorded by the police. This latter difference is discussed by Maguire and Corbett (1987), who suggest that the survey technique, which demands instant answers from respondents on a wide range of subjects, will normally produce fewer admissions or assertions of adverse effects than a lengthy, specialized interview in which people have time to focus their thoughts and memories. There is also evidence elsewhere (Waller 1986) that telephone interviews tend to reveal a lower incidence of emotional distress than interviews conducted in person.

Self-reported effects are, by definition, subjective; ultimately, there is no "correct" measure of their seriousness or incidence. Nevertheless, when account is taken of sampling and methodology, figures produced in this way fall consistently enough within a broad range to allow some meaning to be attached to them. Moreover, some offenses emerge consistently as more disruptive to victims' lives than others.

The best sources of "rank order" of the damage inflicted by different crimes are victim surveys, as they include the widest range of offense types. Table 2 shows findings from the 1984 British Crime Survey, based on answers to the same questions as those quoted above. The two columns show, respectively, among those who did and did not report the offense to the police, the percentages considering themselves "very much affected" by the experience. The two most obvious points to emerge are that violent crime has a considerably greater impact than property crime (with the exception of burglary, an offense found in several other studies to upset many people deeply; see Waller and Okihiro 1978; Maguire 1980, 1982; Friedman et al. 1982), and that the crimes that victims report to the police affect them considerably more than those they do not report.

Where the nature of the effects of crime is concerned, several researchers have found that, even where property offenses are involved, the initial experience takes the form of a strong emotional effect. Maguire with Bennett (1982) asked a sample of 322 burglary victims (randomly selected from police records) what they considered to have been the worst aspect of the offense; over 60 percent named either "intrusion upon privacy" or "emotional upset," only 28 percent naming financial loss or damage. Similarly, injuries in assaults are serious enough to require prolonged hospital treatment in only a small minority of cases, and victims tend to report that they are more affected by shock or fear than by the physical pain or damage (Knudten et al. 1977; Shapland, Willmore, and Duff 1985). Nonetheless, questions about victims' "needs" often produce more answers relating to practical problems such as repairing or replacing property than to perceived needs for emotional

TABLE 2

Percentages of Victims Reporting Themselves "Very Much" Affected by Criminal Incidents

Offense Type	Reported to Police (%)	Not Reported to Police (%)
Robbery/"snatch" theft	40	8
Serious assault/wounding	36	11
Burglary with theft	36	23
Threats	36	15
Major vandalism/damage	29	9
Theft from person (pickpocket)	22	6
Minor vandalism/damage	21	4
Theft of motor vehicle	21	*
Attempted burglary	17	7
Bicycle theft	13	7
Household theft	13	3
Minor assault	12	12
Theft from vehicle	10	2
Other theft	10	5

SOURCE.—Maguire and Corbett (1987), p. 45.
* Numbers too small for analysis.

support. This discrepancy clearly has implications for service agencies, which are discussed in Section III.

Typical patterns of emotional response to these offenses at the "medium to serious" end of the spectrum (major crimes like murder and rape are discussed later) are now quite well documented from in-depth interview studies of the kind described above. Strong initial reactions of shock, fear, and anger are reported in middle to high proportions of cases of burglary and robbery, the offenses most often included. At the high end of the estimates, Friedman et al. (1982) found three-quarters of their sample of victims of burglary, robbery, and assault reporting "psychological problems including fear, anxiety, nervousness, self-blame, anger, shame, and difficulty sleeping"; and Bourque et al. (1978) found that 80 percent of a sample of burglary and robbery victims had reacted with "nervousness, crying, or shaking." Maguire and Corbett (1987) found the most common initial reactions among their "composite sample" of burglary and robbery victims to have been anger (67 percent ticking this off on a list given to them), difficulty sleeping (46 percent), and feeling unsettled or uneasy (45 percent). About two-thirds of the sample said that they had experienced four or more such effects "intensely." However, it is worth noting that Maguire with Bennett (1982) found a similar proportion of burglary victims reporting similar initial reactions, but a closer analysis of what they had actually said suggested that the proportion *seriously* shaken was much lower—in the region of 25 percent.

Most studies suggest that initial fear, shock, and anger give way after a few days to a period of lingering effects such as nervousness, depression, fear of a repeat attack, inability to sleep, turning the event over and over in one's mind, and blaming oneself for having allowed it to happen. Where the offender is unknown, as in many burglaries, victims may start suspecting neighbors, wondering why their house was "picked out," and thinking that they are being watched (Maguire with Bennett 1982). Victims of violence tend to report fear of another attack, avoidance of places similar to the location of the incident and, in the case of people assaulted at work, reluctance to put themselves in danger again. These feelings are particularly well documented by Shapland, Willmore, and Duff (1985), who interviewed a random sample of 276 victims of rape, robbery, and assault soon after the event, following up 78 percent of these in up to four subsequent interviews at different stages of the legal process. They found that over half reported persisting emotional effects and that 14 percent of the assault victims had radically changed their patterns of social activity.

Nevertheless, the consensus of opinion from both survey and interview studies is that, at least where offenses of burglary, robbery, and assault are concerned, serious psychological effects rarely persist for more than a few months, by which time some sort of equilibrium is recovered (for summaries, see Burt and Katz 1985; Maguire 1985; Mawby and Gill 1987). While there is a shortage of long-term studies, those who have interviewed samples of victims a year or so later have generally found them coping adequately with their fears (e.g., Brown and Yantzi 1980; Friedman et al. 1982). Even so, there seems to remain a small proportion—perhaps 5 percent—of victims of offenses of medium seriousness (and even a few among victims of quite minor offenses) who do not "recover" in the expected way and whose lifestyles may continue to be disrupted by anxiety or depression (Skogan and Maxfield 1981; Stuebing 1984; Maguire 1985). As Waller (1986) and Mayhew (1985) have pointed out, this may be a small percentage, but as there are many more such offenses committed, they may constitute a larger group in terms of absolute numbers than people whose lives have been shattered by a murder or a rape.

These findings illustrate the more general point that the effects of crime are determined not only by the type of crime involved but also by the characteristics of the victim. Most studies suggest that the impact of crime tends to be greater on people who are socially disadvantaged (Friedman et al. 1982; Davis 1987) or who have prior emotional problems (Cook, Smith, and Harrell 1987), and levels of fear and trauma may be lower among those with strong social or family networks (Skogan 1977; van Dijk 1979). There are also indications that females are more likely than males (Norquay and Weiler 1981; Maguire with Bennett 1982) and the elderly more likely than the young (Davis and Friedman 1985; Leymann 1985) to suffer severe psychological effects from crimes of all kinds. However, not only are the observed differences relatively small, but it is possible that they are exaggerated by, for example, social conventions among males that make them reluctant to admit so readily as females that they are emotionally upset. Again, old people may be more vulnerable by virtue of widowhood or living alone than simply because of their age (Maguire and Corbett 1987). It should also be noted that some studies (Bourque et al. 1978; Friedman et al. 1982) have found no difference according to age, while Stuebing (1984) even found older people to be *less* affected than the young.

Most of the above findings are derived from studies using methodologies similar to those of Friedman et al. (1982) or Maguire and Corbett (1987), and simply compare subsets of victims within the total interviewed population. The occasional contradictory results are to be expected, given my earlier comments about the impossibility of achieving a "true" measure of the effect of crime, but the overall picture is reasonably consistent. From the viewpoint of victim assistance agencies, of course, the $64,000 question is how to identify and reach the relatively small proportion of individuals who are very severely affected over the long term and unquestionably need their support. This question is far from a solution at present.

2. *Homicide.* A category of victims for which it is hardly necessary to conduct research to demonstrate the severity of the effect and the need for support is the relatives of people who have been murdered. There is a large literature on bereavement, and bereavement counseling is a highly developed specialization (for an overview, see Worden [1982] or Osterweis, Solomon, and Green [1984]). Surprisingly little attention has been paid to "ordinary" homicide, however, and, in particular, to the dimensions of pain and anger added by the knowledge that the death was deliberately inflicted by another individual (though for a summary of differences between the effects of crime and accidents in

nonfatal circumstances, see Janoff-Bulman [1985]). One exception is the work of Rynearson (1984, 1986), who argues that conceptual models of bereavement, and consequently therapeutic strategies, have to take careful account of the cause of death. He notes particular psychological problems in intrafamilial murders, where the bereaved experience "dual identification," that is, identification with both the murderer and the victim. He also points to quite different problems in cases where the murder remains unsolved.

Another specific type of homicide in which some research has been carried out recently is the murder of one parent by another and its effect on the children. Malmquist (1986, p. 322) has examined post-traumatic stress disorder in a small number of such children, concluding that the trauma is greater than in adults, owing to the "added element of an underdeveloped psychological state," and often causes recurrent terrifying nightmares. Despite this, children are less likely than adults to receive psychiatric attention. Isaacs and Hickman (1987*a*, 1987*b*) also note the lack of attention paid by social services to this problem, although there may be as many as forty relevant cases each year in England and Wales alone. They explore methods of therapy based on play, arguing that this helps children to express their emotions better than other methods and may reduce anxiety.

More general studies of the psychological effect of homicide on families include those by Burgess (1975) and Magee (1983), both of whom document the depth of the trauma and the need for long-term counseling. Like most studies in this area, they are based on small numbers of cases and concentrate on understanding the problems rather than establishing their incidence. A different theme is introduced by Getzel and Masters (1984) in summarizing early work with relatives by the Victim Services Agency in New York. They report that, although dealing with acute grief reactions is a vital component, over 60 percent of service requests entail assistance with practical problems such as claims for compensation or other financial entitlements, advocacy, housing difficulties, and medical care. Their conclusion that "secondary victimization" is particularly severe in cases of homicide is echoed by a preliminary report on a multiagency project to help families of murder victims currently being developed by Victim Support in various parts of England (Victim Support 1988). Early findings are based on forty-three cases referred to the project by the police (out of a possible fifty-nine in the areas covered). The report lists several practical consequences which victims find particularly difficult to cope with, including heavy publicity (and sometimes hounding by journalists), postmortems, inquests, problems in getting the body released, and, above all, stressful court appearances. They might also have mentioned insensitive notification of death by the police, identifying the body, and making funeral arrangements (National Organization for Victim Assistance 1985*b*). Extreme anger can remain present for a very long time. Relatives often wish to become involved in legal decisions in their case or in general campaigns for victims' rights or capital punishment. Many are also anxious to share their feelings with others who have been through the same trauma (Rosenblott 1983; Getzel and Masters 1984; Rynearson 1984; Miller, Moore, and Lexius 1985).

3. *Rape*. The effects of rape have been closely documented in clinical studies (e.g., Burgess and Holmstrom 1974*a*, 1974*b*, 1976; Nadelson and Notman 1984) and in an increasing number of studies based on interviews with samples of rape victims (e.g., Kilpatrick, Veronen, and Resick 1979; McCahill, Meyer, and Fischmann 1979; Ellis 1983; Orlando and Koss 1983; Resick 1984; Cook, Smith, and Harrell 1987). Only a few of these studies have been based on samples of more than 100 victims and most have lacked a longitudinal element. The clinical studies have tended to use subjects referred because problems have been recognized, hence perhaps exaggerating their incidence among the full population of victims. Interview studies have been based on recorded offenses, thus overrepresenting "stranger" rapes, which are much more likely to be reported than those committed by acquaintances. Even so, there is now ample weight of evidence to show that quite a large proportion of victims undergo a great deal of prolonged suffering.

Common initial physical effects—quite apart from pain caused by direct injuries—include insomnia, nightmares, weight loss, menstrual irregularities, and general complaints such as dizziness, nausea, and muscle tension. There are also risks of pregnancy, venereal disease, and AIDS, which, even if they do not appear, cause immense anxiety. The psychological consequences have been found to be much longer lasting, common reactions including anger, depression, guilt and self-blame, feelings of helplessness, phobias, "flashbacks" to the event, and decreased sexual enjoyment. Equally frequent are major behavioral changes such as moving house, changing jobs, ceasing to go out, abuse of drugs or alcohol, and withdrawal from social contacts. Williams and Holmes (1981) reported that one in four in a sample drawn from police records moved house as the result of the attack. Burgess and Holmstrom (1976) reported that nineteen of forty-five subjects left their jobs within six weeks (see Katz and Mazur 1979, Burt and Katz 1985, and Mezey 1988 for more detailed reviews).

Early studies suggested that, for the majority of women, most of these symptoms tended to get resolved within a period of three to six months (Sutherland and Scherl 1970). Drawing, to some extent, on "crisis theory" (Caplan 1964), Burgess and Holmstrom (1974*a*) postulated the existence of a "rape trauma syndrome." This was manifested in two stages of reaction, labeled "disorganizational" and "reorganizational," which would normally last a few weeks and a few months, respectively. However, they also asserted that more severe and persistent reactions—a "compound" version of the syndrome—were to be found in some women, mainly those who had previous personality difficulties or psychiatric illness. This last point was later supported by larger studies using multivariate analysis: for instance, both Atkeson et al. (1982) and Sales, Baum, and Shore (1984) found "pre-rape symptoms" (measured by psychiatric history or other indicators of the victim's prior level of emotional stability) to be the best predictor of reactions to the event.

Even in the more serious cases, it was assumed by most early researchers and clinicians that the majority of victims would regain their equilibrium within a year or so. However, studies using longer follow-up periods were soon producing evidence of much longer-term effects, by no means restricted to those with prior problems. Patterns of recovery were found to be less smooth and predictable than previously thought, with recurrences of symptoms even years after the event (Kilpatrick and Veronen 1984); indeed, it was suggested that many victims may never "return to normal" (Ellis, Atkeson, and Calhoun 1981; Burt and Katz 1985). In most cases, of course, this implies permanent negative changes, such as recurrent depression, diminished enjoyment of life, or the formation of drug habits. Conversely, some researchers have reported more positive life changes in the long term, including enhanced clarity of goals in life and improved relationships with other women (Williams and Holmes 1981; Veronen and Kilpatrick 1983; Nadelson and Notman 1984).

Finally, while many writers have suggested that the consequences of rape are unique, a few studies have incorporated comparisons with other violent offenses that indicate that victims of the latter may suffer analogous problems. For example, Cook, Smith, and Harrell (1987) found that the "psychological distress" of victims of serious assault was lesser in degree but similar in type to that of victims of rape. Of course, a factor to be considered in comparing the impact of sexual and nonsexual assault is the gender of the victim. The majority of victims of nonsexual violence are male (or at least, of those known to the police; a great deal of domestic violence goes unreported and unrecorded), and most studies have concluded that, other circumstances being equal, women are likely to be more profoundly affected by victimization than men (Davis 1987). However, Resick (1985) found that, while male robbery victims appeared to "recover" more quickly than female victims of either robbery or rape, they reported greater interpersonal problems and showed a sharper decrease in self-esteem.

4. *Child Abuse.* A final category of victim for whom the long-term effects of crime are, without a doubt, often very serious is that of child abuse, both physical and sexual. It is difficult to separate the effects of the abuse from other factors of deprivation or other negative experiences that may be present. Moreover, although the two types of abuse are often separate, some researchers have suggested that violence may accompany sexual behavior in as many as 50 percent of cases (Muldoon 1979; Eve 1985). Even so, there is fairly widespread agreement that sexually abused children tend to exhibit somatic complaints, self-destructive behavior, and learning difficulties, while as adults they are likely to lead isolated lives, to suffer from depression and low self-esteem, to have problems in establishing normal sex lives, and to become involved in drugs, alcohol abuse, or prostitution (Steele and Alexander 1981; Browne and Finkelhor 1984; Conte 1985). Where physical violence is concerned, there has long been evidence of a "cycle of abuse" where children (particularly male) who have been regularly assaulted replicate the behavior on the next generation (Morris and Gould 1963; Kaufman 1985). It may be that similar replication occurs with victims of child sexual abuse (Goodwin 1982; Eve 1985).

III. Services to Victims: Delivery and Effectiveness

In this section, I examine problems facing organizations set up to provide assistance to victims, focusing on those aiming to deliver general welfare services across a broad range of offense types. Questions are asked about the nature and extent of need for such services and about ways of identifying and contacting those individuals in the greatest need. This is followed by a summary of findings related to the effectiveness of services, in particular the appropriateness of the kinds of help offered and the extent to which intervention can be claimed to make any difference. Finally, I look at the particular case of services to rape victims, where there are strong disagreements about the most suitable model of intervention.

A. *Issues in Service Delivery*

While research has greatly increased knowledge about the effects of crime, there remain many practical questions about the provision of services to victims that have yet to be answered conclusively. For example, how many victims should service agencies aim to assist? Given limited resources, how can they identify and reach those most in need? What kinds of services are most appropriate? And what evidence is there that intervention actually "works," in the sense of helping victims to recover in the short or long term, or of increasing their willingness to cooperate with the police and the criminal justice system?

While, in the early days of the victim movement, almost any form of help was seen as a bonus, expectations have risen enormously, and some writers are now arguing that victims have a "right" to proper welfare services (Mawby and Gill 1987). Moreover, victim assistance organizations have become much more professional in their philosophy and approach, and as they receive more government money, they are being asked to prove their efficiency and effectiveness in the use of that money (Corbett and Maguire 1988). These developments make it all the more important to look closely at the evidence relating to each of the above questions.

1. *Level of Need.* Perhaps the most fundamental question that has to be asked about victim assistance organizations concerns the level of need for their services. This affects major decisions about whether to aim for expansion of staff, to try new ways of advertising the available services, to target particular victim groups, and so on. It also affects their relations with funding bodies, who have to be convinced that they are spending money on a service that is necessary, particularly when being asked to pay for expansion.

As pointed out previously, however, "need" is a notoriously slippery concept, and it is immensely difficult to make a firm statement about the number of people who need, would accept, or would benefit from, specialist victim services. Clearly, such a figure cannot be calculated directly from measures of the effect of crime because, however badly victims are affected, they may receive adequate help from other sources, including family and friends. Most of the estimates quoted in the literature are based on interview studies in which respondents were asked what kinds of help they needed following victimization, and to what extent they received it from any source: the remaining "unmet needs" are then put forward as potential work for the specialist agency. This is an extremely crude technique, and it is not surprising that the results vary widely. For example, Brown and Yantzi (1980), Friedman et al. (1982), and Stuebing (1984) concluded, that 30 percent, 10 percent, and 47 percent, respectively, of their samples of victims of a range of medium-serious recorded offenses needed some form of counseling. These differences illustrate the extent to which the way questions are put can affect the results: as pointed out earlier, people do not always perceive needs if they have no knowledge or expectation of a service that might satisfy them. This is particularly true of the need for counseling, as victims may not even associate their current depression or anxiety with an event that occurred some time in the past. As Skogan, Davis, and Lurigio (1990) admit in a recent study of 470 victims of burglary, robbery, and assault, the somewhat leading question they put, "Did you need someone to talk to about the feelings that were troubling you?" was almost bound to produce a higher percentage of positive responses (28 percent in their study) than Friedman et al.'s (1982) question about a need for "counseling," a procedure less familiar to many.

The measurement of practical needs is equally problematic, and estimates of their incidence again vary widely. For example, 39 percent of Friedman et al.'s sample said that they had needed help with changing or repairing locks and 27 percent that they had needed an immediate cash loan, while Brown and Yantzi (1980), with a broadly comparable sample, came up with figures of 27 percent and 8 percent, respectively. Such differences seem to have been caused partly by differences in how the questions were asked (including the degree of prompting) and partly by confusions about the meaning of "need" in this context. Certainly, many people would like and appreciate assistance of this kind, but the great majority will eventually achieve the repairs or recover financially with or without the assistance of a victim support agency. Thus, the time scale is vital to definition and measurement: the level of "unmet need" will change considerably over time.

Generally speaking, the practical needs that have emerged from the literature as most common have been help with repairs or security (probably reflecting the high representation of burglaries in research samples), information about the progress of cases, and advice or assistance in relation to financial problems, including insurance or compensation claims. It is difficult to make a general statement about the overall level of such needs, or even about their frequency in relation to each other, not least because different types of crime cause the victim different practical problems. As there have been several fairly detailed studies of recorded offenses of burglary, robbery, and assault, however, some tentative conclusions can be reached in relation to these crimes. Defining a practical need as a concrete problem that will remain unresolved for at least three weeks (and excluding the desire for information about the progress of police investigations), I have elsewhere estimated from interviews that about a quarter of burglary victims and 10–15 percent of victims of assault or robbery can be said to have such a need (Maguire and Corbett 1987). Support for this estimate was found in the 1984 British Crime Survey, where about 30 percent of victims of burglary and wounding who had reported the incident to the police stated that at least one of a list of possible needs had remained unresolved (those most frequently mentioned being advice about compensation, crime prevention, legal matters, and insurance). Friedman et al. (1982), too, came up with an overall figure of 30 percent of burglary and robbery victims with "unfulfilled needs"; and while their report does not give a global figure of this kind, the findings presented in Skogan, Davis, and Lurigio (1990) suggest a fairly similar conclusion. More concretely, 18 percent of the burglary victims in Maguire and Corbett's (1987) sample who had been visited unannounced said that the volunteer had provided genuinely helpful practical assistance.

Finally, as there is a considerable overlap between victims who express practical and emotional needs (and, anyway, as Shapland, Willmore, and Duff [1985] point out, the distinction is by no means always clear), estimates of the overall level of need for victim services are not much higher than those quoted above. After considering the available evidence from surveys and interview studies, Maguire and Corbett (1987) came to the very broad conclusion that 30–40 percent of victims of the "medium serious" offenses mentioned above could be said to need—or at least would, prima facie, benefit from—some form of help they would not readily obtain elsewhere. Such an estimate was in accord with the subjective experience of several victim support volunteers they interviewed, who felt that they had been needed in 40 percent of the visits they made. Rape and homicide, by contrast, almost always cause such psychological damage that it is wisest to assume that every survivor is a potential case for support. Finally, considering the full range of recorded crimes, Maguire and Corbett (1987) tentatively put the proportion of victims who might benefit from a visit at around 10 percent. However, they stress that there are serious doubts about the validity of attaching any kind of figure to such a subjective concept as "need" in this context.

2. *Methods of Reaching Victims.* In the United States, while victim-witness assistance programs usually contact the people they help through prosecutors' offices, many other service providers have relied on victims to "refer themselves" via systems such as telephone hotlines. The self-referral method obviously gives a chance to a much wider range of victims to avail themselves of help, as it does not depend on the arrest and prosecution of an offender. Hotline services will also normally accept requests from victims who have not reported an offense to the police. When one looks at "take-up rates" for services offered in this way, however, in comparison with the research findings on the effects of crime and victims' needs described above, the discrepancy is large enough to suggest that the great majority of victims who might need help "slip through the net." For example, despite the high incidence of fear and distress reported to researchers by samples of burglary and robbery victims in New York (Friedman et al. 1982), Davis and Henley (1990) inform us that only 2 percent of victims of recorded crime in that city contact the Victim Services Agency for assistance. Even allowing for the facts that the full recorded crime load contains many minor offenses, and that many victims receive help from other sources, this seems an unexpectedly low take-up rate.

Leaving aside the possibility that victims have grossly exaggerated their needs when speaking to researchers—although it is a possibility that certainly exists—the explanation may lie in the reluctance of many victims to ask for help even when they would almost certainly accept it if it were offered directly. This is reflected in the dramatic differences found by Maguire and Corbett (1987) in victims' responses to offers of help made by letter or personal visit. Over 90 percent of those visited "out of the blue" by a victims support scheme volunteer invited the caller in for a talk, and over half of these discussed their feelings in some depth or requested some practical assistance. Letters to victims produced a request for help in no more than 7 percent of cases. The failure to respond, the researchers speculate, may be due partly to lack of knowledge about the kinds of services available, partly to inertia or lack of time, and partly to a common aversion to "asking for charity" (see also Kilpatrick 1983; Reeves 1985).

Efforts have been made by some agencies in the United States to improve take-up rates by means of outreach in the form of letters or telephone calls to selected victims but, as in the United Kingdom, these methods of approach have usually been found to generate relatively few requests for services (Friedman et al. 1982; Skogan and Wycoff 1987). Indeed, the Minneapolis Crime Victim Crisis Center greatly reduced its outreach program after concluding from a poor response that it had overestimated the need for crisis intervention (Chesney and Schneider 1981). It was also found that outreach was expensive in terms of staff time. Similarly, Skogan, Davis, and Lurigio (1990) describe four schemes in which outreach, though still valued, produces low take-up rates. The study provides a little more insight into the possible reasons for this. Samples of those who failed to respond were interviewed by the researchers, who found that while one-half had not replied because they had received all the help they needed from elsewhere, over one-quarter had had no time or transportation to go to the program and most of the remainder had either felt that it "could not give me the help I really needed" or had felt "uncomfortable with participating."

In Britain, in stark contrast to the United States, outreach has always been the standard form of service delivery, and its general efficacy is rarely questioned. In 1989, victims support schemes offered help directly to about 400,000 people (Victim Support 1989*a*). Their normal method of working entails the coordinator telephoning the local police each morning to obtain the details and names and addresses of victims of offenses recorded during the previous twenty-four hours.[3] The coordinator then decides whether to dispatch volunteers to the victim's home, to telephone, or to write offering the scheme's services. The majority of victims are sent letters, but over one-third are visited unannounced. (Victim Support [1989*a*] gives a figure of 37 percent.) Telephone calls are more unusual, as it is generally felt that this method of contact can cause worry and suspicion. Relatively few letters generate requests for assistance, but the strength and unique flavor of the victim support movement stems from the unsolicited visits—its "trademark" since its origins in 1974. It is by presenting oneself on the doorstep as a "good neighbor," it is argued, that "the victim is protected from the

[3] It may be thought that many victims would object to the police passing on details without permission and to volunteers calling uninvited at their homes. (In West Germany, indeed, these procedures are illegal.) However, the number of complaints received has been minimal, rarely amounting to more than three or four per year, even in the largest schemes; Maguire and Corbett (1987) found that well over 80 percent of those visited actively welcomed the call.

necessity of having to ask for help" (Reeves 1985, p. 685); hence the acceptance rate for offers of help is increased dramatically.

3. *Selection of Victims to Contact.* Neither the contacting of large numbers of victims nor the acceptance of services by a high proportion of those contacted necessarily means that a victim assistance agency is using its resources in an effective manner. Those helped may be in much less need than many who are not contacted. To put the work of victims support schemes in perspective, it is useful to regard it as the final stage of a huge "filtering" process (Maguire 1989). It can be calculated from survey results that there are at least 12 million personal and household offenses committed each year in England and Wales. Only about 2.5 million of these are eventually recorded by the police; the police refer about 400,000 of the recorded offenses to schemes; coordinators select about 140,000 of the referred victims for visits by volunteers; and about 90,000 people actually receive some kind of service in the end, if only a brief talk with the visitor (Maguire 1989). Assuming for a moment that this last figure represents roughly the number of victims that schemes can handle in a year with current resources, what remains to be discovered is the extent to which the "lucky" 90,000 (under one percent of the original 12 million) overlap with the 90,000 most in need of support.

This question is impossible to answer with any confidence, although some indications can be obtained from the research on needs and effects described above as well as from the experience of practitioners. In Britain, victims support schemes have gradually revised their priorities as their knowledge has grown. The first scheme in Bristol began by receiving large numbers of referrals of minor and "medium range" offenses and visited their victims indiscriminately. However, it was quickly discovered that only a small proportion of victims of minor theft required any help. Subsequently, the Bristol program and most of its successors gave priority to victims of residential burglary, often dropping minor theft referrals altogether. In the early 1980s, about 90 percent of all referrals involved this offense, and it would not then have been too great an exaggeration to describe most of the groups as "burglary victims support schemes." More recently, they have greatly expanded their services to victims of rape and other major violent crime, and although burglary still constitutes the "bread and butter" work of most schemes, it now represents only 67 percent of referrals (Victim Support 1989*a*). The picture may change further as more and more schemes are finding it necessary to provide long-term—and hence resource-intensive—support to victims of the major crimes. The pressure of work is now forcing some of the larger schemes to consider whether the time consumed by volunteers making unsolicited visits to the homes of large numbers of burglary victims represents an ineffective use of scarce resources.

The research evidence outlined earlier suggests that burglary produces a need for assistance in a fairly high proportion of cases—although markedly lower than rape and serious assault—hence it justifies attention. The offense is a very common one, however, and in order not to be swamped by burglaries at the expense of victims of more serious offenses, the problem is to identify which particular burglary victims most require help. The odds against finding them may be shortened by concentrating on, for example, the elderly or those living alone, but these are not very reliable indicators, and anyway the necessary information on age or household composition may not be mentioned in police reports. In practice, the decision whether to send a volunteer quite often comes down to a "hunch" on the part of the coordinator (Maguire and Corbett 1987).

More than this, it has to be remembered that schemes receive only a selection of all possible offenses from the police. Each scheme has a general agreement with the police as to what kinds of cases will be referred. The most satisfactory system is known as "automatic referral," whereby the names and addresses of all victims in preagreed categories are passed to the scheme. Many schemes still leave considerable discretion with a centrally based police officer, however, who selects cases on the basis of the circumstances of the crime or the characteristics of the victim. In a few areas, too, it is left to patrol officers to recommend people for referral, based on their observations at the scenes of crimes. These latter systems are vulnerable to officers' idiosyncracies and prejudices, resulting in uneven flows of referrals and sometimes the exclusion of groups, such as young male victims of violence, who may be considered "undeserving" of help (Maguire and Corbett 1987).

Despite an inevitable degree of arbitrariness in the selection processes used by schemes, Maguire and Corbett found that, as a group, their sample of victims of burglary, robbery, and assault who were visited by a volunteer rated themselves significantly worse affected than did a sample of victims in the same offense categories who had *not* been visited (see table 1). Similar findings have been reported concerning those who seek help through self-referral to American assistance programs (Friedman et al. 1982; Davis 1987). Even so, Maguire and Corbett found that too many schemes failed to assist victims in the greatest need of all (those hit by murder or rape), and that some categories of victims, potentially in considerable need of help according to research results, tended to be systematically excluded from referral. These included young male victims of street violence, victims of threats, and victims of a series of minor crimes such as "vandalism," which often amounts to a campaign of harassment or persecution (see also Jones, Maclean, and Young 1986; Genn 1988). To their credit, schemes are responding quite quickly to the gaps that have been identified and Victim Support is engaged, through working parties and demonstration projects, in a continuing reassessment of its priorities. The biggest change has been in the development of services to rape victims, but experiments are also being carried out in relation to homicide, racial harassment, and child victims (Victim Support 1988, 1989*a*, 1989*b*).

B. *Appropriateness and Effectiveness of Services*

Leaving aside the question of who receives services, how effective are those that are provided? Evaluations are still in their infancy, but some interesting findings have emerged. The two main questions are whether the type of assistance given is appropriate to victims' needs and wishes and whether the intervention succeeds in ameliorating the effects of crime.

1. *Practical Help or Counseling?* A number of American studies on the first of these questions suggest that there may be some misjudgment by service agencies of what victims really need and want. For example, Brown and Yantzi (1980), Friedman et al. (1982), and Skogan, Davis, and Lurigio (1990) found that assistance with repairs and security improvements, together with emergency financial assistance, were among the most common practical needs expressed by burglary victims in particular, but, as Davis and Henley (1990) point out, these services are not often provided by victim programs in the United States. They quote a survey of 184 programs by Roberts (1987) that found that only 13 percent provided help with security improvements and 24 percent provided emergency financial aid.

This raises a broader question about the relative emphasis that should be placed on practical and emotional forms of assistance or support. Victim surveys clearly find practical needs more frequently expressed than emotional needs (Hough 1985; Maguire and Corbett 1987), but interview studies differ in assessments of their relative importance. Skogan, Davis, and Lurigio (1990) found the need for help with practical problems less likely to be met by friends and neighbors than the need for psychological support. They also found that, even among people who had been assisted by victim programs, practical problems often remained unresolved. Moreover, many victims did not receive assistance until several days or even weeks after the crime, by which time it was often too late to help. Noting the priority usually given by staff and volunteers to counseling, they speak of a "mismatch" between the needs of victims and services they actually receive.

Maguire and Corbett (1987) come to different conclusions, however. Both their study and Maguire (1980) indicate that victims themselves regard the emotional impact as the worst aspect of the incident. These findings, they argue, together with high victim satisfaction levels with the service provided, support the contention of victims support schemes that what is most needed is what they primarily aim to provide—a "listening ear" to allow victims to express fears, anger, and worries about the crime.

Part of the explanation for these differing conclusions may lie in differences in practice and tradition of the two countries. While supporters in the United States are often either paid workers or volunteers thoroughly trained in counseling skills, victims support schemes in Britain have traditionally used volunteers without professional skills or prolonged training. The latter have preferred to present themselves as sympathetic good neighbors rather than as counselors, referring to professional agencies those cases in which more specialized help is deemed appropriate (Reeves 1985; Maguire and Corbett 1987; Mawby and Gill 1987). Although this is changing somewhat in relation to rape and murder, the principle remains strongly held at the grass-roots level. It is also stressed in volunteer training in Britain that emotional support is enhanced through practical assistance, and help with repairs, insurance and compensation claims, and crime prevention are fairly routinely offered. The opportunity for helping in this way is increased by the fact that most visits take place within two days of the crime—the period in which, Maguire and Corbett found, the majority of victims report their needs to be greatest. By contrast, it may be that in the United States, as Davis and Henley (1990) imply, the emphasis on counseling skills in service practice, encouraged by the prominence in the literature of mental health professionals writing about major crime, has led to a tendency to overestimate the proportion of cases in which such skills are really needed and quite often to employ them inappropriately at the expense of more mundane "problem fixing." Nevertheless, while this may justify some change of emphasis in American practice, the British findings suggest that caution should be exercised against "throwing out the baby with the bathwater" by moving too far toward a service geared to practical assistance.

2. *Does Victim Assistance "Work"?* The final, and probably most important, question to be asked in any evaluation of victim assistance is whether there is any evidence that it works, in the sense of aiding or accelerating the victim's recovery or perhaps by limiting the damage in more intangible ways. Certainly, if one takes the word of victims, the answer seems to be in the affirmative. Interviews with the consumers of the kinds of generalist welfare services we have been describing have usually revealed high levels of satisfaction. For example, in Maguire and Corbett's (1987) study, 87 percent of those who had been visited by volunteers made positive comments and only 6 percent expressed any dissatisfaction. Moreover, 82 percent said that they had "felt better" or "had their mind eased" after the visit; 12 percent stated that it had made a "very big difference"; and 50 percent "some difference" as to how they coped with the emotional consequences of the crime. Chesney and Schneider (1981), Norquay and Weiler (1981), and Skogan, Davis, and Lurigio (1990) also reported a considerable degree of appreciation for the help given.

Nevertheless, whether these kinds of services will ever be shown conclusively to make a significant difference to recovery, particularly over the long term, remains in considerable doubt. As Davis (1987) points out, the majority of interventions entail only one visit by or to the victim, while Maguire and Corbett (1987) found the average length of visits by victim support volunteers to be only half an hour. This being the case, one would hardly expect the typical intervention to have a dramatic or lasting effect in enough cases to show up statistically. Indeed, studies comparing samples of victims who have and have not received crisis assistance have generally failed to find any clear differences between them in their psychological state over either the short or the long term. For example, Cook, Smith, and Harrell (1987) compared a group of victims to whom the police had sent a caseworker from the Pima County Victim/Witness Advocate Program with a group not selected for the program. They found no difference between the two groups a few weeks later on any of their measures of "trauma," although they noted that many victims felt that the program had helped them—a finding consistent with that of Maguire and Corbett (1987). A serious weakness of the study, however, was the strong likelihood that the victims selected by the police were worse affected as a group, having been picked out because they seemed in need of help. A much sounder study design was reported in Davis (1987), whose project team assigned 249 victims randomly to either a crisis intervention program or to a control group. The former received counseling or practical help where appropriate, the latter no assistance. Three months later, the researchers found no differences between the two groups on measures of "material adjustment" or on standard psychological scales.

There are, however, a few indications elsewhere of both positive and negative results of intervention, although the findings are not statistically reliable. On the negative side, Steinmetz (1987, 1989) found higher levels of anxiety and stress among victims who had been "helped" by Dutch support schemes than among a group of victims who had not been helped. He speculated that this was because many of the problems of victims of domestic violence in particular, who formed a large proportion of the samples, were incapable of resolution by the support workers, but the victims' hopes had been falsely raised by the offer of help. Unfortunately, the case selection was not random, so the two groups are not strictly comparable. Finally, Maguire and Corbett (1987) produced positive findings from the point of view of victims support schemes. Using twenty-six matched "pairs" of victims, each consisting of one who had and one who had not been visited by a volunteer, they found considerably less anger and hostility three to six weeks after the crime among the twenty-six who had received support. The authors stress, however, that the samples are too small to draw statistically valid conclusions.

These generally negative, or at least inconclusive, findings may be disheartening to workers in the victim services field, but they do not constitute a serious argument for cutting funds to programs. After all, there is no clear clinical or statistical evidence that prolonged counseling by professionals in the mental health field ultimately makes any difference to the recovery of people in serious trauma, whether from crime or any other major crisis (Auerbach and Kilman 1978; Salasin 1981; Mezey 1988). Furthermore, some would argue that victims' own beliefs and perceptions about the value of support are as important as any more objective measure. This view is implicit in the early philosophy of victims support schemes in Britain, which set out first and foremost to make a gesture of "good neighborliness," their main value lying in the demonstration that "someone cares" (Gay, Holtom, and

Thomas 1975; Holtom and Raynor 1988) and one of the main aims being to restore victims' faith in others or help them "regain a sense of community" (van Dijk 1986). The inference is that the value of victim support lies, first and foremost, in its very existence and its tender of an offer of help, and that further demonstration of "effectiveness" is a bonus. Of course, this argument becomes less easy to sustain once, as has happened, major amounts of public money are invested; then the language of "service delivery," "value for money," and "effectiveness" begins to be heard loudly.

C. Services to Rape Victims: Alternative Approaches

A discussion of welfare services to victims would be incomplete without mention of the special case of assistance to women who have been raped. Arguments about the most appropriate form of intervention have been fiercest in this area, and a variety of approaches are in use. A certain amount of work with rape victims has been undertaken by psychiatrists, but there are good reasons why this is unusual. First, many psychiatrists are unfamiliar with the specific problems associated with the offense and may have nothing more to offer than, for example, experienced volunteers working with rape crisis centers or victims support schemes (Durlak 1979; Coates and Watson 1983; Corbett and Hobdell 1988). Second, it is by no means clear that psychiatric help is appropriate, especially at an early stage: raped women are not "ill" but are undergoing a normal response to a terrifying, often life-threatening, event. Moreover, referral to a psychiatrist could well compound the sense of being stigmatized as a result of being raped (Mezey 1988).

This does not mean that no form of counseling is necessary. On the contrary, it is widely believed—if as yet unproven by research—that sensitive and understanding support at an early stage not only can alleviate the initial effect but also can reduce the chances of major long-term effects. It is generally agreed as well that the principal aim of such intervention should be to provide a reassuring, believing, and nonjudgmental presence, giving the woman every opportunity to "talk through" her fear and anger. This may be accompanied by practical assistance, for example, with arranging tests for venereal disease or finding temporary accommodation.

Following pilot projects in the late 1970s (McCombie et al. 1976) and a recommendation by the 1982 President's Task Force on Victims of Crime, there has been growth in the United States in professionally staffed rape crisis services based in large hospitals (Duddle 1985; Mezey

1987). However, the bulk of work with rape victims in the United States, and virtually all in the United Kingdom, is still undertaken by trained volunteers. This is provided in a number of distinct styles and in accordance with differing philosophies.

Rape crisis centers have traditionally provided counseling and advice over the telephone, although they will arrange face-to-face meetings if the caller wishes. They usually offer a twenty-four-hour hotline service, accepting calls from women who have been in any way sexually abused, recently or in the distant past, whether or not they have reported the matter to the police: indeed, some have actively discouraged women from becoming involved with the police. They are careful to leave all decision making about further contacts with the center to the "survivor," this being consistent with a central aim of encouraging women to regain a sense of self-esteem and self-determination. The work of many rape crisis centers is guided by a radical feminist perspective that has distanced them from most other agencies. Although in some cities mutually beneficial accommodations have been reached with the police or other victim service groups, on the whole rape crisis centers have ploughed a lone but effective furrow with limited financial resources (Amir and Amir 1979; London Rape Crisis Centre 1979; Gornick, Burt, and Pittman 1983; Anna "T." 1988).

In Britain, services to rape victims are increasingly being provided by victims support schemes. This has been a relatively recent development for most schemes as it was received wisdom for some years that volunteers were insufficiently trained to take on such victims—despite the fact that rape crisis centers, often with even less training, had been doing so for years—and that the long-term support they were likely to need was incompatible with the philosophy of providing only short-term or crisis intervention. Moreover, even when they wished to become involved, schemes were often refused access to rape victims by the police, who doubted the capacity of volunteers to deal with them competently. As schemes do not normally operate hotlines (the vast majority—around 98 percent—of the victims they see are referred by the police), this constituted a major obstacle to development.

Schemes gradually identified serious gaps in the available services and began to react more forcefully, however. First, although rape crisis centers were already counseling large numbers of women, it was argued that others were unwilling to contact the centers owing to their radical feminist image (Corbett and Hobdell 1988). Second, the idea that victims with special needs could be referred to professional social work or mental health agencies for counseling proved in practice grossly overoptimistic: many such agencies either pleaded pressure of work or had no staff with the relevant expertise in the effects of sexual crime. Consequently, a number of schemes with volunteers who had counseling experience in other fields persuaded the local police to refer rape victims, on the understanding that they would be supported by these better-qualified helpers. Over time, particularly in London (Corbett and Hobdell 1988), such volunteers built up a reservoir of skills, knowledge, and experience unrivaled even in the few professional agencies with an interest in the area. Their lead was followed by increasing numbers of schemes, and a standard training manual has recently been produced by NAVSS (Victim Support 1989*a*). In the fiscal year 1988–89, 1,324 rape victims were referred to schemes—45 percent of the complainants in all rapes recorded by the police in England and Wales (Victim Support 1989*a*).

The approach adopted by scheme volunteers in supporting rape victims differs from that of rape crisis centers in that feminist ideology is largely absent, the services are personally offered to victims rather than waiting for the latter to make contact, and regular long-term support is encouraged. Critics have argued that raped women are treated too much like passive recipients of "treatment" and that there is a danger of creating dependency on the volunteer. These messages have clearly been received, however, and strenuous efforts have been made by Victim Support at the local and national levels to avoid these pitfalls through training in nondirective counseling. National training standards have been drawn up, and few if any volunteers are now allowed to take on cases without attending special courses (Victim Support 1989*b*).

A final kind of service to rape victims has been offered by self-help organizations, which tend to use the techniques of group meetings to share experiences. Proponents claim that these not only provide a less institutional and more personalized response than state-sponsored programs but also avoid false assumptions made by those who have not experienced the offense about the mental state of victims and hence about the treatment that is best for them (Chelimsky 1981; Katz 1981; Coates and Watson 1983; B. Smith 1985). Victim Support has argued that there is a danger in self-help groups of reinforcing peoples' identity as victims, which goes against the aim of reintegrating them into normal life (Mawby and Gill 1987).

In the absence of any convincing research to show that any one response to serious victimization of this kind is more effective than any other (or, indeed, than no response) in reducing the negative consequences, it is very difficult, except on ideological grounds, to make any judgment about their relative merits. The absence of any strong research-backed orthodoxy may be regarded as beneficial, in that there is less of a threat to the coexistence of a number of alternative programs, each perhaps appropriate for women of different temperaments or beliefs.

IV. Concluding Remarks

In many respects, the short history of the victims' movement can be said to represent a success story from the point of view of its proponents. They have clearly succeeded in putting victims on the political agenda; they can point to real reforms that are backed up by legislation; and, although many small groups, in the United States particularly, have come and gone, organizations offering welfare services to victims are much better established, more securely funded, and better "connected" (both with each other and with official agencies) than would have seemed possible twenty years ago.

While the old cry of "something should be done for victims" has become out of date, the questions remain whether what is now being done represents the best use of the good will and the resources that have been won, whether political commitment to the victim's cause will remain at its present high level, and whether the more controversial directions in which some members of the movement would like to see it progress deserve the support of uncommitted outsiders.

Welfare services constitute probably the least controversial area of the victims' debate. Even so, they involve the expenditure of large sums of public and private money and if they are ineffectively presented, inappropriate to victims' true needs, or delivered to the "wrong" victims, strong criticism is in order. The research findings presented here are inconclusive on these scores, although it is fairly clear that the problem of identifying and contacting those in the greatest need has not yet been solved satisfactorily. Methods that rely on victims themselves contacting an assistance program to ask for help—even when they have been sent a letter inviting them to do so—produce very low take-up rates, while direct referrals from the police and unsolicited visits to selected homes reflect possibly false assumptions on the part of those making the choices about the kinds of people who need (or even "deserve") help. It is interesting that victim services in Britain started at the "less serious" end. Many schemes excluded survivors of rape, homicide, and other grave offenses as well as people suffering continuing victimization such as domestic violence and racial harassment and have only recently begun to give these the priority over burglary and theft that they almost certainly merit. In the United States, by contrast, the major crimes received attention from the start, but a possible negative consequence of this has been an exaggeration of the need for professional counseling, allowing insufficient recognition of the value of simple practical help and the sympathetic presence of a volunteer to victims of less serious crimes. Government-funded services in the United States, too, were handicapped for several years by the overriding importance attached to getting victims to testify in court—a factor that not only excluded the majority who were not required in court, but often blinded those running the programs to their clients' own expressed needs and wishes.

The future of victim services certainly looks more secure than in the past, but the level at which they will be maintained is unclear. In Britain, Victim Support has often expressed the goal of contacting, at least by letter, the victim of every recorded personal or household offense (recently, too, there are moves to include small businesses hit by crime). Whether the organization can convince the government to provide the considerable funds needed to achieve this aim is in doubt, as the need for such a comprehensive service has not been established. Many other social service agencies and voluntary groups can make equally or more convincing cases for funds to meet other pressing needs: should victims come before the sick, the homeless, the handicapped, and so on? Moreover, until some hard evidence, beyond the satisfaction of those who have received the service, can be found that victim support actually alleviates the effects of crime, the success of the organization in maintaining or increasing funding will depend on the insecure foundation of political lobbying. If victims "go out of fashion" in the political world, Victim Support will have few cards left to play.

Where victims' rights are concerned, the future is equally unclear. State compensation is now widely accepted as a proper response to victims of serious violence, but governments have generally been careful to ensure that eligibility is hedged around with sufficient restrictions to keep expenditure from getting out of hand. There are few countries—New Zealand being a notable exception (Miers 1978)—where compensation is a statutory right, and fewer still where it is extended to other categories of victim. The symbolic value of having a compensation scheme is probably strong enough to maintain the gains that have been achieved, but recent experience in the United Kingdom, where the government seems to be having second thoughts about putting the criminal injuries compensation scheme on a statutory footing, suggests that further major advances are unlikely.

Developments in other areas associated with victims' rights are interesting, not so much from the funding angle but in their implications for principles of justice and the rights of offenders. Several legal commentators have expressed misgivings about developments such as "victim impact statements" and restitution from offender to victim. It is argued that the sentencing of offenders is founded on long established notions of culpability and intent, which are quite different from the sometimes fortuitous effect of the crime on the victim; to take the latter into account or to treat restitution as a sentence in its own right is to confuse civil and criminal law, and hasty or ill-thought-out changes could have serious and undesirable consequences for the whole legal system (Gitler 1984; Ashworth 1986; Duff 1988). Some critics have also seen the demand for victim participation in criminal justice as part of a conservative law-and-order political agenda (Henderson 1985; see also Fattah 1986). Writers such as Davis, Kunreuther, and Connick (1984) and Kelly (1990) have countered such arguments with evidence that few victims actually exercise their rights, while those who do so are often far less vindictive than expected. French and West German victims have always had a right to a say in court, through the systems of *partie civile* (mainly geared to restitution claims) and *Nebenkläger* (which allows penal demand to be made). Neither of these countries has notably punitive penal policies, and the strengthening of both systems in recent years does not seem to have created many problems or aroused serious opposition (Maguire and Shapland 1990). Even so, the possibility remains of a gradual undermining of the basic principles of justice that protect accused persons, and vigilance and caution are clearly demanded before rushing into superficially desirable reforms to promote the victim's cause.

Finally, clashes of interests are also evident in the areas of intrafamilial crime, particularly domestic violence, where demands for mandatory arrest and prosecution have been heeded in several American states (Friedman and Shulman 1990), and child sexual abuse. In the latter field, outrage at the effects on victims has fueled a trend away from informal welfare-based approaches toward the prosecution and imprisonment of offending male relatives (Summit and Kryso 1978; Chapman and Smith 1988; Smith 1990), even though there is no evidence that the court solution has any beneficial effects on the children and may, indeed, damage them further (Goodman, Golding, and Haith 1984; Goldstein 1987). This, in turn, has led to calls for safeguards to accused persons to be relaxed by allowing children to give evidence on video rather than in court (e.g., Adler 1988), another move that gives pause for thought about its implications for basic principles of justice.

Whether the shift in attitudes and the initiatives described in this essay really herald the beginning of a long-lasting "sea of change" in responses to crime across most of the Western world (and perhaps beyond—see Waller 1988) is impossible to say at this time. However, what the "victims' movement," however defined, has achieved within a short space of time can only be described as remarkable, and there are few signs of a waning of enthusiasm. In the short term, what remains particularly interesting is whether the very different approaches that have been adopted in different countries will give way to a broad international consensus on policies toward victims. Certainly, prominent members of the victims' movement, through international organizations, journals, and regular conferences involving academics and practitioners alike, are now well informed about developments in many countries, and a considerable amount of cross-fertilization has occurred. Thus there are signs in the United States, where the struggle for rights has dominated the movement, of a greater interest in generalist welfare services for victims, while the reverse process is taking place in Britain, where welfare has previously remained the priority. Above all, however, the international impetus—and the development of consensus—is being maintained by important agreements in such bodies as the Council of Europe and the United Nations, where a series of conventions and guidelines and a major declaration have established sets of general principles that individual countries are taking steps to implement (Council of Europe 1987; Waller 1988; Maguire and Shapland 1990; United Nations 1990). All this is a far cry from the poorly funded local groups of volunteers and campaigners who started the movement off less than twenty years ago.

REFERENCES

Adler, S. 1988. "Prosecuting Child Sexual Abuse: A Challenge to the Status Quo." In *Victims of Crime: A New Deal?* edited by M. Maguire and J. Pointing. Milton Keynes: Open University Press.

Amir, M., and D. Amir. 1979. "Rape Crisis Centres: An Arena for Ideological Conflicts." *Victimology* 4:247–57.

Anna "T." 1988. "Feminist Responses to Sexual Abuse: The Work of the Birmingham Rape Crisis Centre." In *Victims of Crime: A New Deal?* edited by M. Maguire and J. Pointing. Milton Keynes: Open University Press.

Appley, M., and R. Trumbull. 1967. *Psychological Stress: Issues in Research*. Englewood Cliffs, N.J.: Prentice-Hall.

Armstrong, P. 1982. "The Myth of Meeting Needs in Adult Education and Community Development." *Critical Social Policy* 2(2):24–37.

Ash, M. 1972. "On Witnesses: A Radical Critique of Criminal Court Procedures." *Notre Dame Lawyer* 48:386–425.

Ashworth, A. 1986. "Punishment and Compensation: Victims, Offenders and the State." *Oxford Journal of Legal Studies* 6:86–122.

Atkeson, B., K. Calhoun, P. Resick, and M. Ellis. 1982. "Victims of Rape: Repeated Assessments of Depression." *Journal of Consulting and Clinical Psychology* 50(1):96–102.

Auerbach, S., and P. Kilman. 1978. "Crisis Intervention: A Review of Outcome Research." *Psychological Bulletin* 84:1189–1217.

Baker, A., and S. Duncan. 1985. "Child Sex Abuse: A Study of Prevalence in Great Britain." *Child Abuse and Neglect* 9:457–67.

Baluss, M. 1975. *Integrated Services for Victims of Crime*. Washington, D.C.: National Association of Counties.

Bard, M., and D. Sangrey. 1979. *The Crime Victims' Book*. New York: Basic.

Barkas, J. 1978. *Victims*. New York: Scribner's.

Beard, D. 1988. "Congress Begins Review of Victim Service Programs." *NOVA Newsletter*. (February). Washington, D.C.: National Organization for Victim Assistance.

Berger, M. 1980. *Taking the Fifth*. Lexington, Mass.: Heath.

Biderman, A., L. Johnson, J. McIntyre, and A. Weir. 1967. *Report on a Pilot Study in the District of Columbia on Victimization and Attitudes towards Law Enforcement*. President's Commission on Law Enforcement and Administration of Justice, Field Surveys I. Washington, D.C.: U.S. Government Printing Office.

Binney, V., G. Harkell, and J. Nixon. 1985. "Refuges and Housing for Battered Women." In *Private Violence and Public Policy*, edited by J. Pahl. London: Routledge & Kegan Paul.

Blagg, H. 1985. "Reparation and Justice: The Corby Experience." *British Journal of Criminology* 25:1–15.

Blair, I. 1985. *Investigating Rape*. Beckenham, Kent: Croom Helm.

Bolin, D. 1980. "The Pima County Victim Witness Program: Analyzing Its Success." *Evaluating Change* (special issue), pp. 120–26.

Bourque, B., G. Brumback, R. Krug, and L. Richardson. 1978. *Crisis Intervention: Investigating the Need for New Applications*. Washington, D.C.: American Institutes for Research.

Breen, B., and D. Rottman. 1985. *Crime Victimisation in the Republic of Ireland*. Paper no. 121. Dublin: Economic and Social Research Unit.

Brown, S., and M. Yantzi. 1980. *Needs Assessment for Victims and Witnesses of Crime*. Ontario: Mennonite Central Committee.

Browne, A., and D. Finkelhor. 1984. *The Impact of Child Sexual Abuse: A Review of the Research.* Durham: University of New Hampshire, Family Violence Research Program.

Burgess, A. 1975. "Family Reactions to Homicide." *American Journal of Orthopsychiatry* 45(3):391–98.

Burgess, A., and L. Holmstrom. 1974*a*. "Rape Trauma Syndrome." *American Journal of Psychiatry* 131:981–86.

———. 1974*b*. *Rape: Victims of Crisis.* Bowie, Md.: Brady.

———. 1976. "Coping Behavior of the Rape Victim." *American Journal of Orthopsychiatry* 46(2):413–17.

Burt, M., and B. Katz. 1985. "Rape, Robbery and Burglary: Responses to Actual and Feared Criminal Victimization, with Special Focus on Women and the Elderly." *Victimology* 10:325–58.

Canadian Federal-Provincial Task Force. 1983. *Justice for Victims of Crime.* Ottawa: Canadian Government Publishing Centre.

Caplan, G. 1964. *Principles of Preventive Psychiatry.* London: Tavistock.

Carrington, F., and G. Nicholson. 1984. "The Victims' Movement: An Idea Whose Time Has Come." *Pepperdine Law Review* 11:1–13.

Chambers, G., and A. Millar. 1983. *Investigating Sexual Assault.* Edinburgh: H.M. Stationery Office, Scottish Office.

Chapman, J., and B. Smith. 1988. *Child Sexual Abuse: An Analysis of Case Processing.* Washington, D.C.: American Bar Association.

Chelimsky, E. 1981. "Serving Victims: Agency Incentives and Individual Needs." In *Evaluating Victim Services*, edited by S. Salasin. Beverly Hills, Calif.: Sage.

Chesney, S., and C. Schneider. 1981. "Crime Victim Crisis Centers: The Minnesota Experience." In *Perspectives on Crime Victims*, edited by B. Galaway and J. Hudson. St. Louis: Mosby.

Christie, N. 1977. "Conflicts as Property." *British Journal of Criminology* 17:4–17.

Coates, D., and T. Watson. 1983. "Counteracting the Deviance of Depression: Peer Support Groups for Victims." *Journal of Social Issues* 39:169–94.

Cohn, Y. 1976. "Crisis Intervention and the Victim of Robbery." In *Victimology: A New Focus*, edited by R. Drapkin and E. Viano. Lexington, Mass.: Heath.

Colao, F., and T. Hosansky. 1983. *Your Children Should Know.* New York: Bobbs Merrill.

Conte, J. 1985. "The Effects of Sexual Abuse on Children: A Critique and Suggestions for Future Research." *Victimology* 10:110–30.

Cook, R., B. Smith, and A. Harrell. 1987. *Helping Crime Victims: Levels of Trauma and Effectiveness of Services.* Washington, D.C.: U.S. Department of Justice.

Corbett, C., and K. Hobdell. 1988. "Volunteer-based Services to Rape Victims: Some Recent Developments." In *Victims of Crime: A New Deal?* edited by M. Maguire and J. Pointing. Milton Keynes: Open University Press.

Corbett, C., and M. Maguire. 1988. "The Value and Limitations of Victims Support Schemes." In *Victims of Crime: A New Deal?* edited by M. Maguire and J. Pointing. Milton Keynes: Open University Press.

Council of Europe. 1987. *Assistance to Victims and the Prevention of Victimization. Recommendation of the Council of Europe*. Strasbourg: Council of Europe.

Cronin, R., and B. Bourque. 1981. "Assessment of Victim/Witness Assistance Projects." Final report to the National Institute of Justice. Washington, D.C.: American Institutes for Research.

Culyer, A., R. Lavers, and A. Williams. 1972. "Health Indicators." In *Social Indicators and Social Policy*, edited by A. Shonfield and S. Shaw. London: Heinemann.

Daniels, R. 1977. "Battered Women: The Role of Women and Refuges." *Social Work Today* 9:12.

Davis, G., J. Boucherat, and D. Watson. 1987. "A Preliminary Study of Victim Offender Mediation and Reparation Schemes in England and Wales." Research and Planning Unit Paper no. 42. London: Home Office.

Davis, R. 1987. *Providing Help to Victims: A Study of Psychological and Material Outcomes*. New York: Victim Services Agency.

Davis, R., and L. Friedman. 1985. "The Emotional Aftermath of Crime and Violence." In *Trauma and Its Wake*, edited by C. Figley. New York: Brunner/Mazel.

Davis, R., and M. Henley. 1990. "Victim Service Programs." In *Crime Victims: Problems, Programs and Policies*, edited by A. Lurigio, W. Skogan, and R. Davis. Beverly Hills, Calif.: Sage.

Davis, R., F. Kunreuther, and E. Connick. 1984. "Expanding the Victim's Role in the Criminal Court Dispositional Process: The Results of an Experiment." *Journal of Criminal Law and Criminology* 75:491–505.

Dobash, R. E., and R. Dobash. 1979. *Violence against Women*. London: Free Press.

Du Bow, F., and T. Becker. 1976. "Patterns of Victim Advocacy." In *Criminal Justice and the Victim: An Introduction*, edited by W. McDonald. Beverly Hills, Calif.: Sage.

Duddle, M. 1985. "The Need for Sexual Assault Centres in the United Kingdom." *British Medical Journal* 290:771–73.

Duff, P. 1988. "The 'Victim Movement' and Legal Reform." In *Victims of Crime: A New Deal?* edited by M. Maguire and J. Pointing. Milton Keynes: Open University Press.

Durlak, J. 1979. "Comparative Effectiveness of Paraprofessional and Professional Helpers." *Psychological Bulletin* 86(1):80–92.

Dussich, J. 1976. "Victim Service Models and Their Efficacy." In *Victims and Society*, edited by E. Viano. Washington, D.C.: Visage.

———. 1981. "Evolving Services for Crime Victims." In *Perspectives on Crime Victims*, edited by B. Galaway and J. Hudson. St. Louis: Mosby.

Edelhertz, H., and G. Geis. 1974. *Public Compensation to Victims of Crime*. New York: Praeger.

Edmunds, C., K. McLaughlin, M. Young, and J. Stein. 1985. *Campaign for Victim Rights: A Practical Guide, 1985*. Washington, D.C.: National Organization for Victim Assistance.

Eitinger, L. 1964. *Concentration Camp Survivors in Norway and Israel*. Oslo: Universities Press.

Eitinger, L., and A. Strom. 1973. *Morbidity and Mortality after Excessive Stress*. New York: Humanities Press.

Elias, R. 1983. *Victims of the System*. New Brunswick, N.J.: Transaction.

———. 1986. *The Politics of Victimization: Victims, Victimology and Human Rights*. New York: Oxford University Press.

Elliott, D. S. 1989. "Criminal Justice Procedures in Family Violence Crimes." In *Family Violence*, edited by L. Ohlin and M. Tonry. Vol. 11 of *Crime and Justice: A Review of Research*, edited by M. Tonry and N. Morris. Chicago: University of Chicago Press.

Ellis, M. 1983. "A Review of Empirical Rape Research: Victim Reactions and Response to Treatment." *Clinical Psychology Review* 3(4):473–90.

Ellis, M., B. Atkeson, and K. Calhoun. 1981. "An Assessment of Long-Term Reaction to Rape." *Journal of Abnormal Psychology* 90:263–66.

Ennis, P. 1967. *Criminal Victimization in the United States*. President's Commission on Law Enforcement and Administration of Justice, Field Surveys III. Washington, D.C.: U.S. Government Printing Office.

Eve, R. 1985. "Empirical and Theoretical Findings concerning Child and Adolescent Sexual Abuse: Implications for the Next Generation of Studies." *Victimology* 10:97–109.

Even-Zohar, A., V. Russell, C. Reys, and R. Davis. 1976. *An Evaluation of the Victim/Witness Project's Court-based Services*. New York: Vera Institute of Justice.

Fattah, E. 1986. "Prologue: On Some Visible and Hidden Dangers of Victims Movements." In *From Crime Policy to Victim Policy*, edited by E. Fattah. London: Macmillan.

Fields, R. 1981. "Research on Victims: Problems and Issues." In *Evaluating Victim Services*, edited by S. Salasin. Beverly Hills, Calif.: Sage.

Finkelhor, D. 1979. *Sexually Victimized Children*. New York: Macmillan.

Finn, P., and B. Lee. 1987. *Serving Crime Victims and Witnesses*. Washington, D.C.: U.S. Department of Justice, National Institute of Justice.

Fleming, J. 1979. *Stopping Wife Abuse*. New York: Doubleday.

Friedman, L. 1985. "The Crime Victim Movement at Its First Decade." *Public Administration Review* (November), pp. 790–94.

Friedman, L., L. Bischoff, R. Davis, and A. Person. 1982. *Victims and Helpers: Reactions to Crime*. Washington, D.C.: U.S. Government Printing Office.

Friedman, L., and M. Shulman. 1990. "Domestic Violence: The Criminal Justice Response." In *Crime Victims: Problems, Programs and Policies*, edited by A. Lurigio, W. Skogan, and R. Davis. Beverly Hills, Calif.: Sage.

Galaway, B., and J. Hudson, eds. 1981. *Perspectives on Crime Victims*. St. Louis: Mosby.

Gay, M., C. Holtom, and S. Thomas. 1975. "Helping the Victims." *International Journal of Offender Therapy and Comparative Criminology* 19(3):263–69.

Genn, H. 1988. "Multiple Victimization." In *Victims of Crime: A New Deal?* edited by M. Maguire and J. Pointing. Milton Keynes: Open University Press.

Getzel, G., and R. Masters. 1984. "Serving Families Who Survive Homicide Victims." *Social Casework* 65:138–44.

Gill, M. 1986. "Wife Battering: A Case Study of a Women's Refuge." In *Crime Victims*, edited by R. Mawby. Plymouth, Devon: Plymouth Polytechnic.

Gill, M., and R. Mawby. 1990. *Volunteers in the Criminal Justice System*. Milton Keynes: Open University Press.

Gilley, J. 1974. "How to Help the Raped." *New Society* 28:756–58.

Gittler, J. 1984. "Expanding the Role of the Victim in a Criminal Action: An Overview of Issues and Problems." *Pepperdine Law Review* 11:117–82.

Goldstein, S. 1987. *The Sexual Exploitation of Children: A Practical Guide to Assessment, Investigation and Intervention*. New York: Elsevier.

Goodman, G., J. Golding, and H. Haith. 1984. "Jurors' Reactions to Child Witnesses." *Journal of Social Issues* 40(2):139–56.

Goodwin, J., ed. 1982. *Incest Victims and Their Families*. Boston: John Wright.

Gordon, J. 1977. "Alternative Human Services in Crisis Intervention." *Victimology* 2:22–30.

Gornick, J., M. Burt, and K. Pittman. 1983. "Structure and Activities of Rape Crisis Centers in the Early 1980s." *Crime and Delinquency* 31:247–68.

Grayson, R. 1983. *Crime Victims Aid: A Regional Directory of Crime Victim Services for New York, New Jersey and Pennsylvania*. Newark, N.J.: Bloom.

Harding, J. 1982. *Victims and Offenders: Needs and Responsibilities*. London: Bedford Square.

Harland, A. 1983. "One Hundred Years of Restitution: An International Review." *Victimology* 8:190–203.

Henderson, L. 1985. "The Wrongs of Victims' Rights." *Stanford Law Review* 37:937–51.

Hillenbrand, S. 1990. "Restitution and Victim Rights in the 1980s." In *Crime Victims: Problems, Programs and Policies*, edited by A. Lurigio, W. Skogan, and R. Davis. Beverly Hills, Calif.: Sage.

Holmstrom, L., and A. Burgess. 1978. *The Victim of Rape: Institutional Reactions*. New York: Wiley.

Holtom, C., and P. Raynor. 1988. "Origins of Victims Support Policy and Practice." In *Victims of Crime: A New Deal?* edited by M. Maguire and J. Pointing. Milton Keynes: Open University Press.

Home Office. 1990. *Victim's Charter: A Statement of the Rights of Victims of Crime*. London: Home Office.

Horowicz, M. 1980. "Psychological Response to Serious Life Events." In *Human Stress and Cognition*, edited by V. Hamilton and D. Warburton. New York: Wiley.

Hough, M. 1985. "The Impact of Victimization: Findings from the British Crime Survey." *Victimology* 10:488–97.

Hough, M., and P. Mayhew. 1985. "Taking Account of Crime: Key Findings from the 1984 British Crime Survey." Home Office Research Study no. 85. London: H.M. Stationery Office.

Howley, J. 1982. "Victim-Police Interaction and Its Effects on Public Attitudes to the Police." M.Sc. thesis, Cranfield Institute of Technology, United Kingdom.

Hudson, J., and B. Galaway, eds. 1975. *Restitution in Criminal Justice*. Lexington, Mass.: Heath.

———. 1980. *Victims, Offenders and Alternative Sanctions.* Lexington, Mass.: Heath.

Humphreys, J., and W. Humphreys. 1985. "Mandatory Arrest: A Means of Primary and Secondary Prevention of Abuse of Female Partners." *Victimology* 10:267–80.

Isaacs, S., and S. Hickman. 1987*a*. "Double Loss." *Community Care* 656:22–24.

———. 1987*b*. "Communicating with Children after a Murder." *Adoption and Fostering* 11(4):32–35.

Janoff-Bulman, R. 1985. "Criminal vs. Non-criminal Victimization: Victims' Reactions." *Victimology* 10:498–511.

Janoff-Bulman, R., and I. Frieze. 1983. "A Theoretical Perspective for Understanding Reactions to Victimization." *Journal of Social Issues* 39(2):1–17.

Jones, T., B. Maclean, and J. Young. 1986. *The Islington Crime Survey*. Aldershot: Gower.

Karmen, A. 1984. *Crime Victims: An Introduction to Victimology*. Monterey, Calif.: Brooks/Cole.

Katz, A. 1981. "Self-Help and Mutual Aid." *Annual Review of Sociology* 7:129–55.

Katz, A., and M. Mazur. 1979. *Understanding the Rape Victim: A Synthesis of Research Findings*. New York: Wiley.

Kaufman, I. 1985. "Child Abuse—Family Victimology." *Victimology* 10:62–71.

Kelly, D. 1990. "Victim Participation in the Criminal Justice System." In *Crime Victims: Problems, Programs and Policies*, edited by A. Lurigio, W. Skogan, and R. Davis. Beverly Hills, Calif.: Sage.

Kilpatrick, D. 1983. "Rape Victims: Detection, Assessment and Treatment." *Clinical Psychologist* 36(4):92–95.

Kilpatrick, D., and L. Veronen. 1984. *The Psychological Impact of Crime: A Study of Randomly Surveyed Victims*. Washington, D.C.: U.S. Department of Justice, National Institute of Justice.

Kilpatrick, D., L. Veronen, and P. Resick. 1979. "The Aftermath of Rape: Recent Empirical Findings." *American Journal of Orthopsychiatry* 49:658–69.

Knudten, M., and R. Knudten. 1981. "What Happens to Crime Victims and Witnesses in the Justice System?" In *Perspectives on Crime Victims*, edited by B. Galaway and J. Hudson. St. Louis: Mosby.

Knudten, R., A. Meade, M. Knudten, and W. Doerner. 1977. *Victims and Witnesses: The Impact of Crime and Their Experiences with the Criminal Justice System*. Washington, D.C.: U.S. Government Printing Office.

Lamborn, L. 1970. "Remedies for the Victims of Crime." *Southern California Law Review* 43:26–34.

Lerner, M. 1980. *The Belief in a Just World*. New York: Plenum.

Leymann, H. 1985. "Somatic and Psychological Symptoms after the Experience of Life Threatening Events: A Profile Analysis." *Victimology* 10:512–38.

Lifton, R. 1961. *Thought Reform and the Psychology of Totalism*. New York: Norton.

London Rape Crisis Centre. 1979. *Sexual Violence: The Reality for Women*. London: Women's Press.

Lowenberg, D. 1981. "An Integrated Victim Services Model." In *Perspectives on Crime Victims*, edited by B. Galaway and J. Hudson. St. Louis: Mosby.

Lurigio, A., W. Skogan, and R. Davis, eds. 1990. *Crime Victims: Problems, Programs and Policies*. Beverly Hills, Calif.: Sage.

McCahill, T., L. Meyer, and A. Fischmann. 1979. *The Aftermath of Rape*. Lexington, Mass.: Heath.

McCombie, S., B. Bassuk, R. Savitz, and S. Pell. 1976. "Development of a Medical Rape Crisis Intervention Program." *American Journal of Psychology* 133:412–18.

McDonald, W., ed. 1976*a*. *Criminal Justice and the Victim: An Introduction*. Beverly Hills, Calif.: Sage.

———. 1976*b*. "Toward a Bicentennial Revolution in Criminal Justice: The Return of the Victim." *American Criminal Law Review* 13(4):649–73.

McGillis, D., and P. Smith. 1983. *Compensating Victims of Crime: An Analysis of American Programs*. Washington, D.C.: U.S. Department of Justice, National Institute of Justice.

Magee, D. 1983. *What Murder Leaves Behind*. New York: Dodd, Mead.

Maguire, M. 1980. "The Impact of Burglary upon Victims." *British Journal of Criminology* 20:261–75.

———. 1984. "Meeting the Needs of Burglary Victims: Questions for the Police and Criminal Justice Systems." In *Coping with Burglary*, edited by R. Clarke and T. Hope. Boston: Kluwer-Nijhoff.

———. 1985. "Victims' Needs and Victim Services: Indications from Research." *Victimology* 10:539–59.

———. 1986. "Victims' Rights: Slowly Redressing the Balance." In *Crime UK 1986*. Newbury: Policy Journals.

———. 1989. "Matching Victim Assistance to Need." In *Guidelines for Victim Support in Europe*. Utrecht: Vereiniging Landelijke Organisatie Slachtofferhulp.

Maguire, M., with T. Bennett. 1982. *Burglary in a Dwelling: The Offence, the Offender and the Victim*. London: Heinemann.

Maguire, M., and C. Corbett. 1987. *The Effects of Crime and the Work of Victims Support Schemes*. Aldershot: Gower.

Maguire, M., and J. Pointing, eds. 1988. *Victims of Crime: A New Deal?* Milton Keynes: Open University Press.

Maguire, M., and J. Shapland. 1990. "The Victims Movement in Europe." In *Crime Victims: Problems, Programs and Policies*, edited by A. Lurigio, W. Skogan, and R. Davis. Beverly Hills, Calif.: Sage.

Malmquist, C. 1986. "Children Who Witness Parental Murder: Post-traumatic Aspects." *Journal of the American Academy of Child Psychiatry* 25:320–25.

Marshall, T. 1984. "Reparation, Conciliation and Mediation." Research and Planning Unit Paper no. 21. London: Home Office.

Marshall, T., and M. Walpole. 1985. "Bringing People Together: Mediation and Reparation Projects in Great Britain." Research and Planning Unit Paper no. 33. London: Home Office.

Mawby, R., and M. Gill. 1987. *Crime Victims: Needs, Services and the Voluntary Sector*. London: Tavistock.

Mayhew, P. 1985. "The Effects of Crime: Victims, the Public and Fear." In *Research on Victimisation*, vol. 23, edited by European Committee on Crime Problems. Strasbourg: Council of Europe.

Mendelsohn, B. 1947. "New Bio-pyschosocial Horizons: Victimology." *American Law Review* 13:649–73.

———. 1974. "The Origin of the Doctrine of Victimology." In *Victimology*, edited by J. Drapkin and E. Viano. Lexington, Mass.: Lexington.

Mezey, G. 1987. "Hospital Based Rape Crisis Programs: What Can the American Experience Teach Us?" *Bulletin of the Royal College of Psychiatrists* 11(2):49–51.

———. 1988. "Reactions to Rape: Effects, Counselling and the Role of Health Professionals." In *Victims of Crime: A New Deal?* edited by M. Maguire and J. Pointing. Milton Keynes: Open University Press.

Miers, D. 1978. *Responses to Victimisation*. Abingdon: Professional.

Miller, K., N. Moore, and C. Lexius. 1985. "A Group for Families of Homicide Victims: An Evaluation." *Social Casework* 66:432–36.

Morgan, J. 1988. "Children as Victims." In *Victims of Crime: A New Deal?* edited by M. Maguire and J. Pointing. Milton Keyes: Open University Press.

Morgan, R., and A. Bronstein. 1988. "Prisoners and the Courts: The U.S. Experience." In *Accountability and Prisons*, edited by M. Maguire, J. Vagg, and R. Morgan. London: Tavistock.

Morris, M., and M. Gould. 1963. "Role Reversal: A Concept in Dealing with the Neglected-Battered Child Syndrome." In *The Neglected-Battered Child Syndrome*. New York: Child Welfare League of America.

Muldoon, L., ed. 1979. *Incest: Confronting the Silent Crime*. Minneapolis: Minnesota Program for Victims of Sexual Assault.

Nadelson, C., and M. Notman. 1984. "Psychodynamics of Sexual Assault Experiences." In *Victims of Sexual Aggression: Treatment of Children, Women and Men*, edited by I. Stuart and J. Greer. New York: Van Nostrand Reinhold.

National Association of Victims Support Schemes. 1988. *The Victim in Court: Report of a Working Party*. London: National Association of Victims Support Schemes.

National Organization for Victim Assistance. 1985*a*. *Program Directory*. Washington, D.C.: National Organization for Victim Assistance.

———. 1985*b*. "Survivors of Homicide Victims." *National Organization for Victim Assistance: Network Information Bulletin* 2(3):1–12.

———. 1988. *The Victim Assistance Movement in the United States: Sunrise or Sunset*. Washington, D.C.: National Organization for Victim Assistance.

National Society for the Prevention of Cruelty to Children. 1987. *Annual Report*. London: National Society for the Prevention of Cruelty to Children.

Norquay, G., and R. Weiler. 1981. *Services to Victims and Witnesses of Crime in Canada*. Ottawa: Canadian Ministry of the Solicitor General.

Ochberg, F. 1980. "Victims of Terrorism." *Journal of Clinical Psychiatry* 41(3):73–74.

Orlando, J., and M. Koss. 1983. "The Effects of Sexual Victimization on

Sexual Satisfaction: A Study of the Negative-Association Hypothesis." *Journal of Abnormal Psychology* 92:104–6.

Osterweis, M., F. Solomon, and M. Green. 1984. *Bereavement: Reactions, Consequences and Care.* Washington, D.C.: National Academy Press.

Pagelow, M. 1977. *Blaming the Victim: Parallels in Crimes against Women.* Chicago: Society for the Study of Social Problems.

Pahl, J. 1978. *A Refuge for Battered Women.* London: H.M. Stationery Office.

———, ed. 1985. *Private Violence and Public Policy.* London: Routledge & Kegan Paul.

Parad, H., ed. 1965. *Crisis Intervention: Selected Readings.* New York: Family Service.

Parad, H., H. Resnick, and L. Parad, eds. 1976. *Emergency and Disaster Management.* Bowie, Md.: Charles.

Phipps, A. 1988. "Ideologies, Political Parties and Victims of Crime." In *Victims of Crime: A New Deal?* edited by M. Maguire and J. Pointing. Milton Keynes: Open University Press.

Pizzey, E. 1974. *Scream Quietly or the Neighbours Will Hear.* Harmondsworth: Penguin.

Pointing, J., and M. Maguire. 1988. "The Rediscovery of the Crime Victim." In *Victims of Crime: A New Deal?* edited by M. Maguire and J. Pointing. Milton Keynes: Open University Press.

President's Commission on Law Enforcement and Administration of Justice. 1967. *The Challenge of Crime in a Free Society.* Washington, D.C.: U.S. Government Printing Office.

President's Task Force on Victims of Crime. 1982. *Final Report.* Washington, D.C.: U.S. Government Printing Office.

Reeves, H. 1985. "Victims Support Schemes: The United Kingdom Model." *Victimology* 10:679–86.

Resick, P. 1984. "The Trauma of Rape and the Criminal Justice System." *Justice System Journal* 9(1):52–61.

———. 1985. *Psychological Reactions of Victims of Rape/Robbery.* Rockville, Md.: U.S. Department of Health and Human Services, National Institute of Mental Health.

Roberts, A. 1982. *Sheltering Battered Women.* New York: Springer.

———. 1987. "National Survey of Victim Services Completed." *NOVA Newsletter* 11(9):1–2.

Rock, P. 1986. *A View from the Shadows: The Ministry of the Solicitor-General of Canada and the Justice for Victims of Crime Initiative.* Oxford: Oxford University Press.

———. 1988. "Governments, Victims and Policies in Two Countries." *British Journal of Criminology* 28:44–66.

———. 1990. *Helping Victims of Crime: The Home Office and the Rise of Victim Support in England and Wales.* Oxford: Oxford University Press.

Rose, H. 1978. "In Practice Supported, in Theory Decried: An Account of an Invisible Urban Movement." *Urban Regional Research* 2:521–37.

Rosenblott, P. 1983. "Grief and Involvement in Wrongful Death Litigation." *Law and Human Behavior* (1983), pp. 351–59.

Rosenblum, R., and C. Blew. 1979. *Victim/Witness Assistance*. Washington, D.C.: U.S. Government Printing Office.

Russell, D. 1983. "The Incidence and Prevalence of Intra-familial and Extra-familial Sexual Abuse in Female Children." *Child Abuse and Neglect* 7:133–46.

Rynearson, E. 1984. "Bereavement after Homicide: A Descriptive Study." *American Journal of Psychiatry* 141:1452–54.

———. 1986. "Psychological Effects of Unnatural Dying on Bereavement." *Psychiatric Annals* 16:272–74.

Salasin, S., ed. 1981. *Evaluating Victim Services*. Beverly Hills, Calif.: Sage.

Sales, E., M. Baum, and B. Shore. 1984. "Victim Readjustment following Assault." *Journal of Social Issues* 40(1):117–36.

Samuels, A. 1973. "Criminal Injuries Compensation Board." *Criminal Law Review* (July), pp. 418–31.

Schafer, S. 1968. *The Victim and His Criminal: A Study in Functional Responsibility*. New York: Random House.

Schneider, A., and P. Reiter. 1975. *The Victim and the Criminal Justice System: A County-based Approach*. Washington, D.C.: National Association of Counties Research Foundation.

Schneider, A., and P. Schneider. 1981. "Victim Assistance Programs: An Overview." In *Perspectives on Crime Victims*, edited by B. Galaway and J. Hudson. St. Louis: Mosby.

Schwendinger, J., and H. Schwendinger. 1983. *Rape and Inequality*. Beverly Hills, Calif.: Sage.

Seligmann, M. 1975. *Helplessness: On Depression, Development and Death*. San Francisco: Freeman.

Shapland, J. 1986. "Victims and Justice: Needs, Rights and Services." In *Criminal Law in Action*, edited by J. van Dijk, C. Haffmans, F. Ruter, J. Schutte, and S. Stolwijk. Arnhem: Gouda Quint.

Shapland, J., and D. Cohen. 1987. "Facilities for Victims: The Role of the Police and Courts." *Criminal Law Review* (January), pp. 28–38.

Shapland, J., J. Willmore, and P. Duff. 1985. *Victims in the Criminal Justice System*. Aldershot: Gower.

Sherman, L., and R. Berk. 1984. *The Minneapolis Domestic Violence Experiment*. Washington, D.C.: Police Foundation.

Silver, R., and R. Wortman. 1980. "Coping with Undesirable Life Events." In *Human Helplessness*, edited by J. Garber and H. Seligman. New York: Academic Press.

Skogan, W. 1977. "Public Policy and the Fear of Crime in Large American Cities." In *Public Law and Public Policy*, edited by J. Gardiner. New York: Praeger.

Skogan, W., R. Davis, and A. Lurigio. 1990. "Victims' Needs and Victim Services." Final report to the National Institute of Justice. Washington, D.C.: U.S. Department of Justice, National Institute of Justice.

Skogan, W., and M. Maxfield. 1981. *Coping with Crime: Individual and Neighborhood Reactions*. Beverly Hills, Calif.: Sage.

Skogan, W., and M. Wycoff. 1987. "Some Unexpected Effects of a Police Service for Victims." *Crime and Delinquency* 33:490–501.

Smith, B. 1983. *Non-stranger Violence: The Criminal Courts' Response*. Washington, D.C.: U.S. Department of Justice, National Institute of Justice.

———. 1985. "Trends in the Victims' Rights Movement and Implications for Further Research." *Victimology* 10:34–43.

———. 1990. "The Adjudication of Child Sexual Abuse Cases." In *Crime Victims: Problems, Programs and Policies*, edited by A. Lurigio, W. Skogan, and R. Davis. Beverly Hills, Calif.: Sage.

Smith, C. 1985. "Response to Victims: Are the Institutional Mandates of Police and Medicine Sufficient?" *Victimology* 10:560–72.

Steele, B., and H. Alexander. 1981. "Long-Term Effects of Sexual Abuse in Childhood." In *Sexually Abused Children and Their Families*, edited by P. Mrazek and C. Kempe. New York: Pergamon.

Steinmetz, C. 1987. "Victim Assistance: Fine Tuning to the Existing Need." Mimeographed. The Hague: RODC, Ministry of Justice.

———. 1989. "The Effects of Victim Support." In *Guidelines for Victim Support in Europe*. Utrecht: Vereiniging Landelijke Organisatie Slachtofferhulp.

Stookey, J. 1981. "A Cost Theory of Victim Justice." In *Perspectives on Crime Victims*, edited by B. Galaway and J. Hudson. St. Louis: Mosby.

Straus, M., R. Gelles, and S. Steinmetz. 1980. *Behind Closed Doors: Violence in the American Family*. New York: Doubleday.

Stuebing, W. 1984. "Victims and Witnesses: Experiences, Needs and Community/Criminal Justice Response." Working Paper no. 9. Ottawa: Canadian Department of Justice.

Summit, R., and J. Kryso. 1978. "Sexual Abuse of Children: A Clinical Spectrum." *American Journal of Orthopsychiatry* 48:237–51.

Sutherland, S., and D. Scherl. 1970. "Patterns of Response among Victims of Rape." *American Journal of Orthopsychiatry* 40:166–73.

Symonds, M. 1975. "Victims of Violence: Psychological Effects and Aftereffects." *American Journal of Psychoanalysis* 40:503–11.

———. 1980. "The Second Injury to Victims of Violent Crime." *Evaluation and Change* (special issue), pp. 36–38.

———. 1982. "Victim Response to Terror: Understanding and Treatment." In *Victims of Terrorism*, edited by F. Ochberg and D. Soskis. Boulder, Colo.: Westview.

U.S. Attorney General's Task Force on Family Violence. 1984. *Final Report*. Washington, D.C.: U.S. Attorney General.

U.S. Department of Justice. 1975. *Criminal Victimization Surveys in 13 American Cities*. Washington, D.C.: U.S. Department of Justice.

———. 1979. *Criminal Victimization in the United States, 1979*. Washington, D.C.: U.S. Department of Justice.

United Nations. 1990. *Implementation of the Conclusions and Recommendations of the Seventh United Nations Congress on the Prevention of Crime and the Treatment of Offenders: Declaration of Basic Principles of Justice for Victims of Crime and Abuse of Power*. Vienna: United Nations Committee on Crime Prevention and Control.

van Dijk, J. 1979. "The Extent of Public Information and the Nature of Public Attitudes towards Crime." In *Public Opinion on Crime and Criminal Justice*, vol. 17, edited by the European Committee on Crime Problems. Strasbourg: Council of Europe.

———. 1986. "Regaining a Sense of Order and Community." Paper presented at the sixteenth annual Criminological Research Conference on Victimization, Council of Europe, Strasbourg.

———. 1988. "Ideological Trends within the Victims' Movement." In *Victims of Crime: A New Deal?* edited by M. Maguire and J. Pointing. Milton Keynes: Open University Press.

van Dijk, J., P. Mayhew, and M. Killias. 1990. *Experiences of Crime across the World: Key Findings of the 1989 International Crime Survey*. Boston: Kluwer.

Vereiniging Landelijke Organisatie Slachtofferhulp. 1989. *Guidelines for Victim Support in Europe*. Utrecht: Vereiniging Landelijke Organisatie Slachtofferhulp.

Veronen, L., and D. Kilpatrick. 1983. "Rape: A Precursor of Change." In *Lifespan Development Psychology: Non-normative Life Events*, edited by E. Callahan and K. McClusky. New York: Academic Press.

Viano, E. 1979. *Victim/Witness Services: A Review of the Model*. Washington, D.C.: U.S. Government Printing Office.

Victim Services Agency. 1986. *Research at Victim Services Agency*. New York: Metropolitan Assistance Corporation.

Victim Support. 1988. *Families of Murder Victims Project: First Year Report*. London: Victim Support.

———. 1989*a*. *Annual Report, 1988–1989*. London: Victim Support.

———. 1989*b*. *Supporting Female Victims of Sexual Assault: A Training Manual*. London: Victim Support.

———. 1990. *Annual Report, 1989–1990*. London: Victim Support.

Villmow, B. 1985. "Implications of Research on Victimisation for Criminal and Social Policy." In *Research on Victimisation*, vol. 23, edited by the European Committee on Crime Problems. Strasbourg: Council of Europe.

Von Hentig, H. 1948. *The Criminal and His Victim*. New Haven, Conn.: Yale University Press.

Walker, L. 1979. *The Battered Woman*. New York: Harper & Row.

Walklate, S. 1989. *Victimology: The Victim and the Criminal Justice System*. London: Unwin Hyman.

Waller, I. 1986. "Crime Victims: Orphans of Social Policy. Needs, Services and Reforms." In *Victimology in International Perspective*, edited by K. Miyazawa and O. Minoru. Tokyo: Seibundo.

———. 1988. "International Standards, National Trail Blazing, and the Next Steps." In *Victims of Crime: A New Deal?* edited by M. Maguire and J. Pointing. Milton Keynes: Open University Press.

Waller, I., and N. Okihiro. 1978. *Burglary: The Victim and the Public*. Toronto: University of Toronto Press.

Weisaeth, L. 1985. "Psychiatric Studies in Victimology in Norway: Main Findings and Recent Development." *Victimology* 10:478–87.

Williams, J., and K. Holmes. 1981. *The Second Assault: Rape and Public Attitudes*. Westport, Conn.: Greenwood.

Worden, J. 1982. *Grief Counselling and Grief Therapy*. New York: Springer.

Wright, M. 1982. *Making Good: Prisons, Punishment and Beyond.* London: Burnett.

———. 1985. "The Impact of Victim/Offender Mediation on the Victim." *Victimology* 10:631–44.

Yllo, K., and M. Bograd. 1988. *Feminist Perspectives on Wife Abuse.* Beverly Hills, Calif.: Sage.

Young, M. 1988. "The Crime Victims Movement." In *Post-traumatic Therapy and Victims of Violence,* edited by F. Ochberg. New York: Brunner/Mazel.

Zehr, H., and M. Umbreit. 1982. "Victim Offender Reconciliation: An Incarceration Substitute." *Federal Probation* 46(4):63–68.

Ziegenhagen, E. 1977. *Victims, Crime and Social Control.* New York: Praeger.

Ziegenhagen, E., and J. Benyi. 1981. "Victim Interests, Victim Services and Social Control." In *Perspectives on Crime Victims,* edited by B. Galaway and J. Hudson. St. Louis: Mosby.